AF682860

# The Political Economy of Income Distribution in Mexico

The Political Economy of Income Distribution in Developing Countries
Henry Bienen, General Series Editor

I. Turkey
Ergun Ozbudun and Aydin Ulusan, editors

II. Nigeria
Henry Bienen and V. P. Diejomaoh, editors

III. Egypt
Gouda Abdel-Khalek and Robert Tignor, editors

IV. Mexico
Pedro Aspe and Paul E. Sigmund, editors

The Political Economy of Income Distribution in Developing Countries series is prepared under the auspices of the Research Program in Development Studies
Woodrow Wilson School of Public and International Affairs
Princeton University

# The Political Economy of Income Distribution in Mexico

Edited by

Pedro Aspe and
Paul E. Sigmund

The Political Economy
of Income Distribution in Developing Countries
Henry Bienen, General Series Editor

HM

Holmes & Meier Publishers, Inc.
New York • London

First published in the United States of America 1984 by
Holmes & Meier Publishers, Inc.
30 Irving Place
New York, N.Y. 10003

*Great Britain:*
Holmes & Meier Publishers, Ltd.
131 Trafalgar Road
Greenwich, London SE10 9TX

Copyright © 1984 by Holmes & Meier Publishers, Inc.

ALL RIGHTS RESERVED

ISBN 08419-0907-5

MANUFACTURED IN THE UNITED STATES OF AMERICA

# Contents

# Preface

*The Political Economy of Income Distribution in Mexico* is the fourth and last volume of a series undertaken in Turkey, Nigeria, Egypt, and Mexico. The Mexican study involved scholars from Princeton University's Research Program in Development Studies working with Mexican scholars and policy makers. The design and implementation of research were truly collaborative, as they had been in previous studies. Meetings were held in Mexico City, Akumal, and Princeton, where the major issues were discussed, data sources were enumerated, and research methodology was examined.

We are grateful to the Instituto Tecnológico Autónomo de México (ITAM) for providing facilities for meetings in Mexico and above all for providing the institutional base for research coordination in Mexico. The rector of ITAM, Javier Beristain, has been a major participant in the project. He has also been a helpful colleague and friend in support of all our efforts. Professor Pedro Aspe, the coordinator of the Mexican researchers, has managed to make his essential contributions, to organize research, to teach at ITAM, and to carry out his governmental obligations in Mexico and abroad. We owe Rector Beristain and Professor Aspe special debts.

A number of colleagues were involved in our project who did not write chapters, but whose comments and inputs were important. Special mention should be made of Professor Manuel Camacho of the Colegio de México, who helped organize the project in Mexico at the start and made important contributions at our meetings in Akumal. Professor Ravi Kanbur of Cambridge University and Jeffery Round of Warwick University participated in meetings at Princeton to our benefit while they were Visiting Fellows of the Research Program in Development Studies. Professors Mark Gersovitz, Joseph Stiglitz, Charles Issawi, Michael Danielson, and John Page (now at the World Bank) participated in our meetings in Princeton and Mexico and helped think through all the issues. Mr. Kevin Henry, formerly of the Woodrow Wilson School and now at CARE, Inc., did research for us in Mexico. Ms. Julie Nelson, Ph.D. candidate in economics at Princeton, helped with computer and other analytical work, and she, like Mr. Henry, was a participant in our meetings.

I personally want to express my thanks to the Center for Advanced Study in the Behavioral Sciences, where I was a Fellow in 1976–1977 and started work on the same income distribution series. Princeton University has supported our work in many ways, and personal thanks go to Donald Stokes, dean of the Woodrow Wilson School, Agnes Pearson, business manager of the Woodrow Wilson School, and Ingrid Reed, assistant dean. Above all, the administrative staff of the Research Program in Development Studies has done so much to facilitate our work. Ms. Jerri Kavanagh, Office Coordinator, has been travel agent, contracts officer, administrative assistant, and friend to Princeton and Mexican colleagues. We all owe her very special thanks. Shirley Canty, Michelle Krichten, Michael Padulo, and Maxine Moore have also helped our work along. In Mexico, Tercy Tagle provided crucial administrative help at the Instituto Tecnológico Autónomo de México.

To all colleagues in the project, and especially to Pedro Aspe, I express my warm appreciation for their efforts and good will.

Henry Bienen
Director, Research Program in Development Studies
Princeton University
July 1982

# Abbreviations

| | |
|---|---|
| *AHORRO* | Operating Profit for State Enterprises |
| *BANOBRAS* | National Bank of Public Works |
| *BNHUOPSA* | National Bank of Urban and Public Works Mortgages, Inc. |
| *BRD* | Basic recommended Diet |
| *CEMAE* | Standard Industrial Classification in Mexico |
| *CENIET* | National Bureau of Industrial and Labor Statistics |
| *CFE* | Federal Electric Commission |
| *CONACYT* | National Council of Science and Technology |
| *CONASUPO* | National Company of Popular Subsistence |
| *COPLAMAR* | General Coordination of the National Plan of Depressed Zones and Marginated Groups |
| *CORETT* | Commission for the Regulation of Landholdings |
| *CTM* | Congress for Unification of the Workers of Mexico |
| *DDF* | Department of the Federal District |
| *DESC* | Civil Society of Economic Development |
| *DF* | Federal District of Mexico |
| *DGE* | General Board of Statistics |
| *DGHP* | General Board of Public Housing |
| *DGHP–DDF* | General Board of Public Housing of the Federal District |
| *DICONSA* | State Food Distribution Network for Rural Areas |
| *DIF* | National System for Integral Family Development |
| *FIDEURBE* | Trust for Urban Development of Mexico City |
| *FNV* | National Housing Fund |
| *FOGA* | Fund of Guarantees and Assistance |
| *FOMIN* | National Fund for Industrial Growth (or Development) |
| *FOVI* | Housing Operation and Discount Fund |
| *FOVIMI* | Housing Fund for Members of the Naval Fleet |
| *IDB* | Inter-American Development Bank |
| *IES* | Income and Expenditure Survey |
| *IMSS* | Mexican Institute of Social Security |
| *INDECO* | National Institute for the Development of the Rural Community and Public Housing |
| *INFONAVIT* | Institute of the National Housing Fund for Workers |
| *INV* | National Institute for Housing |
| *ISIM* | Turnover Sales Tax |

| | |
|---|---|
| *ISSFAM* | Social Security Institute for the Armed Forces and the Navy |
| *ISSSTE* | Social Service and Security Institute for State Workers |
| *ISSTESON* | Social Security Institute in the Service of the Workers of the State of Sonara |
| *ITAM* | Independent Mexican Institute of Technology |
| *IVCM* | Invalidity, Old Age, Retirement Age, and Death Pensions |
| *MAMC* | Metropolitan Area of Mexico City |
| *Nac. Fin.* | National Financier |
| *NAFINSA* | National Financing, Inc. |
| *OEA* | Organization of American States |
| *OIT* | International Labor Organization |
| *PEMEX* | Petroleos Mexicanos |
| *PIB y Gasto* | Gross Internal Product and Cost |
| *PNR* | National Revolutionary Party |
| *PRI* | Institutional Revolutionary Party |
| *SAM* | Mexican System for Food Allowance |
| *SARH* | Secretariat of Agriculture and Hydraulic Resources |
| *SEP* | Secretariat of Public Education |
| *SHCP* | Secretariat of Mortgages and Public Credit |
| *SIC* | Secretariat of Industry and Commerce |
| *SOE* | State-owned enterprises |
| *SPFI* | Secretariat of Patrimony and Industrial Growth |
| *SPP* | Secretariat of Planning and the National Budget |
| *SSA* | Secretariat of Health and Public Aid |
| *STPRM* | Oil Workers' Union of the Mexican Republic |
| *UAMC* | Urban Area of Mexico City |
| *UNAM* | National Autonomous University of Mexico |
| *VAT* | Value-Added Tax |
| *VISA* | Industrial Securities (Bonds), Inc. |

# The Political Economy of Income Distribution in Mexico

# CHAPTER 1

# *Introduction*

Pedro Aspe and Paul E. Sigmund

In this volume we attempt to go beyond the earlier debates on income distribution in Mexico which have been concerned with changes over time in the distribution of income in the economy as a whole. While some of the authors review and evaluate earlier studies, most of the chapters in this book focus on the impact of public policy instruments in Mexico upon the distribution of income.

The most striking conclusion to which they point seems to be how difficult it is to produce significant changes in income distributions in a political system that attempts to achieve both equity and growth, social transformation and political stability, through a ruling party which—as its name (Revolucionario Institucional) implies—is both revolutionary in origin and objectives, and committed to working through the established social and political institutional framework.

A second conclusion would be that most of the redistributive efforts that have been made have affected the modern and urban sectors rather than the traditional rural areas (for there is a modern rural sector in Mexico, too). This is understandable because the modern urban sectors are most accessible by government action, but since much, if not most, of Mexican poverty is located in the traditional and rural sectors, it means that however ambitious and well-organized the government programs are, they will have great difficulty reaching those who need them most. This has meant that most of the welfare and benefit programs that the Mexican government has set up have improved the conditions not of the very poor, but of groups that have already been the beneficiaries of Mexican economic development for other reasons—mainly the middle sectors. Thus our analyses of individual programs seem to confirm what the more theoretical and general studies done earlier have tended to demonstrate—that if there has been redistribution in Mexico in recent decades as a result of government action, it has benefited the middle sectors at the expense of the extremes.[1]

The work of Aspe and Beristain in this volume shows that whatever measure of relative position is used (current and permanent income or expenditure, household or personal data) the distribution of income in Mexico has remained basically stable since 1950, but that more recently (1963–1977) the participation of the lowest and highest deciles has declined while the participation of the upper middle class (deciles VII–IX) has advanced.[2] Thus, despite the impressive growth rate of the Mexican economy since the 1970s, not only has the distribution of those achievements been unequal but it has resulted in a relative worsening of the position of the lower income groups.

## Who Are the Poor in Mexico?

The 1977 Household Survey of Income and Expenditure reveals that six decades after the Mexican Revolution 36 percent of Mexican families still found themselves below the poverty line, as defined by the World Bank.[3] According to the Survey, 22 million Mexicans were in this "marginal" group. Eighty-three percent of poor families were located in the rural sector and, among poor urban families, 50 percent lived in the largest cities—Mexico City, Guadalajara, and Monterrey—forming the so-called lost cities *(ciudades perdidas)* of misery that surround those urban areas.

Thirty-nine percent of the marginal poor were less than twelve years of age, while 54 percent were between the ages of twelve and sixty-five. Among the poor, half of the family heads were in agriculture, 17 percent were in the industrial sector, 20 percent were in the service sector, and 11 percent were unemployed, compared with overall national figures of 30 percent, 25 percent, 35 percent, and 10 percent respectively. Fifty-six percent of the group's income came from wages and salaries and 35 percent came from "entrepreneurial rent"—a misleading term that includes income from self-employment and handicraft industries—while the source of income of 70 percent of upper-income families was wages and salaries. Of the total income received by the marginal poor, 70 percent was used for food and beverages, a figure that contrasts with the 34.9 percent spent by the high-income families located in the top two deciles. Only 1.2 percent of the expenditures of the poor was for education; 45 percent did not have any education, and 45 percent had not finished primary school. If we compare these figures with the one for the highest level income group (decile X), we find that 75 percent of the heads of family in the top decile of the population have finished primary education (compared with 10 percent of the poor) and 18 percent have a university degree. (The average income for a person who has finished university studies in Mexico is eight times higher than that received by a person without such education.)

## The Mexican Revolutionary Tradition and Social Justice

The limited accomplishments of the Mexican government in the area of income distribution are all the more striking because a central element in the political tradition derived from Mexico's revolutionary past is a belief in the responsibility of the government for the promotion of social justice. The spark that ignited the revolution was the decision by Porfirio Díaz to run for a sixth term as president in 1910, but the revolution immediately acquired a social content. The programs of the revolutionaries promised land reform, worker welfare rights, and national control of mineral resources.

Two articles of the 1917 constitution, in particular, reflected the commitment of the Revolution to social justice. Article 27 placed limits on private property, calling for the break-up and redistribution of large landholdings and declaring as "inalienable and imprescriptible" the ownership by the nation of natural resources and subsoil minerals and petroleum. Article 123 provided for an eight-hour day, a minimum wage, worker housing, as well as accident, old-age, and unemployment insurance, and guaranteed the right to strike and to organize unions. As the studies in this book indicate, it was often many years before these provisions were translated into effective legislation. In the case of Article 27, it was only with the nationalization of petroleum in 1938 that its provision on subsoil rights was implemented, while the agrarian reform has been carried out with varying degrees of commitment by different presidents down to the present day. Social security legislation under Article 123 was only adopted in the 1940's, while government-promoted worker housing had to wait until the 1970s. Yet since 1917 the Mexican revolutionary tradition has required that all governments of Mexico take action to promote social justice.[4]

Initially, those actions focused especially on two groups—landless peasants and organized workers. In the 1920s this meant principally land distribution under the 1915 agrarian reform law and the establishment of a national educational system. With the advent of Lázaro Cárdenas to the presidency in 1934, the social content of the revolution was translated into the acceleration of agrarian reform, the promotion of labor rights, and the organization of peasants and workers into government-supported peasant and labor federations which were formally affiliated with the official government party that had been created in 1929. Cárdenas nationalized the foreign-owned oil industry, and increased public expenditures on education and health, expanding state intervention in the economy and laying the foundations for the later development of Mexico's mixed economy, in which the public and private sectors have alternately taken the lead in Mexican industrialization, while the "social" sector of the economy, principally the *ejido* cooperatives, has been confined to the traditional and rural areas. Under Cárdenas, the agrarian reform distributed more land to the peasants than under any preceding or subsequent president, but land redistribution alone was not enough to resolve the economic problems of the very poor. The government bureaucracy was enlarged, new state agencies were founded, and the government party was reorganized with functional groups representing the peasants, workers, civil servants and teachers, and (until 1940) the military. By the end of the Cárdenas term in 1940, Mexican ideology and policy had acquired the overall orientation which they have maintained to the present.

Cárdenas's successors continued to appeal to the revolutionary traditions of social justice, but they gave more attention to government promotion of economic growth. Mexican presidents have sometimes been labeled according to the relative priority they have given to economic and social objectives, but all modern presidents have felt it necessary to demonstrate that their programs have both promoted development and increased social justice. Until the late 1970s every president affirmed his continuing commitment to agrarian reform and the extension of the ejidal cooperatives. Similarly, for political and economic reasons all Mexican presidents have given high priority to wage increases for unionized labor. At least until the 1960s social justice in Mexico was understood to mean government support for organized labor and the ejidal sector of agriculture.

The particular ability of the Mexican regime and ruling party to contain within themselves a variety of ideological outlooks has also meant that, besides the often-cited alternation of so-called reformist and conservative presidents, there is a kind of internal balancing of policy objectives that requires more "conservative" presidents to take some "radical" steps to preserve their revolutionary credibility, and those more committed to social reform to reassure their supporters that they are also concerned with stability and growth. (We are aware that most Mexican politicans and many serious observers of Mexican politics would feel uncomfortable with the classification we have used, arguing that policy differences are not the result of differing goals or ideology but only of disagreements as to timing and appropriate methods.)

Stability and growth were two salient characteristics of Mexico in the period of "stabilizing development" *(desarrollo estabilizador)* between the middle 1950s and the early 1970s. From 1954 until 1971 the Mexican economy grew between 6 percent and 8 percent a year, inflation rates averaged less than 5 percent, and the value of the peso in relation to the dollar remained stable. According to the World Bank, although there was little change in income distribution, per capita income increased 45 percent in real terms between 1963 and 1977.[5] The social question was resolved by periodically distributing more land and announcing a new increase in the minimum wage, but more fundamental distributive questions were not faced—often because they were not recognized or documented.

As measured by the main macroeconomic aggregates, the growth of the Mexican economy during the period of stabilizing development was astonishing. Over the longer term, however, the strategy generated its own internal weaknesses—particularly because government subsidies for capital investment distorted the relative prices of the factors of production. As Jesús Reyes Heroles observes in his chapter in this volume, the result was a decrease in the relative price of the scarce resource—capital—relative to labor, which was the abundant factor. As time passed, even though production and the wages of those already employed grew rapidly, employment increased more slowly than output. The paradox of expanded production but inadequate generation of new employment, anticipated by Marx and other economic theorists, was based on the fact that entrepreneurs in search of profit maximization made intensive use of the factor that was relatively cheaper—capital. The system did not seem to be capable of employing those in the bottom deciles. Stabilizing development increased the dichotomy between "traditional" and "modern" Mexico.

At the beginning of the 1970s, the Mexican public sector tried to change the model of development. The government of President Luis Echeverría (1970–76) initiated a shift from a policy of stabilizing development to one of shared development *(desarrollo compartido),* in which the government was to take a more active role in promoting equity and redistribution. Echeverría substantially increased government expenditures for social purposes and expanded the state sector of the economy, but in the absence of corresponding tax increases this led to a government deficit, inflation, and finally devaluation of the peso at the end of his presidential six-year term *(sexenio).*

It is true that many of the structural problems that became evident during the Echeverría period had earlier origins. An example would be the pricing policy of the public enterprise sector followed during the period of stabilizing development which kept the prices of petroleum products, electricity, and transportation artifically low, thus contributing to the growth of the public sector deficit in the early 1970s. The increasing deficit fueled inflationary pressures and the distortion of relative factor prices together with macroeconomic instability and the lack of coherence among government objectives led to a crisis in the Mexican economy in 1976.

The crisis was resolved by the post-1976 oil boom and the renewed emphasis given to economic stabilization and growth by Echeverría's successor, president José Lopez Portillo (1976–82). Mexico's new oil prosperity enabled Lopez Portillo's government to expand employment by 4 million jobs, and to initiate ambitious social programs, such as the extension of health coverage to the rural and urban poor and the improvement of the economic and social conditions of the areas of nonirrigated agriculture that had been largely ignored by earlier presidents.

Unfortunately the Lopez Portillo *sexenio* ended, as had that of his predecessor, with runaway inflation and devaluation of the peso. By the end of 1982, when Lopez Portillo turned over the presidency to Miguel de la Madrid Hurtado, Mexico was in the midst of its worst economic and social crisis since the 1930s with hyperinflation, repeated devaluations of the peso, and soaring unemployment. The renewed economic crisis made it all the more difficult to resolve the continuing dilemma of Mexico's development strategy—how to harmonize the political and social need for government programs in favor of the poor with an overall macroeconomic situation that produces a sustained rate of growth and employment, as well as overall price stability.

Summarizing, then, we can say that in the seventy years since the beginning of the Mexican Revolution there has been a continuing commitment to government action to promote equity and social justice. For reasons related to the revolutionary politics, and to specific provisions in the 1917 constitution, that commitment was initially applied principally in the form of land redistribution programs, usually into ejidal cooperatives, and the promotion of trade unionism and organized labor. However, in more recent years attention has been paid to broader problems of urban and rural poverty and the ways in which the government can take action in this area without sacrificing the economic growth which has provided the resources for such programs. With the emergence since the 1930s of a strong six-year presidency and a dominant ruling party, each administration has attempted to find its own way to demonstrate its continuing adherence to the redistributive goals of the revolution, without undermining what has become a stable and institutionalized social order as well as a complicated web of international political and economic relationships. The discussion of income distribution in Mexico must be seen, therefore, as a recent example of the continuing debate over social policy in a regime that expects the government to play a major role in the economic and social life of the nation, and to take vigorous action to improve the lot of the common people.

## The Impact of Public Policy on Income Distribution

The studies in this volume examine the consequences for income distribution both of programs that had other purposes and of those that were specifically aimed at improving the welfare of low-income groups. In the first category, we find, for example, in the chapter by Raymond Hill ("State Enterprise and Income Distribution in Mexico") that the considerable expansion of the state sector of the economy and the proliferation of state-owned enterprises have had important effects on income distribution. Hill shows that there is a tendency for workers in the state sector to be better paid than those in comparable positions in the private sector. A similar argument is made in Socrates Rizzo's study of the impact of oil revenues, which demonstrates that in the specific case of the state-owned petroleum industry much of the oil surplus has been devoted to raising the income of the petroleum workers. In his chapter, Jesús Reyes Heroles also notes the disparity in wages between the private and public sectors and recommends that it be reduced.

A second conclusion of the Hill study is that prices in the state sector tend to increase more slowly in relation to inflation—or even to remain fixed for political reasons. Again, Rizzo confirms this in his discussion of the subsidization of the prices of petroleum products, electricity and railroads, which has tended to benefit middle- and upper-income groups more than the poor. A third related area of public subsidy that both Rizzo and Hill discuss is also analyzed in the chapter by Leopoldo Solís on food marketing—the National Popular Subsistence Corporation (CONASUPO) which has among its specific purposes the provision of cheap food to low-income families. Again a large government subsidy—Rizzo reports an increase in the CONASUPO deficit from 3.2 billion pesos in 1976 to 27.8 billion pesos in 1980—has financed inefficient programs that, Solís argues, benefit the urban middle sectors more than the urban poor.

Two other studies in this book analyze programs that had other primary goals but also affected income distribution—those by Paul Sigmund in his chapter on the regulation of foreign investment, and by Francisco Gil Díaz in the chapter on taxation. In the case of the Sigmund study, the foreign investment legislation was found to have been inspired by a nationalistic desire to control and direct the pattern of investment by foreigners, and to give Mexicans a larger share of the profits, rather than by a redistributive purpose. Its actual impact may indeed have been more income-concentrating than distributing, although the legislation allows the Foreign Investment Commission to promote distributive goals when it grants exceptions to the Mexicanization requirements of the legislation.

Gil's study clearly demonstrates that the tax reform adopted in 1978 is more progressive in character. However, that progressivity again is located principally in the modern sector—those subject to income tax and those who pay the Value Added Tax (IVA). More substantial redistribution would require measures such as food stamps, a negative income tax, and targeted subsidies, which are discussed in the chapter by Nora Lustig. As in other cases, the tax legislation was directed at the promotion of investment and growth, and at efficient collection of revenue rather than at redistribution *per se*. Similar priorities dominate the consideration of alternative trade policies in Clark Reynolds's chapter on trade. Trade policy has nondistributive goals, although it can also be analyzed from the point of view of income distribution.

An additional contribution of the Gil paper is the analysis of the "inflation tax." He recognizes that to the degree that the government decides to pursue an inflationary fiscal policy, it is also deciding to impose a tax on its population which will affect some groups more than others. It is commonly recognized that those on fixed incomes suffer from inflation as do those who hold time deposits with fixed rates of interest, but Gil has also developed a methodology for measuring the incidence of the inflation tax more broadly—both in its impact on Mexican corporations and on distribution across the income groups. A further effect of inflation, its adverse impact on employment and output, is explored in the chapter by Pedro Aspe and Herminio Blanco.

There is a second group of policy studies in this volume that attempt to evaluate programs that are aimed directly at improving the welfare of low-income groups. Again, for reasons discussed above, they have, on the whole, benefited middle-income groups and organized labor rather than the very poor.

The study of education and health by Pedro Aspe and Javier Beristain is a case in point. It would seem that universal free education is a clear example of a way to invest in the future of the country that will be of immediate benefit to low-income groups. From the Aspe/Beristain study it is evident that two positive effects of this effort have been a considerable reduction in illiteracy—from 58 percent in 1940 to 28 percent in 1970—and, in the current decade, almost universal availability of primary school to the population aged six to fourteen. However, when the expenditures at various levels are compared to the numbers and social-economic backgrounds of their clientele, it appears that, as in other countries studied in this series (Turkey, Nigeria, and Egypt),[6] Mexican educational expenditure is skewed regionally and socially to the benefit of the urban middle-class groups that patronize secondary and university-level education. In the latter case in particular, one might ask whether a system of loans and tuition charges based on real costs in the universities might not release funds from the educational budget which could be used to improve primary education in rural areas where there still is a desperate shortage of schools and teachers. A similar argument could be made for the regional and social distribution of government-financed health programs.

The point can be carried further. Even such an apparently obvious effort to improve the welfare of low-income groups as the minimum wage can be criticized because it affects only the lower-middle- and middle-income groups (about 30 percent of Mexican families receive less than the minimum wage). Other critics have argued that is has made labor more expensive in a labor-surplus economy. When combined with the explicit or implicit subsidies to capital that are criticized by Jesús Reyes Heroles in this volume, it has led to considerable distortion in the allocation of factors of production in Mexico.

Housing policy is another striking example of programs aimed at helping low-income groups that do not reach those most in need of government assistance. Richard Moore's chapter demonstrates that programs of rent control, subsidized credit, and employer-financed worker housing have not been effective in coping with the severe housing needs of the majority of Mexicans, although the last named effort—the construction of housing for industrial workers that is jointly financed by compulsory contributions by employers and employees—has improved the housing situation of organized workers.

One program that has begun to respond to the criticism that government welfare programs do not reach the very poor (in Mexican terminology—the "marginal" population) is the expansion to rural areas of the health coverage of the social security program, analyzed by Emilio Lozoya. Social security was guaranteed to the worker in the 1917 constitution, but as noted earlier, it was not until the end of 1942 that a Social Security Law was adopted. It originally covered only accident and retirement insurance but was later extended to include medical coverage as well. As Lozoya explains in his chapter—in the late 1970s a noncontributory health program for "marginal" and depressed zones (COPLAMAR) added a potential 17 million new beneficiaries to the program. According to the Aspe/Beristain chapter on health and education it increased medical coverage from 20 percent of the population in 1965 to 47.5 percent in 1980. The "solidarity" social security—really health—program is an example of a conscious effort by the Mexican government to reach the very poor and to deal with the problems of infant mortality, infectious and intestinal disease, and regional disparities described by Aspe and Beristain.

Since most of those very poor are located in rural areas, it is now recognized that government programs to aid rural development can have an important impact on income distribution. Carlos Salinas's chapter in this volume summarizes some of the findings of his study of the impact of government programs of roadbuilding and of the introduction of high-yield seeds in areas of rain-fed agriculture. The government of President José Lopez Portillo also focused its attention on the rural population in the areas of rainfed agriculture when it created the Mexican Food System (SAM). As described at the beginning of Nora Lustig's chapter, it was an attempt to improve the production of the nonirrigated sector of Mexican agriculture through programs of price guarantees and subsidies, crop insurance, subsidized fertilizers and seeds, and agricultural technology. With the advent of Miguel de la Madrid Hurtado to the presidency in December 1982, the SAM was reorganized and some of its more costly programs were discontinued.

The measures just mentioned—the extension of health coverage to rural and marginal areas and the program for rainfed agriculture—were responses to the criticisms of earlier government programs for their lack of attention to those who were most in need. They indicate that even when the economy was expanding very rapidly and employment was increasing at a high rate, as occurred during the "oil-boom" years (1977–81), the Mexican government was compelled by ideology and politics to demonstrate its continuing commitment to social justice. The administration of President Miguel de la Madrid Hurtado (1982–88) will find it more difficult to develop expensive new social programs—and both the COPLAMAR health program and the SAM agricultural programs have been very expensive (in overall terms, although not on the basis of the number of those assisted)—because during 1982 the international price of Mexico's petroleum exports declined, Mexican foreign debt rose to over $80 billion, the peso was devalued by 400 percent, inflation reached nearly 100 percent, and the previously impressive growth rate of the Mexican economy turned negative. Since in addition to the need to reaffirm the legitimacy of the government by demonstrating its continued concern for the poor through such programs as public health, education, and housing, it is also politically important to retain the support of the urban middle class, the de la Madrid government may find more difficult the choice between programs favoring one group or the other. What the studies in this book have attempted to do is to make it clear that often, if not always, that choice must be made.

The Mexican experience with government action to promote social justice demonstrates that even with a political tradition that places a great emphasis upon government action against poverty, it is difficult to develop effective programs that alter income distribution. Subsidies have provided some assistance, but oil surpluses are declining while the subsidies have tended to grow out of line with the rest of the budget. Government enterprises find that political pressures limit flexibility in pricing, employment, and wage policies. Price controls are notoriously difficult to administer. Welfare programs often require a large and inefficient bureaucracy. The promotion of economic growth is necessary to finance large government programs of aid to the poor, but the private sector resists expansion of government programs, and incentives for capital formation may operate at cross purposes with the objective of job creation or the encouragement of labor-intensive industries. As increasing economic constraints in Mexico make it more difficult to combine growth and equity, the task of designing rational and efficient economic and social programs becomes more complex. It is the hope of the authors that the studies contained in this book will help to improve the formulation and implementation of such programs.

## Notes

1. In the most influential early study of income distribution Ifigenia Martínez concluded that during the 1950s, the highest income groups lost ground relative to the rest of the population. See Ifigenia Martínez de Navarrete, *La Distribución del Ingreso en México y el*

*Desarrollo Económico de México* (México, Instituto de Investigaciones Economicas, Escuela Nacional de Economia, 1960). In a later study Martinez showed that between 1958 and 1963 the upper deciles regained their earlier position while the share of the lowest income groups declined. See Ifigenia Martínez, "La Distribución del Ingreso en México," in Leopoldo Solís (ed.), *El Perfil de Mexico en 1980* (Mexico City: Siglo XXI, 1970).

2. Pedro Aspe and Javier Beristain, "Towards a First Estimate of the Evolution of Inequality in Mexico" (chapter 3 of this volume).

3. *Encuesta de Ingresos y Gastos de los Hogares* (Mexico City: Dirección General de Estadística, Secretaría de Programación y Presupuesto, 1977).

4 See James Wilkie, *The Mexican Revolution: Federal Expenditures and Social Change Since 1910* 2nd ed., (Berkeley, Cal.: University of California Press, 1970); Roger Hansen, *The Politics of Mexican Development* (Baltimore, Md.: Johns Hopkins University Press, 1971); as well as the multivolume *Historia de la Revolución Mexicana,* published by the Colegio de México under the direction of Daniel Cosío Villegas.

5. Joel Bergsman, *Income Distribution and Poverty in Mexico* (Washington, D.C.: World Bank Staff Working Paper No. 395, June 1980), p. 41.

6. See Ergun Özbudun and Aydin Ulusan (eds.), *The Political Economy of Income Distribution in Turkey* (New York: Holmes and Meier, 1980), chapter 16; Henry Bienen and V.P. Diejomaoh (eds.), *The Political Economy of Income Distribution in Nigeria,* (New York: Holmes and Meier, 1981), chapter 11; and Gouda Abdel-Khalek and Robert Tignor (eds.), *The Political Economy of Income Distribution in Egypt* (New York: Holmes and Meier, 1982), chapter 11.

# CHAPTER 2

# *The Evolution of Income Distribution Policies during The Post-Revolutionary Period in Mexico*

Pedro Aspe and Javier Beristain

## Introduction

If the sustained growth of national income is accepted as a criterion for the evaluation of an economy, the performance of the Mexican economy during the last 40 years would be graded as "very good." Between 1940 and 1980, real gross domestic product (GDP) grew more than ten times, and per capita real gross domestic product approximately tripled. Between 1940 and 1950, the economy grew at an average rate of 6.0 percent; between 1961 and 1970, the rate of growth advanced to 7.0 percent; and between 1971 and 1980, the real growth of GDP reached an annual average of 6.4 percent. Particularly noteworthy are the rates of 8.0, 9.2, and 8.3 percent achieved in 1978, 1979, and 1980, respectively.

In the 1940–1950 period, growth was accompanied by great price instability and double-digit inflation; the decade of the 1950s registered moderate inflation; and during the 1960s, which has been recorded as the era of *stabilizing development* in the economic history of the country, the economy experienced growth with price stability. The 1970s were a period of accelerating inflation accompanied by economic growth. But, to reiterate, the principal aspect of the economy has been one of growth.

In spite of the great economic growth, the country has not solved problems, such as poverty, which affect millions of Mexicans. The "Mexican miracle" has been questioned mainly because it has not had important consequences for income or wealth distribution, the patterns of which have been quite resistant over time as well as to the short-term and even structural changes which the economy has experienced in recent years.

A slight redistribution of income has occurred, adversely affecting some higher-income brackets but also to the detriment of low-income families and individuals and to the benefit of the upper-middle-income groups. For many observers and analysts, the redistribution has not only been slight; it has occurred, at least partly, at the expense of the poorest. In other words, it is asserted that if economic development is defined as a sustained process of increase of per capita income (which has been achieved), accompanied by a redistribution of the national product toward the groups with lower relative incomes (which is yet to be achieved), then the country has grown but not developed.

Another way of expressing this is in terms of efficiency and justice. Thus, it can be said that the Mexican economy has been efficient but not equitable. There has been criticism, especially of the economic development model called *stabilizing,* since it is said that this model subordinated justice to efficiency with the argument that the economy had to grow before attempting a substantial redistribution of income. At this point it is not important to see whether or not this was the intention of the model; it remains a fact that the income distribution pattern in Mexico in 1970 as well as in 1977 was very similar to that of 1950, the first year for which there are accurate indicators of growth and income distribution.[1]

The relationship between income growth and distribution, between efficiency and justice, has been a point of debate and an issue of economic policy. In spite of the importance of the matter, efforts to combine a theory of economic growth with one of income redistribution have been fruitless. Such a theory is required as a necessary condition of a good economic policy. Lacking that, it is understandable that few models have been concerned with growth and redistribution, for it is generally believed that first there must be growth and then redistribution, because it is impossible to combine higher rates of income increase with extensive redistributive policies, since these discourage efficiency. On the other hand, in a few but significant number of cases, it is thought that first there must be redistribution and then growth must be fostered, since concentration of income limits the size of domestic markets and discourages productive investment in the country.

The problem is difficult, but it cannot be avoided. It is not possible to become interested, either at a speculative or political level, in the topic of income and wealth distribution and its relation to growth without bias—in other words, without a preanalytical concept (in the words of Schumpeter) of distributive justice. That the observed evidence is discouraging and moves us to the consideration of redistributive actions suggests that what we see does not agree with our idea of justice. In discussing income distribution in Mexico and the need to relate it to other economic issues, we must think about the understanding of justice which should be our point of reference: either we understand justice as an instrument for achieving a greater goal, be it ethical, political, or economic, or we understand it as an end in itself.

It is evident that the way we deal with income distribution and redistribution depends on whether a greater distributive justice is sought as a means to reach an end, such as stability and economic growth, or whether it is an end in itself. We have chosen the second meaning.

This approach does not mean, of course, an underestimation of economic objectives, such as efficiency and growth. It is, rather, a reordering of priorities and a reminder that growth must have a meaning, an orientation, and a goal. We do not share the belief that efficiency is enough: an efficient but unjust system cannot endure. Neither do we believe that justice can be achieved through stagnation, because stagnation leads to the spread of poverty. We reject the possibility of dealing with efficiency and justice as interchangeable goods; both are to be desired. We propose the search for efficiency as a necessary but not sufficient condition for justice.

There will be justice in distribution when the social, economic, and political institutions:

1. Allow inequalities attributed to the individual characteristics of people, including those derived from free election of occupation, profession, and way of life as well as those derived from personal factors such as age
2. Guarantee each person the same right to have access to sufficient material and spiritual satisfaction we avoid the minimum qualifier—to lead a free and dignified life
3. Allow only the inequalities which will benefit the less able

It is evident that the proposed concept of justice does not mean absolute equality. It must be emphasized that there are two inherent inequalities in a just system. The first one arises from human individuality and consists of different tastes, preferences, and ways of life; the second one has its origin in the desire of society to favor the less able. This form of inequality would disappear as society advances in the equality of opportunities. The inequality of individuality would have to be preserved, taking care only that the diversity of individual conditions not be the result of outside intervention, for example, a class division of work that limits social mobility, preordained sexual roles, or, at the extreme, conditionings by the use of genetic engineering of the type described in George Orwell's *Brave New World* in a just system.

Because of the foregoing, the suggested elements for a just redistributive policy should be those which modify existing institutional arrangements in such a way that 1–3 are feasible. This requires political will and decision, and by this we understand the will and decision of society in general, not just those of the government. Existing arrangements are the result of free actions and governmental decision; hence, the modification of both elements is necessary. In the final analysis, a strong government is needed to receive from society the redistributive assignment as well as the power and resources to carry it out.

## Redistributive Policies and Tools

An overview of the programs, plans, or models of economic development attempted by the Mexican governments since the revolution, especially from the 1930s until the 1970s, may illustrate the theory and practice of redistribution. We shall try to summarize the objectives of those programs and to make at the same time some comments and reflections on the tools of economic policy explicitly used for redistributive purposes. We shall mention mainly those policy instruments which directly or indirectly, in an immediate or deferred way, have had distributive consequences:

The amount and purpose of public expenditure and of public investment

Governmental efforts to create human capital and to support property and production in the social sector, such as the *ejidatarios* (communal farmers)

Direct or indirect action in the labor market, resulting in the creation of employment in sectors of relatively large productivity

Taxation and transfer policies because of their effects on the spending and consumption levels of different income brackets

Redistribution of assets, singling out the case of the agrarian reform and land allocation

It has been said that the Mexican revolution was the last of the so-called bourgeois revolutions. But there are some who state that the Mexican revolution was the first of the great social revolutions of the twentieth century. It is not strange, then, that the 1917 Constitution contains apparently opposing concepts of the relation of the individual and society. The main provisions of the earlier 1857 Constitution, concerning individual rights, establishing universal suffrage, and determining the functions of the federal government, coexist with clauses on education, property, and labor that are of an undeniable social content.

The postrevolutionary history of the Mexican people and their governments can be written around the simultaneous search for two values: personal liberty and social justice.

The constructive era of the Mexican revolution started with the government of President Lázaro Cárdenas (1934–1940) when the revolution was institutionalized in a dominant political party; different political forces were accommodated and adjusted, and national and international economic recovery began. The Cárdenas government formulated the first six-year plan which delineated the following general objectives:

Planned exploitation of national wealth and proper development of human energy

Increase of salaries for labor for their intellectual and moral improvement

Creation of work opportunities, fostering industrialization to promote the interchange of products between country and city[2]

This plan and its immediate successors lacked concrete, objective goals in the matter of growth, distribution, or redistribution of income. We believe that the lack of trustworthy statistical information, on the one hand, together with the absence of an integrated outlook on social development led this government to propose qualitative rather than quantitative objectives in economic matters.

The economic policy tools used, with immediate or medium term effects on the income distribution, were congruent with the outlook of an unequal, poor country. In the first place, there was a significant redirection of public expenditure. Its administrative component was reduced in relative terms, and spending for the creation of a basic economic infrastructure such as transportation and communication became increasingly important. At the same time, a special impetus was given to agricultural development, and attention was paid to social expenditure on education and public health programs.

The Cárdenas government set the following conditions for growth with economic justice: (1) the integration of the territory and its towns, (2) agricultural growth together with a better sharing of its fruits backed by an unprecedented redistribution of agrarian land, (3) improvement of human capital, and (4) the strengthening of the economic action of the government, including nationalization of petroleum.[3]

The second six-year plan, corresponding to the government of President Manuel Avila Camacho (1940–1946), was relatively more explicit in relation to the issues we are confronting. Its most outstanding objectives may be summarized as follows:

Avoiding social injustice in wealth distribution so that the working class might obtain the maximum participation compatible with a reasonable profit which would attract and maintain capital in productive enterprises

Protecting the real income of the people and increasing the salaries of the Mexican workers so as to improve their social and economic conditions

Fostering industrial development in the country[4]

This plan did not contain quantitative goals for growth or distribution, but it is worth noting its objectives in terms of the functional distribution of income.

The expenditures of this government, as well as those of its predecessor, were mainly directed to transportation, communication, and agricultural development. The social sector received relatively less emphasis in comparison to the others. In taking advantage of the situation created by World War II, industrialization was seen as a growth mechanism. Most industrial investment was left to the private sector, whose participation in the total investment of the country increased significantly during the 6-year period. The Mexican Institute of Social Security (IMSS) was established during this period, and the tax system was restructured in such a way that the share of income tax revenue in total government revenue increased.

The goal of redistribution was "achieved" in the following way: In 1940, wages, salaries, and supplements were, at factor costs, 29 percent of the domestic product, while profit income and interest reached 37 percent (the remainder was mixed income from labor, capital, and other sources); in 1946, profit income and interest rose to 42 percent, while wages and salaries fell to 25 percent.[5] Certainly the fight against social injustice was "compatible with the possibility of reasonable profits."

The regime of President Miguel Alemán (1946–1952) did not publish a plan, but there are documents which can be used to describe its major economic policy objectives.[6] In summary they were as follows:

To increase production, not as an end in itself but as the best method to raise the standard of living of the Mexican people

To employ the nation's resources to a maximum and to maintain the highest possible level of employment of both people and capital

To achieve integrated industrialization of the country

To assure that public and private investment act in a complementary fashion

No quantitative goals for growth were set, nor were there qualitative goals for distribution. Industrialization became the magic wand to solve the serious national problems, and the confidence of private enterprise in government became essential. Although during this period public investment grew faster than private investment, a good part of this investment was directed toward creating conditions to support industrialization by the private sector. By encouraging self-sufficiency and decreasing the relative price of fuel, for example, and by investing in the development of agricultural zones such as the northwest, currency, raw materials, and cheap food were generated. Simultaneously, there was a decreasing tendency in social expenditures. The Alemán period produced a further decline in the participation of salaries and wages. The 1950 figures of family income distribution (the point of reference for future discussion) show that the lowest quintile received 5.2 percent of the national income; the next, 7.6 percent; the third and fourth, 11.2 and 17.5 percent, respectively; and the top quintile, 58.5 percent.[7]

The National Investment Program was established during the administration of President Adolfo Ruiz Cortinez (1952–1958). The general objectives of this program, relevant to this study, were as follows:

To maintain economic growth at a 5.9 percent annual rate

To improve the standard of living of the population

To achieve a more coordinated and integrated economic development

To avoid deficit financing

To obtain a certain price stability[8]

For the first time, income growth became an economic policy goal, and this goal was quantified. However, there were still no quantitative objectives in relation to income distribution.

Actual public investment showed important departures from what was originally planned. First, private investment grew faster than public investment, defining the structure which was to endure until the 1970s. Second, investment in agricultural development grew much slower than programmed, initiating a loss in its relative importance that culminated at the end of the 1960s and the beginning of the 1970s.

On the other hand, transportation, communications, and energy continued to be the privileged sectors. The evident support of these sectors for industrialization based on private enterprise was again underscored. The dynamic behavior of private sector investment contributed in an unprecedented way to the growth of industrial employment.

Even though there were no significant changes in participation in functional terms, family income distribution reflected important changes; the share of the upper quintile and especially the upper decile lost importance in favor of all the other quintiles. Without having had an explicit goal in income distribution, this government achieved the only deconcentration of income that has taken place in recent decades.

Between 1959 and 1970, coinciding with the governments of presidents Adolfo López Mateos (1958–1964) and Gustavo Díaz Ordaz (1964–1970), an economic strategy called *stabilizing development* was formulated and carried out.

The economic program of President López Mateos proposed, among other things, the following general objectives:

To improve the general standard of living of the population, particularly that of farmers, laborers, and certain sectors of the middle class such as employees, artisans, small business owners, fishermen, etc.

To increase per capita income and improve its distribution

To achieve a greater integration of the country's economy

To accelerate the diversification process and stimulate regional development

To make better use of productive resources, coordinate public and private investment, increase productivity of all factors, and foster reinvestment of profits

To continue the industrialization process, particularly the production of capital goods and the development of heavy industry[9]

During this government, important efforts in the field of economic projection and planning were made that served to focus the mentioned objectives:

Achieving a sustained growth of gross domestic product at annual rates no lower than 5 percent between 1961 and 1965 and 6 percent between 1966 and 1970

Improving income distribution so as to strengthen the income and purchasing power of the majority, thereby creating a vigorous internal market

Limiting the consumption of high-income groups and making fiscal incentives more effective so as to promote investment

Maintaining price and exchange stability[10]

Again the growth goal, still an objective of the economic policy, was quantified. In the distributive field, in contrast to previous programs, emphasis seemed to be placed on personal and not functional income distribution. Besides recognizing the need to increase the standard of living of social groups with a lower relative income, it was also suggested that this was the way to broaden the market and therefore to encourage investment and stimulate national income growth.

It was suggested that instead of affecting the income of the rich, the use made of personal wealth should be altered so that luxury spending was discouraged and savings and investment fostered.

During this 6-year period, public expenditure and especially public investment in social development and training of human capital received a definite impetus. On the other hand, the relative importance of the agricultural sector continued to decline. Public investment in the industrial sector also grew, and the collaboration of the private and public sectors in the effort to industrialize the country began to take place. The government started to leave some of its traditional economic functions aside such as the creation of infrastructure in communication, transportation, and hydraulic resources, for example, to join the private sector in the production of goods and services along the path of industrialization. This was done for the purpose of creating more productive employment. Through these economic policy measures, this government tried to solve the problem of income distribution.

The government of Gustavo Díaz Ordaz (1964–1970) presented the following general objectives in its Economic and Social Development Plan:

To achieve an annual gross domestic product growth of 6.5 percent

To distribute income more equitably

To improve education, health services, housing, and social welfare

To lessen and correct regional and sectoral inequalities in development

To favor agriculture and livestock and program their accelerated development, attempting to strengthen the internal market

To improve rural living conditions and ensure the provision of food and raw materials for industry and export

To accelerate industrialization so that industry and services would be in condition to absorb the surplus rural population and the increase in the labor force

To maintain the stability of the exchange rate and fight inflationary pressures[11]

There was an explicit concern with regard to the inequity in income distribution and the existence of a surplus labor force.

The results obtained by the mid-1960s from the emphasis given to industrialization since the end of the 1940s as a way to create jobs and those obtained from the repeated commitments to redistribute income and improve the living standard of the majority of the population were obviously not those sought. During 1958–1964, the rate of job creation declined, and income had once again become increasingly concentrated. The Díaz Ordaz government insisted, in words and actions, on industrialization and training of human capital as the great solutions; it insisted in words but not in actions on the improvement of rural life. Public spending in the agricultural sector reached its lowest point proportionally in this period, and even when investments occurred, they were channeled to the modern, export-oriented agricultural sector.

A better view of the decade can be obtained from the paper "Stabilizing Development: A Decade of Economic Strategy in Mexico" by Lic. Antonio Ortíz Mena, Secretary of the Treasury under presidents López Mateos and Díaz Ordaz, in which the strategy or model of economic development followed by the Mexican government from 1959 to 1969 is evaluated and analyzed.[12] The author sets forth the major policy objectives during this period:

A high rate of growth
Stopping inflationary pressures
Increasing savings and domestic investment
Increasing real salaries
Improving the participation of workers in national income
Maintaining the exchange rate

Since the document was written in mid-1969, it was easy to prove that all the objectives mentioned in it had been fulfilled, including an increase in real salaries and in the income share of the working class. This did not mean, though, that family income was distributed more equitably or that the portion of national income earned by the lower-income groups was greater. The figures in this respect demonstrate that the lowest quintile lost almost two percentage points in its participation in national income, from 5.2 percent in 1950 to 3.4 percent in 1968; the following quintile also saw its participation reduced from 7.5 percent to 7.2 percent; the third and fourth quintiles gained, as did the ninth decile; the last decile lost six percentage points.[13] It seems to us that these results—greater participation by the workers of the modern sector of the economy together with less participation by the relatively lower-income groups—confirm that it is not through functional redistribution that the problems of the poor or underprivileged of the country are solved. Furthermore, during the decade industrial employment grew only at the rate of increase of the labor force; thus, it was impossible to absorb the "surplus rural population", as was proposed by the Social and Economic Development Plan. It is easily understandable that the lowest-income group, designated as rural, young, and barely qualified for work, did not have the opportunity to participate in the sharing of the fruits of national income growth.

Public investment, which grew in absolute and relative terms during the decade, could not meet the challenge of creating additional jobs besides those created by the private sector, in spite of the increasing focus on industrial development. This was partly due to the fact that the most dynamic public industries were located in areas with a high capital-labor ratio. On the other hand, during this decade spending on and investment in social development increased notably, but its effects on family income distribution are not observable in the short term.

Thus, at the beginning of the 1970s, President Luis Echeverría proposed the following as the main objectives of his economic policy:

Increase employment
Redistribute income
Improve the quality of living

The maximization of income growth did not appear as an end but as a means. Nor did internal macroeconomic stability and a stable exchange rate appear as goals. The economic framework was renamed *shared development,* not only denying the importance of stability but also criticizing the distributive results of the previous model and explicitly proposing its reorientation.

The economic history of this 6-year period (1970–1976) is being written and rewritten, especially with the publication of the new series of national income accounts, but it is possible to highlight the following major points:

> The country continued to grow in terms of its national product and the labor component from income grew rapidly, reaching an unprecedented level; however, unemployment and underemployment were more acute, affecting mainly the lowest quintile in the distributive scale, a group whose relative share continued to drop and which may have even suffered an absolute decrease in real income.

The participation of the federal government and public enterprises in the economy began to grow significantly, but the lack of fiscal funds, after the postponement of an attempt at structural fiscal reform, required deficit financing, which had inflationary effects. Important elements in public spending during the Echeverría administration were the transfers and subsidies to the rest of the economy, with the expected but hardly measurable effects on consumption.

Tables 2-1 and 2-2 summarize and compare the main objectives of the various programs and plans.

Finally, some observations should be made about the periods just described:

1. Accelerated growth of GDP appears as an objective during the 1953–1958 period and disappears as such during the 1971–1976 period. Before 1953 and

*TABLE 2.1.*
*Main Objectives of the Government from 1934 to 1976*

| | *1934–1940* | *1941–1946* | *1947–1962* | *1953–1958* | *1959–1970* | *1971–1976* |
|---|---|---|---|---|---|---|
| GDP growth | | | | X | X | |
| Wage growth | X | X | | | | |
| Increase of employment | X | | X | | | X |
| Income redistribution | | | | | | |
| Among workers | | X | | | X | X |
| Among social groups | | | | | X[a] | |
| Growth of sectors | | | | | | |
| Industrial | | X | X | X | X[a,b] | |
| Agricultural | | | | X | X[a,b] | |
| Regional growth | | | | X | X[a,b] | |
| Efficiency in the use of resources | X | | X | | X[a] | |
| Economic independence | X | X | | X | | X |
| Encouragement of national capital formation | | | | | X[a,b] | |
| Price stability | | | | X | X | |
| Exchange rate stability | | | | | X | |
| Improvement of standard of living | | | X | X | X[b] | X |

[a] In the economic program announced by the Banking Convention of 1959.
[b] In the social and economic development plan, 1966–1970.

since 1971 (at least until 1976), the goal of improving the standard of living of the population is preferred, and growth is used as a means for achieving this goal.

2. Although concern about the persistence of poverty is present, there is neither agreement nor consistency in goals in this respect. In several plans and models the creation of jobs and increase of wages are emphasized, in others a factor redistribution of income is proposed, and in one a redistribution of income among special groups is mentioned. Redistribution of income among families or persons does not appear as an explicit goal in any of them.
3. It was not until the 1960s that some of the objectives were quantified. In no instance is a quantification of distributive proposals attempted. In the same way it is difficult to believe that there was an authentic attempt in any of the plans or models to provide sufficient information for the effective control and management of the economy or to compare results with programmed goals.

The persistence of the problems of poverty and inequality was one of the main economic concerns of President José López Portillo. His global plan of development, 1980–1982, is quite illustrative, first, of government proposals on distribution and, second, of the conceptual and operational

## TABLE 2.2.

## *Income Redistribution Policies Used by Various Governments*

| | | *% of Public Exp.* | | *% of Public Investment* | | | | | | | |
|---|---|---|---|---|---|---|---|---|---|---|---|
| | | *Education Exp.* | *Health Exp.* | *Investment in Social Welfare* | *Investment in Education* | *Investment in Health* | *Investment in Agricultural Development* | *Tax Burden (% of GDP)* | *Relation of Nondirect to Direct Taxes* | *Number of Major Public Enterprises Created* | *Land Distribution (% of 1934–1978)* |
| 1934–1940 | Lázaro Cárdenas | 12.5 | 2.9 | 9.6 | 1.0 | 1.2 | 17.6 | 7.3 | 6–1 | 13[a] | 23.0 |
| 1940–1946 | M. Avila Camacho | 9.9 | 3.6 | 11.1 | 0.2 | 2.4 | 17.3 | 7.7 | 2.5–1 | 23[b] | 7.6 |
| 1946–1952 | Miguel Alemán | 7.8 | 3.2 | 13.5 | 3.0 | 3.1 | 19.8 | 8.1 | 2–1 | 31[c] | 6.2 |
| 1952–1958 | A. Ruiz Cortines | 8.7 | 3.1 | 14.6 | 2.6 | 1.5 | 13.6 | 8.4 | 2–1 | 23 | 6.4 |
| 1958–1964 | A. López Mateos | 11.4 | 3.6 | 24.1 | 2.7 | 7.3 | 9.9 | 8.5 | 1.33–1 | 37 | 14.7 |
| 1964–1970 | G. Díaz Ordaz | 13.2 | 3.1 | 24.7 | 4.8 | 4.9 | 11.0 | 8.8 | 1.25–1 | 23 | 18.2 |
| 1970–1976 | L. Echeverría | 19.4 | 4.5 | 22.2 | 6.6 | 4.3 | 17.3 | 12.0 | 1.25–1 | 108 | 21.6 |
| 1976–1982 | J. López Portillo | 7.7 | 1.1 | 9.5 | 2.6 | 3.1 | 18.5 | 15.3 | 1.33–1 | [d,e] | 2.3 |

SOURCE: *Cuenta Pública*, SHCP, various years.

[a]Includes Pemex, cooperatives.

[b]Includes IMSS, hospitals, Ceimsa, industrials.

[c]Includes Railroads, hospitals, industrials.

[d]President José López Portillo expropriated the private banks in September 1982.

[e]By the end of 1982, the number of public enterprises, including financial trusts but not the expropriated banks, totaled 849, of which 106 were being liquidated.

difficulties in achieving these proposals. Since the proposals contained in the plan are explicit, we shall quote extensively those sections on justice from the global plan:

> The concept of justice inserted in the Constitutional Project establishes that justice in an unequal society is only possible by setting special conditions for unequals. Thus full realization of social rights is required to achieve equality of opportunity. To obtain this goal it is not sufficient to broaden the concept of justice; transforming society is a necessary condition.
>
> The concept of justice as defined in the Constitutional Project is one of the essential characteristics of its revolutionary spirit. It combines the individual and collective aspects in its three basic concepts: *commutative justice,* which supports a proportional relationship in benefits (rights and obligations) and in the exchange relationships that take place among individuals and groups, whose enforcement is guaranteed through procedures and institutions of a judicial nature; *distributive justice,* which promotes equitable sharing of the fruits of labor; *and social justice,* which obliges the community to ensure to all individuals, without any distinction, participation in collective resources according to their needs by equalizing abilities and opportunities.
>
> From this is derived the mandate of equitable distribution of public wealth, income and social benefits. With our notion of justice, the national society, to the limit of its capabilities and resources, should grant all the ability to satisfy their needs.[14]

To fulfill the proposals of social and distributive justice, the global plan basically proposes the following: the generation of productive jobs at significantly higher rates than the demographic rate of growth and the rate of growth of the labor force: wage increases which produce increased benefits and productivity for the working class; limits on excessive profits; and sectoral, regional, and social policies tending to improve the opportunities and the abilities of the population—mainly those essential to satisfying the needs of the underprivileged.

It is significant, by their omission, that the plan nowhere establishes objectives of a quantitative nature in the income distribution pattern, whether personal or factorial, even though in more than one paragraph the observed concentration is criticized. This omission may mean one of two things:

1. That it is believed that the absolute improvement of low-income groups and the abatement of poverty is a sufficient goal, without granting any importance to relative participation or levels or
2. That it is thought that both goals will be achieved simultaneously

This is disturbing since the first point, the elimination of poverty, does not necessarily mean a redistribution of shares, nor does it necessarily lead to such a redistribution.

Perhaps in these paragraphs are the clues to what Mexican governments, at least partially, have attempted and have achieved. The results of the fight against poverty are visible; moreover, the basic methods used to reduce poverty and gradually increase the income of low-level families are known. On the other hand, the alteration of the distribution pattern in a significant way is a topic for research and debate on the frontiers of economic analysis; furthermore, the term *equitable distribution of income* itself is not susceptible to objective definitions or observable expressions.

The main tools employed by the Lopez Portillo government to obtain redistribution goals may be summarized as follows: (1) reorientation of public spending in development programs, in agriculture and livestock, and in social welfare for underprivileged [the Mexican Food System and the IMSS (COPLAMAR) Program are two good examples of this]; (2) fiscal reforms; (3) relative increase of the cost of capital, and (4) unprecedented expansion of aggregate demand based not only on oil exports but on a rise in external borrowing by the public sector to finance an explosive increase in the fiscal deficit that has resulted, at least during the short run, in an increase in the rate of job creation of the economy far beyond its historical trend. Nevertheless, if this expansion rate is not sustainable from a macroeconomic point of view, many of the achievements of this administration will be seriously reversed in the immediate future. Recent events (such as the 100 percent devaluation in the first quarter of 1982) suggest that an important part of the employment creation program of this administration was not of a "permanent" nature. Also, recent events have shown, once again, that it is not through expansionary aggregate demand policies (both of a fiscal and a monetary nature) that the problems of income redistribution are met and resolved.

## Notes

1. The topic of measurement of inequality is analyzed in detail in Chapter 3. What is said here must be taken as general and provisional information.

2. For a description, analysis, and evaluation of this six-year plan, see L. Solís, *Planes de Desarrollo Económico y Social en México* (Sep. Setentas, Secretaría de Educación Publico, 1975), pp. 11–26, 106–120.

3. Later in this chapter is a statistical table (Table 2-2) concerning the issues dealt with in this paragraph and the tools used by later governments.

4. Solís, *op. cit.*, pp. 27–51, 121–134.

5. L. Solís, *La Realidad Económica Mexicana: Retrovisión y Perspectivas* (Siglo XXI, 1970), table on p. 309.

6. See, for example, the text of the speech, of the Secretary of the Treasury and Public

Credit, Lic. Ramón Beteta, at the XVIII National Banking Convention, Secretaría de Hacienda y Crédito Público, in 1952.

7. Data of I. Martínez, La Distribución del Ingreso en México, Tendencias y Perspectivas," in *El Perfil de México en 1980* Siglo XXI, 1970).

8. L. Solís, *Planes, op. cit.* pp. 52–69, 135–141.

9. Speech of the Secretary of the Treasury, Lic. Antonio Ortíz Mena, before the XXV National Banking Convention, the Secretariat of Mortgages and Public Credit (SHCP), 1959.

10. L. Solís, *Planes, op. cit.*, pp. 70–79, 142–163.

11. *Ibid.*, pp. 80–102, 164–189.

12. Document published in *Trimestre Económico* 146 Fondo de Cultura Económico (1970).

13. See I. Martínez, *op. cit.*, and *Encuesta de Ingresos y Gastos de los Hogares: 1968,* Banco de México S.A., F.C.E., México, 1974.

14. Estados Unidos Mexicanos, Poder Ejecutivo Federal, *Plan Global de Desarrollo: 1980–1982, (México: Secretariat of Planning and National Budget. 1980). p. 24.*

## Bibliography

Martínez, I. "La Distribución del Ingreso en México, Tendencias y Perspectivas," en *El Perfil de México en 1980*. Mexico City: Siglo XXI. Editores, 1970.

Ortíz Mena, Antonio. Speech of the Secretary of the Treasury before the XXV National Banking Convention S.H.C.P., 1959.

Ortíz Mena, Antonio. "Stabilizing Development: A Decade of Economic Strategy in México." *Trimestre Económico* 146 (1970).

Solís, Leopoldo. *Planes de Desarrollo Económico y Social en México.* México: Sep. Setentas, 1975.

# CHAPTER 3

# *Toward a First Estimate of the Evolution of Inequality in Mexico*

Pedro Aspe and Javier Beristain

## Introduction

The traditional way in which economic theory has analyzed the phenomenon of income distribution has been through the so-called functional approach. The approach centers its analysis on the relative shares that the different factors of production receive of total income. In the case in which labor capital and land were the factors of production, their respective payments (wages, profits, and rents), and the share of these payments in national income, would determine the functional distribution of income. Thus it is natural that this type of analysis establishes a relationship between factor payments and the income received by the different social classes. In the words of David Ricardo, "The principal problem in Political Economy" is to determine how "the produce of the earth is divided among three classes of the community, namely, the proprietor of the land, the owner of the stock of capital necessary for its cultivation, and the labourers by whose industry it is cultivated."[1]

A different analysis of the income distribution problem is given by the so-called personal approach. In this approach, emphasis is placed on the distribution of income among persons and families, while no major importance is given to the shares of the different factors of production. In other words, the personal approach does not consider social classes as explanatory variables of the distribution of income. In most economic models based on the personal approach, economic agents (workers, landlords, and capitalists) do not have as an objective the maximization of their relative share in national income even though the share in income of a factor of production such as labor equals its wage divided by its average product.

Quoting Mark Blaug,[2] it can be said that in this approach the relative shares of the different factors in total income are ex post quantities that are the result of a series of constrained maximizations of the behavioral variables but that in no way affect directly the behavior of economic agents. In the personal approach, the emphasis in explaining the distributional phenomenon has to be based on the study of the determination of factor prices (like wages and the price of capital) and on the quantitative and qualitative distribution of different factor endowments among the population.

It is obvious that each approach used by economic theorists to analyze income distribution, although not necessarily having different premises, aims at explaining different "angles" of the distribution problem. If inequality in the distribution of income depends on the distribution of wages, on the concentration of nonhuman wealth, and on the relative importance of earned and property income, a global explanation of inequality should include, in principle, both approaches.

However, there are a number of empirical and institutional reasons that convince us to make use of the personal approach in our attempt to explain the distributive phenomenon of our country.

The direct association made by the classics between the payments to the factors of production and the social classes of the community has already been mentioned. During the times of Ricardo, and even during those of Marx, it was adequate to postulate such a link. Thus the emphasis placed on the distribution of income among workers, capitalists, and landowners was evident. However, a series of changes has taken place in the socioeconomic structure such that the unambiguous link established by the classics is no longer clearly correct. This change of structure has made the relationship between factor shares and the distribution of income among persons more complicated.[3]

A beginning point for the analysis of these changes relates to those which have taken place with respect to the ownership of capital. The Ricardian classification is based on the assumption that only the *capitalist class* owns capital. Today however, a large share of total capital belongs to the *working class,* which is composed not only of workers but also of employees. The latter is due to the fact that the working class saves for reasons related to the life cycle, that is, in order to be able to consume when old. Furthermore, it is important to point out that although a large percentage of the savings of this class is voluntary, an important part is compulsory or contractual, as in the case of the contributions to the social security system. In some modern legislation, such as the Mexican, it is even stipulated that a certain fraction of business profits must be distributed among workers.[4]

The issue of capital income becomes even more complicated when one considers institutional settings like the Mexican in which an important share of total capital and profits belongs to the government.[5] Due partly to this fact and to the fact that interest payments from the government domestic debt are counted as part of personal income, without having any counterpart in the private productive sector of the economy, it is obvious that a discrepancy between national and personal income occurs.

On the other hand, it is evident that rents are not received only by landlords. As a result of home ownership by the working class, a substantial part of the imputed rent from housing belongs to this class whether acquired through the market (as in the case of most employees and managers) or through the social security system [as in the case of the Institute of the National Housing Fund for Workers (INFONAVIT) and the Social Service and Security Institute for State Workers (ISSSTE).]

Finally, there is the conceptual and accounting problem in reference to the allocation of the income of the self-employed among factors of production. In principle, this income represents a return to several factors, and it is practically impossible to assign it correctly on the basis of the functional distribution of income.

For the previously mentioned reasons (the mixed income of the different classes and the crucial role played by the state in economic matters and social security), it is obvious that the Ricardian association between factor payments and social classes is no longer readily apparent. Although a large part of the Ricardian association has been lost due to the structural changes that have occurred in the socioeconomic system, its most dramatic manifestation takes place at the empirical level, where the conceptual problems mentioned are combined with the usual statistical problems of the national income accounts.

To make this even more obvious, we shall present a short case study for Mexico based on data on the functional and personal distribution of income from the *Encuesta de Ingresos y Gastos de los Hogares: 1977* (Household Survey on Income and Home Expenditure: 1977).

From the discussion of the functional approach, two results that have direct relevance to personal distribution of income can be deduced[6]: (1) The larger an individual's income is on the average, the smaller should be the proportion of income derived from wages and salaries; and (2) any measure that increases the labor share on the functional distribution must increase, pari passu the equality of the personal distribution of income.

In Table 3-1 and its corresponding graph, Figure 3-1, empirical information for Mexico (1977) concerning the first proposition is presented. As can be observed, the data contradict the first proposition: in general terms, as the average income grows, the share of labor earnings becomes larger, not smaller. In fact, the evolution of labor earnings from total income is particularly contradictory to the first proposition up to the seventh decile due to the quantitative importance of the number of "capitalists" or "businessmen" with relatively low incomes. Note, for instance, that 63 percent of the families located in the first decile declared themselves to be at least partially "capitalists" by reporting income from business dividends, while only 39.8 percent did so with respect to wages and salaries. Paradoxically, in the higher-income decile, only 34.8 percent

*TABLE 3.1.*
*Share of Monetary Income by Sources (Percentages)*

| *Decile* | *Monetary Current Income* | *Earnings from Labor* | *Business Dividends* | *Property Rent* | *Other Income* | *Transfer Payments* |
|---|---|---|---|---|---|---|
| I | 100.0 | 37.2 | 49.7 | 0.4 | 1.3 | 11.3 |
| II | 100.0 | 49.5 | 40.0 | 0.2 | 0.4 | 9.8 |
| III | 100.0 | 57.8 | 34.1 | 0.3 | 0.2 | 7.6 |
| IV | 100.0 | 61.4 | 30.3 | 0.1 | 0.2 | 8.0 |
| V | 100.0 | 67.3 | 24.3 | 0.2 | 0.3 | 7.9 |
| VI | 100.0 | 77.7 | 17.8 | 0.3 | 0.4 | 3.8 |
| VII | 100.0 | 74.4 | 20.2 | 0.1 | 0.3 | 5.0 |
| VIII | 100.0 | 73.2 | 21.3 | 0.1 | 0.5 | 4.8 |
| IX | 100.0 | 75.1 | 18.9 | 0.5 | 0.5 | 5.1 |
| X | 100.0 | 68.4 | 22.0 | 2.2 | 2.6 | 4.8 |

SOURCE: *Encuesta de Ingresos y Gastos de los Hogares: 1977,* Secretariat of Planning and the National Budget, Federal District of Mexico, 1977.

of the families declared that they had received some type of business income, while 85.7 percent declared that they had received labor income.

It is important to observe the evolution of the so-called business dividends in Figure 3-1. From a maximum income share of 49.7 percent for the poorest household decile, it decreases as the level of income grows until reaching a minimum of 17.8 percent on the sixth decile. Note that for the higher-income deciles, this share is relatively "stable." This behavior is in accordance with the one described dealing with the evolution of labor earnings in the higher deciles.

There are different facts that explain these apparently paradoxical results: the 1977 survey states that among the country's total households, 43.1 percent had some type of business income (besides other income), so that according to conventional definitions, this high percentage of households could be considered at least partially capitalist. To illustrate how exaggerated this figure is, we shall concentrate on its implications concerning the lowest-decile households. For these, the survey reports average earnings and business income of 2,276.0 and 1,943.0 pesos, respectively for the half year. A simplistic interpretation of the data would imply that for that income bracket, capitalist income was smaller than labor income.

However, what the data really show is that there is a group of households and persons traditionally included in the definition of entrepreneurs whose per capita income and whose economic behavior must, in fact, be similar to that of the working class. Consequently, "independent" activities such as self-employment in agriculture should not be included as business activities but should be considered some form of paid labor. There are different forms of adjusting business dividends and mixed income data in order to get a more comprehensible economic meaning.[7] Nevertheless, and as should be obvious to the reader, all these adjustments are, because of their construction, arbitrary.[8]

**Figure 3-1. Percentage of Income by Source.**

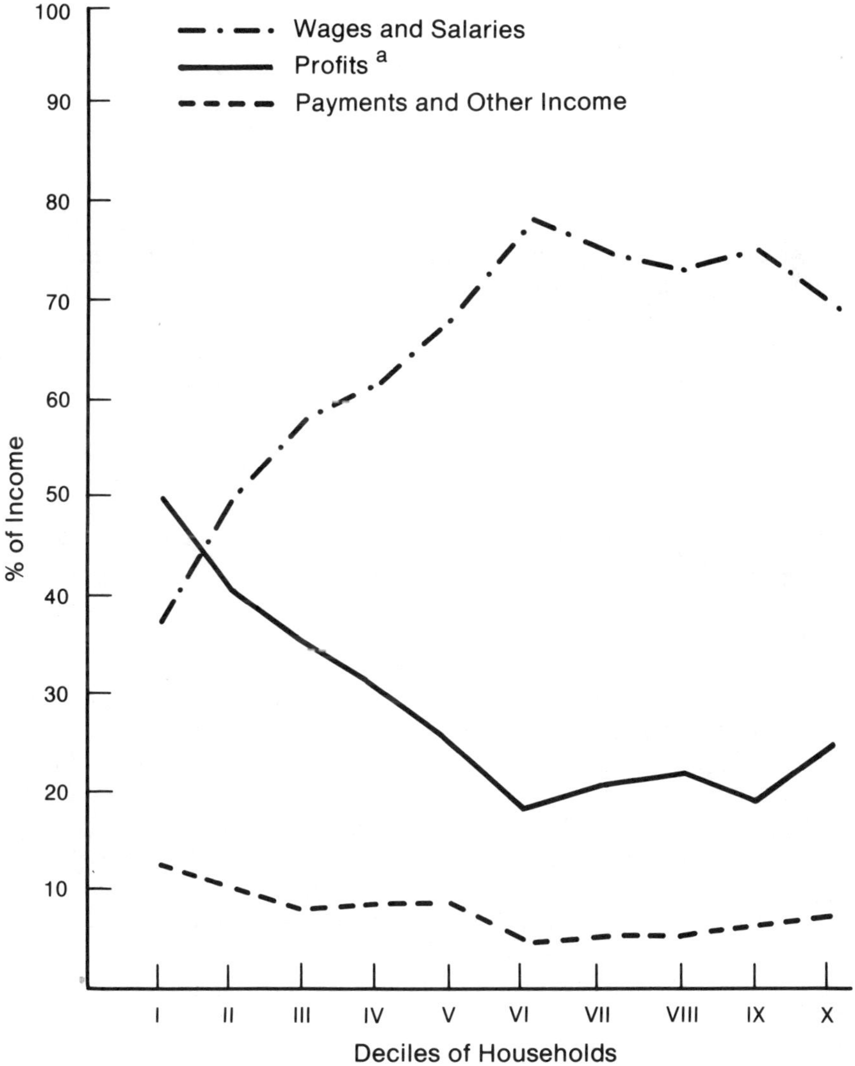


[a] Includes Property Income

SOURCE: Data from Table 3-1.

Concerning the second proposition derived from the functional theory, "that a larger share of labor income should result in a more equitable personal income distribution," it can be said that it will be true only under very special circumstances. First, for this proposition to be true, all other variables must be held constant. It would be especially necessary that the amount of income to be distributed remain constant. Moreover, the proposition is true only under the assumption that labor is a homogeneous factor so that the same wage rate is paid to every worker. In the more general case in which labor of several degrees of qualification exists, the proposition is not necessarily true. For example, in the case that a redistribution in income proceeds from a rise in the income share of the more skilled labor at the expense of the income share of business dividends, it cannot be said, a priori, whether the personal income distribution improved, worsened, or remained constant.

The preceding discussion points toward one of the causes of the unequal income distribution in Mexico: the unequal income share received by the different kinds of labor, a fact that originates in the differences in abilities, training, and skills within the factor. For example, the figures for the country in 1977 show that the average per capita income of the labor force was more than thirty-five times larger between the individuals located in the first decile than those located in the last one.

## The Measurement of Income Distribution Inequality in Mexico

### *Implications of the Meaning of Inequality*

The meaning of inequality that we have adopted in this chapter distinguishes between two types of inequalities: those that are considered *just* because they are derived from human individual characteristics or because they favor the least advantaged and those that are considered *unjust* because they imply the existence of different opportunities among equals.[9] In this section we should point out some of the relevant features that constitute those inequalities considered just, so that once we have identified and analyzed them, we can proceed to separate them in our attempt to measure unjust inequalities.

We acknowledge that individuals differ in tastes, preferences, and degree of risk aversion, which implies that while facing the same type of opportunities, their decisions vary. For instance, two persons facing the same opportunities over their life cycle can make different decisions concerning the fraction of income they want to save: one may decide on maintaining the same pattern of consumption throughout his or her life cycle, while the other, based on personal preferences, may decide on consuming more while young. This distinction leads us again to recognize that the distribution of opportunities during a given period of time is a function, among other factors, of the observed age differentials among the population.

It can be said, again due to life-cycle behavior, that an individual of older age has had more opportunities to save than an individual who has just entered the labor force. Hence, at a given moment of time, the distribution of opportunities among these individuals, while enormous, is not necessarily unjust, since it is still possible that both will face the same opportunities over their life cycles.

The impossibility of making comparisons between the opportunities that households of different sizes face should also be acknowledged. For instance, it is obvious that an adequate aggregate level of consumption for a family of three may be insufficient for a larger family. Hence, the degree of inequality depends on individual needs and not on what could be judged as sufficient for an imaginary average family.

Summing up, we will try to consider factors such as age and number of household members in order to isolate these facts, so we can measure insofar as possible the actual degree of unjust inequality that exists.

An additional problem which will be treated in this section concerns the fundamental difference between the ex ante opportunities that people face and their ex post level of welfare. To the extent that the data used in quantifying the degree of inequality derive from ex post results, the random factors derived from chance will limit the opportunity of obtaining a unique link with the ex ante inequality of opportunities.

Finally, we want to point out from the beginning that despite the fact that from the point of view of individual welfare we have been referring to the inequality of opportunities, we shall consider the distribution of income as a *proxy* indicator of the distribution of opportunities and of individual welfare levels. This is done following a standard assumption made in economic theory. Precisely because of our previous discussion on taste differences and the effects of the life cycle, parallels between opportunity levels and current monetary income are not valid. However, in support of our simplifying assumption, we shall first try to isolate the effects of factors such as age and household size in accordance with the life-cycle and permanent income theories. This will be complemented by other chapters in this volume which will analyze and estimate the endowments and quality of the individual's human and nonhuman wealth and analyze the relative importance of factors that condition their opportunities to attain different levels of welfare.

### *The Trend in Inequality Based on Current Income*

To examine the concepts in our previous discussion we shall use information on the level and distribution of current income as an indicator of economic welfare. Specifically, we shall use information on income from the household budget surveys of 1963, 1968, and 1977. In these surveys, the current income of a household for a given period is defined as the sum of "normal" monetary income plus transfers in kind and money, plus

*TABLE 3.2.*
*Income Distribution among Households*

| | *Percentage Share in Total Income* | | | | | | | | | |
|---|---|---|---|---|---|---|---|---|---|---|
| *Year* | *Decile* I | *Decile* II | *Decile* III | *Decile* IV | *Decile* V | *Decile* VI | *Decile* VII | *Decile* VIII | *Decile* IX | *Decile* X |
| 1963 | 1.3 | 2.2 | 3.1 | 3.7 | 4.9 | 6.1 | 8.0 | 11.8 | 17.0 | 41.9 |
| 1968 | 1.2 | 2.2 | 3.1 | 4.1 | 5.1 | 6.5 | 8.3 | 11.3 | 16.2 | 42.0 |
| 1977 | 0.9 | 2.0 | 3.1 | 4.3 | 5.8 | 7.4 | 9.5 | 12.5 | 17.8 | 36.7 |

SOURCE: *Encuesta de Ingresos y Gastos de los Hogares: 1977,* Secretariat of Planning and the National Budget, Federal District of Mexico, 1977. *Encuesta de Ingresos y Gastos de los Hogares: 1968,* Banco de México, S.A., Fondo de Cultura Económica, Federal District of Mexico, 1974. *Encuesta de Ingresos y Gastos de los Hogares: 1963,* Banco de México, S.A., Federal District of Mexico, 1966.

imputed rent from home ownership, plus capital income obtained during the period.[10]

Table 3-2 shows the figures on income shares among different household groups, arranged according to reported income levels.

As can be observed, the share of the lowest income decile declined from 1.3 percent in 1963 to 1.2 percent in 1968 and 0.9 percent in 1977. At the same time, the share of the highest-income group (decile X) changed from 41.9 percent in 1963 to 42.0 percent in 1968 and 36.7 percent in 1977. Finally, it is worth noting that the joint share of the 30 percent of households included in deciles VII, VIII, and IX was 36.8 percent in 1963 and 35.8 and 39.8 percent in 1968 and 1977, respectively.

Nevertheless, there are several reasons for not considering the data presented in Table 3-2 as definitive. In the first place, there are the usual statistical problems that affect this type of survey. Specifically, we should point out the likelihood of underreporting in income figures of the lower-income households. This probability, which arises from the fact that reported figures of expenditure for households of the lower deciles are consistently larger than their reported income, has made many researchers *adjust* the figures related to this variable.[11] However, it should be obvious that any effort to close the gap between reported income and expenditure is arbitrary.[12]

Apart from the statistical problem concerning these figures, it is difficult to interpret them, since at least for those households who report current dissaving, it can be said that they violate the standard economic definition of income.[13]

An additional problem concerning the figures in Table 3-2 is that they are biased indicators of the evolution of income distribution, because changes in variables such as age and family composition which affect such distribution are not taken into account.

With those problems in mind, we face two alternatives. The first is to adjust the reported income figures of the surveys making use of life-cycle theory so that we can obtain a more realistic picture of the evolution of the distribution. The second consists in designing a new indicator of the inequality trend.

Due to the statistical problems previously mentioned, we have decided first to make some adjustments in the reported income figures, so that once we know how far we can get in our analysis using these estimates we may proceed to obtain alternative indicators. As already stated, the information shown in Table 3-2 provides us with a first approximation of the evolution of the inequality trend in Mexico.

Another way of presenting such figures is by making use of the so-called Lorenz curve. The Lorenz curve of a given income distribution is the line that links the points relating the cumulative percentage of households and their cumulative percentage of income. The curve is a useful indicator of the inequality of a given distribution because those curves closer to the diagonal represent distributions with a lower degree of inequality.[14] In the extreme case of inequality (one household or one person receives all the income), the Lorenz curve would follow the horizontal axis until reaching the last household and would rise vertically because the last household would receive 100 percent of income.

Figure 3-2 shows the Lorenz curve of the distribution of reported income for 1977.

As can be observed from Figure 3-2, the Lorenz curve of the 1977 distribution is below the diagonal, indicating the presence of inequality. In fact, the ratio of the area lying between the Lorenz curve and the diagonal and the area below the diagonal represents a common indicator of the degree of inequality known as the Gini coefficient. The Gini coefficient can vary from a minimum value of zero, as in the case of perfect equality, to a maximum value of 1, as in the case of extreme inequality.

It should be obvious that a larger Gini coefficient would indicate the existence of greater inequality. An alternative way of interpreting the Gini coefficient is the following: imagine that we choose at random two households of the distribution and that we express the difference between their incomes as a proportion of the average income of households; then on average the expected value of this variable would be twice the Gini coefficient. For instance, if in analyzing a certain distribution we obtain a Gini coefficient equal to 0.45, it will mean that on the average, the value of the difference of income of two households chosen at random would equal 90 percent of the average income. The measurement of the Gini coefficient for 1977 gives a value equal to 0.50.

Figure 3-3 compares the Lorenz curves for 1963, 1968, and 1977.

To interpret Figure 3-3, some additional explanation is required. First, it should be noted that the reported Gini coefficients change from a value of 0.53 for 1963 to 0.50 in 1968 and 0.50 in 1977.[15] This result would seem to indicate, at first sight, that the distribution of income in Mexico has remained basically constant in the last decades. However, such an inference is *not* valid. To understand why it is impossible to make any judgment about the trend of inequality from the reported Gini coefficient, we have to go back to Figure 3-3 where we see that the different Lorenz curves intersect. When a Lorenz curve rotates counterclockwise like those in the figure, we observe that, although the areas between the curves and the diagonal do not change much and hence the Gini coefficients remain basically stable, there have been important changes in the distribution of income among the different groups of households. For instance, if we divide the population into groups of low, middle, and high income, we can observe that the relative share of the low- and high-income groups of households has been decreasing at the expense of the growth in the share of the middle-income households.

In this way, the share of income of the group of households from the first three deciles declined from 6.6 percent in 1963 to 6.5 percent in 1968 and 6.0 percent in 1977. At the same time, the share of income of the households in the tenth decile corresponding to the highest income level

**Figure 3-2. Lorenz Curve for 1977 (Reported Income).**

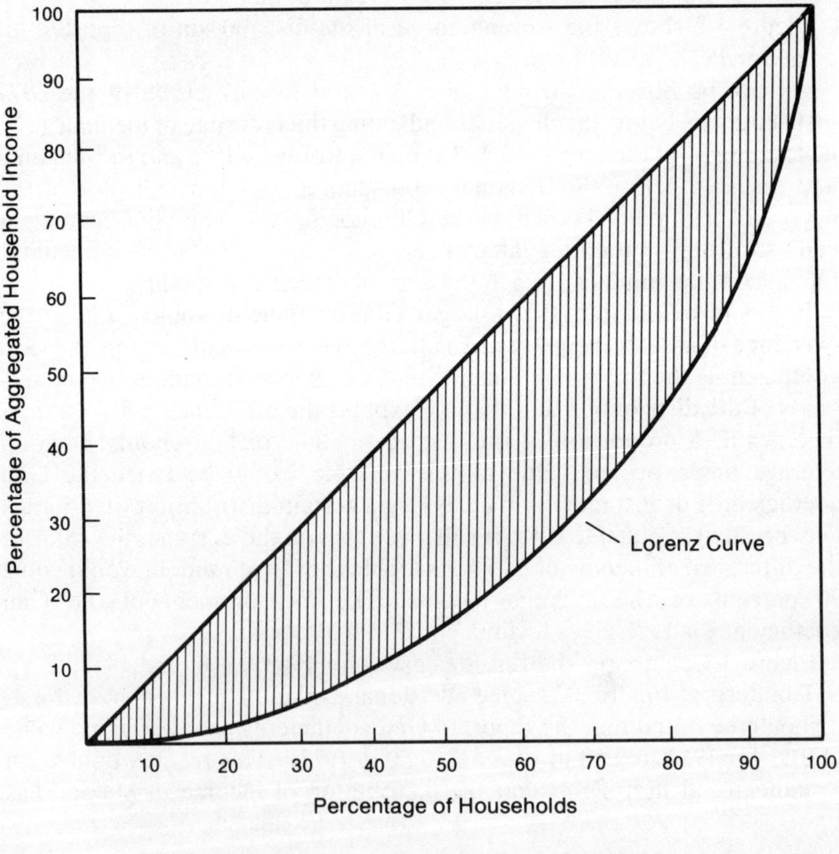

changed from 41.9 percent in 1963 to 42.0 and 36.7 percent in 1968 and 1977, respectively. In contrast, the group of households located between the fourth and the ninth deciles increased their share from 51.5 percent in 1963 and 1968 to 57.3 percent in 1977.

The relation between the existence of major changes in the distribution of income among different groups of households and "stable" Gini coefficients is a useful reminder that although this coefficient appears to be a purely mechanical indicator of the degree of inequality, it in fact implicitly contains some value judgments in reference to the weights it attaches to the existent inequality along the different points on the income scale.[16] It is also an important reminder that if we are interested in obtaining an indicator of the welfare of the community, the measurement of the degree of inequality cannot be obtained without the introduction of value judgments.

Only in those cases where the Lorenz curves do not intersect is it possible to postulate that the distribution whose Lorenz curve lies farther

**Figure 3-3. Lorenz Curve (Deciles of Reported Income).**

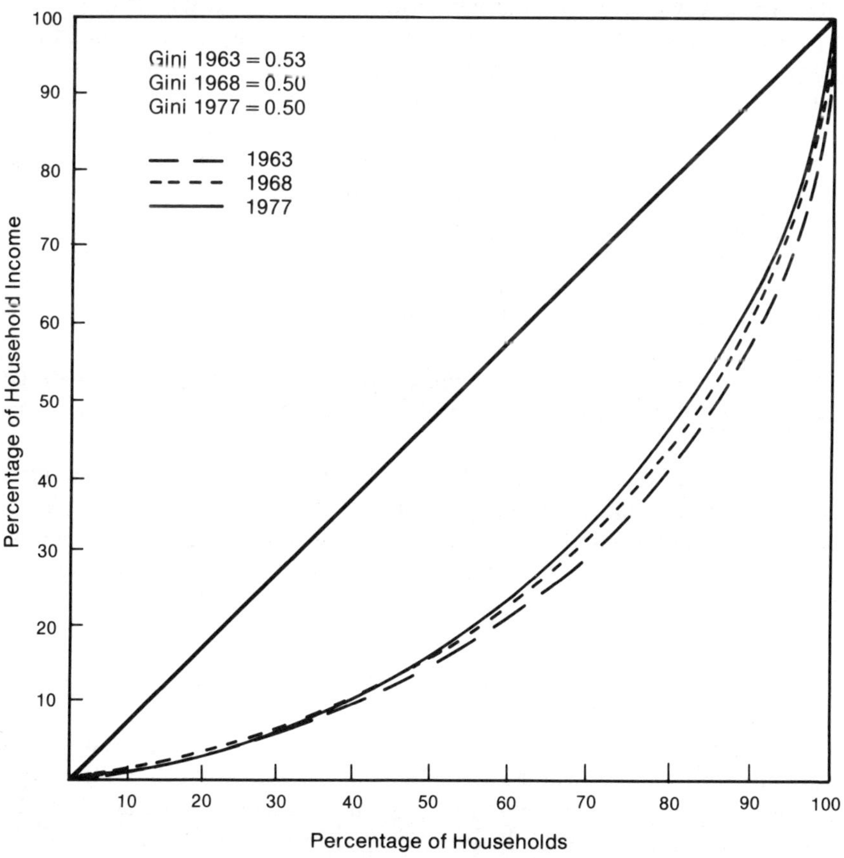

from the diagonal is more unequal than one whose curve is nearer the line of perfect equality. In the cases where the Lorenz curves intersect, the Gini coefficient cannot rank the different distributions correctly, and its values are not valid indicators of the evolution of inequality.

From our previous discussion, an obvious question concerning the Mexican experience is raised: starting with the known fact that the middle class has been obtaining a larger share of income at the expense of households with low and high income, are we able to make any statement about the evolution of income distribution in Mexico in recent decades? The answer to this question depends on the normative assumptions that we are prepared to formulate. This result should not be surprising given that the problem we face concerns the comparison of levels of welfare and utility among different groups of society.

In view of the fact that on the one hand traditional statistical indicators implicitly assume certain value judgments and on the other the Lorenz curves of the relevant distributions for Mexico intersect each other, a possible solution would be to consider these value judgments explicitly. One way to do so is to adopt the proposal of A. B. Atkinson[17] that postulates a social welfare function which depends on a parameter *(E)* which represents the weight that society attaches to inequality. The value of this parameter ranges from zero, which means that society is totally indifferent with respect to the degree of inequality, to infinity, which means that the only concern of society is the relative position of the lowest-income group. In other words, the value of the coefficient *(E)* represents the degree of aversion that a society has toward inequality.

The specific measure of inequality *(I)* proposed by Atkinson is

$$I = 1 - \left[ \sum_i \left( \frac{Yi}{\mu} \right)^{1-E} f(Yi) \right]^{\frac{1}{1-E}} \tag{1}$$

where $E \geq 0$ and $f(Yi)$ is the frequency function of income, $\mu$ is average income, and $E$ denotes the degree of aversion of society toward inequality.

Another way of interpreting the $E$ value from the social welfare function is the following: If the same social weight is assigned to a marginal peso ($1.00) in the hands of a given person or household with an income equal to $Y$, as $X$ pesos is to a person or household with an income equal to $\lambda Y$, then

$$X = \lambda^E \tag{2}$$

For instance, in the case where $E = 0.5$, one peso extracted from a person with an income equal to twice the average would have the same social value as giving 50 cents to a person with half the average income. For $E = 1.0$, the corresponding figure would be only 25 cents.

*TABLE 3.3.*
*Atkinson's Coefficients for Income Distribution in Mexico*

| E | *1963* | *1968* | *1977* |
|---|---|---|---|
| 0.5 | 0.22 | 0.22 | 0.20 |
| 1.0 | 0.41 | 0.40 | 0.40 |
| 1.5 | 0.51 | 0.51 | 0.53 |
| 2.0 | 0.60 | 0.60 | 0.64 |
| 3.0 | 0.70 | 0.71 | 0.76 |
| 5.0 | 0.78 | 0.79 | 0.85 |

The measure of inequality proposed by Atkinson was estimated for Mexico. Table 3-3 shows the results for different values of society's aversion toward inequality.

From Table 3-3 two important results can be obtained: first, for small values in the degree of aversion toward inequality, Atkinson's measure remains basically stable, while for a larger degree of aversion, the evolution of income distribution in the country shows a slight increase in inequality.[18]

A second result, according to the figures reported in Table 3-3, is that the potential benefits of an income redistribution in Mexico are enormous. For instance, for the year 1977 and taking a value of 1.5 for the aversion of society toward inequality, Atkinson's measure would point out the possibility of attaining with perfect distribution the same level of social welfare actually attained with only $1.00 - 0.53 = 47$ percent of that year's national income. Alternatively, the potential benefits of a redistributive policy designed to attain perfect equality would be equivalent to raising the total income of the population by 53 percent. In other words, in 1977, national income could have been half what it was, but an equitable distribution would have provided the same level of social welfare that the country actually reached with a higher but unequally distributed national income. The arbitrariness of the last example should be noted. If a value of 0.5 instead of one of 1.5 in the degree of aversion toward inequality would have been chosen, then the redistribution possibilities would not have been as large as they were in the last exercise. The *redistribution possibilities* fundamentally depend on the chosen degree of inequality, which in turn depends on a value judgment.

Until now we have tried to give a preliminary approximation of the country's inequality trend by using the reported figures of household income. With that same raw data, we shall now proceed to modify the methodology used so far in order to take into account the difference between the inequality of the income of households and that of persons to then make some adjustments based on the life-cycle theory.

The flow of income received by an individual should be judged against his or her needs, which depend, among other factors, on family size. In

**Figure 3-4. Lorenz Curve (Income per Capita).**

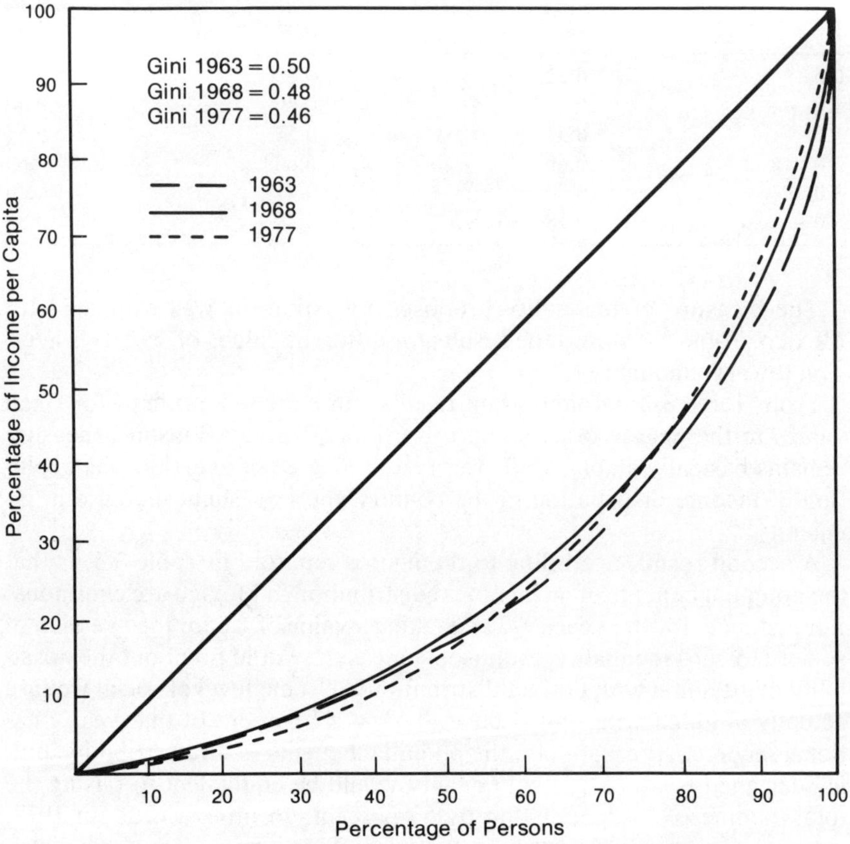


this sense, an income viewed as sufficient for a three-member household would be completely inadequate for an eight-member family. Following this distinction, the per capita income of a household was obtained to determine whether this adjustment modifies our previous results. In general, data from the household surveys show that low-income households are, on the average, smaller in size, so that a ranking based on their per capita income differs from that based on their income.

In Figure 3-4 the corresponding Lorenz curves and the respective Gini coefficients for per capita income are reported.

Two conclusions can be drawn from Figure 3-4. First, the intersection of the Lorenz curves, derived from the continuing redistributive changes that have taken place among different groups of persons, is confirmed. Second, it is clear that each of these curves is closer to the diagonal than those based on household income (see Figures 3-3 and 3-4). We can confirm this by looking at the different values of the Gini coefficient. For instance, the 1977 Gini coefficient for per capita income was 0.46, while that for the household income was 0.50. This means that the use of the Gini coefficient based on household income exaggerated the degree of inequality for that period by 8.6 percent.

As noted earlier, it is evident that we cannot make any statement about the evolution of inequality by comparing the different Gini coefficients. Thus, we proceed to estimate Atkinson's measure of inequality to find out whether for the chosen values of aversion toward inequality the redistributive possibilities are greater or less.

The figures in Table 3-4 confirm our previous results: for small values of *E*, inequality has remained basically constant.

Another important adjustment that needs to be made is to explicitly introduce into the analysis the age differentials of the population. An interesting proposal regarding this issue is the one recently made by M. Paglin.[19] For him, the greatest problem in using the Lorenz curve and the Gini coefficient to measure inequality lies in the implication of the so-called perfect equality line. Assuming no economic growth for the moment, the constancy of the Lorenzian equality requires on one hand that life-cycle income of different households be equal and on the other that the average age of households also be alike.

In other words, the line of perfect equality implicitly assumes that a young family with young children has to have the same income as that of an older one which is near the age of retirement. These conditions concerning the equality of life-cycle income and the same age structure of households are implicit in the 45° line, because along that line all households with different ages ought to have the same current income in the period analyzed. This in turn can be true only if we are prepared to assume that the behavior of a household in respect to consumption is independent of its average age and of its relative position over the life cycle. In other words, the line of equality implicitly assumes that households show a *horizontal* behavior with respect to the relationship between income and age over the life cycle. But is this true?

The data for the Mexican case on this matter, based on the 1968 and

*TABLE 3.4.*

*Atkinson's Coefficients for Per Capita Income Distribution*

| E | *1963* | *1968* | *1977* |
|---|---|---|---|
| 0.5 | 0.20 | 0.16 | 0.17 |
| 1.0 | 0.36 | 0.32 | 0.33 |
| 1.5 | 0.45 | 0.42 | 0.44 |
| 2.0 | 0.53 | 0.50 | 0.54 |
| 3.0 | 0.62 | 0.62 | 0.67 |
| 5.0 | 0.70 | 0.73 | 0.78 |

**Figure 3-5. Age-Income Profiles**

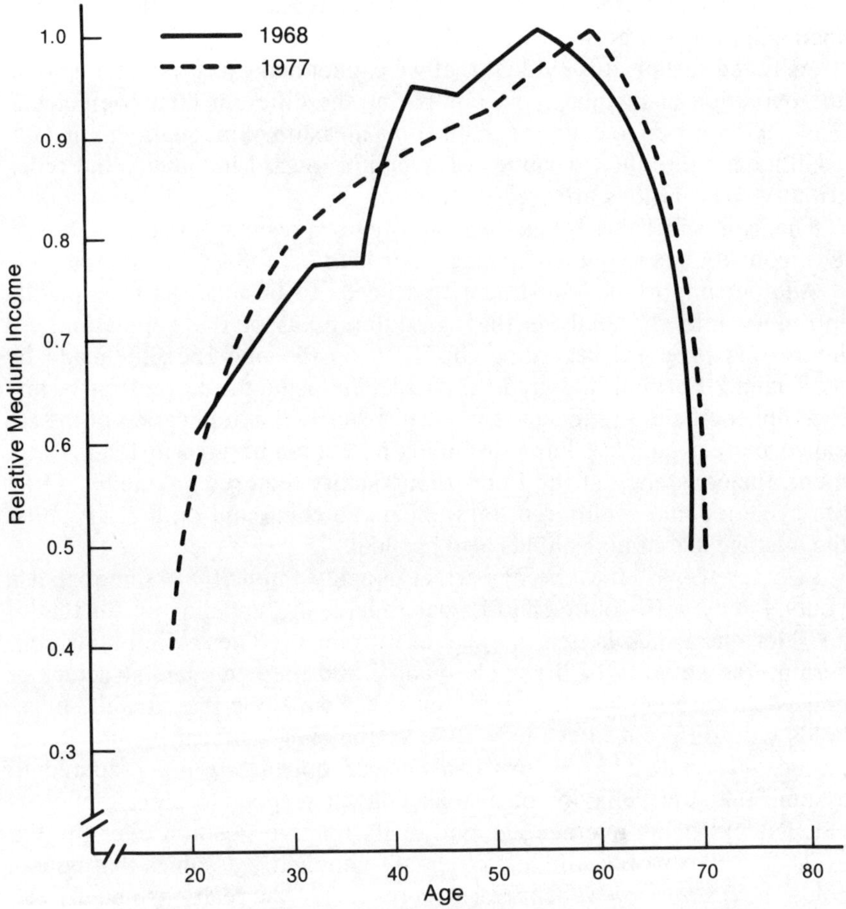


SOURCE: *National Survey on Income and Home Expenditure (Mexico City: S.P.P., 1977). National Survey on Income and Household Expenditure (Mexico City: Bank of Mexico, 1974).*

1977 household budget surveys, is shown in Figure 3-5. As can be seen, the income age structure for households [20] takes the form of an inverted "U," in accordance with the life-cycle theory.

In light of this, Paglin's line of equality requires only that life-cycle incomes be the same, without making the additional assumption, implicit in the 45° line of equality, that the age-income relationship be independent of time.

Based on the above-mentioned methodology, we proceeded to estimate the adjusted line of equality to find Paglin's curve. To this end, we grouped all households by age of head of household and ranked them by their average income. The data show that based on this ranking, and in accordance with the life-cycle theory, the households with the smallest incomes were those whose heads were younger than 20 years of age, followed by those whose heads exceeded 65. With regard to the ranking of households by their income, for which the ages of their heads fell between 20 and 65 years, we obtained a positive correlation between age and income up to the age of 55, when maximum income is attained, for the 1977 distribution.[21]

In Figure 3-6 the Lorenz and Paglin curves for 1968 and 1977 are shown.[22]

From the previous estimation the following results are obtained: the Gini coefficients adjusted by Paglin's method were equal to 0.43 for 1968 and 0.41 for 1977. Hence we observe that the estimation of inequality based on the uncorrected Gini coefficients overestimates the degree of inequality of 16.2 and 20.0 percent for 1968 and 1977, respectively. If we add this correction to those obtained from the estimation based on per capita terms, we may conclude that the uncorrected Gini cofficients based

**Figure 3-6. Lorenz and Paglin's Curves of Income.**

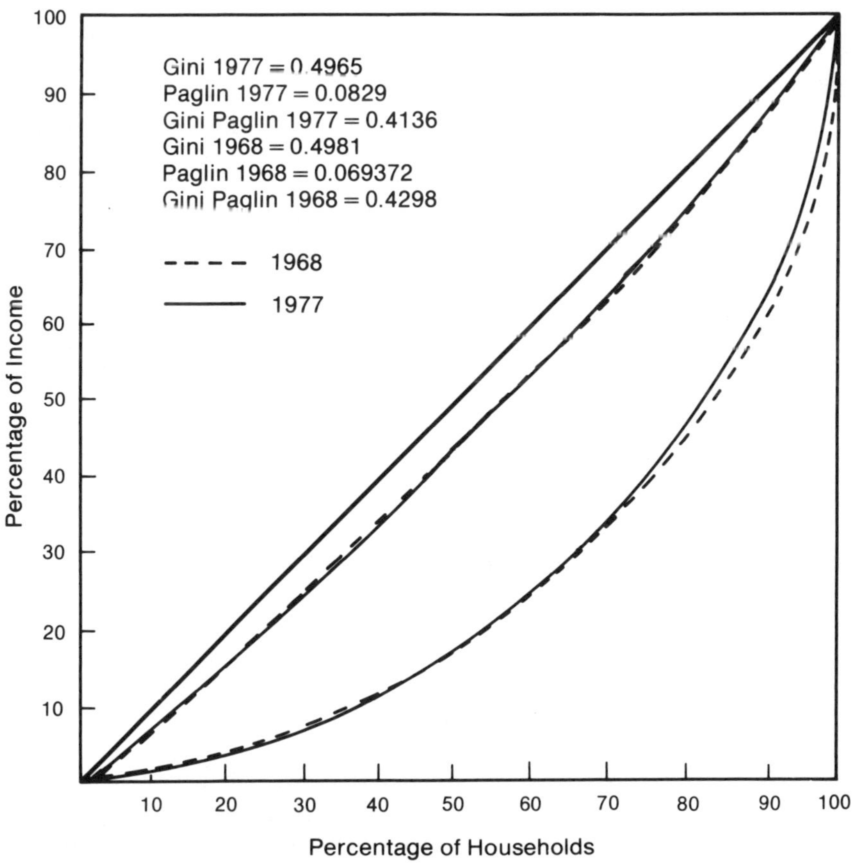

**Figure 3-7.**

**Share of Income of 40 Percent of Lower-Income Households.**

**1970**

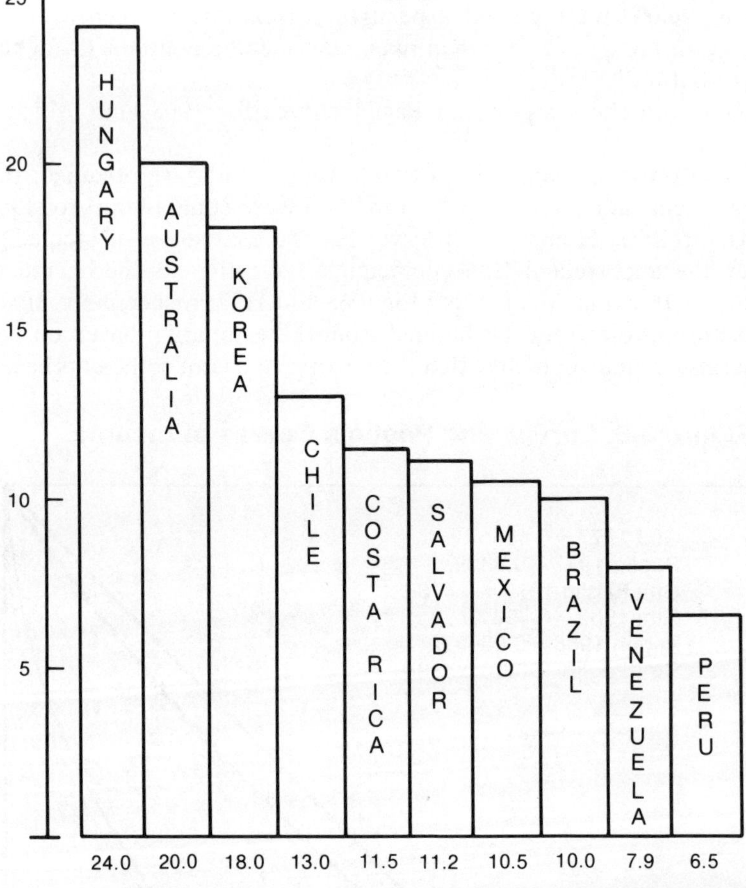


on household incomes overestimated the degree of inequality for 1968 and 1977 by 22.7 and 32.6 percent, respectively. However, note that the previous changes do not modify the basic result. Due to the fact that the Lorenz curves continue to intersect, it is not valid to make any judgment about the evolution of inequality. Up to this point, the only thing we can say about this trend is that, in lieu of the estimation of Atkinson's measure, the trend of inequality has remained basically constant or it has even increased slightly and that the potential gains from a redistributive policy in the Mexican economy are large.

Two additional comparisons are worthwhile: one that relates to the income inequality in the country's rural and urban areas and another which compares the degree of inequality in Mexico with that of other countries. To abbreviate this section we report only the most salient findings concerning the regional distribution of income. It can be said that the degree of inequality in rural areas was similar to that of the urban areas during 1977. The simple Gini coefficient estimated for the rural areas for that year was 0.48, and the one for the urban areas was 0.47. In Figure 3-7 some international comparisons are made regarding the share of income of the 40 percent households of lower income [23] for different countries.

As Figure 3-7 shows the share of the poorest households in Mexico is not only below those of the industrialized countries but also below some of the less developed countries (LDCs) such as Korea, Chile, Costa Rica, and El Salvador.

Finally, it is interesting to compare the potential benefits of redistribution of Atkinson for different countries. Since we had only international information for 1962, we show data for 1963 and 1977 for Mexico (see Table 3-5). The results confirm our previous findings about the relative inequality that exists in Mexico.

### *An Alternative Indicator of Inequality*

In the preceding section we presented some general results of the evolution of inequality in Mexico using as basic data the information on reported household current income. However, as was made clear to the readers, the data had serious statistical problems. Specifically, we faced the problem that the reported current income for some household groups was smaller than the reported expenditure. This violated the standard definition of income and signaled the probable existence of underreporting. An additional problem faced was that of taking information on current income as an indicator of economic welfare instead of taking life-cycle income. Although the information was corrected making use of Paglin's approach, we observed that such a correction was only valid if the reported data had no major statistical problems.

Given the conceptual and statistical problems mentioned, this section presents an alternative indicator that will correct some of the previous

*TABLE 3.5.*
*International Comparison of Atkinson's Coefficient of Inequality*

| | *United Kingdom* | *Germany* | *Mexico* | |
|---|---|---|---|---|
| *E Value* | *1962* | *1962* | *1963* | *1977* |
| 0.5 | 0.12 | 0.17 | 0.22 | 0.20 |
| 1.0 | 0.24 | 0.29 | 0.41 | 0.40 |
| 1.5 | 0.34 | 0.38 | 0.51 | 0.53 |
| 2.0 | 0.43 | 0.45 | 0.60 | 0.64 |

SOURCE: A. B. Atkinson, *The Economics of Inequality,* (London: Oxford University Press, 1978).

problems but will, in turn, introduce new ones. We specifically refer to the use of figures on reported household and per capita expenditure as an indicator of welfare. The level of economic welfare of a household or an individual is attained through the access that they have to economic resources. This access can have different dimensions such as income, expenditure, or wealth.[24]

The income of households and persons in a given period is derived from different sources such as wages and salaries, income from property of real and financial assets, government transfer payments, and capital transfer payments as in the case of bequests. From the uses that a household or a person can give to such income, we can distinguish among the payment of taxes, expenditure for personal consumption, the use of capital transfers, and savings aimed at raising the level of wealth.

If we ignore for a moment the possibility of capital transfer payments, we conclude that a person's net income after taxes can be directed either to consumption or to savings. If an individual saves, which means postponing his or her consumption, the intertemporal benefits he or she will gain will turn into the possibility of having a higher level of consumption in the future, which means that in fact net savings over the life cycle would be equal to zero. In this sense, a natural measure of the degree of access that a person or a household has toward economic resources is his or her level of expenditure, since it represents the acquisition of goods and services that directly provided utility.

An obvious question that arises from the preceding discussion refers to the type of income that a person uses to make decisions concerning the level of his or her current expenditure. The modern economic theories of consumption point out that current consumption not only depends on current income but on the expectation of life-cycle income or permanent income. In this sense, in considering information about current consumption of households and persons, we shall be using de facto an indicator of expected lifelong income or permanent income.[25]

Although the use of reported expenditure may solve some of our conceptual and statistical problems such as those concerning a correct reference period for income and the underreporting of current income, it is important to point out that we shall face the problem of not having considered the existence of capital transfer payments. For instance, if such transfer payments are not considered, problems may arise such as that of a millionaire who lives a life of poverty. From the viewpoint of expenditure, this person will appear "poor," while from the viewpoint of his or her current and permanent income, he or she will appear "rich."

With this problem in mind, the figures on shares of different deciles of households in total expenditure are shown in Table 3-6.[26]

As may be observed in Table 3-6, the share of households of lowest expenditure (decile I) declined from 1.5 percent in 1968 to 1.2 percent in 1977. On the other hand, the share of households of the highest expendi-

*TABLE 3.6.*
*Percentage Shares of Expenditure of Households*

| Year | Decile I | Decile II | Decile III | Decile IV | Decile V | Decile VI | Decile VII | Decile VIII | Decile IX | Decile X |
|---|---|---|---|---|---|---|---|---|---|---|
| 1968 | 1.5 | 2.6 | 3.4 | 4.3 | 5.7 | 7.1 | 9.1 | 11.7 | 16.6 | 38.0 |
| 1977 | 1.2 | 2.3 | 3.4 | 4.5 | 6.0 | 7.6 | 10.0 | 12.6 | 17.2 | 35.2 |

SOURCE: Same as Table 3.2.

ture level (decile X) also declined from 38.0 percent in 1968 to 35.2 percent in 1977. Obviously, the shares of the intermediate deciles (IV–IX) grew through those years. This change in shares means that the Lorenz curves of the 1968 and 1977 distributions intersect.

In Figure 3-8 we show the Lorenz curves for 1968 and 1977 along with the one for the 1963 distribution which was plotted from the reported shares of different brackets (instead of deciles) of expenditure.

From Figure 3-8 we can obtain two important results concerning the evolution of inequality in the country: first, we should note that no intersections between the Lorenz curve of expenditure for 1963 and the corresponding ones for 1968 and 1977 occur. Second, the Lorenz curve for 1963 lies unambiguously closer to the equality line than those of 1968 and 1977.

These two results are important because they show, unambiguously, that according to reported expenditure figures, the distribution of income for 1968 and 1977 has deteriorated in respect to that of 1963. In this sense, the Gini coefficient of the distribution of household expenditure for 1963 changed from 0.39 to 0.49 in 1968 and 0.48 in 1977. Although it is valid to say that the distribution of income of 1968 and 1977 deteriorated with respect to that of 1963, we cannot say anything about what happened with the distribution of income between 1968 and 1977 since their Lorenz curves cross each other.

To study what happened to income distribution between those years, we must retake Atkinson's measure. This information is given in Table 3-7.

The results of Table 3-7 confirm in a significant way the results concerning the increase in inequality between 1963 and 1968 and 1977. It is important to note that even for very low values of the degree of aversion toward inequality the potential benefits from redistribution in 1968 and 1977 are significantly higher than those obtained for 1963. In opposition to this result, only for very high values of the degree of aversion toward inequality was the inequality observed in 1977 worse compared to the one observed in 1968.

The previous results are so important that it is necessary to analyze whether they hold in the case of expenditure in per capita terms. In Figure 3-9 the Lorenz curves on per capita income for 1963, 1968, and 1977 are shown. As can be seen, the results obtained confirm those from household expenditure; that is, the distribution of per capita expenditure worsened between 1963 and 1968 and 1977. It is clear that there has been a tendency toward inequality during the period even though there have been considerable changes in the composition of Mexican families. Atkinson's estimation of inequality based on per capita expenditure also confirms the previous result (see Table 3-8).

## Conclusions

Even if the growth of the Mexican economy since the 1940s has been considerable, generally sustained, without precedent, and equaled by that of very few nations, the distribution of the achievements of this growth has been unequal. The higher-income groups continued to have an exaggerated share from a sociopolitical and moral point of view or when international comparisons are made. At the same time, the relative share

**Figure 3-8. Lorenz Curves for Expenditure of Households.**

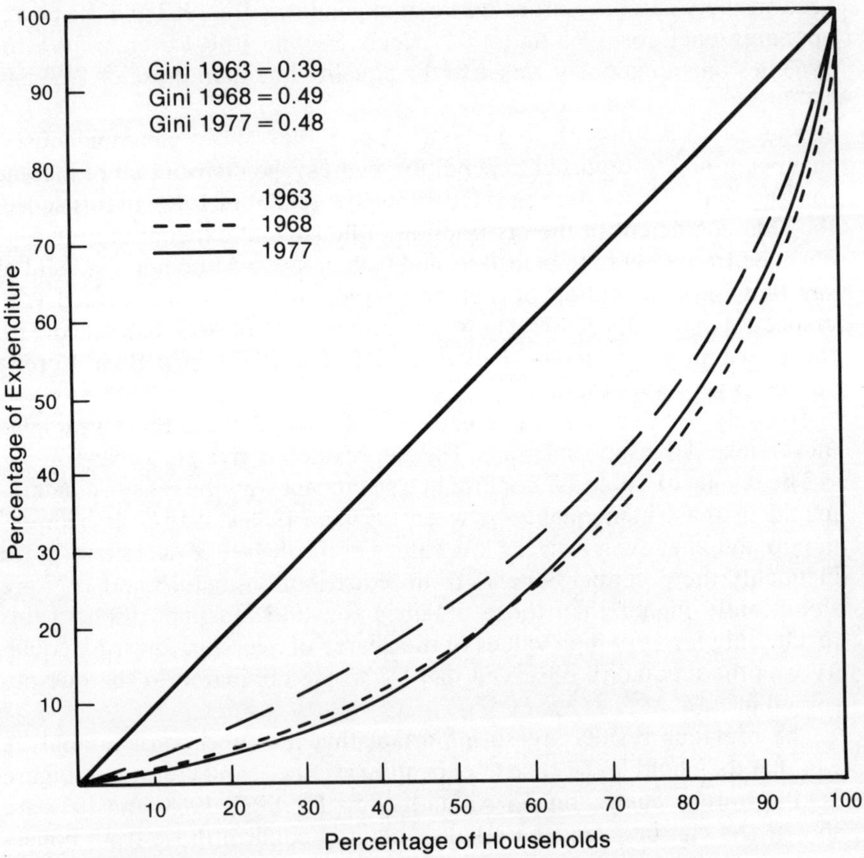

*TABLE 3.7.*
*Coefficients of Atkinson for the Distribution of Expenditure of Households*

| *E* | *1963* | *1968* | *1977* |
|---|---|---|---|
| 0.5 | 0.12 | 0.18 | 0.18 |
| 1.0 | 0.23 | 0.35 | 0.36 |
| 1.5 | 0.30 | 0.45 | 0.48 |
| 2.0 | 0.35 | 0.54 | 0.58 |
| 3.0 | 0.42 | 0.65 | 0.70 |
| 5.0 | 0.50 | 0.75 | 0.80 |

**Figure 3-9. Lorenz Curves, Expenditure per Capita.**

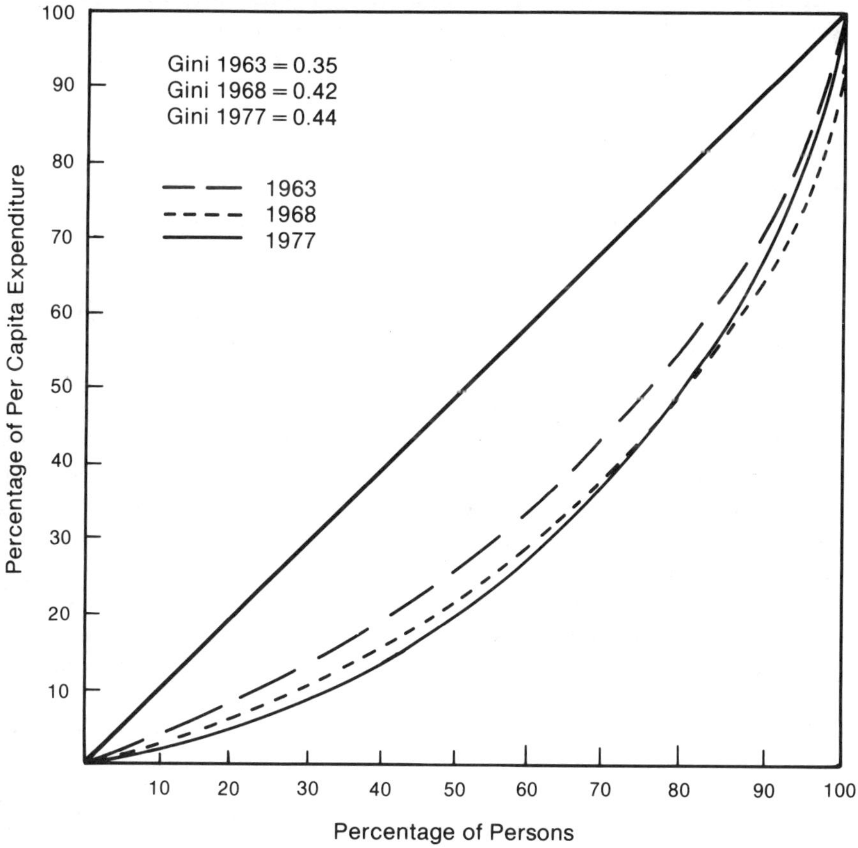

*TABLE 3.8.*
*Coefficients of Atkinson for the Distribution of Per Capita Expenditure*

| *E* | *1963* | *1968* | *1977* |
|---|---|---|---|
| 0.5 | 0.10 | 0.11 | 0.15 |
| 1.0 | 0.19 | 0.25 | 0.30 |
| 1.5 | 0.24 | 0.33 | 0.39 |
| 2.0 | 0.29 | 0.41 | 0.48 |
| 3.0 | 0.36 | 0.52 | 0.60 |
| 5.0 | 0.43 | 0.63 | 0.71 |

of the lower-income groups not only did not improve but in fact worsened.

Whatever measure of inequality is observed and whatever indicator of relative position is used, whether income or expenditure, current or permanent, the main conclusion of this chapter is that the income distribution structure of the country remained basically unaltered between 1950 (the first year for which data on personal and household income and expenditure are available) and 1977 (the year when the last household budget survey was carried out).

It is important to point out that during this period opposite trends in the evolution of income distribution were observed. From 1950 to 1958 the higher-income groups lost participation in favor of the rest of the population, while from 1958 to 1977 the upper deciles regained their position almost fully, and the lower-income groups found themselves below their initial situation.

For us to be able to separate statistically the so-called *just* inequalities, we made use of the following two variables: number of members of a family and the average age of a household. The exercise was carried out with the 1968 and 1977 data on household income and expenditure. From the results obtained, we were able to conclude that the unadjusted Gini coefficient *overestimated* in each of those years the degree of inequality by 22.7 and 32.6 percent, respectively. These results must be taken as a first and therefore hypothetical and provisional approximation of the degree of just inequality in the structure of distribution.

After these adjustments were made, we found again that the income distribution structure remained basically unaltered and that the advantages and benefits of redistribution are considerable, even in the case of a small aversion of society toward the existence of inequality.

The resistance that the redistributive structure has shown to time and above all to economic growth suggests that the problem cannot be solved through subsidies and transfer payments given to expenditure. These tools are just a palliative helping to prevent a discrediting of the system.

Policy measures that affect the structure and have a permanent effect on distribution are needed. They include the following.

First, there must be a reorientation of public expenditure to help attain the distributive change that the country requires. Public expenditure on human capital formation must be redirected so that the productivity of lower-income workers is raised. To achieve this, public effort in elementary and technical schooling must increase in a qualitative way. Given the lag in education, serious efforts must also be made to increase job training programs.

It is necessary to remember that expenditure on education, by increasing the stock of capital of the least favored groups, creates permanent wealth which by itself generates income along the life cycle. This type of expenditure grants political legitimacy by increasing the opportunities for social mobility which make present wealth and income concentration more tolerable.

Another complementary proposal would be to continue the correction of factor price distortions that make the use of labor-intensive techniques unattractive. Therefore, it is of high social priority to dismantle the legal, fiscal, and international trade distortions that tend to make wages relatively more expensive than other factor payments. Additionally, subsidies should be eliminated for the use of other factors such as energy and capital.

As a last comment, it is important to note that, paradoxically, Mexico has one of the lowest capacity utilization rates among the group of intermediate developed countries. The elimination of trade, administrative, and labor policies that hinder the creation of second and third shifts in the industrial sector is highly necessary from a social point of view. This should be accompanied by a special tax treatment designed to increase the use of capacity.

We do not have any illusions at all that the above-suggested measures will have any immediate effects if implemented. However, we hope that if they are carried out over a sufficiently long time a gradual but substantial change in the observed structure will take place.

Finally, the way income is distributed should be considered an indispensable objective in our development model and should no longer be considered the unavoidable result of a growth process. This demands will, tenacity, and decision from a society that gives its government the powers and resources to carry out the distributive mandate.

## Notes

1. David Ricardo, *The Principles of Taxation and Political Economy* (London: Kent, 1821).

2. Mark Blaug, *The Cambridge Revolution: Success or Failure?*, 2nd ed., (London: Hobart Paperback, 1975).

3. For an excellent argumentation of this subject, see A. B. Atkinson, *The Economics of Inequality* (London: Oxford University Press, 1975).

4. In Mexico, 8 percent of total business profits have to be distributed.

5. See, for instance, the work of Socrates Rizzo in Chapter 5 concerning the size of state property from oil.

6. For an excellent treatment of this subject, see J. E. Stiglitz, "Distribution of Income and Wealth Among Individuals," *Econometrica* 37 (1969), pp. 382–97.

7. See M. Brofenbrenner, *Income Distribution Theory* (Chicago: Aldine, 1971).

8. As M. Blaug *(The Cambridge Revolution, op. cit.)* mentions, "depending on how we allocate the income of the self-employed between wages and profits, we can make the aggregate figures come out almost as we like."

9. For a discussion on this topic, see Chapter 2.

10. Although in the surveys the usual problems of comparability are found, it must be said that according to some researchers, they are of a better quality than those of most developed countries. For this point, see J. Bergsman, "Income Distribution and Poverty in Mexico," *World Bank Staff Working Paper No. 395* (World Bank: Washington, D.C., June 1980).

11. Given the magnitude and the persistence of the reported negative savings for these households, it is likely that in fact there is a problem of underreporting of declared income. For a summary on different adjustments made to correct such figures, see the work of J. Bergsman, "Income Distribution," *op. cit.*

12. For a related discussion, see the work of Pedro Aspe, *Una Visión Panorámica de la Distribución del Ingreso en México* (Mexico City: Independent Mexican Institute of Technology, July 1980).

13. In general, income is defined as the maximum amount that can be consumed by a household during a period of time without reducing its level of wealth.

14. This comment is valid only if the Lorenz curves of the distribution do not cross each other. This point will be analyzed in further detail later.

15. The corresponding values of the Gini coefficients for 1950 and 1957 were 0.50 and 0.52, respectively.

16. The Gini coefficient has the serious disadvantage of conferring a relatively greater weight to transfers that affect the income of the middle class in relation to the ones affecting the extremes (whether "rich" or "poor") of the distribution.

17. A. B. Atkinson, "On the Measurement of Inequality," *Journal of Economic Theory* II (1970), pp. 244–63.

18. It is obvious that these results are valid only to the point that the income data reported in the surveys are also valid.

19. Morton Paglin, "The Measurement and Trend of Inequality: A Basic Revision," *American Economic Review* 65 (Sept. 1975).

20. The age of the head of the household was taken as a proxy for the average age of a household.

21. This statement is valid for 1977. For the 1968 distribution we did not obtain the same results concerning continuity, as can be seen in Figure 3-6.

22. Relevant data for 1963 were not found; that is why only the graphs for 1968 and 1977 are shown.

23. The figures related to Mexico shown in Figure 3-7 are for 1968.

24. For a theoretical discussion of this subject, see A. B. Atkinson, *The Economics of Inequality, op. cit.*

25. The income and expenditure surveys of Mexico include information on expenditure levels of household and persons. The conceptual difference between current consumption and current expenditure is that the latter includes the purchases of durable goods, while *consumption* would include only the depreciation of the durable goods of a household or person. Since the household surveys include data on total expenditure, they include purchases of durable goods. However, if we consider that the surveys are random, then the reported purchases of such goods in the given period (6 months) can be taken as a good proxy for the imputed depreciation of durable goods, which due to statistical problems is not included as current expenditure. Hence, the use of household expenditure data is a good indicator of current consumption, which in turn may be viewed as a proxy for life-cycle of permanent income.

## Bibliography

Aspe P. *Una Visión Panorámica de la Distribución del Ingreso en México*. Mexico City: Independent Mexican Institute of Technology, 1980, mimeo.

Atkinson, A. B. "On the Measurement of Inequality." *Journal of Economic Theory* II (1970). pp. 244–263.

Atkinson, A. B. *The Economics of Inequality*. London: Oxford University Press, 1975.

Banco, de México, S. A. *Encuesta de Ingresos y Gastos de los Hogares: 1963*. Federal District of Mexico: 1966.

Banco de México, S. A. *Encuesta de Ingresos y Gastos de los Hogares: 1968*. Federal District of Mexico: Fondo de Cultura Económica, 1974.

Bergsman, J. "Income Distribution and Poverty in Mexico," *World Bank Staff Working Paper No. 395*. Washington, D.C.: World Bank, June 1980.

Blaug, M. *The Cambridge Revolution: Success or Failure?* 2nd ed. London: Hobart Paperback, 1975.

Brofenbrenner, M. *Income Distribution Theory*. Chicago: Aldine, 1975.

Paglin, Morton. "The Measurement and Trend of Inequality: A Basic Revision." *American Economic Review* 65 (Sept. 1975). pp. 598–609.

Ricardo, David. *The Principles of Taxation and Political Economy*. London: Kent, 1821.

Secretariat of Planning and the National Budget. *Encuesta de Ingresos y Gastos de los Hogares*. Mexico City: SPP, 1977.

CHAPTER 4

# *The Incidence of Taxes in Mexico: A Before and After Comparison*

Francisco Gil Díaz

## Introduction

In the years 1978–1981 a tax reform was undertaken in Mexico. At the end of 1978 the first stage of the reform was begun with proposals for changes in the individual income tax and the adoption of a value-added tax. Other legislative proposals and their implementation continued up to 1982. The cumulative effect of the changes since 1978 amounts to a major reform. The consequences of some of the changes can already be seen in the broad tax figures.

For instance, despite yearly adjustments in the personal income tax schedule, which fully compensated for inflation, the distribution of collections per income bracket evolved in the manner shown in Table 4-1.

*TABLE 4.1.*

*Tax Collections Per Labor Income Bracket as Percentage of Total Labor Income Tax Collections*

| *Income Bracket*[a] | *1977* | *1978* | *1979* | *1980* | *1981* |
|---|---|---|---|---|---|
| 1 | 0 | 0 | 0 | 0 | 0 |
| 1 to 5 | 58 | 57 | 40 | 37 | 28 |
| 5 to 10 | 20 | 19 | 32 | 29 | 26 |
| 10 to 15 | 14 | 15 | 19 | 18 | 21 |
| More than 15 | 8 | 9 | 9 | 16 | 25 |

[a] Expressed as multiples of national average minimum wage.

My appreciation for their invaluable help in all stages of this work to Fernando Sánchez Ugarte, Arturo Fernández Pérez, Rafael Ros Torres, Juan Manuel Pérez Porrúa, Alejandro Beuchot, Jesús Romo y García, Lorenza Illanes and to my secretaries Rocío García and Laura Haro.

*TABLE 4.2.*
*Percentage of Income Tax Paid by Capital and Labor*

| | *1975* | *1976* | *1977* | *1978* | *1979* | *1980* | *1981* |
|---|---|---|---|---|---|---|---|
| Capital | 63.7 | 60.4 | 57.6 | 57.2 | 64.9 | 68.5 | 69.2 |
| Labor | 36.3 | 39.6 | 42.4 | 42.8 | 35.1 | 31.5 | 30.8 |

Before 1979, the year the tax reform began to take effect, collections were concentrated in the income bracket of one to five times the minimum wage. As the tax reform started to take hold, this bracket dropped from 58 percent of labor income tax collections to only 28 percent, while the highest bracket went up from a mere 8 percent of the total to 25 percent.

Table 4-2 contains aggregated information which shows other structural changes brought about by the recent reform.

The classification of taxes paid by capital and labor does not pretend to prove by itself a more equitable distribution of the tax burden. Anyone who has carefully inspected the factorial composition of income in family cross-section data knows that there is no merit to class classifications, i.e., the poor getting wages and the rich rents, interest, and profits. This class distinction does not even hold empirically as a pattern of higher relative capital income as income increases.

Table 4-3 is shown for another reason. As Table 4-1 showed, before the tax reform the lower-income brackets were contributing the greater portion of the labor income tax. Table 4-2 shows that while this was occurring, major corporations, the primary contributors of the figure in the "capital" line, were, until 1978, declining in their share of income tax paid.

*TABLE*
*Capital—Labor Income after Taxes 1970–1981*

| *Year* | *(1) GDP* | *(2) Depreciation* | *(3) Indirect Taxes* | *(4) Net National Product (1 − (2 + 3))* | *(5) Gross Payments to Labor Minus Indirect Taxes (3)* | *(6) Labor Share in Net National Product (5/4)* | *(7) Gross Payments to Capital Minus Indirect Taxes Minus Depreciation* | *(8) Capital Share in Net National Product (7/4)* | *(9) Direct Taxes* |
|---|---|---|---|---|---|---|---|---|---|
| 1970 | 296,530 | 20,333 | 14,731 | 261,466 | 104,637 | 40.02 | 156,829 | 59.98 | 13,047 |
| 1971 | 306,712 | 21,673 | 15,881 | 269,158 | 110,908 | 41.20 | 158,249 | 58.80 | 13,852 |
| 1972 | 329,030 | 23,381 | 18,059 | 287,590 | 124,396 | 43.25 | 163,194 | 56.75 | 15,834 |
| 1973 | 354,057 | 24,926 | 23,041 | 306,090 | 130,638 | 42.70 | 175,452 | 57.30 | 17,315 |
| 1974 | 374,977 | 26,707 | 25,955 | 322,315 | 137,370 | 42.62 | 184,944 | 57.38 | 19,881 |
| 1975 | 390,632 | 30,401 | 29,710 | 330,521 | 149,917 | 45.36 | 180,604 | 54.64 | 24,376 |
| 1976 | 398,572 | 33,908 | 30,411 | 334,255 | 163,396 | 48.88 | 170,857 | 51.12 | 26,192 |
| 1977 | 411,575 | 38,687 | 31,092 | 341,796 | 161,640 | 47.29 | 180,156 | 52.71 | 30,363 |
| 1978 | 441,606 | 41,606 | 32,825 | 367,175 | 168,041 | 45.77 | 199,134 | 54.23 | 35,650 |
| 1979 | 476,905 | 45,961 | 34,788 | 396,146 | 175,315 | 44.26 | 220,831 | 55.74 | 39,769 |
| 1980 | 522,300 | 50,347 | 38,099 | 433,854 | 192,003 | 44.26 | 241,851 | 55.74 | 59,315 |
| 1981 | 561,400 | 54,116 | 40,951 | 466,333 | 206,377 | 44.26 | 259,956 | 55.74 | 68,744 |

Source: Banco de México, National Accounts, 1960–1979.

The trend is reversed in 1979 because of inflationary corrections introduced in the personal income tax which reduced the tax burden mainly on labor income and as a result of legislative changes which improve the enforcement of the corporate income tax.

Another way of looking at these results is the distribution of after-tax disposable national income between capital and labor. In Table 4-3 one can observe that capital's share falls from 59.15 percent in 1970 to 49.9 percent in 1981 in column 19, mainly as a result of an increase in taxes, since capital's gross tax share[1] in the net national product falls from 60 percent in 1970 to only 55.7 percent in 1981 (column 8).

Finally, Table 4-4 shows how the composition of direct versus indirect taxes has evolved as a result of a lower ratio of direct taxes to GDP and a higher ratio of income taxes to GDP.

Tables 4-1 through 4-4 show a partial outcome of the reform. A more comprehensive analysis should present full incidence per income bracket, and income should include all its sources, not only labor income. The construction of such a table is one of the main objectives of this chapter.

It would have also been desirable to assess the incidence of government expenditures per income bracket. However, that is beyond the scope of the present analysis. There is a previous study[2] on the overall incidence of the Mexican tax system which shows the incidence per family income level of government expenditures in 1968. For that year government expenditures turned out to be progressive, i.e., to be a greater proportion of lower incomes declining as income increases. The main explanation for this pattern lies in government expenditures on primary and secondary education and on health services. Since the structure of government expenditures has changed in the direction of expanded social services, this pattern should still hold.

The following research is based on household expenditures on goods

*4.3.*

*(Millions of Pesos at 1960 Prices)*

| (10) Social Security | (11) National Disposable Income 4−(9+10) | (12) Direct Taxes Paid by Labor | (13) Social Security Payments by Labor | (14) Net Payments to Labor (5−(12+13)) | (15) Net Share of Labor Income in Disposable Income (14/11) | (16) Direct Taxes Paid by Capital | (17) Social Security Payments by Firms | (18) Net Payments to Capital (7−(16+17)) | (19) Net Share of Capital Income in Disposable Income (18/11) |
|---|---|---|---|---|---|---|---|---|---|
| 4,954 | 243,465 | 4,000 | 1,189 | 99,448 | 40.85 | 9,047 | 3,765 | 144,017 | 59.15 |
| 5,393 | 249,913 | 4,491 | 1,294 | 105,123 | 42.06 | 9,361 | 4,099 | 144,789 | 57.93 |
| 7,396 | 264,360 | 5,080 | 1,578 | 117,738 | 44.54 | 10,754 | 5,818 | 146,622 | 55.46 |
| 8,473 | 280,302 | 5,507 | 1,624 | 123,507 | 44.06 | 11,818 | 6,849 | 156,795 | 55.94 |
| 9,685 | 292,749 | 6,184 | 1,882 | 129,304 | 44.17 | 13,697 | 7,803 | 163,444 | 55.83 |
| 10,653 | 295,492 | 7,687 | 2,071 | 140,159 | 47.43 | 16,689 | 8,582 | 155,333 | 52.27 |
| 11,507 | 296,554 | 9,123 | 2,246 | 152,027 | 51.26 | 17,069 | 9,261 | 144,527 | 48.74 |
| 11,527 | 299,906 | 10,364 | 2,223 | 149,053 | 49.70 | 19,999 | 9,304 | 150,853 | 50.30 |
| 12,029 | 319,496 | 12,380 | 2,309 | 153,352 | 48.00 | 23,270 | 9,720 | 166,144 | 52.00 |
| 12,830 | 343,547 | 11,197 | 2,464 | 161,654 | 47.05 | 28,572 | 10,366 | 181,893 | 52.95 |
| 14,881 | 359,658 | 11,914 | 2,861 | 177,228 | 49.28 | 47,401 | 12,020 | 182,430 | 50.72 |
| 15,903 | 381,686 | 12,092 | 2,991 | 191,294 | 50.12 | 56,652 | 12,912 | 190,392 | 49.83 |

*TABLE 4.4.*
*Percentage of Indirect and Direct Taxes on Tax Collections (Excluding Oil Taxes)*

| | *1971* | *1976* | *1977* | *1978* | *1979* | *1980* | *1981* |
|---|---|---|---|---|---|---|---|
| Direct taxes | 46.15 | 46.52 | 48.49 | 51.53 | 50.85 | 52.42 | 54.65 |
| Indirect taxes | 53.85 | 53.48 | 51.51 | 48.47 | 49.15 | 47.58 | 45.35 |

and services and on the different sources of family income. The data are drawn from the income expenditure survey conducted by the Secretaría de Programación y Presupuesto in 1977.

To infer income tax paid in 1977, the information was handled at the individual level by applying a tax model which iterated until it generated a gross income figure consistent with the net income figure reported in the survey. There is no income-expenditure survey for 1980. The analysis for that year was done simulating the new tax code on the gross income figures obtained with the 1977 data. Expenditure taxes were calculated by applying the diverse tax rates to reported family expenditures. Other taxes such as social security contributions, import taxes, and the inflation tax were also assigned.

The characteristics of the research are the following: the use of the general equilibrium implications of a tax incidence model, the recognition of the inflationary tax as a real command over resources by the government and its distribution per income bracket, the use of permanent income as the variable to measure tax incidence, and the comparison of 2 years, one before and one after a major tax reform, to evaluate tax incidence per family income bracket.[3]

## Description of the Tax Reform

The objectives of the major overhauling of Mexico's tax structure in the past 4 years were as follows: to make the tax system more equitable, to eliminate or reduce important distortions related to labor supply, to make more efficient the allocation of capital resources, to simplify legislation, and to give legal support to a new administrative model which has substantially improved tax administration and taxpayer compliance.

At the level of personal income, the tax reform implied changing the form of taxation on practically all sources of income. The taxation of labor was radically redefined. The global income tax schedule that applied to individuals was also revised, achieving substantial reductions in marginal tax rates. Individuals who formerly faced a 57 percent marginal tax rate now pay a 40 percent marginal tax on the same real income. Those with a 39.9 percent marginal tax rate now pay 26.2 percent, and lower-income individuals barely above the minimum wage threshold who, because of a constitutional exemption of the minimum wage from income tax, formerly faced a starting marginal rate above 50 percent, now pay only 3.1 percent on their marginal income above the minimum wage.

Personal income tax deductions were changed, simplifying considerably a system which allowed only a small basic deduction to low-income individuals and larger, itemized deductions to middle- and high-income individuals.

The new system consists of a single deduction, approximately equal in amount in constant prices to the previous one for middle- and higher-income taxpayers and about three times larger for low-income individuals. The amount of the new deduction is the annual minimum wage, which, besides simplifying the tax, has automatically increased with price and productivity increases. This system also solves the serious problem mentioned above introduced by the exemption of the minimum wage from income tax.

The new system is compatible with the exemption of the minimum wage and allows workers a smooth entry into the income tax schedule. Because the result is a lowering of the marginal rate for this particular class of workers from 55 percent in the old system to 3.1 percent today, a disincentive for overtime or seasonal two shifts is removed.

The tax on capital gains was also subject to a substantial revision. They are now taxed on a real basis, allowing the purchase cost and reinvestments on the asset to be adjusted for price increases.

Since capital gains are a nonrecurrent event for many people and can therefore be taxed at too high a marginal rate if the total gain is simply added to other taxable income, a simple averaging procedure is used to smooth the impact of their accumulation. It is assumed that the capital gain was realized in five equal parts in each of the four years preceding the taxpayer's tax return and the other fifth in the year of the tax return. To determine the tax the taxpayer takes 20 percent of the capital gain and adds it to his or her other taxable income. He or she then calculates the marginal tax rate and applies it to the whole capital gain. Another way to interpret this procedure is to say that 20 percent is the permanent income stream from the asset and that this is the income that should be added to other income in order to calculate the tax rate. In fact this assumption seems to be a rather neat averaging scheme which does away with life-averaging-type complications. However, a much lower figure ought to have been used for this interpretation to hold, such as a 10 percent real rate of interest.

Besides the adjustment for inflation, the cost of corporate shares can also be increased by adding to it reinvested earnings, which may in turn be corrected for inflation.

These changes provide a definition of taxable capital income more closely related to true income. The economic effect is a more equitable treatment of income and offers greater efficiency in the allocation of capital resources.

Assets previously locked in are now more actively traded, and tax collections have actually increased. The reason is perhaps that firms and individuals preferred to keep old shares in their portfolios, showing an asset valued at current market prices and failing to include in their balance sheets the tax liability contingent upon the sale of the asset. This presumably helped their borrowing potential.

The only tax-exempt capital gains remaining are those obtained in the stock market by individuals.

The tax exemption for individuals on gains from listed stocks is not new; it has been in effect for several years and has almost no fiscal consequences since, once corrections are made for inflation and reinvested earnings, the tax base generated by true capital gains turns out on the average to be negative.

Dividends were also subject to an important new definition. At the taxpayer's option, dividends paid to individuals (interfirm dividends are not taxed) may be taxed at a fixed 21 percent rate, or the individual may choose not to pay the 21 percent but will accumulate the grossed-up dividend, getting full credit for the corporate income tax (42 percent paid by most corporations). Partnership profits and taxes are also integrated into the income and the personal taxes of their owners. The objective of this reform is to tax equitably medium- and lower-income individuals and to eliminate the economic distortions on equity versus debt financing which result from separation, for tax purposes, of corporate profits from individual income.

There were numerous other changes introduced on the individual income tax with the objective of making it more equitable as well as closing some important loopholes, but all were made keeping in mind the important objective of not interfering with an efficient allocation of resources.

The other very substantial reform in the tax code was done on federal sales taxation, which was based on a turnover tax which taxed every sale, including interfirm sales. This tax was eliminated, as were more than 30 federal excise taxes, close to 400 municipal and state taxes, and the federal "stamp" tax (which dated from colonial days). All these taxes were replaced by a value-added tax of the consumption type. This tax has one basic exemption which is a zero rate on food and on inputs to agriculture, livestock, fishing, and forestry. The zero rate on agricultural inputs allows human food consumption to be completely exempt from the value-added tax, giving the tax a progressive incidence rarely found in indirect taxes, since food expenditures account for a large proportion of the expenditures of poor people.

Basing the tax on consumption means that investment is not taxed. High levels of investment may even generate tax refunds for some firms. Unlike the previous tax, which was on production, this tax will therefore not interfere with capital formation.

We believe this tax has provided for better resource allocation and a simpler administration and that it has had a tremendous effect on taxpayer compliance.

Federal revenue sharing with the states also underwent a substantial revision. Formerly, revenue sharing to the states resulted in their receipt of about half of federal sales taxes. But since geographical distribution of value added differs from the geographical distribution of sales, the revenue-sharing formula had to be changed. The new law has increased the relative amount of federal revenues going to the states, and it will reward those states with faster economic development and better than average collection efforts.

As will be seen from the contents of this chapter and as suggested by the broad tables already presented, the reform has already had a substantial impact. The tax reform has broadened the taxable income concept, helping to make the tax system a more equitable one. However, one should not expect too much in terms of justice or a better income distribution from a tax system. The greater equity the reform has achieved is more a consequence of better tax enforcement resulting from an expanded definition of taxable income than from theological virtues which could be ascribed to income as a taxable base.

As is well known, income is widely proposed as a basis for taxation on the argument that by taxing it one comes closer to the ideals of equity. While the argument is not necessarily correct (because no income tax system takes into account life-cycle income), in practice so many income concepts remain beyond the definition and reach of fiscal authorities in government administrations that the practical concept of income falls quite short of true income and generates substantial inequities and distortions. However, as in the case of taxes on alcoholic beverages, beer, and tobacco, highly moral arguments are presented to defend taxes which can be defended merely on practical grounds. In the case of beer, tobacco, and liquor one can at least say that the practicality (high revenue raising and low collection costs) goes together with small distortions on resource allocation.

## Incidence Analysis of Taxes in a Small Open Economy

The analysis of the incidence of taxes in Mexico should take into account the size of the economy and its openness to trade in goods and in factors of production.

The relative size of the Mexican economy suggests it is a price taker in all world commodity markets.

Capital is freely mobile. No restrictions are imposed on capital flows between Mexico and other countries. This fact and the relative size of the economy assure that the net rate of return to capital is given internationally.

Most developed capital-exporting countries tax income earned abroad but allow a tax credit up to an amount equivalent to the tax to which such income would be liable at home. This means that capital-importing countries will not be able to attract foreign capital by cutting income tax rates, since profit taxation and provisions about tax credits in the legislation of capital-exporting countries will offset such policies.[4]

Since a small country's net rate of capital return is determined internationally, it will only lose taxes paid by foreign investment if it reduces its profits taxes below the international average. In this case the optimal corporation tax rate becomes the average international tax rate. But who bears the burden of the world tax rate on capital?

If world savings are fixed regardless of the rate of return on savings, capital owners will bear the burden of the tax. This conclusion would be modified if world savings responded to variations in their net rate of return.

In summary, if we can conclude that capital will bear the average world rate of taxation, we only have to concern ourselves with deviations of domestic tax rates from the average world tax rates.

In the framework of a small open economy like Mexico's, where domestic prices of traded goods are given and factor mobility ensures that factor returns are at the world level, the incidence of taxes above or below the world tax rate are shifted and cannot be borne or enjoyed by capital owners. Therefore, the tax is borne by domestic capital at a rate equal to the average world rate, but when the domestic tax rate exceeds the average world rate, the difference is shifted back to land—a nontradable factor—and forward to the price of nontraded goods. Land prices will have to decrease to absorb the tax through a fall in the demand for all factors of production. The fall in land prices brings a benefit to consumers of nontradable goods whose prices are lower.

It is important to emphasize that capital bear a larger burden, since its net rate of return is given. So capital will flow out until its net internal rate of return is back at the world level.

When the domestic tax rate is below the international level, no additional capital will be invested, since domestic savings are basically inelastic with respect to their net of tax yield and because foreign investors cannot get a bigger return due to the taxation policies of their countries.[5] Domestic investors will get a bigger after-tax rate of return, but foreign investors will still bear the original burden, bringing a redistribution of tax revenues to foreign treasuries. In this case domestic investors will bear a lower burden (the domestic tax rate), and the foreign investors' rate will remain the same.

Even if domestic savings respond significantly to changes in the net rate of return, the consequence of a lower domestic income tax will be to substitute domestic savings for foreign capital at a loss, since tax revenue will be lost on the whole stock of foreign capital.

The Mexican corporation income tax rate of 42 percent, coupled with a withholding tax on dividends of 21 percent, reflects international tax levels. This implies that these taxes are fully borne by the owners of those factors.

A similar analysis can be done for labor. International mobility of Mexican labor is quite high. This implies that factor movements should offset significant tax differentials. An analysis of the Mexican income tax schedule shows a strong resemblance to a combination of U.S. federal and local tax rates. Therefore, under a high degree of international labor mobility, with similar income tax schedules, and with a relatively inelastic world supply of labor, we can conclude that the labor income tax is borne by labor.

In the case of indirect taxes, the recent tax reform eliminated several excises and the turnover sales tax and replaced them with a value-added tax.

Before and after the reform, indirect taxes followed the *destination principle:* Border tax adjustments were made. This implies that they are consumption taxes and borne by consumers.

### Incidence of the Mexican Tax System: Analysis of the Results

This section presents the tables which are the end result of the procedures, assumptions, tax model, and figures found in the appendices at the end of the chapter.

In describing the results contained in Tables 4-5 through 4-11, it will be useful to comment first on the incidence of taxes without considering the contribution of the inflation tax and then to add the latter's contribution.

Table 4-6 has a subtotal before the inclusion of the inflation tax which shows the percentage of taxes in relation to permanent income. It can be seen that in 1977 they go from 9.37 percent of income in the first decile to 35 percent in the upper half decile, although the progressiveness is sometimes uneven. For instance, the tax falls slightly when going from the ninth to the tenth half decile; this happens again from the eleventh to the twelfth, from the thirteenth to the fourteenth, from the fifteenth to the sixteenth, and from the seventeenth to the eighteenth.

The reason for this can be found in the column of direct taxes, since excise taxes are basically proportional, and other indirect taxes are also fairly proportional, except for the last half decile, where there is some progressivity.

If we look at Table 4-9, which has a breakdown of direct taxes, we shall find that the jumps mentioned in Table 4-6 originate in the individual income tax.

On the other hand, these jumps are no longer found in the individual income tax column for 1980 (column 2 in Table 4-11).

This is a result partly of a more comprehensive definition of income resulting from the tax reform, because the jumps in the 1977 figures are

*TABLE 4.5.*
*Tax Incidence: 1977–1980*

| *Half Income Deciles* | *1977* | *1980* |
|---|---|---|
| 1 | 10.6 | 9.8 |
| 2 | 11.4 | 9.2 |
| 3 | 13.0 | 11.4 |
| 4 | 13.5 | 11.4 |
| 5 | 14.4 | 12.2 |
| 6 | 15.0 | 12.1 |
| 7 | 16.3 | 13.5 |
| 8 | 16.7 | 13.4 |
| 9 | 17.5 | 14.0 |
| 10 | 16.4 | 16.2 |
| 11 | 21.9 | 18.3 |
| 12 | 21.0 | 21.9 |
| 13 | 25.3 | 21.9 |
| 14 | 22.7 | 24.7 |
| 15 | 26.1 | 24.6 |
| 16 | 26.0 | 27.6 |
| 17 | 27.8 | 28.5 |
| 18 | 25.1 | 29.2 |
| 19 | 26.7 | 30.2 |
| 20 | 41.7 | 48.8 |

attributable to differences in the composition of income sources as one goes from one half decile to another.

Looking in more detail at the 1977 information, column 3 comes from the sum of columns 3 and 4 in Table 4-8 which shows the incidence of the real estate tax, which is mainly progressive, and car ownership taxes, which show the same if uneven pattern.

Import taxes, on the other hand, are negligible in amount and are basically proportional except for the last decile. Excise taxes are the combined result of several small taxes, the basic 4 percent turnover sales tax and excises on beer, tobacco, liquor, telephone services, soft drinks, etc. They are basically proportional, as already mentioned, representing between 6 and 7 percent of permanent income. Going back to Table 4-9, we can see that all direct taxes are progressive, although some are erratic, especially in the case of the corporate income tax. The net effect of all of them is shown in Table 4-6 and, except for the jumps already mentioned, can be described as progressive. With the inclusion of the inflation tax (column 6) the tax burden goes from 10 percent tax on income to 41.7 percent (column 7).

In 1980 the most important changes are in the individual income tax, which was broadened in scope. It is progressive except in the last three half deciles where it becomes regressive. This regressivity is more than compensated for by the corporate income tax and the social security tax for the overall net effect in these same last half deciles. In all cases, however, the individual income tax in the upper strata is higher in 1980 than in 1977 and lower in the lower-income levels.

The corporate income tax also shows more progressivity in 1980 and definitely a higher percentage of income in the upper-income levels.

The tax on interest income is practically the same in 1980; the inflation tax is simply higher and slightly more progressive because it affects interest income more in that year. Automobile taxes are the same as well as social security taxes.

The total effect is to make direct taxes more progressive, as can be seen in column 4 of Table 4-7, and smoother than was the case in 1977.

Other indirect taxes show basically the same pattern, although the burden is lighter, since, as already explained, indirect taxes as a percentage of the GDP are smaller after the reform.

Excise taxes, which include value-added taxes (VATs) show in 1980 a definite progressive pattern instead of a proportional one as a result of the

*TABLE 4.6.*
*Tax Incidence Across Half Deciles in 1977*

| *(1) Half Deciles* | *(2) Excise Taxes* | *(3) Other Indirect Taxes* | *(4) Direct Taxes* | *(5) Subtotal* | *(6) Inflation Tax* | *(7) Total* |
|---|---|---|---|---|---|---|
| 1 | 6.18 | 0.82 | 2.37 | 9.37 | 1.27 | 10.64 |
| 2 | 6.66 | 0.63 | 3.29 | 10.58 | 0.85 | 11.43 |
| 3 | 7.13 | 0.61 | 3.54 | 11.28 | 1.73 | 13.01 |
| 4 | 7.06 | 0.51 | 4.77 | 12.34 | 1.14 | 13.48 |
| 5 | 7.47 | 0.62 | 5.26 | 13.35 | 1.07 | 14.42 |
| 6 | 6.81 | 0.55 | 6.48 | 13.84 | 1.18 | 15.02 |
| 7 | 7.13 | 0.64 | 7.22 | 14.99 | 1.26 | 16.25 |
| 8 | 7.59 | 0.94 | 6.71 | 15.24 | 1.44 | 16.68 |
| 9 | 7.39 | 0.71 | 7.65 | 15.75 | 1.71 | 17.46 |
| 10 | 7.25 | 0.84 | 6.32 | 14.41 | 1.95 | 16.36 |
| 11 | 7.41 | 0.75 | 11.77 | 19.93 | 1.92 | 21.85 |
| 12 | 7.52 | 0.71 | 10.74 | 18.97 | 1.95 | 20.92 |
| 13 | 6.99 | 0.78 | 15.01 | 22.78 | 2.55 | 25.33 |
| 14 | 7.34 | 0.85 | 12.55 | 20.74 | 1.95 | 22.69 |
| 15 | 7.07 | 0.84 | 15.59 | 23.50 | 2.62 | 26.12 |
| 16 | 7.37 | 0.86 | 14.69 | 22.92 | 3.03 | 25.95 |
| 17 | 7.10 | 0.96 | 17.31 | 25.37 | 2.41 | 27.78 |
| 18 | 7.88 | 1.07 | 13.74 | 22.69 | 2.41 | 25.10 |
| 19 | 7.79 | 0.95 | 14.91 | 23.65 | 3.06 | 26.71 |
| 20 | 6.18 | 2.68 | 26.22 | 35.09 | 6.62 | 41.70 |

*TABLE 4.7.*
*Tax Incidence Across Half Deciles in 1980*

| (1) Half Deciles | (2) Excise Taxes | (3) Other Indirect Taxes | (4) Direct Taxes | (5) Subtotal | (6) Inflation Tax | (7) Total |
|---|---|---|---|---|---|---|
| 1 | 4.27 | 0.93 | 2.33 | 7.53 | 2.27 | 9.80 |
| 2 | 4.33 | 0.74 | 3.07 | 8.14 | 1.08 | 9.22 |
| 3 | 4.76 | 0.69 | 3.16 | 8.61 | 2.79 | 11.40 |
| 4 | 5.16 | 0.58 | 4.17 | 9.91 | 1.44 | 11.35 |
| 5 | 5.70 | 0.71 | 4.43 | 10.84 | 1.31 | 12.15 |
| 6 | 4.78 | 0.63 | 5.19 | 10.60 | 1.46 | 12.06 |
| 7 | 5.36 | 0.72 | 5.85 | 11.93 | 1.55 | 13.48 |
| 8 | 5.73 | 1.06 | 4.82 | 11.61 | 1.81 | 13.42 |
| 9 | 5.47 | 0.79 | 5.43 | 11.69 | 2.30 | 13.99 |
| 10 | 5.56 | 0.96 | 6.83 | 13.35 | 2.82 | 16.17 |
| 11 | 5.63 | 0.82 | 9.33 | 15.78 | 2.54 | 18.32 |
| 12 | 5.92 | 0.84 | 12.52 | 19.28 | 2.63 | 21.91 |
| 13 | 5.15 | 0.93 | 12.24 | 18.32 | 3.56 | 21.88 |
| 14 | 5.90 | 0.98 | 15.24 | 22.12 | 2.54 | 24.66 |
| 15 | 5.51 | 0.98 | 14.35 | 20.84 | 3.79 | 24.63 |
| 16 | 5.84 | 1.03 | 16.14 | 23.01 | 4.63 | 27.64 |
| 17 | 6.07 | 1.15 | 17.83 | 25.06 | 3.44 | 28.50 |
| 18 | 6.61 | 1.31 | 17.94 | 25.86 | 3.30 | 29.16 |
| 19 | 6.85 | 1.19 | 17.37 | 25.41 | 4.82 | 30.23 |
| 20 | 6.18 | 1.17 | 29.80 | 37.15 | 11.60 | 48.75 |

zero rate on food consumption in the value-added tax, since food consumption is a declining share of permanent income as income increases.

The net effect of the tax reform is a more progressive pattern of taxation, with a smoother transition from one half decile to another in 1980 compared to 1977. It can also be seen that the tax ratio is lower in 1980 in the eleven lower half deciles and consistently higher from the twelfth half decile on up. So the net result is a more progressive and smoother pattern of taxation in 1980 compared to 1977. Figure 4-1 sets out this result more strikingly than numbers.)

### *A Note on the Income Concept*

As is well known, measured income introduces serious biases underestimating true income in the case of below-average incomes and overestimating true income in the case of incomes above the average. Therefore, permanent income was used to calculate the incidence of Mexican taxes on family income.

The traditional results in income distribution studies are substantially modified when a more appropriate concept of income is used. In the case of Mexico, the recent important contributions of Aspe and Beristain in this volume and of Cervantes[6] take this into account.

In the case of tax incidence studies, one would expect that the use of permanent income will reduce the regressivity or increase the progressivity of indirect taxes when measured against current income tax, while a proportional corporate income tax may turn out basically the same in both approaches.[7] However, in the case of the income tax on individuals there is no straightforward way in which the tax can be grossed up since some sources of income are more variable, and they are subject to diverse tax treatments. For instance, if the source is labor income, one would have to calculate permanent gross income, taking into account the progressivity of the income tax schedule as compared to interest income where grossing up would have to consider the average tax on interest. But should transitory income be allocated mostly to labor income, or should it be allocated proportionally to the shares of the different sources of net income? To avoid tackling these questions, a simple

*TABLE 4.8.*

*1977*

| *(1)* *Half Deciles* | *(2)* *Incidence of Excise Taxes* | *(3)* *Incidence of Taxes on Real Estate and Car Ownership* | *(4)* *Incidence of Import Tariffs* |
|---|---|---|---|
| 1 | 6.178 | 0.611 | 0.214 |
| 2 | 6.665 | 0.406 | 0.229 |
| 3 | 7.132 | 0.391 | 0.221 |
| 4 | 7.063 | 0.276 | 0.239 |
| 5 | 7.475 | 0.393 | 0.227 |
| 6 | 6.811 | 0.314 | 0.240 |
| 7 | 7.128 | 0.402 | 0.236 |
| 8 | 7.593 | 0.682 | 0.263 |
| 9 | 7.388 | 0.452 | 0.257 |
| 10 | 7.253 | 0.579 | 0.262 |
| 11 | 7.414 | 0.465 | 0.284 |
| 12 | 7.520 | 0.463 | 0.252 |
| 13 | 6.995 | 0.541 | 0.242 |
| 14 | 7.336 | 0.587 | 0.259 |
| 15 | 7.067 | 0.594 | 0.246 |
| 16 | 7.369 | 0.608 | 0.257 |
| 17 | 7.101 | 0.716 | 0.243 |
| 18 | 7.876 | 0.806 | 0.262 |
| 19 | 7.793 | 0.700 | 0.247 |
| 20 | 6.180 | 0.718 | 1.962 |

*TABLE 4.9.*

*Incidence of Direct Taxes in 1977*

| (1) Half Deciles | (2) Individual Income Tax | (3) Corporation Income Tax | (4) Tax on Interest Income | (5) Inflationary Tax | (6) Payroll Tax | (7) Social Security Tax |
|---|---|---|---|---|---|---|
| 1 | 0.043 | 0.993 | 0.033 | 1.273 | 0.043 | 1.256 |
| 2 | 0.212 | 1.136 | 0 | 0.851 | 0.068 | 1.872 |
| 3 | 0.369 | 1.012 | 0.025 | 1.729 | 0.071 | 2.062 |
| 4 | 0.597 | 1.222 | 0.009 | 1.141 | 1.001 | 2.845 |
| 5 | 0.890 | 0.694 | 0.001 | 1.069 | 0.141 | 3.539 |
| 6 | 1.252 | 0.868 | 0.001 | 1.183 | 0.147 | 4.162 |
| 7 | 1.401 | 0.936 | 0.002 | 1.257 | 0.176 | 4.712 |
| 8 | 1.985 | 0.792 | 0.002 | 1.439 | 0.130 | 3.800 |
| 9 | 2.376 | 0.656 | 0.008 | 1.710 | 0.155 | 4.451 |
| 10 | 1.993 | 1.046 | 0.023 | 1.948 | 0.114 | 3.145 |
| 11 | 5.835 | 0.534 | 0.008 | 1.922 | 0.185 | 5.203 |
| 12 | 4.847 | 0.942 | 0.011 | 1.954 | 0.166 | 4.764 |
| 13 | 8.483 | 0.523 | 0.016 | 2.551 | 0.216 | 5.773 |
| 14 | 6.715 | 1.000 | 0.011 | 1.946 | 0.176 | 4.653 |
| 15 | 8.957 | 0.511 | 0.030 | 2.616 | 0.207 | 5.888 |
| 16 | 8.547 | 0.517 | 0.064 | 3.033 | 0.201 | 5.361 |
| 17 | 9.524 | 0.304 | 0.046 | 2.410 | 0.274 | 7.163 |
| 18 | 6.599 | 0.522 | 0.068 | 2.410 | 0.222 | 6.330 |
| 19 | 6.779 | 0.513 | 0.071 | 3.063 | 0.286 | 7.253 |
| 20 | 3.369 | 16.888 | 0.372 | 6.620 | 0.213 | 5.383 |

solution was adopted: To consider the gross figure of income tax calculated from measured income with the procedure explained in Appendix I. This tax figure was grossed up with the same factor expenditures grossed up, as will be explained later. The basic relationship is the proportion of permanent consumption $C$ to net of income taxes permanent income $Y_{pn}$:

$$C = \alpha Y_{pn}$$

From it a permanent gross income is obtained equal to

$$Y_{pg} = \frac{C}{\alpha} + \frac{\text{income taxes}}{\alpha}$$

As mentioned, this new variable was generated at the percentile level, not at the family or individual level. Information will be presented aggregated into half income deciles.

TABLE 4.10.
*1980*

| (1) Half Deciles | (2) Incidence of Excise Taxes | (3) Incidence of Taxes on Real Estate and Car Ownership | (4) Incidence of Import Tariffs |
|---|---|---|---|
| 1 | 4.267 | 0.725 | 0.207 |
| 2 | 4.331 | 0.510 | 0.226 |
| 3 | 4.762 | 0.462 | 0.229 |
| 4 | 5.158 | 0.327 | 0.256 |
| 5 | 5.701 | 0.466 | 0.242 |
| 6 | 4.781 | 0.375 | 0.252 |
| 7 | 5.362 | 0.480 | 0.241 |
| 8 | 5.732 | 0.807 | 0.256 |
| 9 | 5.471 | 0.538 | 0.249 |
| 10 | 5.562 | 0.691 | 0.271 |
| 11 | 5.631 | 0.557 | 0.260 |
| 12 | 5.922 | 0.558 | 0.278 |
| 13 | 5.149 | 0.648 | 0.277 |
| 14 | 5.896 | 0.701 | 0.275 |
| 15 | 5.513 | 0.721 | 0.262 |
| 16 | 5.843 | 0.742 | 0.285 |
| 17 | 6.068 | 0.882 | 0.269 |
| 18 | 6.615 | 0.997 | 0.309 |
| 19 | 6.854 | 0.881 | 0.312 |
| 20 | 6.184 | 0.924 | 0.245 |

*TABLE 4.11.*

*Incidence of Direct Taxes in 1980*

| *(1) Half Deciles* | *(2) Individual Income Tax* | *(3) Corporation Income Tax* | *(4) Tax on Interest Income* | *(5) Inflationary Tax* | *(6) Payroll Tax* | *(7) Social Security Tax* |
|---|---|---|---|---|---|---|
| 1 | 0 | 0.989 | 0.037 | 2.271 | 0.043 | 1.256 |
| 2 | 0 | 1.130 | 0 | 1.081 | 0.068 | 1.872 |
| 3 | 0 | 1.012 | 0.029 | 2.787 | 0.071 | 2.062 |
| 4 | 0 | 1.222 | 0.004 | 1.441 | 1.001 | 2.845 |
| 5 | 0 | 0.693 | 0.015 | 1.312 | 0.141 | 3.539 |
| 6 | 0.016 | 0.868 | 0.012 | 1.458 | 0.147 | 4.162 |
| 7 | 0.035 | 0.936 | 0.002 | 1.545 | 0.176 | 4.712 |
| 8 | 0.098 | 0.792 | 0.002 | 1.809 | 0.130 | 3.800 |
| 9 | 0.173 | 0.655 | 0.009 | 2.295 | 0.155 | 4.451 |
| 10 | 0.344 | 3.210 | 0.025 | 2.815 | 0.114 | 3.145 |
| 11 | 1.352 | 2.582 | 0.009 | 2.539 | 0.185 | 5.203 |
| 12 | 1.741 | 5.829 | 0.126 | 2.633 | 0.166 | 4.764 |
| 13 | 3.208 | 3.022 | 0.184 | 3.562 | 0.220 | 5.773 |
| 14 | 3.026 | 7.349 | 0.121 | 2.543 | 0.176 | 4.653 |
| 15 | 4.499 | 3.719 | 0.034 | 3.794 | 0.207 | 5.888 |
| 16 | 6.543 | 3.971 | 0.072 | 4.625 | 0.201 | 5.361 |
| 17 | 7.930 | 2.457 | 0.052 | 3.444 | 0.274 | 7.163 |
| 18 | 7.209 | 4.059 | 0.078 | 3.299 | 0.222 | 6.330 |
| 19 | 5.582 | 4.173 | 0.080 | 4.820 | 0.286 | 7.253 |
| 20 | 4.001 | 19.792 | 0.423 | 11.600 | 0.213 | 5.383 |

**Figure 4-1. Tax Incidence: 1977-1980.**

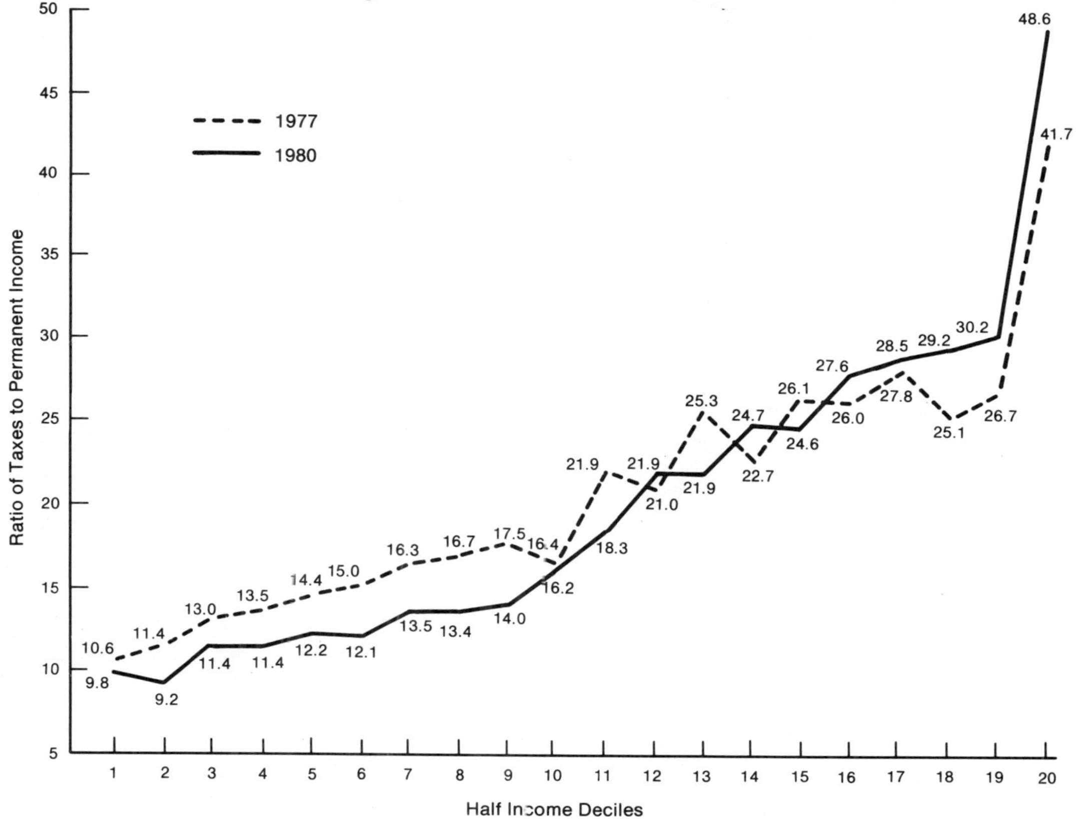

# APPENDIX I

# *The Inflation Tax*

### Definition

In an inflationary situtation the government can obtain an important amount of revenue through a reduction in the real value of its debt. The inflation tax should be included in a study on government finance and on the effect of taxes on income distribution. Even though the inflation tax is not legislated, a democratic society will either accept it or demand its elimination or reduction. Either way it ought to be taken into account because of the simple fact that it taxes the wealth of individuals.

The gain the government derives from inflation depends on the extent to which nominal interest rates do not rise to compensate government lenders for inflation and to provide them a real rate of return. The prime examples are cash balances which pay a zero nominal interest rate.

It will be assumed that the real rate of return in an inflationary situation ought to be the same as that prevailing in a period with reasonable price stability.

The inflation tax occurs even if it is unexpected in the same way a head tax is considered a tax by the elementary fact that it provides revenue for the government. An unexpected inflation tax may not produce all the distortions related to it at the beginning of the inflationary process, but it increases the command of the government over real resources and will be paid in different amounts depending on the financial position of individuals. Thus it will have an effect on the incidence of the tax system.

The inflation tax has an effect of the first order of magnitude on the efficiency and on the equity of the entire tax system. In 1980 in Mexico it accounted for 18.0 percent of total tax revenues and was equivalent to 47.3 percent of the amount raised by the income tax.

This appendix will present the method employed to calculate and assign the inflation tax. It will focus on the budget restraint of the government to derive from it the sources of its inflation income.

The point of departure will be a simplified definition of government accounts used to construct the government's budget constraint. The government and the central bank will be consolidated for analytical purposes.

$$I + R_aA + R'_aA'e + \dot{B} + \dot{B}'e = G + R_bB + R'_bB' + \dot{A} + \dot{A}'e$$

$I$: consolidated ordinary income of the government and of the central bank
$G$: expenditure on goods and services
$A, A'$: peso denominated and dollar denominated assets respectively
$B, B'$: Debt
$R_a, Ra', R_b, R_b'$: nominal interest rates applicable to the respective debts or assets
$e$: exchange rate
· : time derivative

All variables are in current prices.

Equation (1) is an identity. It simply states that cash outflow equals cash inflow. A second definition will be obtained from the net consolidated position in real terms of the government and the central bank:

$$W = \frac{A + A'e - B - B'e}{P}$$

where $P$ is the general price level.

By taking time derivatives of Eq. (2), an expression that can be grouped in two terms is derived. The first reflects the change in wealth resulting from net purchases (which could be negative in sign) of real assets.

The second term captures the depreciation of the value of real assets which results from the increase in prices:

$$\dot{W} = \frac{\dot{A} + \dot{A}'e + A'e\hat{e} - \dot{B} - \dot{B}'e - B'e\hat{e}}{P} - \frac{A + A'e - B - B'e}{P}\pi$$

$$\pi = \frac{\dot{P}}{P}, \quad \hat{e} = \frac{\dot{e}}{e}$$

From Eq. (1), $\dot{A} + \dot{A}'e - \dot{B} - \dot{B}'e$ is derived and substituted into Eq. (3) to give

$$W = \frac{I}{P} + (R_a - \pi)\frac{A}{P} + (R'_a - \pi + \hat{e})\frac{A'e}{P} - \frac{G}{P}(R_b - \pi)\frac{B}{P} - (R'_b - \pi + \hat{e})\frac{B'e}{P}$$

Using the purchasing power parity theorem, we obtain

$$P = eP' \quad \text{or} \quad \pi = \hat{e} + \pi'$$

where $\pi'$ is world inflation,

$$\pi' = \frac{\dot{P}'}{P'}.$$

$$W = \frac{I}{P} + (R_a - \pi)\frac{A}{P} + (R_a' - \pi')\frac{A'}{P} - \frac{G}{P} - (R_b - \pi)\frac{B}{P} - (R_b' - \pi')\frac{B'}{P'}$$

The parity theorem implies that assets yield the same real rate of return provided comparisons among assets denominated in different currencies take into account real rates of return expressed in a currency of a particular denomination. Interest rates applicable to foreign debts and assets are real foreign interest rates which coincide with nominal foreign interest rates expressed as real returns on national currency corrected for exchange rate movements, as shown by Eq. (4).

From Eq. (5) we can derive an expression for the permanent income of the government making $\dot{W} = 0$. The cash flow available for its expenditures will then be

$$\frac{G}{P} = \frac{I}{P} + (R_a - \pi)\frac{A}{P} + (R_a' - \pi')\frac{A'}{P'} - (R_b - \pi)\frac{B}{P} - (R_{b'}' - \pi')\frac{B'}{P'}$$

This equation merely expresses an elementary cash flow definition, but it is useful to analyze the inflation tax because real returns and costs are defined as the difference between nominal interest rates and inflation rates.

The only interesting term for our purposes is $-(R_b - \pi)\frac{B}{P}$. The terms with $\acute{A}$ and $\acute{B}$ in them reflect the extent to which world inflation is imposing an inflation tax in the case of $\acute{A}$ or an inflation yield in the case of $\acute{B}'$ whenever $R_b' - \pi'$ falls below its normal real level. But since in a small economy without an international currency $\pi$ will not influence $\pi'$, these possibilities are uninteresting in relation to the national inflationary tax.

Going back to $-(R_b - \pi)\frac{B}{P}$ when $R_b = 0$ as in the case of currency, the government gets $\pi\frac{B}{P}$ from the inflation tax. Even when government debt pays interest, there will be an inflation tax whenever $R_b - \pi$ falls below the normal real rate of return. If the noninflationary real yield on the government debt is $\rho$, then savers will be taxed at the rate $-(R_b - \pi - \rho)$, so that only when $R_b - \pi = \rho$ will this particular tax equal zero.

If income tax schedules and deductions are not adjusted for inflation, then $I/P$ would be a function of $\pi$. The assumption will be that the appropriate inflationary corrections are made so that $I/P$ is not a function of $\pi$. Inflation will also tax firms through the reduction in the real value of their depreciation and benefit them on their net indebtedness, because normal interest payments and receipts are taxable income or deductible expenditures.

An analysis of the balance sheets of Mexican corporations showed that these effects produced a net gain to Mexican firms, which arises mainly from their foreign debts. However, there is no tax involved here, only a redistribution of wealth within the private sector.

From the definition of government income, one can see that the government can finance a level of real expenditures. All it has to do is issue the amount of money necessary to keep its real debt constant. This is the nature of the inflationary tax, which differs from the income the government obtains from its seigniorial power which allows it to increase the real monetary base in a growing economy. The well-known negative relationship between the real monetary base asset holders will demand and inflation is ignored for these purposes.

## Measurement

### *Broad Aggregates*

To give an idea of the importance of the inflation tax as a source of revenue, a broad exercise is presented before going into the details on how it was distributed among family groups.

The values of the following concepts were considered:

1. Currency in circulation
   a. In the hands of the public
   b. In the portfolio of credit institutions
2. Deposits without interest at Banco de México
   a. From firms and individuals
   b. From credit institutions
3. Interest-paying deposits of financial institutions at Banco de México

Item 3 takes into account the borrowing of the government from the public which in Mexico takes place through the central bank. An open market was recently initiated in treasury bills. Both treasury bills and item 3 yield an inflation tax equal to the difference between inflation and the nominal interest rate plus a "normal" real interest rate, as already explained.

The inflation rate is calculated by taking the average rate of increase of the consumer price index. The normal real rate of interest is assumed to be 3.5 percent.

### *Distribution of the Inflation Tax Across Income Classes*

The income expenditure survey (IES) has data on individual interest income and time deposits but not data on cash balances, except for the increase in cash during the period covered by the survey. To make an estimate of household cash balances, a constant income velocity of cash balances was assumed equal to the aggregate velocity of circulation. Gross household income was divided by this constant to give an estimate of average cash balances. The aggregate estimate of the inflation tax on cash balances was distributed across households in proportion to their estimated cash balances.

The inflation tax on time deposits was first calculated from aggregated data (Table A-1) and then distributed across households in proportion to their individual holdings of total time deposits.

*TABLE A.1.*

*Inflation Tax in Mexico*

*(Balances at the Beginning of the Period in Millions of Current Pesos)*

| | *1976* | *1977* | *1978* | *1979* | *1980* |
|---|---|---|---|---|---|
| 1. Currency in circulation | 56,708.8 | 84,706.1 | 94,512.2 | 120,876.4 | 159,151.9 |
| a. In the hands of the public | 52,263.6 | 79,873.5 | 88,632.3 | 114,810.5 | 149,582.3 |
| b. In the portfolio of credit institutions | 4,445.2 | 4,832.6 | 5,879.9 | 6,005.9 | 9,569.6 |
| 2. Deposits without interest at Banco de México | 1,109.3 | 1,423.9 | 6,448.8 | 5,773.5 | 3,508.8 |
| a. From firms and individuals | 856.1 | 559.8 | 1,862.5 | 817.7 | |
| b. From credit institutions | 253.2 | 864.1 | 5,086.3 | 4,955.8 | 3,508.8 |
| 3. Interest-paying deposits and government bonds in the current account of financial institutions at Banco de México | 114,158.7 | 128,193.9 | 173,860.3 | 232,207.6 | 323,847.9 |
| Sum of items 1 and 3 | 57,818.1 | 86,130.0 | 101,461.0 | 126,699.9 | 162,660.7 |
| Inflationary tax rate on items 1 and 2[a] | 27.2 | 20.7 | 16.2 | 20.0 | 29.8 |
| Inflationary tax rate on item 3[b] | 18.9 | 11.3 | 7.5 | 11.5 | 21.3 |
| Total inflation tax | 17,884.3 | 32,297.6 | 29,476.2 | 52,177.4 | 117,355.2 |

[a] December–December percent increase in consumer price index.

[b] Difference between normal real interest rate in the noninflationary state (3.5 percent) and the actual real interest rate paid by Banco de México on item 3.

# APPENDIX II

# *Methodology for Calculating the Incidence of Taxes across Family Income Groups for Year 1977*

## *Direct Taxes*

Survey[8] information on the different types of income is net of income taxes and was reported for the first semester of 1977. Thus the data were first annualized[9] and then grossed up so families could be classified according to gross income. Income sources reported were individual income and income from firms.

### *Individuals*

Income was reported as labor income; professional income; income from the rental of property; income from ownership of patents, trademarks, and copyrights; and interest income.

Labor income was in turn reported as follows:

1. Wages, salaries, tips, and overtime
2. Year-end bonus
3. Vacation pay
4. Dividends
5. Retirement income

In the case of labor income, an annualization factor for each type of income was obtained from *Estadística Industrial Mensual,* published by the Secretaría de Programación y Presupuesto. These factors were 2.169 for concepts 1–4 and 2 for concept 5.

The annualization factor for professional income was 1.919 and was obtained from the monthly professional income tax series. A 2-month lag was included to capture the delay in the payment of the tax (professional payments for this tax have to be made, at the most, 2 months ater receiving the income). These data were obtained from *Indicadores Tributarios*

*1977*, published by the Dirección General de Política de Ingresos, Secretaría de Hacienda y Crédito Público.

In the case of income from the rental of property, the annualization factor of 2.077 was obtained from the seasonality of the rental price index for 1977 published by Banco de México.

Since there is not an a priori consideration for thinking that some kind of seasonality must exist in income from the ownership of patents, trademarks, and copyrights, only 75 percent of this income was considered as taxable because copyrights are tax exempt.

For interest income the annualization factor was 2.1015, taking the seasonal pattern of the series of financial expenditures by the banking sector published by Banco de México.

The main problem in this study consisted in grossing up net income, already mentioned, which, in turn, depends on the tax treatment derived from the Income Tax Law for 1977. There are two cases: one corresponding to Article 75 and the other corresponding to Article 86. Article 75 is used when the individual receives only labor income and it is less than 90,394.00 pesos[10] (100,000.00 pesos of gross income in Article 86 are equivalent to 90,394 pesos of net income in Article 75). In this case, the individual can deduct from his or her gross income 20 percent of the income. As can be seen, deductions are a function of gross income, the variable we are trying to determine. Other components of gross income are social security contributions, which are also a function of gross income. Thus an iterative method was used in order to make the following equation equal to zero:

$$G - N - ssG - f(G) - 0.2G$$

where

*G:* gross income from labor
*N:* net income from labor
*ssG:* social security contributions (a function of gross salary)
*fG:* tax payment (a function of gross income from labor)

The process consists of an iterative method where in the first step gross salary (*G*) is made equal to net salary (from the survey). Obviously, in this first step the equation will not be zero, so the process continues until its value is zero.

Article 86 is used when

1. Net income from labor exceeds 90,394.00 pesos
2. Net income from labor does not exceed 90,394.00 pesos but the individual has any other source of income (labor or otherwise).

Interest income is not relevant for this procedure because it is received net of taxes, and it is not accumulated to other types of income.

Interest income is simply grossed up by a factor of

$$\frac{1}{1 - 0.1739} = 1.2106$$

where 0.1739 is the average tax rate on interest.

Tax-exempt incomes also constitute gross income, so they were also considered:

1. *Income from small family industries.* It was annualized according to the seasonal pattern of economic activity present in 1977, based on the value of production series published in Estadística Industrial Mensual. The resulting factor was 2.1306.
2. *Income from scholarships, donations, and alimonies.* Since there is no a priori consideration for seasonality, the factor used was 2.
3. *Risk insurance indemnifications.* For the same reason as in 2, the factor used was 2.
4. *Other indemnifications.* A factor of 1 was used, based on the assumption that they are only received once a year. The minimum wage is exempt.

*Firms*

Firms can be classified into two large groups according to their gross income: small taxpayer and major taxpayer. If their gross income is more than 1.5 million pesos, they are considered major. But again the problem was that gross income was not available so an equivalence between gross and net income had to be established. It was assumed that 300,000 pesos of net income is equivalent to 3 million pesos of gross income from sales (assuming a 10 percent profit margin). Because of tax evasion, a firm was considered a major taxpayer if its annualized gross income was estimated larger than 3 million pesos. The corresponding annualization factor was 2.0883 obtained from *Estadística Industrial Mensual.*

Net income from dividends was not treated as direct income of the individual. It was grossed up to obtain the corresponding corporation taxable income. The tax was calculated multiplying gross income by the average tax for corporations in 1977 (40 percent).

The factor for grossing up dividends[11] was 111.41. This factor is the proportion of taxable income to net income from dividends. It was calculated considering the 8 percent ratio of profits sharing to workers on gross profits, the percentage of net corporate income profits reinvested by the corporation, and the 21 percent witholding tax on dividends.

According to the classification of firms made before, the factor for grossing up net income of small taxpayers was then:

$$\frac{1}{1 - 0.05} = 1.0526$$

where 0.05 is the average tax rate for small taxpayers. Taxable income is obtained by multiplying this factor by the net income of small taxpayers.

In the case of major taxpayers the net income from owned firms was grossed up as follows:

$$taxable\ income = \frac{after\text{-}tax\ income}{1 - 0.4 - 0.08} = \frac{after\text{-}tax\ income}{0.52}$$

Disposable income from business = 0.5 after-tax income, assuming that the proportion of income left after reinvestment is 0.5. This ratio is much higher than the dividend profits ratio of 2.18 percent used above because in owner- or family-managed firms dividends are basically a salary as a result of tax considerations.

Then

$$0.5\ (0.52)\ taxable\ income \quad disposable\ income$$

and

$$\frac{1}{0.52 \times 0.5} = 3{,}846$$

The corporate income tax was calculated by multiplying taxable income by the average tax rate for corporations (= 40 percent).

Total tax payments by corporations were obtained by adding up the three calculations described.

*Social Security Contributions*

The relevant income for calculating social security contributions is gross wage or salary. The rates of contribution differ whether the worker works for the government or for a private institution. If the worker is in the first category, he or she will pay 8 percent of the gross salary, and the government will pay 12.75 percent. If the worker works for a private company, he or she will pay 3.75 percent, and the employer will pay 10.875 percent, including the ordinary risk premium.

Other employer contributions are a 1 percent payroll tax and 5 percent of the total amount paid in salaries for the workers' housing fund [Institute of the National Housing Fund for Workers (INFONAVIT)]. The minimum wage is exempt from these contributions. If this is the case, the employer will pay the employee's part.

*Inflation Tax*

The calculation of the inflation tax was done as follows: the velocity of money was calculated using national income data and money average monthly balances for the whole year. Total household gross income was divided by this estimated velocity of money to obtain the average balances held by each household. The total amount of inflation tax collections for this concept was distributed according to the proportion of money balances that each household held of the total.

There is another inflation tax which corresponds to time deposits. Again, the proportion of time deposits that each household held within the total reported in the survey was obtained. Tax collections for this concept were distributed according to this proportion. The amount of tax collected was obtained by multiplying the difference between the real rate of interest in a noninflationary situation (3.5 percent) and the real rate of interest paid by Banco de México on deposits of financial institutions and government bonds held by financial institutions at the Central Bank.

### *Indirect Taxes*

For estimating the indirect tax burden in 1977, tax rates by sector of origin, that is, by sector where the tax is originated, were determined. This 1 × 72 line vector was postmultiplied by the direct and indirect requirements matrix (input-output) to obtain a vector of tax rates by sector of destiny. This vector was multiplied by a 72 × 100 matrix: 72 sectors of expenditure and 100 percentiles of income. A 1 × 100 line vector of indirect tax collections was obtained. This vector was transformed into another which showed the proportion of tax collections paid by each percentile within total tax collections estimated by this method. Actual revenue for indirect taxes that have an incidence on private consumption was distributed according to this proportion to obtain the final 1 × 100 vector of tax collections, so that the *i*th element corresponds to the total indirect taxes paid by the *i*th percentile. These taxes are mainly represented by the turnover sales tax (ISIM), which also has an incidence on investment and public consumption, though its possible incidence on exports is discarded because Mexico acts as a price taker. In this sense these taxes would be a combination of indirect taxes that are passed on to future consumers through a greater depreciation because of the tax that is borne by investment and a tax on income for exporters.

Therefore, it would be necessary to calculate also the tax contents in the actual depreciation that are carried from other periods to present consumers.

The difficulty of doing these calculations makes it preferable not to shift the incidence of these taxes to the future, so that past taxes reflected in depreciation expenditures were not considered. If it is assumed that the proportion of present investment for replacement purposes is large, then taxes having an incidence over investment can be allocated in the current period.

As to exports, in 1977 indirect tax rebates compensate the indirect tax burden that was borne by exporters. This consideration justifies that the turnover sales tax not be partially allocated as an income tax on exporters.

## *Import Taxes*

The estimate of the incidence of import tariffs on each branch of economic activity was made taking into account direct purchases of final products and inputs abroad as well as foreign inputs of domestic inputs and outputs and so on.

We start with the price equation of the input-output matrix without any tariff:

$$P_0 = A' P_0 q^{-1} M' P_0^e n \tag{1}$$

where

- $P_0$: $n \times 1$ column vector with the price index of each branch without tariffs.
- $A$: $n \times n$ direct requirements matrix of domestic inputs
- $q$: $n \times n$ diagonal matrix of the gross production value of each sector.
- $M$: $n \times n$ matrix of imports value (each $M_{ij}$, $i, J = 1 \ldots n$, shows the import value of branch $j$ from sector $i$ abroad)
- $P_0^e$: $n$-element column vector of the foreign import price index for each branch.
- $n$: $n$-element column vector of value added per unit of gross production in each branch

With the tariffs, the price vector becomes

$$P_1 = A' P_1 + q^{-1} M' (I + tmo) P_0^e + n \tag{2}$$

where $tmo$ is a diagonal matrix of tariffs by sector of origin.

Subtracting Eq. (2) from Eq. (1), we get the tariff effect on prices:

$$P_1 - P_0 = A' (P_1 - P_0) + q^{-1} M' \, tmo \, P_0^e \tag{3}$$

Taking the foreign import price index (1 = 100) as $P_0^e = i$, where $i$ is a column vector consisting of $n$ unit elements, and postmultiplying $tmo$ by $i$, we obtain an $n$-element column vector $tmo$. Defining an $n$-element column vector $t = P_1 - P_0$, we can express Eq. (3) as

$$t = A' t + q^{-1} M' \, tmo \tag{4}$$

Solving for $t$, we obtain

$$t = (I - A')^{-1} q^{-1} M' \, tmo \tag{5}$$

which shows each sector tariff payment accruing direct as well as indirect imports. This point could become clearer by denoting $tmd = q^{-1} M' \, tmo$ as an $n$-element column vector of tariff payments as a proportion of gross output in each branch. Since $(I - A')^{-1}$ can be approximated as an infinite series $I + A' + A'^2 + A'^3 + A'^4 + \ldots$, Eq. (5) can be rewritten as

$$t = tmd + A'\,tmd + A'^2\,tmd + A'^3\,tmd + \ldots \qquad (6)$$

in which we can identify the tariff effect on prices at each stage: *tmd*, the direct tariff payment, $A'$ *tmd*, the tariff payment of foreign content in domestic imputs; $A'^2$ *tmd*, the tariff payment of inputs of these inputs; and so on. Now we have the tariff effect according to each sector of final destination.

### *Empirical Estimation*

For the purpose of empirical estimation, the input-output table for 1970 was used. It has the necessary information for estimating Eq. (5) for seventy-two branches of economic activity. Vector *tmo* was estimated with the reallocation of imports and import tax collections by ninety-nine chapters of the Tariff to the General Tax on Imports by seventy-two branches, with information for the year 1978, taking the tax rate as the ratio of tax collection and value of imports for each branch according to the mentioned reclassification.

The matrices $(I - A')^{-1}$, $q$, and $M'$ were taken directly from the input-output information for 1970.

Up to this point, only the intermediate import tax rates by sector of final destination have been calculated. The calculation of import tax rates on consumption goods was done by multiplying each element of the *tmo* vector by the proportion of consumption of imports and total consumption of each of the seventy-two sectors. The $n \times 1$ *tmd* vector was multipled by 1 minus the proportion mentioned. Thus the final import tax rates are a weighted average of import tax rates on intermediate goods and import tax rates on consumption goods.

This vector was postmultiplied by the $72 \times 100$ matrix containing household expenditure by percentile of gross income for each of the seventy-two branches of economic activity to obtain a $1 \times 100$ line vector containing total import tax collection by percentile of household gross income.

## *Real Estate Tax and Car Owner's Tax*

Real estate and car owner's taxes were taken directly from the survey. The real estate tax had an annualization factor of 2 because there is no a priori consideration for thinking that some pattern of seasonality should exist. The annualization factor for car owner's tax was 1 because this tax is paid once a year.

## Methodology for Calculating Fiscal Incidence Across Family Income Groups for the Year 1980

All fiscal burdens obtained for 1980 have the same base as in 1977. For instance, in calculating income tax on individuals and firms, this incidence model answers the following question: How would direct tax burdens for 1977 be modified if the 1980 Income Tax Law is used, applying it to the incomes observed in 1977, and how would the indirect tax burdens be modified if the indirect fiscal system is applied to the consumption expenditures observed in 1977?

### *Methodology for Calculating Direct Taxes*

#### *Individuals*

LABOR INCOME

Labor income includes wages, salaries, tips, overtime, vacation pay, year-end bonus, etc. For calculating the annual tax, Article 98 of the 1980 Income Tax Law is used. This article contains the tax rates and amounts that have to be paid according to the different brackets of income. Thus the brackets and the amounts to be paid have to be deflated in order to use 1980 pesos together with 1977 pesos.

The tax treatment of labor income says that if this income does not exceed 167,261.00 pesos, which correspond to 300,000.00 deflated pesos of 1980, the individual can deduct from his or her gross income the amount of 33,170.00 pesos, which corresponds to the deflated minimum wage of 1980. If this income does exceed the amount stated, the individual will have other deductions: medical and funeral expenses. Article 98 is again used for the calculation of the annual tax.

PROFESSIONAL INCOME

The calculation for the annual tax is done using Article 98 without taking into account the amount of professional income. These individuals can deduct the concepts mentioned plus expenses necessary for obtaining this income. Thus a total deduction of 50 percent is assumed because of the lack of information concerning these expenses.

INCOME FROM THE RENTAL OF PROPERTY AND INCOME FROM OWNERSHIP OF PATENTS, TRADEMARKS, AND COPYRIGHTS

Again, Article 98 is used, but no deductions are considered because the income that was obtained from 1977 (net income by grossing it up) was taxable income and not gross income.

INTEREST INCOME

It was considered that 98.85 percent of total interest income comes from time deposits. The rest, 1.15 percent, is derived from savings accounts. The former was multiplied by the average rate on interest for

1980. This procedure was followed because it is a definite payment, so no calculations for the annual tax had to be done; that is, Article 98 was not necessary for this calculation.

*Firms*

The 1980 Income Tax Law says that if a firm's gross income is greater than 1.5 million pesos, the firm is a major taxpayer. The firm is a small taxpayer if its gross income is below 1.5 million pesos. But this criterion could not be applied because the incomes that we had for 1977 were taxable incomes, so they had to be grossed up by a factor of 20, because 5 percent of gross income corresponds to taxable income. After this, the tax treatment was applied. If gross income was less than 836,307.00 pesos (1.5 million deflated pesos), the tax for small taxpayers was obtained by multiplying gross income by the average tax rate for these taxpayers, 5 percent. If, on the contrary, the firm is a mayor taxpayer, its gross income was multiplied by 0.4305.

This rate incorporates the 42 percent that these firms pay on their taxable income, the percentage of dividends that firms distribute among shareholders (10 percent), the percentage of profit sharing to workers, (8 percent), and the 21 percent withholding tax on dividends.

*Social Security Contributions*

Social security contributions are the same as in 1977 because the social security treatment in 1980 with respect to 1977 did not change.

*Inflation Tax*

The calculation for 1980 was exactly the same as in 1977, taking the corresponding tax collections for 1980.

## *Methodology for Calculating Indirect Taxes*

For 1980 the methodology for indirect taxes is substantially different with respect to 1977. Instead of using input-output information, all the different taxed items of expenditure were considered, multiplying their value by their corresponding indirect tax rate (value-added tax and excise tax).

This was done for every household to determine the amount of indirect taxes paid by each family. Indirect tax collection from national accounts was distributed according to the proportion of indirect taxes that each household paid within the total collection obtained by the method mentioned before.

The value-added tax revenue derived from the food sector was substracted from the total value-added tax collection of 118,908 million pesos because, since September 1980, they became taxed at a zero rate.

### *Methodology for Calculating Import Taxes*

The calculation of import taxes is exactly the same as in 1977, using data for 1980.

# APPENDIX III

## *A General Equilibrium Model to Determine Tax Incidence in a Small Open Economy*

The traditional theory of tax incidence must be qualified in the presence of factor mobility and trade flows among countries or regions.

The Harberger[12] model (which assumes a closed economy) is valid for evaluating the incidence of the average world tax rate on one factor, or on one factor in one sector for a large country like the United States. The possibility of capital movements and trade flows is sufficient to allow a significant share of the burden of taxation to be transmitted abroad.

The case is even more extreme for a small open economy, because here it must be assumed that world prices of final products and of many factor inputs must be taken as fixed i.e., beyond the control of the country in question.

The discussion about the "old" versus the "new" view of the incidence of the property tax has pointed to the need for defining the level (or relative size) of the region where such a tax is imposed before one can make inferences about its incidence. Each of the two views can be correct when applied to the right problem.

The old view (that the property tax is essentially an excise tax) is correct for a small region or, more precisely, what is relevant for this approach are deviations from the "average" world tax rate. The new view is relevant to determine the incidence of the average world tax rate.

The small open economy (be it a country or a region) produces two outputs, $X$ and $Y$; $X$ is tradable and $Y$ is nontradable. This duality can also be used to distinguish between the factor receiving a tax credit for regional development versus other factors.

We assume there are three factors of production: capital $(K)$, labor $(L)$, and land $(A)$. Capital and labor are traded internationally and are perfectly mobile among national regions and sectors. Land is tradable only among the sectors of a region.

The model is presented in differential notation, with its usual implications: only small changes are valid; discrete changes are only local approximations. It is assumed that the point of departure is an undistorted equilibrium. This summarized version of the general equilibrium model discusses only the problems involved with the issue of incidence, so material irrelevant for this purpose is excluded.

It is appropriate to verify the tax equivalences that hold in the small open economy model.

With perfect factor mobility only the price equations are relevant to determine the incidence of taxation:

$$p_x = f_k p_k + f_l p_l + f_a p_a \tag{1}$$
$$P_y = g_k p_k + g_l p_l + g_a p_a \tag{2}$$

Totally differentiating, we obtain:

$$dp_x = f_k (dp_k + t_k) + f_l \, dp_l + f_a \, dp_a \tag{3}$$
$$dp_y = g_k (dp_k + t_k) + g_l dp_l + g_a dp_a \tag{4}$$

Where $p_x$ is an international price. Thus $dp_x = 0$. $p_k$, and $p_l$ and $p_a$ are prices for factors. Because of the small country assumption,

$$dp_k = dp_l = 0$$

The $f_i$'s are the intial factor shares in total cost.

Taxing all factors used to produce $x$ is equivalent to a tax on $x$ at the same rate; from Eq. (3);

$$0 = f_k t + f_l t + f_a (dp_z + t)$$

Therefore $dp_a = -t/f_a$ and $dp_y = -tg_a/f_a$.

From Eq. (3)

$$0 = t_x + f_a \, dp_a$$
$$dp_a = t_x/f_a$$

and hence

$$dp_y = tg_a/f_a$$

Therefore, they are equivalent.

Taxing all factors of production is equivalent to a tax on both outputs at the same rate:

$$\text{Q} = f_k t + f_l t + f_a t + f_a \, dp_a$$
$$dp_a = -t/f_a; \text{ since } f_k + f_l + f_a = 1,$$
$$dp_y = g_k t + g_l t = g_a \, dp_a = t(f_a - g_a)/f_a \tag{5}$$

Taxing both outputs, we obtain:

$$\text{Q} = t + f_a \, dp_a, \qquad dp_a = -t/f_a$$
$$dp_y = t + g_a \, dp_a = t(f_a - g_a)/f_a \tag{6}$$

The last scheme is nonneutral with respect to relative commodity prices unless both sectors have the same share of land in total costs. Additionally, the last scheme, either a tax on both outputs or a tax on all inputs used (a GNP or a value-added tax), is equivalent (except for revenue) to a tax at the same rate on capital and labor, as a general tax on land is fully capitalized into land prices.

It is very important to realize the institutional framework for factor taxation in the world. The "tax credit system" and taxation of income earned abroad induces the small country to tax mobile factors at the average international tax rate. If it is not done, the small country will lose rents from factor taxation because lower tax rates do not induce a foreign inflow of capital. (Tax havens may offset this conclusion). Therefore, the next analysis will focus on differential taxation around the international level.

The analysis of incidence is straightforward. Land and consumers of the nontradable good bear all the burden. In the following analysis, it is assumed that the traded sector is the corporate sector and the nontraded sector is noncorporate (i.e., housing).

The incidence of the corporation income tax in excess of the world level falls exclusively on land owners, who bear more than the full burden of the tax.

$$\phi = f_k t_{kx} + f_a dp_a, \qquad dp_a = t_{kx}(f_k / f_a)$$

and hence

$$A_x(dp_a) = K_x t_{kx}$$

therefore, the total burden is larger than 100 percent:

$$dp_a\,(A_x + A_y) = -K_x\,(A_y + A_x / A_y) t_{kx}$$

The difference between the burden borne by land and the tax collections is enjoyed by consumers of $Y$, the price of which has fallen:

$$dPy = \frac{-g_a f_k T_k x}{f_a}$$

This would be equivalent to, say, a tax credit for regional development that will be enjoyed by landowners, and the consumers of $Y$ will loose.

The incidence of the excess of the property tax (a tax on capital and land in both sectors) over the world level falls on landowners and may also fall on consumers of nontradables:

$$0 = f_k T + f_a T + f_a\,dP_a, \qquad dP_a = \frac{-(f_k + f_a)T}{f_a}$$

and

$$dPy = (g_k - f_a f_k / f_a)T$$

A general property tax is equivalent to a tax on capital at the same rate, but with a smaller revenue for allocation purposes.

Property taxes are usually imposed at differential rates or only on the housing sector, which can be identified with the nontraded sector. In such a situation:

$$dp_a = 0 \quad \text{and} \quad dp_y = (g_k + g_a)\, t$$

implying that the full burden of the differential property tax rate is borne by consumers of housing. Thus it could be tested whether differential property taxes are fully reflected in housing prices or rents. Taxes on the production of the nontraded good will be fully borne by consumers of that good:

$$dp_y = t_y$$

Taxes on production of the traded good will be more than fully borne by the inmobile factor:

$$0 - t_x = f_a dp_a, \qquad dp_a = -t_x/f_a$$
$$A_x dp_a = -t_x X$$

and consumers of *Y* will receive a transfer from landowners equal to the difference between the tax burden on land and the tax revenue.

A general production tax or a value-added tax of the income type will be fully borne by land if $f_a = g_a$, more than fully borne if $g_a > f_a$ (with a transfer to consumers of *Y*), and less than fully borne if $g_a < f_a$ (with consumers of *Y* sharing in the burden).

## Notes

1. However, capital income is smaller than the amounts shown in national accounts. The so-called payments to capital or *superávit de explotación* in the national accounts contain a substantial portion of payments to labor. For instance, the income of all self-employed persons, about one-half of the labor force, is included here.

2. Jesús Reyes Heroles, "Política Fiscal y Redistribución del Ingreso," Licenciado Thesis prepared for the Instituto Technoógico Autónomo de México, 1976.

3. The contribution regarding the assumptions on general equilibrium is drawn from Arturo Fernández from whose Ph.D. thesis proposal I borrowed and who helped me prepare this section. Arturo Fernández, "Essays on Taxation in a Small Open Economy," Ph.D. Thesis Proposal, University of Chicago.

4. Bilateral tax treaties with tax-sparing provisions would change this result. Such is not the case in Mexico, nor are the countries from which it imports capital likely to agree to such a clause.

5. This can be modified due to the "deferral possibility"; i.e., income is taxed abroad until it is sent back home or more likely through the successful use of tax havens.

6. Jesús Cervantes, "México: Análisis de la Distribución del Ingreso," *Comercio Exterior* 3, No. 1 (Jan. 1982), pp. 43–50.

7. There are complications, however, when trying to use the permanent income concept in connection with taxes in defining permanent gross income. The problem is relatively simple in the case of excise taxes because reported expenditure already includes the tax paid by consumers on their purchases of goods and services.

8. From the Household Income Expenditure Survey of 1977.

9. By using a factor that captures each item's particular seasonal pattern.

10. The law stipulated that individuals with annual gross labor incomes above 125,000 had to file a return and were taxed according to the tariff and deductions of Article 86. However, in 1977 an individual could opt for Article 86 if he or she had an annual gross income as low as 62,500 pesos. While Article 86 was more attractive because of its larger itemized deductions, in practice on the average only individuals with incomes above 100,000 pesos actually took advantage of this option. Then:

$$\frac{P}{D} = \frac{1}{(1 - t - s)\, r\, (1 - d)} = \frac{1}{(1 - 0.4 - 0.08)\, 0.02185\, (1 - 0.21)} = 111.41$$

*t:* corporation income tax
*s:* profit-sharing ratio to workers
*r:* dividend/profits ratio
*d:* dividend tax rate

11. For grossing up dividends, let *P* be gross corporation profits.

12. Arnold C. Harberger, "The Incidence of the Corporation Income Tax," *Journal of Political Economy* LXX (June 1972), 215–240.

# CHAPTER 5

# *Generation and Allocation of Oil Economic Surpluses*

Socrates C. Rizzo

## Introduction

Mexico's oil reserves (including natural gas and crude oil) have grown more than 1000 percent in the past 6 years (1975–1981) from 6.3 billion barrels in 1975 to 72 billion in 1981. Mexico now occupies fourth place in the world in proven oil reserves.

According to the policy outlined in the Mexican government's energy program, natural gas and crude oil production will not exceed 10 million barrels a day. By the end of 1980 the average daily production of oil and natural gas was 2.8 million barrels; that is 28 percent of the proposed platform of 10 million barrels a day.

Petroleos Mexicanos' (PEMEX's) gross value added expressed as a percentage of gross domestic product (GDP) went from 1.5 percent in 1975 to 5.2 percent in 1979 and above 7.5 percent in 1980, and if the final product is evaluated at international prices, the value added accounts for 11.5 percent in 1975 and 18 percent in 1979. Regarding employment, the rate that PEMEX generates increased employment is an annual average of 6.3 percent between 1975 and 1979, compared with the average total annual increase of production of 29.3 percent.

Even though the energy program of the federal government (1980) suggests that the intention is to reduce the gap between international prices and national prices in a period of 10 years by approximately 70 percent, the average international price in 1979 with respect to hydrocarbon prod-

I am grateful for the contribution of Ricardo Luna to this paper, especially in the cost of capital estimations and for checking all the calculations. I am grateful also for the contribution of Fernando González in the estimate of Mexico's oil wealth.

ucts was 2.13 times the average internal prices. This ratio diminished at the end of 1981 due to a rise in the domestic price of gasoline, but it increased after the February 1982 devaluation of the Mexican peso.

The outstanding growth in oil production and its contribution to the national wealth will produce a significant change both in sectoral income distribution (agricultural and industrial sector) and between the public and private sectors. The contribution of the oil sector to national income has surpassed that of the agricultural sector, and Mexico's oil wealth is much greater than nonoil wealth. As a result, the relative role of land in income distribution policies will be reduced.

The contribution of the oil sector to GDP in 1980 was 7.6 percent, greater than that of the agricultural sector (5 percent). However, PEMEX employed only 0.5 percent of the labor force, while in agriculture 35 percent of the labor force was employed.

If the exploitable oil reserves, amounting to 101 billion[1] barrels, are valued at the international price of $31.25 per barrel and if the extraction cost is subtracted (estimated at $900 million), the result is a net value of $2.3 trillion, an amount which is 13.6 times 1980's gross domestic product ($168.6 billion)[2] and 5.7 times the total estimated physical capital during this same period.

Those who are in favor of a radical distribution of wealth affecting the ownership of the means of production usually consider that fiscal mechanisms produce only marginal changes without any quantitative importance. This approach does not take into consideration the role that oil plays in the hands of the state, because if we add the estimated value of the hydrocarbons to the national wealth, the Mexican state would own 85 percent of the total wealth, a much greater percentage than that owned by the state in some socialist countries. This fact substantially increases the role of the state in Mexico's mixed economy and implies greater significance for budgeting technologies and fiscal mechanisms in the distribution of income.

This research has a dual purpose: first to examine the implications that oil has for the distribution of wealth between the public and private sector and second to understand the consequences of the use of the oil surplus for intergenerational income distribution.

With respect to the second purpose of this study, the way in which oil wealth is used will determine the level of income for future generations. If the oil surplus (the net income flow from extraction) is utilized for subsidizing consumption or increasing current expenditures of the public sector, the result would be greater current consumption. On the other hand, if the oil surplus is transformed into a permanent income stream or if it is used to reduce external debt, income would be transferred into the future.

In the case of a closed economy, if oil extraction were increased beyond the investment capacity of the economy, this would reduce the rate of return of investment. As a result, the rate of reserve extraction should be diminished so that interest rates fall below the expected increases in the price of hydrocarbons. On the other hand, in an open economy the oil surplus can be channeled abroad in the form of direct or indirect investment, advance repayment of public debt, or a reduction in the rate of increase of foreign indebtedness. In the latter two cases, the relevant opportunity cost to be used in a comparison with the expected growth of oil prices would be the interest that the country would save by advance payment of public external debt.[3]

If the internal consumption of oil is less than its optimum rate of production, as seems to be the case in Mexico, oil wealth will be used for the purchase of other foreign goods or other international assets: imported goods, capital exports, or the accumulation of reserves.

Another important factor in the distribution of income is the effect of oil production on the creation of employment. The direct effect can be seen more clearly since the extraction and production of oil is a relatively capital-intensive activity.

One of the important indirect effects of energy policy on employment is the subsidization of energy costs. Cheap oil promotes the substitution of capital for labor because inexpensive energy goes hand in hand with the use of machinery and increases the relative cost of manpower. Another indirect effect is the overvaluation of the currency caused by the excess foreign exchange earned from oil exports. As a result, labor-intensive exports become uncompetitive, and as hydrocarbon exports increase their participation in foreign markets, Leontief's paradox comes into play: the exports of Mexico, a country with relative abundance of labor force, will be highly capital intensive.

This study covers the period from 1973 to 1980 and is divided into three major parts: the first section is an analysis of the importance of oil production in the foreign market and public finance and a discussion of estimates of the oil wealth; the next part estimates the oil surplus priced at official and shadow prices; the final part analyzes the national consumption of energy and the redistribution of the federal surplus toward the parastatal firms experiencing a deficit and toward the private sector.

## The Importance of Oil in the National Accounts and Total Wealth

Since 1977 oil has become a key factor in the Mexican economy. Not only has it changed the role of the foreign sector and of public finance; it offers a new perspective to the problem of employment and income distribution.

### *Hydrocarbons in Foreign Trade and Public Finance*

The share of exports of crude oil in total revenues in the current account has increased substantially in the last 5 years: from 1.9 percent in

*TABLE 5.1.*
*Exports*
*(Millions of Dollars)*

| | *1970* | *1972* | *1974* | *1977* | *1978* | *1979* | *1980* |
|---|---|---|---|---|---|---|---|
| 1. Goods and services | 3,147.7 | 4,828.3 | 6,342.5 | 8,404.1 | 11,653.1 | 16,652.1 | 24,819.5 |
| 2. Goods | 1,373.0 | 2,070.5 | 2,850.0 | 4,418.4 | 6,063.1 | 8,798.2 | 15,307.5 |
| 3. Oil | 38.0 | 24.7 | 123.2 | 1,029.4 | 1,798.9 | 3,862.0 | 10,304.7 |
| 4. (3/1) × 100 | 1.2 | 0.5 | 1.9 | 12.2 | 15.4 | 23.9 | 41.5 |
| 5. (3/2) × 100 | 2.8 | 1.2 | 4.3 | 23.3 | 29.7 | 43.9 | 67.3 |

SOURCE: Calculations made with data of the Banco de México, S.A., *Informe Anual,* 1970–1980.

1974 to 12 percent in 1977 and 41.5 percent in 1980. Oil sold abroad constituted 1.2 percent in 1973. Since then, its growth has been uninterrupted, representing 29.7 percent in 1978 and 67.3 percent in 1980, as shown in Table 5-1.

In view of the extraordinary growth of exports of hydrocarbons, the role of the foreign sector in the economy has changed considerably. In the past, the country's growth was limited by the scarcity of foreign exchange[4]; today the principal restrictions are the lack of internal resources, such as transportation and skilled labor.[5]

The extraordinary growth in oil production has caused a change in the public sector's balance of payments, whose deficit in the current account went from 51.7 billion pesos in 1977 to a surplus of 17.5 billion pesos in

*TABLE 5.2.*
*PEMEX Contribution to the Balance of Payments*
*(Millions of Dollars)*

| | *1978* | *1979* | *1980* |
|---|---|---|---|
| Current account | −2,693.0 | −4,856.4 | −6,596.6 |
| Commercial balance | −2,273.5 | −3,797.4 | 4,209.4 |
| PEMEX | 512.2 | 2,652.2 | 8,642.6 |
| Nonoil products | −2,785.5 | −6,449.6 | −12,852.1 |
| Exports of goods | 6,063.1 | 8,798.2 | 15,307.5 |
| PEMEX | 1,789.9 | 3,861.0 | 10,305.7 |
| Nonoil products | 4,264.2 | 4,937.2 | 5,001.8 |
| Imports of goods[a] | 8,336.6 | 12,595.6 | 19,517.0 |
| PEMEX | 1,286.9 | 1,209.8 | 1,779.3 |
| Nonoil products | 7,049.7 | 11,386.8 | 17,737.7 |

SOURCE: Calculations made with data of the Banco de México, S.A., *Informe Anual,* 1978–1980.

[a]Capital goods are not included.

*TABLE 5.3.*
*Openness Coefficient*

| | X + M *(Totals/GDP)*[a] | | X + M *(Goods/GDP)* | |
|---|---|---|---|---|
| | A | B | A | B |
| 1965–1975 | 20.9 | 20.8 | 11.8 | 11.6 |
| 1976 | 16.8 | 16.1 | 11.8 | 11.1 |
| 1977 | 24.8 | 23.8 | 13.9 | 12.6 |
| 1978 | 27.9 | 26.0 | 15.0 | 13.1 |
| 1979 | 30.7 | 27.1 | 17.1 | 14.0 |
| 1980 | 34.7 | 27.1 | 17.1 | 14.0 |

SOURCE: See Table 5.2.

[a] *X* = exports; *M* = imports; *A* = includes oil exports; *B* = excludes oil exports.

1980. The foreign currency balance, including capital movements, moved from a surplus of 16.9 billion pesos in 1977 to a surplus of 112.8 in 1980. The current account balance of PEMEX showed an annual average deficit of $278 million for the period 1970–1976; since 1977 it has registered a positive balance that has increased to $8.6 billion in 1980. See Table 5-2.

While oil activity in Mexico is important, the situation is not similar to that existing in nations whose economy is based solely on oil. In Saudi Arabia, Iran, and Kuwait, oil-producing nations par excellence, more than 90 percent of total exports are oil based.

The recent openness of the economy of Mexico can be attributed to the growth of oil exports. The coefficient of openness of the economy for the period from 1965 to 1975 remained around 20 percent, and beginning in 1977 it increased, reaching 34.1 percent in 1980 (see Table 5.3).

The foreign sector openness of Mexico, like other oil-producing countries, has been an endogenously determined change which is quite different from countries such as Chile and South Korea that have promoted an exogenous commercial openness.

Until 1977, the relative contribution of the oil sector to public savings and to GDP stayed constant. During the most recent inflationary period (1978–1980), the contribution of the non-PEMEX public enterprises to public savings has been reduced because the growing inflation affected the cost of these entities, while their prices remained relatively constant due to public regulation,[6] and the increased deficit fed back into the inflationary process. However, PEMEX prices for foreign sales showed extraordinary growth until the second quarter of 1981. See Table 5-4.

The contribution of PEMEX to the revenues of the federal government has grown rapidly; while during the 1960s and until 1976 the oil sector contributed only 5.2 pecent of current revenues, in 1980 it was about 25.4 percent (see Table 5.5).[7]

The national oil company generates a surplus of income in relation to current expenditure after the payment of taxes. PEMEX, therefore, went

*TABLE 5.4.*
*Wholesale Index Price and Price Index of the Public Enterprises (Base 1970 = 100): 1970–1980*

| | *Price Index for Current Income Budget-Controlled Public Enterprises* | *Annual Growth Rate* | *Wholesale Index Prices* | *Annual Growth Rate* |
|---|---|---|---|---|
| 1970 | 100.0 | — | 100.0 | — |
| 1971 | 101.4 | 1.4 | 103.7 | 3.7 |
| 1972 | 104.2 | 1.7 | 106.6 | 2.8 |
| 1973 | 113.7 | 9.1 | 123.5 | 15.8 |
| 1974 | 163.0 | 43.4 | 151.2 | 22.4 |
| 1975 | 196.1 | 20.3 | 167.1 | 10.5 |
| 1976 | 198.9 | 1.4 | 204.2 | 22.2 |
| 1977 | 282.5 | 42.0 | 188.3 | 41.2 |
| 1978 | 107.9 | 8.9 | 333.8 | 15.8 |
| 1979 | 332.2 | 7.9 | 334.9 | 18.3 |
| 1980 | 298.9[a] | 20.1 | 491.6 | 24.5 |

SOURCE: Calculations made from data of the Banco de México, S.A. *Informe Anual*, 1970–1980.

[a] Oil prices were subtracted for this year.

*TABLE 5.5.*
*PEMEX Participation in Federal Revenues (%)*

| | *1977* | *1978* | *1979* | *1980* |
|---|---|---|---|---|
| Federal government current income | 100.0 | 100.0 | 100.0 | 100.0 |
| Taxation | 95.3 | 95.5 | 95.9 | 95.4 |
| PEMEX | 8.0 | 9.3 | 11.6 | 25.4 |
| Rest | 87.3 | 86.2 | 84.2 | 70.2 |
| Nontax revenues | 4.7 | 4.5 | 4.1 | 3.6 |

SOURCE: Dirección de Estadística Hacendaria, DGPH, Ministry of Finance.

from current savings of 14,500 million pesos in 1977 to 63,600 million pesos in 1980, while the rest of the budget-controlled public enterprises had negative current savings that increased from 21,000 million pesos in 1977 to more than 44.8 billion pesos in 1980 (see Table 5-6).

The importance of hydrocarbons in the last years for the generation of the GDP has grown considerably. In 1965 the value added of PEMEX represented only 1.6 percent of the GDP and 2 percent in 1970; from 1977 this coefficient has grown until it reached 8.1 percent of the GDP in 1980, as shown in Table 5-7.

*TABLE 5.6.*
*Current Savings of Budget-Controlled Public Enterprises*
*(Billions of Pesos)*

| | *1977* | *1978* | *1979* | *1980* |
|---|---|---|---|---|
| Revenue[a] | | | | |
| Total | 205.9 | 280.0 | 389.8 | 642.6 |
| PEMEX | 69.5 | 105.4 | 171.9 | 357.3 |
| Rest | 136.4 | 174.6 | 217.9 | 285.3 |
| Expenditure[b] | | | | |
| Total | 212.4 | 268.6 | 358.4 | 623.8 |
| PEMEX | 55.0 | 77.5 | 125.6 | 293.7 |
| Rest | 157.4 | 191.1 | 232.8 | 330.1 |
| Current savings | | | | |
| Total | −6.5 | 11.4 | 31.4 | 18.8 |
| PEMEX | 14.5 | 27.9 | 46.3 | 63.6 |
| Rest | (21.0) | (16.5) | (14.9) | (44.8) |

SOURCE: Ministry of Finance, *Situación Financiera de Organismos y Empresas Controladas,* Mexico City, 1980.

[a]Includes sales of goods and services, employer and employee fees, and other current income.

[b]Composed of salary and wages, acquisition of goods and services, interest, federal taxes, and other current expenditures.

*TABLE 5.7.*
*PEMEX's Participation in Gross Domestic Product*
*(Millions of Pesos and %)*

| | *1977* | *1978* | *1979* | *1980* |
|---|---|---|---|---|
| PEMEX, value added[a] | 49,782 | 91,327 | 144,761 | 314,800 |
| GDP | 1,574,700 | 2,122,800 | 2,767,000 | 3,863,285 |
| PEMEX added value GDP × 100 | 3.0 | 4.3 | 5.2 | 8.1 |

SOURCE: Calculations done with data from Secretaría de Programación y Presupuesto, *Cuenta Pública Federal,* 1977–1980; Banco de México, *Producto Interno Bruto y Gasto,* 1970–1980.

[a]The estimated value added includes payment for personal services, interest, and current savings before taxes paid by PEMEX.

## *Potential Oil Wealth*

The importance of hydrocarbons in the generation and distribution of wealth can best be appreciated when a comparison is made between the potential oil wealth and the physical capital of the economy and GDP. The

*TABLE 5.8.*
*Crude Oil Production Areas*
*(Thousands of Barrels Per Year)*

| | *1979* (1) | *1980* (2) | $\Delta q^b$ (3) |
|---|---|---|---|
| Golfo de Campeche | 52 | 754.8 | 702.8 |
| Chiapas-Tabasco | 1,067 | 1,040.6 | — |
| Others | 342 | 344.6 | — |
| Total | 1,461 | 2,130.0 | 702.8 |

SOURCE: Jaime Corredor, *El Petróleo en México,* Mexico City, 1980.

purpose of this section is to estimate the oil wealth. This is a complicated task, and here we aim only to approximate the order of magnitude of the net value of oil reserves and the implications this has for the distribution of income.

This study considers oil wealth as the surplus obtained by subtracting the current cost of extraction from the reserve value calculated at international prices ($31.25 per barrel).

The reserves taken into account amount to 101.3 billion barrels, consisting of part of the probable and all the proven reserves.[8] Proven reserves in fields now in operation equal 54.5 billion barrels, 17.5 billion barrels are available in fields that are not functioning, and current profitable probable reserves are 29.3 billion barrels.[9]

The marginal cost of extraction, in general, is increasing for two reasons: first due to the fact that the most profitable deposits are generally exploited first, and second due to the drop in the volume of production of each deposit because of diminishing internal pressure, once the contents begin to be removed.

To isolate the two factors that explain the growing cost, a division was made between the proven oil reserves located in fields already operating and those not yet exploited. With respect to the former, the loss in pressure causes a drop in the rate of production and increases its operational cost, but with respect to the latter the marginal cost will increase exponentially until it equals the price when reserves are exhausted, and it ceases to be profitable.

The cost functions were first derived having previously calculated the decline in production, which is explained as follows. The declining rate *(a)* is defined as the absolute decline *(A)* of production in the operating fields with respect to the previous year total net output.[10]

Since the absolute decline *(A)* in production is equal to the gross increase ($\Delta q^b$) in production (especially in the expanding fields) minus the net increase of production ($\Delta q^n$),[11] the declining rate is given by

$$a = \frac{\Delta q^b - q_t + q_t - 1}{q_t - 1}$$

Table 5-8 is a description of the crude oil production areas. The last column indicates the increase in the expansion zone ($\Delta q^b$). The third column shows the positive increase of crude oil production from 1979 to 1980. The total of this column (702.8) is the gross increase in production, while the net variation (669) is the difference between the sum of the columns: (2) minus (1). Therefore the falling rate of production is equal to 2 percent.[12] This does not include gas production, because it would underestimate the gross increase in the productive zones with which gas is not associated to oil production.

Once the rate of fall was calculated, we proceeded to estimate the investment and operating costs.[13]

To estimate the present value of the investment costs in the exploitation of a new field, it is assumed that the rate of production will exponentially decrease until the deposits are exhausted. An investment *(I)* is required which will initially produce ($q_0$), and the opportunity cost of capital for the economy was estimated equal to 11.8 percent.[14] Therefore the present value of investment (PVI) costs will be

$$PVI = \int_0^T k_t q_t e^{-rt}\, dt$$

By incorporating $q_t = q_0 e^{-at}$, the integral will be solved through $k$:

$$k = \frac{PVI}{q_0} \frac{r + a}{1 - e^{-(r + a)t}}$$

The present value of investment is 141.7 billion pesos and $q_0$, the initial production, is 828.7 million barrels a day. Hence, $K_t$, the capital unitary cost, is 6.65 pesos a barrel.

The total operating costs are considered constant each year. Given an initial production level ($q_0'$) and the initial opening cost per barrel equal to $s/q_0'$, the discounted value of the operating costs will be

$$DVC = \int_0^T Ce^{-rt}\, dt$$

Now including the falling *(a)* and solving the integral, we obtain

$$DVC = \frac{C}{q_0} \frac{a + r}{r} \frac{1 - e^{-rt}}{1 - e^{-(a + r)t}}$$

When $t \to \infty$,

$$DVC = \frac{c}{q_0} \frac{a + r}{r}$$

The unitary operating cost is equal to 98.47 pesos per barrel.[15] The total cost (investment and operation) in productive fields therefore will be 6.65 + 98.47 = 105.1 pesos per barrel, equivalent to U.S. $4.57.

And the total cost of extracting the probable reserves (54.514 million barrels) located in actual productive fields will be

$$C_t = 4.57 \times 54{,}514.3 = \$249.2 \text{ billion}$$

For those reserves (46.91 billion barrels) located in the fields that are still not producing, it is assumed that these deposits will begin to be exploited at a unitary cost (including capital) of \$4.57 per barrel and will grow exponentially until it equals the price, at which point economically exploitable deposits will be exhausted.

The following cost function is also assumed:

$$C = \int_0^T C_0 e^{XV}\, dt$$ [16]

By making the volume of production $(V)$ equal to the total reserves, 46.91 billion barrels $(V_f)$, the accumulated final cost will be

$$C_F = C_P = \int_0^{VF} C_0 e^{XV} f\, dt$$

Therefore the total cost equation for these reserve fields can be expressed as

$$C_{T_2} = C_0 \frac{e^{XV} f - 1}{X}$$

and will be equal to \$650.9 billion or U.S. \$13.90 per barrel.

If it is considered that the real price $(P_0)$ of oil will grow at the same rate as the opportunity cost of capital $(r)$, the gross present value of reserves will be

$$\text{GPV} = \int_0^T P_t q_t e^{-\text{rt}}\, dt$$

Where

$$P_t = P_0(1 + r)^t$$

therefore

$$GPV = P_0 \int_0^T q_t dt = P_0 R$$

Hence the gross oil wealth will be

$$GPV = 31.25 \times 101{,}422 = \$3.169 \text{ trillion}$$

and subtracting the present value cost of extraction, we obtain the net value of oil reserves:

$$\begin{aligned} R_{pn} &= \text{GPV} - C_{t_1} - C_{t_2} \\ &= 3{,}169{,}438 - 249{,}154 - 650{,}875 \\ &= \$2.269 \text{ trillion} \end{aligned}$$

*TABLE 5.9.*
*Oil Wealth*
*(Millions of 1960 Pesos)*

| *Variable* | *1980 Value* |
|---|---|
| 1. Gross domestic product | 512,191 |
| 2. Capital | 1,211,492 |
| 3. Net oil wealth | 6,973,468 |
| 4. 2/1 | 2.4 |
| 5. 3/2 | 5.7 |
| 6. 3/1 | 13.6 |

Therefore, the net oil wealth represents 13.6 times the GDP and 5.7 times capital, as shown in Table 5-9.

## Generation of Oil Surpluses

Here we distinguish between social and private prices and several kinds of surpluses. A first kind is equal to the financial deficit, that is, to the net indebtedness of the company. A second type is the consolidated financial surplus, which measures the financial surplus before taxes. Both the cash and financial concepts involve the valuing of output and production costs at their market prices.

If *shadow prices* or the opportunity cost are used instead, the *economic* surplus is obtained. Two kinds of economic surplus can be distinguished, gross and net. For the former, the operating and manpower costs are subtracted from the value of output, all in *social* terms. In the case of the net economic surplus, the opportunity cost of capital is also subtracted.

### *Generation of the Financial Surpluses*

PEMEX's current income in 1980 was 18 times that of 1973; it increased from 18.3 to 357.3 billions of current pesos, compared with a fourfold rise in output. In real terms average income per barrel has increased 3.2 times.[17]

External prices of Mexican crude oil have increased considerably in recent years until early 1981. At the time of the first oil boom (1973), when prices increased by 300 percent, Mexico was not able to generate oil surpluses; however, surpluses were generated during the second boom period, when the increase in the international price was more than 150 percent during 1979–1980.

As opposed to the dynamic behavior of external prices, which have increased more than world inflation, domestic prices of oil have remained proportional relative to domestic inflation and external prices.[18] The inter-

*TABLE 5.10.*
*Current Savings*
*(Billions of Pesos)*

| | *1973* | *1974* | *1975* | *1976* | *1977* | *1978* | *1979* | *1980* |
|---|---|---|---|---|---|---|---|---|
| 1. Total revenues | 18.3 | 29.9 | 36.6 | 42.2 | 70.2 | 105.4 | 171.9 | 357.3 |
| 2. Current expenditure | 15.7 | 25.5 | 32.5 | 34.6 | 55.0 | 77.5 | 125.6 | 293.6 |
| 3. Monetary surplus (current savings) | 2.6 | 5.4 | 4.1 | 11.6 | 15.2 | 27.9 | 46.3 | 63.6 |
| 4. (3/1) × 100 | 14.2 | 17.5 | 11.2 | 25.1 | 21.7 | 26.5 | 26.9 | 17.8 |
| 5. Net flow of debt | 3.9 | 2.3 | 16.2 | 10.9 | 13.8 | 33.6 | 38.9 | 65.8 |
| 6. Total resources | 6.5 | 7.7 | 20.3 | 22.5 | 29.0 | 61.5 | 85.2 | 129.4 |

SOURCE: Ministry of Finance, *Situación Financiera de los Organismos y Empresas Controladas,* Mexico City, 1980.

national price of oil in 1974 was 2.3 times the domestic price and 4.6 times the domestic price in 1980.

Calculations of the financial surpluses were made for the period 1973–1980 and, as described in Table 5-10, they are defined as the difference between total revenue and current expenditures. Principally, revenues include sales and capital revenues, whereas expenditure comprises wages and salaries, interest payments, federal taxes, and the purchase of goods and services.

As Table 5-10 shows, total revenues increased significantly in the 1976–1980 period, rising at an annual rate of 67 percent, compared with an annual rate of 22 percent for inflation. The increase is explained mainly by exports which grew 123 percent (in U.S. dollar terms) per annum in the same period. In Figure 5-1 the behavior of PEMEX's current income and the contribution of domestic and foreign sales are described.

PEMEX's current expenditures (including taxes), valued at market prices, have increased since 1973 as well. From 1973 to 1980 expenditures increased 17.7 times as compared to an 18.5 times rise in sales revenue which produced 23.4 times growth in the cash surplus for the same period.

The *consolidated financial surplus,* which excludes federal taxes from current expenditures, represents the surplus of oil activity for the public sector as a whole, since taxes paid by PEMEX do not represent cost but merely a transfer payment.[19] That financial surplus increased from 18.1 billion pesos in 1976 to 220.8 billion pesos in 1980—that is, it increased over 10 times—whereas the cash surplus increased 4.4 times, because taxes grew 20 times in the same period. As a proportion of revenues, financial surpluses represented 21 percent in 1973 and 71 percent in 1980; as a share to total expenditures they increased from 26.2 to 241 percent (see Table 5-11).

The real consolidated financial surplus, deflated by the GDP price index, increased from 6.3 to 30.0 billion pesos in 1976–1980, that is, an increase of 480 percent.

Net indebtedness of PEMEX has increased at a slower rate than its own resources. Further, the composition of the total debt has been predominantly external. In 1980, external debt equalled 100 percent of total debt. As a result, PEMEX is able to obtain foreign loans at low interest rates.

## *Gross Economic Surplus*

In the previous section the generation of the monetary and financial surpluses were estimated and analyzed according to an accounting approach which considers only market prices. By valuing domestic sales at official prices, the firm's cash flow is obtained, which is useful in financial planning. However, this calculation does not mirror the value that oil production has for the economy as a whole, which is obtained by using shadow prices in the calculation of cost and incomes. The difference between foreign and domestic prices indicates the amount of the subsidy that is granted to domestic consumption. This estimation of the firm's

**Figure 5-1.**

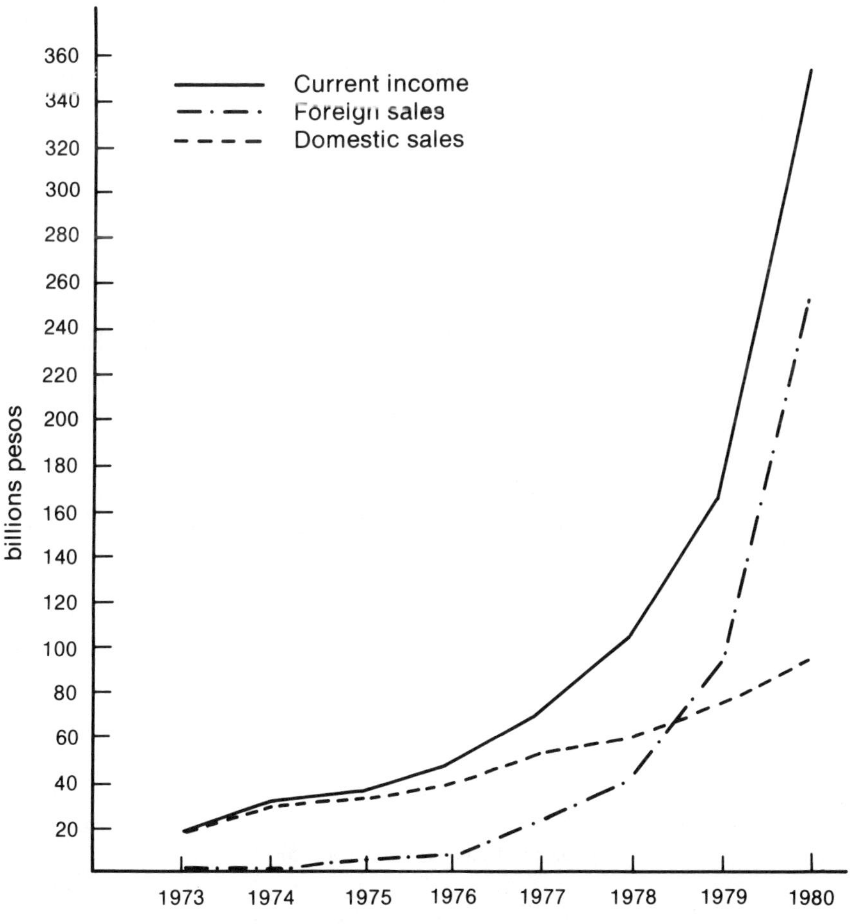

*TABLE 5.11.*
*Financial Surplus*
*(Billions of Pesos)*

| *Concepts* | *1973* | *1974* | *1975* | *1976* | *1977* | *1978* | *1979* | *1980* |
|---|---|---|---|---|---|---|---|---|
| 1. Sales revenue | 18.3 | 30.9 | 36.6 | 46.2 | 70.2 | 105.4 | 171.9 | 357.3 |
| 2. Current expenditure | 14.5 | 20.6 | 23.9 | 26.8 | 36.8 | 49.2 | 77.4 | 131.4 |
| 3. Financial surplus[a] | 3.7 | 10.4 | 4.3 | 18.1 | 37.0 | 57.6 | 101.5 | 220.8 |
| 4. Total resources[b] | 7.6 | 12.7 | 20.5 | 29.0 | 50.8 | 91.2 | 140.2 | 284.4 |
| 5. (3/1) × 100 | 21.0 | 33.3 | 34.7 | 42.0 | 47.6 | 53.3 | 54.6 | 70.7 |
| 6. (3/2) × 100 | 26.2 | 50.0 | 53.1 | 72.4 | 91.0 | 114.3 | 122.1 | 240.5 |
| 7. Federal taxes | 1.2 | 4.9 | 8.6 | 7.8 | 18.3 | 28.3 | 48.2 | 162.3 |
| 8. Investment | 5.9 | 8.0 | 12.5 | 21.5 | 35.6 | 62.7 | 90.5 | 121.8 |
| 9. Changes in cash balances | 0.5 | −0.2 | −0.6 | −0.3 | −3.1 | 0.2 | 1.4 | 0.3 |
| 10. Uses | 7.6 | 12.7 | 20.5 | 50.8 | 50.8 | 91.2 | 140.2 | 284.4 |

SOURCE: Calculation based on data from Ministry of Finance, *Situatión Financiera de los Organismos y Empresas Controladas,* Mexico City, 1980.

[a] Adjusted for foreign accounts.

[b] Includes net debt.

inflow reflects the *true value* of oil production and is the basis for the determination of the economic surplus.

To determine the true value, the prices which PEMEX can obtain abroad have been taken as the alternative value of domestic sales. Table 5-12 describes the relationship between average international and domestic prices which was utilized to correct total domestic sales. The significant growth that the former had during the oil boom of 1973 and the recent one of 1979–1980 can be observed.

Once domestic sales are adjusted for the premium in the international

*TABLE 5.12.*
*Relative Average Prices of the Products of PEMEX*

| *Year* | *Relative Price (Weighted Average)[a]* |
|---|---|
| 1973 | 1.2944 |
| 1974 | 2.2970 |
| 1975 | 1.9039 |
| 1976 | 2.9341 |
| 1977 | 3.1673 |
| 1978 | 3.4870 |
| 1979 | 4.0561 |
| 1980 | 4.6785 |

SOURCE: Calculation based on data from PEMEX, *La Industria Petrolera en México,* Mexico City, 1980.

[a] Estimated according to its participation in oil products in internal sales.

*TABLE 5.13.*
*Internal Sales Revenue*
*(Billions of Pesos)*

| | *1973* | *1974* | *1975*[a] | *1976* | *1977* | *1978* | *1979* | *1980* |
|---|---|---|---|---|---|---|---|---|
| 1. Adjusted internal sales | 23.4 | 70.5 | 63.1 | 112.7 | 167.5 | 206.1 | 302.6 | 446.3 |
| 2. Internal sales without adjustment | 18.0 | 30.7 | 33.1 | 38.4 | 52.9 | 59.1 | 74.6 | 95.4 |
| 3. (1/2) × 100 | 129.4 | 230.0 | 190.6 | 293.5 | 316.6 | 348.7 | 405.6 | 467.7 |

SOURCE: See Tables 5.11 and 5.12.

[a]In this year adjusted domestic sales decreased because the gasoline price rose by 50 percent.

price of oil, an important difference arises with respect to the original figures; for example, in 1979 adjusted domestic sales were 406 percent greater than nonadjusted sales (see Table 5-13).

Adjusted domestic sales grew at an average annual rate of 53.2 percent in 1973–1979. Obviously this rate is directly related to the growth of international prices.

The coefficient of deviation of adjusted and unadjusted sales described in Table 5-13 reflects the undervaluation of domestic consumption, which is certainly greater in years such as 1973 and 1979–1980 when the opportunity cost of domestic consumption rose considerably.[20]

Regarding foreign sales, they have been adjusted by the shadow prices of the exchange rate, estimated by the purchasing power parity of the peso, obtained as the difference between the wholesale prices of Mexico and the United States using 1956 as the base year.

By applying the shadow price of foreign exchange to PEMEX's imports and exports, an adjusted figure for foreign sales and purchase is obtained (see Table 5-14).

The relation between adjusted and unadjusted foreign sales provides an index of the undervaluational exports. In 1975 when currency overvaluation amounted to 26.9 percent, the index of export underestimation was 27.6 percent, whereas in 1977, when the nominal exchange rate was nearer to equilibrium, underestimation was only 9.0 percent. Domestic currency overvaluation has increased since 1977, and, accordingly, export revenue underestimation has increased: 16.6 percent in 1978, 22.1 percent in 1979, and 32.9 percent in 1980.

Wages and salary outlays, which in 1977 and 1978 were 9.2 percent of current expenditures, imply an average wage greater than that observed in other modern industrial sectors; for example, in 1980, the former was twice the latter. To adjust PEMEX's wage expenditures to their opportunity cost, the average wage rate of modern manufacturers was taken as a proxy, as shown in Table 5-15.

*TABLE 5.14.*
*External Sales Revenue*
*(Billions of Pesos)*

| | *1973* | *1974* | *1975* | *1976* | *1977* | *1978* | *1979* | *1980* |
|---|---|---|---|---|---|---|---|---|
| 1. Without adjustment | 0.4 | 1.7 | 5.9 | 7.0 | 23.4 | 41.8 | 91.7 | 239.2 |
| 2. Adjusted through foreign exchange shadow prices | 0.6 | 2.1 | 7.4 | 8.4 | 25.6 | 48.8 | 111.8 | 316.0 |
| 3. 2/1 | 1.0 | 1.2 | 1.3 | 1.2 | 1.1 | 1.2 | 1.2 | 1.3 |
| 4. Shadow price of exchange market (pesos/dollars) | 15.2 | 15.7 | 15.8 | 18.5 | 24.6 | 26.5 | 27.8 | 30.4 |
| 5. Official exchange rate (pesos/ dollars) | 12.5 | 12.5 | 12.5 | 15.4 | 22.5 | 22.7 | 22.8 | 22.9 |

SOURCE: L. Solís and S. Rizzo, "Excedentes Petroleros y Apertura Externa: El Caso de México," (Forthcoming); PEMEX, *La Industria Petrolera en México,* Mexico City, 1980.

*TABLE 5.15.*
*Average Salary and Wages*
*(Thousands of Pesos)*

| | *1973* | *1974* | *1975* | *1976* | *1977* | *1978* | *1979* | *1980* |
|---|---|---|---|---|---|---|---|---|
| 1. PEMEX | 65.6 | 85.6 | 104.2 | 128.1 | 169.0 | 200.5 | 242.6 | 351.2 |
| 2. Modern manufacturing industry | 43.9 | 55.1 | 66.8 | 83.2 | 108.0 | 125.1 | 145.1 | 179.0 |
| 3. 1/2 | 1.5 | 1.6 | 1.6 | 1.5 | 1.7 | 1.6 | 1.7 | 2.0 |

SOURCE: Secretaría de Programación y Presupuesto, *Boletín Mensual de Información Económica,* Mexico City, several years, PEMEX, *La Industria Petrolera en México,* Mexico City, 1980.

Gross economic surplus is then equal to total income minus current expenditures, both in social terms, as described in Table 5-16.

Domestic sales revenues were adjusted by international prices and foreign sales revenues by the exchange rate which is compatible with purchasing power parity. Within outlays, PEMEX's imports are adjusted in the same way as exports; the cost of the labor force is valued at its opportunity cost, and all other variables are valued at market prices.

As described in Table 5-16, the gross economic surplus increased at an average rate of nearly 61.5 percent per annum since 1976. As a percentage of income it represented 74.1 percent in that year, increasing to 80 percent in 1980. As a percentage of gross domestic product it increased from 1.1 percent in 1973 to 19.6 percent in 1980.

*TABLE 5.16.*
*Gross Economic Surplus*
*(Billions of Pesos)*

| | *1973* | *1974* | *1975* | *1976* | *1977* | *1978* | *1979* | *1980* |
|---|---|---|---|---|---|---|---|---|
| 1. Corrected total income | 24.6 | 74.1 | 70.7 | 123.6 | 214.1 | 263.5 | 432.6 | 771.3 |
| 2. Expenditures | 17.6 | 25.8 | 25.2 | 32.0 | 52.3 | 61.5 | 89.5 | 148.2 |
| 3. Gross surplus | 7.0 | 48.3 | 45.5 | 91.6 | 161.8 | 202.0 | 343.1 | 623.1 |
| 4. (3/1) × 100 | 28.4 | 65.2 | 64.3 | 74.1 | 75.6 | 76.7 | 79.3 | 80.8 |
| 5. (3/2) × 100 | 39.8 | 187.2 | 180.6 | 286.3 | 309.4 | 328.4 | 383.4 | 420.4 |
| 6. 3/GDP × 100 | 1.1 | 5.9 | 21.7 | 13.4 | 5.3 | 4.7 | 6.8 | 19.6 |

SOURCE: Calculation based on data from Ministry of Finance, *Situación Financiera de los Organismos y Empresas Controladas,* Mexico City, several years, and Tables 5.13, 5.14, and 5.15.

## *Net Economic Surplus*

The gross surplus reflects the remainder after paying for the cost incurred by society in carrying out oil exploitation.[21] However, at this point the opportunity cost of capital invested by PEMEX has not been considered.

The concept *net economic surplus* is equal to the surplus that is available once the opportunity cost of capital and operating cost have been deducted. That is, it indicates the surplus produced by the resources used by PEMEX in oil exploitation over the amount that they could have generated if they had been utilized in the rest of economy.[22] It represents an additional net income, and the present value of the expected flow of the net surplus, until reserves are exhausted, is equivalent to net oil wealth.

The opportunity cost of capital was obtained by applying the average rate of return of the economy to the value of PEMEX's net fixed assets for each of the years considered here (1973–1980).

The estimate of capital consumption that PEMEX carries out is made for accounting purposes and is therefore hardly reliable as a basis for this study; a more useful estimate would require a much deeper analysis which is outside the scope of this study. Therefore, the concept of net economic surplus adopted here does not exclude depreciation. In further research examining the distribution of the surplus, an item for gross investment including replacement expenses will be included.

To obtain the opportunity cost of capital, its net rate of return was estimated for the economy. For that purpose the Banco de México data on capital stocks and the operating surplus was adjusted. In particular, an effort was made to separate labor earnings which are included in the latter, since in the national acounts this comprises mixed earnings of

*TABLE 5.17.*
*Net Economic Surplus*
*(Billions of Current Pesos)*

| | *1973* | *1974* | *1975* | *1976* | *1977* | *1978* | *1979* | *1980* |
|---|---|---|---|---|---|---|---|---|
| 1. Gross economic surplus | 7.0 | 48.3 | 45.5 | 91.6 | 161.8 | 202.0 | 343.1 | 623.1 |
| 2. Capital cost (without depreciation) | 3.0 | 3.7 | 4.7 | 5.3 | 9.3 | 13.8 | 33.3 | 41.6 |
| 3. Net economic surplus | 4.0 | 44.6 | 80.8 | 86.3 | 152.5 | 188.2 | 309.8 | 581.5 |
| 4. 3/GDP × 100 | 5.6 | 1.5 | 1.9 | 2.4 | 4.7 | 4.1 | 9.3 | 18.5 |

SOURCE: PEMEX, *La Industria Petrolera en México,* Mexico City, 1980.

capital and labor. This was made by imputing a salary to non-salary-earning groups in all economic sectors.

Thus the net rate of return to capital was obtained as the ratio between net operating surplus (excluding that part which corresponds to labor earnings as mentioned above and subtracting depreciation from the surplus) and net fixed assets.

The net economic surplus increased 144 times from 1973 to 1980, and it grew at an annual rate of 61 percent between 1976 and 1980; in real terms the corresponding rate was 77.7 percent (see Table 5-17). As a percentage of gross domestic product it rose from 5.9 percent in 1973 up to 18.5 percent in 1980.

While in 1974 the net economic surplus represented 60.2 percent of adjusted (own) income, in 1980 it rose to 75.4 percent. Figure 5-2 shows the several concepts of economic surplus that have been discussed here.

## The Uses of Oil Surplus

As mentioned earlier, the generated net economic surplus of PEMEX represented 18.5 percent of GDP in 1980, and potential net wealth of hydrocarbons amounted to more than five times the physical capital of the Mexican economy in that year. As a result the government is the owner of 85 percent of national wealth. The utilization of the surplus through budget and public pricing policies will affect significantly the distribution of income between public and private sectors as well as transfers to future generations.

The subsidy to domestic consumption has been intended as an instrument to promote industrialization. However, this policy has clear implications in terms of employment creation and therefore clear adverse consequences for the comparative advantage of Mexico in labor-intensive activities. Further, the behavior of public expenditures and the allocation of these between investment and consumption, as a response to the growth of oil revenues, will affect national wealth and income distribution.[23]

In this section, we shall analyze the direct use of PEMEX revenue surpluses as well as the distribution between internal investment and transfers to the federal government, consumers, industry, and transportation.

The economic surplus was defined as the net value that PEMEX adds to gross domestic product once the output that scarce resources devoted to oil exploitation would have produced in the nonoil sectors is deducted from the former.

One part of that surplus is allocated to capital formation in PEMEX in order to increase output capacity as well as to replace worn-out capital stock. Another portion is transferred to the government in the form of taxation and to hydrocarbon consumers by means of a subsidized price.

### *Investment in PEMEX*

PEMEX's gross fixed investment grew from 5.9 to 90.5 billion pesos (15.3 times) in 1973–1979. Real investment changed from 3.6 to 17.4 billion pesos (4.8 times) in the same period. In the period under examination here the net surplus was more than enough to cover investment require-

**Figure 5-2.**

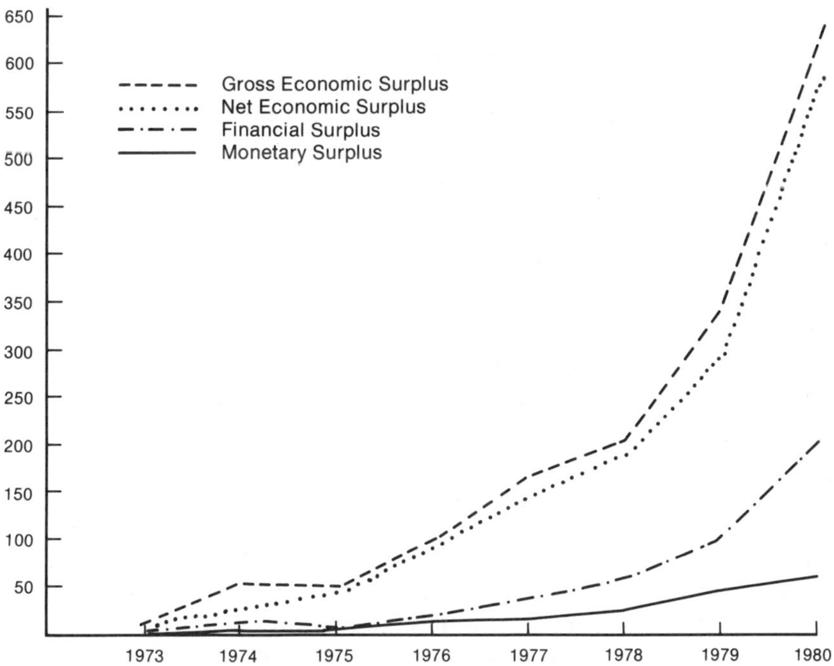

TABLE 5.18.
*Investments, Taxes, and Transfers out of the Public Sector (Billions of Pesos and %)*

| | *1973–1980* | *%* |
|---|---|---|
| 1. Net economic surplus | 1,376.0 | 100.0 |
| 2. Gross fixed investment | 358.5 | 26.0 |
| 3. Transfers out of PEMEX (1 – 2) | 1,017.5 | 74.0 |
| 4. Federal taxes | 279.6 | 20.3 |
| 5. Transfer out of the public sector (3 – 4) | 737.9 | 53.7 |

SOURCE: See Tables 5.11 and 5.17.

TABLE 5.19.
*Employment-Investment Ratio*

| | *1973* | *1974* | *1975* | *1976* | *1977* | *1978* | *1979* | *1980* |
|---|---|---|---|---|---|---|---|---|
| 1. Employed personal (thousands) | 79.1 | 80.0 | 83.7 | 90.7 | 94.7 | 89.9 | 106.8 | 112.3 |
| 2. Gross fixed investment (billions of pesos) | 5.9 | 8.0 | 12.5 | 21.5 | 35.6 | 62.7 | 90.6 | 121.9 |
| 3. Employees per million pesos of investment (2/3) | 13.4 | 10.0 | 6.7 | 4.2 | 2.7 | 1.7 | 1.8 | 1.2 |

SOURCE: PEMEX, *La Industria Petrolera en México,* Mexico City, 1980.

ments; the latter represented only 26 percent of the former; see Table 5-18.

The investment of PEMEX is one of the most profitable activities in the economy because of the great productivity of new oil fields and the extraordinary rise in the international price of crude oil. However, in terms of employment creation, PEMEX has a very poor record. Its direct effect on income distribution is, therefore, unfavorable relative to investment in other sectors. In 1973 PEMEX had 79,000 employees; in 1980 that figure had increased to only 112,300, an increase of 5 percent per annum (see Table 5-19). However, output increased 21.2 percent per annum during the same period.

### *Transfers to the Federal Government*

By deducting PEMEX's internal investment from the net surplus, the amount that is transferred to the rest of the economy is obtained. This amount increased from 36.6 to 459.7 billion pesos in 1974–1980; as a percentage of GDP it rose from 4.5 to 18.7 percent.

A growing part of the oil surplus has been transferred to the federal government through tax payments. In 1973 domestic sales were taxed at 11.1 percent and crude exports at 0.0 percent, whereas in 1980 the corresponding figures were 24.8 and 59.3 percent, respectively. As a percentage of the surplus, taxes paid to the federal government were 17.1 percent in 1973 and 28.0 percent in 1980; the average for the period as a whole was 20.3 percent. (See Table 5-18).

Transfers from the government have been utilized to subsidize state-owned enterprises such as Comisión Federal de Electricidad, the National Company of Popular Substances (CONASUPO), and Ferrocarriles Nacionales, all of which have experienced increasing deficits, as shown in Table 5-20.

### *Subsidy to Domestic Consumption*

If, in addition to internal investment expenditures, taxes paid by PEMEX are deducted, one obtains that part of the surplus which is transferred out of the public sector. For the whole period 1973–1980, this amount was 53.7 percent of total net economic surplus.

The principal use of the surplus is to subsidize domestic consumption by means of a domestic pricing policy well below the international prices movements. A permanent subsidy on domestically consumed energy gives rise to several major problems. First, it has indirect effects on the use of the factors of production of the economy to the extent that it modifies the relative prices of capital to labor, and as a result it induces an intensive use of capital. Second, a hydrocarbon-intensive technology would be adopted, which in the not-too-distant future would become obsolete, since present technological development is geared toward the saving of energy, particularly oil and natural gas. Furthermore, it influences the geographical location of economic activity and population,

*TABLE 5.20.*
*Budget-Controlled Public Enterprises, Current Savings*
*(Millions of Pesos)*

| | *1974* | *1976* | *1978* | *1980* |
|---|---|---|---|---|
| Comisión Federal de Electricidad | −559 | −1,806 | −7,542 | −20,934 |
| Companía Nacional de Subsistencias Populares (CONASUPO) | −5,654 | −3,264 | −10,533 | −27,836 |
| Ferrocarriles | −1,907 | −2,745 | −3,274 | −6,658 |
| PEMEX | +5,385 | +11,642 | +27,928 | +63,609 |
| Rest | −4,011 | −3,739 | +4,826 | +10,566 |
| Total | −6,746 | −88 | +11,405 | +18,847 |

SOURCE: Ministry of Finance, *Situación Financiera de los Oranismos y Empresas Controladas,* Mexico City, 1980.

*TABLE 5.21.*
*The Price of the Principal Hydrocarbon Products*
*(Pesos Per Amount)*

| | *1960* | *1965* | *1970* | *1975* | *1979* | *1980* | *1980/1960* |
|---|---|---|---|---|---|---|---|
| Regular gasoline (liters) | 1.00 | 1.00 | 1.00 | 2.10 | 2.80 | 2.80 | 2.8 |
| All gasoline (weighted average) (liters) | 0.82 | 0.32 | 1.06 | 1.54 | 1.88 | | 2.3 |
| Fuel oil ($m^3$) | 126.50 | 126.50 | 126.50 | 215.00 | 294.41 | | 2.3 |
| Diesel (liters) | 0.32 | 0.32 | 0.32 | 0.32 | 0.50 | 1.00 | 3.1 |
| Liquid gas (kg) | 0.85 | 0.85 | 0.85 | 2.08 | 2.40 | | 2.8 |
| Kerosene (liters) | 0.45 | 0.49 | 0.42 | 0.94 | 1.81 | | 4.0 |
| Mexican implicit GDP deflactor | 100.00 | 118.70 | 141.20 | 253.20 | 580.20 | 754.26 | 7.5 |
| International price of the Mexican crude oil (pesos/barrel) | 20.00 | 22.50 | 22.50 | 142.40 | 447.10 | 766.73 | 38.3 |

SOURCE: PEMEX, *Anuario Estadístico,* Mexico City, 1979.

biasing toward urban concentration since big cities require a high per capita consumption of energy for transportation, given the long distances of travel.

The main subsidy appears in the form of the consumption of gasoline, which in 1979 represented 30 percent of the total value of oil products, followed by fuel oil (25.4 percent), diesel (23.2 percent), and liquid gas (10 percent). From 1960 until 1980 the price of domestically consumed regular gasoline increased 2.8 times, while the international price of oil rose 37 times. For the same period the price of diesel increased three times. (See Table 5-21.)

In 1980 total domestic sales revenue amounted to 95.4 billion pesos if valued at official prices and 446.3 billion if valued at international prices. Accordingly, domestic consumers received a 79 percent subsidy rate (see Table 5-22).

The subsidy on gasoline benefits mainly the higher-income brackets. According to the income-expenditure survey of 1968, 70 percent of total gasoline produced by PEMEX was consumed by 11 percent of Mexican families, whose earnings were more than seventeen times the minimum wage. Furthermore, the same families owned 61.1 percent of the total number of automobiles in that year. (See Table 5-23).

The subsidy on fuel oil benefits, in particular, the manufacturing industries and the Comisión Federal de Electricidad.[24] For diesel the main consumer is the transport sector. Liquid gas is used almost exclusively by households.

The distribution of the total subsidy according to the product structure

*TABLE 5.22.*
*Consumer Subsidy*
*(Billions of Current Pesos)*

| | *1973* | *1974* | *1975* | *1976* | *1977* | *1978* | *1979* | *1980* |
|---|---|---|---|---|---|---|---|---|
| 1. Total internal sales valued at international prices | 23.4 | 70.5 | 63.1 | 112.7 | 167.5 | 206.7 | 302.6 | 446.3 |
| 2. Internal sales valued at official prices | 18.0 | 30.6 | 33.1 | 38.4 | 52.8 | 59.1 | 74.5 | 95.4 |
| 3. Subsidy (1 – 2) | 5.4 | 39.9 | 30.0 | 74.3 | 114.7 | 147.0 | 228.1 | 350.9 |
| 4. Net economic surplus | 3.3 | 43.9 | 40.6 | 86.6 | 144.9 | 185.7 | 291.6 | 579.5 |
| 5. (3/2) × 100 | 30.0 | 130.4 | 90.6 | 193.5 | 217.2 | 248.7 | 306.2 | 367.8 |
| 6. (3/4) × 100 | 163.6 | 91.0 | 74.0 | 85.6 | 79.2 | 79.2 | 78.2 | 60.6 |
| 7. (3/1) × 100 | 23.1 | 56.6 | 47.5 | 66.0 | 68.5 | 71.3 | 75.4 | 79.0 |

SOURCE: PEMEX, *La Industria Petrolera en México,* Mexico City, 1980.

*TABLE 5.23.*
*Percentage Distribution of the Family Expenditure in the Use of Energy Per Bracket Income*

| *Expenditure* | *Bracket 1 (up to Twice the Average Minimum Wage Per Year)* | *Bracket 2 (More than Twice and Until 17 Times the Average Minimum Wage Per Year)* | *Bracket 3 (More than 17 Times the Average Minimum Wage Per Year)* |
|---|---|---|---|
| Gasoline | 2.71 | 26.46 | 70.83 |
| Purchasing of automobiles | 1.00 | 8.54 | 90.46 |
| Electricity | 18.34 | 44.41 | 37.16 |
| Automobile distribution | 5.44 | 33.43 | 61.13 |
| Number of families in the universe | 55.70 | 33.30 | 11.00 |

SOURCE: Banco de México, S.A., *Encuesta Ingreso Gasto,* Mexico City 1968, and Jesus F. Reyes Heroles, *Política Fiscal y la Redistribución del Ingreso,* Tesis de Licencíado, Instituto Tecnológico Autónomo de México (ITAM), 1976.

was calculated by taking the differential between their corresponding external and domestic prices. This is shown for the year 1980 in Table 5-24.

The allocation of subsidies by economic sectors was calculated by distributing it according to PEMEX's structure of sales. The subsidy received by the Comisión Federal de Electricidad was, in turn, allocated

*TABLE 5.24.*
*Subsidy Calculations of the Different Oil Products in 1980*

| | *Consumer Prices (Pesos/ECMCO[a]* | | *Subsidy* |
|---|---|---|---|
| | *National* | *International* | *(Millions of Pesos)* |
| Natural gas | 295.6 | 3,728.5 | 58,702.6 |
| Fuel oil | 265.7 | 4,092.4 | 64,288.0 |
| Diesel | 872.6 | 7,101.1 | 90,313.0 |
| Liquid gas | 2,088.6 | 6,706.6 | 23,020.2 |
| Gasoline | 3,365.0 | 7,706.9 | 75,028.0 |
| Kerosene | 510.9 | 7,794.4 | 14,927.0 |
| Total | | | 362,278.8 |

SOURCE: PEMEX, *Memoria de Labores,* Mexico City, 1980.

[a] Equivalent to cubic meters of crude oil.

*TABLE 5.25*
*Implicit Subsidy from PEMEX to the Economy by Sectors[a]*
*(Million of Pesos): 1980*

| *Concepts* | *Implicit Subsidy* | *%* |
|---|---|---|
| Transports | 154,693.1 | 42.7 |
| Agriculture | 19,953.6 | 5.5 |
| Services | 9,057.0 | 2.5 |
| Industry | 138,415.1 | 38.2 |
| Household | 40,160.1 | 11.1 |
| Total | 362,278.9 | 100.0 |

SOURCE: Calculations based on data from PEMEX, *La Industria Petrolera en Mexico,* Mexico City, 1980.

[a] The subsidy to the energy sector, Comisión Federal de Electricidad, was 94,917 million pesos for 1980. Since this economic sector is not a final consumer of energy, the subsidy is transferred to the sectors to which this industry sells: 21.7 percent to the household sector, 71.4 percent to industry, and 6.9 percent to the agricultural sector.

among the other sectors by taking into account the latter's sale structure in 1980. This exercise was done for 1980. The subsidy amounted to 362.3 billion pesos. The sectors which received the greatest part were manufacturing and transportation which absorbed 38.2 and 42.7 percent, respectively. Both sectors are characterized as capital intensive and labor saving. It can be concluded accordingly that PEMEX's subsidies to other activities further bias the economy to a greater utilization of capital than of labor. (See Table 5-25.)

To show that the subsidy on energy promotes the substitution of capital for labor, we shall establish that there is a certain degree of complementarity between capital and energy. For this purpose, a cross-section analysis based on data from the industrial census of 1975 was carried out and the following regression equation obtained:

$$\text{COBEN} = \underset{(-6.4416)}{-3.4813} + \underset{(23.162)}{1.0284\text{ACFTO}} + \underset{(1.194)}{0.2348\text{LIDT}}$$

where the figures in parentheses are significant measured by students' t tests.

COBEN = natural log of fuel, lubricant, and electric energy

ACFTO = natural log of net fixed asset

LIDT = natural log of the index of utilization of capital

The coefficients of the independent variables of this equation proved to have the expected signs, but only that of ACFTO was significant at the 5 percent level. The coefficient of ACFTO is positive and implies that an increase of 1 percent in the use of capital produces an increase of just 1 percent in the use of energy. This illustrates the degree of complementarity that there is between energy and capital, and so we shall expect a substitution between labor and energy.

### *Subsidy to Importer and Labor Force Working in PEMEX*

There are still two further ways in which the surplus is used, namely, a subsidy to importers through the foreign exchange surplus generated by PEMEX and a subsidy to labor employed by PEMEX which receives a wage higher than the average observed for labor with a similar degree of qualification in the rest of the economy.

If the rate of exchange is kept below the parity of the purchasing power of the peso, importers get a subsidy when they buy foreign exchange, and exporters are the ones who provide that subsidy; for them it is like a tax. This is how PEMEX produces a foreign exchange surplus which is part of its economic surplus and is transferred to the rest of the economy.[25]

The amount of the total subsidy to importers was obtained as the difference between the adjusted (by the purchasing power parity) and the adjusted PEMEX foreign exchange balance (current and capital account). In 1975 this subsidy was 0.7 billion pesos and increased to 66.0 billion pesos in 1989. (See Table 5-26.)

The increasing subsidy to importers indicates that the burden of the peso overvaluation is supported mainly by the public sector, except for 1976.[26]

The subsidy to PEMEX employees is determined by the difference between the wage rate they receive and the one paid in the manufacturing industries. The latter is a proxy for the relevant shadow price of labor. This subsidy was 1.7 billion pesos in 1973 and 10.4 in 1979, which means a 6.1 times increase. (See Table 5-27.)

*TABLE 5.26.*
*Subsidy to Importers*
*(Billions of Pesos)*

| | *1973* | *1974* | *1975* | *1976* | *1977* | *1978* | *1979* | *1980* |
|---|---|---|---|---|---|---|---|---|
| Total subsidy given to importers (excluding PEMEX) | −2.5 | −4.5 | 6.9 | −2.2 | 0.2 | 13.1 | 15.7 | 66.0 |

SOURCE: Calculations based on data from PEMEX, *Institucional de Pemex,* Mexico City, 1980.

*TABLE 5.27.*
*Subsidy Given to the Labor Force Employed by PEMEX*
*(Billions of Pesos)*

| | *1973* | *1974* | *1975* | *1976* | *1977* | *1978* | *1979* | *1980* |
|---|---|---|---|---|---|---|---|---|
| Salary and wage bills paid by PEMEX | 5.2 | 6.9 | 8.7 | 11.6 | 16.0 | 19.8 | 25.9 | 39.4 |
| Alternative use of the salary and wage fund | 3.5 | 4.5 | 5.6 | 7.6 | 10.2 | 12.3 | 15.5 | 20.1 |
| Subsidy | 1.7 | 2.4 | 3.1 | 4.1 | 5.8 | 7.5 | 10.4 | 19.3 |

SOURCE: Calculations based on data from PEMEX, *La Industria Petrolera,* Mexico City, 1980, and Secretaría de Programación y Presupuesto, *Boletín Mensual de Información Económica,* several years.

### *Consolidated Generation and Uses of Oil Economic Surpluses*

The gross economic surplus plus the net debt, adjusting the external portion by the shadow price of foreign exchange, comprise the total amount of resources managed by PEMEX. In turn, this figure is allocated among the investments, tax payments, and subsidies to consumers, importers, and workers.

Table 5-28 was elaborated to assess the preceding and shows the way in which the oil surplus is allocated. Most of the surplus, through subsidies, is granted to consumption directly or through import and to PEMEX's labor force. This, of course, has a negative effect on the income level of future generations. This chapter does not take into account Mexico's most recent situation. Recent devaluations, changes in the international price of oil, and changes in government's participation in financial institutions will affect Mexico's use of the oil surplus. These trends cannot be evaluated as of mid-1982.

*TABLE 5.28.*
*Consolidated Generation and Uses of Oil Economic Surplus*

| | *1973* | *1974* | *1975* | *1976* | *1977* | *1978* | *1979* | *1980* |
|---|---|---|---|---|---|---|---|---|
| 1. Total revenue | 24.6 | 74.1 | 70.7 | 123.6 | 214.1 | 263.5 | 432.6 | 771.3 |
| 2. Internal sales | 23.4 | 70.4 | 63.1 | 112.7 | 167.5 | 206.1 | 302.6 | 446.3 |
| 3. External sales | 0.6 | 2.1 | 7.4 | 7.4 | 25.6 | 48.8 | 111.8 | 316.0 |
| 4. Other revenue | 0.6 | 1.5 | 0.2 | 3.5 | 21.0 | 8.6 | 18.2 | 9.0 |
| 5. Total expenditure | 17.6 | 25.8 | 25.2 | 32.0 | 52.3 | 61.5 | 89.5 | 148.2 |
| 6. Gross economic surplus | 7.0 | 48.3 | 45.5 | 91.6 | 161.8 | 202.0 | 343.1 | 623.1 |
| 7. Net debt | 5.0 | 2.5 | 16.2 | 13.3 | 15.7 | 56.6 | 50.6 | 86.0 |
| 8. Total resources | 12.0 | 50.8 | 61.7 | 104.9 | 177.5 | 258.6 | 393.7 | 709.1 |
| 9. Uses of economic surplus | 12.0 | 50.8 | 61.7 | 104.9 | 177.5 | 258.6 | 393.7 | 709.1 |
| 10. Subsidy, domestic consumption | 5.2 | 39.8 | 30.0 | 73.4 | 114.6 | 147.0 | 227.4 | 350.9 |
| 11. Subsidy to workers of PEMEX | 1.7 | 2.4 | 3.1 | 4.1 | 5.7 | 7.4 | 10.4 | 7.8 |
| 12. Subsidy to importers[a] | −2.5 | −4.5 | 6.9 | −2.2 | 0.2 | 13.1 | 15.7 | 66.0 |
| 13. Investment | 5.9 | 8.0 | 8.6 | 21.5 | 35.6 | 62.7 | 90.6 | 121.7 |
| 14. Taxes | 1.2 | 4.9 | 12.5 | 7.8 | 18.3 | 28.3 | 48.2 | 162.4 |
| 15. Changes in cash balances | +0.5 | +0.2 | +0.6 | +0.3 | +3.1 | +0.1 | +1.4 | +0.3 |

[a]This subsidy was obtained by adjusting the foreign exchange balance, of PEMEX's balance of payments, by an index of purchasing power parity.

## Notes

1. These reserves are composed of 54.5 billion barrels of proven reserves in operating fields and 46.9 billion barrels corresponding to probable and proven oil reserves in fields presently unexploited.

2. In 1980 the GDP was 3.863 trillion pesos; this amount priced at the market exchange rate of 22.9 pesos per dollar is equal to $168.6 billion.

3. The possibility of perfectly elastic outward supply of capital makes easier the trade-off between oil extraction and its uses because a supply of capital at a fixed interest rate would guarantee a minimum earning, which should be the ceiling for the internal rate of return of domestic investment. The supply price of capital would become the relevant discount rate. If the marginal rate of time preference (of consumption) is greater than the foreign interest rate, then the population favors current consumption of oil wealth until the rate of time preference equals the foreign interest rate.

4. In mid-1981 the external crude oil sales price fell $4 per barrel. However, this does not invalidate the long-run perspectives of this chapter since this is a transitory phenomenon.

5. See Asesoria del Presidente, *Encuesta Sobre la Actividad Empresarial 1981*, Mexico, 1981, mimeo.

6. During the period 1976–1980 the price index of public enterprise increased 50 percent, and the wholesale price index increased 141 percent.

7. Tax payments by PEMEX include taxes on domestic sales (15 percent), exports (59.35 percent), production (27 percent), value added (10 percent), and imports (the tariff depends on the imported items). In 1981 PEMEX paid 102 million pesos of daily tax for value added and production and 65 million pesos for 1980.

8. The president stated in his fifth annual report to the nation on September 1, 1981 that there were 72 billion barrels of proven oil reserves and 58.6 of probable reserves. The probable reserves are found in fields that are not yet in operation.

9. Only 50 percent of the probable reserve was taken into account in our oil wealth estimates. According to PEMEX declarations, only 50 percent of those reserves can be profitably produced at current prices and costs of extraction.

10. The declining rate is equal to $a = \frac{A}{q^n_{t-1}}$

11. The net increase ($\Delta q^n$) is equal to the crude oil production in $t$ ($q_t$)minus all the productive areas production in $t-1$: $\Delta q^n = q_t - q_t - 1$.

12. The declining rate is equal to a = (702.8 − 2130.0 + 1461.0) /1461.0 − 2%

13. Investment excludes capital expenditure on petrochemical production and for exploring activities.

14. The opportunity cost of capital was calculated by the ratio of *operating surplus* (net domestic product minus labor earnings), taken from Banco de México, *Producto Interno Bruto y Gasto*, 1970–1979, Mexico City, 1980, and the stock of capital. The operating surplus includes mixed earnings from capital and labor. Therefore, the labor portion was subtracted to assess only the earnings of capital. For the agricultural and the rest of the economy sectors the self-employed economically active population was calculated *(trabajadores por cuenta propia)*, and a salary was imputed for each sector. The imputed salary in agriculture was 80 percent higher than the average wage income in that sector; for the nonagricultural sectors the imputed salary was 32 percent of average wage income. These figures (80 percent, 32 percent) were estimated from the income earned by the self-employed workers relative to average wage income, according to *Encuesta Ingreso de Gasto de 1975*. The capital series was developed by adding the next fixed investment and stock variations figures to the initial 1959 stock of capital. The figures on investment and inventories were taken from Banco de México, *PIB y Gasto*, 1970–1979, Mexico City, 1980. The flows of investment and the stock variation were deflated by the corresponding price deflator according to Banco de México estimations:

*Opportunity Cost of Capital*
*(Millions of Pesos of 1960)*

| | *Net Fixed Investment* | *Stocks Variations Inventories* | *Total Capital Stock* | *Adjusted Operational Surplus* | *Average of Return of Capital (%)* |
|---|---|---|---|---|---|
| 1960 | 15,337 | 4,157 | 249,315 | 59,914 | 24.0 |
| 1965 | 24,939 | 9,230 | 376,010 | 82,065 | 21.8 |
| 1970 | 40,112 | 8,971 | 578,547 | 102,439 | 17.7 |
| 1975 | 59,219 | 7,896 | 856,315 | 106,277 | 12.4 |
| 1979 | 65,244 | 15,666 | 1,125,958 | 132,642 | 11.8 |

15. For the January–November period of 1980 the variable costs were equal to 76.5 billion pesos, and the initial productive level for the same period was 1.003 billion barrels.

16. $C$ is the initial cost, which is equal to $4.57 per barrel; $X$ is the rate of growth (0.0004098), and it will rise until it equals its price. $V_0$ is the initial volume, and since it is calculated in 1980, its initial value is zero.

17. The income is deflated through the GDP implicit price deflator index.

18. The domestic price of the *nova* gasoline (regular) did not suffer any variation from 1960 to 1972 nor did the *extra* (unleaded) gasoline from 1965 to 1972. During 1973–1979 both gasoline prices increased 100 percent, while the wholesale price index increased 220%.

19. The term *consolidated* refers to the inclusion of the federal government and all the budget-controlled entities.

20. For a better adjustment one must use the permanent or expected international price. Otherwise, a drastic and temporary increase of international prices would require a drastic fall in domestic consumption in order to increase exports.

21. Expenditures are calculated at their opportunity cost.

22. Considering average rate of return of investment and the average productivity of labor in modern industry.

23. Similarly, there would also be an impact on savings in terms of how the population perceives the expected income from oil surplus.

24. In 1977 the Comisión Federal de Electricidad, a public enterprise, consumed 52.5 percent of industrial fuel oil consumption, and 47.5 percent was consumed by the remaining industrial sector.

25. It was valued at international prices and adjusted by the social cost of foreign exchange.

26. This argument is reinforced by the price inflexibility (or lag in price adjustment with respect to inflation) in electricity, fertilizers, and other public enterprise goods. Therefore the public sector price index is below the price index of the rest of the economy.

# CHAPTER 6

# *The Distribution of Labor Income in Mexico*

Jesús F. Reyes Heroles

## I. Introduction

As in most developing economies, the share of labor income in total income has been increasing rapidly in Mexico; it grew from 27.3 percent in 1950 to 49.4 percent in 1976.[1] The Mexican experience in this area is also consistent with the expected long-run outcome that arises from the main neoclassical growth models.[2] It should be said, however, that the short-run outcome may differ from the long-run prediction in response to a specific set of income policies. The behavior of the share of earnings in GDP during the last 4 years in Mexico provides empirical support to this possibility. Although analyzing this type of shift is extremely important for understanding the welfare effects of short-run economic policies, this chapter does not deal with them.[3] In other words, it proceeds under the assumption that the share of labor income in total income has been increasing more or less steadily over the last three decades and will continue to do so over the next.

If labor income is becoming relatively more important as the Mexican economy develops, then its size distribution increases its influence in shaping the size distribution of total income.[4] Therefore it is necessary to analyze what determines the current shape of the size distribution of labor income in Mexico and how it may evolve in the near future.

It is convenient to note that the overall size distribution of labor in-

I want to thank Gabriel Vera Ferrer and Blanca García, at the Bank of Mexico, for providing the survey data needed for this paper, Roberto Seira for his research assistance, and Alicia Alvarado for her typing.

come, or earnings, as they will be called interchangeably in this chapter, results from adding up the corresponding sectoral distribution.[5] This disaggregation introduces, in turn, two main determinants of the distributive outcome: (1) transformations in the distribution of earnings within an industry and (2) alterations in the output mix and the sectorial allocation of employment.

Relatively little research has been done, in general but especially for the case of Mexico, on the differences in the earnings frequency distribution across industries. It is possible that further work in this area can contribute to a better understanding of the distributive issue in Mexico and shed some light on current controversies in labor, income distribution, and development economics. Analyzing interindustry differences in the frequency distributions of earnings can, among other things, help to establish the medium-term distributive implications of Mexico's current development pattern.

To say that little attention has been paid to interindustry differences in the frequency distribution is not to say that there has been little attention to interindustry differences in earnings levels.[6] The former is meant to cover not only median or average earnings but also their dispersion and, further, the shape of their distribution.

Although some studies deal with interindustry differences in earnings, they do so in order to show the effects of sex, race, schooling, or union membership on the level of earnings but rarely on its distribution.[7] Furthermore, most of the work dealing with interindustry differentials responds to the need to use cross-section methodologies, but it is only rarely the result of a specific interest in industry differences.[8]

This chapter gives a good deal of attention to the specific factors determining the intraindustry distributions of earnings and therefore the differences in the Mexican earnings distributions by industry. It does so to evaluate their implications, taking into account the relative importance of sectorial employment to the distribution of labor income in a static and dynamic context. Section II presents the evidence on the Mexican size distribution of earnings, with special emphasis on its sectorial composition for the year 1977. Section III briefly reviews some theoretical aspects of income distribution and development economics dealing with the frequency distribution of earnings. Section IV analyzes some processes shaping the intraindustry distribution of earnings in Mexico, relating them to the structure of the labor market. Section V analyzes the implications of this evidence for the overall distribution of labor income in the course of economic development. Finally, Section VI presents some final remarks on the probable net effect of simultaneous transformations in the intraindustry distribution of earnings and in the structure of sectorial employment. It also makes an effort to specify the main policy implications of the analysis.

## II. The Distribution of Labor Income in Mexico: Empirical Evidence

According to the most recent income expenditure survey, earnings constituted, on average in 1977, 71.6 percent of total personal income in Mexico.[9] Further, they represented no less than 53.5 percent and up to 82.0 percent for different income brackets.[10] This highlights how the shape of the distribution of earnings constitutes a primary determinant of income distribution.

Research on earnings differentials, the wage structure, and the distribution of labor income in Mexico is scarce. Stinson Ortiz (1979) and Montemayor (1980), among others, deal with the effects of education on earnings from a human capital perspective, but do not fully relate their findings with the overall distribution of earnings. Everett (1967) analyzed the effects of unionism on earnings for the 1950s and early 1960s, finding a premium for membership in strong national unions.[11]

Available evidence suggests that interindustry wage differentials in the manufacturing sector are smaller today than what they were approximately three decades ago. Table 6-1 traces the movement in distribution over the period 1940–1978, as measured by the unweighted coefficient of variation of average wages across sectors. The pattern they follow suggests increased distribution up to the late 1950s and reduced thereafter.

In their international wage comparisons, Gregory (1974) and Salazar-Carrillo (1977) included occupational wage differentials for Mexico, finding them to be large in relation with those of other Latin American countries. Eriksson (1966) worked with occupational wage differentials for Mexico in the early 1960s, pointing out their tendency to decrease over time. Reyes Heroles (1980) confirmed this tendency for the 1960s and provided evidence of a previous period of widening occupational wage differentials in the manufacturing sector during the 1940s and part of the 1950s.

Previous work on occupational wage differentials, however, cannot provide a complete picture of the evolution of the earnings distribution, since it only focuses on the wage structure and not the job structure. Furthermore, the data used are confined to the modern segment of the manufacturing sector. Although this research is useful, additional work has to be done in order to deal with the overall distribution of earnings, that is, covering all sectors and segments of the labor market.

This chapter undertakes the task of analyzing the distribution of earnings in a more comprehensive way. To do so it uses data on the distribution of earnings from the income expenditure survey of 1977.

It is convenient to initiate the analysis of the size distribution of *labor income* in Mexico by relating it to the level and distribution of *total income*. At least four concepts of income have to be distinguished[12]:

TABLE 6.1.
*Intersectorial Distribution of Hourly Wages in the Industrial Sector: 1940–1977 (Current Pesos)*

| *Year* | $\bar{W}$ | $\sigma_w$ | $CV = \sigma_w/w$ | *Number of Observations (Industries)* |
|---|---|---|---|---|
| 1940 | 0.57 | 0.18 | 0.316 | 22 |
| 1942 | 0.61 | 0.21 | 0.344 | 27 |
| 1943 | 0.78 | 0.25 | 0.321 | 28 |
| 1944 | 0.82 | 0.27 | 0.329 | 28 |
| 1947 | 1.12 | 0.42 | 0.375 | 28 |
| 1948 | 1.35 | 0.47 | 0.348 | 28 |
| 1949 | 1.30 | 0.47 | 0.362 | 28 |
| 1951 | 1.51 | 0.58 | 0.384 | 28 |
| 1952 | 1.69 | 0.62 | 0.367 | 28 |
| 1953 | 1.76 | 0.57 | 0.324 | 28 |
| 1954 | 2.11 | 0.64 | 0.303 | 28 |
| 1955 | 2.24 | 0.76 | 0.339 | 28 |
| 1956 | 2.51 | 0.91 | 0.363 | 28 |
| 1957 | 2.64 | 0.92 | 0.349 | 28 |
| 1958 | 2.97 | 1.23 | 0.414 | 28 |
| 1959 | 3.17 | 1.30 | 0.410 | 28 |
| 1960 | 3.47 | 1.33 | 0.383 | 28 |
| 1961 | 3.57 | 1.09 | 0.305 | 28 |
| 1962 | 4.08 | 1.66 | 0.407 | 28 |
| 1963 | 4.28 | 1.36 | 0.318 | 28 |
| 1964 | 4.41 | 1.36 | 0.308 | 47 |
| 1965 | 4.93 | 1.49 | 0.302 | 49 |
| 1966 | 5.48 | 1.57 | 0.287 | 49 |
| 1967 | 5.76 | 1.56 | 0.271 | 49 |
| 1968 | 6.01 | 1.59 | 0.265 | 49 |
| 1969 | 6.47 | 1.59 | 0.246 | 49 |
| 1970 | 7.00 | 1.74 | 0.249 | 49 |
| 1971 | 7.59 | 1.89 | 0.249 | 49 |
| 1972 | 8.28 | 1.94 | 0.234 | 49 |
| 1973 | 10.09 | 2.42 | 0.240 | 49 |
| 1974 | 13.35 | 3.29 | 0.246 | 49 |
| 1975 | 14.69 | 4.17 | 0.284 | 49 |
| 1976 | 21.36 | 5.72 | 0.268 | 49 |
| 1977 | 24.12 | 6.69 | 0.277 | 49 |

SOURCE: Calculated by the author from Secretariat of Planning and the National Budget (SPP Mexico City), *Trabajo y Salarios Industriales*, several issues.

1. *Total income per participant (YP),* which includes all types of income for any individual reporting a positive income
2. *Labor income per participant (WP),* which considers only wages, salaries, and other types of income related with earnings for individuals reporting a positive income
3. *Total income per employee (YE),* which includes all types of income *only* for those individuals reporting having received wages and salaries
4. *Labor income per employee (WE),* which considers wages, salaries, and other types of income related with earnings *only* for those individuals reporting positive wages and salaries

Each of these concepts has different implications for the analysis, and therefore it is convenient to present how these concepts of income, and income recipients, relate to each other and especially to labor income per employee. This constitutes the primary interest of this chapter.

The relative number of employees by sector reflects the sectorial importance of wage-earning employment; the remaining labor force is considered here as self-employed. As can be seen in the last column of Table 6-2, self-employment seems to be relatively more important in handicrafts, "all other", machinery repairs, cattle raising, cleaning and laundry, clothing and apparel, and agriculture. For these sectors the distribution of earnings is relatively less important in shaping the distribution of total income. The number of self-employed found in agriculture (1,734,542) represents 10.1 percent of the total number of participants. This part of the work force, which accounts for 38.6 percent of the total in agriculture, did not receive wages or salaries. In terms of the sectorial location of self-employment, the commerce sector is also very important; it is estimated that in 1977 there were 868,827 self-employed in this sector. For the remaining sectors employees represent over 66 percent of the work force; at the aggregate level about 70 percent of the work force received wages and/or salaries.

Another basic feature of the Mexican labor market results from the distribution of employees across income brackets. As can be seen in Table 6-3, self-employment is relatively more concentrated in low-income brackets. Families located in the lowest-income category had 1,759,777 working members who did not receive wages or salaries in 1977; this figure represents 48.2 percent of the participants found in that income bracket. For other brackets, however, over 63 percent and up to 84.1 percent of the working members were employees.

A third piece of evidence which provides some useful clues on the relative importance of the labor market in shaping the distribution of total income is the structure of income of the different types of income recipients. It can be observed in Table 6-4 that the share of total income of employees in total income of each bracket first rises and then decreases as average family income increases. In other words, employees are relatively more important as providers of income for the families located

TABLE 6.2.

*Income Recipients by Sector: 1977*
*(Absolute Number and Percentages)*

| | Participants | | Employees | | Employees/ Partici- pants |
|---|---|---|---|---|---|
| | Absolute (1) | % (2) | Absolute (3) | % (4) | (5) |
| 1. Agriculture | 4,492,849 | 26.1 | 2,758,307 | 23.0 | 61.4 |
| 2. Cattle raising | 288,488 | 1.7 | 172,361 | 1.4 | 59.7 |
| 3. Forestry | 29,903 | 0.2 | 19,095 | 0.2 | 63.9 |
| 4. Fishing | 86,099 | 0.5 | 72,231 | 0.6 | 83.9 |
| 5. Mining | 58,556 | 0.3 | 52,855 | 0.4 | 90.3 |
| 6. Oil and gas | 77,829 | 0.5 | 77,829 | 0.6 | 100.0 |
| 7. Food | 500,084 | 2.9 | 417,083 | 3.5 | 83.4 |
| 8. Beverages and tobacco | 115,847 | 0.7 | 112,016 | 0.9 | 96.7 |
| 9. Textiles | 160,674 | 0.9 | 147,253 | 1.2 | 91.6 |
| 10. Clothing and apparel | 506,772 | 2.9 | 309,973 | 2.6 | 61.2 |
| 11. Footwear | 127,926 | 0.7 | 108,089 | 0.9 | 84.5 |
| 12. Wood | 98,501 | 0.6 | 74,023 | 0.6 | 75.1 |
| 13. Handicrafts | 105,893 | 0.6 | 11,708 | 0.1 | 11.1 |
| 14. Furniture, except metallic | 144,191 | 0.8 | 132,324 | 1.1 | 91.8 |
| 15. Leather | 33,977 | 0.2 | 28,696 | 0.2 | 84.5 |
| 16. Paper and related products | 46,683 | 0.3 | 37,209 | 0.3 | 79.7 |
| 17. Printing and editorial | 90,661 | 0.5 | 86,891 | 0.7 | 95.8 |
| 18. Rubber and plastic | 115,564 | 0.7 | 107,420 | 0.9 | 93.0 |
| 19. Pharmaceuticals and cosmetics | 63,189 | 0.4 | 62,399 | 0.5 | 98.7 |
| 20. Chemicals | 45,616 | 0.3 | 45,616 | 0.4 | 100.0 |
| 21. Nonmetallic mineral products | 178,896 | 1.0 | 148,453 | 1.2 | 83.0 |
| 22. Basic metals | 153,682 | 0.9 | 150,902 | 1.3 | 98.2 |
| 23. Metallic products | 258,420 | 1.5 | 230,131 | 1.9 | 89.1 |
| 24. Machinery | 42,381 | 0.2 | 37,497 | 0.3 | 88.5 |
| 25. Electrical and electronic equipment | 133,458 | 0.8 | 128,675 | 1.1 | 96.4 |
| 26. Transportation equipment | 91,403 | 0.5 | 88,563 | 0.7 | 96.9 |
| 27. Other manufactures | 169,075 | 1.0 | 150,991 | 1.3 | 89.3 |
| 28. Construction | 972,553 | 5.6 | 847,345 | 7.1 | 87.1 |
| 29. Electricity | 58,244 | 0.3 | 58,244 | 0.5 | 100.0 |
| 30. Commerce | 2,146,355 | 12.5 | 1,277,528 | 10.6 | 59.5 |
| 31. Hotels and lodging | 69,242 | 0.4 | 61,917 | 0.5 | 89.4 |
| 32. Restaurants and bars | 387,580 | 2.3 | 266,916 | 2.2 | 68.9 |
| 33. Radio, TV, and amusement | 144,920 | 0.8 | 122,774 | 1.0 | 84.7 |
| 34. Telephonic and telegraphic services | 37,898 | 0.2 | 37,898 | 0.3 | 100.0 |
| 35. Education and research | 529,122 | 3.1 | 519,347 | 4.3 | 98.2 |
| 36. Credit, insurance, and finance | 179,987 | 1.0 | 176,156 | 1.5 | 97.9 |
| 37. Medical services | 333,744 | 1.9 | 309,646 | 2.6 | 92.8 |
| 38. Cleaning and laundry | 116,082 | 0.7 | 76,511 | 0.6 | 65.9 |
| 39. Domestic service | 608,088 | 3.5 | 459,025 | 3.8 | 75.5 |

*TABLE 6.2.* (Continued)

| | *Participants* | | *Employees* | | *Employees/Partici-pants* |
|---|---|---|---|---|---|
| | *Absolute (1)* | *% (2)* | *Absolute (3)* | *% (4)* | *(5)* |
| 40. Professional services and leasing | 199,651 | 1.2 | 150,029 | 1.3 | 75.1 |
| 41. Automobile repairs | 217,684 | 1.3 | 180,751 | 1.5 | 83.0 |
| 42. Machinery repairs | 168,379 | 1.0 | 100,676 | 0.8 | 59.8 |
| 43. Other services | 165,461 | 1.0 | 124,740 | 1.0 | 75.4 |
| 44. Railroad | 68,897 | 0.4 | 66,462 | 0.6 | 96.5 |
| 45. Transportation, passengers | 244,403 | 1.4 | 191,169 | 1.6 | 78.2 |
| 46. Transportation, freight | 159,807 | 0.9 | 136,018 | 1.1 | 85.1 |
| 47. Other transportation | 86,540 | 0.5 | 77,329 | 0.6 | 89.4 |
| 48. Federal government | 437,383 | 2.5 | 437,383 | 3.6 | 100.0 |
| 49. Other government | 154,008 | 0.9 | 149,589 | 1.2 | 97.1 |
| 50. All other | 1,522,257 | 8.8 | 403,375 | 3.4 | 26.5 |
| Total | 17,224,902 | 100.0 | 11,999,418 | 100.0 | 69.7 |

SOURCE: Elaborated by the author based on the household survey of 1977.

toward the middle-income ranges. For example, income of this group constituted 83.8 percent of the total income of the families classified within the seventh bracket, making self-employment a relatively unimportant source of income.

A related issue is how important labor income is as a source of total income for the employees and what other types of income they receive. The data presented in Table 6-5 show that labor income constitutes on average at least 88.7 percent and up to 97.6 percent of total income of the employees. Changes of this share across income brackets indicate that, on average, other types of income are a relatively small supplement of earnings for low-income employees. Mixed income represents on average only 3.8 percent of total income of the employees of the lowest bracket. This suggests that there is a fairly clear division between those income recipients in self-employment and those working as employees. Mixed income tends to be relatively more important as a source of total income for employees at the bottom and top of the distribution. On the other hand, the share of pure capital income in total income rises as wage earners attain a higher income. Employees with moderate labor income complement their earnings with self-employment, while those with high salaries increase their access to capital income as total income rises.

Before proceeding with the analysis of the distibution of labor income, it is convenient to examine how diverse income concepts are distributed among corresponding populations. The statistics in Table 6-6 indicate that labor income of employees is less concentrated than any other type of

TABLE 6.3.
*Income Recipients by Income Bracket: 1977*
*(Absolute Number and Percentages)*

| *Income Bracket*[a] | *Participants* Absolute | % | *Employees* Absolute | % | *Self-employed* Absolute | % | *Employees/ Participants* |
|---|---|---|---|---|---|---|---|
| 1 | 3,651,222 | 21.2 | 1,891,369 | 15.8 | 1,759,853 | 33.7 | 51.8 |
| 2 | 1,618,622 | 9.4 | 1,027,913 | 8.6 | 590,709 | 11.3 | 63.5 |
| 3 | 1,330,705 | 7.7 | 885,369 | 7.4 | 445,336 | 8.5 | 66.5 |
| 4 | 1,591,254 | 9.2 | 1,110,242 | 9.3 | 481,012 | 9.2 | 69.8 |
| 5 | 1,660,664 | 9.6 | 1,208,102 | 10.1 | 452,562 | 8.7 | 72.8 |
| 6 | 1,755,679 | 10.2 | 1,373,046 | 11.4 | 382,633 | 7.3 | 78.2 |
| 7 | 2,181,854 | 12.7 | 1,834,303 | 15.3 | 347,551 | 6.7 | 84.1 |
| 8 | 1,270,423 | 7.4 | 1,029,100 | 8.6 | 241,323 | 4.6 | 81.0 |
| 9 | 909,281 | 5.3 | 724,425 | 6.0 | 184,856 | 3.5 | 79.7 |
| 10 | 605,987 | 3.5 | 445,329 | 3.7 | 160,658 | 3.1 | 73.5 |
| 11 | 298,736 | 1.7 | 229,936 | 1.9 | 68,800 | 1.3 | 77.0 |
| 12 | 184,886 | 1.1 | 133,305 | 1.1 | 51,581 | 1.0 | 72.1 |
| 13 | 165,589 | 1.0 | 106,979 | 0.9 | 58,610 | 1.1 | 64.6 |
| Total | 17,224,902 | 100.0 | 11,999,418 | 100.0 | 5,225,484 | 100.0 | 69.7 |

SOURCE: Computed by the author from the household survey of 1977.
[a] See definition of brackets in Appendix 1.

TABLE 6.4.
*Contribution of Employees to Total Income by Bracket: 1977*
*(Millions of Pesos and Percentages)*

| *Income Bracket*[a] | *(1) Total Income* | *(2) Total Income of Employees* | *(3) Total Income of Self-employed* | *2/1 (%)* | *3/1 (%)* |
|---|---|---|---|---|---|
| 1 | 1,325.4 | 739.6 | 585.8 | 55.8 | 44.2 |
| 2 | 1,421.8 | 903.7 | 518.1 | 63.6 | 36.4 |
| 3 | 1,584.8 | 1,050.9 | 533.9 | 66.3 | 33.7 |
| 4 | 2,521.2 | 1,756.7 | 764.5 | 69.7 | 30.3 |
| 5 | 3,517.2 | 2,566.2 | 951.0 | 73.0 | 27.0 |
| 6 | 4,939.2 | 3,876.7 | 1,062.5 | 78.5 | 21.5 |
| 7 | 7,955.9 | 6,667.5 | 1,288.4 | 83.8 | 16.2 |
| 8 | 6,244.3 | 5,059.6 | 1,184.7 | 81.0 | 19.0 |
| 9 | 5,859.8 | 4,661.0 | 1,198.8 | 79.5 | 20.5 |
| 10 | 5,321.2 | 3,909.8 | 1,411.4 | 73.5 | 26.5 |
| 11 | 3,492.4 | 2,675.4 | 817.0 | 76.6 | 23.4 |
| 12 | 2,862.8 | 2,070.1 | 792.7 | 72.3 | 27.7 |
| 13 | 4,528.0 | 2,703.5 | 1,824.5 | 59.7 | 40.3 |
| Total | 51,574.0 | 38,640.6 | 12,933.4 | 74.9 | 25.1 |

SOURCE: Computed by the author from the household survey of 1977.
[a] See definition of brackets in Appendix 1.

income. It is followed, in terms of the Gini coefficient, by the distribution of total income per employee.

Summarizing, labor income is the major source of income for the work force. Of all income recipients, 69.7 percent received wages or salaries, and their earnings represented 74.9 percent of personal income in 1977. Those income recipients without earnings, considered here as self-employed, are concentrated in a few sectors; agriculture, commerce, and all other are those where self-employment was more frequent. Labor income is relatively more important as the source of income for families with middle incomes. It was also observed that there seems to be a fairly clear division between self-employed and employees. For the last category labor income constituted, on average, 95.2 percent of total income. Finally, labor income of the employees is less concentrated than total income. All this illustrates the importance of the earnings distribution in determining the distribution of total income.

Figure 6-1 depicts the frequency distribution of labor income per employee for selected economic sectors, and Table 6-7 presents the parameters of the sectorial distributions for this concept.[13] To get an idea of the relationship between the shape of the distribution and their corresponding parameters, it is convenient to focus on some extreme cases.

As can be seen in Figure 6-1 and in the coefficient of skewness (SKWE) in Table 6-7, agriculture (sector 1) and domestic service (sector 39) have very skewed distributions.[14] Average labor income (WE) in both sectors is the lowest.[15] The coefficient of variation (CVWE) of domestic service is the second highest, and that of agriculture is also relatively high. As can be seen in Figure 6-1, the frequency distributions for these two sectors are very flat around their corresponding means. The last characteristic is captured by the coefficients of excess kurtosis (KUWE).[16] Finally, these sectors show a Gini coefficient higher that for the overall distribution of labor income.

On the other hand, the frequency distributions of machinery repairs (sector 42) and of cleaning and laundry (sector 38) tend to resemble a normal distribution. The coefficients of skewness are closer to zero than for any other sector. The degree of peakedness of the distributions around their mean, closer to that of the normal, is adequately captured by the relatively low coefficients of excess kurtosis. These two sectors also have relatively low average labor income and a low dispersion of earnings, as indicated by the coefficient of variation. Finally, concentration of earnings is lower than in most sectors, as captured by the Gini coefficient.

The figure and the table indicate that the distribution of labor income is skewed to the right for every sector, as is the economy-wide size distribution. It also stands out that several of the sectorial distributions depicted in Figure 6-1, including the overall distribution of earnings, are bimodal.[17] Furthermore, one of the modes usually indicates a relatively large number

*TABLE*

*Income Sources of Employees*

*(Percentages)*

| Bracket | *Labor Income* | | | | | | *Mixed Income* | | | | | *Capital* | |
|---|---|---|---|---|---|---|---|---|---|---|---|---|---|
| | *(1)*[a] | *(2)* | *(3)* | *(4)* | *(5)* | *Total* | *(6)* | *(7)* | *(8)* | *(9)* | *Total* | *(10)* | *(11)* |
| 1 | 94.59 | 0.07 | 0.03 | 0.53 | 0.07 | 95.29 | 3.18 | 0.26 | 0.32 | 0.02 | 3.78 | 0.05 | 0.04 |
| 2 | 95.05 | 0.04 | 0.04 | 0.10 | 0.02 | 95.23 | 3.07 | 0.11 | 0.78 | 0.00 | 3.96 | 0.02 | 0.00 |
| 3 | 94.38 | 0.10 | 0.07 | 0.06 | 0.00 | 94.61 | 3.39 | 0.12 | 0.39 | 0.04 | 3.94 | 0.03 | 0.04 |
| 4 | 94.59 | 0.17 | 0.05 | 0.27 | 0.13 | 95.21 | 2.53 | 0.39 | 0.67 | 0.02 | 3.61 | 0.14 | 0.03 |
| 5 | 95.37 | 0.20 | 0.06 | 0.09 | 0.23 | 95.95 | 2.39 | 0.12 | 0.56 | 0.05 | 3.12 | 0.12 | 0.00 |
| 6 | 96.19 | 0.26 | 0.27 | 0.10 | 0.46 | 97.28 | 1.61 | 0.06 | 0.31 | 0.02 | 2.00 | 0.02 | 0.02 |
| 7 | 95.90 | 0.45 | 0.62 | 0.08 | 0.57 | 97.62 | 0.88 | 0.14 | 0.27 | 0.03 | 1.32 | 0.06 | 0.00 |
| 8 | 92.30 | 0.97 | 1.31 | 0.11 | 0.91 | 95.60 | 1.27 | 0.10 | 0.66 | 0.11 | 2.14 | 0.42 | 0.04 |
| 9 | 92.62 | 0.99 | 1.18 | 0.11 | 1.29 | 96.19 | 0.56 | 0.04 | 0.75 | 0.04 | 1.39 | 0.57 | 0.00 |
| 10 | 91.83 | 1.23 | 1.16 | 0.06 | 1.80 | 96.08 | 0.43 | 0.02 | 0.73 | 0.04 | 1.22 | 0.65 | 0.01 |
| 11 | 87.99 | 1.60 | 1.28 | 0.03 | 0.89 | 91.79 | 3.10 | 0.00 | 0.69 | 0.19 | 3.98 | 1.13 | 0.00 |
| 12 | 87.85 | 1.17 | 1.33 | 0.06 | 0.92 | 91.33 | 4.51 | 0.00 | 2.10 | 0.00 | 6.61 | 0.36 | 0.01 |
| 13 | 85.85 | 0.97 | 0.85 | 0.11 | 0.90 | 88.68 | 3.78 | 0.01 | 1.59 | 0.08 | 5.46 | 0.56 | 0.00 |
| Total | 92.79 | 0.74 | 0.79 | 0.10 | 0.80 | 95.22 | 1.81 | 0.01 | 0.70 | 0.06 | 2.58 | 0.36 | 0.00 |

SOURCE: Computed by the author from the household survey of 1977.

of employees with average monthly earnings lower than a thousand pesos and therefore inferior to the lowest minimum wage.[18] This is the result of the interaction of two main causes: temporary employment and the dual structure of production in Mexico. The first represents a problem for the analysis, since it is not possible to approximate the "true" (full-time equivalent) job-wage structure.[19] The second is one of the basic features of the Mexican labor market; its implications for economic development will be examined in section IV-2.

A brief review of the sectors contributing to the first mode of the overall distribution is in order. Of all employees with monthly earnings lower than 700 pesos (first bracket), 47.8 percent were located in agriculture, 14.2 percent in domestic service, and 8.0 percent in commerce.[20] The relative importance of employees with earnings within the second bracket follows the same ranking. The association between these sectors and those believed to function as residual employers of the underemployed is clear. It is evident that economic development is associated with a decrease in low-earnings employees, especially in these sectors. It is also apparent that other sectors, like basic metals, hardly show a traditional segment. Of all participants in this sector 98.2 percent are employees, and the distribution indicates that relatively few of them earned less than its modal wage.

6.5

*by Income Bracket: 1977*

*(Percentages)*

| *Income* | | | *Other Income* | | | | | | | | *Total* | *Total* |
|---|---|---|---|---|---|---|---|---|---|---|---|---|
| *(12)* | *(13)* | *Total* | *(14)* | *(15)* | *(16)* | *(17)* | *(18)* | *(19)* | *(20)* | *Total* | *(%)* | *Income*[b] |
| 0.00 | 0.00 | 0.09 | 0.00 | 0.00 | 0.02 | 0.00 | 0.00 | 0.03 | 0.80 | 0.85 | 100.0 | 739.6 |
| 0.00 | 0.00 | 0.02 | 0.00 | 0.00 | 0.00 | 0.00 | 0.00 | 0.00 | 0.77 | 0.77 | 100.0 | 903.7 |
| 0.01 | 0.00 | 0.08 | 0.00 | 0.00 | 0.14 | 0.00 | 0.14 | 0.00 | 1.07 | 1.35 | 100.0 | 1,050.9 |
| 0.05 | 0.00 | 0.22 | 0.00 | 0.00 | 0.03 | 0.00 | 0.00 | 0.01 | 0.92 | 0.96 | 100.0 | 1,756.7 |
| 0.02 | 0.00 | 0.14 | 0.00 | 0.01 | 0.06 | 0.04 | 0.03 | 0.00 | 0.60 | 0.79 | 100.0 | 2,566.2 |
| 0.00 | 0.00 | 0.04 | 0.00 | 0.00 | 0.05 | 0.08 | 0.02 | 0.00 | 0.52 | 0.67 | 100.0 | 3,876.7 |
| 0.03 | 0.00 | 0.09 | 0.00 | 0.01 | 0.06 | 0.02 | 0.21 | 0.00 | 0.66 | 0.96 | 100.0 | 6,667.5 |
| 0.05 | 0.00 | 0.51 | 0.02 | 0.02 | 0.07 | 0.02 | 0.54 | 0.05 | 1.01 | 1.75 | 100.0 | 5,059.6 |
| 0.18 | 0.00 | 1.26 | 0.04 | 0.07 | 0.20 | 0.02 | 0.26 | 0.04 | 1.02 | 1.65 | 100.0 | 4,661.0 |
| 0.19 | 0.00 | 0.85 | 0.00 | 0.02 | 0.34 | 0.07 | 0.11 | 0.23 | 1.10 | 1.87 | 100.0 | 3,909.8 |
| 0.13 | 0.00 | 1.26 | 0.00 | 0.03 | 0.23 | 0.27 | 0.69 | 0.07 | 1.78 | 2.98 | 100.0 | 2,675.4 |
| 0.29 | 0.37 | 1.03 | 0.00 | 0.08 | 0.19 | 0.00 | 0.05 | 0.00 | 0.71 | 1.04 | 100.0 | 2,070.1 |
| 2.17 | 0.57 | 3.30 | 0.44 | 0.00 | 1.58 | 0.06 | 0.00 | 0.00 | 0.45 | 2.53 | 100.0 | 2,703.5 |
| 0.23 | 0.06 | 0.65 | 0.04 | 0.02 | 0.23 | 0.05 | 0.21 | 0.04 | 0.87 | 1.46 | 100.0 | 36,640.6 |

TABLE 6.6.

*Distribution of Diverse Income Concepts*[a]

*(Percentages)*

| | *Participants* | | *Employees* | | |
|---|---|---|---|---|---|
| *Bracket* | *Population* | *Total Income* | *Population* | *Labor Income* | *Total Income* |
| 1 | 21.2 | 2.6 | 15.8 | 1.9 | 1.9 |
| 2 | 9.4 | 2.8 | 8.6 | 2.3 | 2.3 |
| 3 | 7.7 | 3.1 | 7.4 | 2.7 | 2.7 |
| 4 | 9.2 | 4.9 | 9.3 | 4.6 | 4.6 |
| 5 | 9.6 | 6.8 | 10.1 | 6.7 | 6.6 |
| 6 | 10.2 | 9.6 | 11.4 | 10.2 | 10.0 |
| 7 | 12.7 | 15.4 | 15.3 | 17.7 | 17.3 |
| 8 | 7.4 | 12.1 | 8.6 | 13.1 | 13.1 |
| 9 | 5.3 | 11.4 | 6.0 | 12.2 | 12.1 |
| 10 | 3.5 | 10.3 | 3.7 | 10.2 | 10.1 |
| 11 | 1.7 | 6.8 | 1.9 | 6.7 | 6.9 |
| 12 | 1.1 | 5.6 | 1.1 | 5.1 | 5.4 |
| 13 | 1.0 | 8.8 | 0.9 | 6.6 | 7.0 |
| Total | 100.0 | 100.0 | 100.0 | 100.0 | 100.0 |
| Gini | | 0.517 | | 0.475 | 0.479 |

SOURCE: Computed by the author from the household survey of 1977.

[a] Fractions may not coincide due to rounding.

**Figure 6-1.**

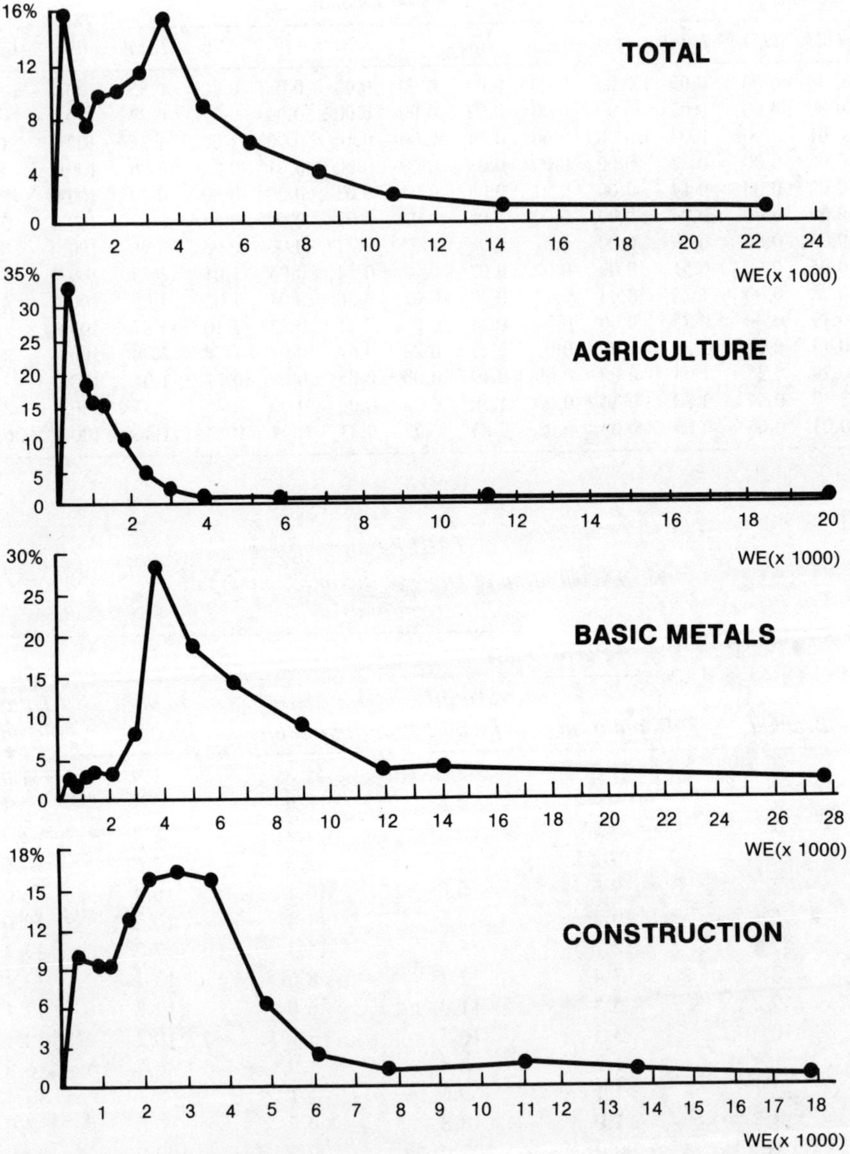
TOTAL
16%
12
8
4
0
2
4
6
8
10
12
14
16
18
20
22
24
WE(x 1000)
AGRICULTURE
35%
30
25
20
15
10
5
0
2
4
6
8
10
12
14
16
18
20
WE(x 1000)
BASIC METALS
30%
25
20
15
10
5
0
2
4
6
8
10
12
14
16
18
20
22
24
26
28
WE(x 1000)
CONSTRUCTION
18%
15
12
9
6
3
0
1
2
3
4
5
6
7
8
9
10
11
12
13
14
15
16
17
18
WE(x 1000)

**Figure 6-1 (continued)**

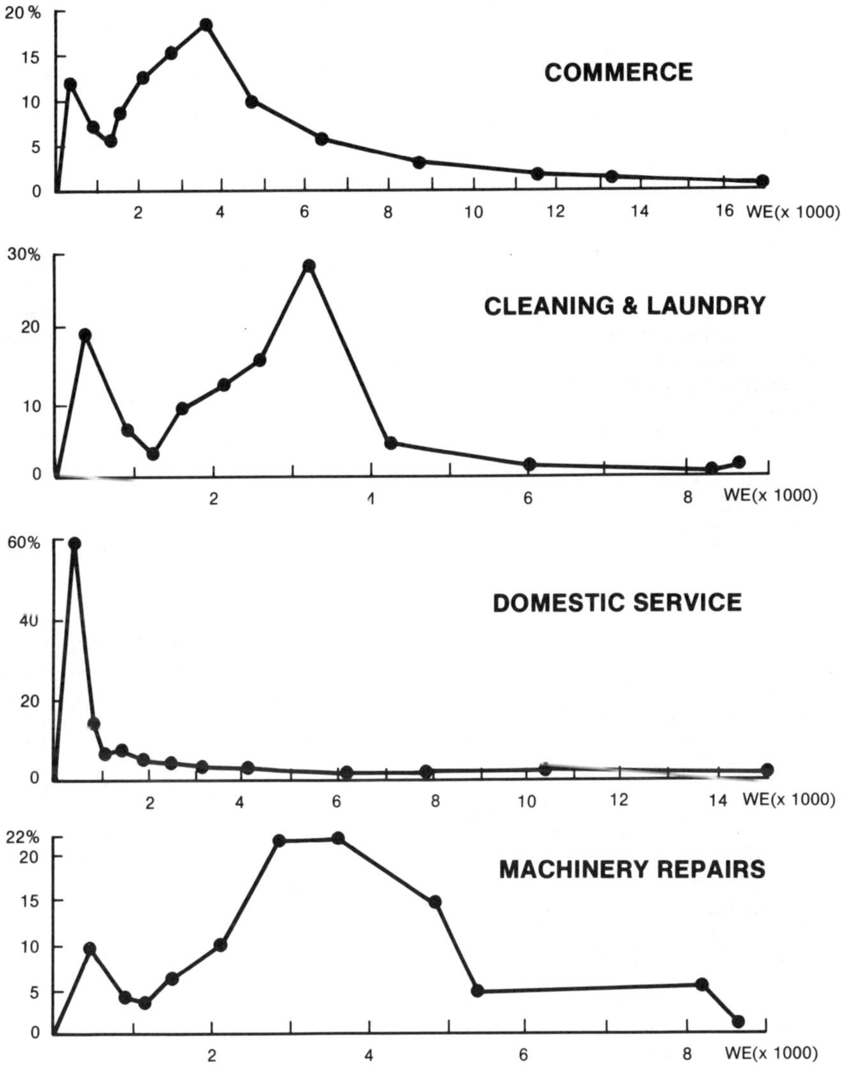

## *TABLE 6.7.*

## *Parameters of the Sectorial Distribution of Labor Income Per Employee*

| | *WE* | *SDWE* | *CVWE* | *SKWE* | *VLWE* | *KUWE* | *GWE* |
|---|---|---|---|---|---|---|---|
| 1. Agriculture | 1138 | 1,192 | 1.05 | 5.23 | 0.84 | 44.61 | 0.422 |
| 2. Cattle raising | 1977 | 1,738 | 0.88 | 2.31 | 0.69 | 7.17 | 0.405 |
| 3. Forestry | 2509 | 0 | 0 | 1.81 | 1.99 | 2.82 | 0.479 |
| 4. Fishing | 2263 | 1,931 | 0.85 | 1.30 | 0.79 | 0.89 | 0.414 |
| 5. Mining | 7028 | 13,848 | 1.97 | 2.40 | 1.35 | 3.87 | 0.644 |
| 6. Oil and gas | 6720 | 5,484 | 0.82 | 1.93 | 0.64 | 4.53 | 0.370 |
| 7. Food | 3416 | 2,967 | 0.87 | 2.63 | 0.81 | 9.08 | 0.388 |
| 8. Beverages and tobacco | 4010 | 2,923 | 0.73 | 2.08 | 0.65 | 7.30 | 0.338 |
| 9. Textiles | 3913 | 4,184 | 1.07 | 2.87 | 1.23 | 8.98 | 0.433 |
| 10. Clothing and apparel | 2536 | 1,863 | 0.73 | 1.92 | 0.92 | 8.46 | 0.366 |
| 11. Footwear | 2489 | 1,638 | 0.66 | 2.17 | 0.55 | 12.81 | 0.311 |
| 12. Wood | 2338 | 2,004 | 0.86 | 1.33 | 1.14 | 2.18 | 0.417 |
| 13. Handicrafts | 1079 | 0 | 0 | 2.17 | 1.63 | 6.58 | 0.521 |
| 14. Furniture, except metallic | 2646 | 1,721 | 0.65 | 3.22 | 0.63 | 22.69 | 0.283 |
| 15. Leather | 2614 | 2,204 | 0.84 | 2.58 | 0.43 | 9.84 | 0.315 |
| 16. Paper and related products | 4957 | 5,482 | 1.11 | 2.41 | 0.51 | 4.95 | 0.402 |
| 17. Printing and editorial | 3838 | 3,019 | 0.79 | 2.19 | 0.69 | 7.34 | 0.355 |
| 18. Rubber and plastic | 4559 | 4,713 | 1.03 | 3.34 | 0.83 | 14.58 | 0.404 |
| 19. Pharmaceuticals and cosmetics | 5456 | 6,627 | 1.21 | 3.68 | 1.02 | 15.46 | 0.430 |
| 20. Chemicals | 5422 | 6,243 | 1.15 | 2.88 | 0.54 | 8.52 | 0.406 |
| 21. Nonmetallic mineral products | 3094 | 2,525 | 0.82 | 1.85 | 0.60 | 5.16 | 0.394 |
| 22. Basic metals | 5590 | 4,895 | 0.88 | 4.24 | 0.52 | 30.47 | 0.354 |
| 23. Metallic products | 3650 | 3,019 | 0.83 | 2.93 | 0.82 | 14.08 | 0.367 |
| 24. Machinery | 4822 | 6,417 | 1.33 | 3.49 | 0.70 | 13.18 | 0.441 |
| 25. Electrical and electronic equipment | 5344 | 4,222 | 0.79 | 2.80 | 0.32 | 9.12 | 0.325 |
| 26. Transportation Equipment | 4670 | 2,477 | 0.53 | 1.44 | 0.25 | 3.13 | 0.257 |
| 27. Other manufactures | 4143 | 2,773 | 0.67 | 1.45 | 0.77 | 4.68 | 0.336 |
| 28. Construction | 2650 | 2,504 | 0.94 | 3.70 | 0.76 | 19.59 | 0.397 |
| 29. Electricity | 7318 | 6,447 | 0.88 | 1.55 | 0.86 | 2.24 | 0.404 |
| 30. Commerce | 3117 | 2,743 | 0.88 | 2.40 | 0.96 | 8.54 | 0.415 |
| 31. Hotels and lodging | 3412 | 2,908 | 0.85 | 1.50 | 0.68 | 2.19 | 0.394 |
| 32. Restaurants and bars | 2906 | 2,176 | 0.75 | 1.28 | 1.09 | 2.20 | 0.388 |
| 33. Radio, TV, and amusement | 3480 | 2,876 | 0.83 | 1.34 | 0.83 | 1.46 | 0.408 |
| 34. Telephonic and telegraphic services | 5408 | 4,126 | 0.76 | 2.19 | 0.30 | 6.21 | 0.307 |
| 35. Education and research | 5132 | 3,380 | 0.66 | 1.89 | 0.54 | 6.22 | 0.324 |
| 36. Credit, insurance, and finance | 6073 | 4,624 | 0.76 | 2.94 | 0.55 | 12.67 | 0.331 |
| 37. Medical services | 5539 | 4,317 | 0.78 | 2.21 | 0.59 | 7.29 | 0.368 |
| 38. Cleaning and laundry | 2184 | 1,487 | 0.68 | 0.84 | 0.80 | 2.23 | 0.344 |
| 39. Domestic service | 1007 | 1,452 | 1.44 | 4.70 | 1.16 | 30.99 | 0.526 |
| 40. Professional services and leasing | 5370 | 5,673 | 1.06 | 4.44 | 0.84 | 45.75 | 0.455 |
| 41. Automobile repairs | 2999 | 2,717 | 0.91 | 2.07 | 1.04 | 6.43 | 0.431 |
| 42. Machinery repairs | 3181 | 2,023 | 0.64 | 0.83 | 0.65 | 0.71 | 0.325 |
| 43. Other services | 2543 | 2,535 | 1.00 | 1.61 | 1.79 | 3.16 | 0.484 |
| 44. Railroad | 4611 | 3,499 | 0.76 | 2.58 | 0.42 | 8.44 | 0.310 |
| 45. Transportation, passengers | 4004 | 2,516 | 0.63 | 1.74 | 0.40 | 4.67 | 0.308 |
| 46. Transportation, freight | 3740 | 3,322 | 0.89 | 2.86 | 0.93 | 14.30 | 0.401 |
| 47. Other transportation | 6700 | 5,886 | 0.88 | 1.63 | 0.82 | 2.63 | 0.408 |
| 48. Federal government | 4983 | 3,832 | 0.77 | 3.03 | 0.38 | 12.39 | 0.330 |
| 49. Other government | 3177 | 2,201 | 0.69 | 1.58 | 0.58 | 3.66 | 0.341 |
| 50. All other | 3364 | 3,629 | 1.08 | 3.49 | 1.04 | 16.70 | 0.466 |
| All | 3066 | 3,317 | 1.08 | | 1.20 | | |

SOURCE: Calculated by the author from the household survey of 1977.

Finally, it is worthwhile to point out that of those employees with the highest earnings (bracket 13), 12.2 percent were located in medical services (includes public sector institutions) and 10.6 percent in federal government, the two sectors with more high-earnings employees. These figures support the frequently cited existence of a privileged beaucracy in Mexico.

Although all sectorial distributions are skewed to the right and several are bimodal, there are significant differences in their shape. The location of their mode and mean differ, as does the dispersion of earnings and the degree of skewness. It is necessary to identify some factors determining these differences in the intraindustry distributions of earnings, as well as their contributions in shaping the overall distributions. This, in turn, is required for the evaluation of past and future effects of economic development on the distribution of earnings and total income.

## III. Factors Shaping the Distribution of Earnings: Theoretical Antecedents

For analytical purposes it is convenient to divide changes in the overall distribution of earnings into two parts. The first refers to alterations in the intraindustry distributions, while the second refers to the effects of changes in output mix and sectorial employment on the overall distribution of earnings.

The main analytical work dealing with the distribution of earnings has been carried out within the fields of income distribution and development economics. Research within the first field has given more attention to the processes determining intraindustry distributions, without giving much consideration to how the relative weight of employment in each sector affects the overall distribution. On the contrary, the work in development economics has stressed the effects of changes in output mix and sectorial employment on the overall distribution; little attention has been given to the intrasectorial alterations that most probably accompany the intersectorial changes in output and employment.

To explain the observed skewed distribution of earnings at a moment of time has been a constant goal of income distribution theorists. Attempts to reach this goal have resulted, for example, in theories based on racial and sexual discrimination, the distribution of innate abilities, the nature of the organizational pyramid within the firm, and even stochastic processes.[21] Recent research has focused on the relationship between the distribution of earnings and the distribution of jobs.

The theory of job competition constitutes the best example of the last line of research.[22] It advances some hypotheses about the mechanisms used by the economic system to assign different workers to available jobs. Based on propositions forwarded earlier by labor economists,[23] this theory presents three sets of factors affecting job distribution: the distribution of technical knowledge, the sociology of wage determination, and the distribution of labor costs. It should be stressed that the propositions of this theory refer to the economy-wide distribution; little attention has been given to how it may correspond to specific sectors or to how sectorial features may alter the general propositions.

Research on the shape of the intraindustry earnings distribution, based on its relationships with the job distribution by sector, can help explain the distribution of earnings both at a moment of time and over time. Cross-section studies can identify the technological characteristics of the firms and the demographic characteristics of workers in various industries and then evaluate the relative importance of these factors in shaping the economy-wide earnings distribution. It is conceivable that if the main causes shaping intraindustry earnings distribution are found, then special policies by sector or industry could be designed to alter it in the desired direction.

To explain the distribution of income in the course of economic growth has been a task undertaken by development economics.[24] The most favored line of thought is that trends in income distribution can be traced back to changes in employment shares by industry. If industries which increase their share in total employment have relatively more unequal earnings distributions, the economy-wide distribution will probably become more concentrated as the economy grows or vice versa.

These ideas, put forward by Kuznets (1955) a quarter of a century ago, have been a basic element of non-Marxist research on the growth-equity relationship since they appeared. Although work in this line has become more refined as it proceeds, there has been little attention to factors determining the intraindustry distributions and their evolution. The approach is, however, helpful. It focuses on the process by which, given an initial income distribution and technology, changes in output mix, resulting from those in preferences, the composition of exports, etc., gradually modify the sectorially derived demand for labor and the level and distribution of rewards to the working force.

The attention given by development economics to the relationship between structural change (i.e., output mix) and income distribution is warranted since it is unavoidable when dealing with dual economies. The basic model of Lewis (1954) is constructed around such a transformation, although sectors are defined differently. With minor qualifications a segment of agriculture, handicrafts, commerce, and domestic service of the Mexican economy could be added to Lewis's traditional sector.

The first step in attempting to profit from these insights and to analyze the distribution of earnings in Mexico is to briefly review the factors that the theory of job structure determination suggests play a role in shaping the intraindustry distributions of earnings and to confront them with the Mexican experience.

## IV. Some Factors Shaping the Intraindustry Distributions of Earnings in Mexico

This section reviews some elements of income distribution economics regarding the distribution of earnings. It then advances hypotheses on how the basic postulates may need to be modified in order to deal with the case of a developing economy. Finally, it contrasts these hypotheses with the Mexican experience.

### *IV–1 Income Distribution Economics and the Distribution of Jobs and Earnings in a Developed Economy*

Within the core of income distribution and labor economics the issue of the determination of the job structure continues to be of overwhelming interest, because it constitutes a summary representation of labor market stratification and the point of entry into the problem of earnings distribution determination.

Scholars have found it difficult to establish a single way to represent the job structure. Number of tasks, level of skills, type of activity or occupation, and earnings levels have been used interchangeably to describe the *job distribution*. It is worth noting that none of these concepts is optimal for the representation of the distribution of what is commonly understood as *job content;* it is also true, however, that taken together they give an acceptable picture of it. In what follows the standard simplifying assumption that the earnings distribution reflects the job structure, is made. Throughout this chapter the number of tasks, skills, type of activity or occupation and any other relevant element of the job content are mapped into a single variable called level of earnings. Its magnitude, along with its relative position in the distribution, should characterize a job. Given these assumptions, the graphical representation of the job distribution will show the number of tasks undertaken and/or level of skills and/or earnings level on the horizontal axis and frequency on the vertical axis (see Figure 6-2).

Two main lines of thought can be identified within the existing theories of job structure determination. The first gives more importance to the supply side of the labor market in determining job structures. When the worker, given the market conditions, "chooses" according to his or her preferences what job to perform, he or she is able to induce changes in job distributions by altering the job content. Human capital theory is the prime example of this line of reasoning. Also some theories of union behavior consider these organizations as elements acting on the job structure from the supply side.

The second line of reasoning gives more attention to the other side of the coin, stressing the demand side determinants of the job structure. Two subgroups can be further differentiated: those who find social control to

**Figure 6-2.**

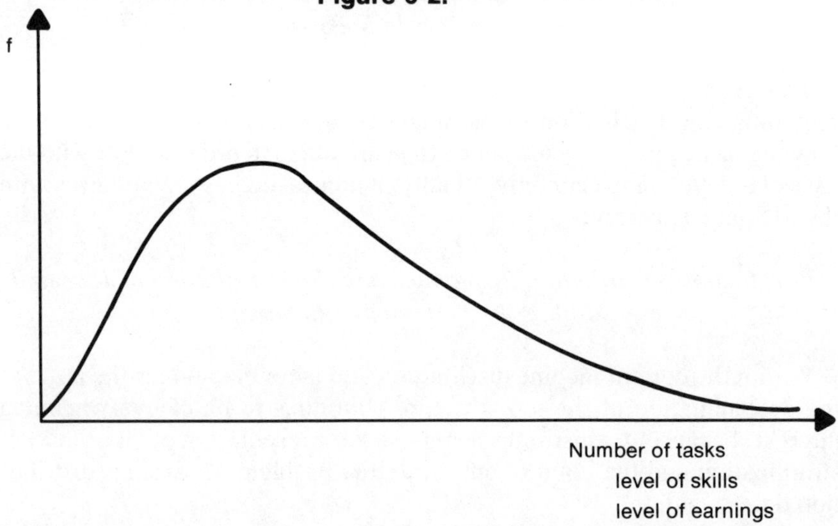


be the main force shaping the job structure, and those who find product market and technological factors to be dominant. Examples of the first approach are Marglin (1971) and Stone (1974). In their view, the job structure reflects and results from the hierarchical structure of society, which, in turn, is brought about by the need for social control. The second approach, which finds its roots in Adam Smith's theory of the division of labor, has been expanded and applied to the theory of job structures by Piore (1973).

The theory of job competition, in its current version, holds an intermediate position. Although it recognizes the importance of demand factors affecting the job distributions, it allows that the supply side induces some alterations in it.[25] Changes in background characteristics of the labor force (such as education and experience) affect training costs, and this induces changes in the job distribution. It is beyond the scope of this chapter to review these theories.[26] Some of the propositions of the technological theory of job structure determination are used here, however, as elements in the explanation of the earnings distribution by industry.[27] Before proceeding, it is convenient to stress that the primary intention of this theory is to give a historical, dynamic explanation of the process of division of labor and job structure determination. A static interpretation must, therefore, be done cautiously.

The theory of the technological determination of the job structure follows Adam Smith's theory of the division of labor, which basically states the following: (1) The division of labor increases productivity as a result of the separation of work into a series of component parts, improved dexterity of workers, saving of time, application of machinery, and increases in the machines' productivity with specialization. (2) The extent of the market limits the division of labor. The first of these statements has been the subject of academic discussion.[28] However, for the purpose of this chapter it is only necessary to accept that division of labor tends to be associated with the application of machinery and therefore with increased use of physcial capital.

The second statement has been generally accepted. Furthermore, in the extended version of the technological theory, the division of labor is limited by the extent of the market, by the degree of product standardization, and by the stability and uncertainty in the demand of the final product. The larger the extent of the market (at the micro level, i.e., the size of the firm), the more standardized the product and the more stable and less uncertain the demand, the more advanced the division of labor will be.

In summary, for operational purposes it can be hypothesized that the division of labor will be greater in industries with higher capital intensity and with a larger average size for its establishments. It can also be hypothesized that more specialized industries, and those with relatively more stable and predictable demands, will present a greater division of labor. Finally, since the job structure determination theory is mainly designed to explain industrial production, it can be hypothesized that the larger the fraction of production workers in total employment, the greater the possibility of industrial-type division of labor.

According to this theory, relatively low-skilled, single-tasked, low-paid jobs will result from division of labor over time. The job distribution brought about by this process will show, in terms of number of tasks and/or skill level, a statistical mode lower than the statistical mean. Furthermore, granting an unavoidable need for intermediate and highly skilled jobs (multitasked) for production and supervisory purpose, the job distribution will be skewed to the right. It also follows that, for such distribution, the higher the modal frequency, the lower will be the relative number of semi- or highly skilled jobs (see Figure 6-3).

The transformation illustrated can apply to the economy-wide distribution or to that of particular sectors. As presented, it is mainly determined by demand factors, although supply factors could be incorporated. Such transformation would be associated, according to this theory, with the process of industrial growth and modernization.

It illustrates, in summary, a plausible theoretical link between product market, technological factors, and the shape of the distribution of jobs, as implied by the extended version of the technological theory of division of labor. The distributive outcome, a shift toward concentration of earnings, requires careful consideration.[29]

In addition to the caution that should be exerted when giving a static interpretation to the technological theory of job structure determination, it should be stressed that the main goal of this theory is to explain the job structure of currently developed economies. Furthermore, according to this theory, the observed distribution results from a gradual process of

**Figure 6-3.**

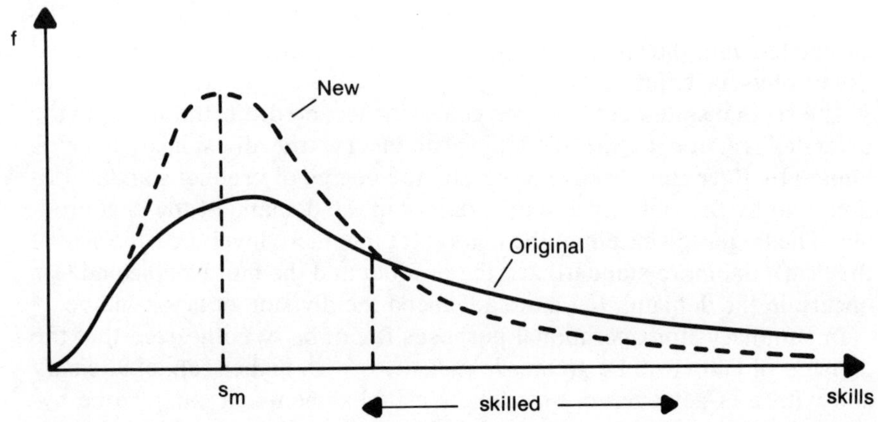


industrialization. This constrains severely its explanatory power for dealing with developing economies where "modern" firms are found in a "traditional" environment, giving rise to the well-known dual structure of production. The process of "modernization" by transplant and not by evolution may modify or even invalidate some of the propositions of the technological theory of the job structure when they are considered in regard to a developing economy. The theory introduces, however, some processes relevant for explaining either developed or developing cases.

### *IV–2. The Distribution of Jobs and Earnings in a Developing Economy*

One might think that some elements of this general process of the job structure evolution would also be observed in developing economies. This may be so for "modern" firms within the modern core of the economy but not for a sector or industry as a whole.

In a dual semiindustrialized economy, such as Mexico's, the emergence of a new modern firm within an industry implies, in general, its coexistence with "traditional" firms within the same industry. The essential characteristic of the process of modernization would be a gradual domination by modern of traditional firms. Only in the long run, and for mature firms or industries, can a transformation of the job structure such as the one described in the previous section take place. But that is not the dominant change observed in the job-wage structure of an industry in the process of modernization.

Modern firms in a developing country resemble closely their counterparts in a developed economy. It is clear that mechanization, the size of the market, specialization, and the stability and uncertainty of demand intervene in shaping the technology used in production and the internal job-wage structure. But it should be stressed that adequate conditions in

*TABLE 6.8.*

*Distribution of Establishments and Employment by Establishment Size (Percentages)*

<table>
<tr><th rowspan="2">Size of Establishment by Number of Employees</th><th colspan="2">1960</th><th colspan="2">1965</th><th colspan="2">1970</th><th colspan="2">1975</th></tr>
<tr><th>Est.</th><th>Emp.</th><th>Est.</th><th>Emp.</th><th>Est.</th><th>Emp.</th><th>Est.</th><th>Emp.</th></tr>
<tr><td>1–5</td><td>79.1</td><td>13.1</td><td>67.3</td><td>9.4</td><td>62.9</td><td>7.2</td><td>59.2</td><td>5.6</td></tr>
<tr><td>6–25</td><td>12.1</td><td>9.9</td><td>20.9</td><td>12.3</td><td>22.9</td><td>11.1</td><td>25.1</td><td>9.9</td></tr>
<tr><td>26–100</td><td>6.1</td><td>19.3</td><td>8.1</td><td>20.7</td><td>9.7</td><td>20.4</td><td>10.4</td><td>18.2</td></tr>
<tr><td>101–350</td><td>2.3</td><td>31.2</td><td rowspan="2">3.3</td><td rowspan="2">57.7</td><td>3.5</td><td>26.4</td><td>4.0</td><td>25.4</td></tr>
<tr><td>351 and over</td><td>0.0</td><td>25.9</td><td>1.1</td><td>35.0</td><td>1.5</td><td>41.1</td></tr>
<tr><td>Total</td><td>100.0</td><td>100.0</td><td>100.0</td><td>100.0</td><td>100.0</td><td>100.0</td><td>100.0</td><td>100.0</td></tr>
</table>

SOURCE: *Industrial Census,* several issues.

relation to each of these factors affect the emergence of modern firms and modern industries. The analytical problem stems from the fact as these firms appear, they are, in most cases, inserted within sectors which have a traditional segment of considerable size. A continuous inflow of such modern units will alter the shape of the sectorial job-wage structure, and they may eventually constitute the only or the dominant type of production unit.

The basic process by which traditional or craft activities are shrinking, whatever their sectoral location, while modern activities gain relative importance, is one of the fundamental characteristics of economic development, as Lewis (1954) pointed out. Some studies have shown that the experience of developing countries conforms with the dualism model.[30]

Available evidence also indicates that such processes have been associated with economic growth in Mexico. For consistency with the theories reviewed in the previous section, modernization should be associated with the gradual domination of larger establishments (in terms of employment), the use of more capital-intensive techniques, and larger markets (at the micro level). There has been a clear decrease in the relative importance of employment in small establishments in the Mexican industrial sector. Table 6-8 indicates that firms with less than five employees which accounted for 13.1 percent of employment in 1960 accounted for 5.6 percent in 1975. On the other hand, firms of over 350 increased their share in employment from 25.9 to 41.1 percent over the same period. A rapid decrease in the relative number of establishments of the smaller size has also taken place.

Additionally, it is observed that for every establishment size fixed capital per employee was higher in 1975 than in 1960, as Table 6-9 shows.[31] Furthermore, the data in the table indicate that capital intensity is higher

TABLE 6.9.
*Fixed Total Net Assets Per Employee in the Industrial Sector*[a]
*(Thousands of Pesos at 1960 Prices)*

| *Size of Establishment by Number of Employees* | *1960* | *1965* | *1970* | *1975* |
|---|---|---|---|---|
| 1–5 | 11.0 | 9.3 | 15.3 | 11.9 |
| 6–25 | 37.0 | 33.8 | 40.6 | 29.4 |
| 26–100 | 52.2 | 53.4 | 65.0 | 45.4 |
| 101–350 } 351 and over } | 68.3 | 83.8 | 86.2 | 64.2 |
| | | | 104.9 | 92.4 |
| Total | 54.5 | 64.4 | 78.2 | 66.4 |

SOURCE: *Industrial Census,* several issues.

[a] Figures were deflated using the deflator for gross fixed investment.

TABLE 6.10.
*Average Value Added Per Establishment in the Industrial Sector*[a]
*(Thousands of Pesos at 1960 Prices)*

| *Size of Establishment by Number of Employees* | *1960* | *1965* | *1970* | *1975* |
|---|---|---|---|---|
| 1–5 | 29.3 | N.A. | 37.7 | 41.9 |
| 6–25 | 155.3 | | 273.9 | 282.7 |
| 26–100 | 1,125.2 | | 1,598.1 | 1,755.4 |
| 101–350 | 5,225.8 | | 7,555.3 | 8,236.5 |
| 351 and over | 39,421.9 | | 38,698.3 | 45,693.5 |
| Total | 855.1 | | 936.0 | 1,296.4 |

SOURCE: *Industrial Census,* several issues.

[a] Figures were deflated using the deflator for value added in manufacture.

the larger the establishment. Finally, fixed capital per employee has grown faster in large establishments, which, in turn, have increased their share in total employment.

There is also evidence that firms have been able to increase their scale of production in the course of development. Table 6-10 shows that average production per establishment of every size has grown over the last decade and a half. This enlargement of the market at the micro level allows craft production units to modernize and modern firms to enter the market.

This evidence supports the idea that recent Mexican growth, at least in the industrial sector, has been associated with a process of modernization. The issue is to establish the following: first, how this process of modernization may alter intraindustry job-wage structures; second, how it may modify the overall earnings distribution through these intrasectorial variations; third, how changes in intersectorial employment could affect the economy-wide distribution; and, fourth, how these changes relate with the observed distribution of earnings in Mexico.

Consider the change that would occur in the intraindustry job-wage structure of some sector with the creation of a considerable number of modern firms, some of them replacing traditional firms while some others introducing new lines of products within the same industry. Figure 6-4 illustrates the type of transformation that is expected.

Several factors bring about this transformation in the intraindustry distribution of earnings in countries like Mexico. One which plays an important role is the existence of minimum wages (*WM* in Figure 6-4 represents the average general legal minimum). Modernization implies easier enforcement of binding minimum wages and an increase in the relative number of employees with earnings in the neighborhood of *WM*. That would reduce the positive skewness of the distribution. As Tables 6-8 through 6-10 indicate, new firms in Mexico are characterized as being relatively more capital intensive than previous ones and larger. They also pay relatively higher average wages, both because of their higher productivity and because of the impossibility of paying wages below the legal minimum *(WM)*. If in a particular industry the relative size of the traditional segment (with wages below the statutory) is shrinking, the relative number of jobs (frequency) with earnings higher than the legal minimum will increase (range II), while simultaneously the relative number of jobs with a pay in range I will decrease. This will reduce the number of observations clustered to the left of the mean while leaving the relative number of extreme cases (highly skilled and supervisory jobs) located to the right of the mean (i.e., range III) about constant, making the intraindustry distribution less skewed. The frequency distribution will also become less peaked than it was before the introduction of modern firms.

In more detail, the expected effects of modernization on the intraindustry distribution of earnings are the following:

**Figure 6-4.**

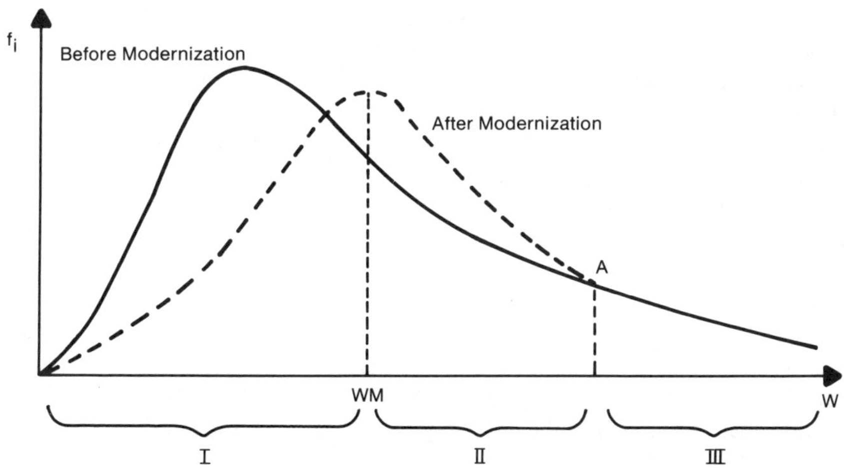

First, average earnings *(WE)* will be higher, because of increased productivity and the fact that relatively more workers are earning above the minimum wage. It is clear that increased modernization can be associated with a deeper division of labor in the modern sector.

Second, increased modernization will concentrate a large number of workers within a small range of middle-low earnings, in the neighborhood of the average minimum wage. In doing so, it will reduce the relative number of low-pay jobs. Hence, the net effect of modernization on the variance of intraindustry earnings (or the unitless coefficient of variation CVWE = $\sigma_w/WE$) is to reduce it. The variance of the logarithms of wages (VLWE), which gives relatively more weight to earnings at the lower end of the distribution, will also tend to decrease along with modernization.

Third, if the range of possible earnings does not increase much with larger size and further modernization, the concentration of a relatively high number of workers toward the middle-lower part of this range (close to *MW*) will reduce the positive skewness of the intraindustry earnings distribution. The deeper the modernization, the smaller the (positive) coefficient of skewness of earnings (SKWE).

Fourth, given a skewed distribution of earnings, its mode is expected to be located to the left of its mean. That implies that the distribution will, in general, be flat around its mean. A relative measure of this is the coefficient of excess kurtosis of the earnings distribution (KUWE); positive values imply that it is flatter than the normal distribution around its mean and negative values that it is more peaked than the normal.[32] Modernization will tend to move the mode of the distribution to the right, closer to the mean. That will make the distribution more symmetric and peaked around the mean, reducing the coefficient of excess kurtosis.

Fifth, the probable net effect of modernization on earnings inequality of one sector (as measured by the Gini coefficient GWE) is to reduce it.[33] On one side, average earnings increase; on the other, modernization bunches a larger proportion of workers on the middle-low range of the earnings scale. Given a probable upper bound for the highest earnings $WE^+$, as a result of institutional conditions or of the international market, the difference between it and average earnings $(WE^+ - WE)$ would decrease as modernization deepens and *WE* increases. The last tendency would tend to reduce the Gini coefficient.

In summary, the general idea is that besides social control some economic, sociological, technological, and demographic factors influence the shape of the intraindustry distribution of earning in a predictable way. In a developing economy, however, the process of modernization tends to be the dominant force in shaping the intraindustry distribution of earnings.

A final point has to be made. If one believes in a complete technological (or social control) determination of the job distribution, then the distribution of background characteristics of the employees would mirror the job distribution. Given the physical and economic characteristics of the final product, the relative number and nature of the jobs required to produce for a given technology, and the market wage needed to hire somebody for a job with these characteristics, the earnings distribution is obtained. The nature of some jobs may require specific sex, training, schooling, or a combination of background characteristics, but the mix of these characteristics may be technologically bounded.

If on the other hand the possibility of some independent contribution of background characteristics and other factors in shaping the earnings distribution is accepted, then they should be included in the analysis. Examples of factors having probably an independent effect on earnings distribution are collective bargaining coverage, education, experience, and sexual discrimination.

As mentioned previously, there is some evidence that union membership in Mexico tends to yield a wage premium. The effect of collective bargaining coverage on the shape of the earnings distribution is, however, harder to establish. It is probable that, for a given state of modernization, a higher degree of coverage will tend to stretch wage differentials within the modern subsector and between it and the traditional one. This is true for as long as there is a traditional segment within the sector, the gap between earnings of those workers belonging to that segment and those belonging to strong unions will widen. Therefore, the greater the relative union membership, the more concentrated the earnings distribution.

Since firms most probably use education as a screening device for selecting new employees and since more modern firms have been able to choose workers from a labor force with higher average schooling, education has to be positively associated with higher average earnings. This association between schooling and modernization also implies that higher average education will be correlated with reduced inequality. Note, however, that a relatively high average schooling could imply the presence of a few highly educated, and probably well remunerated, employees. This would tend to reduce the correlation between education and diminished concentration of earnings.

The relationship between experience and the shape of the earnings distribution is harder to establish unambiguously a priori. On the one hand, modern firms most probably have longer career ladders than craft production units. A positive correlation would emerge between experience and equality. On the other hand, available evidence on Mexico indicates that employees in sectors with a relatively large craft sector tend to have an average experience higher than the national average. For example, Table 6-11 indicates that all five primary sectors have higher average experience than the national average of 24.9 years.[34] This is also the case of handicrafts, construction, cleaning and laundry, other services, etc. The net effect has, therefore, to be determined empirically.

The effects of sex composition of employees on the earnings distribution is also hard to establish unambiguously. Some sectors with a traditional segment of considerable size are clearly characterized by female employment. That is the case, as Table 6-11 shows, of clothing and ap-

TABLE 6.11.

*Sex, Education, and Experience of Income Recipients*

| | *Sex* | | | *Education* | | | *Experience* | | |
|---|---|---|---|---|---|---|---|---|---|
| | *Partici-pants (1)* | *Employ-ees (2)* | *2/1 (3)* | *Partici-pants (4)* | *Employ-ees (5)* | *5/4 (6)* | *Partici-pants (7)* | *Employ-ees (8)* | *8/7 (9)* |
| 1. Agriculture | 0.97 | 0.98 | 1.01 | 0.83 | 0.87 | 1.05 | 32.55 | 28.77 | 0.88 |
| 2. Cattle raising | 0.89 | 0.94 | 1.06 | 1.11 | 1.24 | 1.12 | 32.92 | 26.63 | 0.81 |
| 3. Forestry | 0.99 | 0.99 | 1.00 | 0.89 | 1.19 | 1.34 | 30.79 | 27.44 | 0.89 |
| 4. Fishing | 0.91 | 0.90 | 0.99 | 0.73 | 0.73 | 1.00 | 26.24 | 26.13 | 1.00 |
| 5. Mining | 0.96 | 0.98 | 1.02 | 2.15 | 2.16 | 0.16 | 28.27 | 28.00 | 0.99 |
| 6. Oil and gas | 0.88 | 0.88 | 1.00 | 3.37 | 3.37 | 1.00 | 24.07 | 24.07 | 1.00 |
| 7. Food | 0.73 | 0.78 | 1.07 | 1.86 | 2.01 | 0.90 | 26.08 | 24.20 | 0.93 |
| 8. Beverages and tobacco | 0.86 | 0.86 | 1.00 | 2.41 | 2.47 | 1.02 | 23.44 | 22.77 | 0.97 |
| 9. Textiles | 0.74 | 0.81 | 1.09 | 2.14 | 2.30 | 1.07 | 25.31 | 24.51 | 0.97 |
| 10. Clothing and apparel | 0.28 | 0.32 | 1.14 | 1.78 | 1.81 | 1.02 | 24.63 | 22.08 | 0.90 |
| 11. Footwear | 0.88 | 0.86 | 0.98 | 1.71 | 1.70 | 0.99 | 23.95 | 21.36 | 0.89 |
| 12. Wood | 0.95 | 0.96 | 1.01 | 1.60 | 1.57 | 0.98 | 25.75 | 23.97 | 0.93 |
| 13. Handicrafts | 0.24 | 0.67 | 2.79 | 0.81 | 0.94 | 1.16 | 32.57 | 27.47 | 0.84 |
| 14. Furniture, except metallic | 0.92 | 0.91 | 0.99 | 1.78 | 1.80 | 1.01 | 23.22 | 22.30 | 0.96 |
| 15. Leather | 0.93 | 0.94 | 1.01 | 2.10 | 2.07 | 0.99 | 22.61 | 21.72 | 0.96 |
| 16. Paper and related products | 0.77 | 0.85 | 1.10 | 2.20 | 2.27 | 1.03 | 29.32 | 25.81 | 0.88 |
| 17. Printing and editorial | 0.75 | 0.75 | 1.00 | 2.95 | 2.89 | 0.98 | 24.51 | 23.90 | 0.98 |
| 18. Rubber and plastic | 0.65 | 0.66 | 1.02 | 2.48 | 2.57 | 1.04 | 24.23 | 23.92 | 0.99 |
| 19. Pharmaceuticals and cosmetics | 0.53 | 0.52 | 0.98 | 3.43 | 3.53 | 1.03 | 21.62 | 21.56 | 1.00 |
| 20. Chemicals | 0.87 | 0.88 | 1.01 | 3.39 | 3.28 | 0.97 | 22.95 | 23.24 | 1.01 |
| 21. Nonmetallic mineral products | 0.89 | 0.92 | 1.03 | 1.96 | 2.02 | 1.03 | 24.77 | 22.43 | 0.91 |
| 22. Basic metals | 0.94 | 0.94 | 1.00 | 2.96 | 2.97 | 1.00 | 24.17 | 24.11 | 1.00 |
| 23. Metallic products | 0.97 | 0.96 | 0.99 | 2.04 | 2.02 | 0.99 | 23.78 | 22.86 | 0.96 |

| | | | | | | | | | |
|---|---|---|---|---|---|---|---|---|---|
| 24. Machinery | 0.76 | 0.75 | 0.99 | 3.18 | 3.42 | 1.08 | 21.65 | 20.43 | 0.94 |
| 25. Electrical and electronic equipment | 0.70 | 0.69 | 0.99 | 3.52 | 3.54 | 1.01 | 23.68 | 23.62 | 1.00 |
| 26. Transportation equipment | 0.94 | 0.95 | 1.01 | 2.53 | 2.45 | 0.97 | 23.00 | 22.79 | 0.99 |
| 27. Other manufactures | 0.72 | 0.74 | 1.03 | 3.17 | 3.41 | 1.08 | 22.72 | 20.96 | 0.92 |
| 28. Construction | 0.98 | 0.98 | 1.00 | 1.30 | 1.29 | 0.99 | 28.18 | 26.96 | 0.96 |
| 29. Electricity | 0.95 | 0.94 | 0.99 | 3.33 | 3.37 | 1.01 | 25.42 | 25.07 | 0.99 |
| 30. Commerce | 0.63 | 0.66 | 1.05 | 2.13 | 2.55 | 1.20 | 27.72 | 21.56 | 0.78 |
| 31. Hotels and lodging | 0.61 | 0.67 | 1.10 | 2.07 | 2.05 | 0.99 | 27.81 | 26.96 | 0.97 |
| 32. Restaurants and bars | 0.45 | 0.53 | 1.18 | 1.73 | 1.99 | 1.15 | 27.58 | 23.08 | 0.84 |
| 33. Radio, TV, and amusement | 0.84 | 0.85 | 1.01 | 2.20 | 2.23 | 1.01 | 30.21 | 28.38 | 0.94 |
| 34. Telephonic and telegraphic services | 0.65 | 0.66 | 1.02 | 4.29 | 4.18 | 0.97 | 18.77 | 18.52 | 0.99 |
| 35. Education and research | 0.45 | 0.45 | 1.00 | 5.38 | 5.41 | 1.01 | 22.36 | 22.20 | 0.99 |
| 36. Credit, insurance, and finance | 0.66 | 0.65 | 0.98 | 4.44 | 4.45 | 1.00 | 20.88 | 20.81 | 1.00 |
| 37. Medical services | 0.37 | 0.36 | 0.97 | 4.58 | 4.65 | 1.02 | 22.20 | 21.28 | 0.96 |
| 38. Cleaning and laundry | 0.47 | 0.50 | 1.06 | 1.62 | 1.63 | 1.01 | 28.63 | 26.61 | 0.93 |
| 39. Domestic service | 0.10 | 0.12 | 1.20 | 1.07 | 1.15 | 1.07 | 26.81 | 24.05 | 0.90 |
| 40. Professional services and leasing | 0.75 | 0.67 | 0.89 | 5.14 | 4.65 | 0.90 | 24.01 | 20.74 | 0.86 |
| 41. Automobile repairs | 0.99 | 0.99 | 1.00 | 2.23 | 2.28 | 1.02 | 21.94 | 19.82 | 0.90 |
| 42. Machinery repairs | 0.93 | 0.91 | 0.98 | 2.31 | 2.34 | 1.01 | 26.04 | 20.35 | 0.78 |
| 43. Other services | 0.70 | 0.68 | 0.97 | 2.49 | 2.64 | 1.06 | 28.95 | 26.77 | 0.92 |
| 44. Railroad | 0.87 | 0.91 | 1.05 | 2.79 | 2.82 | 1.01 | 28.99 | 28.76 | 0.99 |
| 45. Transportation, passengers | 0.98 | 0.98 | 1.00 | 1.97 | 2.04 | 1.04 | 28.30 | 26.59 | 0.94 |
| 46. Transportation, freight | 0.98 | 0.98 | 1.00 | 1.50 | 1.58 | 1.05 | 29.10 | 27.87 | 0.96 |
| 47. Other transportation | 0.98 | 0.93 | 0.95 | 2.92 | 2.84 | 0.97 | 26.25 | 25.77 | 0.98 |
| 48. Federal government | 0.76 | 0.76 | 1.00 | 3.71 | 3.72 | 1.00 | 25.72 | 25.70 | 1.00 |
| 49. Other government | 0.79 | 0.79 | 1.00 | 3.19 | 3.25 | 1.02 | 25.16 | 24.96 | 0.99 |
| 50. All other | 0.48 | 0.74 | 1.54 | 1.96 | 2.48 | 1.27 | 39.53 | 26.25 | 0.66 |
| All | 0.74 | 0.78 | 1.05 | 1.94 | 2.19 | 1.13 | 29.00 | 24.93 | 0.80 |

SOURCE: Computed by the author from the household survey of 1977.

parel, handicrafts, commerce, cleaning and laundry, and domestic service. Insofar as female employees are willing to accept lower wages for equivalent jobs than men, due to sexual discrimination or any other reason, and/or they are mostly confined to low-paying jobs, the higher the percentage of male employment in total employment, the less inequitable will be the distribution of earnings. Another possibility, acting in the same direction, is that females find employment in *residual* sectors, such as those mentioned.

## *IV-3 Empirical Evidence*

It is necessary to see if these propositions on how modernization alters the intraindustry distribution of earnings conform with the Mexican data; this is required to deal with policy issues.

The ideal procedure to test the basic hypothesis that modernization improves the intraindustry distributions of earnings would be to follow the evolution of these distributions for each sector over a considerable period of time. Available data do not allow the testing of this proposition in that way. Therefore, a cross-section analysis based on data for 1977 is used here as a substitute for that procedure.[35] For the medium-run perspective of this chapter, it is regrettable that the sectorial earnings distributions are available only for 1977, since this is an atypical year in terms of Mexico's economic performance. It is the year following the devaluation of August 1976 and the fourth of growth below historical average. This macro outcome has to reflect necessarily on the job-wage structure, most probably raising the relative number of employees with low earnings.

The first four moments around the mean are used here as the main statistical characteristics of the earnings distribution in each industry. The variables to be explained are the mean and the coefficients of variation, skewness, and excess kurtosis.[36] Also the variance of the logarithms of earnings and the Gini coefficient help to represent sectorial distributions. Although each of these statistics gives only a partial characterization of the frequency distribution, together they provide a more complete representation of it.

Given the impossibility of determining a detailed specific functional form based on theoretical priors, after some experimentation the following model was found to yield the best fit and is therefore used in the exercise of this section[37]:

$$\begin{aligned} lnX = {} & \alpha + \beta_1 \ln KLT + \beta_2 \ln AS + \beta_3 \ln VD + \beta_4 \ln SPE + \beta_5 \ln PRW \\ & + \beta_6 \ln DUE + \beta_7 \ln COV + \beta_8 \ln EDE + \beta_9 \ln EXE + \beta_{10} \ln SXE \\ & + u \end{aligned}$$

where $\bar{X}$ represents any one of

WE: average labor income per employee (monthly)
CVWE: coefficient of variation of labor income per employee
SKWE: parameter of skewness of the size distribution of labor income per employee
VLWE: variance of the logs of labor income per employee
KUWE: parameter of excess kurtosis of the size distribution
GWE: Gini coefficient for labor income per employee

and where

1. *KLT:* capital per employee
2. *AS:* average size of establishments
3. *VD:* coefficient of variation of product's demand
4. *SPE:* specialization ratio in production
5. *PRW:* percentage of production workers in total employment
6. *DUE:* degree of duality in production
7. *COV:* degree of collective bargaining coverage
8. *EDE:* average schooling of employees
9. *EXE:* experience of employees
10. *SXE:* sex of employees; percentage of males
11. *u:* random error term

Although the double log specification allows a straightforward interpretation of the estimated parameters as elasticities, no attempt will be made in this section to infer quantitative predictions based on the parameters' values. Neither the data base nor the cross-section procedure would warrant such inferences. The focus will be on qualitative implications of modernization, based exclusively on sign estimates.

The first four RHVs included in the equation have a straightforward relationship to the technological theory of job-structure determination. The fifth (PRW) was introduced because it seems reasonable that the greater the fraction of production workers over total workers, the greater the chance that modernization has taken place. The sixth introduces the magnitude of the traditional segment of each sector into the estimations. To capture the "independent" effect of personal characteristics of employees on the earnings distribution, the last four RHVs were included. The OLS estimations were done with data for twenty-three industrial sectors. The results are presented in Table 6-12.

According to expectations about sign of the coefficients, based on the previous section's presumptions, *KLT, AS, SPE, PRW, COV, EDE, SXE,* and probably *EXE* should have a positive effect on average monthly earnings *(WE)*.

As can be seen in column 1 of Table 6-12, only KLT and EDE fulfill those sign expectations. It is not possible to reject the null hypothesis for the coefficients of other variables expected to have a positive sign.[38] The variability of product's demand *(VD)* and sectorial dualism show, as expected, negative signs but do not pass the rejection test.

The results in column 2 of Table 6-12 indicate that, according to expec-

*TABLE 6.12.*
*Probable Effects of Modernization on Intrasectorial Earnings Distribution: Regression Results*[a]

| | (1) LWE | (2) LCVWE | (3) LSKWE | (4) LVLWE | (5) LKUWE | (6) LGWE |
|---|---|---|---|---|---|---|
| C | 3.56 | | 6.60 | | 20.69 | |
| | (1.65) | | (1.43) | | (1.97) | |
| LKLT | 0.15[b] | 0.21 | 0.10 | 0.08 | −0.01 | 0.12 |
| | (2.00) | (1.64) | (0.64) | (0.44) | (−0.02) | (1.25) |
| LAS | −0.0 | −0.24[b] | −0.24 | −0.34[b] | −0.29 | −0.10 |
| | (−0.05) | (−1.88) | (−1.45) | (−1.77) | (−0.76) | (−1.02) |
| LVD | −0.03 | −0.10 | −0.25 | −0.39 | −0.43 | −0.09 |
| | (−0.22) | (−0.43) | (−0.86) | (−1.16) | (−0.65) | (−0.52) |
| LSPE | 0.00 | −0.24[c] | −0.28[c] | −0.26[b] | −0.42 | −0.18[c] |
| | (0.07) | (−2.84) | (−2.23) | (−2.06) | (−1.46) | (−2.69) |
| LPRW | 0.12 | −0.55[c] | −0.68[b] | −0.47 | −0.93 | −0.30 |
| | (0.73) | (−2.27) | (−2.01) | (−1.29) | (−1.21) | (−1.62) |
| LDUE | −0.05 | −0.32[c] | −0.34[b] | −0.29 | −0.44 | −0.15 |
| | (−0.61) | (−2.37) | (−1.94) | (−1.45) | (−1.10) | (−1.41) |
| LCOV | 0.09 | 0.24[b] | 0.32[b] | 0.50[c] | 0.66[b] | 0.19[c] |
| | (1.15) | (2.11) | (2.00) | (3.00) | (1.78) | (2.23) |
| LEDE | 0.71[c] | −0.38 | −0.30 | −0.84[b] | −0.73 | −0.46[c] |
| | (3.30) | (−1.45) | (−0.66) | (−2.14) | (−0.70) | (−2.27) |
| LEXE | 0.87 | 0.88[b] | −0.52 | 1.05 | −3.98 | 0.21 |
| | (1.32) | (1.80) | (−0.36) | (1.44) | (−1.23) | (0.54) |
| LSXE | −0.02 | −0.03 | 0.08 | −0.37 | 0.06 | −0.08 |
| | (−0.14) | (−0.14) | (0.27) | (−1.07) | (0.09) | (−0.42) |
| $R^2$ | 0.94 | 0.59 | 0.48 | 0.62 | 0.36 | 0.49 |
| Number of observations | 23 | 23 | 23 | 23 | 23 | 23 |

[a] $t$ statistics are in parentheses.
[b] Reject the null hypothesis $H_0$:$ß_i = 0$ at a 10 percent significance level.
[c] Reject the null hypothesis $H_0$:$ß_i = 0$ at a 5 percent significance level.

tations, the larger the establishment, the more specialized production, and the greater the proportion of production workers, the smaller will be intraindustry earnings variation. Capital intensity tends, on the contrary, to increase it.[39] For a given degree of modernization, collective bargaining coverage and experience increase the relative variation of sectorial earnings.

Column 3 indicates that the larger the average establishment, the more specialized production is, and the greater the proportion of production workers, the less skewed will be the distribution. These results indicate, according to expectations, that the shape of sectorial earnings distributions tends toward that of the normal distribution as modernization occurs. They further suggest that other background characteristics have a negligible effect on skewness of the distribution. A broader membership in unions is, however, an exception; for given modernization and demographic characteristics, it tends to make the distribution more skewed to the right.

Column 4 helps to evaluate the effects of modernization on the left tail of the earnings frequency distribution. This measure of dispersion gives relatively more weight to low earnings. The results indicate that, with the exception of the capital-labor ratio, the variables tracing sectorial modernization have the expected sign. Sectorial earnings concentration tends to be lower for relatively more modern industries. As for the results on the coefficient of variation, additional coverage and experience raise earnings dispersion, while education and a relatively male composition of employees tend to diminish it.

The results of column 5 are the worst of all in terms of the goodness of fit. They reflect the difficulties found in an unambiguous interpretation of the coefficient of excess kurtosis. Although the signs of the estimated coefficients do not contradict expectations, there is little that can be said with acceptable confidence about the effects of modernization on the peakedness of the earnings distribution. The results only suggest a shift toward symmetry around the mean, which would be consistent with the estimations of columns 2–4.

The final column of Table 6-12 basically summarizes the results previously analyzed. It indicates that, with the exception of KLT, other variables associated with modernity tend to reduce intrasectorial earnings concentration as they rise. On the other hand, for a given degree of sectorial modernity, collective bargaining coverage tends to increase concentration, while average schooling tends to be negatively associated with it.

A result which requires further analysis is the effect of capital intensity (assets per employee) on earnings distribution; its effect on its shape is contrary to expectations. This variable was introduced in the regressions based on evidence that modernity tended to be associated with increased use of capital—more specifically, more capital per worker. This, by itself, would raise the worker's productivity, and if there exists an upper bound on possible highest earnings $(WE^{+})$ (dictated by custom, international standards, fiscal factors, etc.), the difference $(WE^{+} - WE)$ would decrease. The process would, simultaneously, increase the relative number of workers with earnings slightly higher than minimum wage.

The empirical results suggest, however, that capital is complementary to skilled workers and substitutes for unskilled. As the value of equipment used by workers increases, a cost-minimizing employer would upgrade the quality (skills, responsibility, etc.) of his or her workers to meet the standards required by equipment. Furthermore, the employer would also improve the "quality" of his or her personnel to avoid unnecessary damage of equipment, as long as the wage premium required to get this type of labor is lower or equal to maintenance and replacement costs that would have been caused by the use of less skilled labor. If this is true, after a certain level further increases in capital intensity would raise the relative number of highly skilled workers and the skewness of earnings distribution. The substitution of highly skilled for unskilled workers would tend to increase the coefficient of excess kurtosis, making the distribution less peaked around its mean *(WE)*. This may be the channel through which higher capital intensity affects the earnings distribution in a developing economy, increasing its concentration.

## V. Output-Mix and the Overall Distribution of Earnings

As mentioned in Section III, it is convenient, for analytical purposes, to divide changes in the overall earnings distribution into two parts. The first refers to alterations in intraindustry distributions, while the second refers to effects of changes in output mix and sectorial employment on the overall earnings distribution.

The previous section indicates that the process of modernization affects the intrasectorial earnings distributions in a fairly predictable way. The results, although restricted because of the cross-section sample they were drawn from, further suggest that, starting from an already existing dual structure of production and up to a certain stage, modernization does not seem to have a perverse effect on the intrasectorial earnings distributions.

This section presents an exercise to illustrate what could be the individual effect of changes in sectorial employment on the overall earnings distribution. To do so, it assumes that the intrasectorial job-wage structures stay constant, so that the distributive outcome is exclusively determined by alterations in the relative importance of each sector in total employment.

To make the exercise realistic, we examine observed changes of sectorial employment in Mexico for the period 1960–1975. Table 6-13 presents the sectorial employment share elasticities estimated for that period.[40] It indicates, for example, that a 10 percent increase in total participants would be associated with a 9.4 percent decrease in the *share* of participants working in agriculture over total participants.

Table 6-13 reflects how Mexican development over the period has been associated with a rapid decrease in the relative importance of employment in most primary sectors. Agriculture, for its large absolute size, has been the primary provider of labor force to the rest of the economy. For the purpose of this chapter the sectorial employment share elasticities for wage earners, or employees, as they are called here, are more relevant. The figures signal a sectorial reallocation quite similar to that observed by participants. With the exception of forestry, employment in primary sectors has been losing relative importance in relation to other sectors. That is also the case of some industries, such as textiles, which began to expand early. On the other hand, capital goods industries such as machinery, electrical appliances, transportation equipment, and especially automobiles have been gaining relative importance rapidly.

These changes in sectorial employment closely reflect variations in output mix. These, in turn, follow changing patterns of domestic and foreign demand. It is beyond the scope of this chapter to address the issue of what type of development pattern, in relation to the income distribution-consumption cycle and structure of foreign trade, is implied by the output-mix outcome. Some work in this area suggests, however, that a perverse cycle may underly this outcome.[41]

What transformation will the overall earnings distribution experience if sectorial employment of wage earners increases according to historical patterns, given constant intrasectorial job-wage structures?

The results of a simulation assuming an increase in employment of approximately 20 percent, the intrasectorial job-wage structures of Table A-1-1, and the sectorial employment share elasticities of Table 6-13 are presented in Tables 6-14 and 6-15.[42] The assumed expansion in employment would be roughly equivalent to 6 years of growth at the average rate of 3.1 percent observed over the period 1960–1975.[43] The results suggest a reduction of earnings concentration as indicated by the Gini coefficient. This outcome, however, is wanting. Although it implies a reduction in the relative number of low-earnings employees, there is an increase in the absolute number. For example, about 300,000 additional employees reach monthly earnings lower than 700 pesos.

There are two cases which can illustrate the kind of intersectorial shifts playing an important role in this outcome. The first refers to changes in agricultural employment. Although the share of agriculture in total employment decreased from 23.0 to 20.6 percent, still out of all the newly employed 8.0 percent found a job in agriculture. Furthermore, given the intrasectorial job-wage structure in that sector, about 140,000 employees reached earnings within the first three low-income brackets. These additional "journeymen" represent 5.3 percent of total newly created employment. Similar cases are cleaning and laundry and domestic service.

The second illustrative shift is that observed in relation with the commerce sector. For it, contrary to agriculture, the employment share elasticity is positive and relatively high (1.12). The expansion of overall employment makes the share of commerce in total employment increase from 10.6 to 13.0 percent. With an unchanged intrasectorial job-wage structure, this brings about an increase in low-earnings employees. Out of

*TABLE 6.13.*
*Employment Share Elasticities of Sectorial Participants and Employees: 1960–1975*

| | *Participants,*[a] *Share in Total Employment*[b] | | *Employment Share Elasticity* | *Employees,*[c] *Share in Total Employment*[b] | | *Employment Share Elasticity* |
|---|---|---|---|---|---|---|
| | *1960* | *1975* | | *1960* | *1975* | |
| 1. Agriculture | 50.1 | 36.2 | −0.94 | 40.8 | 32.1 | −0.52 |
| 2. Cattle raising | 1.5 | 1.7 | 0.43 | 1.6 | 1.8 | −1.55 |
| 3. Forestry | 0.6 | 0.7 | 0.57 | 0.4 | 0.6 | 0.69 |
| 4. Hunting and fishing | 0.2 | 0.1 | −0.94 | 0.2 | 0.1 | −0.60 |
| 5. Metallic mines | 0.7 | 0.3 | −2.28 | 1.1 | 0.4 | −1.99 |
| 6. Nonmetallic minerals | 0.5 | 0.3 | −1.59 | 0.7 | 0.4 | −1.45 |
| 7. Petroleum and petrochemicals | 0.5 | 0.9 | 1.56 | 0.9 | 1.3 | 0.89 |
| 8. Meats and poultry | 0.3 | 0.4 | 1.09 | 0.4 | 0.5 | 0.57 |
| 9. Wheat grinding | 1.3 | 1.7 | 0.69 | 1.4 | 1.6 | 0.19 |
| 10. Other food | 1.1 | 1.3 | 0.64 | 1.7 | 1.9 | 0.23 |
| 11. Beverages | 0.7 | 0.7 | 0.43 | 0.9 | 1.0 | 0.22 |
| 12. Tobacco | 0.1 | 0.1 | −0.11 | 0.1 | 0.1 | −0.32 |
| 13. Textiles and soft fibers | 1.4 | 0.7 | −1.70 | 2.1 | 1.0 | −1.52 |
| 14. Other textiles | 0.6 | 0.2 | −2.99 | 0.9 | 0.3 | −2.51 |
| 15. Shoes, apparel, and other textiles | 2.7 | 2.9 | 0.35 | 2.8 | 3.0 | 0.21 |
| 16. Wood and cork | 1.7 | 1.8 | 0.19 | 1.7 | 1.7 | 0.15 |
| 17. Paper and paper products | 0.3 | 0.4 | 0.74 | 0.5 | 0.6 | 0.17 |
| 18. Printing and editorial | 0.5 | 0.6 | 0.08 | 0.7 | 0.7 | −0.21 |
| 19. Leather | 0.2 | 0.2 | −0.12 | 0.2 | 0.2 | −0.19 |
| 20. Rubber products | 0.2 | 0.3 | 1.22 | 0.3 | 0.4 | 0.62 |
| 21. Basic chemicals | 0.2 | 0.2 | −0.11 | 0.2 | 0.2 | −0.32 |
| 22. Synthetic fibers | 0.1 | 0.2 | 2.72 | 0.1 | 0.3 | 1.73 |

| | | | | | | |
|---|---|---|---|---|---|---|
| 23. Fertilizers | 0.1 | 0.1 | 0.90 | 0.1 | 0.1 | 0.42 |
| 24. Soap and detergents | 0.1 | 0.1 | −0.57 | 0.1 | 0.1 | −0.65 |
| 25. Pharmaceuticals | 0.3 | 0.4 | 0.52 | 0.5 | 0.5 | 0.14 |
| 26. Perfumes and cosmetics | 0.1 | 0.1 | 2.37 | 0.1 | 0.2 | 1.56 |
| 27. Other chemical industries | 0.1 | 0.2 | 1.85 | 0.1 | 0.2 | 1.09 |
| 28. Nonmetallic mineral products | 1.0 | 1.4 | 1.18 | 1.3 | 1.7 | 0.60 |
| 29. Basic metallic industries | 0.5 | 0.7 | 1.07 | 0.8 | 1.0 | 0.61 |
| 30. Metallic products | 1.0 | 1.5 | 3.32 | 1.5 | 1.8 | 0.45 |
| 31. Machinery | 0.5 | 1.1 | 1.93 | 0.6 | 1.3 | 1.22 |
| 32. Electrical appliances | 0.6 | 1.4 | 2.37 | 0.8 | 1.7 | 1.70 |
| 33. Transportation equipment | 0.7 | 1.6 | 2.06 | 0.9 | 1.7 | 1.28 |
| 34. Automobile industry | 0.2 | 1.0 | 4.31 | 0.3 | 1.1 | 2.99 |
| 35. Other manufactures | 1.0 | 1.2 | 1.44 | 0.8 | 1.4 | 0.80 |
| 36. Construction | 4.6 | 6.3 | 0.76 | 6.8 | 7.4 | 0.04 |
| 37. Electricity | 0.4 | 0.6 | 0.85 | 0.6 | 0.7 | 0.38 |
| 38. Radio, TV, and amusement | 0.8 | 1.0 | 0.96 | 0.8 | 0.9 | 0.40 |
| 39. Transportation | 3.3 | 3.6 | 0.30 | 4.5 | 4.0 | −0.32 |
| 40. Communication | 0.3 | 0.6 | 1.70 | 0.5 | 0.8 | 1.01 |
| 41. Commerce | 9.3 | 10.7 | 0.50 | 6.0 | 9.4 | 1.12 |
| 42. Leasing of real estate | 0.0 | 0.1 | 1.01 | 0.1 | 0.1 | 0.45 |
| 43. Restaurants and lodging | 1.6 | 2.7 | 1.51 | 1.9 | 2.8 | 0.84 |
| 44. Financial services | 1.0 | 1.2 | 1.07 | 1.1 | 1.5 | 0.53 |
| 45. Other services | 7.7 | 10.8 | 0.96 | 10.0 | 9.5 | −0.10 |
| Total | 100.0 | 100.0 | | 100.0 | 100.0 | |

SOURCE: Computed by the author from employment data contained in Secretaría de Patrimonio y Fomento Industrial (1979).

[a]It refers to the economically active population remunerated (PEAR).

[b]Percentages.

[c]It refers to salaried workers.

*TABLE 6.14.*
*Distribution of Earnings Before and After Expansion in Total Employment*[a]

| | *Employees* | | | | | | | |
|---|---|---|---|---|---|---|---|---|
| | *Original* | | *New* | | *Difference* | | *Earnings* | |
| *Bracket* | *Absolute* | *%* | *Absolute* | *%* | *Absolute* | *%* | *Original* | *New* |
| 1 | 1,891,369 | 15.8 | 2,192,290 | 15.0 | 300,921 | 11.5 | 1.9 | 1.8 |
| 2 | 1,027,913 | 8.6 | 1,207,720 | 8.3 | 180,000 | 6.9 | 2.3 | 2.2 |
| 3 | 885,369 | 7.4 | 1,039,590 | 7.1 | 154,221 | 5.9 | 2.7 | 2.6 |
| 4 | 1,110,242 | 9.3 | 1,318,050 | 9.0 | 207,808 | 8.0 | 4.6 | 4.4 |
| 5 | 1,208,102 | 10.1 | 1,474,440 | 10.1 | 266,338 | 10.2 | 6.7 | 6.6 |
| 6 | 1,373,046 | 11.4 | 1,724,410 | 11.8 | 351,364 | 13.5 | 10.2 | 10.4 |
| 7 | 1,834,303 | 15.3 | 2,276,400 | 15.6 | 442,097 | 16.9 | 17.7 | 17.8 |
| 8 | 1,029,100 | 8.6 | 1,299,010 | 8.9 | 269,910 | 10.3 | 13.1 | 13.4 |
| 9 | 724,425 | 6.0 | 923,128 | 6.3 | 198,703 | 7.6 | 12.2 | 12.5 |
| 10 | 445,329 | 3.7 | 563,501 | 3.9 | 118,172 | 4.5 | 10.2 | 10.4 |
| 11 | 229,936 | 1.9 | 288,660 | 2.0 | 229,936 | 8.8 | 6.7 | 6.8 |
| 12 | 113,305 | 1.1 | 171,111 | 1.2 | 57,806 | 2.2 | 5.1 | 5.3 |
| 13 | 106,979 | 0.9 | 131,048 | 0.9 | 24,069 | 0.9 | 6.6 | 5.8 |
| Total | 11,999,418 | 100.0 | 14,609,358 | 100.0 | 2,609,940 | 100.0 | 100.0 | 100.0 |
| Gini | | | | | | | 0.475 | 0.462 |

SOURCE: Computed by the author; see comments in text.
[a]Fractions may not coincide due to rounding.

the 590,695 additional hirings in this sector, over 143,000 reached earnings within the three low-earnings brackets.

These results indicate that although intersectorial shifts could bring about a reduction in earnings concentration, most probably this outcome would imply an increase in the absolute size of low-earnings employment and the poverty segment. To avoid the last feature of expanded employment, "benevolent" transformations in the intrasectorial job-wage structures are needed. The type of transformations required is that which previous sections associated with intrasectorial modernization.

The detailed working of the labor market becomes the final determinant of the distributive outcome. If market forces are such that labor demand in the modern segment, regardless of its sectorial location, grows faster than the labor force, the relative and absolute number of low-paying jobs would decrease. Actually, the shape of the overall distribution of earnings, especially its left tail, heavily depends on the *equilibrium* conditions of the labor market. If there is an excess supply of labor, mainly unskilled, the absolute and relative number of low-paying jobs will increase. The figures suggest that this expansion will mostly occur in a few sectors which previously had relatively large traditional segments, such as commerce and some services. This process would also be accompanied by an increase in subsistence self-employment.[44]

## *TABLE 6.15.*
## *Sectorial Employment After Expansion in Total Employment*

| | *Original Employment* | | *Employment Share Elasticity* | *New Employment* | |
|---|---|---|---|---|---|
| | *Absolute* | *%* | | *Absolute* | *%* |
| 1. Agriculture | 2,758,307 | 23.0 | −0.52 | 2,967,408 | 20.61 |
| 2. Cattle raising | 172,361 | 1.4 | −1.55 | 139,097 | 0.97 |
| 3. Forestry | 19,095 | 0.2 | 0.69 | 32,773 | 0.23 |
| 4. Fishing | 72,231 | 0.6 | −0.60 | 76,028 | 0.53 |
| 5. Mining | 52,855 | 0.4 | −1.72 | 37,784 | 0.26 |
| 6. Oil and gas | 77,829 | 0.6 | 0.89 | 101,774 | 0.71 |
| 7. Food | 417,083 | 3.5 | 0.26 | 530,182 | 3.68 |
| 8. Beverages and tobacco | 112,016 | 0.9 | 0.17 | 134,000 | 0.93 |
| 9. Textiles | 147,253 | 1.2 | −1.75 | 112,315 | 0.78 |
| 10. Clothing and apparel | 309,973 | 2.6 | 0.21 | 390,106 | 2.71 |
| 11. Footwear | 108,089 | 0.9 | 0.21 | 135,037 | 0.94 |
| 12. Wood | 74,023 | 0.6 | 0.15 | 140,825 | 0.98 |
| 13. Handicrafts | 11,708 | 0.1 | −0.52 | 12,902 | 0.09 |
| 14. Furniture, except metallic | 132,324 | 1.1 | 0.15 | 163,144 | 1.33 |
| 15. Leather | 28,696 | 0.2 | −0.19 | 27,704 | 0.19 |
| 16. Paper and related products | 37,209 | 0.3 | 0.17 | 44,667 | 0.31 |
| 17. Printing and editorial | 86,891 | 0.7 | −0.21 | 96,562 | 0.67 |
| 18. Rubber and plastic | 107,420 | 0.9 | 0.62 | 145,663 | 1.01 |
| 19. Pharmaceuticals and cosmetics | 62,399 | 0.5 | 0.55 | 79,916 | 0.56 |
| 20. Chemicals | 45,616 | 0.4 | −0.32 | 53,911 | 0.37 |
| 21. Nonmetallic mineral products | 148,453 | 1.2 | 0.60 | 193,527 | 1.34 |
| 22. Basic metals | 150,902 | 1.3 | 0.61 | 210,028 | 1.46 |
| 23. Metallic products | 230,131 | 1.9 | 0.45 | 298,210 | 2.07 |
| 24. Machinery | 37,497 | 0.3 | 1.22 | 53,738 | 0.37 |
| 25. Electrical and electronic equipment | 128,675 | 1.1 | 1.70 | 212,246 | 1.47 |
| 26. Transportation and equipment | 88,563 | 0.7 | 1.95 | 140,105 | 0.97 |
| 27. Other manuactures | 150,991 | 1.3 | 0.80 | 217,141 | 1.51 |
| 28. Construction | 847,345 | 7.1 | 0.04 | 1,030,529 | 7.16 |
| 29. Electricity | 58,244 | 0.5 | 0.38 | 77,468 | 0.54 |
| 30. Commerce | 1,277,528 | 10.6 | 1.12 | 1,868,223 | 12.97 |
| 31. Motels and lodging | 61,917 | 0.5 | 0.84 | 84,092 | 0.58 |
| 32. Restaurants and bars | 266,916 | 2.2 | 0.84 | 370,001 | 2.57 |
| 33. Radio, TV, and amusement | 122,774 | 1.0 | 0.40 | 155,512 | 1.08 |
| 34. Telephonic and telegraphic services | 37,898 | 0.3 | 1.01 | 51,924 | 0.36 |
| 35. Education and research | 519,347 | 4.3 | −0.10 | 606,787 | 4.21 |
| 36. Credit, insurance, and finance | 176,156 | 1.5 | 0.53 | 228,124 | 1.58 |
| 37. Medical services | 309,646 | 2.6 | −0.10 | 366,894 | 2.55 |
| 38. Cleaning and laundry | 76,511 | 0.6 | −0.10 | 84,668 | 0.59 |
| 39. Domestic service | 459,025 | 3.8 | −0.10 | 536,230 | 3.72 |
| 40. Professional services and leasing | 150,029 | 1.3 | 0.45 | 204,038 | 1.42 |
| 41. Automobile repairs | 180,751 | 1.5 | −0.10 | 211,670 | 1.47 |
| 42. Machinery repairs | 100,676 | 0.8 | −0.10 | 112,891 | 0.78 |
| 43. Other services | 124,740 | 1.0 | −0.10 | 141,113 | 0.98 |
| 44. Railroad | 66,462 | 0.6 | −0.32 | 80,866 | 0.56 |
| 45. Transportation, passengers | 191,169 | 1.6 | −0.32 | 215,644 | 1.50 |
| 46. Transportation, freight | 136,018 | 1.1 | −0.32 | 148,255 | 1.03 |
| 47. Other transportation | 77,329 | 0.6 | −0.32 | 80,866 | 0.56 |
| 48. Federal government | 437,383 | 3.6 | −0.10 | 508,007 | 3.53 |
| 49. Other government | 149,589 | 1.2 | −0.10 | 169,336 | 1.18 |
| 50. All other | 403,375 | 3.4 | 1.00 | 587,492 | 4.08 |
| Total | 11,999,418 | 100.0 | | 14,667,426 | 102.05 |

SOURCE: Computed by the author; see comments in text.

## VI. Final Remarks and Policy Implications

One might erroneously conclude from this chapter that growth will automatically produce a reduction in earnings concentration or in income inequality. No conclusion could be more misleading than that.

For analytical purposes this chapter has abstracted from what happens with the size distribution of mixed and capital income while the earnings distribution is changing. It is clear that nothing prevents capital income from concentrating in the course of economic development. Little is known about the Mexican experience in this regard. It is not clear if rapid population growth and the process of wealth subdivision associated with inheritance have been able to counteract concentrating tendencies. Among the last tendencies it is possible to think of rising economic control of financial and industrial groups and of rapid accumulation via quasi-rents granted by the government to supporting groups and the bureaucracy.

The results of Section IV, on the probable transformations that the intraindustry job-wage structures will experience in the course of modernization, and those of Section V, on the effects of changes in sectorial employment, do not mean that such benevolent transformations have actually taken place. To support such a conclusion we would need to demonstrate that modern employment (i.e., with earnings higher than the minimum wage) has been growing faster than traditional employment. This, in turn, would imply that modern employment has been growing faster than the labor force.

Available statistics suggest that one ought to be quite skeptical about associating such a rapid increase in modern employment with Mexican development over the last decades. The basic "guesstimates" establish the annual rate of growth of labor supply between 3.1 and 3.7 percent over the last decade and forecast an annual rate in the range of 3.4–3.7 percent during the 1980s.[45] On the other hand, employment of all kings (participants) has been growing at average annual rates in the range 2.3–2.4

*TABLE 6.16.*
*Growth of Employment: 1950–1975*
*(Average Annual Rates in Percentages)*

| *Source* | *1950–1960* Partici-pants | *1950–1960* Employees | *1960–1970* Partici-pants | *1960–1970* Employees | *1970–1975* Partici-pants | *1970–1975* Employees |
|---|---|---|---|---|---|---|
| SPFI | 2.6 | 4.6 | 2.4 | 3.3 | 2.2 | 2.7 |
| Altimir | 2.8 | 4.7 | 2.3 | 2.8 | N.A. | N.A. |

SOURCE: Secretaría de Patrimonio y Fomento Industrial (1979) and Altimir (1974).

percent during the 1970s (see Table 6-16). During that decade the number of wage earners (employees) seems to have grown at an average annual rate of 2.8–3.3 percent.

These figures suggest it would have been very difficult for the Mexican economy to have absorbed the new labor force into employment. It is impossible to say, from available figures, if modern employment grew faster than craft or traditional, bringing about a reduction in the relative size of the traditional segment of the labor market.[46] Although the number of wage earners seems to have grown faster than that of participants, it is not possible to rule out that this expansion implied a proportional (or even more than proportional) growth of low-paying jobs.

As for policy implications of this study, they can be divided in to two broad categories: (1) implications for macroeconomic policies and (2) implications for microeconomic policies.

The matter becomes more simple, however, if it is realized that although growth is not a sufficient condition for reducing earnings concentration, it is a necessary condition. This is brought about by the need to keep modern employment expanding faster than the labor force. This is the only state which is compatible with a reduced relative and absolute size of the traditional sector. Therefore the implications for macroeconomic policy, simply stated, are to advocate the provision of the needed conditions for sustained growth at a pace capable of generating such expansion in modern employment. The specific and general policies that have to be implemented for such an outcome are complex and controversial. The literature on this is abundant, and we shall not deal with the issue here.[47]

If this is accepted as the main objective for reducing earnings inequality, then there are three kinds of implications for micro policies. The first would include those measures needed for reaching the growth goal; these policies form part of the macro policy package. The second covers those policies oriented toward causing growth to be associated with maximum generation of modern employment. Finally, the third subsumes those micro policies aimed at preventing "perverse" transformations of the job-wage structure. Theoretical work and concrete experiences of developing economies indicate that there may be conflicts and/or trade-offs among these policy goals. There is no way to specify, in general and a priori, a set of internally non-contradictory policy measures. For the sake of completeness, however, some of those most broadly accepted may be briefly reviewed.

Among those policies which attempt to make growth generate maximum modern employment, one of the traditional recipes always deserves careful consideration: the attempt to make relative factor prices reflect as closely as possible true scarcity prices. For the Mexican case this implies, on the side of physical capital, that we should be more careful in granting implicit subsidies to capital acquisition (such as an overvalued exchange rate) or explicit subsidies, such as accelerated depreciation. On the cost of labor side the typical proposition is to eliminate taxes and other charges above the basic wage in order to reduce the user's cost of labor. Steps in this direction would raise the relative price of physical capital and increase employment. Closely related to this issue is the prescription to reduce the amount of paper work, the bureaucratic delays, and other obsolete governmental requirements to existing and, more important, incipient "modern" firms. Some of these requirements are related to employment.

Another basic recipe in relation to the second sort of micro policy implications refers to "managing" the incremental output mix. Recommendations boil down to fostering growth of (hopefully unskilled) labor-intensive sectors (hopefully relatively modern). The argument usually ends, by means of the Heckscher-Ohlin-Samuelson theorem, proposing export-led growth. There is some empirical evidence that even in the presence of wage differentials this strategy is still advisable.[48] How this fits into the macro package is something we shall not examine in this chapter.

In relation to the third kind of implication for micro policy, the guidelines are less clear. To prevent perverse transformations in the job-wage structure implies orienting the technologies used in production and intervening in the process of attaching wages to the jobs brought about by technology. The literature on choice of technique and "appropriate" technologies has found it hard to pass from its theoretical analysis to the prescription of feasible policies.[49] The problem stems from the fact that the scope for choice is quite restricted in the real world, even if relative factor prices reflect true scarcities. The institutional restrictions for adapting or generating the appropriate technologies are huge, and most programs of this sort require resources most probably not available in LDCs. Efforts are being made in Mexico in this direction, but it has to be recognized that any substantial result will not appear in the short or medium run.

Intervening successfully in the wage-setting process, including the occupational wage structure, is certainly a difficult task. The social mores and the political factors affecting this process may be changed only slowly. An abrupt dislocation of the prevailing equity rules can easily lead to the rupture of the production process. There is, however, some scope for action. Ironically enough, it is in relation to the earnings of the high bureaucracy and government officials that the effort has to start. Recall that even with the rough data of the household survey of 1977, the federal government has a leading role in the determination of earnings for employees with the highest labor income. The government's wage policy, in reference to its own employees, surely feeds back to other sectors' wage policies. Casual empiricism suggests that earnings of this part of the bureaucracy, even excluding the well-known existence of nonpecuniary rewards and side payments, do not correspond to Mexico's economic reality. Some would argue that altering this "compensation" policy would endanger the political system and future development of the country. It is possible to understand the argument but certainly not possible to justify it. Furthermore, the contrary argument could be sounder, so that actual conditions constitute a serious threat to stability and to future social development.

# Appendix 1

# *Data from the Household Survey of 1977*

It was possible to use the original data of the household survey of 1977, at the questionnaire level, to obtain the information required for this chapter. The data used, however, have been subject to some "adjustments" for "missing" information and other problems by a team at Banco de México, S.A. For details, see Diez-Canedo and Vera (1981).

Table A-1-1 provides raw data used to derive labor income characteristics of employees by income bracket.

Tables A-1-2 through A-1-4 provide derived parameters for labor and total income for employees and participants.

### Income Definitions

Total income and labor income were defined as stated in the notes to Table A-1-1.

### Definition of Participants

Any individual older than 12 years declaring a positive income, that is, a positive value for any of the twenty income concepts of Table A-1-1, was defined as a participant.

TABLE

*Income Sources of "Participants"*
*Fuentes de Ingreso de los "Participantes"*
*(Percentages)*

| *Bracket* | *Labor Income* | | | | | | *Mixed Income* | | | | | *Capital* | |
|---|---|---|---|---|---|---|---|---|---|---|---|---|---|
| | *(1)*[a] | *(2)* | *(3)* | *(4)* | *(5)* | *Total* | *(6)* | *(7)* | *(8)* | *(9)* | *Total* | *(10)* | *(11)* |
| 1 | 52.78 | 0.11 | 0.01 | 0.54 | 0.10 | 53.54 | 24.15 | 1.09 | 7.79 | 0.14 | 36.97 | 0.29 | 0.08 |
| 2 | 60.41 | 0.03 | 0.03 | 0.18 | 0.08 | 60.73 | 21.20 | 2.03 | 6.40 | 0.21 | 30.64 | 0.22 | 0.22 |
| 3 | 62.59 | 0.08 | 0.05 | 0.27 | 0.10 | 63.09 | 21.14 | 1.15 | 5.00 | 0.22 | 28.31 | 0.64 | 0.05 |
| 4 | 65.91 | 0.23 | 0.04 | 0.59 | 0.10 | 66.87 | 17.71 | 1.21 | 5.27 | 0.04 | 24.23 | 0.62 | 0.23 |
| 5 | 69.58 | 0.14 | 0.05 | 0.20 | 0.17 | 70.14 | 15.03 | 1.09 | 5.65 | 0.19 | 21.96 | 0.84 | 0.08 |
| 6 | 75.50 | 0.20 | 0.21 | 0.29 | 0.36 | 76.56 | 12.29 | 0.96 | 4.14 | 0.03 | 17.42 | 0.64 | 0.09 |
| 7 | 80.37 | 0.42 | 0.52 | 0.16 | 0.53 | 82.00 | 10.15 | 0.69 | 2.69 | 0.03 | 13.83 | 0.46 | 0.08 |
| 8 | 74.78 | 0.80 | 1.06 | 0.16 | 0.76 | 77.56 | 11.82 | 0.31 | 3.79 | 0.13 | 16.05 | 1.40 | 0.03 |
| 9 | 73.68 | 0.79 | 0.94 | 0.36 | 1.94 | 76.81 | 11.95 | 0.42 | 4.48 | 0.07 | 16.92 | 1.30 | 0.07 |
| 10 | 67.47 | 0.91 | 0.85 | 0.10 | 1.41 | 70.74 | 15.83 | 0.28 | 6.29 | 0.13 | 22.53 | 1.02 | 0.01 |
| 11 | 67.41 | 1.29 | 1.02 | 0.03 | 0.68 | 70.43 | 14.43 | 0.16 | 3.15 | 0.26 | 20.00 | 3.02 | 0.07 |
| 12 | 63.52 | 0.84 | 0.96 | 0.11 | 0.67 | 66.10 | 21.25 | 0.00 | 7.34 | 0.00 | 28.59 | 0.89 | 0.20 |
| 13 | 51.26 | 1.36 | 0.51 | 0.08 | 0.59 | 53.80 | 25.48 | 0.85 | 4.29 | 0.05 | 30.67 | 0.66 | 0.00 |
| Total | 69.52 | 0.65 | 0.60 | 0.21 | 0.63 | 21.61 | 15.54 | 0.76 | 4.66 | 0.10 | 20.96 | 0.99 | 0.07 |

*A.1.1*

*by Income Bracket, 1977*

*(Percentages)*

| *Income* | | | *Other Income* | | | | | | | | *Total* | *Total* |
|---|---|---|---|---|---|---|---|---|---|---|---|---|
| *(12)* | *(13)* | *Total* | *(14)* | *(15)* | *(16)* | *(17)* | *(18)* | *(19)* | *(20)* | *Total* | *(%)* | *Income*[b] |
| 0.06 | 0.00 | 0.43 | 0.00 | 0.00 | 0.38 | 0.30 | 0.02 | 0.04 | 6.23 | 9.05 | 100.0 | 1,325.4 |
| 0.05 | 0.00 | 0.49 | 0.04 | 0.00 | 1.32 | 0.15 | 0.02 | 0.06 | 7.00 | 8.59 | 100.0 | 1,421.8 |
| 0.01 | 0.00 | 0.70 | 0.00 | 0.03 | 2.20 | 0.04 | 0.15 | 0.16 | 5.32 | 7.90 | 100.0 | 1,584.8 |
| 0.09 | 0.00 | 0.94 | 0.00 | 0.01 | 2.23 | 0.15 | 0.18 | 0.04 | 5.36 | 7.97 | 100.0 | 2,521.2 |
| 0.07 | 0.00 | 0.99 | 0.00 | 0.14 | 2.20 | 0.20 | 0.14 | 0.06 | 4.14 | 6.90 | 100.0 | 3,517.2 |
| 0.11 | 0.00 | 0.84 | 0.00 | 0.00 | 1.58 | 0.11 | 0.12 | 0.25 | 3.27 | 5.33 | 100.0 | 4,919.2 |
| 0.12 | 0.02 | 0.48 | 0.01 | 0.02 | 1.01 | 0.07 | 0.22 | 0.01 | 2.16 | 3.50 | 100.0 | 7,955.9 |
| 0.07 | 0.00 | 1.50 | 0.04 | 0.05 | 1.52 | 0.14 | 0.62 | 0.35 | 2.14 | 4.88 | 100.0 | 6,244.3 |
| 0.25 | 0.00 | 1.42 | 0.03 | 0.06 | 1.39 | 0.01 | 0.21 | 0.03 | 2.92 | 4.55 | 100.0 | 5,859.8 |
| 0.43 | 0.00 | 1.44 | 0.01 | 0.01 | 1.54 | 0.00 | 0.17 | 0.59 | 2.68 | 5.00 | 100.0 | 5,321.2 |
| 0.42 | 0.30 | 3.51 | 0.00 | 0.46 | 1.34 | 0.20 | 0.46 | 0.05 | 3.55 | 6.06 | 100.0 | 3,492.4 |
| 0.55 | 0.48 | 2.12 | 0.00 | 0.05 | 1.78 | 0.00 | 0.04 | 0.00 | 1.32 | 3.19 | 100.0 | 2,862.8 |
| 4.50 | 1.56 | 0.72 | 0.24 | 0.00 | 4.79 | 0.04 | 0.45 | 0.00 | 1.27 | 6.81 | 100.0 | 4,528.0 |
| 0.77 | 0.17 | 2.00 | 0.04 | 0.06 | 1.78 | 0.10 | 0.26 | 0.15 | 3.05 | 5.44 | 100.0 | 51,574.0 |

[a] Key:

(1) Wages, salaries, commissions, tips, and overtime
(2) Christmas bonus
(3) Vacation and other bonuses
(4) Payment in kind
(5) Share in profits
(6) Net income from own business
(7) Net income from household industries
(8) Gross income from room and board
(9) Net income from services rendered
(10) Net income from rent on buildings and other leasing
(11) Net income from land leasing
(12) Net income from interest
(13) Net income from stocks
(14) Net income from risk insurance
(15) Indemnity from noninsurance sources
(16) Pension income
(17) Income from institutional scholarships and benefits
(18) Indemnity from layoffs and accidents at work
(19) Divorce allowances
(20) Cash transfers received

[b] Millions of current pesos.

*TABLE A.1.2.*

*Frequency Distributions of Labor Income Per Employee by Sector*
*(Percentages)*

| | Earnings Bracket | | | | | | | | | | | | |
|---|---|---|---|---|---|---|---|---|---|---|---|---|---|
| | *1* | *2* | *3* | *4* | *5* | *6* | *7* | *8* | *9* | *10* | *11* | *12* | *13* |
| 1. Agriculture | 32.8 | 17.9 | 15.6 | 14.9 | 9.8 | 4.7 | 2.2 | 0.9 | 0.3 | 0.4 | 0.2 | 0.2 | 0.01 |
| 2. Cattle raising | 8.7 | 11.5 | 3.0 | 21.0 | 17.8 | 8.3 | 9.2 | 6.2 | 1.3 | 1.4 | 1.0 | 0 | 0.4 |
| 3. Forestry | 20.1 | 10.2 | 14.3 | 4.1 | 8.8 | 13.7 | 15.6 | 4.5 | 0 | 8.7 | 0 | 0 | 0 |
| 4. Fishing | 18.3 | 7.7 | 12.7 | 15.3 | 8.5 | 13.6 | 11.2 | 2.9 | 9.7 | 0 | 0 | 0 | 0 |
| 5. Mining | 2.8 | 1.0 | 15.9 | 16.7 | 11.8 | 11.1 | 9.4 | 16.5 | 2.6 | 1.0 | — | — | 11.2 |
| 6. Oil and gas | 2.7 | 2.5 | 0 | 6.2 | 0 | 11.1 | 11.8 | 11.5 | 21.3 | 19.4 | 4.4 | 4.6 | 4.4 |
| 7. Food | 7.2 | 4.1 | 5.7 | 8.3 | 14.3 | 14.1 | 22.3 | 9.6 | 5.6 | 4.0 | 1.9 | 2.1 | 0.3 |
| 8. Beverages and tobacco | 7.2 | 3.1 | 4.1 | 1.6 | 7.8 | 16.2 | 18.0 | 19.4 | 14.7 | 4.9 | 1.0 | 1.6 | 0.5 |
| 9. Textiles | 9.0 | 4.8 | 6.1 | 8.4 | 4.9 | 13.7 | 26.1 | 12.6 | 5.7 | 2.9 | 0.7 | 0.4 | 4.5 |
| 10. Clothing and apparel | 11.8 | 10.4 | 2.8 | 9.6 | 20.1 | 15.3 | 15.7 | 5.0 | 8.0 | 0.8 | 0.2 | 0.3 | 0 |
| 11. Footwear | 13.0 | 2.7 | 7.3 | 7.4 | 23.7 | 19.2 | 18.2 | 4.6 | 2.6 | 1.0 | 0 | 0.2 | 0 |
| 12. Wood | 14.9 | 13.6 | 13.2 | 10.2 | 4.7 | 16.5 | 14.0 | 4.8 | 7.4 | 0 | 0.6 | 0 | 0 |
| 13. Handicrafts | 53.6 | 16.9 | 0 | 4.6 | 8.3 | 6.4 | 8.7 | 0 | 1.5 | 0 | 0 | 0 | 0 |
| 14. Furniture, except metallic | 8.5 | 2.5 | 11.1 | 4.6 | 10.8 | 21.4 | 3.3 | 5.7 | 1.0 | 0.5 | 0.2 | 1.2 | 0 |
| 15. Leather | 5.4 | 3.0 | 4.4 | 30.4 | 12.3 | 18.7 | 11.9 | 9.4 | 2.4 | 0 | 2.1 | 0 | 0 |
| 16. Paper and related products | 2.3 | 0 | 0 | 13.4 | 11.4 | 13.7 | 23.1 | 15.2 | 9.3 | 3.0 | 0 | 2.4 | 6.4 |
| 17. Printing and editorial | 3.6 | 4.9 | 9.7 | 5.0 | 6.0 | 18.1 | 19.2 | 13.2 | 12.2 | 3.6 | 0.7 | 2.2 | 1.8 |
| 18. Rubber and plastic | 8.6 | 2.6 | 0 | 0.8 | 9.9 | 12.2 | 34.4 | 7.0 | 10.8 | 8.4 | 0 | 3.2 | 2.0 |
| 19. Pharmaceuticals and cosmetics | 6.1 | 2.7 | 0 | 5.0 | 7.0 | 9.8 | 24.2 | 16.0 | 12.5 | 5.6 | 7.0 | 1.3 | 2.8 |
| 20. Chemicals | 2.1 | 0 | 2.2 | 9.4 | 1.3 | 16.5 | 30.2 | 18.7 | 4.4 | 2.4 | 3.9 | 5.4 | 3.5 |
| 21. Nonmetallic mineral products | 8.7 | 9.1 | 4.7 | 13.5 | 15.3 | 11.6 | 12.2 | 11.8 | 6.6 | 4.7 | 1.2 | 0.6 | 0 |
| 22. Basic metals | 2.4 | 1.5 | 2.8 | 3.3 | 3.0 | 7.8 | 28.1 | 18.6 | 14.1 | 8.9 | 3.6 | 3.7 | 2.2 |
| 23. Metallic products | 6.0 | 1.9 | 4.1 | 9.4 | 13.7 | 11.8 | 27.3 | 12.8 | 5.2 | 3.1 | 3.5 | 0.6 | 0.6 |

| | | | | | | | | | | | | | |
|---|---|---|---|---|---|---|---|---|---|---|---|---|---|
| 24. Machinery | 1.1 | 6.8 | 7.4 | 4.7 | 0 | 13.6 | 21.3 | 14.0 | 19.1 | 5.5 | 2.4 | 0.5 | 3.6 |
| 25. Electrical and electronic equipment | 0 | 0.5 | 1.6 | 3.8 | 3.5 | 13.6 | 32.5 | 16.0 | 11.8 | 5.4 | 6.5 | 1.1 | 3.7 |
| 26. Transportation equipment | 0.9 | 0 | 2.3 | 1.7 | 4.3 | 14.7 | 23.3 | 22.5 | 17.7 | 10.0 | 1.2 | 1.4 | 0 |
| 27. Other manufactures | 7.7 | 2.4 | 1.5 | 6.5 | 6.2 | 10.0 | 26.5 | 13.6 | 13.9 | 8.0 | 1.6 | 1.8 | 0.36 |
| 28. Construction | 9.7 | 9.1 | 9.0 | 12.5 | 15.5 | 16.2 | 15.6 | 6.2 | 2.2 | 1.0 | 1.5 | 1.0 | 0.5 |
| 29. Electricity | 1.4 | 8.0 | 1.9 | 0 | 5.5 | 3.6 | 7.3 | 18.3 | 20.1 | 9.7 | 13.0 | 4.9 | 6.4 |
| 30. Commerce | 11.8 | 6.9 | 5.6 | 8.5 | 12.3 | 15.2 | 18.3 | 9.8 | 5.5 | 3.0 | 1.5 | 1.4 | 0.5 |
| 31. Hotels and lodging | 10.7 | 4.2 | 2.5 | 7.7 | 15.2 | 21.8 | 15.7 | 4.1 | 8.4 | 6.8 | 2.6 | 0.3 | 0 |
| 32. Restaurants and bars | 11.6 | 6.3 | 6.6 | 11.1 | 10.6 | 14.3 | 15.9 | 14.2 | 4.2 | 4.8 | 0.4 | 0 | 0 |
| 33. Radio, TV, and amusement | 11.7 | 5.0 | 2.3 | 7.1 | 12.7 | 15.1 | 20.3 | 7.1 | 4.9 | 9.7 | 3.2 | 1.0 | 0 |
| 34. Telephonic and telegraphic services | 0 | 0 | 0 | 3.5 | 1.5 | 8.3 | 25.9 | 31.0 | 7.0 | 13.4 | 5.1 | 3.3 | 1.0 |
| 35. Education and research | 2.2 | 2.5 | 2.3 | 4.3 | 4.1 | 10.2 | 19.6 | 20.5 | 16.9 | 8.2 | 6.7 | 1.6 | 1.0 |
| 36. Credit, insurance, and finance | 3.8 | 1.3 | 0.8 | 1.2 | 1.7 | 11.4 | 20.1 | 15.8 | 20.3 | 14.2 | 3.6 | 2.4 | 3.6 |
| 37. Medical services | 2.0 | 2.8 | 1.7 | 3.3 | 7.7 | 10.6 | 19.2 | 17.0 | 13.2 | 11.0 | 3.9 | 3.5 | 4.2 |
| 38. Cleaning and laundry | 19.1 | 6.7 | 3.8 | 9.0 | 12.3 | 15.9 | 27.9 | 4.2 | 0.5 | 0.2 | 0.6 | 0 | 0 |
| 39. Domestic service | 58.7 | 13.2 | 6.2 | 6.8 | 5.4 | 3.5 | 2.7 | 1.3 | 1.2 | 0.3 | 0.5 | 0.2 | 0 |
| 40. Professional services and leasing | 3.9 | 5.8 | 3.7 | 7.5 | 8.4 | 11.1 | 18.8 | 6.5 | 10.0 | 7.3 | 7.7 | 5.3 | 4.2 |
| 41. Automobile repairs | 14.7 | 11.0 | 8.4 | 4.6 | 9.2 | 9.3 | 21.6 | 8.7 | 7.6 | 2.1 | 1.7 | 0.9 | 0.2 |
| 42. Machinery repairs | 9.4 | 4.0 | 3.4 | 6.0 | 9.9 | 21.4 | 21.6 | 14.5 | 4.2 | 5.1 | 0.5 | 0 | 0 |
| 43. Other services | 19.7 | 11.6 | 2.9 | 10.5 | 9.2 | 15.1 | 9.9 | 8.7 | 5.7 | 4.3 | 2.4 | 0.3 | 0 |
| 44. Railroad | 3.1 | 4.2 | 1.3 | 1.3 | 0.5 | 16.2 | 29.6 | 18.3 | 11.0 | 7.6 | 3.8 | 1.3 | 1.9 |
| 45. Transportation, passengers | 1.0 | 3.2 | 4.8 | 3.6 | 9.9 | 21.3 | 21.3 | 13.1 | 14.4 | 5.6 | 0.2 | 1.7 | 0 |
| 46. Transportation, freight | 7.8 | 3.5 | 6.2 | 11.0 | 9.9 | 13.1 | 18.6 | 8.4 | 9.1 | 7.7 | 0.3 | 3.8 | 0.5 |
| 47. Other transportation | 1.9 | 2.7 | 1.9 | 2.1 | 5.2 | 7.3 | 20.9 | 12.8 | 17.1 | 7.2 | 12.7 | 2.9 | 5.4 |
| 48. Federal government | 1.1 | 1.5 | 1.6 | 1.5 | 5.3 | 16.5 | 30.1 | 14.8 | 9.0 | 10.2 | 4.7 | 1.2 | 2.6 |
| 49. Other government | 5.7 | 4.9 | 5.3 | 5.1 | 21.7 | 15.1 | 16.3 | 12.6 | 5.7 | 3.3 | 4.2 | 0.3 | 0 |
| 50. All other | 12.6 | 7.1 | 6.7 | 9.4 | 8.7 | 13.2 | 19.9 | 8.7 | 6.1 | 2.9 | 2.3 | 1.2 | 1.2 |

SOURCE: Computed by the author from the household survey of 1977.

*TABLE A.1.3.*

*Parameters of the Sectorial Distributions of Total Income Per Employee*

| | *YE* | *SDYE* | *CVYE* | *SKYE* | *VLYE* | *KUYE* |
|---|---|---|---|---|---|---|
| 1. Agriculture | 1,276 | 1,324 | 1.04 | 5.22 | 0.77 | 43.52 |
| 2. Cattle raising | 2,183 | 2,119 | 0.97 | 3.32 | 0.68 | 17.34 |
| 3. Forestry | 2,510 | 0 | 0 | 1.81 | 1.99 | 2.82 |
| 4. Fishing | 2,286 | 1,927 | 0.84 | 1.27 | 0.79 | 0.85 |
| 5. Mining | 7,350 | 14,792 | 2.01 | 2.59 | 1.20 | 5.46 |
| 6. Oil and gas | 6,820 | 5,453 | 0.80 | 1.92 | 0.63 | 4.53 |
| 7. Food | 3,540 | 3,048 | 0.86 | 2.49 | 0.81 | 7.94 |
| 8. Beverages and tobacco | 4,178 | 3,015 | 0.72 | 1.92 | 0.66 | 6.22 |
| 9. Textiles | 3,972 | 4,245 | 1.07 | 2.79 | 1.24 | 8.34 |
| 10. Clothing and apparel | 2,621 | 1,948 | 0.74 | 1.85 | 0.93 | 7.21 |
| 11. Footwear | 2,521 | 1,663 | 0.66 | 2.13 | 0.55 | 12.01 |
| 12. Wood | 2,348 | 1,998 | 0.85 | 1.33 | 1.13 | 2.20 |
| 13. Handicrafts | 1,239 | 0 | 0 | 1.93 | 0.88 | 4.50 |
| 14. Furniture, except metallic | 2,748 | 2,029 | 0.74 | 4.17 | 0.66 | 28.56 |
| 15. Leather | 2,657 | 2,188 | 0.82 | 2.57 | 0.42 | 9.95 |
| 16. Paper and related products | 5,007 | 5,515 | 1.10 | 2.37 | 0.50 | 4.72 |
| 17. Printing and editorial | 4,065 | 3,518 | 0.87 | 2.41 | 0.74 | 7.58 |
| 18. Rubber and plastic | 4,625 | 4,681 | 1.01 | 3.38 | 0.78 | 14.85 |
| 19. Pharmaceuticals and cosmetics | 5,507 | 6,621 | 1.20 | 3.67 | 0.94 | 15.41 |
| 20. Chemicals | 5,536 | 6,328 | 1.14 | 2.76 | 0.55 | 7.78 |
| 21. Nonmetallic mineral products | 3,124 | 2,555 | 0.82 | 1.83 | 0.61 | 4.95 |
| 22. Basic metals | 5,763 | 5,992 | 1.04 | 7.08 | 0.53 | 76.46 |
| 23. Metallic products | 3,744 | 3,052 | 0.82 | 2.85 | 0.80 | 13.31 |
| 24. Machinery | 5,613 | 8,284 | 1.48 | 4.10 | 0.68 | 17.09 |
| 25. Electrical and electronic equipment | 5,462 | 4,341 | 0.79 | 2.68 | 0.33 | 8.15 |
| 26. Transportation equipment | 4,791 | 2,485 | 0.52 | 1.34 | 0.25 | 2.94 |
| 27. Other manufactures | 4,365 | 3,158 | 0.72 | 1.64 | 0.79 | 4.19 |
| 28. Construction | 2,757 | 2,756 | 1.00 | 4.23 | 0.77 | 27.87 |
| 29. Electricity | 7,534 | 6,640 | 0.88 | 1.58 | 0.81 | 2.40 |
| 30. Commerce | 3,251 | 2,939 | 0.90 | 2.65 | 0.94 | 10.54 |
| 31. Hotels and lodging | 3,521 | 2,961 | 0.84 | 1.45 | 0.67 | 1.88 |
| 32. Restaurants and bars | 2,983 | 2,184 | 0.73 | 1.26 | 1.03 | 2.12 |
| 33. Radio, TV, and amusement | 3,630 | 3,022 | 0.83 | 1.52 | 0.83 | 2.58 |
| 34. Telephonic and telegraphic services | 5,761 | 4,117 | 0.71 | 2.12 | 0.26 | 5.60 |
| 35. Education and research | 5,340 | 3,510 | 0.66 | 1.80 | 0.54 | 5.45 |
| 36. Credit, insurance, and finance | 6,300 | 5,094 | 0.81 | 2.81 | 0.57 | 10.30 |
| 37. Medical services | 5,931 | 5,024 | 0.85 | 2.35 | ’.63 | 6.92 |
| 38. Cleaning and laundry | 2,326 | 1,611 | 0.69 | 1.27 | 0.80 | 5.60 |
| 39. Domestic service | 1,069 | 1,487 | 1.39 | 4.37 | 1.18 | 27.44 |
| 40. Professional services and leasing | 5,707 | 6,155 | 1.08 | 3.80 | 0.87 | 32.90 |
| 41. Automobile repairs | 3,043 | 2,791 | 0.92 | 2.20 | 1.04 | 7.59 |
| 42. Machinery repairs | 3,260 | 2,065 | 0.63 | 0.94 | 0.60 | 1.25 |
| 43. Other services | 2,796 | 2,717 | 0.97 | 1.51 | 1.70 | 2.31 |
| 44. Railroad | 4,962 | 3,767 | 0.76 | 2.24 | 0.46 | 6.19 |
| 45. Transportation, passengers | 4,097 | 2,520 | 0.62 | 1.68 | 0.36 | 4.39 |
| 46. Transportation, freight | 4,013 | 3,790 | 0.94 | 2.49 | 0.99 | 9.07 |
| 47. Other transportation | 6,864 | 5,824 | 0.85 | 1.63 | 0.66 | 2.64 |
| 48. Federal government | 5,359 | 4,427 | 0.83 | 3.13 | 0.42 | 12.98 |
| 49. Other government | 3,513 | 2,712 | 0.77 | 1.89 | 0.60 | 4.57 |
| 50. All other | 3,488 | 3,812 | 1.09 | 3.47 | 1.01 | 16.19 |
| All | 3,220 | 3,540 | 1.10 | | 1.14 | |

SOURCE: Calculated by the author from the household survey of 1977.

*TABLE A.1.4.*

*Parameters of the Sectorial Distributions of Total Income Per Participant: 1977*

| | *YP* | *SDYP* | *CVYP* | *SKYP* | *VLYP* | *KUYP* |
|---|---|---|---|---|---|---|
| 1. Agriculture | 1,380 | 1,796 | 1.30 | 6.56 | 0.94 | 68.81 |
| 2. Cattle raising | 2,309 | 2,623 | 1.14 | 3.47 | 1.01 | 17.45 |
| 3. Forestry | 2,457 | 3,053 | 1.24 | 2.11 | 1.69 | 3.49 |
| 4. Fishing | 2,150 | 1,719 | 0.80 | 1.40 | 0.74 | 1.29 |
| 5. Mining | 6,771 | 12,789 | 1.89 | 2.77 | 1.37 | 6.48 |
| 6. Oil and gas | 6,820 | 5,091 | 0.75 | 1.92 | 0.63 | 4.53 |
| 7. Food | 3,373 | 3,028 | 0.90 | 2.34 | 1.02 | 7.16 |
| 8. Beverages and tobacco | 4,178 | 2,901 | 0.69 | 1.85 | 0.70 | 5.78 |
| 9. Textiles | 3,658 | 4,059 | 1.11 | 2.79 | 2.01 | 8.68 |
| 10. Clothing and apparel | 2,229 | 2,641 | 1.18 | 3.81 | 2.00 | 22.73 |
| 11. Footwear | 2,911 | 2,293 | 0.79 | 2.49 | 0.63 | 8.36 |
| 12. Wood | 2,366 | 1,849 | 0.78 | 1.27 | 1.06 | 1.89 |
| 13. Handicrafts | 565 | 798 | 1.41 | 2.74 | 2.59 | 10.57 |
| 14. Furniture, except metallic | 2,846 | 2,041 | 0.72 | 3.44 | 0.70 | 20.97 |
| 15. Leather | 3,386 | 3,079 | 0.91 | 2.35 | 0.70 | 5.59 |
| 16. Paper and related products | 6,633 | 11,043 | 1.16 | 3.18 | 1.12 | 9.39 |
| 17. Printing and editorial | 4,420 | 4,503 | 1.02 | 4.19 | 0.84 | 26.33 |
| 18. Rubber and plastic | 4,634 | 4,565 | 0.99 | 3.39 | 0.96 | 14.72 |
| 19. Pharmaceuticals and cosmetics | 5,346 | 5,977 | 1.12 | 3.76 | 0.93 | 16.18 |
| 20. Chemicals | 5,644 | 5,686 | 1.01 | 2.68 | 0.57 | 7.31 |
| 21. Nonmetallic mineral products | 3,005 | 2,509 | 0.83 | 1.74 | 0.72 | 4.09 |
| 22. Basic metals | 5,748 | 5,731 | 1.00 | 7.16 | 0.52 | 78.14 |
| 23. Metallic products | 3,906 | 3,910 | 1.00 | 5.20 | 0.80 | 39.92 |
| 24. Machinery | 4,733 | 2,910 | 0.61 | 1.04 | 0.63 | 1.73 |
| 25. Electrical and electronic equipment | 5,472 | 4,363 | 0.80 | 2.59 | 0.37 | 7.25 |
| 26. Transportation equipment | 4,817 | 2,401 | 0.50 | 1.23 | 0.28 | 2.42 |
| 27. Other manufactures | 4,295 | 3,391 | 0.79 | 1.66 | 1.50 | 3.84 |
| 28. Construction | 2,799 | 2,767 | 0.99 | 4.10 | 0.81 | 25.77 |
| 29. Electricity | 7,418 | 6,047 | 0.82 | 1.58 | 0.84 | 2.42 |
| 30. Commerce | 3,295 | 3,625 | 1.10 | 5.60 | 1.16 | 77.47 |
| 31. Hotels and lodging | 3,482 | 2,689 | 0.77 | 1.47 | 0.66 | 1.99 |
| 32. Restaurants and bars | 2,853 | 2,386 | 0.84 | 1.54 | 1.21 | 3.43 |
| 33. Radio, TV, and amusement | 3,661 | 3,200 | 0.87 | 2.19 | 0.88 | 7.70 |
| 34. Telephonic and telegraphic services | 5,811 | 3,511 | 0.60 | 2.08 | 0.26 | 5.56 |
| 35. Education and research | 5,315 | 3,484 | 0.66 | 1.79 | 0.54 | 5.33 |
| 36. Credit, insurance, and finance | 6,199 | 4,919 | 0.79 | 2.82 | 0.58 | 10.46 |
| 37. Medical services | 5,800 | 4,911 | 0.85 | 2.30 | 0.78 | 6.84 |
| 38. Cleaning and laundry | 2,086 | 1,794 | 0.86 | 2.36 | 1.13 | 11.89 |
| 39. Domestic service | 1,043 | 1,730 | 1.66 | 9.96 | 1.22 | 163.98 |
| 40. Professional services and leasing | 8,486 | 10,746 | 1.27 | 3.35 | 1.14 | 14.20 |
| 41. Automobile repairs | 3,355 | 2,915 | 0.87 | 1.88 | 1.02 | 4.98 |
| 42. Machinery repairs | 3,622 | 2,849 | 0.79 | 2.19 | 1.04 | 8.61 |
| 43. Other services | 2,699 | 2,690 | 1.00 | 1.67 | 1.81 | 3.12 |
| 44. Railroad | 4,823 | 3,457 | 0.72 | 2.27 | 0.47 | 6.38 |
| 45. Transportation, passengers | 4,612 | 4,672 | 1.01 | 6.59 | 0.55 | 58.95 |
| 46. Transportation, freight | 4,049 | 3,675 | 0.91 | 2.36 | 1.02 | 8.14 |
| 47. Other transportation | 6,840 | 5,372 | 0.79 | 1.63 | 0.63 | 2.55 |
| 48. Federal government | 5,359 | 4,379 | 0.81 | 3.13 | 0.42 | 12.95 |
| 49. Other government | 3,445 | 2,613 | 0.76 | 1.89 | 0.64 | 4.64 |
| 50. All other | 2,570 | 4,161 | 1.62 | 7.14 | 1.93 | 81.48 |

SOURCE: Calculated by the author from the household survey of 1977.

*TABLE A.1.5.*

*Parameters of the Sectorial Distributions of Labor Income Per Participant: 1977*

| | WP | *SDWP* | *CVWP* | *SKWP* | *VLWP* | *KUMP* |
|---|---|---|---|---|---|---|
| 1. Agriculture | 709 | 1,087 | 1.53 | 5.04 | 10.92 | 46.40 |
| 2. Cattle raising | 1,182 | 1,625 | 1.37 | 2.41 | 13.10 | 8.16 |
| 3. Forestry | 1,602 | 2,328 | 1.45 | 2.19 | 13.35 | 4.85 |
| 4. Fishing | 1,900 | 1,839 | 0.97 | 1.31 | 7.65 | 1.11 |
| 5. Mining | 6,343 | 12,029 | 1.90 | 2.56 | 6.84 | 4.73 |
| 6. Oil and gas | 6,720 | 5,119 | 0.76 | 1.20 | 0.64 | 4.53 |
| 7. Food | 2,849 | 2,963 | 1.04 | 2.45 | 9.12 | 8.60 |
| 8. Beverages and tobacco | 3,878 | 2,835 | 0.73 | 1.20 | 2.70 | 6.82 |
| 9. Textiles | 3,586 | 4,016 | 1.12 | 2.85 | 5.81 | 9.20 |
| 10. Clothing and apparel | 1,559 | 1,889 | 1.21 | 1.84 | 13.90 | 6.57 |
| 11. Footwear | 2,103 | 1,694 | 0.81 | 1.64 | 8.03 | 8.52 |
| 12. Wood | 1,757 | 1,906 | 1.08 | 1.42 | 10.96 | 2.28 |
| 13. Handicrafts | 119 | 520 | 4.37 | 6.73 | 4.13 | 59.90 |
| 14. Furniture, except metallic | 2,426 | 1,739 | 0.72 | 2.63 | 4.98 | 17.90 |
| 15. Leather | 2,388 | 2,034 | 0.85 | 1.66 | 8.12 | 4.66 |
| 16. Paper and related products | 3,856 | 4,646 | 1.20 | 2.47 | 11.35 | 5.91 |
| 17. Printing and editorial | 3,685 | 2,881 | 0.78 | 2.07 | 3.20 | 6.90 |
| 18. Rubber and plastic | 4,248 | 4,497 | 1.06 | 3.24 | 5.07 | 14.26 |
| 19. Pharmaceuticals and cosmetics | 5,310 | 5,997 | 1.13 | 3.74 | 1.78 | 16.02 |
| 20. Chemicals | 5,525 | 5,611 | 1.02 | 2.80 | 0.56 | 8.02 |
| 21. Nonmetallic mineral products | 2,588 | 2,504 | 0.97 | 1.73 | 8.65 | 4.62 |
| 22. Basic metals | 5,463 | 4,747 | 0.87 | 4.15 | 1.76 | 29.75 |
| 23. Metallic products | 3,397 | 3,574 | 1.05 | 3.62 | 6.85 | 20.72 |
| 24. Machinery | 3,550 | 2,707 | 0.76 | 0.90 | 6.98 | 1.27 |
| 25. Electrical and electronic equipment | 5,143 | 4,142 | 0.81 | 2.66 | 2.80 | 8.55 |
| 26. Transportation equipment | 4,507 | 2,428 | 0.54 | 1.21 | 2.33 | 2.77 |
| 27. Other manufactures | 3,664 | 2,771 | 0.76 | 1.18 | 6.89 | 3.67 |
| 28. Construction | 2,320 | 2,505 | 1.08 | 3.47 | 6.83 | 18.32 |
| 29. Electricity | 7,203 | 5,873 | 0.82 | 1.55 | 0.88 | 2.26 |
| 30. Commerce | 1,860 | 2,604 | 1.40 | 2.52 | 14.70 | 9.56 |
| 31. Hotels and lodging | 3,042 | 2,732 | 0.90 | 1.45 | 6.42 | 2.13 |
| 32. Restaurants and bars | 2,029 | 2,217 | 1.09 | 1.36 | 12.63 | 2.13 |
| 33. Radio, TV, and amusement | 3,018 | 2,839 | 0.94 | 1.29 | 8.80 | 1.44 |
| 34. Telephonic and telegraphic services | 5,463 | 3,523 | 0.64 | 2.14 | 0.30 | 6.10 |
| 35. Education and research | 5,034 | 3,389 | 0.67 | 1.82 | 1.79 | 5.92 |
| 36. Credit, insurance, and finance | 5,949 | 4,501 | 0.76 | 2.87 | 1.72 | 12.43 |
| 37. Medical services | 5,127 | 4,347 | 0.85 | 2.05 | 5.33 | 6.65 |
| 38. Cleaning and laundry | 1,437 | 1,525 | 1.06 | 1.01 | 12.68 | 1.23 |
| 39. Domestic service | 762 | 1,322 | 1.73 | 5.01 | 8.30 | 36.42 |
| 40. Professional services and leasing | 4,216 | 5,398 | 1.28 | 3.97 | 12.90 | 39.36 |
| 41. Automobile repairs | 2,489 | 2,655 | 1.07 | 2.03 | 8.98 | 6.27 |
| 42. Machinery repairs | 1,889 | 2,154 | 1.14 | 1.06 | 15.13 | 0.57 |
| 43. Other services | 1,950 | 2,393 | 1.23 | 1.77 | 10.88 | 3.70 |
| 44. Railroad | 4,424 | 3,270 | 0.74 | 2.45 | 2.71 | 8.09 |
| 45. Transportation, passengers | 3,138 | 2,712 | 0.86 | 1.31 | 11.27 | 3.03 |
| 46. Transportation, freight | 3,223 | 3,235 | 1.00 | 2.62 | 8.32 | 12.88 |
| 47. Other transportation | 5,948 | 5,579 | 0.94 | 1.61 | 7.50 | 2.67 |
| 48. Federal government | 4,981 | 3,791 | 0.76 | 3.02 | 0.39 | 12.36 |
| 49. Other government | 3,065 | 2,176 | 0.71 | 1.46 | 2.76 | 3.33 |
| 50. All other | 897 | 2,367 | 2.64 | 5.38 | 11.92 | 42.23 |

SOURCE: Calculated by the author from the household survey of 1977.

*TABLE A.1.6*

*Criterion for Aggregating Sectors from the Household Survey of 1977*

| | *Number of Observations* |
|---|---|
| 1. Agriculture | 3,847 |
| 2. Cattle raising | 297 |
| 3. Forestry | 36 |
| 4. Fishing | 71 |
| 5. Mining | 60 |
| 6. Oil and Gas | 77 |
| 7. Food | 524 |
| 8. Beverages and tobacco | 158 |
| 9. Textiles | 169 |
| 10. Clothing and apparel | 525 |
| 11. Footwear | 181 |
| 12. Wood | 99 |
| 13. Handicrafts | 81 |
| 14. Furniture, nonmetallic | 148 |
| 15. Leather | 51 |
| 16. Paper and related products | 56 |
| 17. Printing and publishing | 82 |
| 18. Rubber and plastic products | 123 |
| 19. Pharmaceutical and cosmetics | 78 |
| 20. Chemicals | 60 |
| 21. Nonmetallic mineral products | 212 |
| 22. Basic metals | 234 |
| 23. Metallic products | 248 |
| 24. Machinery | 52 |
| 25. Electrical and electronic equipment | 137 |
| 26. Transportation equipment | 103 |
| 27. Other manufactures | 187 |
| 28. Construction | 1,130 |
| 29. Electricity | 73 |
| 30. Commerce | 2,385 |
| 31. Hotels and lodging | 92 |
| 32. Restaurants and bars | 393 |
| 33. Radio, TV and amusement | 158 |
| 34. Telephonic and telegraphic services | 45 |
| 35. Education and research | 578 |
| 36. Credit, insurance, and finance | 199 |
| 37. Medical services | 407 |
| 38. Cleaning service | 676 |
| 39. Domestic service | 676 |
| 40. Professional services and leasing | 219 |
| 41. Automobile repairs | 247 |
| 42. Machinery repairs | 204 |

*TABLE A.1.6* (Continued)

| | Number of Observations |
|---|---|
| 43. Other services | 175 |
| 44. Railroad | 87 |
| 45. Transportation, passenger | 280 |
| 46. Transportation, freight | 201 |
| 47. Other transportation | 92 |
| 48. Federal government | 435 |
| 49. Other government | 191 |
| 50. All other | 1,714 |

**Definition of Employees**

Any individual older than 12 years declaring a positive income for concepts 1–5 of Table A-1-1 was defined as an employee.

**Definition of Sectors**

The ninety-nine sectors originally considered in the survey had to be combined to fifty to guarantee having "sufficient" observations for each sector. The reclassification of sectors involved in this aggregation was required to make the final sectors coincide with the standard industrial classification in Mexico (CEMAE). The list included at the end of this appendix presents the original and final aggregations and the number of observations in each sector (Table A-1-6)

**Definition of Education (EDE)**

EDE refers to average schooling based on values attached to each original category as follows:

| | | Value |
|---|---|---|
| A | No schooling | 0 |
| B | Some primary school | 3 |
| C | Completed primary | 6 |
| D | Some intermediate | 8 |
| E | Completed intermediate | 9 |
| F | Some high school | 10 |
| G | Completed high school | 11.5 |
| H | Some university | 14 |
| I | Completed university | 18 |
| K | Graduate study | 20 |
| Z | Not specified | |

Then sectorial averages were taken.

**Definition of Sex (SXE)**

SXE refers to the percentage of males in total employment, either participants or employees.

**Definition of Experience (EXE)**

EXE was calculated at the individual level as

$$EXE = AGE - EDE - 6$$

Then sectorial averages were taken.

**Definition of Brackets**

Brackets refer to the monthly flow of the corresponding concept in pesos.

| | |
|---|---|
| 1. | 0.1– 700.0 |
| 2. | 700.0– 1,000.0 |
| 3. | 1,000.0– 1,350.0 |
| 4. | 1,350.0– 1,800.0 |
| 5. | 1,800.0– 2,400.0 |
| 6. | 2,400.0– 3,150.0 |
| 7. | 3,150.0– 4,300.0 |
| 8. | 4,300.0– 5,725.0 |
| 9. | 5,725.0– 7,500.0 |
| 10. | 7,500.0–10,150.0 |
| 11. | 10,150.0–13,400.0 |
| 12. | 13,400.0–18,000.0 |
| 13. | 18,000.0 and over |

# Appendix 2

# *Independent Variables: Definitions and Sources*[50]

As mentioned in the text, the source for most independent variables was the economic census of 1975. Only education, sex, and experience were estimated from the household survey of 1977 according to the definitions presented in Appendix 1.

The specific sources and definitions are as follows:

*KT:* Value of total assets *(acervos totales).* Sources: *Census of Commerce,* Table 7; *Census of Services,* Table 1; *Industrial Census,* Table 3; *Transportation Census,* several tables.

*LT:* Total labor *(personal ocupado total promedio).* Sources: *Agricultural Census,* Table 32; *Census of Commerce,* Table 7; *Census of Services,* Table 1; *Industrial Census,* Table 3; *Transportation Census,* several tables.

EES: Employees; excludes self-employed *(obreros más empleados).* Sources: *Agricultural Census,* Table 17; *Census of Commerce,* Table 16; *Census of Services,* Table 15; *Industrial Census,* Vol. 2, Table 6; *Transportation Census,* several tables (includes drivers, operators, crew members, and workers).

EST: Establishments *(establecimientos).* Sources: same as for *LT.*

*AS:* Average size of establishment. Definition: *AS* = *LT*/EST.

DUE: Duality measured by establishments. Definition: establishments without salaried employees, as percentage of total establishments. Sources: *Census of Commerce,* Table 7; *Census of Services,* table 7; *Industrial Census,* table 8.

PRW: Percentage of production workers in total employment. Definition: PRW = EES/*LT.*

*VD:* Variability of product's demand. Definition: coefficient of variation of the monthly rates of growth of gross production in every sector. Source: *Index of Industrial Production,* Banco de México, S.A.

KLT: Total capital per participant. Definition: KLT = *KT*/*LT.*

# Notes

1. This figure refers to the share of total payments to labor in total net value added at factor cost.

2. The basic model is Solow-Swan. For a brief presentation of it, see Dixit (1976).

3. For research in this area, see Reyes Heroles (1980).

4. We use the term *size* distribution as a convention to distinguish the shape of the frequency distribution from the *functional* or *factorial* distribution.

5. It is clear that the decomposition of the overall distribution can follow other criteria, e.g., regional.

6. The literature on the U.S. case illustrates the path taken by research. Relative effects of unionism on earnings by industry have been studied by, among others, Weiss (1966) and Freeman (1978) and have generally obtained a positive differential. For a brief review of the literature on this topic, see G. E. Johnson (1978). Relative effects of sex and race on earnings by industry have occupied the attention of Welch (1974) and W. R. Johnson (1978), who found evidence of sexual and racial discrimination. The relative effects of education and experience on earnings are the subject of Mincer (1974) and Eckaus (1973) among others.

7. A counterexample is Freeman (1978).

8. Among the exceptions are Reynolds and Taft (1956), Culley (1956), and Estrin (1981).

9. For the definitions of earnings and personal income, see Appendix 1. This figure is significantly higher than the share of labor payments in GDP reported in the national accounts since it seems the survey underreported capital income. For details, see Diez Canedo and Vera (1981).

10. Source: Table A-1-1.

11. See especially Chapter VIII.

12. Detailed definitions are provided in Appendix 1.

13. Table A-1-2 in Appendix 1 presents the data of the frequency distributions of Figure 6-1 and Tables A-1-3 and A-1-5 present the parameters for the sectorial distributions of total income per employee and per participant and of labor income per participant.

14. The coefficient of skewness is defined as SKWE $= m_3/(\sigma_w)^3$, where $m_3$ is the third moment around the mean of the distribution of earnings and $\sigma_w$ its standard deviation.

15. With the exception of handicrafts. Recall, however, that the prevalent mode of production in this sector is self-employment.

16. The coefficient of excess kurtosis, with respect to the normal distribution, is calculated as follows: KUWE $= m_4/(\sigma_w)^4) - 3$, where $m_4$ is the fourth moment around the mean of earnings. This coefficient measures the relative peakedness of the curve; a normal distribution will have a coefficient of excess kurtosis of zero.

17. Table A-1-2 indicates other cases of bimodality.

18. The average monthly general minimum wage was 2414.17 pesos in 1977; such wage falls between the fifth and sixth income brackets used in this research. The lowest general and agricultural minimum wages were 1432.63 and 1237.96 pesos, respectively; they fall within the third and fourth brackets. Table A-1-2 shows that a substantial fraction of workers had earnings below this level.

19. The income expenditure survey of 1977 does not allow distinguishing earnings from part-time and full-time employment.

20. 4.3 percent were located in construction, probably as a result of part-time employment.

21. For research on the effects of the organizational pyramid, see Lydall (1959).

22. See Thurow (1972, 1975).

23. See Piore (1973).

24. For a survey, see Cline (1974).

25. See Thurow (1975).

26. For a review of these theories, see Carter and Carnoy (1974).

27. See Piore (1973).

28. See Toharia (1978).

29. An exercise developed by the author based on U.S. data suggests that such tendency may conform with the experience of that country. A cross-section analysis for forty-five three-digit manufacturing sectors, similar to the one for Mexico presented in Section IV-3, indicated that intraindustry earnings concentration increased with deeper division of labor. See Reyes Heroles (1978).

30. For example, see Nelson (1968) on Colombia.

31. The decrease from 1970 to 1975 most probably responds to short-run problems. Private investment was extremely sluggish during this period.

32. See Mood et al. (1974, p. 76). For research questioning this traditional interpretation of kurtosis, see Darlington (1970). In his view the kurtosis is a measure of unimodality versus bimodality.

33. For a summary of the statistical characteristics of the Gini coefficient and the other statistics, see Szal and Robinson (1971, p. 491).

34. For the definition of the variables displayed in Table 6-11, see Appendix 1.

35. The variables to be explained, the sectorial earnings distributions, were estimated based on the household survey of 1977. However, most of the explanatory variables, i.e., technological, refer to 1975; they were estimated based on the economic census of that year, especially the industrial.

36. See Mood et al. (1974, p. 74).

37. See detailed definitions and sources of the independent variables in Appendix 2.

38. Note that the result on average size *(AS)* is contrary to what is generally known as the Masters' effect of size on earnings. See Masters (1969).

39. This result is contrary to Freeman's (1978).

40. The definition of sectorial *employment share elasticity* is

$$ESE_i = \frac{d \ln \frac{EI}{TE}}{d \ln TE}$$

where $E_i$ represents employment in sector $i$ (either participants[i] or employees) and $TE$ total employment. They were estimated with OLS.

41. The most recent example is Lustig (1981).

42. Since the sectorial classifications of Table A-1-2 and Table 6-13 differ, an arbitrary matching had to be made. It basically required grouping sectors or the use of some sectorial employment share elasticities more than once, especially for services. It was observed, however, that the main result did not change with alternative sets of sectorial employment share elasticities. The adopted sectorial elasticities appear in Table 6-15. Note, additionally, that since each sectorial share was modified according to estimated elasticities they do not add up to 1. Therefore overall employment actually increases 21.8 percent instead of 20.0 percent, as assumed for estimating the new shares.

43. Based on employment data of Secretaría de Patrimonio y Fomento Industrial (1979).

44. For a similar but more detailed argument based on the results of a general equilibrium model for the Mexican economy see Reyes Heroles (1980).

45. See Rosenzweig (1975) and Levy (1981).

46. Figures for enrollment in social security institutions are frequently used for this purpose. Inferences based on these figures can be quite misleading, since sectorial coverage of social security has been increasing, so that increased enrollment includes previously existing employment.

47. For a survey, see Morawetz (1974), and for the Mexican case, see Levy (1981).

48. See Sidaoui (1979).

49. See, for example, Steward (1977) and Eckaus (1977).

50. Complete references are given in the Bibliography.

## References

Altimir, O. "La medición de la población económicamente activa de México, 1950–1970." *Demografía y Economía* VIII, No. 1 (1974), 50–83.

Carter, M., and M. Carnoy. *Theories of Labor Markets and Labor Productivity*. Palo Alto, Calif.: Center for Economic Studies, 1974, mimeo.

Cline, W. "Distribution and Development." *Journal of Development Economics* 1, No. 4 (Feb. 1974), 359–400.

Culley, J. "The Inter-industry Wages Structure, 1899–1950." *The American Economic Review* 46 (1956), 353–359.

Darlington, R. "Is Kurtosis Really Peakedness?" *The American Statistician* (April 1970), 19–20.

Diez-Canedo, J., and G. Vera. "La distribución del ingreso en México en 1977," *Serie Documentos de Investigación,* No. 37. Federal District of Mexico: Banco de México, S.A., Sept. 1981.

Dixit, A. *The Theory of Equilibrium Growth*. Oxford: Oxford University Press, 1976.

Eckaus, R. *Estimating the Return to Education*. Berkeley: Carnegie Commission on Higher Education, 1973, especially Chap. 2.

Eckaus, R. *Appropriate Technologies for Developing Countries*. Washington, D.C.: National Academy of Sciences, 1977.

Eriksson, J. R. "Wage Structure and Economic Development in Selected Latin American Countries: A Comparative Analysis," unpublished doctoral dissertation in economics, University of California, Berkeley, 1966.

Estrin, S. "Income Dispersion in a Self-Managed Economy." *Economica* 48 (May 1981), 181–194.

Everett, M. D. "The Role of the Mexican Trade Unions, 1950–1963," unpublished doctoral dissertation in economics, Washington University, St. Louis, 1967.

Freeman, R. B. "Changes in the Labor Market for Black Americans, 1948–72." *Brookings Papers on Economic Activity* I (1973), 67–131.

Freeman, R. B. *"Unionism and the Dispersion of Wages," discussion paper No. 629*. Cambridge, Mass.: Harvard Institute of Economic Research, 1978.

Freeman, R. B., and J. L. Medoff. *New Estimates of the Industrial Locus of Unionism in the U.S.* Cambridge, Mass.: Harvard University, June 1978, mimeo.

Freeman, R. B., and J. L. Medoff. *The Effect of Percent Organized on Union and Nounion Wages*. Cambridge, Mass.: Harvard University, July 1978, mimeo.

Garbarino, J. W. "A Theory of Inter-industry Wage Variation." *Quarterly Journal of Economics* (May 1950), 299–305.

Gregory, P. "Wage Structures in Latin America." *The Journal of Developing Areas,* 8, No. 8 (July 1974), 557–579.

Hill, T. P. "An Analysis of the Distribution of Wages and Salaries in Great Britain." *Econometrica* 27 (June 1959), 355–381.

Johnson, G. E. "Economic Analysis of Trade Unionism," in L. Reynolds, S. Masters, C. Moser et al. (eds.), *Readings in Labor Economics and Labor Relations*. Englewood Cliffs, N.J.: Prentice-Hall, 1978.

Johnson, W. R. "Racial Wage Discrimination and Industrial Structure." *The Bell Journal of Economics* 9 (Spring 1978), 70–80.

Kuznets, S. "Economic Growth and Income Inequality." *The American Economic Review* vol. 45 (March 1955), 1–28.

Levy, S. *El problema del empleo en México: reorientación de la estrategia económica."* Federal District of Mexico: Banco Nacional de México, S.A., 1981.

Lewis, W. A. "Economic Development with Unlimited Supplies of Labour." Reprinted in A. Argarwala, and S. Singh (eds.). *The Economics of Underdevelopment*. New Delhi: Oxford University Press, 1976, pp. 400–449.

Lustig, N. *Distribución del Ingreso y Crecimiento Económico en México; un Análisis de las Ideas Estructuralistas*. Federal District of Mexico: El Colegio de México, 1981.

Lydall, H. F. "The Distribution of Employment Incomes." *Econometrica* 27 (1959), 110–115.

Marglin, S. "What Do Bosses Do?" *The Review of Radical Political Economics* 6, No. 2 (1971), 33–60.

Masters, S. "Wages and Plant Size: An Inter-industry Analysis." *Review of Economics and Statistics* (Aug. 1969), 51, 341–348.

Mincer, J. *Schooling, Experience and Earnings*. National Bureau of Economic Research, New York, 1974.

Montemayor, A. "Educación y distribución del ingreso en México." *Re-*

*vista Latinoamericana de Estudios Educativos* X, No. 2 (1980), 33–68.

Mood, A., F. Graybill, and D. Boes. *Introduction to the Theory of Statistics*. New York: McGraw-Hill, 1974.

Morawetz, D. "Employment Implications of Industrialization in Developing Countries: A Survey." *Economic Journal* vol. 84 (Sept. 1974), 491–542.

Nelson, R. "A Diffusion Model of International Productivity Differences in Manufacturing Industry." *American Economic Review,* 58, (Dec. 1968), 1229–1284.

Nugent, J., and F. Tarawneh. *The Anatomy of Changes in Income Distribution and Poverty Among Mexico's Economically Active Population Between 1950 and 1970*. Los Angeles: University of Southern California, April 1981, mimeo.

Piore, M. J. "On the Technological Foundations of Economic Dualism," Working Paper No. 110. Cambridge, Mass.: Massachusetts Institute of Technology, May 1973.

Rees, A., and M. T. Hamilton. "Changes in Wage Dispersion," in J. F. Burton et al. (eds.), *Readings in Labor Market Analysis*. New York: Holt, Rinehart and Winston, 1971, pp. 484–488.

Reyes Heroles, J. F. *Industrial Structure and the Distribution of Earnings: The U.S. Case*. Cambridge, Mass.: Massachusetts Institute of Technology, Oct. 1978, mimeo.

Reyes Heroles, J. F. "Welfare Effects of Short-Run Macroeconomic Policies in a Dual Economy: The case of Mexico," unpublished doctoral dissertation in economics, Massachusetts Institute of Technology, Cambridge, Aug. 1980.

Reynolds, L., and C. Taft. *The Evolution of Wage Structure*. New Haven, Conn.: Yale University Press, 1956.

Rosenzweig, F. "Política agrícola y generación del empleo en México." *El Trimestre Económico* 42 (Oct.–Dec. 1975), 837–855.

Salazar-Carrillo, J. "Labor Income Differentials Within the Latin American Free Trade Area." *Review of Income and Wealth 23,* No. 3 (Sept. 1977), 217–237.

Secretaría de Patrimonio y Fomento Industrial. *Plan Nacional de Desarrollo Industrial, 1979–82*. Federal District of Mexico, March 1979.

Secretaría de Programación y Presupuesto, Dirección General de Estadísticas. *V Censos Agrícola-Ganadero y Ejidal 1970. Resumen General*. Federal District of Mexico, 1975.

Secretaría de Programación y Presupuesto. *VII Censo de Servicios. Resumen General*. Federal District of Mexico, 1978.

Secretaría de Programación y Presupuesto. *VIII Censo de Transportes y Comunicaciones*. Federal District of Mexico, 1979.

Secretaría de Programación y Presupuesto. *X Censo Industrial, Resumen General*. 2 vols. Federal District of Mexico, 1979.

Secretaría de Programación y Presupuesto. *VII Censo Comercial. Resumen General*. Federal District of Mexico, March 1980.

Secretaría de Programación y Presupuesto. *X Censo Industrial: Desgloce de productos obtenidos por clase de actividad*. Federal District of Mexico, April 1981.

Secretaría del Trabajo y Previsión Social. *Directorio General de Agrupaciones Sindicales*. Federal District of Mexico: Departamento de Registro de Asociaciones, 1970.

Sidaoui, J. "Factor Market Distortions in a Multisectorial Model: A Case Study of Mexico," unpublished doctoral dissertation in economics, George Washington University, Washington, D.C., Feb. 1979.

Steward, F. "Choice of Technique in Developing Countries." *Journal of Development Studies* 9, No. 11 (Oct. 1977), 99–121.

Stinson Ortiz, Yvonne. *"Los determinantes del ingreso laboral: El enfoque de rendimientos a la escolaridad,"* tesis profesional, Nueva León: Universidad Autónoma, 1979.

Stone, K. "The Origins of Job Structures in the Steel Industry." *The Review of Radical Political Economy* 6, No. 2 (Summer 1974), 61–97.

Szal, R., and S. Robinson. "Measuring Income Inequality," in C. Frank, R. Webb et al. (eds.), *Income Distribution and Growth in Less-Developed Countries*. Washington, D.C.: The Brookings Institution, 1971, pp. 491–533.

Thurow, L. "Education and Economic Equality." *Public Interest* 28 (Summer 1972), 66–81.

Thurow, L. *Generating Inequality*. New York: Basic Books, 1975.

Toharia, L. *The Division of Labor in a Nineteenth Century Factory: The McCormick Works*. Cambridge, Mass.: Massachusetts Institute of Technology, Sept. 1978, mimeo.

Van Ginneken, W. and M. Garzuel. *Mexico's Income Distribution (1968); An Essay to Make Survey Data Comparable with National Accounts and Population Estimates*. Geneva: ILD's Income Distribution and Employment Programme, May 1981.

Wabe, S., and L. Dennis. "Relative Earnings in UK Manufacturing: A Reconsideration of the Evidence." *The Economic Journal* 88 (June 1978), 296–313.

Weiss, L. "Concentration and Labor Earnings." *The American Economic Review* 56 (March 1966), 96–117.

Welch, F. "Education and Racial Discrimination," in O. Aschenfelter and A. Rees (eds.), *Discrimination in Labor Markets*. Princeton: Princeton University Press: 1974, pp. 43–87.

Williamson, J. G. "The Sources of American Inequality." *The Review of Economics and Statistics* LVIII (Nov. 1976), 387–397.

Zazueta, C., and S. Geluda. *Población Planta Industrial y Sindicatos*. Federal District of Mexico: Centro Nacional de Información y Estadísticas del Trabajo, 1981, mimeo.

# CHAPTER 7

# *Macroeconomic Uncertainty and Employment: The Case of Mexico*

Pedro Aspe and Herminio Blanco

### Introduction

There is some intuitive appeal to the hypothesis that massive increases in uncertainty widely defined would tend to affect negatively the distribution of income by hurting the poor more than the rich. The basis of this idea is that rich people either are better informed and/or have access to and possess a more diversified portfolio of assets. Modeling and testing this hypothesis is a challenging and interesting area of research.

Our approach to uncertainty is somewhat indirect. It considers increases in employment as a proxy for improvements in the distribution of income. For this reason it focuses on the effects of changes in uncertainty upon the level of employment of the economy and, indirectly, on the overall distribution of income.

The motivation of this approach is that in a *dual* economy, one of the most pressing features of income distribution is the observed disparity between those employed in the *modern* sector and those unemployed or underemployed in the *traditional* sector. In this sense, increases in employment in the modern sector should tend to decrease overall income inequality. Some light on this hypothesis has been shed by simulation studies. The procedure is to compute the effects on the overall personal distribution of income of incorporating different percentages of the unemployed or underemployed into the occupied labor force of the modern sector.[1]

In the last three decades Mexico has witnessed two different periods from a macroeconomic point of view: a very stable period with low inflation and steady growth that extends from the devaluation of 1954 up to 1972 and a second period from 1973 to the present, which has been characterized by high and variable inflation and by two massive devaluations. In this aggregate sense, it would seem that since 1973, individuals and firms have been facing an increase in the uncertainty of their economic environment. From the point of view of the management of economic policy, these two periods also mark a drastic change of policy. In the first period, the authorities pegged the nominal exchange rate to the dollar and subordinated fiscal and monetary policies to that objective.

In the second period, the government directed its fiscal and monetary mix toward increasing social welfare and employment. As a result of this change, there was an increase in the level and variability of aggregate demand.

The working hypothesis of this chapter is that, notwithstanding the government achievements on the social welfare front,[2] economic uncertainty has increased since 1973. Furthermore, we argue that this increase has negatively affected the output and employment potential of the economy.

The organization of the chapter is as follows: in the next section, we review the literature on the relationship between uncertainty and employment. Then we present two operational measures of uncertainty that are proposed and estimated. In the following section, we analyze the relationship between one of these measures and the rate of inflation. The final section presents empirical tests of the effects of uncertainty upon employment and output.

## The Relationship Between Uncertainty and Employment

The basic theoretical apparatus to analyze the effects of increases in uncertainty on economic decisions was developed by Rothschild and Stiglitz (1971). The problem is stated as follows: an economic agent desires to maximize the expected value of some objective function by setting the level of some control variables. Let V $(\alpha,\lambda)$ be such a function where $\lambda$ is a random variable and $\alpha$ is the vector of control variables. Then the problem can be formally represented as follows:

$$\max_{\alpha} \int V(\alpha,\lambda)\, dF\lambda = \max_{\alpha} EV(\alpha,\lambda)$$

The first-order conditions for an optimal $\alpha$ are as follows:

$$E\frac{\delta V(\alpha,\lambda)}{\delta\alpha} = EV_{\alpha}(\alpha,\lambda) = 0$$

Assume that $\alpha^*$ is the unique solution to this set of equations and that they are decreasing in the vector $\alpha$.

An increase in uncertainty is formalized by adding to the stochastic variable under consideration another variable with a positive variance and zero expected value. This is known as a mean-preserving spread.

Then if $\alpha$ undergoes a mean-preserving spread and $\partial V(\alpha,\lambda)/\partial\alpha$ is concave on $\lambda$, $E_\alpha V(\alpha,\lambda)$ would become negative.[3] To reestablish the first-order conditions, $\alpha$ has to be decreased. The reverse is true for cases in which $\partial V(\alpha,\lambda)/\partial\alpha$ is convex.

All the reviewed papers on uncertainty and the demand for inputs can be thought of as presenting different scenarios in which $\partial V(\alpha,\lambda)/\partial\alpha$ is either concave or convex.

For the case of flexible factors, Sandmo (1971) and Batra and Ullah (1974) have shown that if the firm maximizes the expected value of profits, increases in uncertainty do not have any effect on the demand for factors. The effect on employment could only be negative if firms behave as risk averters; that is, they maximize the expected value of a utility function which is concave on profits.

The risk-averse behavior by firms may be a good assumption for owner-controlled firms or even for firms that maximize their market value in the presence of bankruptcy costs and implicit subsidies for debt financing.[4]

If capital is assumed to be a fixed factor and labor is assumed to be flexible (i.e., the level of employment is decided after the realization of the random variables, which may be either wages or prices), then the effects of uncertainty are ambiguous. Hartman (1976) shows that the sign of the effects depends on the characteristics of the production function and of the implicit utility function of the firm.

A more general approach would consider the reactions to uncertainty of both firms and workers. If the number of hours worked becomes more uncertain, then either workers have to be compensated by a higher wage or they negotiate contracts with lower wages but less uncertainty about the amount of working hours. This problem can be analyzed from the point of view of the theory of implicit contracts and wage bargaining of Azariadis (1975), Baily (1974), and Hall and Lilien (1979). We have not pursued this approach. In general the net effect on employment of an increase in uncertainty is ambiguous, depending on the relative risk aversion and bargaining power of both parties.

In summary, the effect of uncertainty on employment appears to be ambiguous. It depends on the shape of the production function and of the implicit utility functions.

A complete empirical test would involve deriving a demand for and a supply of labor from stochastic intertemporal optimization models of the firm and workers' behavior. These models should be rich enough to let the data determine the shapes of the above-mentioned functions jointly with the effect of uncertainty on employment.

Unfortunately, explicit solutions for stochastic nonlinear intertemporal models exist only for very restrictive cases. Primarily, analytical solutions exist for quadratic models. These are useless for our purposes since Theil (1957) has shown that certainty equivalence holds for these models; i.e., only the expected values of variables enter the decision rules.

## Measuring Uncertainty

From the review of the literature, it is apparent that changes in uncertainty about prices of inputs and outputs[5] will have some effect on the demand for labor. For workers, uncertainty about wages, hours worked, and prices of consumer goods is relevant in determining the supply of labor.

Therefore, there is some presumption that indeed uncertainty about these variables will affect the level of employment.

We propose two operational measures of uncertainty: the variance of the forecasting error in a time-series framework and the cross-section variability of relative prices.

### *A Time-Series Measure of Uncertainty*

The variance of the forecasting error is an attractive measure of uncertainty. It simply represents the degree of confidence with which economic agents can forecast the variables relevant to their decisions. Lower confidence in their forecast implies higher uncertainty about the future. To define this measure, we first present some standard notation.

Let $X_\tau$ be a stationary stochastic process generated by the following structure[6]:

$$X_\tau - \phi_1 X_{\tau-1} - \cdots - \phi_p X_{\tau-p} = \mu + \epsilon_\tau + \theta_1 \epsilon_{\tau-1} + \cdots + \theta_q \epsilon_{\tau-q}$$

where $\epsilon_t$ is the one-step-ahead forecasting error, with expected value equal zero and variance defined by $\sigma^2_\epsilon$. The multistep-ahead variance of the forecasting error is defined as

$$\sigma^2_F b_j = E_\tau (X_{\tau+j} - E_\tau X_{\tau+j})^2$$

where $X_{\tau+j}$ and $E_\tau X_{\tau+j}$ are the actual and forecasted values of $X_\tau$. $\sigma^2_{Fj}$ depends positively on $\sigma^2_\epsilon$.[7]

An additional component of the forecasting error is the error in estimating the parameters $\phi$ and $\theta$.

Furthermore, unanticipated shifts in the $\phi$s and $\theta$s would also increase the variance of the forecasting error. Such an increase would be transitory, and it would fade away as additional information to estimate the new

*TABLE 7.1.*
*Tests of Stability*[a] *(1969–1972 and 1973–1980)*

| | Calculated $\chi^2$ | $\chi^2$ for $\alpha = 0.05$ |
|---|---|---|
| *CP* | 44.52 | 5.99 |
| *WP* | 33.33 | 5.99 |
| *MS* | 9.40 | 9.49 |

[a] *CP, WP,* and *MS* are the consumer price index, the wholesale price index, and the money supply.

parameter values becomes available. Tests for changes in $\sigma_\epsilon^2$ and in the parameters $\phi$ and $\theta$ were performed with monthly data for the money supply and consumer and wholesale price indexes.

These tests are intended to shed some light on the behavior of macroeconomic uncertainty in the 1969–1980 period. The forecasting variances of many other variables are relevant for economic decisions in different sectors of the economy. Specifically, the forecasting variance of different relative prices should be considered. A measure that is related to such variance is presented in the next section.

The exact selection of the subperiods for these tests was somewhat arbitrary. It is based on visual inspection of the series and on some evidence of the changes in fiscal policy during the second year of Echeverría's government. The subperiods are from 1969 to 1972 and from 1973 to 1980.

Table 7-1 reports the tests of the stability of the parameters $\phi$ and $\theta$.[8] The $\chi^2$ calculated for these likelihood ratio tests[9] are significantly higher than the $\chi^2$ for $\alpha = 0.05$. Therefore, a significant change in the parameters did occur. This implies that there was a temporary increase in the variance of the forecasting error somewhere around 1973.

A change in the one-step-ahead variance of the forecasting error is also evident from Table 7-2. Therefore, it can be argued that there was a permanent increase in the variance of the forecasting error.

Our two tests provide some evidence of an increase in the variance of the forecasting error between the compared subperiods.

*TABLE 7.2.*
*Test for Changes in Variances*

| | Calculated *F* | *F* ($\alpha = 0.05$)[a] |
|---|---|---|
| *CP* | 7.97 | 1.69 |
| *WP* | 4.88 | 1.47 |
| *MS* | 2.32 | 1.39 |

[a] *CP, WP,* and *MS* are the consumer price index, the wholesale price index, and the money supply.

A full explanation of these changes in parameters requires the specification of a macro model. However, the reduced forms of many specifications would imply a positive relation between the forecasting variance of monetary and fiscal variables (as well as aggregate supply variables) and the forecasting variance of inflation.

### *A Cross-Section Measure of Uncertainty*

In the last section we showed some evidence of a worsening in the quality of aggregate variables forecast. Even if these variables have an important role in the economic environment, it is hard to see their direct relevance for economic decisions at the industry level.

Indeed, for a constant structure of relative prices an increase in the variance of the forecasting error of inflation would have little impact on production and employment decisions. Formally speaking, if the contemporaneous correlation of the forecasting errors of disaggregated nominal prices is 1 (high), then increases in the forecasting variance of inflation would have no (small) first-order effects on production.

Instead of undertaking the estimation of the stochastic structure of a large number of prices of different industries, we proceeded to use an alternative method. Theil[10] proposes a measure of the cross-section variability of relative prices.[11]

Let $P_{it}$ be the price of the $i$th commodity in time period $t$. The rate of change in the $i$th price between periods $t - 1$ and $t$, measured as the difference in the logarithms, will be denoted by $DP_{it}$. The aggregate price level (as in the case of the consumer price index) is denoted by $Pt$.

We define the aggregate inflation of the consumer price index as follows:

$$DP_t = \sum_{i=1}^{M} \frac{w_i P_{it}}{P_t} DP_{i,t}$$

where the $w_i$ stands for the fixed weight of the $i$th commodity in the consumer basket.

The measure of the variability of relative price changes between periods $t - 1$ and $t$ proposed by Theil is

$$VP_t = \sum_{i=1}^{M} w_i P_{it}(DP_{it} - DP_t)^2$$

The larger the variability of relative prices $(VP_t)$, the more nonproportional are the changes in prices relative to the common $DP_t$.

In Figure 7-1 we present the evolution of the inflation rate (as measured by the consumer price index) and the variance of relative price changes obtained from the disaggregated data on consumer prices. A correlation

**Figure 7-1. Consumer Price Index (Aggregate Series).**

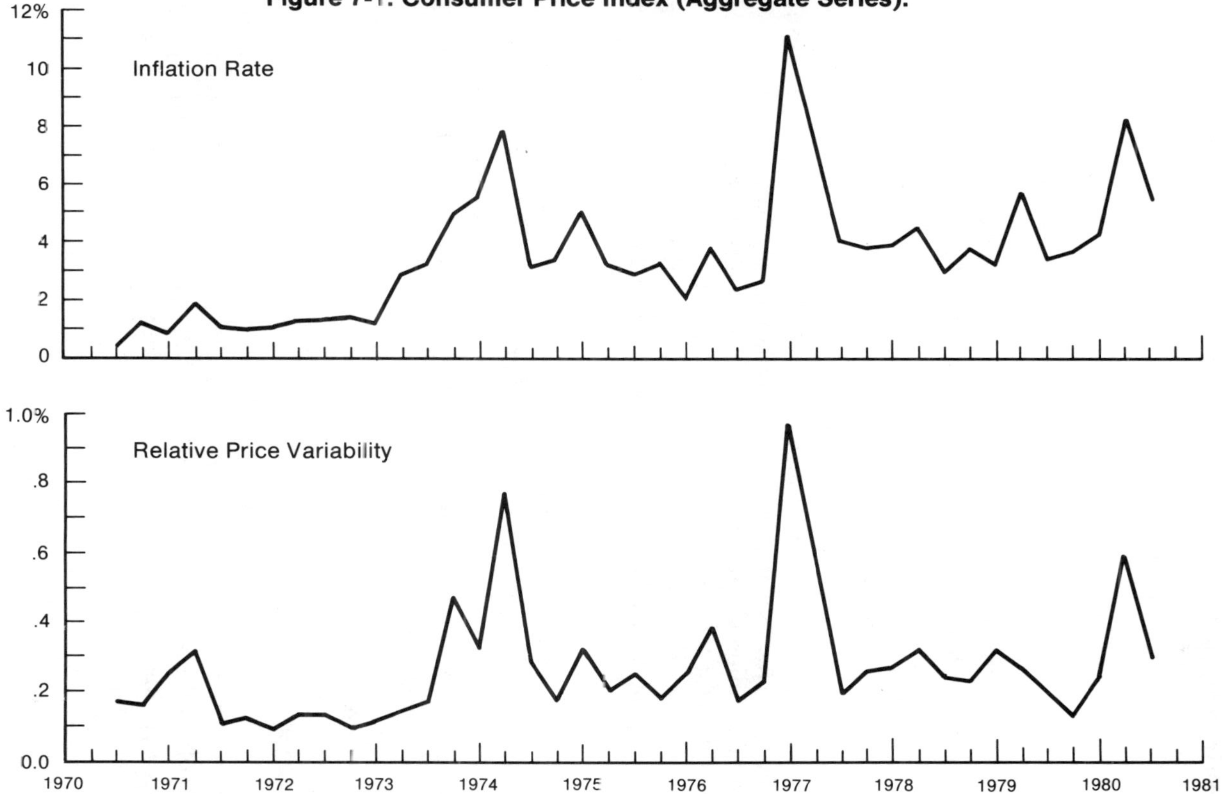


SOURCE: Banco de México, National Consumer Price Index.

between the average rate of inflation and the variability of relative price changes is apparent.

An increase in the average of the variability measure can be observed in Figure 7-1 after 1972. The hypothesis of stability of this measure across subperiods divided by 1972 is rejected by the data.[12]

## The Relationship Between the Rate of Inflation and the Variability of Relative Price Changes

One of the main hypotheses of modern macroeconomic theory (i.e., the theory of rational expectations) is that the behavior of the real variables of an economy (particularly the production of goods, employment, and relative prices) is independent of the anticipated movements of the nominal variables of the system.

In contrast to this anticipated or "pure" inflation, it has recently been postulated that due to the existence of imperfect information, the resulting unanticipated inflation affects the variability of relative prices.[13]

In this section we present some empirical results on the validity of this hypothesis for the case of the Mexican economy.

Our results validate the hypothesis that unanticipated inflation has an effect on the variability of relative prices. However, and in contrast to other studies for some industrial economies, we find that even the fully anticipated rate of inflation also affects relative prices. A plausible explanation of this fact is the existence of price controls. However, as will be seen below, our preliminary results are ambiguous.

The visual observation from Figure 7-1 is corroborated by the estimates with quarterly data of the following equation for the period $1969_{I}$–$1980_{II}$:

$$VP_t = \underset{(2.03)}{0.0003} + \underset{(9.77)}{0.0691}\, DP_t^2 + u_t$$

$$SSR = 0.00004$$
$$DW = 1.59$$
$$R^2 = 0.79$$

where the numbers in parentheses are the values for the $t$ test of the null hypothesis, $a_0 = 0$, $a_1 = 0$, respectively.

Table 7-3 reports our tests of the implications of the rational expectations hypothesis for the behavior of relative price variability. The estimated equation is

$$VP_t = b_0 + b_1[DP_t - E_{t-1}(DP_t)]^2 + b_2E_{t-1}(DP_t)^2$$

where $E_{t\text{-}1}$ (DP$_t$) is the inflation rate forecasted with the information available at $t$-1. Therefore, $DP_t - E_{t\text{-}1}$ DP$_t$ is the unexpected inflation rate. The forecasts of $DP_t$ were obtained from the following autoregressions:

$$E_{t-1}DP_t = \underset{(3.06)}{0.015} + \underset{(4.47)}{0.56}DP_{t-1} \quad \text{(Aggregate consumer price index)}$$
$$DW = 2.07 \quad R^2 = 32$$

$$E_{t-1}DP_t = \underset{(2.99)}{0.017} + \underset{(3.65)}{0.484}DP_{t-1} \quad \text{(controlled series)}$$
$$DW = 1.93 \quad R^2 = 0.23$$

$$E_{t-1}DP_t = \underset{(2.90)}{0.013} + \underset{(5.19)}{0.62}DP_{t-1} \quad \text{(free series)}$$
$$DW = 2.23 \quad R^2 = 0.39$$

Equations a, b, and c are, respectively, the estimates when *VP* and *DP* is computed using all the commodities, only those subject to control, and only those not subject to control of the consumer price index basket.

As predicted by the rational expectations hypothesis, the results of the first line of Table 7.3 show a $b_I$ that is positive and significantly different from zero; however, $b_2$ is also positive and significantly different from zero.

This puzzling result could be due to the existence of price controls. See Figures 7.2 and 7.3. To test this hypothesis, we separated the basket of commodities into those that were subject to controls and those that were not.

If indeed price controls are the explanation of our results, we should find that $b_2$ is positive for the first set of commodities and not significantly different from zero for the second one.

The results of the second and third lines of Table 7-3 do not reject our hypothesis, i.e., expected inflation is relevant only in determining relative price variability for commodities subject to price controls. However, preliminary testing with monthly data tends to reject our hypothesis. Further research into the dynamic structure and the functional form of this relation is needed before conclusive statements can be made.

*TABLE 7.3.*
*Quarterly Data: $1969_I$–$1980_{II}$*[a]

| *Equation* | $b_0$ | $b_1$ | $b_2$ | *SSR* | $R^2$ | DW |
|---|---|---|---|---|---|---|
| a. Aggregate index | 0.0016<br>(6.39) | 1.0410<br>(5.59) | 0.0660<br>(1.79) | 0.00006 | 0.49 | 2.09 |
| b. Controlled series | 0.0009<br>(2.50) | 0.4925<br>(4.14) | 0.8365<br>(4.69) | 0.00011 | 0.50 | 1.95 |
| c. Free series | 0.0023<br>(7.72) | 1.55<br>(5.81) | 0.035<br>(0.20) | 0.00006 | 0.45 | 1.64 |

[a] Estimation procedure: ordinary least squares.

**Figure 7-2. Consumer Price Index (Free Series).**

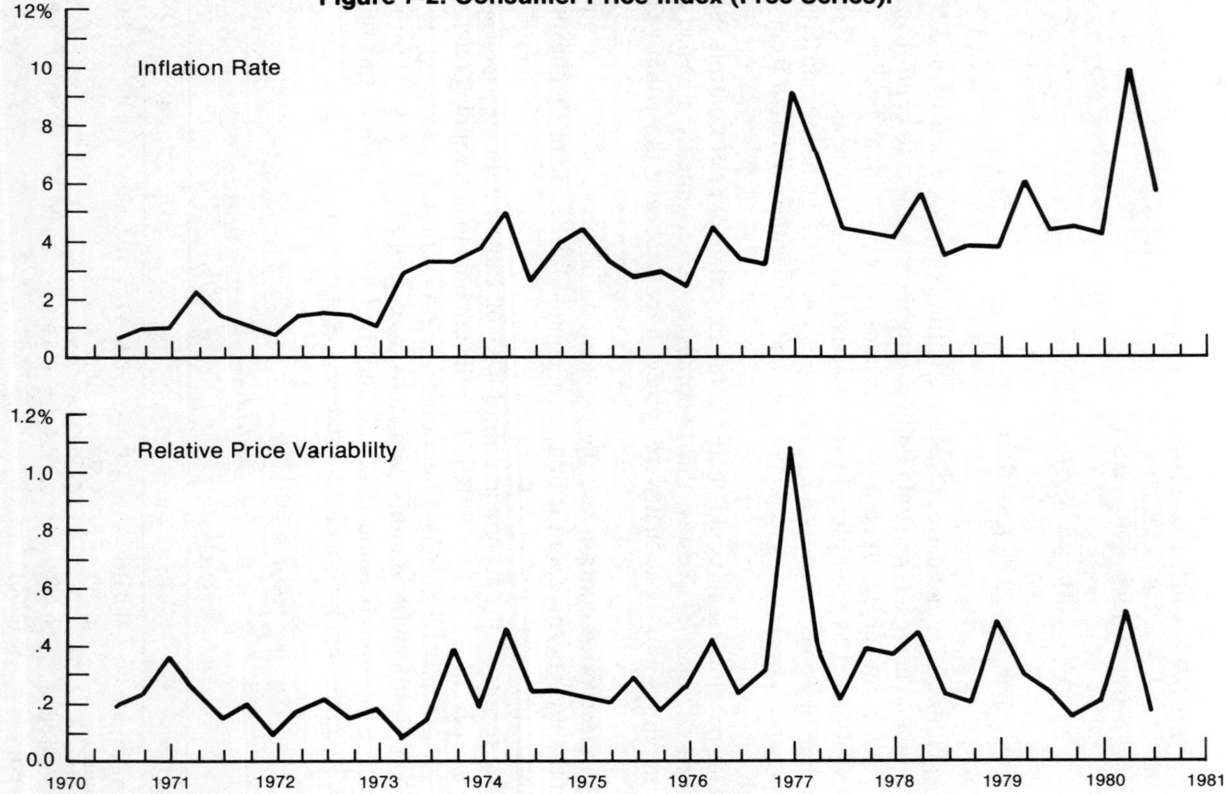


SOURCE: Banco de México, National Consumer Price Index.

**Figure 7-3. Consumer Price Index (Series of Prices Subject to Controls).**

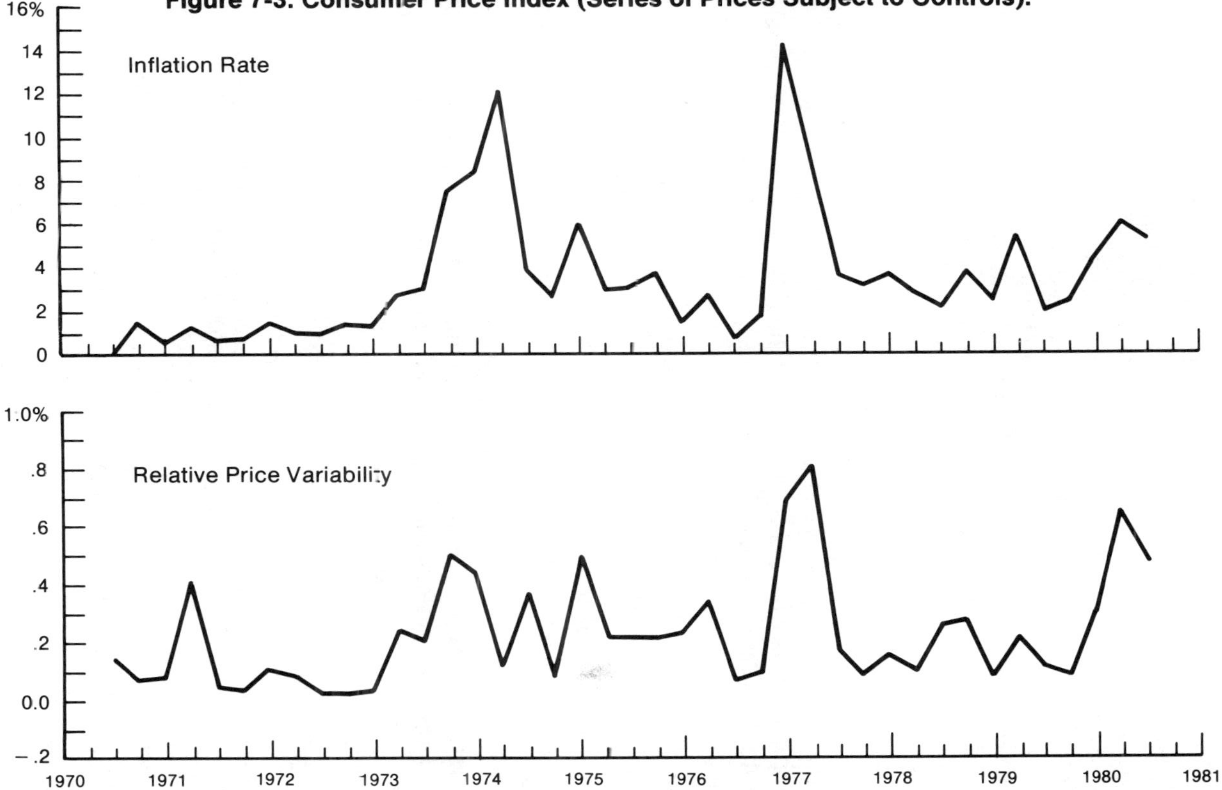


SOURCE: Banco de México, National Consumer Price Index.

## The Variability of Relative Prices and the Evolution of Output and Employment

The possibility that output and employment could be negatively correlated with the volatility of relative prices was originally pointed out by J. M. Keynes in his treatise on monetary reform (1924). Here Keynes postulated that large fluctuations in the relative values of commodities increase the costs associated with specialization and hence would provoke a slackened productive process. Along the same lines, Milton Friedman (1977) observed in his Nobel lecture that an increase in the volatility of the rate of inflation could cause an increase in the average level of unemployment through the occurrence of institutional changes which require the use of scarce resources and through the increased amount of noise in market signals which cause errors and use resources. However, as we argued in the first section, formal models that analyze the effects of increases in uncertainty yield ambiguous results.

Initially we perform a bivariate test of the relation between the variability of relative prices and output and employment:

$$Y_t = a_0 + a_1 VP_t + a_2 VP_{t-1} + a_3 T + u_t \quad (7)$$
$$h_t = b_0 + b_1 VP_t + b_2 VP_{t-1} + b_3 T + u_t \quad (8)$$

where $Y_t$ and $h_t$ denote the logs of real GDP and of working hours, respectively.[14] The estimates of the parameters of this regression are presented in Table 7-4.[15]

These results show that the variability of relative prices has a significantly negative effect both on output and employment. An additional test was performed using another version of the aggregate supply function[16]:

*TALBE 7.4.*
*The Effects of Relative Price Variability on Real Output and Employment: $1969_{III}$–$1980_{II}$ (Quarterly Data)*

| Dependent Variable | Constant | Time Trend | $VP_{t-1}$ | $R^2$ | SSR | SER | DW |
|---|---|---|---|---|---|---|---|
| Y | 10.80 | 0.013 | −6.51 | 0.97 | 0.024 | 0.026 | 2.35[a] |
| | (274.2) | (17.41) | (−2.34) | | | | |
| h | 9.93 | 0.009 | −6.80 | 0.94 | 0.026 | 0.027 | 1.93[a] |
| | (166.9) | (8.77) | (−1.76) | | | | |

[a]The equations were estimated by OLS and corrected by first-order serial correlation using the Cochrane-Orcutt procedure.

*TABLE 7.5.*

| *Equation* | $b_0$ | $b_1$ | $b_2$ | $b_3$ | $b_4 + b_5$ | *SSR* | $R^2$ | *Dh* |
|---|---|---|---|---|---|---|---|---|
| *(9)* | 6.3<br>(3.91) | 0.007<br>(3.93) | −0.09<br>(−0.74) | 0.41<br>(2.75) | −2.62<br>(−1.57) | 0.027 | 0.97 | −2.8 |

The equation incorporates the following hypothesis: 1 ($b_1 > 0$). As capital accumulates, the quantity of output produces increases ceteris paribus: 2 ($b_2 > 0$). Firms do not immediately adjust their level of output or employment due to costs of adjustments. Instead it is optimal to adjust them gradually: 3 ($b_3 > 0$). The rational expectations-natural rate or the long-term contracts hypothesis implies that firms will respond positively to errors in forecasting prices: 4 ($b_4 + b_5 < 0$). Uncertainty, as represented by the variability of relative prices, negatively affects the level of output.

The results of Table 7-5 show that $b_4 + b_5$ is negative and significantly different from zero.

Two additional results are worth mentioning. The Chow test rejects the null hypothesis of stability of the parameters across the subperiods, divided by 1972, and the unexpected change in the price level does not affect the level of output.[17] A plausible explanation is the simultancity problem[18] since the unanticipated inflation is not independent of the aggregate supply shocks which are included in $u_t$.

## Conclusions

The main achievement of this chapter is the evidence that it provides on two important questions: (1) Is the change in government economic policy that has occurred since 1972 correlated with higher economic uncertainty? (2) Is this increase in uncertainty correlated with decreases in aggregate output and employment?

Taking for granted the limitations of our theoretical and statistical work, we answer affirmatively to both questions. However, we want to emphasize that the evidence presented refers only to correlations and not necessarily to causality. Nevertheless, the evaluation of the financing of government expenditures should consider potential social costs implied by increases in economic uncertainty.

One of the main hypotheses of this chapter is that there is a positive correlation between employment in the modern sector and equality in personal income distribution. If indeed such a correlation exists, the potential social costs of government expenditure would not only involve the loss of output but also increases in the inequality of the distribution of income.

## Notes

1. See Pedro Aspe, *Una Visión Panorámica de la Distribución del Ingreso en México,* Independent Mexican Institute of Technology (ITAM), Mexico City, May 1980, mimeo.

2. For the evaluation of some of these programs, see Chapter 2.

3. This follows from Jensen's inequality. A proof appears in Hartman (1972).

4. The existence of bankruptcy costs limits the optimal debt-capital ratio. By decreasing the risk involved in its operation, the firm can raise its debt-capital ratio and take advantage of the tax subsidies for debt financing.

5. For firms behaving as monopsonists and/or monopolists, the uncertainty about variables shifting the supply of inputs and the demand for output would be relevant.

6. These parametrizations have been made popular by Box and Jenkins (1970). Alternative parametrizations such as multivariate autoregressions or multivariate Auto Regressive Moving Average models were not performed.

7. See Box and Jenkins (1970).

8. In the Box and Jenkins terminology the models that passed the different diagnostic checkings are the following: for *CP* an Auto Regressive Integrated Moving Average (1,1,12), for *WP* an ARIMA (1,1,0), and for *MS* an ARIMA (0,13,13). Autoregression for these three variables were also estimated. The results concerning the stability tests are the same. More extensive testing for other relevant variables is left for further research.

9. Define

$$\lambda = \frac{\max L_R}{\max L_u}$$

where $L_R$ and $L_u$ are the values of the likelihood function for the restricted and unrestricted cases, respectively. $-2\ln\lambda$ is distributed $\chi^2_K$, where $K$ is the number of restrictions.

10. Theil (1967).

11. This measure was used by Parks (1978).

12. A heuristic $t$ test (i.e., assuming that the variability measure is a well-behaved random variable) was performed and the null hypothesis at the 95 percent confidence level was rejected:

| Period | $VP_t$ |
|---|---|
| $1965_4$–$1972_{12}$ | 0.000629 |
| $1973_1$–$1980_6$ | 0.0011422 |

Estimated $t$ statistic: 139.57.

13. See Barro (1976). Causality in the other direction is possible. If one of the sources of information is to settle prices observed in the markets in which agents trade, then as *VP* increases, less information is obtained which could worsen the aggregate variables forecast.

14. The data on working hours were taken from the information provided by the *Encuesta Industrial Mensual,* published by the S.P.P.

15. The Chow test does not reject the null hypothesis at the 95 percent significance level.

16. Blejer and Leiderman (Nov. 1980) test this hypothesis for the United States assuming that $b_3 = 0$.

17. The last result differs from that of Blejer and Leiderman (July 1980), which was performed with annual data. Their paper came to our attention after the final draft of this chapter was finished.

18. Several econometric methods which deliver consistent estimators have been proposed in the literature. Work on this together with the respecification of the functional form and of the dynamic structure is left for future research.

## Bibliography


Azariadis, C. "Implicit Contracts and Underemployment Equilibria." *Journal of Political Economy* 83 (Dec. 1975), 1183–1202.

Baily, M. N. "Wages and Employment Under Uncertain Demand." *Review of Economic Studies* 41 (Jan. 1974), 37–50.

Banco de México, S.A. "Disaggregated Consumer Price Index and Wholesale Price Index," 1969–1980 (not published).

Barro, R. J. "Rational Expectations and the Role of Monetary Policy." *Journal of Monetary Economics* II (1976), pp. 1–32.

Batra, R. N., and Q. Ullah. "Competitive Firm and the Theory of Input Demand Under Price Uncertainty." *Journal of Political Economy* 82 (May 1974), 537–48.

Blejer, M., and Leiderman, L. "On the Real Effects of Inflation and Relative Price Variability: Some Empirical Evidence." *Review of Economics and Statistics* 62 (Nov. 1980), 539–544.

Blejer, M., and Leiderman, L. "Relative Price Variability and Output-Inflation Tradeoffs in the Mexican Economy," *Discussion Paper Series No. 43*. Boston: Center for Latin American Development Studies, Boston University, July 1980.

Box. G. E. P., and G. M. Jenkins. *Time Series Analysis: Forecasting and Control*. San Francisco: Holden-Day, Inc., 1970.

Friedman, Milton. "Nobel Lecture: Inflation and Unemployment." *Journal of Political Economy* 58 (June 1977), 451–472.

Hall, R. E., and D. M. Lilien. "Efficient Wage Bargains Under Uncertain Supply and Demand." *American Economic Review* 69 (Dec. 1979), 868–879.

Hartman, R. "The Effects of Price and Cost Uncertainty on Investment." *Journal of Economic Theory* 5 (1972), 258–266.

Hartman, R. "Factor Demand with Input Price Uncertainty." *American Economic Review* 66 (Sept. 1976), 675–681.

Keynes, J. M. *Monetary Reform*. New York: Harcourt, Brace, 1924.

Lucas, R. E., Jr. "Some International Evidence of Output-Inflation Tradeoffs." *American Economic Review* 63 (June 1973), 326–334.

Parks, R. W. "Inflation and Relative Price Variability." *Journal of Political Economy* 86 (Feb. 1978), 79–96.

Rothschild, M. and J. E. Stiglitz. "Increasing Risk II: Its Economic Consequences." *Journal of Economic Theory* 197, No. 3 (1971), 66–84.

Salih, N. "A Time Series Analysis of the Real Wages—Employment Relationship." *Journal of Political Economy* 86, No. 2, Pt. 1 (April 1978), 281–291.

Sandmo, A. "Competitive Firm Under Price Uncertainty." *American Economic Review* 61 (March 1971), 65–73.

Sargent, T. J. "Rational Expectations, and Real Rate of Interest and the Natural Rate of Unemployment." *Brookings Papers on Economic Activity* 4 (1973), 429–479.

Secretariat of Planning and National Budget. *Estadística Industrial Mensual.* Federal District of Mexico, 1969–1981, monthly publication.

Taylor, J. B. "On the Relation Between the Variability of Inflation and the Average Inflation Rate." *Carnegie Rochester Conference Series on Public Policy* 15 (1981), 57–86.

Theil, H. "A Note in Certainty Equivalence in Dynamic Planning." *Económetrica* 25 (April 1957), 316–349.

Theil, H. *Economics and Information Theory*. Chicago: Rand McNally, 1967.

# CHAPTER 8

# *The Impact of Foreign Trade and Export Strategies on Distribution of Income for Low-Income Households in Mexico*

Clark Reynolds, Raul Ramos, and Robert McCleery

Our conclusions are twofold: As of the end of 1980, Mexico had allowed the peso-dollar exchange rate to appreciate to a level which seriously diminishes both the profitability of exporting and the positive effect of nonpetroleum export sector job creation on the incomes of Mexico's poor. A mitigating factor is that altering the current structure of protection could give rise to a substantial increase in employment of unskilled labor. The bottom line is that even with a very optimistic forecast of unskilled labor demanded by the Mexican economy to the year 1990, estimated supply will exceed demand by at least two million workers. The events of 1982 strengthen both the analysis and the policy implications of the study.

The present study is a composite of several components of analysis dealing with the pattern of relationships among economic growth and structural change, trade patterns and policies, and the level and distribution of income of unskilled labor. The analysis pursues a general model which may be termed *full exchange* in which a range of degrees of openness of the economy is considered, from zero trade in goods and services, migration, finance and direct international investment, and technological transfers (complete autarky) to completely free exchange in all these areas (full exchange). Clearly neither extreme is acceptable to those wishing to protect national or regional interests in terms of economics, culture, social structure, or political power. The crucial issue is the degree to which exchange should be opened in the several areas and what are the complementarities or competitive elements associated with the various flows among themselves. In this chapter, one particular dimension is highlighted, that of income of so-called "unskilled" labor. It is certain the term *unskilled* is inappropriate, since it is often made synonymous with labor whose skills command almost no market value (e.g., van Gogh in his lifetime). It is clear that the relationship between value and skill needs more attention than can be given here. However, without going into such issues, we are concerned, on a more pedestrian level, with the income of labor receiving the lowest income, both rural and urban in origin, and the way in which a variety of policies pursued or contemplated in comtemporary Mexico might affect the wages and incomes of Mexico's poor.[1] Section I treats the concept of full exchange and its implications for Mexican employment under a variety of exchange relationships through trade, migration, and investment. Here the employment impact is measured very roughly, by broad sectorial categories, and without distinguishing between skilled and unskilled labor. It is shown that the direct employment impact of trade in goods and services is rather small, except in the case of *maquiladoras* (plants which process intermediate imports for reexport),where there has been substantial growth and where future growth prospects are significant. By the same token, investment by the United States and other foreign countries has had little direct employment impact except through the *maquiladora* program.

Migration, most of which is temporary rather than permanent, is shown to have a large and growing direct impact on lower-income households as well as indirectly on those with the lowest incomes through the consumption multiplier of remittances of migrant workers (since migrant workers are generally at an income level somewhat higher than the poorest socioeconomic stratum). Migration is almost certain to remain an important element in the tightening of the market for unskilled labor since it responds to the large absolute wage differential for similar work between the United States and Mexico.[2] Section II (prepared by Raul Ramos) presents a general equilibrium model of growth and employment in Mexico based on a comprehensive analysis of the interindustry relations (using the 1970 input-output table updated to 1978) and the implications of the industrial plan projections of investment and output for employment of unskilled labor through 1990 under two alternative simulations. The first simulation maintains current patterns of relative prices and protection of tradeables; the second moves toward more equal rates of protection by reducing protection in the heavily protected sectors such as metals and machinery and increasing protection (often a decrease in negative effective protection) afforded to agriculture, mining, food, and wood products. Prices in the nontradeables sectors are allowed to equilibrate in response to market forces. While this model does not directly address the questions of overall trade policy or income distribution, it does provide important insights into those intersectorial relationships that lead to a tightening or slackening of demand for unskilled labor. We regard the wage impact of the adjustment of the labor market for unskilled workers to be one of the most important mechanisms through which policies affecting structural changes in the economy as a whole are able to raise the income of low-income households.

This section examines some implications of various degrees of interdependence between the two countries given their respective economic and political goals. Special attention is paid to the fact that interdependence proceeds from very different levels of wages, per capita income, and wage shares of national income north and south of the border. The implications of varying degrees of interdependence on the level and distribution of wages, profits, and rents are of particular concern. Changes in these factor shares are likely to arise through the process of international interdependence, just as they have occurred regionally through national integration of the two economies. What implications will this have on the welfare of both partners? Are wages in the two countries likely to converge during this process, and, if so, how sensitive might such a process of leveling be to alternative policies affecting international trade, migration, investment, and technology transfer? Finally, how might their respective policies be expected to deal with increasing interdependence?

## I. From Zero to Full Exchange: A Conceptual Framework[3]

The method of analysis used in this study employs at one extreme an approach to the effect of trade and development on wages and profits introduced by the Swedish economists, Heckscher and Ohlin. In their view, trade occurs in response to differences in relative factor prices of the trading partners which reflect their respective endowments of labor, capital, land, technology, and tastes providing gains from specialization along the lines of comparative advantage. Formalized versions of their approach were developed by Samuelson and Lerner to show that under certain highly restrictive assumptions trade alone might cause wages and profit rates to equalize between trading partners even in the absence of migration or capital flows.[4] While these formalizations of the *factor price equalization theorem* abstract considerably from reality, the original Heckscher and Ohlin approach was more dynamic, based at least in part on the economic history of Sweden. Over the past several hundred years, Sweden has advanced from medieval agrarianism, through the export of copper, iron ore, timber, and other primary products, to the present stage of highly advanced industrialization. This growth of production and trade in Sweden was accompanied by a demographic explosion in the nineteenth to early twentieth centuries as overwhelming in relative terms as that of Mexico today. However, in the last century opportunities existed for Swedish labor to migrate to the United States, Canada, and other newly opening areas.

In addition to increased trade and outmigration of "excess" labor, Sweden possessed an economic and social system capable of generating significant technological innovation. With these innovations came considerable local entrepreneurship and financial capital capable of transforming technology and ideas into profitable ventures. Resource rents and profits from innovations permitted Sweden's evolution from an initially raw material and primary product-based economy to one which specialized in the manufacture of intermediate and final goods. Much of the surplus generated by the process was accumulated and invested in further development of the economy as well as in productivity-enhancing economic and social infrastructure including highly advanced public education. As a result, Sweden's initially low real wages and incomes rose to among the highest in the world in little more than a century. Not surprisingly, Heckscher and Ohlin attributed much of this progress to the gains from trade. But migration, capital mobilization, and improved technology were essential complements to the exchange of goods and services.

For Sweden, the process of exchange, while never laissez-faire, was relatively free. But its rapid growth took place in a different economic and political era from the politically charged and economically interdependent world of today. Even if this economic miracle could be repeated today, it would involve significant noneconomic costs. All we are trying to do is estimate the economic benefit to increased exchange, so that it can be compared to the noneconomic costs, leading to an informed decision by policymakers.

The case of complete freedom of movement of goods, services, labor, capital, and technology may be termed *full exchange*. In practice, every economy finds itself somewhere between the extremes of zero and full exchange given its location, size, income, tastes, and policies affecting trade, migration, and investment. Stated in its broadest form, the Heckscher-Ohlin proposition might read as follows: As two markets approach full exchange, their respective wage and profit rates will tend to converge until they are separated only by an amount reflecting transport and other relocation costs of goods and factors, including the subjective preferences of workers in the low-wage and low-income economy not to migrate to the high-wage economy and the discounts placed by capital holders on international relocation of their assets. Hence for wages of unskilled labor, migration may be said to be the ultimate equalizing factor. Labor will tend to migrate from a lower- to a higher-wage economy even after both have approached complete specialization in production in their respective areas of comparative advantage if wages have not yet converged. The original perspectives of Heckscher and Ohlin that a historical process of structural change would lead to a gradual equalization of factor prices was not static. Such a dynamic perspective is most applicable to contemporary relations between Mexico and the United States.

The concepts of zero to full exchange are employed here to accommodate the full range of possibilities of exchange between two economies through trade, labor migration, finance and direct investment, and technology transfer. The expansion of the concept of *free trade* to one of *full exchange* recognizes that the latter is simply an extreme in the range of degrees of exchange. Its use is by no means designed to advocate laissez-faire but rather to provide a framework within which the effects of various types of exchange can be examined and the consequences of various degrees of openness tested. Indeed, one of the basic issues to be explored is the degree of exchange that would be socially and politically optimal for the two countries, given their different situations, institutions, and values. While no consensus is either intended or expected, the object is to encourage a range of economic and sociopolitical analyses in order to clarify the options. Policymakers may then draw on these studies as they seek to harmonize the development of the two countries while minimizing frictions that are bound to arise as forces of interdependence clash with those of autarky.

## *The Four Dimensions of Economic Exchange*

While the exchange of values, tastes, and ideology may well prove to be one of the most important elements in the evolving relationship between the United States and Mexico, we shall stress the four more basic economic dimensions of exchange: trade, migration, finance, and technology transfer. Though no more than an introduction of the problem is possible in the scope of this chapter, it is hoped that the issues raised will stimulate further research. The main focus here is upon the employment implications of the process of exchange, including the likely effect of tightness or slackness of the respective labor markets on the wages of unskilled workers in both countries. It is assumed that only if the labor market tightens at the lower end will the wage component of *factor price equalization* occur for unskilled labor both within Mexico and between Mexico and the United States. Hence development policies affecting labor demand in both countries are seen to be central to the goal of growth with equity which underlies both Mexican and United States development policy. As a result, policies affecting the four dimensions of exchange are viewed primarily in terms of their impact on the demand for unskilled labor.

### *Trade*[5]

A fundamental premise of the full exchange approach used here is that the processes of trade and migration cannot be completely separated in the case of the two adjacent economies such as Mexico and the United States where labor is relatively free to move. The formalized Heckscher-Ohlin model argues that given common technologies, factor qualities, production of tradeable goods, and incomplete specialization (plus a number of other strong assumptions), increased trade will lead to factor price convergence even without the need for movement of factors between the two economies. When one adds the possibilities of migration of labor to the capital-abundant economy and of capital to the labor-abundant economy, as in the case of Mexico and the United States, and in the absence of major differences in resource endowments, factor price convergence should accelerate. Why, then, have the wages of unskilled labor between Mexico and the United States remained at a gap of seven to one or moreover so many generations?

First, there has never been completely free trade between the two countries at any point in history and especially today. In the past, barriers of distance, culture, transport costs, and language stood between the two economies even when legal barriers to migration or investment were minimal. Today both the United States and Mexico impose considerable obstacles to trade, with the degree of effective protection higher in the latter, and both have restricted labor migration with Mexico protecting skilled labor and the United States attempting to limit the inflow of unskilled labor.

In addition, a large and growing share of the output and employment of the two economies is in the production of nontradeables such as services, so that the United States is becoming a high-wage service economy and Mexico a low-wage service economy. Without migration there is less of a tendency for the price of nontradeables to converge between the two countries or for the prices of factors employed in such markets to converge unless employment conditions tighten considerably within Mexico or slacken within the United States. Also the technologies of the two countries are far from equal. Finally, in the past, natural resource endowments have tended to favor the United States especially in agriculture, though in the future Mexico's vast mineral and hydrocarbon reserves may shift the balance.

The existence of multiple factors of production, including labor of varied skills, natural resources, and capital of different vintages and qualities, greatly complicates the applicability of simple factor price equalization theories. In addition, different patterns of accumulation, investment, and research and development change the structure of each economy from period to period, providing additional complications. Mexico's current development plans, which call for a fourfold increase in GNP in 20 years, plus a demographically induced doubling of the work force are sure to generate wage and employment effects that will eclipse the results of present trade policy or reasonable alternatives. But when one combines the employment effects of alternative trade policies with their implications for growth and productivity in the long run, the degree of efficiency in use of the nation's resources will almost certainly have a substantial impact upon eventual employment, income distribution, and welfare. If strategies are pursued which favor a pattern of growth that overutilizes capital and underutilizes abundant labor and distorts the distribution of income away from the working class, this will increase pressures for

*TABLE 8.1.*
*Sectorial Definitions, Employment, and Labor Intensity: 1970*

| *Sector* | *Activity* | *Workers (Thousand Man-years)* | *Man-years of Labor Per Million Pesos of Product* |
|---|---|---|---|
| 1 | Agriculture, hunting, forestry, and fishing | 4,466.8 | 43.0 |
| 2 | Mining and quarrying (excluding petroleum extraction) | 74.5 | 7.9 |
| 3 | Extraction and refining of petroleum and natural gas | 89.3 | 6.8 |
| 4 | Food products, beverages, and tobacco | 450.1 | 24.2 |
| 5 | Textiles, articles of clothing, and other products | 341.2 | 14.5 |
| 6 | Wood related industries and products | 99.7 | 19.2 |
| 7 | Fabrication of paper and paper products | 92.9 | 12.7 |
| 8 | Fabrication of chemicals, rubber, and plastics | 174.5 | 8.7 |
| 9 | Fabrication of nonmetallic minerals except the derivatives of petroleum and carbon | 122.4 | 11.4 |
| 10 | Basic metal industries | 63.1 | 6.3 |
| 11 | Fabrication of metallic products, machinery, and equipment | 362.5 | 11.2 |
| 12 | Nontradeable goods | 6,121.2 | 14.2 |
| Total | | 12,458.2 | 17.5 |

SOURCE: The 1970 sectorial labor force breakdown was obtained from Mexican government sources. The labor intensities in the final column are estimates obtained by completely inverting a twelve-sector input-output table of the Mexican economy aggregated from Table I.1 in *Matriz de Insumo-Productor de Mexico año 1970,* Banco de México, p. 73.

migration and expand the demand for foreign investment, defeating Mexico's goal of national autonomy and lessened external dependence.

We have made some rough estimates of the employment implications of recent trends in Mexico's foreign trade. The figures indicate that although exports remain relatively labor intensive, the pattern of trade may well have retarded the growth of employment as a whole. Table 8-1 provides data on the labor used to generate one million pesos of final product in the different sectors of the Mexican economy in 1970. Agriculture (1) is the most labor-intensive sector, using 43 man-years of labor per million pesos of product, almost twice as much as the sector of next highest intensity, 24.2 man-years in processed foods (4). The only other sector whose labor

TABLE 8.2.

*Exports and Employment Generated: 1960–1975*

| | *1960* | | *1970* | | *1975* | |
|---|---|---|---|---|---|---|
| | *Value of Exports (Millions of 1970 Pesos)* | *Estimated Labor Embodied (Thousand Man-years)* | *Value of Exports (Millions of 1970 Pesos)* | *Estimated Labor Embodied (Thousand Man-years)* | *Value of Exports (Millions of 1970 Pesos)* | *Estimated Labor Embodied (Thousand Man-years)* |
| 1. Agriculture | 5,009 | 215.4 | 5,461 | 234.8 | 5,552 | 238.7 |
| 2. Mining and quarrying | 1,370 | 10.9 | 914 | 7.3 | 1,397 | 11.1 |
| 3. Petroleum and natural gas | 343 | 2.4 | 480 | 3.3 | 3,472 | 23.8 |
| 4. Food, tobacco, and beverages | 690 | 16.7 | 2,274 | 55.0 | 1,777 | 43.0 |
| 5. Textiles | 3,523 | 50.9 | 609 | 8.8 | 1,104 | 16.0 |
| 6. Wood and wood products | 72 | 1.0 | 96 | 1.8 | 137 | 2.6 |
| 7. Paper and paper products | | | 336 | 4.3 | 239 | 3.0 |
| 8. Chemicals (rubber, plastic, etc.) | 245 | 2.1 | 1,778 | 15.5 | 1,998 | 17.4 |
| 9. Nonmetallic mineral fabrication | 108 | 1.2 | 224 | 2.5 | 285 | 3.2 |
| 10. Basic metals | 988 | 6.3 | 1,618 | 10.3 | 2,084 | 13.2 |
| 11. Machines and equipment | 436 | 4.9 | 2,242 | 25.0 | 2,605 | 29.1 |
| Total | 12,784 | 311.8 | 16,016 | 368.7 | 20,649 | 401.2 |
| Export sector ratio | 24.4 | | 23.0 | | 19.4 | |
| Ratio for entire Mexican economy | 17.5 | | | | | |
| Ratio for tradeable goods sector of Mexican economy | 17.3 | | | | | |

SOURCE: Total value of exports and their sectorial breakdown are from *United Nations Trade Statistics*, 1978, 1973, and 1963. 1960 and 1975 figures have been converted to 1970 pesos by means of a sectorial implicit price deflator series found in *Información Económica-Producto Interno Bruto y Gasto*, Banco de México, 1979. Labor embodied is computed from export values by means of the sectorial labor ratios in Table 8 1. Estimates of labor embodied for 1960 and 1975 are computed assuming no growth in the productivity of labor. See Table 8 5 for estimates which reflect likely growth of labor productivity.

intensity exceeds the average for the economy as a whole is wood processing (6), which, like food processing, is a heavy user of agricultural output as inputs into its production process. The sectors which stand out as the least labor intensive are basic metal industries (10) at 6.3 man-years per million pesos and the petroleum sector (3) at 6.8. Both sectors are well under half the average of 17.5 man-years for the Mexican economy as a whole.

Table 8-2 extends the analysis to estimate the amount of labor required to produce the observed level of exports, by production sector, for 1960, 1970, and 1975. Without taking into consideration likely productivity growth, labor embodied in Mexican exports is estimated to have grown by 1.3 percent per annum between 1960 and 1975. This compares unfavorably, in terms of labor absorption, with an estimated 2.8 percent average growth rate of employment in the economy as a whole over the same period. In other words, in terms of labor utilization, the export sector expanded at half the rate of the economy at large. Although it did remain relatively more labor intensive, it was becoming less so. Since the same (1970) labor coefficients are used for each year in Table 8-2 despite likely productivity growth, labor use is probably understated in 1960 and overstated in 1975.

Table 8-3 extends the analysis of Table 8-2 to the years 1979 and 1980, for which the data are more preliminary and in more aggregate form, and to 1990, for which projections based on recent trends are made. Again, these tables do not reflect the growth of labor productivity Mexico experienced and will continue to experience over this period, as reflected in Table 8-5. But it is clear that despite a brief surge following the devaluation, both agricultural and manufacturing exports, which have traditionally employed the majority of export sector workers, are declining. Through 1980, the strong growth in petroleum exports and employment more than made up for this decline. The employment rise, however, has been much less than the phenomenal growth in export value might indicate, as non-labor-intensive exports replace those which are labor intensive.

Table 8-4 shows the period 1975–1981 in more detail. Three 2-year subperiods suggest themselves: rapid rise in nonextractive exports from 1975 to 1977 reflecting the 1976 devaluation, slower growth in 1978–1979 as the peso began to become overvalued, and absolute decline thereafter as the appreciation of the peso relative to Mexico's major trading partners continued. The devaluation of the peso in February 1982 went beyond purchasing power parity limits. If subsequent exchange rate policy permits the real devaluation to be maintained, our projections for 1990 may yet be reached. However, if the real exchange rate is once again permitted to appreciate, it is unlikely that nonextractive exports will become the dynamic employment generators they were in 1975–1977.

Table 8-5 takes into account the approximate level of productivity

TABLE 8.3.

*Exports and Employment Generated: 1979–1990*

| | *1970* | | *1980* | | *1990* | |
|---|---|---|---|---|---|---|
| | *Value of Exports (Millions of 1970 Pesos)* | *Estimated Labor Embodied (Thousand Man-years)* | *Value of Exports (Millions of 1970 Pesos)* | *Estimated Labor Embodied (Thousand Man-years)* | *Projected Value of Exports (Millions of 1970 Pesos)* | *Estimated Labor Embodied (Thousand Man-years)* |
| Agriculture (1) | 10,284 | 442.21 | 7,207 | 309.9 | | |
| Mining (2) | 1,835 | 14.6 | 2,347 | 18.6 | | |
| Petroleum (3) | 21,767 | 149.1 | 46,104 | 315.8 | | |
| Manufacturing (4–11) | 16,976 | 211.7 | 15,769 | 196.7 | | |
| Total | 50,870 | 817.5 | 71,442 | 841.0 | 175,000 | A: 2046.2<br>B: 1537.7 |
| Average man-years per million pesos of exports | 16.07 | | 11.77 | | A: 11.77<br>B: 8.79 | |

SOURCE: Table 8 1. and Banco de México, *Indicadores Económicos* for the relevant years. Estimates A and B are based on the extractive and nonextractive breakdown in Table 8 4. The total value of exports estimate is a projection first done in "Labor Market Projections for the United States and Mexico and Their Relevance to Current Migration Controversies" by C. W. Reynolds in *Food Research Institute Studies* 17, No. 2 (1979) Stanford University, Stanford.

TABLE 8.4.

*Value of Extractive and Nonextractive Exports and the Appreciation of the Real Exchange Rate*

| | 1975 | 1976 | 1977 | 1978 | 1979 | 1980 | (est.) 1981 | (est.) 1996 |
|---|---|---|---|---|---|---|---|---|
| Nonextractive exports | | | | | | | | |
| Value (millions of pesos) | 17,150 | 22,000 | 26,960 | 27,850 | 29,100 | 25,340 | 23,500 | A: 62,000<br>B: 25,000 |
| Percent increase or decrease | | 28 | 33 | 3 | 4 | −13 | −7 | |
| Extractive exports | | | | | | | | |
| Value (millions of 1970 pesos) | 3,500 | | | | 21,770 | 46,100 | 61,500 | A: 113,000<br>B: 150,000 |
| End-of-period actual peso/dollar exchange rate | | | 22.74 | 22.72 | 22.80 | 23.36 | 23.7 | |
| Ratio of Mexican consumer price index to the U.S. consumer price index | | | $\frac{100}{100}$ | $\frac{117.5}{109.0}$ | $\frac{138.9}{123.5}$ | $\frac{175.4}{137.5}$ | $\frac{203.5}{148.4}$ | |
| Correct nominal exchange rate if no change in the real rate occurs | | | 22.74 | 24.52 | 25.57 | 29.02 | 31.2 | |
| Percentage appreciation in the real exchange rate since 1977 | | | | 8 | 12 | 28 | 37 | |

SOURCE: Banco de México, *Indicadores Económicos*, and *The Economic Report of the President* (U.S.), for the U.S. Consumer Price Index. Line 6 is equal to line 5 multiplied by 22.74. Line 7 is equal to line 5 minus 1. Projections A and B are as in Table 8-1.

*TABLE 8.5.*
*Labor Embodied in Exports: 1970–1990*
*(Assuming a 2 Percent Productivity Growth Rate)*

| | *1970* | *1975* | *1979* | *1980* | *1990* |
|---|---|---|---|---|---|
| Value of exports (millions of 1970 pesos) | 16,016 | 20,649 | 50,870 | 71,442 | 175,000 |
| Labor multiplier | 23.0 | 18.5 | 14.7 | 9.7 | A: 7.9<br>B: 5.9 |
| Labor embodied (thousand man-years) | 368.7 | 363.4 | 684.1 | 690.0 | A: 1,386.4<br>B: 1,034.8 |
| Trade share of GDP (export value/GDP) (percent) | 7.35 | | | 7.55 | 9.85 |

SOURCES AND ASSUMPTIONS: Value of export figures are from Tables 8.2 and 8.3. Estimates A and B are defined as in Tables 8.1 and 8.4. It is assumed that growth of labor productivity is constant through time and across sectors at 2 percent per year or that deviations from this trend are small and nonsystematic. A simple approximation of the growth of labor productivity can be obtained by dividing an index of real gross domestic product (GDP) by an index of the labor force. For Mexico during the period from 1971 to 1980, this yields an approximate yearly labor productivity growth rate of 2.5 percent. 1990 GDP is estimated by projecting a growth rate of 6.6 percent per year for the period 1980–1990.

growth experienced by Mexico in the last decade and projects this growth to 1990. Of course, the effect on productivity growth is to reduce the amount of labor required to produce a given amount of product.

Estimates A and B in the last column of Tables 8-3 and 8-5 present two possible scenarios leading to year 1990. In case A, revenue from petroleum exports continues to expand as a needed source of foreign exchange but is not allowed to swamp the growth of other exports which are more effective in utilizing unskilled labor, the basis of Mexico's comparative advantage with the developed world. The export sector, in this case, contributes more than its share to rapid employment growth, absorbing both the multitude of new entrants and returning migrants from the United States. This is not to say that the export sector alone can solve Mexico's coming challenges, but it can be a strong, positive force instead of a drag on employment creation.

In estimate B, revenue from petroleum is allowed to dominate total exports, with the exchange rate diverging from the ratio of the purchasing power of the two currencies at the same rate as between 1976 and 1982. In this scenario, the rapid (9.5 percent per year) growth of exports would yield only a modest (4 percent per year) growth of employment, in the same manner that 16 percent annual export growth generated only 6.5

percent employment growth in the prior decade. Thus projected employment growth in the export sector in this scenario is below not only the rate of growth necessary for the economy as a whole to absorb new entrants plus returning migrants (6 percent per year) but below that rate which will employ simply the new entrants plus those currently unemployed or underemployed (4.4 percent per year). There is also the problem that the jobs being made available in the petroleum sector do not match the skills of the people looking for work, which would exacerbate the degree of structural unemployment and necessitate major training programs. In conclusion, it seems that trade policy is strongly linked to the degree of employment of unskilled labor and to the income share of the Mexican poor. The export sector has the potential to play a greater role in factor price narrowing between the two countries, a role largely assumed by migration. Trade make the benefits of foreign markets available even to those too poor to relocate physically to another country.

Since increasing reliance on oil-related exports will exacerbate the shift factor, it is clear that the recent trend in Mexican trade away from labor-intensive exports, including agricultural commodities, toward oil and gas should be slowed or mitigated by strong programs of job creation subsidized by the petroleum rents.[6] While the government ceiling for petroleum export contracts was 1.5 million barrels per day in February 1981, actual exports were somewhat less. There is a continuing debate on whether the export platform should be increased significantly, and as of mid-1982 it did not appear that exports would exceed 2 million barrels per day in the near future. Until February 1982, foreign exchange earnings generated by hydrocarbon exports plus associated borrowing permitted the peso exchange rate to be supported at a level which, given high and rising rates of domestic inflation relative to the major industrial countries, progressively overvalued its purchasing power relative to other international currencies. This gradual revaluation of the peso since 1976 worked against nonpetroleum exports and offset policies designed to protect import-competing activities. Though this, too, is debated, Mexican trade appears to be relatively price elastic. Evidence for the 1976 devaluation showed sharply increased exports and reduced imports (though the deflationary effect of devaluation on the economy as a whole also had a major negative effect on import demand that is difficult to separate from the price effect of devaluation). If trade is to have a significant impact on employment in the future, oil export revenues cannot be allowed to distort the exchange rate or to permit a continuation of relative price bias against agriculture and other labor-intensive activities. A blessing in disguise may be the fact that the foreign debt as of 1982 will virtually exhaust oil revenues. Oil has been substituting for other, more labor-intensive, exports, but with a real appreciation of the exchange rate in February and August 1982, plus the imposition of exchange controls, it is possible that nonoil exports can recover and grow at impressive rates, provided that the peso is allowed to adjust to inflation in the future in a more consistent manner than in the past.

Not only do oil exports create relatively few jobs per unit of final output, but the types of jobs created do less to help the distribution of income in Mexico than job creation in any other tradeable goods sector. Of 1000 jobs created by increased oil exports, 108 of them are for highly skilled technical and professional people, and only 716 are for unskilled laborers. Clearly, Mexico's secondary concern is to upgrade the quality and pay of unskilled labor, but its primary concern must be to employ the unemployed, including those laid off by the collapse of inefficient industries and government infrastructure projects in the 1982 crisis. Increased demand for the highly skilled has had the negative effect of increasing wages of the already well-to-do and causing some technicians to be imported from foreign countries. At the opposite end of the spectrum is the agricultural sector in which every 1000 new jobs are divided between highly skilled and unskilled in the proportion of 4 to 987. Increasing production in the agricultural sector brings about a larger increase in total employment and favors that type of employment which helps tighten the labor market at the lower end thereby improving the distribution of income. Section II deals directly with this skilled-unskilled dichotomy.[7]

Oil could become a useful source of foreign exchange, without sacrificing the goals of employment and improved income distribution, if and when the peso exchange rate is allowed to move in relation to its relative purchasing power vis-à-vis other international currencies and especially the dollar (since over 60 percent of Mexico's trade is with the United States).[8] While some might argue that overvaluation of the peso could act as a brake on domestic price inflation by placing a ceiling price on tradeables, this would only occur in a pure state of free trade or with rapidly declining effective protection and reasonably competitive markets. It would work at the expense of import-competing production, which will lose markets to imports at least in the short and medium run. The sophisticated argument based on the analysis of Blejer and others is that domestic prices rise in an open economy in equilibrium in proportion to the rate of external inflation plus the rate of exchange devaluation.[9]

The current (September 1982) full embargo on the availability of pesos for other than "essential" imports is of course inconsistent with such an approach. While it is theoretically attractive, because lower-priced imports substitute for inflationary-priced domestic goods, driving down the internal rate of inflation, in a fixed-exchange-rate regime, or one with preannounced devaluation, the adjustment occurs at the expense of a growing balance of trade deficit and unemployment in tradeables production which Mexico in its current dollar crisis cannot contemplate. In an economy such as Mexico's with a large and growing nontradeables sector (the tertiary sector now employs over 40 percent of the work force) and with minimum wages, certain prices regulated by government decree, a trade regime that relies heavily on nontariff barriers, and where a large and growing injection of liquidity and foreign exchange derives from petroleum export rents, the effectiveness of such an approach is severely restricted. Moreover, the political and social costs of underemployment of labor and capital in these sectors that would obviously be affected during the adjustment process cannot and would not be ignored, for in Mexico both industrial labor and management have significant political voice. While the approach has been applied with some success in strictly economic terms in Chile under an authoritarian regime, it has been much less successful in Argentina where both employment and output of import-substituting industries are of greater concern to policymakers.

*Maquiladoras*

The *maquiladora* program is one exception to the trend toward lower labor intensity of exports. In 1981, those plants that process intermediate imports for reexport provided over 120,000 jobs annually the majority of which were for young women. Most of the *maquiladoras* are located in the border region, although the program is being expanded to favor the interior of Mexico and especially the new industrial centers located near its "development ports." The major industrial centers, Mexico City, Monterrey, and Guadalajara, are specifically excluded to avoid even greater concentration in those areas. Estimates of likely growth of employment under the program in the next 5 years suggest at least a doubling of the number of jobs, or another 120,000, which compares favorably with the roughly 700,000 jobs to be generated directly by the export sector in the 1980s. While at present the multiplier effect of *maquiladora* value added on Mexican production and employment is relatively low since, at least until the 1982 devaluation, a significant share of earnings was spent across the border, there remains a great potential for expanding linkages with the rest of the Mexican economy.[10] It is estimated that from one to three jobs are created in the United States for every Mexican job in the border plants through the demand for imports from suppliers and expenditures of income by Mexicans north of the border. But if and when the program moves south and jobs become more skilled, this employment multiplier may be expected to decline. In addition, the sponsors of the program argue that the training effect and possibilities for vertical mobility of the labor force are increasing over time on the Mexican side. We feel that, especially in the wake of the 1982 crisis, these linkages can and will develop, leading to the integration of the *maquiladoras* into the Mexican domestic eonomy, provided that U.S. policy remains favorable. However, if Mexico is eventually able to recover its rapid growth of output and achieve significant increases in wages over the next decade, this will erode Mexico's competitive position vis-à-vis other labor surplus economies, forcing *maquiladoras* into new stages of sophistication if they are to remain competitive.

As real wages rise during the process of exchange, less competitive *maquiladoras* will be forced either to integrate forward and backward into more complete production-sharing activities or to move to cheaper labor areas if they are not to be driven out of business. Although Mexican wages are low (about $0.80 an hour under the August 1982 peso exchange rate) by United States standards, they are in the midrange for similar industries in the Third World. (By comparison Haiti's labor cost is $0.50 per hour or less.) A strategy that continues growth with equity is essential in Mexico to achieve the kind of political stability that is vital if *maquiladoras* and direct foreign investment are to be attracted to Mexico to play a role in its push toward wage and income parity with its northern neighbor.

The *maquiladoras* are criticized for adding little more than the unskilled labor share of value added to Mexico's economy, of primarily employing young women rather than the severely underemployed male work force, and of resisting unionization. In addition, it is claimed that they are enclaves with little integration into the national economy and are "footloose," tending to move elsewhere when local employment conditions tighten. They are not regarded as a firm foundation for the integrated development of the national economy. Notwithstanding these criticisms, the Mexican government views the benefits *maquiladoras* provide through employment creation as outweighing their other disadvantages and for this reason strongly supports the program. It could be argued that every effort should be made to further the integration of such activities into the domestic economy. If this were possible, such highly efficient operations which are heavily labor intensive could then begin to provide Mexico's population with basic goods at a fraction of the cost of those supplied by highly protected and inefficient "import-competing industries" that currently monopolize the national market. So far the interests of import-competing industries and economic nationalists have bitterly opposed attempts to open the domestic market to *maquiladoras*.

*Migration*

Trade policy is closely linked to migration pressures. Measures designed to protect the United States market from imports of labor-intensive goods and services exacerbate slack conditions in the Mexican labor market, leading to increased pressures for emigration as job opportunities become relatively more attractive in "protected industries" north of the border. In addition to the competitive nature of export jobs versus migration, exchange rate policy designed to favor exports may have a complementary effect on migration since devaluation of the peso makes both peso exports and dollar earnings abroad more attractive. Thus in 1976, the

*TABLE 8.6.*

*A Comparison of the Employment Effects of Migration and Exports: 1960–1980*

| | *1960* | *1970* | *1975* | *1980* |
|---|---|---|---|---|
| 1. Migrants working in the U.S. (thousands) | 1710 | 2620 | 3475 | 4300 |
| 2. Export sector jobs (thousands) | 312 | 369 | 363 | 690 |
| Ratio of migrant workers to export jobs (½) | 5.5 | 7.1 | 9.6 | 6.2 |

SOURCE: Table 8.5 and 8.7 except for the 1980 migration estimates which were contructed using the same methodology as for table 8.7.

sharp decline in the peso stimulated migration at the same time that it encouraged exports, although the accompanying domestic recession almost certainly added to migratory pressures. Table 8-6 shows that the ratio of migrant jobs to export jobs rose steadily between 1950 and 1975 but fell between 1975 and 1980, although the absolute increase in migrants still exceeded the growth in export sector jobs for this period. Much of the 1970–1975 rise in this ratio is probably attributable to progressive overvaluation of the peso which tended to discourage exports, as we have seen.

In Table 8-7 estimates are made of Mexican migration.[11] They indicate a steady increase in the number of Mexican workers that have joined the U.S. labor pool as temporary or permanent workers. The figure amounts to a significant percentage of the Mexican-born work force. Projections of the demand for labor in Mexico (Table 4a, Reynolds, *op. cit.*) indicate that a 6.6 percent sustained growth of GNP by the year 2000 would be able to absorb the new workers coming into the job market between 1980 and 2000 but would *not* be sufficient to mop up existing underemployment, including those employed abroad, which together amount to around eight million workers. In short, an optimistic 6.6 percent average rate of growth for the next 20 years will not tighten the labor market sufficiently for real wages of unskilled labor to begin to approach the U.S. level. And if GNP were to grow at only 6 percent annually (an impressive 20-year average for any country), the labor surplus over and above underemployment and the number now employed in the United States would amount to from 3.3 to 4.3 million workers by the year 2000, or as high as 10 percent of the work force in that year.

These projections assume that growth will tend to follow Mexico's Global Development Plan, which places a heavy emphasis on capital-intensive manufacturing production, though at a somewhat slower rate. That strategy is also an important element of the industrial plan of President Lopez Portillo. Without calling into question those objectives or the ability of forecasts such as this to project accurately employment consequences over two decades under conditions of major structural change, there is strong evidence that unless plan strategies shift drastically, migratory pressures will not diminish significantly during the next 20 years and will probably increase. This is due not only to domestic underemployment but to a growing absolute gap in real wages between the two countries, a gap that is bound to increase still further unless Mexico's labor market

*TABLE 8.7.*
*Mexican Contributions to the U.S. Labor Pool for Selected Years*
*(Thousand Workers)*

| | *1940* | *1950* | *1960* | *1970* | *1975* |
|---|---|---|---|---|---|
| 1. Mexican labor force | 5858 | 8345 | 10213 | 12955 | 15,400 est. |
| 2. Legal and undocumented temporary migrant workers (per year) | 300 | 500 | 500 | 600 | 900 |
| 3. Cumulative stock of permanent undocumented workers (beginning in 1940) | | 500 | 1000 | 1550 | 1,925 |
| 4. Cumulative stock of legal immigrant workers (beginning in 1940) | | 30 | 210 | 470 | 650 |
| 5. Total Mexican workers in U.S. labor pool | 300 | 1030 | 1710 | 2620 | 3,475 |
| 6. Mexicans working in U.S. as share of Mexican work force (5 ÷ 1 = 6) | 5.1 | 12.3 | 16.7 | 20.2 | 22.6 |

SOURCE: Mexican labor force totals for 1940, 1950, and 1970 are from the census data on economically active population age 12 and over (including unemployed). The 1960 census figure was adjusted to correct for overcounting of rural workers [for details, see C. W. Reynolds, "Labor Market Projections for the United States and Mexico and Current Migration Controversies," *Food Research Institute Studies* 17, no. 2 (1979) Stanford University. (1979)]. A detailed discussion of Mexican labor force and employment data is in D. B. Keesing, "Employment and Lack of Employment in Mexico, 1900–1970] in J. W. Wilkie and K. Ruddle, *Quantitative Latin American Studies* (Los Angeles: UCLA Latin American Center, 1977); his adjusted labor force total for 1950 is 8272 and for 1960 is 9691. For 1940 and 1970 they are the same as the census figures. The estimates in row 2 are based on the number of legal temporary workers (including Braceros from 1942 to 1964) plus an estimate of undocumented workers during the previous 5-year period (double the number of illegals deported reduced by one-fourth for nonparticipants in the work force). The figure is reduced by 20 percent more in 1975 to provide the most conservative possible estimate in view of the speculative nature of the methodology used. Row 3 is based on the assumption that 10 percent of the seasonal migrants in row 2 elect to remain in the United States each year. Row 4 represents the net cumulative legal migration of workers assuming that legal migrants from Mexico have an 0.65 labor force participation rate and a 5 percent attrition rate.

tightens enough to permit real wages to accelerate rapidly south of the border or unless real wages for unskilled labor in the United States fall significantly (something that would be socially and politically destabilizing).

The Mexican government's food and agricultural development program, Sistema Alimentario Mexicano (SAM), may help to absorb labor in the rural areas, slowing the rate of urbanization and raising real wages. However, it is certain that at least 7 million young job seekers will be emerging from the rural sector in the next 20 years. To absorb those workers in productive employment will require—at current levels of technology—$20,000 per additional job or a total of $140 billion in new investment.[12] This amounts to a good share of the surplus (estimated at $20 per barrel) from oil exports of 1.23 million barrels per day throughout the period 1980–2000 and ignores the real problems of recycling foreign exchange earnings into expanded domestic employment on that scale without severe inflation as well as the commitment of much of that surplus to service existing debt. It also ignores the additional need for investment in infrastructure, education, and social expenditures to complement direct investment in productive capacity. Finally,the estimate does not include the cost of expanding capacity to provide jobs for an additional 13 million young people entering the labor market from the nonagricultural sector, not to mention the need for higher productivity employment for the presently underemployed, unemployed, and those working abroad who may wish to return to Mexico.

It would seem that a conscious national emigration policy must become an essential complement to Mexico's employment, income distribution, and trade strategies if real wages are to rise significantly at home and if labor income convergence between Mexico and the United States is gradually to occur.[13] Exports, however free they are to adjust along the lines of Mexico's comparative advantage, will not begin to generate the same job-creating capacity as migration, at least until well into the next century. Nevertheless, migration does represent a cost to Mexico in terms of the education, training, and skills formation of those workers who migrate abroad. They add to U.S. productivity by more than their wages while detracting from the productive capacity of Mexico's domestic economy.

The remission of foreign earnings may be estimated at from $500 million to $1 billion per year. This amounts only to less than 1 percent of Mexico's 1980 GNP (in 1978 prices), but for certain geographical areas and poor households the contribution could be one-eighth or more of family income. The opportunities which such employment provides for the income and wealth expectations of Mexican families are extremely important, together with even the limited exposure most migrants get to U.S. technology, work habits, and culture, which may provide productive benefit to Mexico. While the balance may favor the United States, though some groups debate this, both countries have benefited from Mexican migration. It has reduced factor scarcities in the United States and relieved unemployment in Mexico while remitting foreign exchange to the poorer Mexican households.[14]

*Finance, Foreign Direct Investment, and Technology Transfer*

Capital and technology flows to Mexico may be seen to be interdependent with trade and migration, and this is becoming increasingly so over time as investors make locational decisions in terms of access to labor as well as markets. As changes in Mexican law seek to increase the national benefits from imported technology, some U.S. firms prefer to import labor rather than export the industrial location. For others, the *maquiladora* program and related trade policies encourage them to serve the U.S. market from plants located on Mexican soil. Finally, financial flows in both directions in response to relative yields on investment have become highly sensitive to the effect of trade and migration policy on the balance of payments, exchange rate, wage level, and political stability, as they affect project and country risk. While it is not possible to unravel all the threads of interdependence in this brief section, some of the salient features are touched upon.

United States direct investment is 80 percent of total direct foreign investment in Mexico and has a long history in that country. In the early part of the century such investment tended to favor extractive industries, railroads, and infrastructure including telecommunications and electric power. Following expropriation of the petroleum industry in 1938, and the enforcement of restrictive policies on foreign ownership of mining plus the nationalization of power, telecommunications, and transport industries, foreign direct investment has shifted toward those import-competing industries which have benefited from import protection to serve the domestic market. Demand for the products of such industries is still highly concentrated, primarily in the major urban areas and among the top 20 percent of households whose average incomes approximate those of the U.S. middle class (the top 5 percent of Mexican households today have an average family income of $27,000). The effective demand generated by this small minority of the population provides a market for a wide array of products which are virtually identical to those manufactured and marketed in the United States although sold at a significantly higher price.

Today the pattern of foreign investment in Mexico is again changing. First with the border assembly plants and more recently through production sharing (in which Mexican subsidiary firms of a U.S. parent company produce part of the value added of goods sold in both Mexican and U.S. markets) an open economy orientation is beginning to emerge for at least some of the more productive firms.

Over time, foreign direct investment has increased the U.S. share of ownership in the leading manufacturing industries in Mexico, and such firms have tended to enjoy preferential access to external sources of financial capital, especially in times of domestic credit stringency. Since one of the policies of the Mexican government is to reduce rather than increase the relative power of foreign (and especially U.S.) firms, this raises a number of problems. Transnational enterprises have access to the widest range of technology. However, they also demand compensation for their patents, licenses, and know-how. Until recently, such firms have tended to rely on sources of research and development in the home country, rather than to expend funds for this purpose in Mexico, in part to secure control over the returns to intellectual property.

The new phase of production sharing into which Mexico is entering means that transnational firms portion out different stages of production between countries in terms of relative factor costs. This provides an opportunity for such firms to increase their degree of Mexicanization, to strengthen Mexico's exports along lines of comparative advantage, and to increase employment. Here is an area in which trade and foreign investment are highly complementary and where migration may be reduced by production sharing. However, such a process requires considerable openness to trade, including access to intermediate products at a quality and price sufficient to make reexports competitive on the world market.[15] For maximum benefit such firms must also be permitted to compete with less efficient suppliers in the local market. In view of the relative market power and financial leverage of transnational firms with their greater scale economies relative to domestic firms, greater openness is likely to lead to more concentration, less domestic control of industry, and further inroads on national economic autonomy. This is the price that may have to be paid for rapid growth and employment, but it is certain to create internal social and political conflicts as well as increased friction with the United States.[16]

### *Is Full Exchange Necessary or Sufficient for Development with Equity?*

In conclusion, Section I has touched on a number of key aspects of exchange between Mexico and the United States. It is evident that properly designed strategies for trade, migration, investment, and technology transfer, while increasing absolute interdependence, may also permit an increase in the relative independence and power of Mexico. Indeed, they may be essential to the achievement of full employment and increased social participation in the economy, which are among the goals of government policy. Migration in particular may permit greater degrees of freedom for domestic development policy which could ultimately eliminate the need for large-scale emigration of unskilled labor 20 years hence. On the other hand, shortsighted closed-door trade, migration, and investment policies could constrain the economy's potential for growth *with* distribution by worsening the slack in the labor market, pushing down real wages, and increasing the gap between rich and poor.

However, complete full exchange implies an extreme set of strategies which carries with it a loss of autonomy and national control over the economy that would be unacceptable to either country. Free migration would generate immense opposition from those groups in the United States struggling to raise or at least maintain their real wages. This would include service workers, blue-collar workers, unskilled labor, and minorities. If allowed to operate fully, the iron law of factor price equalization could cut in two directions, lowering real wages in the United States even as it raised wages in Mexico.

A certain consequence is that if social justice and political stability are to be secured in Mexico, wage, wealth distribution, and employment policies must be far more direct and drastic than they have ever been in the United States, requiring measures that go well beyond the present program of the Mexican government. And if the United States is to preserve its economic power and social progress in an increasingly interdependent world, it must be prepared to exchange goods and services, labor, capital, and technology, with Mexico on a scale unprecedented in history.

Row 2 is based on figures on legal and undocumented migration and labor participation rates from Marshall (1978), Domestic Council Committee on Illegal Aliens (1976), and Cornelius (1978). The figures in Table 8-7 represent estimated numbers of workers who will participate in the U.S. labor market at some time during the year cited, whether as temporary or permanent additions to the stock of manpower and do not represent man-years of labor. Hence, row 2 includes workers who might have been employed in Mexico as well as in the United States during that year, since the average period of employment of temporary Mexican workers in the United States is from 3 to 6 months (Cornelius [1978]).[17]

## II. A General Equilibrium Model of the Mexican Economy[18]

This section is more specific, focusing directly on the employment of unskilled labor, which we feel is the key variable in predicting the path of income distribution. Yet it is also more general in that the effects of trade policy change are viewed in terms of the entire economy and not just via the impact on the *export sector* per se. The procedure used next is to estimate a matrix of general equilibrium employment and output elasticities with respect to key exogenous variables. These elasticities show the responsiveness of output and employment in the various sectors to changes in rates of tariff protection. First, several important assumptions and potential difficulties are addressed. Then certain conclusions are drawn from the results of the estimation and two simulations. Due to their more technical nature, the formal model and a more detailed presentation of the results are reported in the Appendix. One may infer from the model that increasing the protection afforded the food processing, textile, and machinery sectors and decreasing the trade bias against agriculture both tend strongly to increase employment of unskilled labor, while increasing the degree of protection in other sectors tends to have a negligible to adverse effect on unskilled labor employed. The agricultural sector in particular, due to its size and the intensity with which it uses unskilled labor, should be a focus for the attention of policymakers. This conclusion parallels that of the previous section in which we emphasize the importance of import substitution and export of agricultural products as a key to the absorption of unemployed and underemployed labor and a check on the internal pressure for migration abroad.

### *Assumptions and Limitations of the Model*

The law of one price holds for all tradeable goods as modified by trade restrictions. A critical consequence of this assumption is that Mexico can sell all its surplus agricultural output at a given world price (to the United States, for example). A dual labor market is assumed in the sense that wages adjust to clear the market for skilled workers and the quantity of unskilled labor employed adjusts to clear the unskilled labor market. While this is true in the short run, for small changes in the variables, these assumptions are only approximations of reality over the longer period of time covered by the simulations. Mexico does not have an infinite number of unskilled workers, and the ranks of skilled workers are augmented through time both by advancement of formerly unskilled workers and by new entrants into the labor force.

The model uses estimates of effective protection of 1975, adjusted for exchange rates. Since many export incentives were eliminated after the 1976 devaluation, this is clearly incorrect, but the magnitude of the error and its effect on the results are not clear. The use of National Plan estimates of investment, employment, and government expenditures reflects an overly ambitious and hopeful version of Mexico's economic future in the light of 1982 events, but the relative merits of different policy options should not be seriously affected.

There is no binding foreign exchange constraint in the model, nor is there a balanced trade condition. To the extent that oil exports are politically free to adjust to finance imports, this is not a harmful assumption. Sectors are assumed to operate under constant returns to scale except in agriculture where decreasing returns to scale exist. Zero technological change is posited, so that, as discussed in the first section, labor requirements are somewhat exaggerated if technological advancement takes place. The first of these assumptions is standard practice in economic modeling and is no less appropriate here. An ex post adjustment is made to the results of the simulations to allow comparison with Table 8-5 in which projections incorporating a yearly labor productivity growth rate of 2 percent are shown.

*TABLE 8.8.*
*The Unskilled Labor Employment-Tariff Relationship*[a]

| *Sector* | *Elasticities of Total Employment of Unskilled Labor with Respect to Tariffs* | *Maximum Employment Increase from a 1% Increase in the Sector's Tariff* |
|---|---|---|
| | | *(man years)* |
| *Agriculture | 1.728 | 81,112 |
| Mining | 0.029 | 19 |
| Oil | 0.057 | 49 |
| *Food | 0.547 | 2,343 |
| *Textiles | 0.546 | 2,472 |
| Wood | 0.073 | 221 |
| Chemicals | −0.099 | −124 |
| Nonmetals | 0.155 | 248 |
| Metals | 0.210 | 162 |
| *Machinery | 0.422 | 3,208 |

SOURCE: See the Appendix.
[a] See the text regarding the sectors preceded by an asterisk.

## *Conclusions of the Exercise and Simulations*

In Section I we classified agriculture (1), processed foods, (4), and wood products (6) as labor-intensive sectors. Section II adds two further considerations: the proportion of unskilled workers to the total labor force in a sector and the responsiveness of output and ultimately employment to changes in tariff rates. The results show in Table 8-8 emphasize even more strongly the dominance of agriculture as a potential employer. The machinery and textiles sectors join processed foods as other promising prospective employers of unskilled labor.

In relation to goods that can be traded internationally (the output of sectors 1–10), the model can be viewed as being driven by supply side considerations in the following sense. An increase in exogenous demand results only in increased imports, so that neither domestic output nor employment is substantially affected. But changes that affect supply such as changes in the inputs of capital or skilled labor cause significant increases in output and employment in the sector receiving the increase and small declines in the other tradeables sectors as resources are bid away from them to the growing sector. Sectors hurt most by this reallocation are those that compete strongly for resources with the growing sector.

Tables 8-9 and 8-11 indicate that the nontradeable sectors (11–15) are both quite dissimilar to the tradeable sectors and a nonhomogeneous group. In general, changes affecting demand are more important and changes affecting supply less important than for tradeables. An example from Table 8-9 is the service sector (14). A 1 percent rise in the capital

*TABLE 8.9.*

*General Equilibrium Elasticities of Sectorial Output with Respect to Selected Exogenous Variables*[a]

| Sector | Changes in Own Capital Stock | | Changes in Own Exogenous Demand | | Changes in Labor Supply | | | Neutral Technological Change |
|---|---|---|---|---|---|---|---|---|
| | | | | | Skill 1 | Skill 2 | Skill 3 | |
| Agric. | 0.7214 | (10) | 0.0008 | (14) | −0.0001 | 0.0056 | 0.0085 | 1.4783 |
| Min. | 0.9525 | (4) | 0.0023 | (11) | 0.0301 | 0.1021 | 0.0957 | 1.9761 |
| Oil | 0.9638 | (2) | 0.0007 | (15) | 0.0547 | 0.0194 | 0.0568 | 1.4321 |
| Food | 0.9023 | (8) | 0.0060 | (8) | 0.0333 | 0.0473 | 0.1096 | 1.6257 |
| Text. | 0.9218 | (6) | 0.0070 | (7) | −0.0050 | 0.0095 | 0.1872 | 2.2429 |
| Wood | 0.9639 | (2) | 0.0037 | (10) | 0.0117 | 0.0280 | 0.1158 | 1.7493 |
| Chem. | 0.9322 | (5) | 0.0057 | (9) | 0.0366 | 0.0335 | 0.1875 | 1.6706 |
| Nonmet. | 0.9665 | (1) | 0.0020 | (12) | 0.0461 | 0.0492 | 0.2820 | 2.7934 |
| Met. | 0.9026 | (7) | 0.0116 | (5) | 0.1492(1) | 0.0445 | 0.3692 | 3.1017 |
| Mach. | 0.8289 | (9) | 0.0114 | (6) | 0.0466 | 0.0364 | 0.2724 | 2.0519 |
| Elec. | 0.0513 | (14) | 0.0674 | (3) | 0.0519 | 0.0500 | 0.2022 | 0.1099 |
| Comm. | 0.2141 | (11) | 0.0017 | (13) | 0.0920 | 0.1062(1) | 0.4349(1) | 0.5786 |
| Transp. | 0.0924 | (13) | 0.0267 | (4) | 0.0550 | 0.0634 | 0.2401 | 0.2810 |
| Serv. | 0.1692 | (12) | 0.2132 | (2) | 0.0612 | 0.0631 | 0.1953 | 0.4076 |
| Const. | 0 | (15) | 1 | (1) | 0 | 0 | 0 | 0 |

[a]The numbers in parentheses indicate the ranking of sectors ordered by the magnitude of the elasticities.

*TABLE 8.10.*

*General Equilibrium Output Elasticities with Respect to Changes in Tariffs*

| *Sector* | *Tariff 1* | *Tariff 2* | *Tariff 3* | *Tariff 4* | *Tariff 5* | *Tariff 6* | *Tariff 7* | *Tariff 8* | *Tariff 9* | *Tariff 10* |
|---|---|---|---|---|---|---|---|---|---|---|
| Agric. | 0.0251 | −0.0038 | −0.0124 | −0.0633 | −0.0166 | −0.0064 | −0.0244 | −0.0054 | −0.0112 | −0.0274 |
| Min. | −0.0067 | 1.5126 | −0.1033 | −0.2732 | −0.1513 | −0.0799 | −0.0780 | −0.0588 | −0.1158 | −0.2413 |
| Oil | −0.0061 | −0.0286 | 0.8500 | −0.1561 | −0.0879 | −0.0219 | −0.0483 | −0.0358 | −0.0851 | −0.1987 |
| Food | −0.8935 | −0.0453 | −0.0649 | 1.9162 | −0.1649 | −0.0707 | −0.0623 | −0.0510 | −0.1038 | −0.2517 |
| Text. | −0.2029 | −0.0603 | −0.0650 | −0.4058 | 2.5281 | −0.0872 | −0.5195 | −0.0744 | −0.1571 | −0.3488 |
| Wood | −0.0971 | −0.0379 | −0.0533 | −0.2522 | −0.1892 | 1.3887 | −0.1112 | −0.0528 | −0.1113 | −0.2499 |
| Chem. | −0.0478 | −0.0942 | −0.2205 | −0.4273 | −0.2456 | −0.1395 | 1.6719 | −0.0806 | −0.1774 | −0.3654 |
| Nonmet. | −0.0319 | −0.6263 | −0.1690 | −0.5308 | −0.3072 | −0.1612 | −0.1482 | 3.3375 | −0.2408 | −0.4995 |
| Met. | −0.0680 | −1.0162 | −0.2437 | −0.9236 | −0.5401 | −0.2001 | −0.2475 | −0.1891 | 4.9344 | −1.0906 |
| Mach. | −0.0355 | −0.1128 | −0.0997 | −0.5025 | −0.2991 | −0.1188 | −0.1555 | −0.1077 | −0.5608 | 2.1662 |
| Elec. | −0.0120 | −0.0043 | −0.0395 | 0.0727 | 0.0676 | 0.0182 | 0.0077 | 0.0452 | 0.2866 | 0.0223 |
| Comm. | 0.1814 | 0.0882 | −0.0689 | 0.2722 | 0.2185 | 0.0359 | −0.0176 | 0.0536 | 0.1490 | 0.3015 |
| Transp. | 0.0938 | 0.0368 | −0.0097 | 0.1451 | 0.1063 | 0.0037 | 0.0031 | 0.0615 | 0.0820 | 0.1394 |
| Serv. | 0.0875 | 0.0377 | −0.0185 | 0.0961 | 0.0787 | 0.0240 | −0.0024 | 0.0436 | 0.0475 | 0.0999 |
| Const. | 0 | 0 | 0 | 0 | 0 | 0 | 0 | 0 | 0 | 0 |

stock would cause only a 0.17 percent increase in output, compared with an average of about 0.9 for tradeable goods, but a 1 percent increase in exogenous demand would induce a 0.21 percent increase in output, whereas the highest output response among tradeable goods is the 0.0057 increase in the chemicals sector. The behavior of the commerce sector seems to be a mix of that of a tradeable sector and a nontradeable sector by the above criteria, reflecting the strong linkages between it and foreign trade.

The response of output and employment to changes in the trade tariffs is the focus of this chapter and is shown in detail in Tables 8-10, 8-11, and 8-12. Table 8-10 might lead one to believe that nonmetallic minerals (8) and basic metals (9) could be important sources of unskilled labor employment, due to the strong positive output effect caused by tariff increases in these sectors. A 1 percent increase in the tariff protection afforded the base metals sector would, as shown in Table 8-10, increase output in the base metals sector by 4.9 percent, increase output in electricity and communication by 0.29 and 0.15 percent, respectively, and decrease output by 0.24 percent in nonmetallic metals, by 0.18 percent in chemicals, and so forth. Agriculture, on the other hand, has the smallest output response to an increase in its tariff (0.625), and the processed food sector contracts sharply (−0.89) due to this rise in price of its most important input. But, as can be seen in Table 8-8, the size and unskilled labor intensiveness of the agriculture sector causes this relatively small percentage output response to lead to the largest unskilled employment increase in terms of both percentages and absolute man-years. The reverse is true for items 8 and 9, whose small size and less intensive use of unskilled labor make the employment effects much less significant than the output effects.

In addition to agriculture, which clearly represents the most important potential employer of unskilled labor, the processed foods, textiles, and machinery sectors may provide substantial help. A breakdown of the elasticities of unskilled labor employed between agriculture and nonagriculture is available in Tables 8-11 and 8-12.

Table 8-8 shows elasticities of total employment with respect to increases in sectorial tariffs. Since these abstract from the small negative effects in the nontraded sectors, they represent maximum amounts of labor. Those sectors marked by asterisks, agriculture, food processing, textiles, and machinery, are ones in which tariff increases clearly lead to net employment gains.

The two simulations use the matrix of elasticities estimated as shown in the Appendix, in concert with the Global Plan estimates of capital formation and growth rates of other exogenous variables through the year 1990. The first simulation assumes no change in the current structure of tariffs and the exchange rate, while the second simulates a 10 percent rise in the protection of agriculture, mining, food processing, and wood processing and a 10 percent fall in protection of all other tradeable goods sectors,

TABLE 8.11.
*General Equilibrium Elasticities of the Total Employment of Nonskilled Agricultural Labor with Respect to Selected Exogenous Variables*

| *Sector* | *Changes in Own Capital Stock* | *Neutral Technological Change* | *Trade Tariffs* | *Exogenous Demand* |
|---|---|---|---|---|
| Agric. | 0.7051 | 1.4449 | 1.854 | 0.0017 |
| Min. | −0.0098 | −0.0203 | −0.009 | 0.0005 |
| Oil | −0.0096 | −0.0144 | −0.032 | 0.0002 |
| Food | −0.0196 | −0.0353 | −0.161 | 0.0013 |
| Text. | −0.0102 | −0.0249 | −0.035 | 0.0009 |
| Wood | −0.0075 | −0.0137 | −0.016 | 0.0008 |
| Chem. | −0.0086 | −0.0154 | −0.068 | 0.0007 |
| Nonmet. | −0.0032 | −0.0092 | −0.011 | 0.0002 |
| Met. | −0.0051 | −0.0175 | −0.024 | 0.0006 |
| Mach. | −0.0170 | −0.0419 | −0.060 | 0.0012 |
| Elec. | 0.0042 | 0.0089 | — | −0.0002 |
| Comm. | 0.0214 | 0.0579 | — | −0.0001 |
| Transp. | 0.0027 | 0.0082 | — | −0.0001 |
| Serv. | 0.0097 | 0.0232 | — | −0.0025 |
| Const. | 0.0001 | 0.0003 | — | 0.0092 |
| Inves. | — | — | — | 0.0099 |

TABLE 8.12.
*General Equilibrium Elasticities of the Total Employment of Nonskilled, Nonagricultural Labor with Respect to Selected Exogenous Variables*

| *Sector* | *Changes in Own Capital Stock* | *Neutral Technological Change* | *Trade Tariffs* | *Exogenous Demand* |
|---|---|---|---|---|
| Agric. | 0.1958 | 0.4011 | −0.100 | −0.0112 |
| Min. | 0.0707 | 0.1467 | 0.031 | −0.0033 |
| Oil | 0.0821 | 0.1219 | 0.071 | −0.0018 |
| Food | 0.1803 | 0.3248 | 0.566 | −0.0085 |
| Text. | 0.1286 | 0.3130 | 0.465 | −0.0062 |
| Wood | 0.0671 | 0.1219 | 0.071 | −0.0052 |
| Chem. | 0.0579 | 0.1038 | −0.025 | −0.0050 |
| Nonmet. | 0.0345 | 0.0998 | 0.133 | −0.0014 |
| Met. | 0.0427 | 0.1470 | 0.187 | −0.0042 |
| Mach. | 0.1456 | 0.3604 | 0.386 | −0.0079 |
| Elec. | 0.0192 | 0.0412 | — | −0.0016 |
| Comm. | −0.0046 | −0.0126 | — | 0.0006 |
| Transp. | 0.0063 | 0.0192 | — | 0.0001 |
| Serv. | 0.0494 | 0.1190 | — | −0.0168 |
| Const. | −0.0224 | −0.1020 | — | 0.0399 |
| Inves. | — | — | — | −0.0591 |

except the petroleum sector, whose protection remains unchanged. The sectors whose levels of protection we chose to increase for the second simulation are those either in which current rates of protection are well below the average for tradeable goods (mining) or which have high labor-product coefficients (food and wood processing) or both (agriculture). The opposite is true for those sectors in which we wished to simulate a decrease in protection.

In Table 8-13, some of the results of the simulations are presented. In simulation I, unskilled nonagricultural employment increases by 11.67 percent, or by about 649,000. Unskilled agricultural employment rises by 4.09 percent, or 180,000, for a total rise of 829,000, or 8.3 percent. New job creation will take place at a ratio of 3.6 nonagricultural jobs per job in agriculture in contrast to the current 5 to 4 ratio if the Global Plan investment pattern is followed.

The results of simulation II show even more job creation for unskilled labor. In aggregate, 1,331,000 jobs would be created for unskilled labor, a rise of about 13.3 percent, 60 percent more than in simulation I. In this case, the increase would be biased 3 to 1 toward agricultural job creation. The 60 percent additional employment growth is an impact effect of the

*TABLE 8.13.*

*Values of Some Endogenous Variables in the Simulations (All Figures Are Annual Percentage Changes)*

| | *1. Prices* | | | *3. Output* | |
|---|---|---|---|---|---|
| | *Simulation 1 (%)* | *Simulation 2 (%)* | | *Simulation 1 (%)* | *Simulation 2 (%)* |
| Agric. | 0 | 10.0 | Agric. | 5.18 | 11.55 |
| Min. | 0 | 10.0 | Min. | 6.02 | 24.01 |
| Oil | 0 | 0 | Oil | 14.16 | 16.59 |
| Food | 0 | 10.0 | Food | 6.58 | 21.98 |
| Text. | 0 | −10.0 | Text. | 12.67 | −9.17 |
| Wood | 0 | 10.0 | Wood | 3.57 | 20.73 |
| Chem. | 0 | −10.0 | Chem. | 8.42 | −6.69 |
| Nonmet. | 0 | −10.0 | Nonmet. | 3.06 | −31.84 |
| Met. | 0 | −10.0 | Met. | −1.27 | −52.02 |
| Mach. | 0 | −10.0 | Mach. | 8.77 | −9.35 |
| Elec. | 5.99 | 1.20 | Elec. | 8.45 | 4.88 |
| Comm. | 2.28 | −0.29 | Comm. | 15.87 | 14.60 |
| Trans. | 2.59 | −0.17 | Trans. | 9.68 | 3.85 |
| Serv. | 4.04 | 0.91 | Serv. | 10.05 | 9.83 |
| Const. | 0.31 | −2.48 | Const. | 11.57 | 11.57 |
| | | | Inves. | 11.57 | 11.57 |

| | *2. Wage Rates* | | | *4. Total Employment of Unskilled Labor* | |
|---|---|---|---|---|---|
| | *Simulation 1 (%)* | *Simulation 2 (%)* | | *Simulation 1 (%)* | *Simulation 2 (%)* |
| Skill class 1 | 4.23 | 0.18 | Nonagric. | 11.67 | 5.89 |
| Skill class 2 | 6.71 | 3.47 | Agric. | 4.09 | 22.76 |
| Skill class 3 | 7.13 | 1.64 | | | |

trade policy changes, and employment growth would revert back to that described in simulation I. One can safely conclude that lessening the relative price distortions in the Mexican economy by moving rates of effective protection closer together should increase the amount of unskilled labor employed. After most of the unemployed and underemployed are absorbed, this pressure will then be translated to increases in wages in the agricultural sector and for unskilled labor as a whole. The employment projections in simulation I (8.2 million jobs if no productivity growth occurs but only 6.1 million jobs assuming 2 percent growth of productivity) can be compared with a projection of the number of job seekers in 1990 (8.6 million new entrants, 6 to 7 million of which will be unskilled, plus 1 to 2 million currently unemployed or underemployed, plus those of the approximately 4 million migrants working in the United States that wish to return, less unskilled workers who can upgrade their status to skilled).[19] We see that the degree of freedom of exchange is an important policy instrument in an effort to increase wages of unskilled labor. Trade liberalization of the extent proposed here may be important in helping Mexico move toward growth with equity by 1990, even if the ambitious domestic growth plans of 8 to 10 percent per annum on which the simulations are based must be cut back to an average of 6–6.5 percent over the decade.

In conclusion, in Section II we obtain strong evidence from the general equilibrium approach favoring the role of trade in raising the incomes of Mexico's poor. In Section I it was shown that trade will not go far toward absorbing surplus labor given policy measures in effect through the end of 1981. But Section II points out that the employment-generating potential for trade could be very responsive to changes in trade restrictions, especially in certain sectors such as agriculture, labor-intensive manufacturing, and tourism. The Mexican economy grew rapidly through 1981, and despite the current crisis at the time the book goes to press, the prospects for future growth look bright. But the key policy questions in the interim seems to be the extent to which migration will be able to bear the short- to medium-run burden in equilibrating the labor market and how much of this burden can be shifted to export-oriented trade policy without undue loss of economic and political control.

# Appendix

## The Model

1. The objective of this exercise is to analyze what difference (if any) a trade liberalization policy would make on the employment effects of the development plans elaborated by the Mexican government. More concretely, the changes in labor employment that would result from the investment programs of the Industrial Development National Plan (PLAN) are compared with the changes resulting from such programs if they were combined with a generalized reduction in tariffs.

2. To achieve the preceding, a general equilibrium model of the kind originally proposed by Johansen (1974) is formulated and estimated. In general, solving explicitly a walrasian equilibrium system requires complex algorithms because the system may not be linear. The Johansen model gets around this difficulty since it is a log-linear approximation to the walrasian system: differentiating totally with respect to time the original system of equilibrium conditions, one can obtain a system of linear equations of the following form:

$$Ax + By = 0 \qquad \text{(A-1)}$$

where $A$ and $B$ are $n \times n$ and $n \times m$ matrices, respectively, of behavioral parameters, $x$ is an $n \times 1$ vector of rates of change of the endogenous variables (prices, production levels, etc.), and $y$ is an $m \times 1$ vector of rates of change of the exogenous variables (tax rates, factor endowments, etc.). Solving = (A–1) for $x$, one obtains

$$x = Cy \qquad \text{(A-2)}$$

where $C \equiv A^{-1}B$. The *fundamental objective* of the analysis is to estimate matrix $C$, whose $ij$th element represents the *general equilibrium elasticity of the ith endogenous variable with respect to the jth exogenous variable*. Once $C$ is estimated, it becomes possible to analyze different policies by giving different values to the $y$ vector. Nevertheless, it must be kept in mind that because of the way in which the model is built, its predictions are strictly valid for only "small" changes in $y$.

3. This exercise follows Taylor and Black's formulation (1974) of the

Johansen model. This means that we conceive the Mexican economy as a "small" open economy that also produces nontraded goods. We use the following sectorial classification (the composing sectors, according to the 45-sector classification, appear in parentheses):

1. Agriculture (1–4)
2. Mining (5, 6)
3. Petroleum (7)
4. Food (8–12)
5. Textiles (13–15, 19)
6. Wood and paper (16–18)
7. Chemicals (20–27)
8. Nonmetallic minerals (28)
9. Basic metals (29)
10. Machinery (30–35)
11. Electricity (37)
12. Commerce (41)
13. Transportation (39, 40)
14. Services (38, 42–45)
15. Construction (36)
16. Investment goods (except buildings and construction)

We shall assume that the first 10 sectors produce goods that are traded internationally; therefore, their prices are determined by the international arbitrage condition. Sectors 11–15 produce nontraded goods. Sector 16 is an artificial sector whose value added is zero by definition; it produces a composite "investment-good" by combining in fixed proportions goods produced by sectors 1–14.[20]

Moreover, we shall assume that all sectors behave as profit maximizers and that competition prevails throughout the economy. Production takes place under fixed-coefficients conditions insofar as the use of intermediate goods are concerned, but labor and capital can be combined according to Cobb-Douglas production functions in the production of value added. Capital is immobile between sectors, so the rate of return on capital is not equalized across sectors.

Following Sidaoui (1978), we assume the existence of five labor skill classes, each with a different production elasticity:

1. Professional workers (includes engineers, chemists and other scientists, economists, teachers, lawyers, doctors with or without titles but with full university training or equivalent)
2. Technical workers (comprises all types of professional or technical workers except the ones already defined)
3. White collar workers
4. Blue collar workers
5. Agricultural workers

Sectors 2–15 employ workers of the first four skill classes. Sector 1 hires workers of skill classes 1, 2, 3, and 5.

The private sector's demand for consumption goods is a function of prices and income. Furthermore, we assume that it is derived from a separable utility function. Thus, Frisch's method (1959) is used to estimate all price elasticities from knowledge of only the income elasticities, the mean income propensities to consume, and the *flexibility of the mar-*

*ginal utility of money* parameter. The demand for investment goods (including construction), the government's consumption demands, and the changes in inventories are all exogenously determined.

4. The system of equations of the model, the derivation of each equation, and the corresponding symbols are available from the authors on request. The first group of equations applies the international arbitrage conditions, which are used to determine the prices of the traded goods. According to these conditions, the internal price of traded goods can change only if the exchange rate, the international prices, and/or tariffs change. The second group of equations comprises the sectorial labor demand functions for each skill category. These demand functions are derived from the profit maximization assumption under conditions of pure competition. The third group is formed by the *structural form* sectorial output supply functions; from the Cobb-Douglas form of the production functions it follows that the percentage change in output is equal to a weighted sum of the percentage changes in inputs used. The fourth group of equations comprises the equilibrium conditions for the labor markets and the fifth equilibrium conditions for the goods markets. In the markets for tradeable goods, the value of net imports (or net exports) adjusts so as to clear any gap between production (determined in the third group of equations) and the sum of private consumption demand and exogenous demand. In the markets for nontradeable goods, prices are the adjusting variables. Note that in the case of the two sectors that produce investment goods (i.e., sectors 15 and 16) all demand is assumed to be exogenous; changes in prices generated by increments in demand will not result in partially offsetting reductions. This makes the demand for investment goods one of the driving forces of the model, as will be seen below. The last equation is the balance of trade equilibrium condition.

5. Since this walrasian model can determine only relative prices, we can choose any wage rate or price (say $w_s$) as numeraire of the system, thus defining its rate of change as being identical to zero. Therefore, the model has 194 variables and 107 equations, so 87 variables must be determined exogenously. Natural choices to play this role are the rates of technological change, the indirect tax rates, tariffs, international prices, and the autonomous components of sectorial output demands. Moreover, as already mentioned, instead of assuming free capital mobility (and thus including a market-clearing condition for capital), we suppose that the government determines exogenously not only the rate of growth of the overall capital stock but the growth of the stock utilized in each sector.

Given these assumptions there are still several ways of closing the model. Since our main interest is the analysis of labor employment, we use a *Keynesian* alternative: we let the rate of growth of employment of labor of types 4 and 5 be endogenously determined by the model by fixing the wage rate $w_4$, the exchange rate $e$, and the net balance of the current account Δ. This specification simplifies considerably the model since in effect it renders exogenous the rate of change of the prices of traded goods. Alternatively, a *classical* specification could be used by letting the rate of growth of employment of all types of labor be exogenously fixed from the supply side. Then the model would be closed either by fixing the net balance of the trade accounts and letting the exchange rate adjust or vice versa.

6. There are several *conceptual* problems with the formulation of the model that are worth mentioning. First, it would be highly desirable to specify different demand systems for different income groups or for different productive facors, closing the model with the appropriate budgetary restrictions. This would allow us to analyze the second-order effects on the distribution of income that come about due to changes in the consumption structure. Solving this problem, however, would drastically increase the informational requirements of the model.

Second, there is the question of "how far we can push the law of one price." This problem about the adequacy of the usual *small open economy* specification is quite fundamental, and in the case of Mexico it is aggravated by the magnitude of the nontariff trade barriers that protect the domestic industry. As McKinnon (1979) has noted, the effects of a devaluation, for example, in an economy extensively protected by quotas may be completely different from its effects on an economy protected by equivalent tariffs. The study by Cavazos (1977) for 1975 shows evidence of the existence of water in the tariff in many sectors of the Mexican economy, due to the prevalence of low quotas. However, the importance of this problem in evaluating our results and the way to solve it if necessary are not clear matters.

Third, Taylor and Black (1979) have shown that the estimations of the employment effects of changes in tariffs are sensitive to the specification of the production functions, in particular to the assumption of fixed coefficients for the intermediate inputs and of unitary elasticity of substitution between labor and capital. Here the problem is simply one of availability of data.

Finally, it would be very desirable to introduce an adequate description of the budgetary process of the government and of the private sector's savings behavior.

7. Clearly, there are several short-run and long-run problems that cannot be analyzed with the technique used in this chapter: in the short run, very important monetary questions are involved in the transition from one trade strategy to another; in the very long run, issues concerning the way in which the changes in factor prices resulting from the modification of trade barriers affect the choices of technology and investment. Thus, it is important to clarify the meaning of our estimations. To this end, it is worth quoting Johansen (1974, pp. 57–58) at length:

As a mental experiment we may conceive of a dynamic system, involving stochastic terms, which would describe completely the actual development of the variables in which we are interested. We could then consider the following types of development of the variables:

(a) The development as generated by the complete stochastic dynamic system.
(b) The development which would be generated by the system if the stochastic "error" were neglected.
(c) The development which would correspond to those components of the solution of the system used under (b) which do not vanish in the long run.
(d) Finally we may consider the development which is generated by the system under (b) when also all lags and frictions are ruled out of the model.

It should be observed that (c) and (d) are not equivalent, even when the cyclical parts of the solution are damped. . . .

The development generated by our model belongs clearly to class (d) above. In our application we shall set out from an observed initial point which, equally clearly, must belong to class (a). We shall try to choose a "normal" year to serve as the base point of time. The observations from such a normal year will, however, approximate the conditions of class (c) rather than class (d). This is a difficulty which is not easily overcome. If it were possible, it would also be more interesting, from a point of view of growth analysis, to consider (c) rather than (d). In the present study—in which we apply a system of type (d) to data which are at best approximations to a solution of type (c)—we have to assume that the deviations between (c) and (d) are not *too* important or alternatively that they can be taken care of by modifications of the parameters of a system which formally belongs to class (d).

## The Data

1. The results presented in Tables 8-8 through 8-13 take 1978 as the base year for all estimations. The most recent year for which the data set required by the model is available entirely is 1970. However, the profound changes that the Mexican economy experienced in the last decade make it indispensable to use more recent information in the analysis. Since 1978 is the only post devaluation, post-oil-discoveries year for which an input-output table is available, it was used as base year. However, as will be seen below, the rest of the information for 1978 is quite incomplete, and it was necessary to make many arbitrary assumptions in order to obtain all the parameters of the model. This rather crucial limitation of our analysis must be kept in mind.

2. The input-ouput matrix for 1978 was elaborated by the Ministry of

TABLE B.1.

*Input-Output Matrix (Technical requirement coefficients 1978)*

| Sector of origin | Destination Sector 1 | 2 | 3 | 4 | 5 | 6 | 7 | 8 | 9 | 10 | 11 | 12 | 13 | 14 | 15 | 16 |
|---|---|---|---|---|---|---|---|---|---|---|---|---|---|---|---|---|
| 1 | .07787 | .00062 | 0 | .32897 | .04820 | .04087 | .00956 | .00045 | 0 | .00178 | .00050 | 0 | 0 | .00090 | 0 | .02598 |
| 2 | .00113 | .15808 | .00844 | .00667 | .00465 | .00509 | .02173 | .15747 | .09556 | .01769 | .00350 | .00007 | .00132 | .00157 | .03005 | .00113 |
| 3 | .01478 | .03218 | .30054 | .00718 | .00418 | .00745 | .07882 | .02353 | .00756 | .00489 | .12400 | .00567 | .07396 | .00440 | .01324 | 0 |
| 4 | .05948 | 0 | 0 | .14908 | .01115 | .00381 | .01767 | 0 | 0 | 0 | 0 | 0 | 0 | .00230 | 0 | .00339 |
| 5 | .00355 | .00219 | .00231 | .00888 | .20174 | .02489 | .01008 | .00136 | .00097 | .00355 | .00100 | .00233 | .00092 | .00385 | .00045 | .01294 |
| 6 | .00532 | .02937 | .00259 | .01654 | .01324 | .24233 | .04399 | .03032 | .01046 | .02073 | .01200 | .00825 | .00815 | .00890 | .03329 | .00318 |
| 7 | .03240 | .02124 | .01429 | .00948 | .14077 | .04087 | .20031 | .02036 | .01287 | .02761 | .00200 | .00455 | .04085 | .01756 | .02447 | .00657 |
| 8 | .00071 | .00250 | .00190 | .00013 | .00023 | .00200 | .00105 | .00905 | 0 | .00274 | .00100 | .00007 | .00031 | .00218 | .10968 | .00051 |
| 9 | .00177 | .00469 | .01497 | .00106 | .00116 | .00618 | .00916 | .00769 | .37017 | .12067 | .00250 | .00197 | .00469 | .00080 | .07353 | .05205 |
| 10 | .00869 | .01000 | .04041 | .01356 | .00720 | .01926 | .01283 | .01176 | .02976 | .23231 | .05200 | .00330 | .06072 | .03145 | .04446 | .54856 |
| 11 | .00532 | .02812 | .00980 | .00761 | .01045 | .01272 | .01270 | .01629 | .02188 | .00777 | .00050 | .00778 | .00326 | .00474 | .00312 | 0 |
| 12 | .03075 | .06186 | .01469 | .05118 | .09605 | .09083 | .10998 | .06380 | .07416 | .10460 | .02400 | .01205 | .05104 | .02315 | .06769 | .29990 |
| 13 | .00609 | .01343 | .05156 | .01407 | .01452 | .01944 | .02972 | .03122 | .01931 | .01806 | .00800 | .00771 | .03545 | .01258 | .03414 | .03645 |
| 14 | .01005 | .04217 | .04966 | .02746 | .02671 | .02961 | .05617 | .06787 | .02847 | .02665 | .04200 | .05755 | .08313 | .10895 | .02044 | .00934 |
| 15 | 0 | 0 | 0 | 0 | 0 | 0 | 0 | 0 | 0 | 0 | 0 | 0 | 0 | 0 | 0 | 0 |
| 16 | 0 | 0 | 0 | 0 | 0 | 0 | 0 | 0 | 0 | 0 | 0 | 0 | 0 | 0 | 0 | 0 |

SOURCE: *Matriz de Insumo-Producto de México año 1970,* Secretaría de Programación y Presupuesto, Banco de México, Mexico City, 1976, pp. 73, updated to 1978 as detailed in text.

*TABLE B.2.*
*Parameters of the Production Functions*

| *Sector* | $\beta i$ | $\alpha i$ | $\alpha_{1i}$ | $\alpha_{2i}$ | $\alpha_{3i}$ | $\alpha_{4i}$ | $\alpha_{5i}$ |
|---|---|---|---|---|---|---|---|
| 1 | .488 | .337 | .0008 | .0052 | .0102 | — | .3208 |
| 2 | .482 | .518 | .0199 | .0592 | .0889 | .3500 | — |
| 3 | .673 | .327 | .0388 | .0183 | .0717 | .1982 | — |
| 4 | .555 | .445 | .0259 | .0380 | .1063 | .2748 | — |
| 5 | .411 | .589 | .0088 | .0192 | .1213 | .4397 | — |
| 6 | .551 | .449 | .0153 | .0283 | .1058 | .2996 | — |
| 7 | .558 | .442 | .0325 | .0373 | .1722 | .2000 | — |
| 8 | .346 | .654 | .0232 | .0303 | .1559 | .4446 | — |
| 9 | .291 | .709 | .0574 | .0360 | .1844 | .4312 | — |
| 10 | .404 | .596 | .0343 | .0357 | .1793 | .3467 | — |
| 11 | .467 | .490 | .0637 | .0340 | .1756 | .2167 | — |
| 12 | .370 | .630 | .0107 | .0161 | .2105 | .3927 | — |
| 13 | .329 | .576 | .0140 | .0280 | .1137 | .4203 | — |
| 14 | .415 | .585 | .0969 | .0863 | .1682 | .2336 | — |
| 15 | .220 | .780 | .0708 | .0371 | .0986 | .5735 | — |

SOURCE: Sidaoui (1978).

Planning and Budget to be used in the formulation of the Global Development Plan (Plan Global de Desarrollo). It was obtained by updating the 72-sector matrix elaborated by Banco de México in 1970 using the RAS ($r_i a_{ij} s_j$) method. This matrix has the great advantage of being a matrix of total requirements *(not* solely of domestic requirements, as are the matrices of 1960 and 1975) and thus allows one to disaggregate imports and exports by sector, instead of creating an additional, artificial imports sector and treating exports as exogenous variables. The matrix is valued in producer prices of 1978.

3. As already mentioned, we chose the Cobb-Douglas form for the production functions of value added of all sectors. Except for sectors 1, 11, and 13 (agriculture, electricity, and transportation) we assumed constant returns to scale in the use of capital and all kinds of labor skills. For sectors, 1, 11, and 13 the sums of the production elasticicities are 0.825, 0.957, and 0.905, respectively. All the production function parameters were taking from Sidaoui (1978, pp. 38–45), and they appear in Table B-2.

4. Estimation of all the consumption price elasticities is based on information about the mean propensities to consume, income elasticities, and the flexibility of the marginal utility of money. The mean propensities were obtained from the input-output table and the income elasticities from Sidaoui (1978, p. 53). For the flexibility of the marginal utility of income we use Sidaoui's value of $-3.3$. We assumed that the construction sector does not produce consumption goods, and given that the proportion of the output of the mining sector that is consumed by the private sector is very

*TABLE B.3.*

*Sectoral price elasticities of demand (Buyers' prices) Mexico 1978*

*Price j*

| *Good i* | *1* | *2* | *3* | *4* | *5* | *6* | *7* | *8* | *9* | *10* | *11* | *12* | *13* | *14* | *15* |
|---|---|---|---|---|---|---|---|---|---|---|---|---|---|---|---|
| 1 | −.1932 | — | −.0040 | −.1545 | −.0528 | −.0096 | −.0132 | −.0017 | — | −.0233 | −.0021 | — | −.0282 | −.1038 | — |
| 2 | — | — | — | — | — | — | — | — | — | — | — | — | — | — | — |
| 3 | −.0219 | — | −.3524 | −.2934 | −.1003 | −.0183 | −.0250 | −.0033 | — | −.0442 | −.0041 | — | −.0536 | −.1971 | — |
| 4 | −.0153 | — | −.0053 | −.4448 | −.0699 | −.0128 | −.0174 | −.0023 | — | −.0308 | −.0028 | — | −.0373 | −.1374 | — |
| 5 | −.0178 | — | −.0062 | −.2391 | −.3628 | −.0149 | −.0204 | −.0027 | — | −.0360 | −.0033 | — | −.0437 | −.1607 | — |
| 6 | −.0206 | — | −.0071 | −.2758 | −.0943 | −.3413 | −.0235 | −.0031 | — | −.0416 | −.0038 | — | −.0504 | −.1853 | — |
| 7 | −.0168 | — | −.0058 | −.2256 | −.0771 | −.0141 | −.2844 | −.0025 | — | −.0340 | −.0031 | — | −.0412 | −.1516 | — |
| 8 | −.0269 | — | −.0094 | −.3612 | −.1235 | −.0225 | −.0308 | −.4285 | — | −.0544 | −.0050 | — | −.0660 | −.2427 | — |
| 9 | — | — | — | — | — | — | — | — | — | — | — | — | — | — | — |
| 10 | −.0329 | — | −.0114 | −.4408 | −.1507 | −.0275 | −.0376 | −.0049 | — | −.5844 | −.0061 | — | −.0805 | −.2962 | — |
| 11 | −.0199 | — | −.0069 | −.2673 | −.0914 | −.0167 | −.0228 | −.0030 | — | −.0403 | −.3178 | — | −.0488 | −.1796 | — |
| 12 | — | — | — | — | — | — | — | — | — | — | — | — | — | — | — |
| 13 | −.0262 | — | −.0091 | −.3518 | −.1203 | −.0219 | −.0300 | −.0039 | — | −.0530 | −.0049 | — | −.4777 | −.2364 | — |
| 14 | −.0237 | — | −.0082 | −.3174 | −.1085 | −.0198 | −.0270 | −.0035 | — | −.0478 | −.0044 | — | −.0580 | −.5862 | — |
| 15 | — | — | — | — | — | — | — | — | — | — | — | — | — | — | — |

SOURCE: Sidaoui (1978).

small, we chose to assume there is no private demand for mining products. Furthermore, following Johansen (1974, pp. 95–98), it was supposed that there is no direct private demand for commerce services. Instead, we derived an *indirect* demand for these services from the assumption of the existence of trade margins which are fixed in real terms for sectors 1–10 (trade margins in the remaining sectors are assumed to be zero). This assumption makes it possible to transform the information about the demand system—expressed originally in consumer prices—to producer prices. The trade margins were estimated following Sidaoui's procedure (1978, pp. 48–50). The matrix of the demand price elasticities appears in Table B-3, and the mean propensities to consume and the income elasticities are in Table B-4.

5. There is no informatin on the levels of tariff protection for 1978. The latest study is that of Cavazos (1977) where implicit levels of protection for 35 sectors in 1975 was estimated. To calculate values of international prices by sector for 1978, Cavazos's data were adjusted for the differential rates of accumulated inflation in Mexico and the United States for the period 1975–1978 (for Mexico, the sectorial GDP deflators were used; for the United States, the indices of producer prices in the *Survey of Current Business* were used). The value of the exchange rate used to convert domestic prices into international prices was 22.767 pesos per dollar (the average value of the exchange rate in 1978). It was assumed that the indirect tax rates were the same as in 1970. These rates and the values of the international prices appear in Table B-4.

*TABLE B.4.*

| Sector | *Demand income elasticities (Buyer's prices)* | *Mean propensities to consume (Buyer's prices)* | *Tariff rates (%)* | *Indirect tax rates (%)* |
|---|---|---|---|---|
| 1 | .5994 | .0235 | −12.66 | 0.41 |
| 2 | — | .0022 | −27.71 | 3.90 |
| 3 | 1.1378 | .0102 | 10.26 | 8.02 |
| 4 | .7930 | .3394 | 13.22 | 2.97 |
| 5 | .9274 | .1226 | 32.14 | 1.22 |
| 6 | 1.0696 | .0238 | 18.22 | 1.53 |
| 7 | .8750 | .0299 | 40.02 | 2.65 |
| 8 | 1.4009 | .0050 | 22.59 | 2.25 |
| 9 | — | .0010 | 29.61 | 1.02 |
| 10 | 1.7095 | .0806 | 37.36 | 2.43 |
| 11 | 1.0367 | .0052 | — | 11.41 |
| 12 | — | — | — | 7.41 |
| 13 | 1.3644 | .0803 | — | 0.99 |
| 14 | 1.2309 | .2763 | — | 2.27 |
| 15 | — | 0 | — | 0.69 |

SOURCES: Cavazos (1977) and Sidaoui (1978).

6. No information on labor employment by productive sector is available for 1978. To estimate the sectorial shares in the total employment for each skill class, we used the PLAN's projections of total sectorial employment for 1978 and assumed that, within each sector, the proportion in which labor of each skill class was used was the same as in 1970.

7. The input-output matrix for 1978 showed that some portion of the output sectors we classified as producers of nontradeable goods was in effect traded internationally. However, since the traded volumes were generally insignificant, we considered them among the exogneous components of demand. In what follows, we shall describe the way in which the values of the exogenous variables used in the simulations were obtained.

8. With the exception of the mining sector—in which case private consumption is included—the exogenous component of demand for sectors 1–14 includes government consumption and changes in inventories (with the adjustments for nontraded goods that have been mentioned). The PLAN includes projections of the total amount of government consumption and of the changes in inventories by sector. To estimate the rates of growth of the exogenous components of demand, we calculated the weighted sums of the growth rates of their components in the period 1980–1990, assuming that the government consumption of the output of all sectors grows at the same rate (13.54 percent). On the other hand, all the demand for the output of the capital goods sectors is exogenous. We assumed that for both sector 14 and sector 15 demand would grow at the same rate,which is the mean rate of growth of total investment in the period 1980–1990 according to the PLAN's projections.

9. The rate of growth of the capital stocks for sectors 2–15 (with the exception of sectors 3 and 9, that is, agriculture and oil) was estimated by applying the mean annual rates of growth of total sectorial investment for the period 1980–1990 projected by the PLAN to the data on gross sectorial investment for 1970 that appear in the document *Acervos y Formacíon de Capital* (ACERVOS), published by Banco de México. Substituting the appropriate provisions for depreciation (estimated from the 1970 data in ACERVOS), we calculated the net additions to the 1970 stock and the resulting mean annual growth rate for the following ten periods. In the cases of the oil and basic metals sectors (sectors 3 and 9) we chose to follow a different procedure because of the special characteristics of the time pattern of investment in these industries in the recent past. In both cases, very considerable investment projects were undertaken in the last years of the past decade; therefore, we decided to use the mean annual rate of growth of total sectorial investment for the period 1978–1990 instead of the corresponding rates for the period 1980–1990.

In ACERVOS there are no estimates of the total capital stock in the agricultural sector. For our simulations, we arbitrarily assumed a growth rate of 8.02 percent (equal to half the mean annual growth rate of investment in this sector).

*TABLE B.5.*
*Values of Exogenous Variables Used in Simulations*

| *Sector* | *Growth of sectorial capital stock* $K_i'$ % | *Growth of exogenous demand* $Z_i'$ % | *Rate of change of tariffs* $T_i'$ % | *Rate of technological change* $\epsilon_i'$ % | *Basic data on growth of "sectorial investment"* % |
|---|---|---|---|---|---|
| 1 | 8.02 | 7.81 | +10.0 | 0 | 16.05 |
| 2 | 10.27 | 6.00 | +10.0 | 0 | 9.39 |
| 3 | 6.49 | 8.69 | 0 | 7.46 | 1.18 |
| 4 | 10.64 | 9.36 | +10.0 | 0 | 11.13 |
| 5 | 17.29 | 15.79 | −10.0 | 0 | 18.99 |
| 6 | 6.73 | 13.39 | +10.0 | 0 | 16.07 |
| 7 | 13.64 | 6.15 | −10.0 | 0 | 12.89 |
| 8 | 10.38 | 14.01 | −10.0 | 0 | 18.27 |
| 9 | 10.46 | 11.49 | −10.0 | 0 | 17.00 |
| 10 | 15.47 | 13.28 | −10.0 | 0 | 19.68 |
| 11 | 6.62 | 13.54 | — | 0 | 9.12 |
| 12 | 18.78 | 13.54 | — | 0 | 15.54 |
| 13 | 10.54 | 13.54 | — | 0 | 14.20 |
| 14 | 9.51 | 13.54 | — | 0 | 10.31 |
| 15 | 17.90 | 11.57 | — | 0 | 20.26 |
| 16 | — | 11.57 | — | — | — |

SOURCE: The Mexican government's industrial plan.

10. A gross estimate of the rates of sectorial neutral techological change could be obtained as the difference between the growth rate of sectorial value added and the weighted sum of the growth rates of the inputs hired by each sector. However, this procedure could not be followed because of the absence of adequate time series for the labor force. Therefore, in the simulations we arbitrarily assumed a zero rate of neutral technological change for all sector, except for the oil sector. For this sector we assumed a mean annual growth rate of 7.46 percent. As in the preceding section positive technological change would reduce the labor required for the production of a given level of output.

11. The growth rates of the first three labor skill classes were taken from Sidaoui (1978, p. 69). Sidaoui's data consist of the projections elaborated by Keesing and Manne (1973) for the period 1968–1980, but for the lack of better information, relevant to the classification of the labor force that we use here, we decided to use them. These data appear in Table B-5.

12. The mean annual growth rate of the net trade balance was taken from the PLAN's projections.

## Bibliography

Cavazos, M. "Evolución del Protecionismo en México." *Commercio y Desarrollo* (Nov.–Dec. 1977). pp. 28–42.

Cornelius, W. A. "Mexican Migration to the United States (with Comparative Reference to Caribbean-Basin Migration): The State of Current Knowledge and Recommendations for Future Research." Working Paper No. 2, San Diego: Center for U.S.-Mexican Studies, University of California, 1978.

Domestic Council Committee on Illegal Aliens. Preliminary Report, Washington, D.C., 1976.

Frisch, R. *A Complete Scheme for Computing All Direct and Cross Demand Elasticities in a Model with Many Sectors, 1959.*

Johansen, L. *A Multi-Sectorial Study of Economic Growth,* 2nd enlarged ed. Amsterdam: North-Holland, 1974.

Keesing, D. and Manne, A. "Manpower Projections," in Louis Goreux and Alan Manne, eds., *Multilevel Planning: Case Studies in Mexico* (North Holland American: Elsevier, 1973).

Marshall, F. R. "Economic Factors Influencing the International Migration of workers," in S. R. Ross, ed., *Views across the Border: The United States and Mexico*. Albuquerque: University of New Mexico Press, 1978.

McKinnon, R. "Foreign Trade Regimes and Economic Development: A Review Article," *Stanford University CREG Reprint No. 178,* 1979.

Reynolds, C., and C. Tello, ed. *United States-Mexico Relations: Social and Economic Aspects*. Stanford, Calif.: Stanford University Press, 1983.

Sidaoui, J. J. "Factor Market Distortions in a Multisectorial Model: A Case Study Mexico," unpublished Ph.D. dissertation, George Washington University, Washington, D.C., 1978.

Taylor, L., and S. Black. *Practical General Equilibrium Estimation of Resource Pulls Under Trade Liberalization*. Vol. 4, pp. 38–58, 1974.

## Notes

1. This chapter was written in 1981. It has subsequently been reviewed in the light of major events affecting the economy of Mexico in 1982. Where relevant, footnotes and slight textual revisions have been made to reflect the implications of the current crisis.

2. Events since the 1982 crisis increase the relevance of this point, since austerity measures including exchange controls have already had a severe dampening effect on do-

mestic employment, while real depreciation of the exchange rate increases the attractiveness of migration.

3. This section draws from concepts developed in a paper by Clark Reynolds entitled "Mexican-U.S. Interdependence: Economic and Social Perspectives," to be published in *United States-Mexico Relations: Social and Economic Aspects,* Clark Reynolds and Carlos Tello (eds.), Stanford University Press, (Stanford, 1983).

4. See P. A. Samuelson, "International Trade and the Equalization of Factor Prices, "*Economic Journal* 58 (June 1948) 163–184. A. P. Lerner, "Factor Prices and International Trade," *Econometrica* 20 (Feb. 1952), 1095 reprinted in *Essays in Economic Analysis* (London: Macmillan, 1953), originally given at a seminar at the London School of Economics in December 1933. For a clear presentation of these and related theories, see M. O. Clement, R. L. Pfister, and K. J. Rothwell, *Theoretical Issues in International Economics,* Houghton Mifflin, Boston, 1967, Chap. 1, "Trade and Relative Factor Prices." More important assumptions underlying the pure (Samuelson) factor price equalization theorem include two homogeneous consumption goods and two factors of production identical in both countries, incomplete specialization in production by either trading partner, perfect competition in both goods and factor markets, fixed supplies of factors in both countries including no net international migration or capital flows, identical tastes in both countries, different factor endowments but common technologies in the two countries, free and costless trade, and constant returns to scale. Clearly these simplifying assumptions depart widely from conditions obtaining in the United States and Mexico. Yet the underlying principles of the model are considered to be a useful point of departure for examining the effects of trade and other aspects of exchange on, e.g., wage level and the pattern of wage convergence between the two countries. By relaxing the more rigid assumptions of the formal model, an attempt is made to return to the broader historical perspective of Heckscher and Ohlin in which trade and welfare are related to the process of growth and structural change.

5. Like all macroeconomic studies, our analysis assumes that one can meaningfully aggregate the different products which compose a sector and the production of a single product for domestic use and export. Changes in the mix of products that compose a sector, or differences in the labor intensity of domestic and export-oriented production, could alter the following results. But these effects are in general small and nonsystematic. For example, some might argue that agricultural production for export takes place disproportionately in those regions of irrigation and greater capital intensity where the labor/value-added ratio is lower than average for the rural sector, much of which involves primitive rainfed cultivation. Actually, however, a number of export cash crops from Mexico are highly labor intensive, including cotton, fruits, and winter vegetables. Such exports have higher labor inputs than average in agriculture, especially when compared with wheat and corn production, which are import-substituting activities. Recent trends in exports have worked against agriculture, while in the past couple of years, food crop imports have accelerated. A more detailed examination of the new Systema Alimentario Mexicano (SAM) self-sufficiency program is required if its consequences for employment generation are to be determined.

6. Here again the post-July 1982 scenario makes this even more imperative, as part of a stabilization-with-restructuring program for the next *sexenio*.

7. A more complete breakdown of employment by skill categories is presented in Sidaoui (citation in the Appendix).

8. See Table 8-4.

9. Mario Blejer, *Dinero, Precios, y la Balanza de Pagos: La Experiencia de México 1950–1973,* Centro de Estudios Monetarios Latino-Americanos (CEMLA), Mexico City, 1977.

10. The 1982 devaluations and exchange controls lowered costs and increased the profitability of *maquiladora* operations but may retard the development of these vital linkages.

11. This section draws heavily on C. W. Reynolds's "Labor Market Projects for the United States and Mexico and Their Relevance to Current Migration Controversies," *Food Research Institute Studies* 17, No. 20 (1979). More recent estimates of temporary and permanent migration by Mexico's Labor Department research program CENIET do not significantly alter the basis of the calculations in Table 8-4. See the paper by Manuel Garcia y Griego in Reynolds and Tello (1983), *op. cit.*

12. This estimate is based on the incremental capital-labor ratio in Mexico taken from official macroeconomic statistics.

13. Surprisingly, the government has remained virtually silent on the question of migration, seeing it as a "nonproblem," even when passage of the controversial Simpson-Mazzoli Act seemed imminent. In 1983, the act remains mired deep in the legislative process and now seems sure to lose support as the U.S. economy recovers.

14. Elsewhere C. W. Reynolds estimated that the benefit of migration of Mexican workers to the U.S. economy in 1975 was at least $16 billion or about $80 per capita on average for all U.S.-citizens: Reynolds, "Analysis of the Impact of the U.S. Economy on the Economy of Mexico and its Border Region" (revised), April 1980. Note that earlier estimates of remittances should be scaled down to reflect the recent work of Juan Diez-Canedo (M.I.T. Ph.D. dissertation, 1980) which estimates remittances through financial institutions (money orders, postal money orders, personal and other checks) to have been only $317 million in 1975. Diez-Canedo argues persuasively that migration to the United States tends to affect that class of rural and urban households which is somewhat above the subsistence level, while the poorest families tend to migrate to Mexico's urban areas. Diez-Canedo's work also reinforces the belief that certain states and municipalities contribute very disproportionately to the total number of Mexican migrants, and the effects of remittances can often be readily seen as oases of relative prosperity.

15. The imposition of exchange controls in 1982 may prove to be a significant setback to development of production sharing and substantially reduce the incentive for foreigners to invest in production targeted for Mexican consumers.

16. Since the beginning of the 1970s, Mexico has introduced a number of laws to restrict the operation of foreign enterprises, to increase the national share of returns from foreign technology, and to expand the degree of Mexicanization of important sectors of the economy. While at first this appeared to discourage foreign direct investment, especially during the Echeverría administration, since the oil bonanza there has been an increase in firms seeking access to the lucrative Mexican market and its labor—which is still low cost by U.S. standards. See Van R. Whiting, Jr., *The Politics of Technology Transfer in Mexico,* Department of Political Science, University of California, Berkeley, 1980, and *Programa Nacional de Ciencia y Tecnología,* 1978–1982, Consejo Nacional de Ciencia y Tecnología, CONACYT, Oct. 1978. Mexico City. Also see Chapter 9 in the volume.

17. When we speak of "Mexicans" in the United States, we refer to all legal and illegal immigrants from Mexico who entered this country between 1940 and the present and their progeny, regardless of place of birth. This is clearly not the same as "people of Mexican origin" as detailed in a recent *Current Population Survey*. The magnitude of the different (about 1.5 million people) can be explained as being all legal and illegal immigrants and their descendants who came before 1940.

18. This section is based on a formal model adopted by Raul Ramos for the purpose of this project.

19. Labor supply projections are from "Labor Market Projections for the United States and Mexico and Their Relevance to Current Migration Controversies." by C. W. Reynolds in *Food Research Institute Studies* 17, No. 2 (1979).

20. The fixed proportions are equal to the proportions of total investment that sectors other than construction produced in 1978.

21. All symbols with apostrophes represent log changes.

# CHAPTER 9

# *The Regulation of Foreign Investment in Mexico and Its Impact on Income Distribution*

Paul E. Sigmund

In many parts of the Third World, the dominant neoclassical argument for the advantages of direct foreign investment has come under increasing attack—not only from Marxist-influenced writers but more generally from the advocates of accelerated national economic and social development through state action.

Three aspects in particular have been emphasized in the critique of foreign investment: the loss of national control over economic policy due to foreign ownership of important elements of the national economy, the long-run negative impact on the balance of payments of the repatriation of profits and payments for royalties and technology, and the adverse effects on income distribution of the capital-intensive character of foreign investment which establishes models of production and consumption that are inappropriate for labor-surplus economies with large proportions of their populations living in poverty.[1]

Two possible policies may be adopted by the capital-importing countries to deal with these problems. On the one hand, they can assert national control, attempt to capture the payments to foreigners, and reorient technology and consumption patterns by nationalizing foreign investment. This is the course that many Third World countries have taken in the area of natural resources, particularly petroleum. However, nationalization can have serious costs, in lessened efficiency, diminished access to international capital, loss of technology and markets, and the politicization of economic relations. Only in Communist countries has state control of the entire economy been seen as desirable, although a number of countries have used nationalization to secure national ownership and control of the "commanding heights" of the economy.[2]

An increasingly common method to secure national control—or at least influence—over the investment policy as well as in some cases a share in ownership and profits of foreign enterprise is the use of screening mechanisms by the government to set conditions upon and regulate the performance of foreign investors. Before a foreign investor is permitted to enter the national economy, he or she must satisfy certain government requirements which are designed to maximize the return to the national economy and to minimize the social costs.[3] The advantage of investment screening over nationalization is that the developing country retains access to the capital, technology, and markets offered by the foreign investor, but—depending on its bargaining power—can set prerequisites of entry and, in some cases, of continuing activity that conform to national priorities.

One of these priorities—although it is not the only one—is the impact of foreign investment on income distribution to labor through job creation and labor-intensive investment, to domestic private capital through a share in ownership and profits, and to government through taxation. Others include development of linkages to other parts of the economy, expansion of exports, training of nationals, and the transfer of technology. In making national investment-screening policy, the capital-importing country must decide how to rank those priorities, conscious of the fact that in some cases they may be in conflict.

This chapter will attempt to analyze the Mexican experience with the regulation of foreign investment. It will argue that the principal condition now placed on the entrance of foreign investment into Mexico—that of 51 percent Mexican ownership—has led to a transfer of income from the foreign investor to a limited number of Mexican private industrialists and investors but that the procedure of granting exemptions from the Mexicanization requirement includes criteria that can have a positive effect on the distribution of income through increases in employment and the promotion of the development of less industrialized areas. A further effect of the investment-screening legislation has been the creation of a regulatory body, the Foreign Investment Commission, to monitor the Mexicanization process and to grant exceptions to it—which has substantially increased the capacity of the Mexican government to control foreign investment and to direct it to government objectives. The chapter therefore concludes that this capacity can be used now to give a greater emphasis to distributional considerations by using the screening process to assure that all foreign investment—not just that desiring exemption from Mexicanization—conforms to government development objectives.

## Regulation of Foreign Investment in Mexico

The Mexican government has attempted to control and direct foreign economic activity ever since the end of the Mexican revolution. In the 1920s, this involved takeovers of foreign-owned land and limits on bank holdings. In the 1930s, railroads and petroleum were nationalized. In

1944, new foreign investors were required by an executive decree to register with the Ministry of Foreign Relations, and the ministry was given the power to require majority ownership by Mexicans in areas which it deemed vital to the national interest. In 1947 an interministerial committee on foreign investment was formed, and it issued twelve decrees before becoming dormant in 1953. In the 1950s the treasury began to examine foreign technology payments for tax purposes and to disallow payments in excess of 3 percent of net annual sales. In 1959 a law gave the government a monopoly on the production and distribution of primary petrochemicals and required 60 percent Mexican ownership in the area of secondary petrochemicals. In 1960 foreign-owned electric companies were nationalized, and in 1961 new mining legislation mandated Mexicanization of the mining industry, sharply reducing taxes on companies that were 51 percent Mexican-owned and granting new concessions to foreign investors only if 66 percent ownership was in Mexican hands. In 1962, the importation of foreign motor vehicles was prohibited, and domestically produced vehicles were required to use a minimum of 60 percent domestically produced parts. In 1967 government pressures forced the sale to Mexicans of foreign-owned sulfur industry, and in 1970 the outgoing Diaz Ordáz administration required 51 percent Mexican ownership in the areas of steel, cement, glass, fertilizer, cellulose, and aluminum, By 1970 foreign investment had moved out of mining and transportation and into manufacturing. Foreign—principally but not exclusively U.S.—investment in Mexico was responsible for a majority of production in the areas of tobacco (97 percent), rubber products (64 percent), chemicals (51 percent), nonelectric (52 percent) and electric (50 percent) machinery, and transportation equipment (64 percent).[4]

With the exception of the nationalization of petroleum in 1938 the Mexican government's actions tended to avoid confrontation with the foreign investor, preferring a bargaining relationship, which has somctimes been compared to negotiations between two monopolists, with one side controlling access to the domestic market, import licenses, legal and tax concessions, etc., and the other offering capital, technology, managerial and production techniques, and access to foreign markets. Few doubted that the foreign investors had something to offer Mexico. The only questions were in what areas, at what cost, and subject to what limits. Mexican legislation and policy governing foreign investment had emerged as a result of a relatively haphazard process without a consistent and integrated vision of the place of foreign investment as a whole in Mexican development—except to encourage foreign investment in import-substituting manufacturing and to force the foreigner out of the extractive industries, utilities, and transportation.

Here, as in so many other areas, things began to change with the advent of the administration of Luis Echeverría in late 1970. Under Echeverría there was a reexamination of the arguments for and against foreign investment—and more generally of the whole model of stabilized development which had dominated the thinking of Mexican policymakers since the early 1950s. While it was admitted that Mexico had grown at a very rapid rate, the social and distributional effects of the earlier policies, particularly in the area of income distribution and employment, were criticized as to a large degree negative. Tariff protection and the encouragement of industrialization had resulted in high profits for industrialists and a pattern of capital-intensive development at a time when Mexico was suffering from massive unemployment and rapid migration to the cities. The impressive 6.6 percent annual growth rate between 1950 and 1970 had only produced an average annual increase in employment of 2.5 percent, while population had grown by 3.4 percent a year.[5] Some of the studies of income distribution did indicate a decrease in share of the very wealthy in favor of the middle and upper-middle classes, but all seemed to agree that the share of the poor had diminished as a result of industrialization. In addition the import substitution program did not seem to have remedied Mexico's chronic balance of payments problem but had only replaced imports of consumer goods with imports of machinery, capital goods, replacement parts and—increasingly in the decade of the 1970s—of basic grains.

Worse still, much of the industrial growth was being carried out by multinational corporations that entered the Mexican market by buying out Mexican firms, often with money borrowed locally, and that benefited from cheap labor and energy costs and complete freedom to repatriate capital and profits, while making their policies on the basis of transnational corporate interests with little or no concern for their impact on Mexican development. The net effect of the remission abroad of profits, royalties, and technology payments, it was argued, far exceeded new capital brought in by foreign investors, thus seriously worsening Mexico's increasingly critical balance of payments. In turn, the defenders of foreign investment pointed to the jobs they had created and the imports that they had saved and decried the illogic of their critics in basing their case for exploitation on a fallacious comparison of net annual inflow of new foreign investment each year with the outflow of payments for profits and royalties which were based on long-standing and productive earlier investment already in Mexico.[6]

The criticisms of the multinationals that were most frequent were that buy-outs by foreign investors of existing Mexican firms were "denationalizing" the Mexican economy, that the multinationals were charging excessively high prices for royalties and technology licensing, and that they relied on capital-intensive technology that was inappropriate for Mexico's labor-surplus economy. Spurred by research by both Mexican and American scholars that appeared to support these charges and urged by the foreign investors themselves to establish a clear set of "rules of the game," the Echeverría administration introduced legislation aimed both at remedying these abuses and at systematizing the haphazard patchwork of controls on foreign investment in Mexico.

## New Regulatory Legislation

On December 20, 1972, a law was adopted establishing the National Registry on the Transfer of Technology to register all existing foreign technology contracts and to review and approve or disapprove all proposed new technology contracts. Contracts involving excessive payments for technology were to be rejected. (The upper limit on such payments was initially the 3 percent of sales used by the Treasury, but most contracts involved a lesser figure, diminishing over a period of 5 to 10 years.) No contracts were permitted for technology already freely available in Mexico, and contractual limits on exports and sales were prohibited. In his last report to the Mexican Congress in September 1976, President Echeverría claimed that between 1973 and 1976 the law had saved Mexico between four and eight billion pesos—an estimate that seems to have included all payments for the life of the contracts. In the first 5 years of the program, 6,904 contracts were approved and 2,109 rejected, principally for excessively high payments. In one well-publicized case a licensor in the chemical industry had his technology payment reduced from $4 million to $100,000 because the registry informed him that similar technology was available from another country at the latter price.[7]

The most important piece of new legislation in the foreign investment field was the Law to Promote Mexican Investment and to Regulate Foreign Investment which came into effect in May 1973. This law created a National Registry of Foreign Investment and required all existing foreign-owned firms to register with it. It reserved to state ownership the areas of petroleum and basic petrochemicals, nuclear energy, electricity, railroads, telephone and telegraphs, and some mining. It also reserved for 100% Mexican ownership radio and television, communications, forestry, gas distribution, and air and sea transportation. The central focus of the law, however, was a requirement that all new investment by foreigners be 51 percent Mexican-owned. This seemingly sweeping extension of the earlier partial Mexicanization policy was, however, qualified by a lengthy article (Article 13) which listed a total of seventeen "considerations" which were to be taken into account by an interministerial National Commission on Foreign Investment in authorizing new investments and granting exceptions to the 51 percent requirement.

The Foreign Investment Law (and the earlier Technology Transfer Law) thus attempted to achieve two goals which could have an impact on income distribution. First, the Mexicanization and technology transfer requirements attempted to secure a share in the profits of foreign firms for Mexican investors which (except for tax revenues) had accrued exclusively to foreigners and to reduce payments abroad for technology. Second, the establishment of registries for foreign investment and technology contracts gave the government instruments to control foreign investment in ways that could be used to protect Mexican industry, promote development, and direct investment in ways that were socially beneficial—including some that could improve the distribution of income. In particular, the provision for granting exceptions to Mexicanization allowed equity and other considerations to be taken into account by Mexican policymakers in deciding when to waive or alter the Mexicanization requirements.

The most important of the factors which the legislation directed the Foreign Investment Commission to consider were the effect of the proposed investment on exports and the Mexican balance of payments, the new technology and specialized training that it brought to the country, and, most significant for the purpose of this chapter, its impact on the generation of new jobs and on the development of less developed parts of the country. The Foreign Investment Commission, which includes, in addition to an executive secretary who is also the Director General of the Foreign Investment Registry, the representatives of the Ministries of the Interior, Foreign Relations, Finance, Commerce, Labor, National Properties (Patrimonio), and Programming and Budget, was empowered to grant exceptions to the 49 percent limit, when "in its judgment it is convenient for the economy of the country" (Article 5). The law was to be applied not only to foreign investment entering the country for the first time but also to the establishment of new product lines and the entry into new but related areas by existing foreign-owned enterprise.[8]

The law also incorporated the previously existing requirements that secondary petrochemicals and auto parts be 60 percent Mexican-owned. It did not affect the auto industry as such, which continued to be largely foreign-owned, mostly on a 100 percent basis. Indeed, shortly before the new law was adopted, Chrysler of Mexico was permitted to buy out its Mexican partner and become a 100-percent-owned subsidiary. Chrysler was allowed to do so because it threatened to close down in Mexico, thus eliminating five thousand jobs if it was not permitted to become a wholly owned subsidiary, since, it argued, that it would only fulfill other government requirements such as expanded exports on the basis of integration into the worldwide Chrysler system.

The automobile industry has always been treated as a special case, both because of its importance in the Mexican economy (in 1980 it employed 56,000 workers directly, and it was estimated that auto-related industry employed nearly 500,000 more) and because of its impact on Mexican relations with the United States and Japan. In the case of automobiles, policy control by the Mexican state and access to foreign technology markets are considered more important than Mexican ownership.[9]

Besides auto assembly, the other significant exceptions to the Mexicanization rule were the border industries which were exempted from the provisions of the Foreign Investment Law at the first meeting of the commission in June 1973. A special provision of U.S. law permitted U.S. companies to take advantage of the lower wage scales in Mexico to establish textile and electronic assembly plants for reexport to the United States with import duties paid only on the value added in Mexico. The Mexican Customs Code in turn exempted from import duties machinery and materials for the border plants provided that the resulting production was exported in its entirety. By the late 1970s, 470 such industries on the border and another 100 located in in-bond locations in the interior and at newly developing ports employed 100,000 Mexicans with that number likely to be doubled or tripled over the next 5 years. The majority of the workers were women, and their official minimum wage was the highest in Mexico, although still well below that in the United States.[10]

The cases of the auto industry and the border plant illustrate the twofold character of the regulation of foreign investment. While on its face it seemed that the 1973 law was primarily concerned with increasing Mexican ownership, exemption from Mexicanization was to be used as an instrument to direct foreign investment to areas of national priority, such as employment, technology transfer, and exports. Moreover, when as in autos or border and in-bond plants the possible impact of job creation was significant, wholesale exceptions were made to the Mexicanization rule. How has the new regime operated in practice in terms of its impact in these areas?

## The Impact of the Foreign Investment Law

Initially the new legislation was greeted critically by the foreign investment community. When the Kimberly Clark Company used the Mexican stock market to reduce its ownership to 43 percent in early 1973 and immediately repatriated the proceeds, this was seen as an indication that the results of Mexicanization might be a large-scale withdrawal of foreign investors from Mexico. In the mid-1970s a sharp drop-off in new foreign investments (from $362 million in 1974 to $295 million in 1975 and $231 million in 1976) seemed to be a further indication of the adverse effect of the law. In fact, it now seems in retrospect that the drop was more a response to the broader problems of the Mexican economy in the period immediately before and after the peso devaluations of the last half of 1976 than to the Foreign Investment Law. It is true that the commission got off to a slow start and maintained a hard line on the Mexicanization requirement, while bureaucratic delays created backlogs of as much as 7 months. However, in early 1978 a new executive secretary was appointed, the Technology Transfer Registry was transferred to his control, and within 4 months a backlog of 300 cases had been eliminated, and the commission was handling 35 cases a month and giving a formal reply to applications within 30 days. The staff information system was computerized and the application form simplfied from fourteen to two pages with considerable emphasis on informal consultations before formal submission. The staff also began to promote foreign investment in priority industries and to develop a file of Mexican investors to assist foreign firms seeking partners.[11]

In 1978 the Mexican economy also staged a recovery from its devaluation-induced depression, and new petroleum finds as well as the increase in the price of oil produced new sources of revenue and investment. Foreign investment increased by 60 percent in 1979 and 35 percent in 1980, and new U.S. investment in manufacturing grew by $276 million in 1978, $560 million in 1979, and $1 billion in 1980.[12] It seemed that the other positive aspects of the economy far outweighed any deterrent effect of the investment regulation legislation. After Brazil, Mexico was the chief recipient of U.S. investment in Latin America, accounting for about 12.5 percent of the total U.S. investment in the area.

The commission is now taking very seriously its role in directing foreign investment toward national priorities. Those priorities are specified in the original law, but at the end of the article spelling them out there is a blanket phrase listing as a final consideration "the level to which [the investment] conforms to the goals and policies of Mexican development." Those goals and policies were more clearly articulated in a series of planning documents including the National Employment Plan and the National Industrial Plan published in 1979 and the Global Development Plan and the National Energy Plan that appeared in 1980. The National Employment Plan set an overall goal of the creation of 2.5 million jobs over a 3-year period, and the job-creating impact of a proposed new investment is very important in the Foreign Investment Commission's thinking. However, those who have dealt with the commission emphasize that other considerations such as export promotion and regional decentralization should also be part of the package if a company wants approval of its proposals to avoid or postpone Mexicanization.

One example that has been publicized is the speedy approval of an $11 million investment by Becton Dickinson to produce medical supplies at a new factory away from Mexico City where its present factory is located. Full foreign ownership was approved by the commission because it created new jobs in a "marginal" area and produced socially useful products with the use of new production technologies and reduced technology fees from 2.5 to 1 percent of sales. Other examples include a Texas Instruments plant in Aguascalientes and an oil drill head plant in Vera Cruz.[13]

In an interview with the author of this chapter, a representative of the Secretariat *(Dirección General)* of the Foreign Investment Commission gave the figures on commission actions in the period between May 1978 and May 1980. Out of 582 applications for exemption from Mexicanization, 421 or 72 percent had been approved. Forty percent of the applications involved the generation of exports, 25 percent replaced imports, 30 percent were located in priority regions that needed economic development, and 40 percent involved the transfer of new technology without the payments of royalties. The approved projects involved the creation of 33,670 jobs.[14]

The Ministry of National Properties and Industrial Development gave another example of the use of the screening process to direct foreign investment to national development goals. A Pepsi-Cola expansion was tied to the manufacture and export of potato chip products, and both linked to job creation in marginal areas and to the production of proteinized food for the school lunch program.

On the other hand, once a foreign investor has Mexicanized (i.e., arranged 51 percent of Mexican ownership), he or she escapes the control of the commission—and judging from the complaints on this score by those interviewed at the Ministry of National Properties, it seems that Mexicanization is seen by the regulators as an obstacle to the attainment of the other national goals embodied in the criteria listed in Article 13 and applied by the commission. The major impact of the law has thus been to force association of Mexican and foreign capital, and investment screening for other purposes has been limited to the cases involving exceptions to Mexicanization, although it can be argued that the wording of Article 13 seems to give the commission a general power "to determine the convenience of authorizing foreign investment" on the basis of the criteria listed.

## Mexicanization Problems

Besides the post-Mexicanization loss of control over the direction and nature of foreign investment, the Mexicanization requirement has also led to a number of difficult problems of implementation.

1. *The use of the stock market and "pulverization."* An easy way to Mexicanize is to float an issue on the Mexican stock market. Government policy and the oil boom prosperity have combined to make the stock market much more important than heretofore, when bank credit was the only financing method used by government and industry.[15] It also provided a means of giving many more groups and individuals a share in Mexican development. Since the commission was interpreting the Mexicanization requirement strictly in connection with expansion and the development of new products, a number of existing American firms including Ralston Purina, Firestone, Hart, Schaffner and Marx, and Scott Paper reduced their ownership to 49 percent by stock market offerings. However, the representative of the Foreign Investment Commission on the National Securities Commission *(Comisioń Nacional de Valores)* began to fear that stock issues would dilute Mexican control so that a minority foreign holder could still exercise effective control while Mexican

capital resources were diverted to purchase the required 51 percent equity. In two cases in 1978, Mexicanization of foreign companies through stock market offerings were delayed until it could be demonstrated that the boards of directors would be structured in a way that would assure Mexican control. (The 1973 law already had unenforced sanctions against the widespread practice of *prestanombres,* the use of Mexican dummy owners to conceal the continued control by foreign investors.)

2. The desire to ensure effective Mexican control, however, created a new problem: *the increasing dominance of a small number of private Mexican industrial groups* that were the only ones capable of entering into agreements with the large multinationals in ways that ensured that Mexican interests were represented. By one estimate sixteen financial groups in Mexico dominate the private side of Mexicanization. Two in particular, the Alfa and VISA (Valores Industriales S.A.) groups, both controlled by members of the Garza Sada family of Monterrey, are particularly visible. Alfa is the largest private company in Latin America. It has entered into joint ventures with General Foods, Dupont, Hercules, Hitachi, Magnavox, Philco, Admiral, and Yamaha and a 75 percent/25 percent joint venture with Ford Motors to manufacture and export aluminum cyclinder heads. Between 1975 and 1979 Alfa's net assets grew from 11 billion pesos to nearly 53 billion pesos, principally through acquisitions and joint ventures. In 1980 it moved from 373rd to 288th in the *Fortune* magazine list of the 500 largest non-U.S. companies. Alfa ranks fifth, behind four state companies in the *Expansión* list of the 500 companies in Mexico. Among the areas in which it has interests are steel, paper, petrochemicals, mining, television, and food. VISA is 15th on the *Expansión* list. It owns the brewery that was the core of the Garza Sada family fortune and includes banking, animal feed, and building materials among its interests.[16]

A number of private Mexican industrial holding companies were established after the adoption of further legislation authorizing the creation of Mexican development corporations *(Sociedades de Fomento)* which were required to be wholly Mexican and to have a dominating interest in the Mexican proportion of any joint venture with foreign investors. The best-known is DESC *(Desarrollo Económico Sociedad Civil)* which is said to be especially interested in arrangements which involve the acquisition of sophisticated technology. It is associated with Monsanto, Phillips, RCA, SKF, and Bosch.[17]

There are no public figures on the impact of Mexicanization on the concentration of income, but one of those interviewed confessed to the author that "It has made me a rich man" and observed that the shortage of Mexican partners had enabled him to dictate terms to large foreign companies which included acquiring shares in existing and highly profitable Mexican operations as part of a package deal involving more risky expansions or new products. Mexicans with access to local capital and contacts with the multinationals have been able to take advantage of their position to secure a share of the monopoly or oligopoly profits of foreign enterprise with little or no risk on their part. The effective monopolization of aspects of the Mexican economy has not been threatened by the existence of an organic law implementing the antimonopoly provisions of Article 28 of the Mexican Constitution, since in practice it has not been enforced. Thus Mexicanization, while it has altered the balance between the foreign and domestic private sectors, has also encouraged further concentration of income and economic power in a small and politically influential group of Mexican businessmen.

An alternative source of Mexicanization capital is the banking sector. Banamex, one of the largest Mexican private banks, has assisted in a number of Mexicanizations, but it prefers to have less than a majority control. The two large government-owned development banks, Nacional Financiera and Somex, are also heavily involved, but there are financial and administrative limits to the degree to which they can become partners of multinational corporations in a way that involves the kind of control that the 1973 legislation contemplates. An increasingly common pattern, according to those interviewed, is a three-way joint venture in which the foreign firm is linked with a Mexican bank and a Mexican industrial firm. Nacional Financiera (Nafinsa) has a specific trust fund, the Fondo Nacional de Fomento Industrial (FOMIN) (National Fund for Industrial Development), to put up to 30 percent equity in new industrial ventures, and it is also involved in coinvestment funds with financial institutions in Britain, France, Germany, Spain, Italy, and Japan. Nafinsa now has eighty affiliate companies of which forty-five are majority-owned, and its total assets as of 1978 were 184 billion pesos. It is said to be especially interested in promoting secondary petrochemicals and the capital goods industry. Somex, the other government bank in the industrial development area, controls thirty-six companies and is a partner of thirteen multinational corporations.[18] The two government banks are possible instruments to limit private economic power, but most Mexicanization is being carried out under private auspices.

3. A further result of the foreign investment legislation seems to have been *to discourage the small and medium-sized foreign (especially American) investor.* The legislation has not led to a decline in new foreign investment since as noted the declines in the mid-1970s seem to be related to other factors. However, the author's interviews with U.S. embassy officials who had been in touch with a number of potential investors indicated that despite the express desire of the Mexican government to attract them—since their investments are thought to be more labor intensive than those of the multinationals—smaller U.S. firms are deterred by the bureaucratic difficulties as well as the cost of complying with the complex Mexican regulations. One source estimated that between

$10,000 and $20,000 in lawyer's fees are required to secure necessary approvals. In the case of smaller firms with no experience in working abroad, a joint venture may also be seen as involving the risk of continual disagreements over policy and profits.[19] Thus if one assumes that some jobs which would have been created by investments by small and medium-sized foreign firms (or by larger firms opposed in principle to joint ventures) have been foregone as a result of the legislation, this would be another adverse effect of the legislation. It is difficult to estimate the overall magnitude involved, but it seems likely that it is not very large.

The Law on the Transfer of Technology that was adopted at the same time as the Foreign Investment Law and the Law on Inventions and Trademarks (1976) may also have had some deterrent effect. While most of the rejections of new technology contracts have been based on excessively high fees, the implementation of the law is reported to have become more flexible in this respect in recent years. However, the real deterrent to the transfer of new technology seems to be the danger that trade secrets will be compromised and the limits (a 10-year maximum is stated in the law, but shorter periods are also mandated) on the duration of the contract after which the technology is to be freely available. The Inventions and Trademarks Law also limits patent protection to 10 years. In areas such as pharmaceuticals and food, it substitutes for patents "certificates of invention" that make the processes available to competitors if royalties are paid—and there are reports of the adoption of such technological advances by competitive Mexican firms even before the foreign investor is able to get his or her product in place. Again it is impossible to measure the impact of foregone investment on jobs and economic growth, but there seems to be at least some trade-off between the objective of avoiding exploitation and monopoly rents and that of attracting new technology and investment.[20]

## Income Concentration and Income Distribution

One may conclude that from the point of view of income distribution there is an inherent tension between the income-concentrating effects of the Mexicanization program with its objectives of domestic control of policy and a share in profits and the possible income-distributing effects of the screening procedures employed by the Foreign Investment Commission in granting exceptions to the Mexicanization requirement for investments that have achieved specified socially beneficial objectives. While the commission does not isolate employment generation as its only goal, it is an important one, and when combined with export promotion and the development of marginal regions, it can have an impact on the resolution of the unemployment problem that is one of the principal reasons for the income distribution problems in Mexico.

One may expect that the creation of jobs would continue to be important to Mexican policymakers since it is estimated that Mexico needs to create 800,000 new jobs every year just to keep up with new entrants into the job market. In his 1980 annual address to Congress, President Lopez Portillo called for an annual increase in jobs of 4.2 percent for the remainder of his term in order to reduce the number of unemployed, which he estimated (on the basis of surveys in large cities) at 5.8 percent. (A more common estimate put 1980 unemployment in the country as a whole at 9 percent and underemployment at 40 percent.) The birth rate has dropped to 2.9 percent and employment rose by 5 percent in 1980 and an estimated 6.5 percent in 1981, but job creation remains a critical priority.[21]

It is clear, however, that means other than investment regulation must be used to promote employment. Foreign investment is much discussed and very visible in certain parts of the economy—such as motor vehicles, pharmaceuticals, food processing, and chemicals—but it represents only about 7.7 percent of the gross national product, and in 1973 majority-owned foreign plants employed only 528,000 people out of a work force of 15 million.[22] Tax measures that allow deductions from the tax bill of Mexican firms that hire additional personnel in priority zones such as the 1981 decree granting a 2-year tax credit of 20 percent of the annual minimum wage for each new worker hired are likely to be more important than investment screening in expanding employment.[23] More generally, the continuing expansion of the economy as a whole along with further declines in the birthrate can do much more over time to alleviate Mexico's unemployment problem than possibly inefficient shifts in the capital-labor mix on the part of foreign enterprise, which are usually located in areas where the capital-labor ratio is high.

## Conclusion

In what appears to be a considerable shift in policy toward the multinational corporation throughout the Third World, developing countries have generally abandoned the stark alternatives of confrontational nationalization or an open door to all foreign investment—opting instead for a bargaining relationship which attempts to secure the advantages of such investment without its disadvantages. Mexico, because of its longer experience in dealing with such investment and its decision that the developmental model of a mixed economy should include an important input from foreign investment, has been in the forefront of such bargaining. In the early 1970s the criticisms of foreign investment's adverse effects produced a battery of regulatory legislation in Mexico. As its title indicates, the most important of these laws, the Law to Promote Mexican Investment and to Regulate Foreign Investment, combined approaches to foreign investment which aimed at distinct objectives and had different effects on the distribution of income. On the one hand, the Mexicanization requirements tended to shift income from the foreign investor to a small number of domestic industrial and financial groups. On the other hand, the provisions for exceptions to the Mexicanization rule made it possible for the Mexican government to force foreigners to demonstrate congruence between their objectives and those of the government. Prominent among those objectives were job creation, regional decentralization, and the promotion of exports—all of which were likely to benefit lower-income groups, principally through their impact on employment.

As a final note, our study also throws some light on the recent discussion of the so-called "triple alliance" of government, multinationals, and domestic business in Latin America. While some of the research on foreign investment in Mexico has emphasized the continuing power of the multinational corporation and others have noted the expansion of the private Mexican business in recent years, the third member of that alliance, the state administrator, appears from our research to have emerged as the strongest in negotiating with the other two. The economic and political power of the Mexican state is now vastly greater than it was a decade ago, and the instruments available to the state policymakers much more effective. An interministerial committee, its 38-year-old executive secretary, and a staff of 190 persons (including secretaries and office personnel) have power to determine the future course of investment by large multinational corporations—and this bargaining power has been enhanced in recent years by the increasing economic attraction of the Mexican market as a result of the new oil discoveries.[24] When the availability of cheap energy, low-priced labor, and, in the case of Mexicanized firms, various fiscal and tax incentives are added to the list, it is not difficult to understand why, despite occasional complaints about the new regulations, foreign investors are willing to meet the demands of the state administration.[25]

With the advent of a new presidential administration in December 1982, one may expect a new look to be taken at current investment legislation. Given the increasing public concern about the distributional impact of Mexico's oil-induced prosperity, serious consideration should be given to extending the scope of the regulatory capacity of the Foreign Investment Commission, so that, for instance, Mexicanization proposals might also be required to demonstrate their conformity to the goals set forth in Article 13 of the Foreign Investment Law and in the National Development Plans. Other mechanisms might also be considered such as regulations on stock offerings so as to promote their wider distribution along lines similar to those initiated in Nigeria following the adoption of the "indigenization" legislation.[26]

Some Marxists would argue that the state bureaucracy will not be capable of effectively regulating the national or international bourgeoisie, but research and the recent Mexican experience seem to demonstrate that such a view is oversimplified. The triple alliance model is more useful since while it assumes common interests it also allows for divergence of objectives and mutual bargaining. This applies not only to the relationship between the state and the foreign investor but also, as an increasing amount of evidence seems to suggest, between the government administrators and the domestic private sector. The investment legislation allows advantages to be given to Mexican investors in some cases and to multinational corporations in others depending—in theory at least—on the view of the national interest taken by government administrators and technocrats. Whether in practice this is or can be the case is the subject of continuing debate, but the 1973 legislation and the development plans provide guidelines as well as institutional mechanisms to apply to them.[27]

A concluding word must be said on one further income distribution effect of the regulation of foreign investment. There is one group that has received far more economic benefit than any other from the new legislation—and it is not the poor, the state administrators, or the foreign and domestic companies. That group—which is also the one that wrote the legislation—is the legal profession.

## Notes

1. For summaries of the debate on foreign investment, see the report of the Group of Eminent Persons, *The Impact of Multinational Corporations on Development and on International Relations* (New York: United Nations, 1974), and Thomas J. Biersteker, *Distortion of Development?: Contending Perspectives on the Multinational Corporation* (Cambridge, Mass.: M.I.T. Press, 1978) (paperback ed., 1981). The best-known discussion of the adverse effects of foreign private investment is Richard J. Barnet and Ronald Muller, *Global Reach: The Power of the Multinational Corporation* (New York: Simon and Schuster, 1974). For a defense, see Raymond Vernon, *Storm over the Multinationals* (Cambridge, Mass.: Harvard University Press, 1977).

2. See the argument in Paul E. Sigmund, *Multinationals in Latin America: The Politics of Nationalization* (Madison: University of Wisconsin Press, 1980).

3. A summary of current investment screening mechanisms in fifteen countries is contained in Richard R. Robinson, *National Control of Business Entry* (New York: Praeger, 1976). See also Department of Legal Affairs, Organization of American States, *A Comparative Study of Latin American Legislation on the Regulation and Control of Private Foreign Investment,* OEA/Ser. G CP/INF, 680/75 (Washington: General Secretariat of the Organization of American States, 1975).

4. The percentages are taken from Fernando Fajnzylber and Trinidad Martínez, *Las Empresas Transnacionales* (Mexico City: *Fondo de Cultura Económica,* 1976) p. 154. On the history of regulation of foreign investment in Mexico, see Harry K. Wright, *Foreign Enterprise In Mexico* (Chapel Hill: University of North Carolina Press, 1971), especially Chapter III: Douglas Bennett, Morris L. Blachman, and Kenneth Sharpe, "Mexico and Multinational Corporations: An Explanation of State Action," in Joseph Grunwald (ed.), *Latin America and the World Economy* (Beverly Hills, Calif.: Sage Publications, 1979), Chapter 12; Jaime Alvarez Soberanis, *La Regulación de las Invenciones y Marcas y de la Transferencia Tecnológica* (Mexico City: Porrua, 1979); and Samuel del Villar, "El Sistema

Mexicano de Regulación de la Inversión Extranjera," *Foro Internacional* XV, No. 3 (Jan.–March 1975), pp. 331–378, as well as del Villar's earlier article, "La Necesidad de Regular la Inversión Extranjera," *Foro Internacional* XV, No. 1 (July–Sept. 1974), pp. 13–52.

5. Comisión Consultiva del Empleo, *Programa Nacional de Empleo, Presentación Resumida* (Mexico City: Secretaria del Trabajo, 1979), p. 15.

6. For the research and critical discussion on the Mexican side, see Bernardo Sepulveda and Antonia Chamucero, *La Inversión Extranjera en México* (Mexico City: Fondo de Cultura Económica, 1973); Bernardo Sepulveda et al., *Las Empresas Transnacionales en México* (Mexico City: El Colegio de Mexico, 1974); Fernando Fajnzylber and Trinidad Martinez, *Las Empresas Transnacionales* (Mexico City: Fondo de Cultura Económica, 1976); and Victor Manuel Bernal Sahagun et al., *El Impacto de las Empresas Multinacionales en el Empleo y los Ingresos. El Caso de México* (Mexico City: UNAM, Instituto de Investigaciones Económicas, 1976). The argument of the Sepulveda-Chamucero study that takeovers by multinationals and foreign control of decision making were increasing is challenged in Gerald Garnier, T. Noel Osborn, Fernando Arias, and Rafael Lecon, "The Decision-Making Relationship Between U.S. Multinationals and Their Mexican Affiliates," in Barry Poulson and T. Noel Osborn (eds.), *U.S.-Mexico Economic Relations,* (Boulder, Col.: Westview Press, 1977), pp. 107–128. On the American side, see Richard S. Newfarmer and Willard F. Mueller, *Multinational Corporations in Brazil and Mexico,* Report to the Subcommittee on Multinational Corporations, Senate Foreign Relations Committee (Washington, D.C.: U.S. Government Printing Office, 1975)—focusing on the "denationalization" of Mexican industry; John M. Connor and Willard F. Mueller, *Market Power and Profitability of Multinational Corporations in Brazil and Mexico,* Report to the Subcommittee on Foreign Economic Policy, Senate Foreign Relations Committee (Washington, D.C.: U.S. Government Printing Office, 1977); and John M. Connor, *The Market Power of Multinationals* (New York: Praeger, 1977). For defenses of foreign investment in Mexico, see José Antonio Fernandez and Herbert May, *The Effects of Foreign Investment in Mexico* (New York: The Council of the Americas, 1971), and Harry Robinson and Timothy Smith, *The Impact of Foreign Investment on the Mexican Economy* (Stanford, Calif.: Stanford Research Institute, 1976). The Fernandez and May study argued that U.S. investment in Mexico benefitted the Mexican economy by $1.5 billion each year in export earnings and import savings and employed 104,000 people in 1966, only 685 of whom were U.S. employees. The Robinson and Smith study claimed that in 1974 foreign investors had contributed $8.6 billion to the development of Mexico and reinvested 72 percent of their profits. The most frequently cited source on the worsening of income distribution is Ifigenia Martínez de Navarrete, "La Distribución del Ingreso en México," in L. Solís (ed.), *El Perfil de Mexico en 1980* (Mexico City: Siglo XXI, 1970). For a bibliography on the subject containing 712 items, principally in Spanish, see Victor M. Soria, "Bibliografía Sobre Empresas Transnacionales," *Iztapalapa* I, No. 2 (Enero–Junio 1980), pp. 194–227.

7. Council of the Americas study cited in Jose Luis Reyna and Richard Weinert (eds.), *Authoritarianism in Mexico* (Philadelphia: Institute for the Study of Human Issues, 1977), p. 122. For a tabulation of applications and rejections, see Jaime Alvarez Soberanis, *La Regulación de las Invenciones y Marcas y de la Transferencia de Tecnología* (Mexico City: Porrua, 1979), pp. 667–669, which also includes the text of the law (pp. 631–636). A revision of the law which adds specific penalties for violations but does not change its essential features was published on December 29, 1981. For the text, see *Mercado de Valores* XLII, No. 3 (Jan. 18, 1982).

8. Secretaría de Patrimonio y Fomento Industrial, *Ley para Promover la Inversión Mexicana y Regular la Inversión Extranjera* (Mexico City: 1980 ed.), *passim.* For the political context in which the law was adopted, see Leopoldo Solís "A Monetary Will-o'-the-Wisp: The Pursuit of Equity Through Deficit Spending," Discussion Paper No. 77 (Princeton, N.J.: Research Program in Development Studies, July 1977).

9. For an account, see "Chrylser de Mexico: El Ascenso de una Estrella Caida,"

*Expansión* (May 16, 1973), pp. 24..38. On the special problems involved in treatment of foreign-owned automotive plants, see Rhys O. Jenkins, *Dependent Industrialization in Latin America: The Automotive Industry in Argentina, Chile, and Mexico* (New York: Praeger, 1977), and Douglas C. Bennett and Kenneth E. Sharpe, "Agenda Setting and Bargaining Power: The Mexican State Versus Transnational Automobile Corporations," *World Politics* XXXII, No. 1 (Oct. 1979), pp.57–89. Bennett and Sharpe are critical of the bargaining model of analysis because it fails to discuss agenda setting and potential versus actual power (p. 59). On the job-creating aspects of the industry, see *Mercado de Valores* XLI, No. 46 (Nov. 16, 1981), p. 1195.

10. Business International, *Investment Strategies in Mexico* (New York: Business International, 1979), p. 25; Clark Reynolds, "Economic and Social Perspectives for Mexico," *Conference on Economic and Social Aspects of Relations Between the United States and Mexico,* November 12–15, 1980, pp. 13–14. See also Victor Manuel Bernal Sahagun, *op. cit.,* pp. 171–186; Jaime Alvarez Soberanis, *op.cit.,* pp. 360–362; and the reports on the border industries in *Mercado de Valores,* XLI, No. 45 (Nov. 9, 1981).

11. Material in this paragraph is taken from *Business International, op.cit.,* pp. 41–54, and from interviews at the Dirección General de Inversión Extranjera in the Ministry of Natural Properties (Patrimonio).

12. Economist Intelligence Unit, *Quarterly Economic Report, Mexico,* 3rd Quarter, 1980, p. 7; *Latin American Weekly Report,* June 13, 1980, p. 6; Department of Commerce, *Survey of Current Business* LX, No. 9 (Sept. 1980), pp. 26–31; and *Survey* LXI, No. 8 (Aug. 1981), pp. 31–33. About two-thirds of the increase in U.S. investment in Mexico was reinvested earnings. In early 1981, fifty-three foreign investment projects involving $1 billion in investment were awaiting government approval, and new foreign investment for the year was expected to exceed $3 billion (*New York Times,* Feb. 23, 1981).

13. *Business Week,* Jan. 15, 1979, p. 70; Interview, Economic Counsellor, U.S. Embassy, Jan. 29, 1981.

14. Interview, Coordinator of Analysis of Foreign Investment, Dirección General de Inversión Extranjera y transferencia de Tecnología, July 15, 1980.

15. The value of shares traded on the Mexican stock exchange rose from 5.8 billion pesos in 1977 to 94 billion pesos in 1979. See *El Mercado de Valores* XL, No. 25 (June 23, 1980), p. 619. Foreign participation in the stock market without stockholder voting rights has been made possible by the creation of the *Fondo México* (Mexican Fund), a closed-end mutual fund with shares quoted on the New York and London stock exchanges. It is described in *Mercado de Valores* XLI, No. 24 (June 15, 1981), pp. 635–636.

16. On the expansion of the Monterrey industrial groups, see *The Financial Times* (London), Aug. 28, 1980; *Forbes,* Oct. 29, 1979; and the summaries of Alfa's annual reports in *Proceso* (Mexico City), Nov. 5, 1979 and May 19, 1980. In the early 1980s Alfa began to have financial problems because of overexpansion. See articles in *The New York Times,* Oct. 21, 1981 and June 21, 1982.

17. Antonio Juarez, *Las Corporaciones Multinacionales y los Trabajadores Mexicanos* (Mexico City: Siglo XXI, 1979), pp. 267–271.

18. Business International, *Investment Strategies in Mexico* (New York: Business International, 1979), pp. 117–133. See also *El Mercado de Valores,* the weekly publication of Nacional Financiera.

19. For case studies and contrasting evaluations of two joint ventures with European firms in Mexico, see R. Montavon, *The Role of Multinational Companies in Latin America, A Case Study of Mexico* (London: Saxon House, 1979).

20. Price controls on pharmaceuticals and basic food stuffs also discourage investment and technical innovation but improve the incomes of the poor.

21. "Cuarto Informe Presidencial," *Comercio Exterior* 30/9 (Sept. 1980), p. 1011; *Mercado de Valores* XLI, No. 45 (Nov. 9, 1981), p. 1174.

22. The 7.7 percent figure is taken from Peter Smith, *Mexico, The Quest for a U.S. Policy* (New York: Foreign Policy Association, 1980), p. 14. The estimate of the number of workers employed by foreign enterprise is drawn from a Banco de Mexico study used in Victor M. Bernal Sahagun, *op. cit.* Another study estimates that foreign investors employed 3.7 percent of the Mexican work force and 16.3 percent of those employed in manufacturing (Jacques Freyssinet, cited in Antonio Juarez, *Las Corporaciones Multinacionales,* p. 108.

23. The decree of June 11, 1981 appears in *Mercado de Valores* XLI, No. 27 (July 6, 1981), pp. 718–720. The government also grants tax subsidies to small industries that tend to be more labor intensive. On the net adverse effects on income distribution of the subsidy program, see Calvin P. Blair, "Economic Development Policy in Mexico," in Richard D. Erb and Stanley R. Ross (eds.), *United States Relations with Mexico* (Washington, D.C.: American Enterprise Institute, 1981), pp. 233–257.

24. For an alternative view, that the 1973 legislation continues to serve the interests of the multinationals by reinforcing their alliance with a dependent national bourgeoisie, see the essays in Alonso Aguilar et al., *Política Mexicana Sobre Inversiones Extranjeras* (Mexico City: National Autonomous University of Mexico, 1977).

25. On the importance of other factors such as stability and economic potential in attracting foreign investment rather than the presence or absence of restrictive regulations, see Richard S. Weinert, "Foreign Capital in Mexico," in Susan Kaufman Purcell (ed.), *Mexico-United States Relations* (New York: Academy of Political Science, 1981), pp. 115–124.

26. See O. Teriba, "Financial Institutions, Financial Markets, and Income Distribution," in Henry Bienen and V. P. Diejomaoh (eds.), *The Political Economy of Income Distribution in Nigeria* (New York: Holmes & Meier, 1981), pp. 485–512. For an estimate that fiscal incentives have created 6,500 new jobs directly and 120,000 jobs indirectly, see *El Mercado de Valores* XL, No. 48 (Dec. 1, 1980), p. 1191.

27. On the triple alliance, see Peter Evans, *Dependent Development* (Princeton, N.J.: Princeton University Press, 1979), which sees the Brazilian "state bourgeoisie" as participating in "a common project with both the multinational and local private capital" (p. 47) but in its empirical evidence seems to demonstrate the dominance of government policymakers. On the differing backgrounds and policy orientations of the private and public sectors in Mexico, see Peter Smith, *Labyrinths of Power: Political Recruitment in Twentieth Century Mexico,* (Princeton, N.J.: Princeton University Press, 1979). The argument for a state interest in Mexico that is different from that of private business is made in John F. J. Purcell and Susan Kaufman Purcell, "Mexican Business and Public Policy," in James Malloy (ed.), *Authoritarianism and Corporatism in Latin America* (Pittsburgh: University of Pittsburgh Press, 1977), pp. 191–226. Critics point out that the executive secretary of the Foreign Investment Commission between 1979 and 1982 came to that position from a position with an organization representing small and medium-sized Mexican private business *(Canacintra)* and was therefore more likely to defend their interests than a separately identifiable state interest.

# CHAPTER 10

# *Distribution of Education and Health Opportunities and Services*

Pedro Aspe and Javier Beristain

## Introduction

### *Personal Income, Education, and Health*

There is no doubt that a person's income, level of education, and health are related. This relationship can be expressed in at least two causal forms: first, that a higher level of personal income determines higher levels of education and health, and second, that the higher education and health levels command a higher level of income. It is likely that, in the short term, the first interpretation may be correct, while, in the longer term, the second version better explains the relationship. But whatever the theoretical interpretation, the fact that there is a relationship among health, education, and personal income is highly significant.

Moreover, a high correlation can be observed between education and health. Again, two causal explanations can be given: that the level of health determines that of education or that the educational level determines that of health. A U.S. study concludes that this second interpretation is correct,[1] at least for that country. Common sense suggests that a more educated person is better prepared to prevent illness and better informed on medical options. Furthermore, the cost of sickness, measured in terms of lost income, is greater at a higher level of education; hence, people in this category strive harder for prevention. Finally, it is quite probable that some activities carried out by less educated people lead to a higher level of poor health.

An explanation of the determinants of personal income, inequality, and poverty distribution would not be complete without a description of the quality and the distribution of opportunities and educational services. We propose that a large number of inequalities observed in income can be attributed to prior inequalities in educational opportunities and to the quality of the health services available. This chapter will deal with this hypothesis, beginning with demographic information which will serve to delineate the severity of the problem and to emphasize the enormous national effort needed for its gradual elimination. Past, present and foreseeable end-of-the-century demographic conditions will no doubt, place a considerable demand on opportunities and on educational and health services. Finally, it should be noted that the desired decrease in educational and health inequalities is not enough, in the short and medium term, to affect significantly the income concentration indexes, but it would still be a powerful instrument in the struggle against poverty and a condition for the gradual reduction of income differentials in the long term.

### *Structure and Dynamics of Population*

During the sixties, Mexico had the dubious distinction of having one of the highest demographic growth rates in the world. This was the result of two forces: a high birth rate and a drastic decrease in mortality rate. In fact, the large increase in the demographic growth rate had begun long before, at least as early as the thirties, but reached its highest point in the sixties. Preliminary information from the 1980 Population Census suggests that both the birth rate and the demographic growth rate began to decrease in the seventies. Table 10–1 shows basic data supporting this point.

One consequence of accelerated population growth is the youthfulness of the population. Mexicans under 15 years were 41.2 percent of the population in 1940 and 46.2 percent in 1980. Between 1970 and 1980, this

*TABLE 10.1.*
*Total Population and Demographic Indexes*

| *Years* | *Total Population (in thousands of people)* | *Demographic Indexes per thousand inhabitants* | | *Annual Growth Index* |
|---|---|---|---|---|
| | | *Birth* | *Mortality* | |
| 1930 | 16,553 | | 25.6 | |
| 1940 | 19,653 | 44.45 | 23.35 | 2.12 |
| 1950 | 25,791 | 45.56 | 16.11 | 2.94 |
| 1960 | 34,923 | 46.05 | 11.53 | 3.45 |
| 1970 | 48,225 | 44.22 | 10.07 | 3.42 |
| 1975[a] | 60,145 | 39.9 | 7.3 | 3.25 |
| 1980[b] | 69,347 | | | 3.29 |

SOURCES: *La Población de México, su ocupación y sus niveles de bienestar* (Mexico City: Secretaría de Programación y Presupuesto [Bureau of Planning and Budget] 1979.). Supplement, Historical Statistics, *Fifth State-of-the-Nation Report,* made by President José López Portillo, Mexico, 1981, on 1980 data.

[a] Preliminary data for 1975, National Population Council.

[b] Preliminary results from the Tenth Population and Housing Census.

*TABLE 10.2.*
*Age Distribution*

| | *1940* | *1950* | *1960* | *1970* | *1980** |
|---|---|---|---|---|---|
| Total Population | 19,654 | 25,799 | 34,923 | 48,225 | 69,347 |
| (in thousands) | 100.0 | 100.0 | 100.0 | 100.0 | 100.0 |
| 0–4 years | 14.6 | 15.4 | 16.6 | 16.9 | 16.1 |
| 5–14 years | 26.6 | 26.3 | 27.8 | 29.3 | 28.7 |
| 15–24 years | 18.0 | 19.1 | 18.6 | 18.9 | 20.0 |
| 25–34 years | 14.8 | 13.4 | 13.1 | 12.2 | 12.5 |
| 35–44 years | 11.8 | 10.7 | 9.4 | 9.2 | 9.0 |
| 45–54 years | 6.9 | 7.4 | 6.6 | 5.9 | 6.0 |
| 55–64 years | 4.3 | 4.2 | 4.4 | 4.0 | 3.8 |
| 65 years and more | 3.0 | 3.4 | 3.4 | 3.7 | 3.8 |

SOURCE: *La Población de México, su ocupación y sus niveles de bienestar.*
*Preliminary Data.

group decreased slightly, to 44.6 percent, in response to the slowdown in demographic growth. This, in turn, has meant a high index of dependence, i.e., the measurement of how many under 15 and over 65 depend on each 100 inhabitants from 15 to 64 years of age. In 1940, this figure was 79.1, rising to 99.7 in 1970, and decreasing slightly in 1980 to 95.0.

This skewed age structure has had some important effects, notably a high demand for basic health and education services, a decrease in the labor force and in the economically productive population, an increase in the number of heads-of-household in the less productive age category showing a higher propensity for consumption in terms of the life cycle, etc.

The distribution by ages of population is presented in Table 10–2.

Another indicator is the rural-urban structure of the population. Defining rural population as residing in areas with less than 2,500 inhabitants, the urban population has risen from 33.5 percent in 1930 to 58.7 percent in 1980.

Table 10–3 presents population distribution for 1970, according to size of localities.

In 1970, the most rural states were Chiapas, Durango, Guerrero, Hidalgo, Michoacan, Oaxaca, Puebla, Queretaro, Quintana Roo, San Luis Potosi, Sinaloa, Tabasco, Tlaxcala, Veracruz, and Zacatecas. These are also among the poorest states of the Republic.[2]

## Education and Schooling of the Population

### *Schooling and Income*

The 1977 Survey on Income and Expenditures offers useful information on the correlation between the levels of schooling and income. In table 10-4, families are ranked according to the level of semiannual monetary

*TABLE 10.3.*
*Population and Size of Localities*

| | *Population (in thousands)* | *%* |
|---|---|---|
| 1 to 499 | 8,360 | 17.3 |
| 500 to 2,499 | 11,556 | 24.0 |
| 2,500 to 4,999 | 4,130 | 8.6 |
| 5,000 to 9,999 | 3,764 | 7.8 |
| 10,000 to 19,999 | 3,410 | 7.1 |
| 20,000 to 49,999 | 3,406 | 7.1 |
| 50,000 to 99,999 | 2,357 | 4.9 |
| 100,000 to 249,999 | 3,735 | 7.7 |
| 250,000 to 499,999 | 1,972 | 4.1 |
| 500,000 and more | 5,535 | 11.5 |
| Total | 48,225 | 100.0 |

SOURCE: *La Población en Mexico, su ocupación y sus niveles de bienestar.*

income of the home with respect to the general minimum wages of statistical regions and metropolitan areas, and information is given on the schooling of the head-of-household at each level.

The numbers speak for themselves. Ninety-five percent of the poorest heads-of-household do not have any schooling or have not finished elementary school; at the other extreme, 50 percent of the richest heads-of-household reach higher secondary level education or more. The average age of the head of family is included as a control variable.

It is difficult to quantify to what degree education helps to ease the transition of a worker from a low to a high income status. Figure 10-1 (based on figures from the 1970 Census) points to the degree of association between lifelong income and education.

Table 10-5 shows the limited amount of schooling that a large part of the population receives despite the notable efforts being made. The first column of Table 10-4 shows the schooling of family heads. In 1977, more than two-thirds of these did not have a complete elementary education and only 3 percent had university or higher degrees. The average schooling for the population of 15 years of age and older, who constitute the labor force of this country, was 3.5 years in 1971, rising to 4.8 years in 1981, a number which is still low.[3]

Table 10-6 presents information on population schooling by states. The differences are noticeable. In 1970, for example, in Chiapas, Guerrero, and Oaxaca more than 50 percent of the population six years of age and older did not have any instruction; in Chiapas and Oaxaca, only 3 percent had completed one year at the secondary level, compared to a national average of 7.8 percent. On the other hand, in the Federal District, 17.6

**Figure 10-1. Typical Inter-Occupational Deviation of Income by Age and Educational Level for the Mexican Republic.**

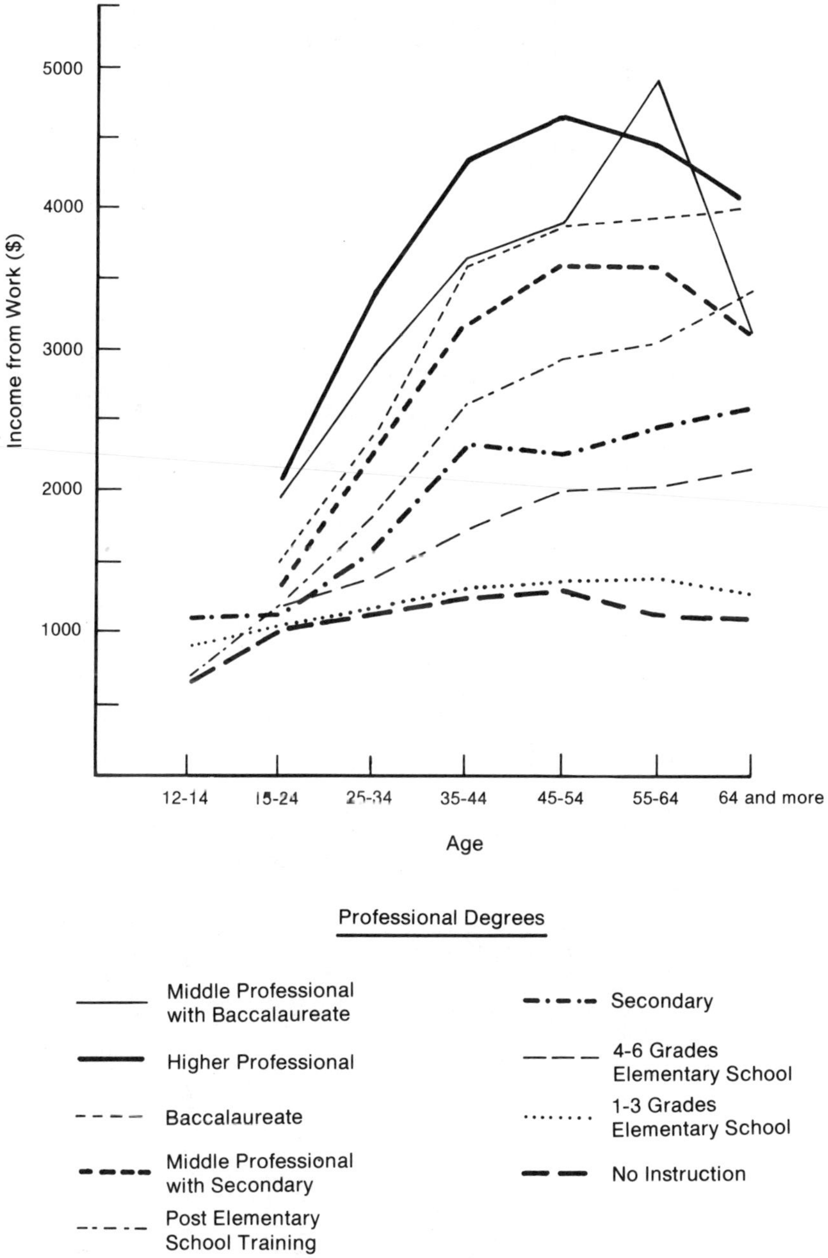


SOURCE: Licentiate Thesis of Raul Ramos Tercero, "The Mobility of the Labor Force in Mexico. A study based on the Human Capital Theory," Instituto Technológico Autónomo de México (ITAM), [Autonomous Technogical Institute of Mexico], 1979.

*TABLE 10.4.*

*Income and Schooling*

*Actual W ÷ Minimum W Income levels times the general minimum wages (percentages)*

| *Head-of-household schooling* | *Total* | *0–0.50* | *0.51–1* | *1.01–1.50* | *1.51–2* | *2.01–3* | *3.01–4* | *4.01–5* | *5.01–6* | *over 6* |
|---|---|---|---|---|---|---|---|---|---|---|
| Total | 100.0 | 100.0 | 100.0 | 100.0 | 100.0 | 100.0 | 100.0 | 100.0 | 100.0 | 100.0 |
| No instruction | 27.7 | 57.9 | 39.5 | 32.7 | 23.7 | 14.8 | 14.5 | 11.1 | 9.7 | 5.3 |
| Incomplete elementary | 40.0 | 37.2 | 51.1 | 48.8 | 44.1 | 42.7 | 34.6 | 26.3 | 38.7 | 17.1 |
| Complete elementary | 15.2 | 3.2 | 6.0 | 12.9 | 21.0 | 24.0 | 23.4 | 24.6 | 20.6 | 17.4 |
| Incomplete middle | 3.2 | .5 | 1.2 | 1.6 | 3.5 | 5.4 | 5.4 | 6.6 | 6.1 | 4.4 |
| Complete middle | 4.6 | .3 | .5 | 2.1 | 4.0 | 6.4 | 9.0 | 12.1 | 10.9 | 10.2 |
| Incomplete middle-high | 1.2 | n.s. | .2 | .4 | 1.2 | 1.2 | 2.3 | 3.5 | 3.2 | 3.5 |
| Complete middle-high | 2.4 | n.s. | .3 | .2 | .9 | 2.9 | 4.8 | 5.8 | 7.7 | 8.6 |
| Incomplete university | 1.7 | n.s. | n.s. | .2 | .4 | 1.5 | 2.8 | 4.4 | 5.4 | 8.3 |
| Complete university | 2.7 | n.s. | .2 | .1 | .4 | .6 | 2.6 | 4.9 | 5.8 | 21.4 |
| Graduate | .3 | n.s. | n.s. | n.s. | .2 | .1 | .1 | .1 | .3 | 2.8 |
| Not specified | .8 | .8 | 1.0 | 1.1 | .8 | .4 | .4 | .5 | 1.5 | .9 |
| Age of the head-of-household | 44 | 49 | 45 | 43 | 42 | 42 | 43 | 43 | 44 | 46 |

SOURCE: Encuesta Nacional de Ingresos y Gastos de los Hogares, 1977 (Mexico City: Secretaría de Programación y Presupuesto [Ministry of Planning and Budget]).

percent of the population six years and older had at least one grade of secondary schooling and 4.8 percent had one year of a university level education, three times the national average. Nuevo León and other states of the north and northeast show relatively high indexes.

### *Illiteracy Indices*

A majority of the people with no instruction are illiterate in the strict sense of the word; that is, they are functionally illiterate.[4] Table 10-7 shows the basic extent of this serious problem.

During the entire period, illiteracy was significantly higher among women than among men. Nevertheless, in this period, illiteracy among women decreased from 70.5 percent to 30.7 percent and among men from 62.7 percent to 25 percent. Illiteracy is highest among those younger than 14 and older than 40, although, as a percentage of the corresponding population, it is higher in the latter group in 1970, as Table 10-8 shows.

The most recent figures on illiteracy show that the illiterate population fifteen years or older has decreased from 6,747,000 in 1971 to 6,594,000 in 1981.[5]

Significant differences exist among the illiteracy of the different states in the Mexican Republic, as is shown in Table 10-9. States with a lower relative development have high illiteracy rates. This is the case of Chiapas, Guerrero, and Oaxaca, states which have a low level of economic development and many non-Spanish speaking indigenous groups. In the northern and northeastern states, as well as in the Federal District, one can see the lowest illiteracy rates. This distribution of results is similar to that observed in schooling.

### *Meeting Educational Demand*

In 1950, 79.5 percent of population between 6 and 24 years of age did not attend any schooling institution. In 1970, this percentage had dropped

*TABLE 10.5.*
*Schooling of Population in 1960 and 1970*

| | *1960* | *1970* |
|---|---|---|
| Population 6 years or older | 100.0 | 100.0 |
| No instruction | 43.6 | 34.8 |
| One or more years of completed schooling | 56.4 | 65.2 |
| Elementary | 50.7 | 55.6 |
| Middle education | 4.8 | 7.8 |
| Higher education | 0.9 | 1.6 |

SOURCE: Dirección General de Estadística, Secretaría de Industria y Comercio, VIII and IV Population Censuses, Mexico.

*TABLE 10.6.*

*Schooling by States as Population Percentages (Population Over 6 Years of Age)*

| States | Pop. with No Instruction | | Population with Some Passed Grade | | | | | | | |
|---|---|---|---|---|---|---|---|---|---|---|
| | | | Any Grade | | Elementary | | Secondary | | Higher | |
| | 1960 | 1970 | 1960 | 1970 | 1960 | 1970 | 1960 | 1970 | 1960 | 1970 |
| Aguascalientes | 33.7 | 26.0 | 66.3 | 74.0 | 61.3 | 66.7 | 4.4 | 6.6 | 0.6 | 0.7 |
| Baja California | 25.5 | 25.9 | 74.5 | 74.1 | 66.4 | 61.5 | 7.3 | 11.2 | 2.8 | 1.4 |
| Baja California Sur | 28.0 | 25.4 | 72.0 | 74.5 | 65.5 | 63.9 | 6.0 | 9.7 | 0.5 | 0.9 |
| Campeche | 39.3 | 33.0 | 60.7 | 67.0 | 56.4 | 60.1 | 4.0 | 6.1 | 0.3 | 0.8 |
| Coahuila | 25.4 | 23.3 | 74.6 | 76.7 | 66.1 | 66.4 | 7.3 | 9.1 | 0.7 | 1.2 |
| Colima | 36.7 | 31.4 | 63.3 | 68.6 | 58.4 | 60.5 | 3.9 | 7.2 | 0.5 | 0.8 |
| Chiapas | 64.6 | 54.3 | 35.4 | 45.7 | 33.9 | 42.2 | 1.3 | 3.0 | 0.2 | 0.5 |
| Chihuahua | 30.5 | 25.7 | 69.0 | 74.3 | 63.0 | 65.4 | 5.9 | 7.9 | 0.6 | 1.0 |
| Distrito Federal | 21.7 | 16.7 | 78.3 | 83.3 | 60.5 | 60.8 | 14.2 | 17.6 | 3.6 | 4.8 |
| Durango | 30.5 | 27.6 | 69.5 | 72.4 | 65.7 | 66.0 | 3.4 | 5.6 | 0.4 | 0.8 |
| Guanajuato | 56.3 | 49.5 | 43.7 | 50.5 | 41.3 | 45.5 | 2.1 | 4.3 | 0.3 | 0.7 |
| Guerrero | 70.7 | 56.7 | 29.3 | 43.3 | 28.0 | 38.4 | 1.1 | 4.4 | 0.2 | 0.5 |
| Hidalgo | 57.4 | 47.6 | 42.6 | 52.4 | 40.3 | 47.1 | 2.1 | 4.6 | 0.2 | 0.7 |
| Jalisco | 41.9 | 32.4 | 58.1 | 67.6 | 54.1 | 59.5 | 3.4 | 6.5 | 0.6 | 1.6 |

| | | | | | | | | | | |
|---|---|---|---|---|---|---|---|---|---|---|
| México | 50.2 | 36.1 | 49.8 | 63.9 | 47.4 | 55.7 | 2.1 | 6.9 | 0.3 | 1.3 |
| Michoacán | 57.0 | 48.0 | 43.0 | 52.0 | 41.0 | 47.0 | 1.8 | 4.3 | 0.2 | 0.7 |
| Morelos | 43.0 | 36.5 | 57.0 | 63.5 | 52.5 | 53.6 | 3.9 | 8.8 | 0.5 | 1.1 |
| Nayarit | 40.4 | 33.2 | 59.6 | 66.8 | 56.8 | 60.1 | 2.6 | 5.9 | 0.2 | 0.8 |
| Nuevo León | 24.0 | 18.6 | 76.0 | 81.4 | 64.9 | 66.8 | 9.4 | 12.0 | 1.7 | 2.5 |
| Oaxaca | 63.9 | 51.2 | 36.1 | 48.8 | 34.9 | 45.1 | 1.0 | 3.1 | 0.1 | 0.6 |
| Puebla | 54.3 | 42.3 | 45.7 | 57.3 | 42.6 | 51.2 | 2.7 | 5.4 | 0.4 | 1.1 |
| Querétaro | 64.0 | 48.6 | 36.0 | 51.4 | 33.6 | 45.1 | 2.1 | 5.3 | 0.3 | 1.0 |
| Quintana Roo | 40.5 | 34.0 | 59.5 | 66.0 | 56.5 | 59.8 | 2.7 | 5.6 | 0.3 | 0.6 |
| San Luis Potosí | 53.9 | 40.6 | 46.1 | 59.4 | 43.4 | 53.7 | 2.4 | 4.8 | 0.3 | 0.9 |
| Sinaloa | 40.8 | 31.9 | 59.2 | 68.1 | 55.6 | 60.6 | 3.2 | 6.6 | 0.4 | 0.9 |
| Sonora | 28.6 | 25.9 | 71.4 | 74.1 | 64.3 | 63.3 | 6.3 | 9.5 | 0.7 | 1.3 |
| Tabasco | 45.3 | 36.0 | 54.7 | 64.0 | 53.2 | 59.1 | 1.3 | 4.2 | 0.2 | 0.7 |
| Tamaulipas | 28.5 | 26.0 | 71.5 | 74.0 | 64.1 | 60.0 | 6.7 | 8.5 | 0.7 | 1.4 |
| Tlaxcala | 44.3 | 31.7 | 55.7 | 68.3 | 53.5 | 61.9 | 2.0 | 5.8 | 0.2 | 0.6 |
| Veracruz | 50.8 | 41.1 | 49.2 | 58.9 | 46.2 | 52.7 | 2.6 | 5.2 | 0.4 | 0.9 |
| Yucatán | 39.6 | 36.7 | 60.4 | 63.2 | 56.2 | 55.3 | 3.7 | 6.8 | 0.5 | 1.0 |
| Zacatecas | 43.7 | 33.0 | 56.3 | 67.0 | 54.9 | 62.9 | 1.3 | 3.5 | 0.1 | 0.6 |
| National Total | 43.6 | 34.8 | 56.4 | 65.2 | 50.7 | 55.6 | 4.8 | 7.8 | 0.9 | 1.6 |

SOURCE: Secretaría de Programación y Presupuesto, *Manual de Estadísticas Básicas Socioedemográficas IV* Sector Educativo (México, 1979).

*TABLE 10.7.*
*Illiteracy Indexes*

| *Year* | *Number of Illiterates six years and older (thousands of people)* | *Number of Illiterates six years and older as percentage of total population six years and older* |
|---|---|---|
| 1930 | 9,018 | 66.6 |
| 1940 | 9,450 | 58.3 |
| 1950 | 8,942 | 43.2 |
| 1960 | 10,573 | 37.8 |
| 1970 | 10,857 | 28.3 |

SOURCE: *La Población de México, su ocupación y sus niveles de bienestar.*

*TABLE 10.8.*
*Illiteracy by Age Groups*
*(in thousands)*

| | *1960* | | | *1970* | | |
|---|---|---|---|---|---|---|
| *Age Groups* | *Population* | *Illiterates* | *%* | *Population* | *Illiterates* | *%* |
| 6–14 | 8,512 | 3,827 | 45 | 12,440 | 4,158 | 33 |
| 15–19 | 3,521 | 909 | 26 | 5,041 | 749 | 15 |
| 20–24 | 2,932 | 825 | 28 | 4,019 | 717 | 18 |
| 25–29 | 2,479 | 772 | 31 | 3,248 | 717 | 22 |
| 30–39 | 3,969 | 1,322 | 33 | 5,111 | 1,314 | 26 |
| 40 and over | 6,575 | 2,918 | 44 | 8,513 | 3,203 | 38 |
| | 27,988 | 10,573 | 38 | 38,372 | 10,858 | 28 |

SOURCE: *La Población de México, su ocupación y sus niveles de bienestar.*

to under 50 percent. Table 10-10 shows the evolution of school service in relation to demand at all levels in the past decade.

The preceding index shows the magnitude of educational opportunities, but says nothing about the extent to which people take advantage of these, a matter that will be dealt with later. In this respect as well there are notable differences among the states. Again Chiapas and Oaxaca, together with Puebla, Veracruz, and Guanajuato, prove to have the lowest rates; the Federal District and Nuevo León, the highest, with rates twice that of Chiapas. Table 10-11 presents this information for 1980.

Distribution of enrollment, by educational level is shown in Table 10–12.

The figures in Table 10–12 show the explosive growth of the national educational system, which has practically doubled its enrollment in ten years. They also underscore the improvement of the service indexes on the elementary and basic secondary levels. But they also indicate that these proportions decreased in the higher secondary cycle because of the insufficient opening of new opportunities on the baccalaureate level, a problem related to the limits set by the Universidad Nacional Autónoma de México [National Autonomous University of Mexico] UNAM, for its growth. Absolute increases are notable, especially those which are related to systems for job training, not only on the post-elementary level but also on the terminal secondary level for clearly technical vocations. How-

*TABLE 10.9.*

*Total Illiterates as a Percentage of the Population Six Years and Older, by State*

| *State* | *1960* | *1970* |
|---|---|---|
| Aguascalientes | 26.8 | 19.3 |
| Baja California | 18.3 | 17.8 |
| Baja California Sur | 21.8 | 17.3 |
| Campeche | 31.8 | 26.5 |
| Coahuila | 19.4 | 16.7 |
| Colima | 31.0 | 24.4 |
| Chiapas | 60.6 | 48.1 |
| Chihuahua | 24.5 | 18.5 |
| Distrito Federal | 16.6 | 12.6 |
| Durango | 24.8 | 19.9 |
| Guanajuato | 49.0 | 40.4 |
| Guerrero | 61.9 | 48.8 |
| Hidalgo | 56.0 | 41.4 |
| Jalisco | 34.0 | 24.7 |
| México | 42.6 | 29.8 |
| Michoacán | 49.0 | 38.8 |
| Morelos | 39.2 | 29.5 |
| Nayarit | 34.0 | 25.8 |
| Nuevo León | 19.3 | 13.4 |
| Oaxaca | 58.8 | 45.1 |
| Puebla | 49.7 | 37.4 |
| Querétaro | 57.1 | 41.7 |
| Quintana Roo | 35.5 | 28.8 |
| San Luis Potosí | 46.6 | 33.4 |
| Sinaloa | 34.0 | 24.9 |
| Sonora | 23.8 | 19.1 |
| Tabasco | 38.3 | 30.5 |
| Tamaulipas | 26.2 | 18.5 |
| Tlaxcala | 38.4 | 27.0 |
| Veracruz | 45.2 | 34.4 |
| Yucatán | 34.4 | 30.6 |
| Zacatecas | 36.4 | 24.7 |
| National Total | 37.8 | 28.3 |

SOURCE: Secretaría de Programación y Presupuesto, *Manual de Estadísticas Básicas Sociodemográficas* IV Sector Educativo, (México, 1979).

*TABLE 10.10*
*Meeting Educational Demand*

| *Scholastic Year* | *Population from 6–24 Years* | *Population Enrolled at All Levels* | *Meeting Demand (%)* |
|---|---|---|---|
| | *(millions of persons)* | | |
| 1971–1972 | 23.1 | 12.3 | 53 |
| 1972–1973 | 23.9 | 13.0 | 54 |
| 1973–1974 | 24.8 | 13.7 | 55 |
| 1974–1975 | 25.7 | 14.5 | 56 |
| 1975–1976 | 26.6 | 15.5 | 58 |
| 1976–1977 | 27.5 | 16.6 | 60 |
| 1977–1978 | 28.4 | 17.4 | 61 |
| 1978–1979 | 29.4 | 19.0 | 65 |
| 1979–1980 | 30.3 | 20.4 | 67 |
| 1980–1981 | 31.3 | 22.0 | 70 |
| 1981–1982 | 32.3 | 23.4 | 72 |

SOURCE: *Supplement, Historical Statistics, Fifth State-of-the-Nation Report.*

ever, the numbers hide the fact that there is still an important percentage of enrolled students who do not finish the cycle, a problem which is especially serious at the elementary school level.

*Elementary Education*

Article 3 of the Constitution of the United Mexican States provides that "elementary schooling will be obligatory." In 1970, however, a third of the population had no instruction whatsoever. The government has doubled its effort, trying on one hand to provide education for children of school age, and on the other, to provide education for adults. Population demand in the corresponding age group has been met satisfactorily and approximately 100 percent are now covered, as shown in Table 10-13.

There is no doubt that the federal and state governments are responsible for the largest share of educational opportunities at an elementary level. The participation of private institutions has decreased from 7.2 percent in 1971–1972 to a 4.6 percent in 1981–1982.

Information by states again shows important differences, as can be observed in Table 10-14. Chiapas has the lowest index, followed by Veracruz, Tabasco, and Guanajuato. It is surprising that response to demand has fallen in the Federal District. Oaxaca and Guerrero reach higher indexes than those of the national average.[6]

Even though there are educational opportunities, the system is not sufficiently efficient to retain the students until the completion of primary grades. An indicator of this is the absorption by grade of elementary school students. Of those enrolled in first grade of the 1971–1972 scholastic year, almost 30 percent did not register for the second grade, and another 30 percent left at later points, so that only 43 percent of those starting primary school enrolled for the sixth grade. Within these statistics one can find important differences among the states, as can be seen in Table 10-15.

A reason for the persistence of high drop-out rates is that a great number of elementary schools do not offer the full six years. In 1973, for

*TABLE 10.11*

*Index of Meeting Educational Demand by State (1980)*

| *State* | *Population from 5–24 Years* | *Scholastic Population* | *Rate of Response to Demand* |
|---|---|---|---|
| Aguascalientes | 164,946 | 87,551 | 53.1 |
| Baja California | 462,332 | 238,562 | 51.6 |
| Baja California Sur | 62,064 | 36,013 | 58.0 |
| Campeche | 121,426 | 60,251 | 49.6 |
| Coahuila | 538,970 | 304,641 | 56.5 |
| Colima | 118,406 | 56,834 | 54.8 |
| Chiapas | 780,133 | 251,235 | 32.2 |
| Chihuahua | 775,624 | 394,218 | 50.8 |
| Distrito Federal | 3,347,031 | 2,107,827 | 63.0 |
| Durango | 426,964 | 225,601 | 52.8 |
| Guanajuato | 1,032,110 | 407,078 | 39.4 |
| Guerrero | 774,240 | 388,793 | 50.2 |
| Hidalgo | 569,106 | 272,089 | 47.8 |
| Jalisco | 1,596,207 | 768,085 | 48.1 |
| México | 1,849,895 | 854,952 | 46.2 |
| Michoacán | 1,143,752 | 512,386 | 44.8 |
| Morelos | 294,566 | 162,881 | 55.3 |
| Nayarit | 265,052 | 148,732 | 56.1 |
| Nuevo León | 765,491 | 493,188 | 64.4 |
| Oaxaca | 937,777 | 413,023 | 44.0 |
| Puebla | 1,178,866 | 508,772 | 43.2 |
| Querétaro | 229,021 | 105,984 | 46.3 |
| Quintana Roo | 42,885 | 43,450 | — |
| San Luis Potosí | 610,743 | 278,135 | 45.5 |
| Sinaloa | 622,752 | 326,280 | 52.4 |
| Sonora | 535,846 | 280,974 | 52.4 |
| Tabasco | 388,543 | 161,126 | 41.5 |
| Tamaulipas | 690,114 | 377,480 | 54.7 |
| Tlaxcala | 201,612 | 102,716 | 50.9 |
| Veracruz | 1,828,732 | 788,845 | 43.1 |
| Yucatán | 355,441 | 181,062 | 50.9 |
| Zacatecas | 462,030 | 208,542 | 45.1 |
| National Total | 23,172,677 | 11,555,306 | 49.9 |

SOURCE: *La Población de México, su ocupación y sus niveles de bienestar,* 1979.

TABLE 10.12

*Enrollment and Service of Demand by Educational Levels*

| *Levels* | *1971–1972 (in thousands)* | *Index %* | *1981–1982 (in thousands)* | *Index %* |
|---|---|---|---|---|
| *Elementary* | | | | |
| Pre-School | 422 | 11.9 | 1,430 | 31.5 |
| Primary | 9,700 | 79.7 | 15,536 | 98.0 |
| *Basic Secondary* | | | | |
| Work Training | 166 | 12.5 | 407 | 17.8 |
| Secondary | 1,225 | 64.2 | 3,647 | 94.1 |
| *Higher Secondary* | | | | |
| Terminal | 42 | 8.4 | 199 | 13.9 |
| Baccalaureate | 329 | 72.2 | 986 | 60.7 |
| Teacher Training | 56 | 7.3 | 198 | 7.8 |
| *Higher* | 316 | — | 978 | — |
| | 12,256 | | 23,381 | |

SOURCE: *Supplement, Historical Statistics, Fifth State-of-the-Nation Report.*

Note: For pre-school and primary instruction the service index refers to the proportion of the corresponding age group actually enrolled; for other levels, it is the percentage of absorption of those coming from the immediately preceding cycle. It can be higher than 100% because of service delay.

TABLE 10.13.

*Matriculation in Elementary Schools and Service Index*

| *Scholastic year* | *Population 6–14 years* Total (in thousands) | *Population 6–14 years* Enrolled in elementary (in thousands) | *Service index* Service % | *Service index* Total in primary (in thousands) |
|---|---|---|---|---|
| 1971–1972 | 13,145 | 9,328 | 79.7 | 9,700 |
| 1972–1973 | 13,630 | 9,765 | 80.6 | 10,113 |
| 1973–1974 | 14,060 | 10,185 | 81.6 | 10,509 |
| 1974–1975 | 14,499 | 10,698 | 83.1 | 10,999 |
| 1975–1976 | 14,954 | 11,184 | 84.5 | 11,461 |
| 1976–1977 | 15,326 | 11,969 | 88.4 | 12,223 |
| 1977–1978 | 15,831 | 12,418 | 89.3 | 12,648 |
| 1978–1979 | 16,224 | 13,441 | 93.4 | 13,647 |
| 1979–1980 | 16,310 | 14,100 | 96.4 | 14,282 |
| 1980–1981 | 17,148 | 14,833 | 98.0 | 14,995 |
| 1981–1982 | 17,844 | 15,412 | 98.0 | 15,555 |

SOURCE: *Supplement, Historical Statistics, Fifth State-of-the-Nation Report.*

*TABLE 10.14.*
*Percentages of Demand Covered in Elementary Education*[a]

| *State* | *1970–1971* | *1976–1977* |
|---|---|---|
| Estados Unidos Mexicanos | 69.7 | 75.9 |
| Aguascalientes | 74.2 | 80.0 |
| Baja California | 77.5 | 79.2 |
| Baja California Sur | 76.2 | 90.3 |
| Campeche | 75.5 | 73.5 |
| Coahuila | 80.8 | 88.7 |
| Colima | 75.2 | 86.6 |
| Chiapas | 47.4 | 76.3 |
| Chihuahua | 74.6 | 76.3 |
| Distrito Federal | 88.0 | 72.1 |
| Durango | 73.5 | 75.8 |
| Guanajuato | 53.6 | 68.5 |
| Guerrero | 69.7 | 82.6 |
| Hidalgo | 69.1 | 83.3 |
| Jalisco | 68.7 | 77.7 |
| México | 66.7 | 80.4 |
| Michoacán | 63.7 | 73.8 |
| Morelos | 69.5 | 80.4 |
| Nayarit | 74.7 | 82.0 |
| Nuevo León | 83.8 | 84.1 |
| Oaxaca | 65.1 | 80.6 |
| Puebla | 59.6 | 71.0 |
| Querétaro | 63.1 | 72.7 |
| Quintana Roo | 74.6 | 97.4 |
| San Luis Potosí | 64.4 | 75.9 |
| Sinaloa | 76.9 | 82.1 |
| Sonora | 74.8 | 79.5 |
| Tabasco | 59.9 | 67.7 |
| Tamaulipas | 79.1 | 78.8 |
| Tlaxcala | 70.8 | 88.6 |
| Veracruz | 62.7 | 65.9 |
| Yucatán | 74.0 | 85.9 |
| Zacatecas | 66.7 | 74.2 |

SOURCE: *La Población de México, su ocupación y sus niveles de bienestar.*

[a]The proportions of attendance a·e smaller than those reported in Table 10-10. since the total population estimates of the 4–16 year age group, used in the data of the Fifth Governmental Report are significantly lower than those used on this chart. It has not been possible to up-date these because of a lack of information from the states.

TABLE 10.15.

*Output by Grade of Elementary Students*[a]

| | 1st Grade | 2nd Grade | | 3rd Grade | | 4th Grade | | 5th Grade | | 6th Grade | |
|---|---|---|---|---|---|---|---|---|---|---|---|
| State | 1970–71[b] | 1971–72 | % | 1972–73 | % | 1973–74 | % | 1974–75 | % | 1975–76 | % |
| Mexican United States | 2,695,202 | 1,921,362 | 71.4 | 1,687,660 | 62.7 | 1,518,616 | 54.5 | 1,270,529 | 47.2 | 1,154,363 | 42.9 |
| Aguascalientes | 17,443 | 14,656 | 84.0 | 13,182 | 75.6 | 11,688 | 67.0 | 10,344 | 59.2 | 8,973 | 51.4 |
| Baja California | 41,838 | 37,116 | 88.7 | 35,159 | 84.0 | 35,001 | 66.2 | 31,689 | 75.7 | 28,561 | 54.8 |
| Baja California Sur | 7,451 | 5,532 | 74.2 | 5,281 | 70.9 | 4,930 | 86.2 | 4,176 | 56.0 | 4,084 | 54.6 |
| Campeche | 17,183 | 10,697 | 62.3 | 9,122 | 53.1 | 7,956 | 46.4 | 6,589 | 38.3 | 6,049 | 35.2 |
| Coahuila | 58,182 | 46,305 | 79.6 | 42,633 | 73.3 | 38,142 | 65.6 | 34,845 | 59.9 | 33,836 | 58.2 |
| Colima | 14,699 | 11,766 | 80.1 | 10,059 | 68.4 | 8,786 | 59.8 | 7,390 | 50.3 | 6,513 | 44.3 |
| Chiapas | 92,076 | 51,842 | 56.3 | 33,677 | 36.6 | 25,263 | 27.4 | 22,271 | 24.2 | 20,197 | 21.9 |
| Chihuahua | 95,301 | 68,288 | 71.7 | 63,198 | 66.3 | 57,516 | 60.4 | 47,589 | 49.9 | 42,624 | 44.8 |
| Distrito Federal | 286,436 | 251,681 | 87.9 | 234,881 | 82.0 | 273,442 | 75.5 | 205,739 | 71.8 | 191,372 | 66.8 |
| Durango | 61,413 | 43,449 | 70.7 | 38,244 | 62.3 | 31,976 | 52.1 | 26,106 | 42.5 | 23,001 | 37.5 |
| Guanajuato | 112,661 | 82,676 | 73.4 | 66,601 | 59.1 | 54,821 | 48.7 | 46,601 | 41.4 | 42,336 | 37.6 |
| Guerrero | 124,205 | 75,186 | 60.5 | 57,290 | 46.1 | 48,392 | 39.0 | 39,987 | 32.2 | 36,586 | 29.5 |
| Hidalgo | 86,942 | 49,573 | 57.0 | 42,613 | 49.0 | 33,610 | 38.7 | 30,414 | 35.0 | 26,568 | 30.6 |
| Jalisco | 190,979 | 127,345 | 66.7 | 116,148 | 60.8 | 100,823 | 52.8 | 85,621 | 44.8 | 77,591 | 40.6 |
| México | 211,070 | 156,604 | 74.3 | 146,259 | 69.3 | 138,975 | 65.8 | 126,280 | 59.8 | 117,346 | 55.6 |

| | | | | | | | | | | | |
|---|---|---|---|---|---|---|---|---|---|---|---|
| Michoacán | 152,607 | 98,303 | 64.4 | 81,954 | 53.7 | 67,739 | 44.4 | 53,359 | 35.0 | 45,386 | 29.7 |
| Morelos | 30,833 | 23,760 | 77.1 | 21,500 | 69.7 | 20,376 | 66.1 | 18,299 | 59.3 | 17,306 | 56.1 |
| Nayarit | 34,470 | 23,082 | 67.0 | 21,028 | 61.0 | 17,280 | 50.1 | 15,470 | 44.9 | 14,088 | 40.9 |
| Nuevo León | 83,588 | 68,532 | 82.0 | 66,226 | 79.2 | 59,080 | 70.7 | 55,760 | 66.7 | 55,325 | 66.2 |
| Oaxaca | 136,329 | 81,618 | 59.9 | 67,877 | 49.8 | 50,469 | 37.0 | 45,191 | 33.1 | 35,970 | 26.4 |
| Puebla | 128,217 | 91,618 | 71.5 | 76,797 | 59.9 | 66,735 | 52.0 | 54,360 | 42.4 | 47,934 | 37.4 |
| Querétaro | 28,896 | 21,000 | 72.7 | 17,264 | 59.7 | 13,202 | 45.7 | 11,239 | 38.9 | 9,973 | 34.5 |
| Quintana Roo | 8,816 | 4,390 | 49.8 | 4,261 | 48.3 | 4,245 | 48.2 | 2,903 | 32.9 | 2,594 | 29.4 |
| San Luis Potosí | 72,567 | 53,902 | 74.3 | 45,593 | 62.8 | 35,846 | 49.4 | 29,399 | 40.5 | 26,034 | 35.9 |
| Sinaloa | 74,869 | 55,055 | 73.5 | 50,150 | 67.0 | 43,893 | 58.6 | 37,529 | 50.1 | 34,507 | 46.1 |
| Sonora | 59,871 | 45,146 | 75.4 | 42,127 | 70.4 | 38,657 | 64.6 | 34,509 | 57.6 | 31,254 | 52.2 |
| Tabasco | 47,600 | 33,194 | 69.7 | 27,441 | 57.6 | 21,125 | 44.4 | 16,156 | 33.9 | 13,507 | 28.4 |
| Tamaulipas | 76,215 | 62,378 | 81.8 | 57,108 | 74.9 | 50,577 | 66.4 | 43,808 | 57.5 | 39,666 | 52.0 |
| Tlaxcala | 24,414 | 17,586 | 72.0 | 15,795 | 64.7 | 14,047 | 57.5 | 12,425 | 50.9 | 11,418 | 46.8 |
| Veracruz | 208,103 | 137,378 | 66.0 | 117,012 | 56.2 | 93,521 | 44.8 | 75,455 | 36.3 | 70,634 | 33.9 |
| Yucatán | 52,757 | 31,367 | 59.5 | 24,837 | 47.1 | 20,158 | 38.2 | 16,182 | 30.7 | 14,356 | 27.2 |
| Zacatecas | 57,171 | 40,337 | 70.6 | 36,343 | 63.6 | 30,345 | 53.1 | 22,854 | 40.4 | 18,774 | 32.8 |

SOURCE: *La Población en México, su ocupación y sus niveles de bienestar.*

[a]Output of a scholastic year is the proportion of students who pass that grade and enroll the next one.
[b]The percentages were calculated with respect to the base year (1970–1971).

*TABLE 10.16.*

*Schools and Enrollment of Elementary Schools, by State, 1973*

| | *Totals* | | | *"Rural Areas" (under 2500)* | | | *"Urban Zones" (over 2500)* | | |
|---|---|---|---|---|---|---|---|---|---|
| | *Schools* | | *Enrollment* | *Schools* | | *Enrollment* | *Schools* | | *Enrollment* |
| *States* | *Compl.* | *Incompl.* | *(thousands)* | *Compl.* | *Incompl.* | *(thousands)* | *Compl.* | *Incompl.* | *(thousands)* |
| Estados Unidos Mexicanos | 19755 | 28332 | 10281 | 8970 | 27206 | 4036 | 10785 | 1126 | 6245 |
| Aguascalientes | 156 | 161 | 85 | 62 | 155 | 34 | 94 | 6 | 51 |
| Baja California | 415 | 127 | 210 | 128 | 38 | 38 | 287 | 39 | 172 |
| Baja California Sur | 92 | 92 | 31 | 56 | 87 | 13 | 36 | 5 | 18 |
| Campeche | 113 | 179 | 57 | 64 | 169 | 25 | 49 | 10 | 32 |
| Coahuila | 707 | 352 | 251 | 340 | 321 | 77 | 367 | 31 | 174 |
| Colima | 126 | 118 | 57 | 44 | 108 | 16 | 82 | 10 | 41 |
| Chiapas | 413 | 1423 | 262 | 224 | 1379 | 172 | 189 | 44 | 90 |
| Chihuahua | 883 | 978 | 355 | 400 | 908 | 107 | 483 | 70 | 248 |
| Distrito Federal | 2075 | 143 | 1386 | — | — | — | 2075 | 143 | 1386 |
| Durango | 468 | 659 | 213 | 305 | 638 | 113 | 163 | 21 | 100 |
| Guanajuato | 537 | 1301 | 335 | 235 | 1280 | 157 | 302 | 21 | 178 |
| Guerrero | 629 | 1592 | 372 | 287 | 1568 | 228 | 242 | 24 | 144 |
| Hidalgo | 513 | 1349 | 263 | 362 | 1332 | 170 | 151 | 17 | 93 |

| | | | | | | | | | |
|---|---|---|---|---|---|---|---|---|---|
| Jalisco | 1421 | 2129 | 731 | 480 | 1970 | 241 | 941 | 159 | 490 |
| México | 1377 | 1032 | 889 | 586 | 961 | 256 | 791 | 71 | 633 |
| Michoacán | 923 | 1891 | 488 | 424 | 1846 | 245 | 499 | 45 | 243 |
| Morelos | 237 | 162 | 127 | 103 | 154 | 48 | 134 | 8 | 79 |
| Nayarit | 250 | 347 | 122 | 128 | 336 | 57 | 122 | 11 | 65 |
| Nuevo León | 841 | 665 | 401 | 416 | 633 | 104 | 425 | 32 | 297 |
| Oaxaca | 864 | 1859 | 435 | 622 | 1839 | 300 | 242 | 20 | 135 |
| Puebla | 971 | 1570 | 470 | 583 | 1524 | 257 | 388 | 46 | 213 |
| Querétaro | 215 | 491 | 99 | 121 | 482 | 60 | 94 | 9 | 39 |
| Quintana Roo | 42 | 147 | 25 | 27 | 146 | 16 | 15 | 1 | 9 |
| San Luis Potosí | 617 | 1192 | 365 | 381 | 1172 | 253 | 236 | 20 | 112 |
| Sinaloa | 638 | 888 | 300 | 348 | 858 | 142 | 390 | 30 | 158 |
| Sonora | 516 | 467 | 251 | 212 | 454 | 67 | 304 | 13 | 184 |
| Tabasco | 300 | 817 | 166 | 194 | 869 | 113 | 106 | 3 | 53 |
| Tamaulipas | 696 | 717 | 321 | 292 | 701 | 92 | 404 | 16 | 229 |
| Tlaxcala | 221 | 173 | 95 | 135 | 172 | 46 | 86 | 1 | 49 |
| Veracruz | 1632 | 3801 | 734 | 891 | 3664 | 374 | 741 | 137 | 360 |
| Yucatán | 331 | 577 | 169 | 119 | 518 | 70 | 212 | 59 | 99 |
| Zacatecas | 536 | 933 | 216 | 401 | 924 | 145 | 135 | 4 | 71 |

SOURCE: Secretaría de Programación y Presupuesto, *Anuario Estadístico de los Estados Unidos Mexicanos: 1975–1976* (México, 1979).

*TABLE 10.17.*
*Secondary Education Enrollment and Rate of Attendance*[a]
*(in thousands of people)*

| *Years* | *Job Training* | | *Secondary* | | | |
|---|---|---|---|---|---|---|
| | *Students* | *%* | *Students* | *%* | *General* | *Technical*[b] |
| 1971–1972 | 166 | 12.5 | 1,225 | 64.2 | 1,041 | 184 |
| 1972–1973 | 180 | 13.1 | 1,348 | 66.3 | 1,126 | 222 |
| 1973–1974 | 194 | 13.1 | 1,498 | 69.4 | 1,229 | 269 |
| 1974–1975 | 204 | 13.4 | 1,644 | 73.4 | 1,318 | 326 |
| 1975–1976 | 243 | 14.3 | 1,898 | 77.8 | 1,512 | 386 |
| 1976–1977 | 244 | 13.4 | 2,153 | 80.3 | 1,700 | 453 |
| 1977–1978 | 247 | 11.9 | 2,305 | 76.3 | 1,805 | 500 |
| 1978–1979 | 251 | 11.7 | 2,560 | 81.4 | 2,012 | 548 |
| 1979–1980 | 276 | 12.0 | 2,927 | 89.4 | 2,312 | 615 |
| 1980–1981 | 371 | 17.5 | 3,229 | 86.6 | 2,536 | 693 |
| 1981–1982 | 407 | 17.8 | 3,646 | 94.1 | 2,851 | 795 |

SOURCE: *Fifth State-of-the-Nation Report.*

[a] Refers to the percentage of graduates absorbed from elementary; index may be higher than 100 because of lag in service.

[b] Includes secondary education for workers and technological secondary schools.

example, only 41 percent of the total elementary schools had all six grades; in villages of less than 2,500 inhabitants, this percentage drops to 25 percent. The numbers by states with the corresponding data on enrolled students are represented in Table 10-16.

The State of Chiapas serves as a good example of the problems mentioned in this section. Of those inhabitants at an age to receive elementary education, 63.9 percent were admitted (1976–1977); of those enrolled in the first grade of elementary school, only 21.9 percent registered for sixth grade (1975–1976). From its 1,836 schools, 77.5 percent did not complete the six years (1973); in the rural areas this percentage was 86 percent (1973). Furthermore, 87.3 percent of its schools and 66 percent of its students are located in the rural zones (1973).

There has been a sustained effort in this decade to give attention to the non-Spanish speaking indigenous population. Thus, while in 1971 education in native dialects was offered to 3,256,000 people, in 1981, non-Spanish instruction was estimated at 3,521,000 people. Adult basic education is also a concern. In 1980, more than 110,000 attended and 37,000 adults finished this program.

The importance of the expansion and completion of elementary education is demonstrated by the relationship between schooling and current and permanent income as presented in the first section of this chapter.

### *Secondary Education*

This cycle includes job training at post-elementary and secondary levels. The basic figures for these groups are presented in Table 10–17 with their corresponding proportions of attendance.

The growth of secondary education can be seen if the data are compared with those of 1958, when only 348,000 students were enrolled in post-elementary education, including advanced secondary and higher education. The growth in enrollment in the system and schools that train for work skills, at a post-primary and secondary level, is of special importance for this study. This preparation is a useful resource, showing immediate effects on the income level of people.

Availability of middle education service, by states, shows several important differences. Table 10-18 demonstrates the abovementioned situation in relative terms and compares it to the population and elementary education. Two results can be clearly observed: higher socioeconomic development is related to greater secondary school enrollment, and greater skills for work. Chiapas illustrates the extreme low case. Elementary enrollment and the participation of inhabitants between 5 and 14 years are higher than the national average. However, at the secondary level the state is clearly underrepresented.

Efficiency in basic secondary education systems can be seen in Table 10-19. Bearing in mind that only 40 percent of those entering first grade complete 6th grade, the result of the table suggests that only 17 percent of these enrolled in the first grade of elementary school will finish secondary school. In some states this number does not reach 10 percent, while in the Federal District and Nuevo León, it is closer to 40 percent.

On the basic secondary level, participation of private schools is higher than on the elementary level. Participation is higher in job training programs and includes mainly training for administrative jobs. On the secondary level the federal and state governments provide 80 percent of the educational programs although in technological secondary programs the government is the sole participant in industrial, poultry, and fishing technological programs, whose importance has grown notably in this decade, as Table 10-20 shows.

The importance for this study of educational effort was suggested in the first section of this chapter, but it should be emphasized that people with a secondary education oriented to job skills have an expectation of greater lifelong income than those with a general traditional secondary education.

### *Higher Secondary Education*

This level includes the terminal secondary education with a technical orientation, the general traditional and technological as well as teacher training programs. The basic figures for the decade are shown in Table 10–21.

In spite of notable absolute growth, additional educational opportunities at this level have not been sufficient. This is why the percentage of attendance as a proportional demand has decreased.

Direct participation of the federal government in baccalaureate and in terminal secondary education is markedly lower than at other educational levels. It is replaced by offerings from autonomous and state institutions of higher education which, in many instances, have studies incorporated in the higher secondary educational systems. This is the case for the

*TABLE 10.18.*
*Availability of Services for Secondary Education by State, in Relative Terms, 1980–1981*

| *States* | *Population* | *Elementary enrollment* | *Registration for job training* | *Registration for secondary* |
|---|---|---|---|---|
| Estados Unidos Mexicanos | 100.0 | 100.0 | 100.0 | 100.0 |
| Aguascalientes | 0.6 | 0.8 | 1.2 | 0.8 |
| Baja California | 2.0 | 1.8 | 4.3 | 2.7 |
| Baja California Sur | 0.3 | 0.3 | 0.3 | 0.4 |
| Campeche | 0.5 | 0.6 | 0.3 | 0.5 |
| Coahuila | 2.1 | 2.3 | 5.5 | 2.9 |
| Colima | 0.5 | 0.5 | 1.6 | 0.6 |
| Chiapas | 3.1 | 3.4 | 0.8 | 1.8 |
| Chihuahua | 3.2 | 3.1 | 7.1 | 3.0 |
| Distrito Federal | 14.2 | 10.1 | 12.7 | 19.7 |
| Durango | 1.8 | 2.0 | 1.9 | 1.6 |
| Guanajuato | 4.5 | 5.1 | 0.8 | 3.0 |
| Guerrero | 3.2 | 3.8 | 1.1 | 2.8 |
| Hidalgo | 2.2 | 2.5 | 0.4 | 2.0 |
| Jalisco | 6.6 | 6.9 | 14.7 | 6.4 |
| México | 10.0 | 10.9 | 4.0 | 8.9 |
| Michoacán | 4.5 | 4.7 | 2.4 | 3.4 |
| Morelos | 1.3 | 1.4 | 2.0 | 1.8 |
| Nayarit | 1.1 | 1.1 | 0.8 | 1.4 |
| Nuevo León | 3.7 | 3.5 | 8.0 | 6.0 |
| Oaxaca | 3.7 | 4.1 | 0.8 | 2.3 |
| Puebla | 4.9 | 4.8 | 4.7 | 3.5 |
| Querétaro | 0.9 | 1.1 | 0.4 | 0.7 |
| Quintana Roo | 0.2 | 0.3 | 0.1 | 0.3 |
| San Luis Potosí | 2.4 | 2.5 | 1.6 | 2.0 |
| Sinaloa | 2.7 | 3.0 | 3.2 | 3.5 |
| Sonora | 2.2 | 2.2 | 4.4 | 3.3 |
| Tabasco | 1.6 | 1.5 | 1.6 | 1.2 |
| Tamaulipas | 3.0 | 2.8 | 3.6 | 3.5 |
| Tlaxcala | 0.8 | 0.9 | 0.5 | 0.9 |
| Veracruz | 7.9 | 7.4 | 3.0 | 5.6 |
| Yucatán | 1.4 | 1.5 | 1.1 | 1.4 |
| Zacatecas | 1.7 | 1.9 | 1.2 | 1.2 |

SOURCE: *Supplement, Historical Statistics, Fifth Government Report,* except for the data on population, whose source is *Población de México*. Data for 1976.

Universidad Nacional Autónoma de México (UNAM), for example. The baccalaureate program under the control of the federal government has a clearly technical orientation, different from the rest. This demonstrates the intention of the federal government to support both vocational and preparatory education. Without decreasing its attention to students who

*TABLE 10.19.*
*Output by Grade*

| *States* | *Registered in 6th grade of elementary 1970–1971* | *Registered in 1st grade of secondary 1971–1972* | *Registered in 3rd grade of secondary 1973–1974* |
|---|---|---|---|
| Estados Unidos Mexicanos | 100.0 | 59.8 | 49.0 |
| Aguascalientes | 100.0 | 54.2 | 47.1 |
| Baja California | 100.0 | 68.9 | 53.9 |
| Baja California Sur | 100.0 | 72.8 | 57.8 |
| Campeche | 100.0 | 55.0 | 46.0 |
| Coahuila | 100.0 | 59.3 | 46.8 |
| Colima | 100.0 | 64.3 | 44.4 |
| Chiapas | 100.0 | 50.3 | 39.9 |
| Chihuahua | 100.0 | 47.9 | 37.1 |
| Distrito Federal | 100.0 | 80.3 | 62.0 |
| Durango | 100.0 | 42.9 | 36.5 |
| Guanajuato | 100.0 | 49.3 | 35.6 |
| Guerrero | 100.0 | 58.7 | 48.3 |
| Hidalgo | 100.0 | 49.2 | 40.5 |
| Jalisco | 100.0 | 47.0 | 38.2 |
| México | 100.0 | 48.0 | 36.9 |
| Michoacán | 100.0 | 51.2 | 37.8 |
| Morelos | 100.0 | 67.7 | 57.1 |
| Nayarit | 100.0 | 67.6 | 54.3 |
| Nuevo León | 100.0 | 73.9 | 65.8 |
| Oaxaca | 100.0 | 39.4 | 30.6 |
| Puebla | 100.0 | 52.5 | 40.9 |
| Querétaro | 100.0 | 59.1 | 46.2 |
| Quintana Roo | 100.0 | 63.5 | 53.8 |
| San Luis Potosí | 100.0 | 47.8 | 44.5 |
| Sinaloa | 100.0 | 59.3 | 46.6 |
| Sonora | 100.0 | 67.9 | 49.9 |
| Tabasco | 100.0 | 53.3 | 38.1 |
| Tamaulipas | 100.0 | 57.7 | 47.5 |
| Tlaxcala | 100.0 | 53.0 | 39.7 |
| Veracruz | 100.0 | 55.9 | 40.4 |
| Yucatán | 100.0 | 73.8 | 58.1 |
| Zacatecas | 100.0 | 30.8 | 24.1 |

SOURCE: *Anuario Estadístico de los Estados Unidos Mexicanos,* various years.

*TABLE 10.20.*
*Enrollment in Technological Secondary Schools*

| | *1971–1972* | *1981–1982* |
|---|---|---|
| For Workers | 55,448 | 148,486 |
| Industrial or business technologies | 110,203 | 364,872 |
| Poultry technology | 27,986 | 269,821 |
| Fishing technology | — | 11,714 |
| Sum | 193,637 | 794,893 |
| As a percentage of the total enrollment for secondary schools | 15% | 22% |

SOURCE: *Supplement, Historical Statistics, Fifth State-of-the-Nation-Report.*

*TABLE 10.21.*
*Enrollment and Attendance in Higher Secondary Education (thousands of people)*

| | | *Attendance* | | | | | | | |
|---|---|---|---|---|---|---|---|---|---|
| | | | *Middle Terminal* | | *Baccalaureate* | | *Teaching* | | |
| *Years* | *Total* | *%* | | *%* | | *%* | | *%* |
| 1971–1972 | 427 | 87.9 | 42 | 8.4 | 329 | 72.2 | 56 | 7.3 |
| 1972–1973 | 514 | 91.5 | 49 | 8.4 | 395 | 75.4 | 70 | 7.7 |
| 1973–1974 | 596 | 91.7 | 59 | 10.0 | 459 | 72.5 | 79 | 9.2 |
| 1974–1975 | 706 | 97.7 | 69 | 9.8 | 547 | 78.4 | 91 | 9.3 |
| 1975–1976 | 798 | 98.4 | 78 | 10.2 | 608 | 77.9 | 112 | 10.3 |
| 1976–1977 | 863 | 89.5 | 78 | 8.5 | 650 | 70.9 | 136 | 10.1 |
| 1977–1978 | 951 | 88.6 | 75 | 8.1 | 719 | 69.5 | 157 | 11.0 |
| 1978–1979 | 1092 | 91.0 | 83 | 7.7 | 812 | 70.9 | 197 | 12.4 |
| 1979–1980 | 1204 | 88.7 | 103 | 8.7 | 886 | 70.5 | 215 | 9.5 |
| 1980–1981 | 1366 | 90.1 | 178 | 14.2 | 972 | 68.2 | 216 | 7.7 |
| 1981–1982 | 1385 | 82.4 | 200 | 13.9 | 987 | 60.7 | 198 | 7.8 |

SOURCE: *Supplement, Historical Statistics, Fifth State-of-the-Nation Report.*
NOTE: The attendance index refers to the absorption of graduates of the lower secondary schools.

wish to prepare for higher levels, it emphasize training for work skills. Of the total baccalaureate enrollment, 23 percent is in technological schools which, together with the terminal secondary education figure means about 25 percent of the educational opportunities at a higher secondary level are for job training.

No important change is observed in the participation of teacher education, and this may affect possibilities of significant short-range improvement in the efficiency of the elementary level teaching. In this type of education, the role of private schools reaches 50 percent.

Distribution of educational opportunities among the states shows a great concentration. The Federal District offers 32 percent of the total baccalaureate openings; Jalisco follows with 8.5 percent and the State of Mexico with a 6.5 percent, although this percentage is lower than the percentage of the State's population in the total population of the country.

There is a notable difference in enrollment for baccalaureates in Chiapas, Guanajuato, Guerrero, Hidalgo, Michoacán, Oaxaca, Puebla, Veracruz, and Zacatecas in relation to the national total and the respective state participation in population.[7] Other programs at this level—terminal secondary education and teaching training—show a somewhat smaller concentration, even though this is still significant. Data on this paragraph are given in Table 10-22.

At this educational level a disparity begins to appear in comparison with other Latin American countries, even those with less economic development. This and other international comparisons are presented in Table 10-26.

*Higher Education*

The national university system covers the effective demand almost entirely, understood as the number of graduates from higher secondary level. Nevertheless, so large is the early attrition rate and so acute is the lack of advancement from one level to the next that the system shows that less than 5 percent of the student population have access to higher education, and of these only half graduate. Moreover, a high percentage of these graduates do not obtain professional degrees.

Growth of this educational level, including higher education for teachers, has also been explosive as can be seen in Table 10-22.

The geographic concentration of the service is also high although it is rapidly devolving because of the federal support given to state universities and because of the creation, in the 1970s, of a subsystem of federal technological institutes established in the states of the Republic. In addition, Universidad Nacional Autónoma de México (UNAM) has voluntarily slowed its growth. These data are shown in Tables 10-24 and 10-25.

An important factor for the purpose of this study is the distribution of university enrollment by areas of study. It can be observed that 37 percent of the total university students are enrolled in social and administrative sciences while 27 percent are enrolled in the area of engineering and technology. Several studies in other Latin American countries with similar proportions concur that there is an excess supply of professionals in the social sciences leading to unemployment and lower relative salaries, while now and for the near future in Mexico there is an excess demand for technicians and engineers. It is also said that there is an excess supply of doctors, whose participation in university enrollment is 21 percent, but perhaps here the problem is more one of geographic concentration: occupation or under-occupation of doctors in the hospital and social service systems of the great cities but scarcity in those from the rural zones of the

*TABLE 10.22.*
*Participation of the States in Higher Secondary Education 1981–1982*

| *States* | *Population* | *Enrollment in terminal secondary education* | *Enrollment in baccalaureate* | *Enrollment in schools for teachers* |
|---|---|---|---|---|
| Estados Unidos Mexicanos | 100.0 | 100.0 | 100.0 | 100.0 |
| Aguascalientes | 0.6 | 0.8 | 0.9 | 1.5 |
| Baja California | 2.0 | 2.6 | 3.0 | 2.4 |
| Baja California Sur | 0.3 | 0.4 | 0.5 | 0.5 |
| Campeche | 0.5 | 0.5 | 0.5 | 1.0 |
| Coahuila | 2.1 | 2.8 | 2.4 | 3.0 |
| Colima | 0.5 | 0.6 | 0.6 | 0.5 |
| Chiapas | 3.1 | 1.9 | 1.0 | 6.5 |
| Chihuahua | 3.2 | 0.8 | 3.0 | 1.6 |
| Distrito Federal | 14.2 | 18.6 | 32.0 | 12.0 |
| Durango | 1.8 | 1.7 | 1.2 | 7.0 |
| Guanajuato | 4.5 | 3.3 | 2.2 | 5.5 |
| Guerrero | 3.2 | 2.9 | 2.0 | 4.6 |
| Hidalgo | 2.2 | 2.1 | 1.5 | 1.4 |
| Jalisco | 6.6 | 5.9 | 8.5 | 4.4 |
| México | 10.0 | 9.5 | 6.5 | 4.5 |
| Michoacán | 4.5 | 3.5 | 1.7 | 2.1 |
| Morelos | 1.3 | 2.1 | 1.0 | 3.0 |
| Nayarit | 1.1 | 1.5 | 1.1 | 0.5 |
| Nuevo León | 3.7 | 6.0 | 4.7 | 7.4 |
| Oaxaca | 3.7 | 1.4 | 1.4 | 2.7 |
| Puebla | 4.9 | 3.6 | 3.0 | 6.9 |
| Querétaro | 0.9 | 0.8 | 0.6 | 0.8 |
| Quintana Roo | 0.2 | 0.3 | 0.2 | 0.5 |
| San Luis Potosí | 2.4 | 2.1 | 1.6 | 4.4 |
| Sinaloa | 2.7 | 3.6 | 2.3 | 2.5 |
| Sonora | 2.2 | 3.2 | 3.6 | 2.4 |
| Tabasco | 1.6 | 1.3 | 1.0 | 1.0 |
| Tamaulipas | 3.0 | 3.7 | 2.5 | 4.3 |
| Tlaxcala | 0.8 | 1.0 | 1.0 | 0.8 |
| Veracruz | 7.9 | 5.8 | 2.9 | 2.3 |
| Yucatán | 1.4 | 1.4 | 1.5 | 1.6 |
| Zacatecas | 1.7 | 1.1 | 0.9 | 1.3 |

SOURCE: *Supplement, Historical Statistics, Fifth State-of-the-Nation Report,* except for the data on population, which was obtained from "La Población de México".

*TABLE 10.23.*
*Enrollment and Efficiency of Higher Education*

| *Years* | *New students in first grade* | *Total enrollment* | *Graduates* | *Efficiency*[a] |
|---|---|---|---|---|
| 1971–1972 | 100,855 | 316,077 | 32,407 | n.d. |
| 1972–1973 | 112,219 | 355,226 | 33,373 | n.d. |
| 1973–1974 | 128,430 | 403,897 | 40,016 | n.d. |
| 1974–1975 | 142,320 | 471,717 | 49,175 | n.d. |
| 1975–1976 | 166,666 | 543,112 | 52,866 | n.d. |
| 1976–1977 | 153,867 | 569,266 | 53,822 | 53.4 |
| 1977–1978 | 197,089 | 609,079 | 51,611 | 46.0 |
| 1978–1979 | 221,844 | 740,050 | 64,823 | 50.4 |
| 1979–1980 | 255,541 | 850,863 | 73,900 | 51.9 |
| 1980–1981 | 290,785 | 934,111 | 79,279 | 47.6 |
| 1981–1982 | 304,805 | 977,960 | 80,333 | 52.2 |

SOURCE: *Supplement, Historical Statistics, Fifth State-of-the-Nation Report.*

[a]Graduate percentages are estimated on the basis of new students having entered five years previously.

country. This is a matter related to the quality and orientation of the national health services, a topic which will be dealt with in the next section of this paper.

### *Some International Comparisons*

To finish this section on demand and meeting of demand for education, Table 10-26 presents some measures for international comparison.

## *Resources Allotted for Education*

### *Schools and Teaching Personnel*

A first indicator of the quality of education at different levels is the relation between the number of students and variables such as the number of schools and number of teachers. This information is presented in Table 10-27.

Perhaps the best indicator is the diminishing number of students per teacher registered in elementary schools; moreover, the index is still high if compared with other countries.

The figures obscure the fact that for a post-elementary education there are a high number of teachers giving only one class or working by the hour, not exclusively engaged as full-time teachers. This explains the relatively low coefficients. The number of students by school, on the other hand, conceals the fact that a higher percentage of elementary schools do not have a complete six-year program. Another reason for small elementary schools is that the dispersion of towns hinders concentration of installations. The figures for Mexico compared with other countries are shown in Table 10-28.

*Financial Resources*

Given the relative importance of public education within the system and the constitutional commitment that "all education provided by the State will be free," the size and use of public expenses and investment in

*TABLE 10.24.*
*Distribution of Higher Educational Opportunities*

| *States* | *1970–1971* | *1975–1976* |
|---|---|---|
| Estados Unidos Mexicanos | 100.0 | 100.0 |
| Aguascalientes | 0.1 | 0.6 |
| Baja California | 0.7 | 1.9 |
| Baja California Sur | — | 0.3 |
| Campeche | n.s. | 0.2 |
| Coahuila | 2.0 | 2.2 |
| Colima | 0.1 | 0.4 |
| Chiapas | 0.2 | 0.5 |
| Chihuahua | 1.8 | 2.6 |
| Distrito Federal | 50.9 | 28.7 |
| Durango | 0.4 | 1.7 |
| Guanajuato | 1.3 | 1.3 |
| Guerrero | 0.9 | 1.7 |
| Hidalgo | 0.4 | 0.6 |
| Jalisco | 10.0 | 9.3 |
| México | 1.3 | 6.1 |
| Michoacán | 2.2 | 3.2 |
| Morelos | 0.7 | 0.9 |
| Nayarit | 1.1 | 1.6 |
| Nuevo León | 8.6 | 8.5 |
| Oaxaca | 0.6 | 1.7 |
| Puebla | 5.7 | 4.7 |
| Querétaro | 0.5 | 0.5 |
| Quintana Roo | — | n.s. |
| San Luis Potosí | 1.7 | 1.5 |
| Sinaloa | 0.9 | 4.0 |
| Sonora | 1.1 | 1.7 |
| Tabasco | 0.4 | 0.6 |
| Tamaulipas | 1.7 | 3.4 |
| Tlaxcala | 0.1 | 0.4 |
| Veracruz | 3.0 | 6.3 |
| Yucatán | 1.2 | 1.3 |
| Zacatecas | 0.5 | 0.6 |

SOURCE: *Supplement, Historical Statistics, Fifth State-of-the-Nation Report.*

*TABLE 10.25.*
*Administrative Control of Higher Education*

| | *1971–1972 Enrollment* | | *1980–1981 Enrollment* | |
|---|---|---|---|---|
| National Autonomous University of Mexico | 85,271 | 29.3 | 163,500 | 19.2 |
| National Polytechnical Institute | 49,607 | 17.1 | 65,630 | 7.7 |
| National Metropolitan Autonomous University | — | — | 20,108 | 2.4 |
| Federal institutions | 8,450 | 2.9 | 55,350 | 6.5 |
| State universities and institutions | 111,385 | 38.3 | 437,448 | 51.4 |
| Private and independent | 35,890 | 12.4 | 109,254 | 12.8 |
| | 290,603 | 100.0 | 851,290 | 100.0 |
| Teaching and higher level subsystem | 25,474 | | 126,660 | |
| Total | 316,077 | | 977,960 | |

SOURCE: *Supplement, Historical Statistics, Fifth State-of-the-Nation Report.*

*TABLE 10.26.*
*Indexes of Meeting Demand*

| | *Income per capita US$* | *Enrolled students, as age group percentages* | | | | | | *Adult literacy index* | |
|---|---|---|---|---|---|---|---|---|---|
| | | *Elementary* | | *Secondary* | | *Higher* | | | |
| *Country* | *1978* | *1960* | *1977* | *1960* | *1977* | *1960* | *1977* | *1960* | *1975* |
| Cuba | 810 | 109 | 122 | 14 | 50 | 3 | 11 | — | 96 |
| Colombia | 850 | 77 | 103 | 12 | 39 | 2 | 9 | 63 | 81 |
| Paraguay | 850 | 98 | 102 | 11 | 25 | 2 | 6 | 75 | 81 |
| Ecuador | 880 | 83 | 101 | 12 | 44 | 3 | 28 | 68 | 74 |
| Guatemala | 910 | 45 | 65 | 7 | 16 | 2 | 5 | 32 | 47 |
| México | 1290 | 80 | 116 | 11 | 39 | 3 | 10 | 65 | 76 |
| Panamá | 1290 | 96 | 86 | 29 | 115 | 5 | 22 | 54 | 82 |
| Chile | 1410 | 109 | 117 | 24 | 50 | 4 | 13 | 84 | 88 |
| Brazil | 1570 | 95 | 90 | 11 | 24 | 2 | 12 | 61 | 76 |
| Uruguay | 1610 | 111 | 85 | 47 | 60 | 8 | 13 | — | 94 |
| Argentina | 1910 | 98 | 110 | 23 | 41 | 11 | 29 | 91 | 94 |
| Spain | 3470 | 110 | 114 | 23 | 76 | 4 | 22 | 87 | — |
| USSR | 3700 | 100 | 97 | 49 | 73 | 11 | 22 | 98 | 99 |
| Japan | 7280 | 103 | 100 | 74 | 93 | 10 | 29 | 98 | 99 |
| France | 8260 | 144 | 108 | 46 | 83 | 10 | 24 | — | 99 |
| U.S.A. | 9590 | 118 | 94 | 86 | 93 | 32 | 56 | 98 | 99 |

SOURCE: *World Development Report, 1980* (Washington, D.C.: The World Bank, 1980).

*TABLE 10.27.*
*Resources by Educational Level*

| | *1970–1971* | | *1980–1981* | |
|---|---|---|---|---|
| | *Students per school* | *Students per teacher* | *Students per school* | *Students per teacher* |
| Pre-school | 130 | 38 | 84 | 33 |
| Elementary | 205 | 48 | 194 | 40 |
| Job training | n.a. | n.a. | 148 | 20 |
| Terminal elementary | 138 | 20 | 130 | 16[a] |
| Basic secondary | 267 | 16 | 319 | 18 |
| Terminal secondary | 151 | 8 | 254 | 14 |
| Higher secondary | 433 | 16 | 546 | 17 |
| Teacher training | 242 | 11 | 449 | 17 |
| Higher[b] | 703 | 11 | 1048 | 13 |

SOURCE: *La Población de México* op. cit. for 1970–1971. *Supplement, Historical Statistics, Fifth State-of-the-Nation Report.*

[a] Numbers for 1979–1980.

[b] Includes higher teacher training.

n.a. Not available

*TABLE 10.28.*
*Students per Teacher and School*
*(Educational Level)*

| | *Pre-school students per* | | *Elementary students per* | | *Secondary students per Teacher* | *Higher students per Teacher* |
|---|---|---|---|---|---|---|
| | *Teacher* | *School* | *Teacher* | *School* | | |
| Mexico | 37 | 135 | 46 | 225 | 17 | 13 |
| Argentina | 19 | 65 | 18 | 170 | 7 | 13 |
| Brazil | 21 | 62 | 22 | 107 | 11 | 15 |
| Japan | 24 | 175 | 25 | 420 | 18 | 13 |
| France | 47 | 208 | 29 | 82 | 15 | n.a. |
| Spain | 37 | n.a. | 29 | 120 | 32 | 16 |
| Cuba | 29 | n.a. | 23 | 115 | 13 | 12 |
| U.S.A. | n.a. | n.a. | 20 | 245 | 18 | 16 |
| U.S.S.R. | 12 | 85 | 15 | 344 | n.a. | 15 |

SOURCE: Secretaría de Programación y Presupuesto, *La Población de México, su ocupación y sus niveles de bienestar* (México: 1979).

n.a. = not available.

education acquire a special importance for the distribution and redistribution of human capital.

A first glance at expenditures on education in the last two decades would indicate that they have increased dramatically. For example, Figure 10-2, based on data from table 10-29, presents expenditures of the public sector on education with respect to the Gross Domestic Product (GDP). As the graph shows, the amount of the product spent on education has been on a constant rise.

Other indicators of expenditures on education in the last two decades seem to indicate that they have also increased dynamically. For example, Figure 10-3 shows that education expenditure has constantly grown in proportion to federal government expenditure. These results contrast with the tendency of the 1940s and part of the 1950s, periods in which the relationship between education and total public expenditure decreased in comparison with the levels reached by the government of President Cárdenas.

If we explore the composition of educational expenditure, however, the results are not encouraging. For example, Figure 10-4 shows the evolution of spending by the Secretariat of Public Education (SEP) on elementary education, as a proportion of its total expenditure, and demonstrates a disturbing decrease. It is especially surprising to find the relative decrease in spending for elementary education—almost 50 percent for the sample period—with respect to the total S.E.P. expenditures.

The decrease suggests an important change in the composition of expenses for the educational sector. In fact, this change in the composition of spending for education is even more evident if we analyze the evolution of spending on elementary education in comparison with that on higher education. Figure 10-5 details this evolution. As can be seen in this graph, since 1962, when the relationship between expenses for elementary and secondary education was highest (3.70), there has been a consistent decline, dropping to lower than 1.0 in 1976. It should be noted that in 1977 this tendency is reversed.

That higher education received a privileged treatment in recent years is reflected in the real expenditure per student at different educational levels shown in Table 10-30.

The recent evolution of federal expenditures for educational and cultural services is shown in Table 10-31. The expenditure made by the Secretariat of Public Education is higher than the federal government's expenditures in this sector since it allots part of its budget to social welfare that is different from education. At the same time the federal government spends on education amounts not channeled through the corresponding Secretariat. The increase in expenditure for elementary education in 1977 was noticeable; unfortunately there is no updated information on this aspect.

To place in perspective the high drop-out rate, at least up to 1976, in

*TABLE 10.29.*

*Evolution of Expenditure and Public Investment in Education (millions of pesos)*

| *Years* | *1 GDP (nominal)* | *2 Federal government expenditures* | *3 SEP expenditures* | *4 Total public investment* | *5 Federal public investment in education and research* | *3/1 %* | *3/2 %* | *5/4 %* |
|---|---|---|---|---|---|---|---|---|
| 1935 | 4,279 | 301 | 38 | 137 | 2 | 0.9 | 12.6 | 1.5 |
| 1936 | 5,038 | 406 | 51 | 168 | 2 | 1.0 | 12.7 | 1.1 |
| 1937 | 6,409 | 479 | 63 | 192 | 2 | 1.0 | 13.3 | 1.0 |
| 1938 | 6,862 | 504 | 64 | 198 | 2 | 0.9 | 12.8 | 1.0 |
| 1939 | 7,337 | 571 | 67 | 233 | 2 | 0.9 | 11.7 | 0.9 |
| 1940 | 7,774 | 610 | 75 | 290 | 3 | 0.9 | 12.3 | 1.0 |
| 1941 | 8,701 | 689 | 77 | 337 | 1 | 0.9 | 11.1 | 0.3 |
| 1942 | 10,066 | 845 | 86 | 464 | 1 | 0.8 | 10.1 | 0.2 |
| 1943 | 12,285 | 1,085 | 94 | 568 | 1 | 0.8 | 8.7 | 0.2 |
| 1944 | 17,719 | 1,505 | 130 | 657 | 9 | 0.7 | 8.6 | 1.4 |
| 1945 | 19,382 | 1,633 | 170 | 848 | 9 | 0.9 | 10.4 | 1.1 |
| 1946 | 26,322 | 1,829 | 199 | 999 | 10 | 0.8 | 10.8 | 1.0 |
| 1947 | 29,237 | 2,343 | 216 | 1,310 | 13 | 0.7 | 9.2 | 1.0 |
| 1948 | 31,196 | 2,773 | 237 | 1,539 | 17 | 0.8 | 8.5 | 1.1 |
| 1949 | 34,316 | 3,741 | 282 | 1,956 | 15 | 0.8 | 7.5 | 0.8 |
| 1950 | 39,736 | 3,700 | 314 | 2,672 | 29 | 0.8 | 8.5 | 1.1 |
| 1951 | 51,245 | 5,075 | 366 | 2,836 | 102 | 0.7 | 7.2 | 3.5 |
| 1952 | 57,482 | 6,603 | 459 | 3,280 | 221 | 0.8 | 7.0 | 6.7 |
| 1953 | 57,172 | 5,825 | 507 | 3,076 | 109 | 0.9 | 8.7 | 3.5 |
| 1954 | 69,680 | 8,471 | 691 | 4,183 | 136 | 1.0 | 8.2 | 3.3 |
| 1955 | 84,870 | 9,255 | 731 | 4,408 | 74 | 0.9 | 7.9 | 1.7 |

| | | | | | | | | |
|---|---|---|---|---|---|---|---|---|
| 1956 | 96,996 | 10,567 | 901 | 4,571 | 131 | 0.9 | 8.5 | 2.9 |
| 1957 | 111,402 | 11,815 | 1,035 | 5,628 | 129 | 0.9 | 8.8 | 2.3 |
| 1958 | 123,815 | 13,841 | 1,273 | 6,190 | 155 | 1.0 | 9.2 | 2.5 |
| 1959 | 132,669 | 14,777 | 1,506 | 6,362 | 108 | 1.1 | 10.2 | 1.7 |
| 1960 | 150,511 | 20,778 | 1,959 | 8,376 | 192 | 1.3 | 9.4 | 2.3 |
| 1961 | 163,265 | 20,946 | 2,196 | 10,372 | 273 | 1.3 | 10.5 | 2.6 |
| 1962 | 176,030 | 21,421 | 2,512 | 10,823 | 175 | 1.4 | 11.7 | 1.6 |
| 1963 | 195,983 | 21,371 | 2,877 | 13,821 | 438 | 1.5 | 13.5 | 3.2 |
| 1964 | 231,370 | 29,660 | 3,728 | 17,436 | 610 | 1.6 | 12.6 | 3.5 |
| 1965 | 252,028 | 36,979 | 4,075 | 13,048 | 774 | 1.6 | 11.0 | 5.9 |
| 1966 | 280,090 | 33,061 | 4,697 | 15,475 | 589 | 1.7 | 14.2 | 3.8 |
| 1967 | 306,317 | 40,860 | 5,260 | 21,057 | 1,021 | 1.7 | 12.9 | 4.8 |
| 1968 | 339,145 | 42,980 | 5,819 | 23,314 | 1,136 | 1.7 | 13.5 | 4.9 |
| 1969 | 374,900 | 49,775 | 7,073 | 26,339 | 1,472 | 1.9 | 14.2 | 5.6 |
| 1970 | 418,700 | 52,656 | 7,817 | 29,205 | 1,060 | 1.9 | 14.8 | 3.6 |
| 1971 | 452,400 | 55,786 | 9,445 | 22,392 | 1,230 | 2.1 | 16.9 | 5.5 |
| 1972 | 512,300 | 77,230 | 11,760 | 33,248 | 2,034 | 2.3 | 15.2 | 6.1 |
| 1973 | 619,600 | 102,241 | 15,140 | 49,778 | 2,199 | 2.4 | 14.8 | 4.4 |
| 1974 | 813,700 | 135,795 | 20,795 | 64,817 | 3,022 | 2.5 | 15.3 | 4.7 |
| 1975 | 988,300 | 200,416 | 31,116 | 95,767 | 4,602 | 3.1 | 15.5 | 4.8 |
| 1976 | 1,227,900 | 238,733 | 42,496 | 108,611 | 4,885 | 3.5 | 17.8 | 4.5 |
| 1977 | 1,674,700 | 355,132 | 61,761 | 140,102 | 5,874 | 3.7 | 17.4 | 4.2 |
| 1978 | 2,122,800 | 442,034 | 77,562 | 217,382 | 8,606 | 3.7 | 17.5 | 3.9 |
| 1979 | 2,767,000 | 652,100 | 102,955 | 313,750 | 5,689 | 3.7 | 15.8 | 1.8 |
| 1980 | 3,760,300 | 1,002,013 | 131,130 | 486,178 | 9,809 | 3.5 | 13.1 | 2.0 |

NOTE: The investment data up to 1964 are those authorized and those from 1965 to date are the actual expenditures. GDP data are from Bank of Mexico, S.A. Data on expenditure and investments have been gathered from different scurces, but basically are those from the accounts of Public Treasury and Secretariat of Programming and Budgeting. The Annual Report 1970–1973, of Nacional Financiera, S.A., (Mexico 1976) was used to complete this series.

Figure 10-2.

Public Sector Expenditure on Education/GDP.

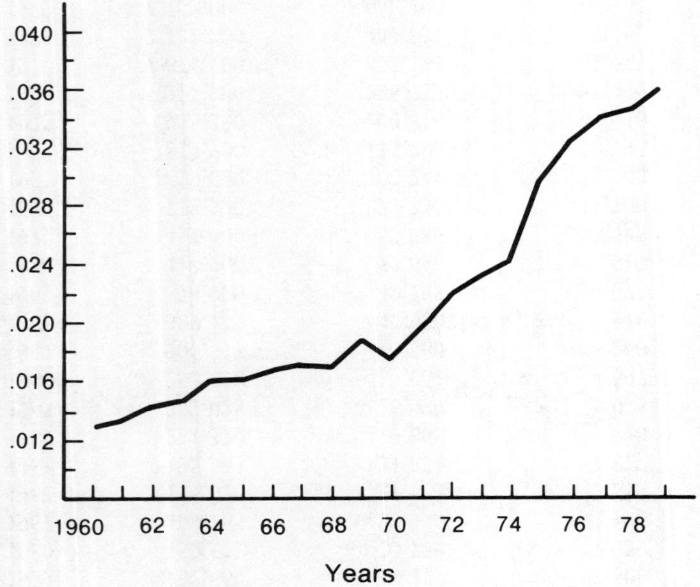


Figure 10-3.

$$\frac{\text{Public Sector Expenditure on Education.}}{\text{Expenditure of the Federal Government}}$$

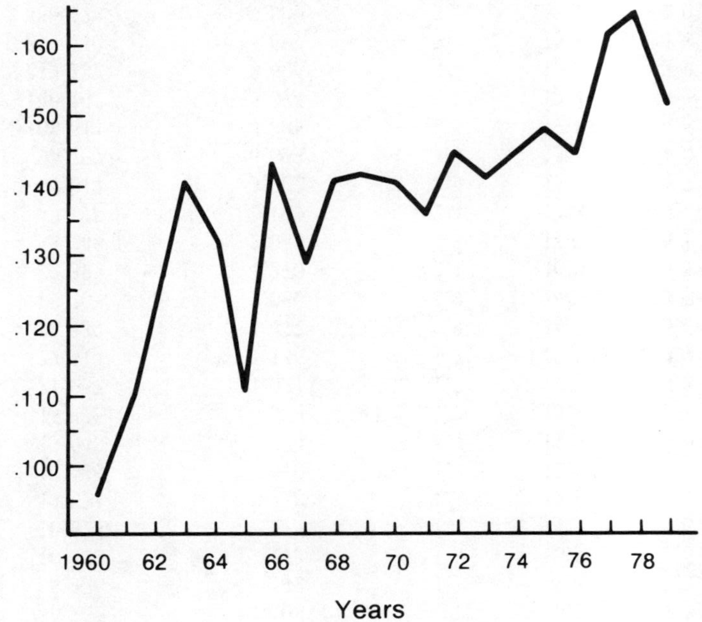


SOURCE: Secretaría de Hacienda y Crédito Público (Office of Public Finance and Credit) and Secretaría de Programación y Presupuesto Statistics, Statistics on the Mexican Economy, Nacional Financiera S.A. (NAFINSA).

**Figure 10-4.**

**Expenditure of the Public Sector on Elementary School**
**Expenditure of the SEP**

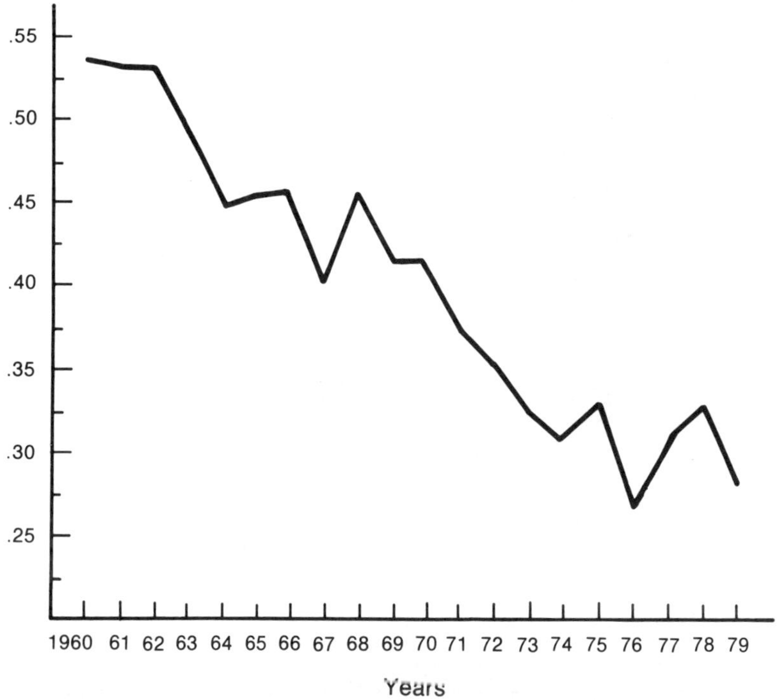


SOURCE: Hacienda Pública, S.H.C.P. and S.P.P. statistics.

elementary education in comparison with higher education, it must be recalled that 50 percent of heads-of-household considered "very poor" (family income from 0 to 0.5 times the general minimum wage) had no instruction whatsoever, while another 45 percent had not finished elementary education (See Table 10-4). If we further consider that 83 percent of those "poor" families are located in towns of under 100,000 inhabitants, we can conclude that, from the viewpoint of personal income distribution of the country, greater efforts in education should be carried out not only in fostering primary education in general, but also in specifically supporting elementary education in the rural sector. It must also be remembered that one of the main causes for 45 percent of the country's "poor" not finishing elementary school is that, even today, there are more elementary schools without full programs than with complete six-year programs. Even though all the children of "elementary" ages have access to educational opportunity, the efficiency of the system is still low. Thus, there is a need to allot greater resources to increase the quality of elementary teaching.

It can be seen from the foregoing that spending for elementary educa-

**Figure 10-5.**

**Expenditure of the Public Sector on Elementary School / Expenditure of the Public Sector on Higher Education**

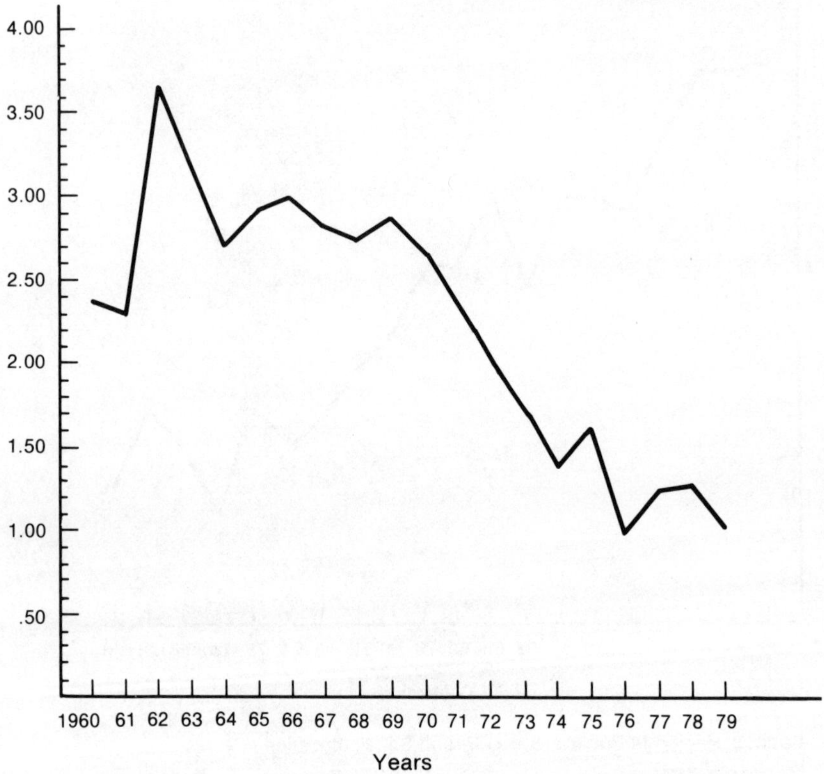


SOURCE: Hacienda Pública, S.H.C.P. and S.P.P. statistics.

tion (especially that for the rural sector) must become a national priority since, although it is long in producing results, this process will provide human capital to those families.[8] The possible effect of reassigning and increasing public spending in this sense could be very significant, especially if it is recalled, that on the one hand, almost all the "poor" heads-of-household of the country lack a formal education and that, on the other, formal education is a prerequisite for finding work in the modern sector of the economy, and its absence greatly hampers social mobility.[9]

It should be mentioned that in contrast to actions that affect the property rights of existing capital, the extension of education to the poor creates new human capital. This fact makes education politically more attractive since in the long run there are clear advantages even for those who enjoy the benefits of physical capital, because of the increase in productivity of labor and the advantage of greater supply of qualified labor. This was specifically important during 1980 and 1981. Because of

*TABLE 10.30.*
*Real Expenditure per Student made by the S.E.P.*

| | *1970* | *1976* |
|---|---|---|
| Pre-school | 522 | 785 |
| Elementary | 477 | 577 |
| Secondary level | 1,672 | 1,376 |
| Teaching level | 8,672 | 6,383* |
| Higher level | 20,516 | 43,947 |
| Total of the system | 735 | 1,156 |

SOURCE: *Manual de Estadísticas Básicas,* op. cit.
*1975 Datum.

the magnitude of the economic recuperation, the economy faced, for the first time in years, bottlenecks in finding not only qualified but also semiqualified labor.

It should be pointed out, finally, that the main political return from investment in education would be to legitimize the social system. If society on the whole believes that there are equal opportunities for all throughout the educational system, then even the most serious differences observed in the income distribution of the country will be more tolerable.

## Health Conditions

### *Life Expectancy and Mortality*[10]

One of the most important indicators of the health level of a population is its "life expectancy at birth." This indicator of the expected number of years of life of the newborn has evolved dynamically.[11] For example, the numbers shown on Table 10-32 indicate that life expectancy has increased from 36.9 years in 1930 to 49.7 years in 1950, reaching 64.4 years in 1975.

From Table 10-32, three different periods can be distinguished: the first from 1930 to 1950, when life expectancy rose dramatically; a second from 1950 to 1960 with a high but smaller growth rate, and a third from 1960 to 1975, when life expectancy rose at much lower rates than those of previous periods.

The continuing rise in life expectancy at birth is explained basically by the reduction in the general mortality rate. This rate, in turn, depends fundamentally on two factors: general preventive and curative measures in public health (such as increase in immunization and more medical attention) and the adoption of sanitary engineering measures (such as drinkable water, garbage disposal, swamp drainage, etc.)

*TABLE 10.31.*

*Federal Spending on Educational and Cultural Services*
*(millions of peso)*

| *Exp. S.E.P.* | *Total* | *Pre-school* | *Elementary* | *Secondary* | *Teaching* | *Higher* | *Other* | *Libraries, newspapers and magazines, museums* | *Investment* | *Other services* |
|---|---|---|---|---|---|---|---|---|---|---|
| 7,073 | 6,958 | 133 | 2,914 | 898 | 162 | 1,014 | 55 | 55 | 1,455 | 272 |
| 7,817 | 7,188 | 145 | 3,184 | 1,265 | 154 | 1,188 | 58 | 71 | 744 | 379 |
| 9,445 | 8,724 | 155 | 3,483 | 1,475 | 129 | 1,474 | 83 | 63 | 1,476 | 385 |
| 11,760 | 11,059 | 177 | 4,110 | 1,624 | 220 | 2,041 | 236 | 122 | 1,973 | 556 |
| 15,140 | 14,091 | 251 | 4,879 | 1,953 | 284 | 2,764 | 436 | 106 | 2,697 | 723 |
| 20,795 | 19,311 | 361 | 6,270 | 2,558 | 403 | 4,486 | 721 | 144 | 3,155 | 1,213 |
| 31,115 | 29,153 | 324 | 9,895 | 2,587 | 367 | 6,197 | 784 | 230 | 4,571 | 4,197 |
| 42,496 | 39,776 | 2,124 | 9,479 | 4,750 | — | 11,906 | 237 | 15 | 5,056 | 6,208 |
| 61,761 | 57,258 | 1,156 | 19,011 | 9,238 | 746 | 15,659 | 330 | 28 | 7,260 | 3,829 |
| 77,562 | | | | | | | | | | |
| 102,955 | | | | | | | | | | |
| 131,130 | | | | | | | | | | |

SOURCE: Secretaría de Programación y Presupuesto, *Información sobre Gasto Público 1969–1978* (México, 1980).

*TABLE 10.32.*
*Life Expectancy at Birth*
*(in years)*

| | |
|---|---|
| 1930 | 36.9 |
| 1940 | 38.9 |
| 1950 | 49.7 |
| 1960 | 57.4 |
| 1970 | 60.2 |
| 1975 | 64.4 |

SOURCE: *La Población de México, su ocupación y sus niveles de bienestar. Anuario Estadístico de los Estados Unidos Mexicanos* (Mexico), Dirección General de Estadística (General Statistics Department), Secretaría de Industria y Comercio, several years. (México: Secretaría de Programación y Presupuesto, 1979).

The figures on mortality rates, an additional indicator of the evolution of the population's health, are shown in Table 10-33.

As Table 10-33 shows, the mortality rate has continually decreased over time. In fact, the rate has decreased almost three-fourths in the sample period.

If we analyze the evolution in Mexico of the gross mortality rate by sexes, it is found that the rate for men is consistently higher than that for women. For example, while the mortality rate for men was 12.4, 10.8, and 7.9 for the years 1960, 1970, and 1975, it was 10.9, 9.3, and 6.5 respectively for women. Obviously, life expectancy at birth for men is lower than that for women. In 1975, life expectancy at birth of females was 66.4 years, while that of males was 62.8 years.

The figures presented in the last two tables show evidence that the

*TABLE 10.33.*
*Gross Mortality Rate**

| | |
|---|---|
| 1930 | 25.6 |
| 1940 | 23.4 |
| 1950 | 16.2 |
| 1960 | 11.5 |
| 1970 | 10.1 |
| 1975 | 7.2 |

SOURCE: Dirección General de Estadística, *Anuario Estadístico de los Estados Unidos Mexicanos,* Secretaría de Industria y Comercio, several years.

*The mortality rate represents the number of people who die every year out of each thousand inhabitants. In reference to these numbers, it should be noted that because of the traditional under-reporting of infant death in rural areas, the rates presented are clearly undervalued. See E. Cordero: "Subestimación de la Mortalidad Infantil en México" (Undervaluation of Infant Mortality in Mexico), *Demografía y Economía,* Vol. II, No. 1. México, 1968.

country has improved substantially the overall health levels of its population.

However, in an economy full of contrasts and inequalities such as Mexico's, it is essential to probe further in order to analyze the composition behind those aggregate numbers and to place them in perspective.

Let us start by comparing the mortality figures from our country with those from other countries of the continent. In order to make a valid comparison, mortality rates should be "corrected" with the international differentials in distribution by age of the population, since those structures have a great influence on the number of deaths. Table 10-34 shows the "corrected" mortality indexes.

As Table 10-34 shows, one of the most important indicators of the state of health in Mexico initially indicates that the advances seen there are not so spectacular when compared with those of other countries. In fact, one can see that the adjusted mortality rates for several of the selected countries with a per capita gross domestic income lower than that of Mexico, are less than the rate in our country.

The comparative numbers in Table 10-34 allow us to evaluate in relative terms the degree of improvement in health conditions of the country, but the most disturbing aspects of these conditions are evident when we analyze the breakdown that is implied in the total figures.

*Mortality by age group*

One of the most trustworthy indicators of a population's health is its infant mortality rate. Table 10-35 shows the indicators of mortality rates by age groups for selected years.

*TABLE 10.34.*

*Gross Mortality Rates Adjusted by Age in Selected Countries for 1971*[a]

| *Country* | *Gross rate* | *Adjusted rate* |
|---|---|---|
| Guatemala | 14.5 | 14.3 |
| Honduras | 7.9 | 8.5 |
| Mexico | 9.0 | 8.4 |
| Chile | 8.6 | 8.1 |
| Venezuela | 6.7 | 6.9 |
| Costa Rica | 5.9 | 6.3 |
| Dominican Republic | 6.2 | 6.2 |
| Cuba | 5.9 | 4.8 |
| U.S.A. | 9.4 | 4.8 |

SOURCE: Dirección General de Estadística, Secretaría de Industria y Comercio, *Imagen Demográfica 1960–1973,* Series: Estadísticas Vitales, (México, 1975).

[a]Rate per 1,000 people

*TABLE 10.35.*
*Mortality Rate by Age Group*[a]

| *Age Groups* | *Rate* 1970 | 1975 |
|---|---|---|
| Under 1 year of age | 68.5 | 49.0 |
| 1– 4 years | 10.9 | 4.3 |
| 5–14 years | 3.4 | 1.0 |
| 15–24 years | 4.0 | 1.9 |
| 25–44 years | 7.8 | 3.9 |
| 45–64 years | 13.5 | 11.6 |
| 65–74 years | 40.3 | 35.4 |
| 75 years and older | 145.5 | 103.8 |

SOURCE: Dirección General de Estadística, Secretaría de Industria y Comercio, *Imagen Demográfica 1960–1973* (México, 1975).

[a] Index per 1,000 people.

As the table shows, the mortality rate for infants (children under one year) is higher than that of other age groups, except those 75 years of age or older.

Because of the importance of the infant mortality rate as an indicator of the degree of the population's health, this evolution over a long period of time is presented in Table 10-36.

The evolution of these rates is surprising, especially when we consider that, for example, in 1975 deaths of children under one year represented 27.3 percent of the total number of deaths in the country.

If the evolution of these rates is one of the first signs for concern, their real magnitude is evident when we set them in an international context in

*TABLE 10.36.*
*Infant Mortality Rate**

| Year | Rate |
|---|---|
| 1930 | 210.6 |
| 1940 | 205.3 |
| 1950 | 96.2 |
| 1960 | 74.2 |
| 1970 | 68.5 |
| 1975 | 49.0 |

SOURCE: La Economica Mexicana en Cifras, Nacional Financiera, (México: 1978), Dirección General de Estadística, Secretaria de Industrie y Comercio (México: 1975).

*Figures refer to deaths of children under one year of age for each 1,000 born alive and registered. It is probable that the numbers one the chart are undervalued as the result of under-reporting of deaths in the rural areas.

*TABLE 10.37.*
*Infant Mortality Rate in Selected Countries (1975)*[a]

| *Country* | *Rate* |
|---|---|
| Guatemala | 81.1 |
| Chile | 55.6 |
| Mexico[b] | 49.7 |
| Venezuela | 43.7 |
| Dominican Republic | 43.5 |
| Costa Rica | 38.2 |
| Honduras | 33.7 |
| Cuba | 27.3 |
| U.S.A. | 16.1 |

SOURCE: *Statistical Abstract of Latin America.* U.C.L.A., Vol. 20, (Los Angeles: 1980).

[a]Number of deaths among children under one year for each 1,000 born alive.

[b]Notice that the number reported for Mexico differs slightly from that presented in Table 10.36.

comparison with countries of a level of total development similar to or less than that of Mexico.

For example, Table 10-37 shows comparative statistics relevant to other countries on the American continent.

The tables show that the infant mortality rate in Mexico is higher than that of not only countries with a similar level of per capita income, but also of countries, such as Honduras and the Dominican Republic, with a lower per capita income than Mexico's.

A second examination of the figures on Tables 10-32 and 10-33 immediately leads us to ask how it can be possible that while the aggregate figures reflect optimistic results in the development of health in Mexico, the figures on infant mortality rate contain clear signs for concern. The answer to this question lies in the enormous segmentation of income levels and regions within the so-called Mexican miracle.

### *Main Causes of General Mortality*

After the brief presentation on infant mortality rates in Mexico, it is evident that we must examine further the composition of the aggregate numbers. We must return to the total mortality figures. Even though the gain in relative terms has already been questioned, there seems to be an undeniable achievement in absolute terms.

For example, we may ask the general causes of death in our country. Table 10-38 shows figures on the main causes of mortality.[12]

From this table we may deduce several items. First, it is clear that the two principal causes of death for 1975 remained the same as those in past decades: infectious and respiratory diseases. These are closely related to the living conditions of the population and therefore, could have been preventable. In fact, it should be noticed that for the year of reference approximately 34.4 percent of deaths resulted exclusively from these two causes.

Furthermore, the evolution of mortality due to chronic degenerative diseases, although relatively important (increasing with time), does not reflect a satisfactory advance in sanitation. In countries of greater relative development, the main cause of death is circulatory system diseases.

Finally, it is surprising to see the absolute and relative importance that accidents from violence have acquired as a cause of aggregate mortality.

Recent analysis of the death rate due to respiratory and intestinal diseases leads us to conclude that the health conditions of the populations have stagnated, at least from the viewpoint of this variable. An indication of this problem is the fact that Mexico is still behind many countries in the same relative developmental level. For example, in Table 10-39 the international comparison on mortality causes adjusted by the age structure of the population is presented.

The international comparison of these figures clearly indicates the country's relative backwardness in health care. It is evident, as well, that the main causes of death are totally preventable since they are derived from an absolute and relative lag of the country in the sanitary hygienic conditions of its population. In this sense, problems such as the lack of potable water and of sewage disposal, as well as malnutrition levels in certain elements of the population, are still the real causes of the high mortality rate.

*TABLE 10.38.*

*Percentage of Deaths by Groups of Diseases (1975)*[a]

| | *Order of importance* | *Percentage* |
|---|---|---|
| Total | — | 100.0 |
| Parasitic and infectious diseases | 1 | 17.7 |
| Respiratory system diseases | 2 | 16.7 |
| Circulatory system diseases | 3 | 14.9 |
| Accidents by poisoning and violence | 4 | 12.4 |
| Symptoms and poorly defined morbid states | 5 | 10.5 |
| Digestive system diseases | 6 | 6.3 |
| Others | — | 21.5 |

SOURCE: Secretaría de Programación y Presupuesto, *La Población de Mexico, su ocupación y sus niveles de bienestar*. Basic Information of the Nation Series, 1979.

[a] Figures according to the Eight Revision of the International Classification of Diseases.

*TABLE 10.39.*
*International Comparison of Mortality Rates Adjusted by the Age Structure from Different Causes of Death (1975)**

| *Country* | *Enteritis and other Diarrheic Diseases* | *Influenza & Pneumonia* | *Heart Diseases* |
|---|---|---|---|
| Guatemala | 218.1 | 190.5 | 6.5 |
| Honduras | 85.4 | 28.4 | 9.9 |
| Mexico | 78.3 | 90.9 | 21.0 |
| Chile | 30.1 | 82.5 | 39.7 |
| Costa Rica | 27.7 | 30.7 | 38.9 |
| Dominican Republic | 41.0 | 16.1 | 16.8 |
| Cuba | 10.1 | 34.2 | 80.1 |
| U.S.A. | 1.1 | 13.5 | 116.9 |

SOURCE: OPS *Health Conditions in the Americas, 1973–1976* (Washington: 1978). U.C.L.A., *Statistical Abstract of Latin America,* Vol. 20, (Los Angeles: 1980).

*Rates per 100,000 inhabitants.

## *Regional Distribution of Health Conditions*

It is possible to locate a first indicator of the distribution of the population's health conditions by analyzing its regional composition.

The 1975 mortality rates of each federal entity of the Republic are indicated on Table 10-40.

It is important to note in Table 10-40 that it is precisely the states with the lowest per-capita income of the country (Oaxaca and Tlaxcala) that have the highest mortality rates. This relation is clearly seen in Figure 10-6, where the negative correlation between mortality and per capita income by state is shown.

It is also interesting to observe in Table 10-41 the distribution of deaths by groups of disease for each state in the country.

The data in Table 10-41 demonstrate previously presented problems in relation to aggregate mortality composition. Thus the individual figures for death causes do not reveal an encouraging view of the health conditions of the population. An analysis of the regional composition makes it clear that the problems are acute. It is only necessary to mention that 48 percent of the total number of deaths in 1975 for the State of Tlaxcala were due to causes associated with infectious and respiratory diseases.

## *Health Services*

### *Material and Human Resources*

During 1976, the country had 5,828 working medical units with a total of 68,846 beds. Of these units 31.7 percent were hospitals and 68.3 percent out-patient medical units. Of the total hospital units, 44.9 percent be-

TABLE 10.40.
*Mortality Rate by State*

| *State* | *Rate*[a] | |
|---|---|---|
| | *1970* | *1975* |
| Aguascalientes | 11.3 | 7.8 |
| Baja California | 8.1 | 5.7 |
| Baja California Sur | 6.5 | 6.2 |
| Campeche | 7.8 | 6.3 |
| Coahuila | 10.4 | 7.4 |
| Colima | 10.2 | 7.5 |
| Chiapas | 11.3 | 7.9 |
| Chihuahua | 8.8 | 6.6 |
| Distrito Federal | 9.6 | 5.9 |
| Durango | 7.4 | 5.8 |
| Guanajuato | 12.3 | 8.8 |
| Guerrero | 8.3 | 6.4 |
| Hidalgo | 12.1 | 9.5 |
| Jalisco | 10.2 | 7.4 |
| México | 10.5 | 7.0 |
| Michoacán | 8.7 | 7.2 |
| Morelos | 8.6 | 6.5 |
| Nayarit | 8.3 | 5.6 |
| Nuevo León | 7.4 | 5.4 |
| Oaxaca | 15.3 | 11.3 |
| Puebla | 14.5 | 10.7 |
| Querétaro | 12.0 | 8.4 |
| Quintana Roo | 5.0 | 3.7 |
| San Luis Potosí | 11.2 | 8.5 |
| Sinaloa | 6.8 | 5.5 |
| Sonora | 8.2 | 6.5 |
| Tabasco | 8.8 | 6.4 |
| Tamaulipas | 7.5 | 5.5 |
| Tlaxcala | 13.6 | 10.8 |
| Veracruz | 9.3 | 6.9 |
| Yucatán | 10.0 | 8.3 |
| Zacatecas | 9.7 | 7.1 |

SOURCE: Secretaría de Programación y Presupuesto, *La Población de Mexico, su ocupación y sus niveles de bienestar,* 1979.

[a] Mortality rate per 1,000 inhabitants.

**Figure 10-6. Mortality Rate in 1975 (per 1,000 inhabitants).**

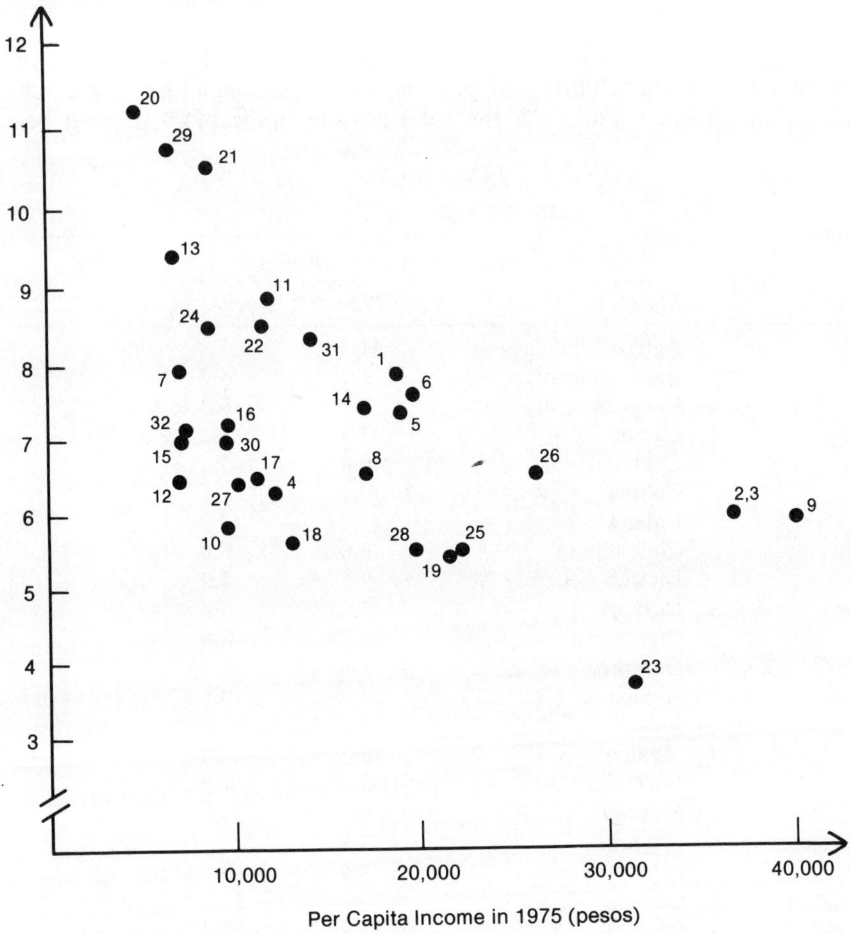


NOTE: The numbers accompanying each of the dots on the graph correspond to the names of the states described in Table 10-41. The figures regarding Northern and Southern Baja California are grouped under point 2,3.

longed to the Social Security Institutions (such as the IMSS, ISSSTE, etc.), 38.7 percent to Social Aid Institutions (SSA and DDF), 11.0 percent to private institutions: and finally, 5.4 percent to other institutions (such as the Red Cross, as well as union, town, and state units).[13]

The equipment of the hospital units comprised 17,464 consultation offices, 1,054 clinical analysis laboratories, 1,213 radiology cubicles, 2,171 operating rooms, and 2,171 childbirth units.

The human resources of this sector in 1976 consisted of 255,916 people, of which 18.0 percent were medical, 48.8 percent paramedic, and 33.2 percent administrative personnel.

The number of doctors per person has continued to grow. In 1970, there were 7.1 doctors for every 10,000 people, while in 1976 this number had risen to 7.4 doctors.

During 1976, of the total number of doctors (46,094), 48.6 percent worked for the Social Security Institutions, 25.6 percent for social aid institutions, and the remaining 25.8 percent for private establishment.[14]

For an idea of the relative advance of the country in this matter, Table 10-42 makes some international comparisons with certain selected countries.

As Table 10-42 shows, the aggregate relationship between doctors and people in Mexico is comparable internationally with developed countries. Nevertheless, the registered data on the number of beds for each inhabitant is lower than the international comparisons.

*Medical Services*

The Mexican government has tried to improve the population's health by providing direct medical services to the people. One of the specific ways in which these services are extended to the community is by out-patient medical care which does not require hospitalization. During 1976, medical institutions reported 83.2 million out-patient consultations. Of these, 78.2 percent corresponded to the social security institutions,[15] 13.3 percent to aid institutions, 2.4 percent to private establishments, and finally, 6.1 percent to other organizations.

Regarding types of consultation given, it can be seen that a great percentage was general (59.8 pecent), followed by pediatric (7.9 percent) and odontological (7.1 percent) care.

As to causes of hospitalization, parasitic and infectious diseases were still the main illnesses, followed by circulatory and digestive diseases.

Even though the number of out-patient consultations and hospitalizations has increased in recent years, it is important to point out that there is still clear evidence that improvement in this area is needed. For example, during 1976, only 40.7 percent of the total births in the country were attended by medical personnel. In the face of this high figure, it is obvious that one of the main causes for the high maternal and newborn mortality in our country is the lack of medical care during most pregnancies and births. In 1975, for example, the main cause of maternal death was hemorrhage.

Finally, in reference to preventive medicine services, it must be noted that the coverage of innoculations against smallpox, poliomyelitis, diphtheria, etc., has increased dramatically. It is sufficient to mention the number of doses administered by the IMSS. These increased by 210 percent between 1971 and 1976.

Considering these figures, one can say without exaggeration that the favorable effect on life expectancy has been due to advances in preventive medicine.

*TABLE 10.41.*

*Percentage Distribution of Deaths by Groups of Diseases and Federal Entity (1975)*[a]

| *State* | *Total* | *Parasitic and infectious diseases* | *Respiratory system diseases* | *Circulatory system diseases* | *Accidents by poisoning and violence* | *Symptoms and poorly defined morbid states* | *Digestive system diseases* | *Others* |
|---|---|---|---|---|---|---|---|---|
| Aguascalientes | 100.0 | 17.6 | 15.5 | 15.8 | 10.4 | 5.7 | 6.9 | 28.1 |
| Baja California | 100.0 | 12.9 | 14.4 | 19.4 | 15.3 | 3.4 | 5.1 | 29.5 |
| Baja California Sur | 100.0 | 18.1 | 13.8 | 15.7 | 12.1 | 2.4 | 4.3 | 33.6 |
| Campeche | 100.0 | 20.9 | 9.8 | 14.4 | 13.0 | 9.8 | 6.0 | 26.1 |
| Coahuila | 100.0 | 15.7 | 14.6 | 19.2 | 10.3 | 6.8 | 5.8 | 27.6 |
| Colima | 100.0 | 20.6 | 11.2 | 14.5 | 17.7 | 4.2 | 7.2 | 24.6 |
| Chiapas | 100.0 | 29.8 | 9.8 | 7.5 | 11.6 | 22.4 | 4.5 | 14.3 |
| Chihuahua | 100.0 | 14.6 | 16.8 | 17.8 | 13.5 | 9.7 | 4.7 | 22.9 |
| Distrito Federal | 100.0 | 13.1 | 17.2 | 19.1 | 8.9 | 2.7 | 10.3 | 29.7 |
| Durango | 100.0 | 12.6 | 13.3 | 19.5 | 17.2 | 12.1 | 4.3 | 21.0 |
| Guanajuato | 100.0 | 18.6 | 22.1 | 13.7 | 10.2 | 8.8 | 5.8 | 20.8 |
| Guerrero | 100.0 | 19.6 | 11.7 | 10.6 | 22.8 | 17.4 | 4.4 | 13.5 |
| Hidalgo | 100.0 | 15.0 | 22.2 | 13.7 | 11.9 | 12.3 | 8.7 | 16.2 |
| Jalisco | 100.0 | 17.3 | 15.1 | 17.4 | 12.5 | 8.6 | 6.5 | 22.6 |
| México | 100.0 | 19.4 | 26.5 | 12.1 | 10.4 | 4.7 | 7.9 | 19.0 |

| | | | | | | | | |
|---|---|---|---|---|---|---|---|---|
| Michoacán | 100.0 | 16.7 | 14.8 | 16.1 | 17.2 | 8.0 | 6.3 | 20.9 |
| Morelos | 100.0 | 14.7 | 12.0 | 17.8 | 20.8 | 6.8 | 7.4 | 20.5 |
| Nayarit | 100.0 | 16.6 | 13.7 | 17.4 | 17.2 | 7.4 | 5.7 | 22.0 |
| Nuevo León | 100.0 | 17.6 | 13.3 | 20.9 | 11.1 | 5.3 | 3.9 | 27.9 |
| Oaxaca | 100.0 | 24.0 | 10.3 | 7.4 | 10.4 | 33.0 | 3.2 | 11.7 |
| Puebla | 100.0 | 16.4 | 22.9 | 9.1 | 11.1 | 17.0 | 6.4 | 17.1 |
| Querétaro | 100.0 | 21.9 | 19.1 | 12.7 | 11.0 | 6.9 | 6.9 | 21.5 |
| Quintana Roo | 100.0 | 16.8 | 11.8 | 12.9 | 19.8 | 8.7 | 4.4 | 25.6 |
| San Luis Potosí | 100.0 | 20.2 | 19.1 | 13.9 | 9.8 | 10.5 | 4.8 | 30.7 |
| Sinaloa | 100.0 | 13.2 | 11.6 | 19.8 | 22.0 | 7.6 | 4.2 | 21.6 |
| Sonora | 100.0 | 13.5 | 14.5 | 22.2 | 14.8 | 4.9 | 3.5 | 26.6 |
| Tabasco | 100.0 | 24.5 | 11.3 | 13.2 | 16.0 | 13.4 | 4.2 | 17.4 |
| Tamaulipas | 100.0 | 15.4 | 12.0 | 21.5 | 13.6 | 4.6 | 4.4 | 28.5 |
| Tlaxcala | 100.0 | 13.7 | 34.3 | 14.9 | 7.9 | 6.0 | 7.0 | 16.2 |
| Veracruz | 100.0 | 19.6 | 10.0 | 15.9 | 13.6 | 12.8 | 6.4 | 21.7 |
| Yucatán | 100.0 | 17.7 | 11.6 | 15.2 | 6.5 | 13.8 | 6.5 | 28.7 |
| Zacatecas | 100.0 | 16.2 | 20.8 | 14.4 | 10.7 | 13.7 | 4.8 | 10.4 |

SOURCE: *La Población de México, su ocupación y sus niveles de bienestar*, 1979.

[a]Data according to the Eighth Revision of the International Classification of Diseases.

TABLE 10.42.
*Medical Personnel, Number of Beds in Relation to Population of Selected Countries (numbers around 1976)*

| Country | Doctors per 10,000 inhabitants | Beds per 1,000 inhabitants |
|---|---|---|
| Guatemala | 2.3 | 2.0 |
| Honduras | 3.4 | 1.7 |
| Mexico[a] | 7.4 | 1.2 |
| Chile | 4.5 | 3.6 |
| Venezuela | 11.5 | 2.9 |
| Costa Rica | 6.6 | 3.8 |
| Dominican Republic | 5.4 | 2.8 |
| Cuba | 8.9 | 4.0 |
| U.S.A. | 16.3 | 6.4 |

SOURCE: O.P.S. *Health Condition of the Americas,* 1973–1976, (Washington: 1978).

[a]The figure for doctors per 10,000 inhabitants of Mexico was taken from *La Población de México, su ocupación y sus niveles de bienestar.*

### Social Security and Aid[16]

The population covered by the social security system has increased in absolute terms as well as in coverage. The percentage of people with social security services increased from 20.1 percent in 1965 to 35.6 percent in 1976. Nevertheless, the most significant advances occurred in the 1977–1981 period when the IMSS increased its 1977 coverage from 26 percent of the total population to almost 37.0 percent (1981). Since the analysis of this important structural change is presented in great detail by Emilio Lozoya in this volume,[17] we will simply note one more point. Even though the total population percentage covered by social security institutions reached a record figure of 47.5 percent in 1980, it must be emphasized that most families still not covered belong basically to the rural zones in which the real poverty of the country prevails. In this sense, the solidarity program of IMSS–COPLAMAR, located precisely in these zones, is the first attempt to correct the health policy in Mexico.

### Regional Distribution of Medical Services

The regional distribution of medical units in 1971 points out the clear concentration of services in the urban zones, especially in the Federal District and the States of Jalisco and Veracruz. However, the greatest concentration problem is related to human resources. Based on figures from the Fourth General Population Census of 1970, the concentration of medical personnel in the Federal District, Jalisco, and Veracruz is alarming since 54.2 percent of the doctors live in these zones. In Table 10-43 the figures on human resource distribution of the health sector by class and federal entity are presented. The disparity between the number of inhabitants per doctor is severe, since it varies from a minimum of 474 in the Federal District to a maximum of 5,612 in Oaxaca. Moreover, this table

*TABLE 10.43.*
*Distribution of the Health Sector Personnel by Class and State (1970)*

| *State* | *Inhabitants per medical personnel* | *Inhabitants per paramedical personnel* | *Inhabitants per administrative personnel* |
|---|---|---|---|
| Aguascalientes | 1,778 | 875 | 1,076 |
| Baja California | 1,599 | 761 | 1,113 |
| Baja California Sur | 1,132 | 649 | 577 |
| Campeche | 1,657 | 863 | 1,105 |
| Coahuila | 1,059 | 517 | 709 |
| Colima | 1,497 | 879 | 960 |
| Chiapas | 4,139 | 2,459 | 2,753 |
| Chihuahua | 1,784 | 938 | 1,185 |
| Distrito Federal | 474 | 231 | 247 |
| Durango | 2,432 | 1,146 | 1,683 |
| Guanajuato | 3,266 | 1,636 | 2,110 |
| Guerrero | 3,713 | 1,938 | 2,898 |
| Hidalgo | 3,363 | 2,013 | 2,080 |
| Jalisco | 1,513 | 884 | 1,294 |
| México | 4,090 | 2,218 | 3,257 |
| Michoacán | 2,520 | 1,802 | 2,140 |
| Morclos | 1,706 | 843 | 1,151 |
| Nayarit | 2,542 | 1,819 | 2,734 |
| Nuevo León | 1,107 | 456 | 763 |
| Oaxaca | 5,612 | 3,432 | 4,315 |
| Puebla | 2,370 | 1,299 | 1,920 |
| Querétaro | 2,292 | 1,179 | 1,659 |
| Quintana Roo | 1,466 | 977 | 1,189 |
| San Luis Potosí | 2,176 | 1,292 | 1,718 |
| Sinaloa | 1,979 | 1,045 | 1,339 |
| Sonora | 1,130 | 585 | 756 |
| Tabasco | 2,742 | 1,630 | 2,182 |
| Tamaulipas | 1,324 | 801 | 823 |
| Tlaxcala | 3,007 | 2,419 | 2,752 |
| Veracruz | 1,963 | 1,139 | 1,273 |
| Yucatán | 1,038 | 692 | 889 |
| Zacatecas | 3,718 | 2,339 | 3,306 |

SOURCE: *La Población de México, su ocupación y sus niveles de bienestar.*

shows the disproportion in the per capita numbers of doctors and paramedic and administrative personnel in the different states.

Given the preceding conditions on regional distribution of medical units and human resources, the existing concentration in medical services is not surprising. For example, Table 10-44 gives information on the per-

*TABLE 10.44.*
*Percentage Distribution of Medically Attended Births per State*

| *States* | *Attended births* | *Attended births per each 100 registered births* |
|---|---|---|
| United Mexican States | 824,275 | 36.9 |
| Aguascalientes | 5,613 | 31.5 |
| Baja California | 22,850 | 57.0 |
| Baja California Sur | 2,763 | 43.5 |
| Campeche | 3,141 | 26.2 |
| Coahuila | 36,498 | 58.7 |
| Colima | 5,135 | 46.3 |
| Chiapas | 5,807 | 8.8 |
| Chihuahua | 29,020 | 42.0 |
| Distrito Federal | 233,373 | 75.4 |
| Durango | 17,084 | 36.3 |
| Guanajuato | 29,766 | 27.6 |
| Guerrero | 11,519 | 14.1 |
| Hidalgo | 12,159 | 21.5 |
| Jalisco | 72,022 | 46.3 |
| México | 25,011 | 17.2 |
| Michoacán | 26,634 | 23.1 |
| Morelos | 9,826 | 32.5 |
| Nayarit | 7,593 | 29.0 |
| Nuevo León | 57,172 | 71.2 |
| Oaxaca | 6,478 | 6.8 |
| Querétaro | 8,225 | 30.9 |
| Quintana Roo | 626 | 12.9 |
| San Luis Potosí | 17,941 | 27.2 |
| Sinaloa | 23,982 | 37.2 |
| Sonora | 32,426 | 62.2 |
| Tabasco | 3,663 | 9.5 |
| Tamaulipas | 30,173 | 51.0 |
| Tlaxcala | 4,103 | 17.6 |
| Veracruz | 37,809 | 25.1 |
| Yucatán | 12,785 | 36.4 |
| Zacatecas | 7,473 | 15.0 |
| Puebla | 25,605 | 30.0 |

SOURCE: Secretaría de Programación y Presupuesto, *Anuario Estadístico de los Estados Unidos Mexicanos* 1972–1974, (México: 1978).

TABLE 10.45.
*Gross Expenditure Allocated for Health by the Public Sector (in millions of 1960 pesos)*

| *Year* | *Total* | *Health, Aid and Hospital Services** | *Welfare and Social Security* |
|---|---|---|---|
| 1969 | 11,071 | 3,177 | 7,894 |
| 1970 | 12,301 | 3,261 | 9,040 |
| 1971 | 13,762 | 3,279 | 10,483 |
| 1972 | 17,054 | 4,112 | 12,942 |
| 1973 | 18,232 | 4,456 | 13,776 |
| 1974 | 20,116 | 4,069 | 16,047 |
| 1975 | 21,953 | 4,630 | 17,323 |
| 1976 | 24,282 | 4,869 | 19,413 |
| 1977 | 23,679 | 4,810 | 18,869 |
| 1978 | 22,445 | 4,927 | 17,518 |

SOURCE: Secretaría de Programación y Presupuesto, *Información sobre Gasto Público* 1969–1978, 1980.

*Figures refer to the functional classification of the gross allocated expenditure of the public sector and have been converted into real terms by the implicit deflator of the Gross Domestic Products (GDP).

centage of births medically cared for in the different states of the republic.

The foregoing table shows once again the great regional differences the country faces in health; while 75.4% of the births in the Federal District were medically attended, only 6.8 percent of the births in the state of Oaxaca were.

*Sanitary Hygiene Condition of the Population and Its Regional Distribution*

It has already been mentioned that since preventive medicine has had a positive impact, an alternative weapon against mortality and disease is the improvement of the sanitary hygienic conditions of the population. Recent data on these conditions in the country are a matter of concern. According to the available Population Census (1970), approximately 40 percent of total housing at a national level did not have piped water. This aggregate figure points clearly to the need for greater national effort in the application of sanitary measures. An analysis of this figure produces even more surprising results. For example, in 1980, 80 percent of housing in urban zones and only 34 percent of those in rural zones had piped water. Only 32 percent of the total housing in 1970 had bathrooms with running water. Sewage drains were found in just 41.5 percent of housing in the entire country. The latter figure is even more disturbing for the rural areas, in which ony 14 percent had sewage disposal.

As must be obvious to the reader, if the foregoing figures are indicators of the underdevelopment in total sanitary hygiene of the country, the

*TABLE 10.46.*
*Public Sector Expenditure on Health*[a]

| *Year* | *Percentage of GDP spent on Health* | *Percentage of Total Public Expenditure spent on Health* |
|---|---|---|
| 1969 | 4.0 | 15.3 |
| 1970 | 4.1 | 15.9 |
| 1971 | 4.5 | 16.7 |
| 1972 | 5.2 | 17.8 |
| 1973 | 5.1 | 15.6 |
| 1974 | 5.4 | 15.8 |
| 1975 | 5.6 | 13.9 |
| 1976 | 6.1 | 15.5 |
| 1977 | 5.8 | 14.0 |
| 1978 | 5.1 | 11.6 |

SOURCE: Secretaría de Programación y Presupuesto, *Información sobre Gasto Público 1969–1978,* 1980.

[a]The figures refer to the public sectors's controlled budget.

distribution differences among the various states of the republic further aggravate this situation.

*Levels and Composition of Public Expenditure in Health*

Because of the enormous importance of the health of the nation's population as one of the necessary conditions for a sustained increase in productivity and lifelong income, resources allocated by the state for this objective must be a national priority. As seen before, most of the material and human resources in the health sector are provided by the public institutions of the country. Moreover, because of poor health conditions in underprivileged areas, public spending for improvement represents a medium *sine qua non* to combat directly the absolute levels of poverty in the country.

The overall evolution of real expenditure by the public sector for health is shown in Table 10-45.

As the table shows, the real public expenditure for health grew 101.4 percent in the sample decade. Basically, these aggregate figures show a dynamic behavior in the evolution of this spending. However, given the real growth of the country, other types of comparisons are necessary. Table 10-46 displays the evolution of the public sector's expenditures on health as a percentage of GDP and of the total spending of the public sector.

As the table shows, spending on health rose in proportion to the GDP during 1969–1976 and decreased in 1977 and 1978. However, the most dramatic variations are seen in relation to total public expenditure. From a sample maximum of 17.8 percent in 1972, this relationship drops to a minimum of 11.6 percent in 1978. The magnitude of the fall in this last proportion clearly demonstrates that, even as a total, public spending on health has lagged as a priority in relation to total public expenditure.[18]

It is interesting to compare the share of public spending on health in respect to the GDP of different countries and periods of time. Table 10-47 makes this international comparison.

Overall figures referring to Mexico are much lower than figures for industrialized and even for some Latin American countries.

Aggregate figures of public spending on health give only a first indicator of the tendencies observed in Mexico in public health services. However, the different components of this expenditure must be analyzed from the viewpoint of the various types of services granted as well as their regional distribution.

The percentage share of public expenditure on health is presented according to functional classification in Table 10-48.

From Table 10-48, different conclusions may be drawn. First, it is interesting to observe that the aggregate "Health, Aid and Hospital Ser-

*TABLE 10.47.*

*International Comparison of the Percentage of Public Expenditure on Health with Respect to the GDP*[a]

| *Country* | *1973* | *1976* |
|---|---|---|
| Italy | 19.4 | 21.2 |
| Federal Germany | 15.6 | 20.2 |
| Denmark | 15.3 | 18.5 |
| United Kingdom | 11.6 | 14.4 |
| Uruguay | 10.8 | 12.9 |
| Chile | 8.9 | 8.4 |
| U.S.A. | 8.0 | 10.3 |
| Israel | 7.7 | 10.8 |
| Mexico | 3.9 | 4.3 |
| Venezuela | 3.4 | 3.7 |
| Peru | 1.1 | 1.1 |

SOURCE: International Monetary Fund, *Government Finance Statistics Yearbook,* Vol. II, 1978. Secretaría de Programación y Presupuesto, *Información sobre Gasto Público 1969–1978,* 1980.

[a]The figures refer to the functional classification of expenditure (Sanitation and Social Security). The figures were not modified to respect international criteria classification, and for this reason differ from those on table 10.48.

*TABLE 10.48.*
*Percentage Share of the Public Sector Expenditure on Health*

| *Total* | *1969* | *1970* |
|---|---|---|
| I. Health, aid and hospital services | 28.7 | 20.3 |
| a) Health, medical aid, and hospital services | 4.6 | 7.1 |
| b) Hospital construction | 1.3 | 1.1 |
| c) Maternity and child aid | 0.5 | 1.7 |
| d) Social aid | 21.1 | 9.1 |
| e) Diverse complementary services | 1.3 | 1.4 |
| II. Welfare and social security | 71.3 | 79.9 |
| a) Medical services to public employees | 6.6 | 15.5 |
| b) Other services to public employees | 9.4 | 8.1 |
| c) Retirement and pensions | 9.5 | 4.1 |
| d) State contribution to IMSS | 5.5 | 5.4 |
| e) Aid to the indigenous nuclei | 0.4 | 2.4 |
| f) Other social expenses | 39.9 | 44.2 |

SOURCE: *Secretaría de Programación y Presupuesto, Información sobre Gasto Público 1969–1978.*

vices" represents only a small percentage of the total expenditure in health and shows a decreasing share, from 28.7 percent in 1969 to 20.3 percent in 1977. The reason for this decrease is the severe reduction reported under the heading, "Social Aid," which changed from 21.1 percent in 1969 to only 9.1 percent in 1977. On the other hand, we find the subheading of social security, "Medical Services for Public Employees" rising from 6.6 percent in 1969 to 15.5 percent in 1977.

It is clear that the relative decrease of the aggregate "Health Aid and Hospital Services" represents a drop in the support given by the public sector to the noninsured population of the country. In fact, during the sample period this figure grew by only 55 percent in real terms, while the heading, "Welfare and Social Security" increased 119 percent. This fact is even more relevant when we remember that during 1976, 64.4 percent of the country's total population was not covered by any social security system. In addition, the budget of Secretariat of Health and Public Aid (Secretaría de Salubridad y Asistencia) which represented 1.7 percent of the total 1972 budget was only 1.3 percent in 1979.

With regard to the distribution of spending on public health, there is an economic classification of these expenses for the federal government.[19] Combining this information with the functional classification, one can obtain a matrix for the composition of health expenditure by the federal government.

A comparison of the figures from Tables 10-49 and 10-50 is of interest

TABLE 10.49.

*Percentage Distribution of Gross Expenditure of the Federal Government on Health According to Functional Economic Classification (1969)*

| | Personal services | Administrative purchases and goods | General services | Transfers | Public works construction | Financial investment | Other expenses | Total |
|---|---|---|---|---|---|---|---|---|
| I. Health, aid, & hospital services | 10.13 | 1.90 | 0.38 | 24.82 | 2.08 | — | .18 | 39.49 |
| a) Health, medical aid, & hospital services | 6.22 | 1.29 | 0.03 | 8.54 | 2.08 | — | .05 | 18.22 |
| b) Hospital construction | 0.01 | — | — | 5.02 | — | — | — | 5.02 |
| c) Maternity & infant aid | 0.65 | — | — | 1.26 | — | — | — | 1.91 |
| d) Social aid | 0.96 | 0.01 | 0.01 | 8.35 | — | — | — | 9.33 |
| e) Complementary services | 2.29 | 0.59 | 0.34 | 1.66 | — | — | .12 | 5.00 |
| II. Welfare & social security | 2.57 | 0.50 | 0.09 | 56.65 | 0.34 | 0.22 | .13 | 50.51 |
| a) Medical services for public employees | 0.51 | 0.32 | 0.01 | 12.60 | 0.21 | — | — | 13.65 |
| b) Other services for public employees | — | 0.03 | 0.01 | 1.79 | 0.13 | — | — | 1.96 |
| c) Pensions & retirement | — | — | — | 16.24 | — | — | — | 16.24 |
| d) State contribution to IMSS | — | — | — | 21.67 | — | — | — | 21.67 |
| e) Aid to indigenous groups | 0.51 | — | 0.01 | 0.94 | — | — | — | 1.46 |
| f) Other social costs | 1.55 | 0.15 | 0.07 | 3.41 | — | 0.22 | .12 | 5.53 |
| Total[a] | 12.70 | 2.40 | 0.47 | 81.47 | 2.42 | 0.22 | .31 | — |

SOURCE: Secretaría de Programación y Presupuesto, *Información sobre Gasto Público 1969–1978*, 1980.

[a]Totals have been rounded off.

*TABLE 10.50.*

*Percentage Distribution of Gross Expenditure of the Federal Government for Health according to its Functional-Economic Classification (1977)*

| | *Personal services* | *Administrative purchases and goods* | *General services* | *Transfers* | *Public works & construction* | *Financial investment* | *Other expenses* | *Total* |
|---|---|---|---|---|---|---|---|---|
| I. Health, aid, & hospital services | 7.66 | 1.27 | 0.40 | 25.23 | 3.32 | — | 0.81 | 38.69 |
| a) Health, medical aid, & hospital services | 4.52 | 0.10 | 0.05 | 14.57 | 1.96 | — | 0.03 | 21.23 |
| b) Hospital construction | — | — | — | 2.11 | 1.23 | — | — | 3.34 |
| c) Maternity & infant aid | 0.71 | 0.01 | — | 4.40 | — | — | — | 5.13 |
| d) Social aid | 0.89 | 0.01 | 0.03 | 4.00 | — | — | — | 4.93 |
| e) Complementary services | 1.54 | 1.15 | 0.32 | 0.15 | 0.12 | — | 0.77 | 4.65 |
| II. Welfare & social security | 6.21 | 0.10 | 0.11 | 51.41 | 0.94 | 2.36 | 0.17 | 61.31 |
| a) Medical services for public employees | 0.04 | 0.01 | — | 17.49 | — | — | — | 17.54 |
| b) Other services for public employees | 0.07 | 0.01 | 0.01 | 7.93 | — | — | — | 8.03 |
| c) Pensions & retirement | — | — | — | 2.08 | — | — | — | 2.08 |
| d) State contribution to IMSS | — | — | — | 16.10 | — | — | — | 16.10 |
| e) Aid to indigenous groups | 4.86 | 0.02 | 0.02 | 2.41 | — | — | 0.01 | 7.31 |
| f) Other social costs | 1.24 | 0.06 | 0.09 | 5.40 | 0.93 | 2.36 | 0.16 | 10.24 |
| Total | 13.87 | 1.37 | 0.51 | 76.64 | 4.26 | 2.36 | 0.98 | 100.00 |

SOURCE: Secretaría de Programación y Presupuesto, *Información sobre Gasto Público 1969–1978*, 1980.

NOTE: Totals have been rounded off.

because they show the changes over time of the composition of spending on health by the federal government.

The positive results in the changes of expenditure composition are a greater effort to help the indigenous population (1.5 percent in 1969, as opposed to 7.3 percent in 1977) and less federal aid for the IMSS (21.7 percent of the 1969 expenditure in contrast to 16.1 percent in 1977). On the negative side there is again a drop in expenditure percentage for "Social Aid" (9.3 percent to 4.9 percent) and there is a dramatic decrease in support for "Pension and Retirement Funds" (16.2 percent to 2.1 percent in 1977). This latter change was due principally to inflationary effects on real income of pensioned and retired people. That is, this is the result of the typical redistributive effect of inflation, penalizing persons and families with fixed incomes.

The percentage of federal public investment in health has been decreasing with time. In 1969, the total public investment allocated for health was 3.8 percent while in 1978 it was only 2.9 percent. Regarding the Secretariat of Public Health and Aid, the IMSS, and the ISSSTE., the following can be said about total investment in health: The IMSS has maintained its same share of about 45 percent of the total in the sample period while the ISSSTE has increased its participation (from 21.4 percent in 1969 to 26.3 percent in 1978) and the Secretariat of Public Health and Aid has decreased its contribution (from 32.7 percent to 29.0 percent). In summary, the total gross capital formation of this sector decreases in relation to that of the public sector as a whole. A drop can also be seen in the share of investment by the Secretariat of Public Health and Aid in relation to that of the public security institutions.

Furthermore, it is important to emphasize that the main share of the sector's investment is devoted to building enormous hospitals with sophisticated equipment, which do not take care of the health problems of the underprivileged.[20]

Finally, it must be added that the regional distribution of expenditure and of public investment in health shows clear signs of concentration in the urban zones, especially in the Federal District, the States of Jalisco, Veracruz, and Nuevo León, thereby perpetuating differentials in health conditions of the population.

## Conclusions

The first conclusion of this descriptive study of health and educational opportunities and services is that they have been unequally distributed throughout the country, corresponding, in general, to the inequalities in income distribution of the states and regions. The greatest significance of this study is a negative one: the educational and health policies have not been corrective and have not diminished the disparity in income, but have, on the contrary, confirmed and reaffirmed these conditions.

It is true that the overall indicators show progress in the evolution of educational and health opportunities. These, although spectacular at first glance, are not too far from those of countries comparable to Mexico in structure and development and are much lower than the achievements of countries with larger relative development, including countries such as Cuba, which have given political priority to satisfying the health and education needs of its population.

The main results of this study concerning education were as follows:

1. Higher education, accesible only to an already privileged minority received an increasingly disproportionate share of fiscal aid; nevertheless, services of many elementary schools continue to be incomplete and contribute to the high school drop-out rates.
2. Job training has become important. This is promising because the harvest from this level of education is significantly higher and more immediate than that of the traditional teaching of a more liberal and general nature.
3. The growing decentralization of educational opportunities at secondary and higher levels is also promising, because it contributes to reducing costs of local studies for students and it tends to keep students in their home towns and states.

Several important results in health are the following:

1. Excessive importance and resources have been awarded to curative in relation to preventive medicine, which perpetuates the high infant mortality rate.
2. Efforts to take care of the underprivileged or of those not covered by formal systems of social security are recent and very promising. The earlier practice of considering health as a right related to participation in organized labor had to be broken and health had to be granted independent importance.
3. There has been little connection of health with education, resulting in an excess of doctors but in a scarcity of paramedical personnel especially in the rural and underprivileged areas.

*TABLE A.1.*
*Real Gross Domestic Income Per Capita, by State*

| *State* | *GDP Per Capita*[a] *1975* |
|---|---|
| Aguascalientes | 7009 |
| Baja California | 14353[b] |
| Campeche | 5332 |
| Coahuila | 7869 |
| Colima | 7124 |
| Chiapas | 2631 |
| Chihuahua | 6832 |
| Distrito Federal | 15467 |
| Durango | 3864 |
| Guanajuato | 4741 |
| Guerrero | 2798 |
| Hidalgo | 2574 |
| Jalisco | 6758 |
| México | 2805 |
| Michoacán | 3825 |
| Morelos | 4290 |
| Nayarit | 5162 |
| Nuevo León | 8313 |
| Oaxaca | 1649 |
| Puebla | 3313 |
| Querétaro | 4754 |
| Quintana Roo | 11707 |
| San Luis Potosí | 3478 |
| Sinaloa | 8761 |
| Sonora | 10635 |
| Tabasco | 3851 |
| Tamaulipas | 7639 |
| Tlaxcala | 2604 |
| Veracruz | 3609 |
| Yucatán | 5873 |
| Zacatecas | 2909 |
| United Mexican States | 6489 |

SOURCE: Secretaría de Programación y Presupuesto, *Anuario Estadístico de los Estados Unidos Mexicanos, 1975–1976* (Mexico: 1979). *Desagregación del PIB por Entidad Federativa* Professional Thesis ITAM, Luis Miguel Alvarez Alonso, (Mexico: 1981).

[a] GDP at constant prices (1960-100)

[b] Northern and Southern Baja California were added.

## Notes

1. Grossman, M, "The Correlation Between Health and Schooling," in Nestor Terlecky, (ed.); *Household Production and Consumption, Studies in Income and Wealth,* No. 40, National Bureau of Economic Research, 1976.

2. Data on 1975 per capita state income appear in Table A.1. This information provides a frame of reference for this chapter.

3. This figure is taken from the supplement, *Historical Statistics of the Fifth State-of-the-Nation Report* made by President José López Portillo, Mexico, 1981.

4. The implication of functional illiteracy is that an individual is unable to perform even basic literacy skills, eg., read bus signs.

5. Supplement, *Historic Statistics of the Fifth State-of-the–Nation Report.*

6. This, together with the limited education of the heads-of household, suggests that youth are emigrating because of a lack of job opportunities.

7. A partial explanation probably lies in the fact that the emigration of youth from these states is higher than the national averages.

8. It must also be noted that the recommendation is made for elementary education for both adults and children in the rural sector. The problem seems to be more serious with respect to adult illiteracy because of the enormous lag in education at present.

9. The proposal for adapting the educational system to human resource employment should be emphasized. See the paper of D. Ibarra in "El Perfil de Mexico en 1980" Siglo XXI Editores, Mexico D.F. 1970.

10. For a further discussion of health care programs of the government, see article by Lozoya in this volume.

11. Life expectancy at birth represents the average number of years that a newborn can expect to live, in relation to the mortality rate of the year of reference.

12. We should clarify that the numbers shown must be carefully analyzed since they are based on death certificates stating the immediate cause of death. Obviously, in a number of cases the "immediate causes are other factors like malnutrition that leaves an individual vulnerable.

13. IMSS stands for Mexican Institute of Social Security; ISSSTE for the Social Service and Security Institute for State Workers, SSA for the Secretariat of Health and Public Aid and DDF for the Department of the Federal District.

14. Although for the year of reference, 74.2 percent of the doctors in the country worked for public sector units (considering the Social Security and Social Aid Institutions as ones of the public sector), it must be noted that a high percentage of those doctors combined their services with the private practice of medicine.

15. The IMSS itself provided 58.7 percent of the total out-patient consultations for said year.

16. See also the discussion by Lozoya in this volume.

17. Emilio Lozoya "Health, Security and Social Solidarity in Mexico" this volume.

18. This tendency becomes of even greater concern when analyzing the public expenditure make-up of the states; in 1969, spending by the states on health represented 5.8 percent of total expenditure, while in 1977, it was 4.8 percent.

19. Controlled expense includes that of the federal government and of budget controlled organisms (IMSS, ISSSTE).

20. In this sense, see the interesting studies of Daniel Lopez Acuña, *La Salud Desigual en México* Siglo XXI Editores; 1980.

# CHAPTER 11

# *Urbanization and Housing Policy in Mexico*

Richard J. Moore

## Introduction

The purpose of the present chapter is to examine the impact of rapid urbanization in Mexico on the distribution of wealth, and more specifically, to examine government action in one sphere—housing policy—in terms of the attempts to ameliorate the condition of poverty for a large portion of the urban population. This analysis begins with a brief examination of the process of rapid urbanization in Mexico in recent decades, and considers both intersectorial (i.e., urban-rural) shifts and regional impacts. The analysis proceeds with an examination of one set of public policy actions—housing policy—and focuses on the institutional development of housing policy and current housing conditions in Mexico City.

The analysis that follows suggests that recent history, particularly recent government action, has seen little amelioration of interregional disparities in income and wealth. Most studies indicate that, at best, these disparities have remained the same. The preponderance of the central valley of Mexico, and especially Mexico City, has exacerbated interregional inequality and, in turn, has been exacerbated by government action. As Barkin (1978, 297) notes, deliberate government strategy in regional development aims at speeding the process of national development and has accelerated the processes of concentration and centralization of capital. One consequence of this concentration has been a concomitant concentration of population.

At another level, it is argued here that government (housing) policy *within* urban areas has failed to reach a major portion of the urban poor. There are several factors that account for this which will be examined in this chapter, among these:

*TABLE 11.1.*
*Mean Annual Increase of Population**

| *Period* | *Total* | *Rural* | *Urban* | *Mexico City* |
|---|---|---|---|---|
| 1900–1910 | 1.1% | 0.9% | 2.2% | 3.1% |
| 1910–1921 | −0.5 | −0.9 | 1.5 | 3.1 |
| 1921–1930 | 1.6 | 1.1 | 3.5 | 5.0 |
| 1930–1940 | 1.7 | 1.4 | 3.0 | 3.9 |
| 1940–1950 | 2.7 | 1.5 | 5.9 | 5.9 |
| 1950–1960 | 3.0 | 1.6 | 5.5 | 4.9 |
| 1960–1970 | 3.4 | 1.7 | 5.4 | 5.2 |

SOURCES: Unikel (1978); and Garza and Schteingart (1978).
*Mean Annual Increase is calculated of the basis of the following formula:

$$MAI = \frac{2(P_1 - P_0)}{P_1 + P_0} \cdot \frac{1}{n} \cdot 100$$

Where $P_1$ and $P_0$ is the population at the end and beginning of the period, and n is the number of years.

1. Perceptions of housing needs have been framed in terms of a "financial problem," requiring government to stimulate (subsidize) private-sector actions to accomodate greater numbers
2. Housing policy for the poor has focused on the "deserving poor," or working poor, who have as their principal need the *refining of access* to existing land and housing markets
3. Perceptions of the preference structures of the poor (and most notably, of squatters) have not focused on the fact that *paying* for land is a low priority and that the provision of "low cost" housing (and I use the term loosely) may imply *added* costs for the poor
4. The problem of "reaching the urban poor" presupposes an understanding of who the urban poor are, of differential needs among segments of the urban poor, and of the mechanism(s) for implementing an appropriate delivery system (or systems) for this population

These questions will be addressed in later sections of this chapter.

## Urbanization Patterns and Inequality in Mexico

As is characteristic of most developing countries, Mexico has experienced extremely rapid rates of urbanization since 1940. In addition to relatively high rates of total population growth—mean annual rates of increase of 2.9 percent since 1940—the rates for urban areas have been 5.6 percent per year for the same time period.[1] Thus, not only have rates of urbanization been rapid, but the urban share of the total populations has grown steadily. This is evident in Table 11-1 and 11-2 which examine changes in population over the course of the twentieth century. The share of population in urban areas more than doubled from 1940 to 1970, increasing from 20 percent to 44.9 percent. Projections for 1980 suggest that more than half of the total population of Mexico now resides in urban areas (Garza and Schteingart 1978).

Urbanization and urban growth have not been distributed equally in Mexico. Several tendencies are observable within the national system of cities. First, there is a notable "macrocephalic" pattern to urban growth in the twentieth century. In both recent historical and in current times, Mexico has experienced a high degree of primate urban development, with the emergent preeminence of Mexico City at the turn of the century as the key to understanding this primacy. By the end of the nineteenth century, Mexico City was three and one-half times the size of the second largest city (Guadalajara). During the twentieth century, this primacy increased to such a degree that by 1950 Mexico City was more than seven times the size of Guadalajara. This same relationship obtains when the growth of Mexico City is compared with that of the next three cities (Guadalajara, Monterrey, and Puebla). Indeed, Mexico City alone is larger than the next thirty cities in the country combined.

Thus, the most spectacular manifestation of the urban growth of Mexico is the growth of the capital city. Throughout history the city has played a critical role in national development. At various points in history, Mexico City has served as the seat of the indigenous empire (Tenochtitlán during the precolonial days), the capital city of the viceroyalty of New Spain (in colonial days), the center of the French occupation of Mexico (in the nineteenth century), and finally, the decision center of modern Mexico. It has been estimated that as early as 1750 the city had a population of 100,000 (Wibel and de la Crux 1971). However, the growth of the city throughout the eighteenth and nineteenth centuries was slow, and a relative demographic balance in the urban hierarchy existed until the end of the 19th century.[2] The current level of dominance of Mexico City is of relatively recent origin. The city adjoined the "million club" by

*TABLE 11.2.*

*Population: Total, Urban, Rural, and Largest 35 Cities, 1900–1970 (thousands)*

| *Year* | *Total* | *Urban* | *% Urban* | *Rural* | *% Rural* | *35 Largest* | *% of Total Urban* |
|---|---|---|---|---|---|---|---|
| 1900 | 13,607 | 1,434 | 10.5 | 12,173 | 89.5 | 1,284 | 89.5 |
| 1910 | 15,160 | 1,783 | 11.8 | 13,377 | 88.2 | 1,627 | 91.3 |
| 1921 | 14,335 | 2,100 | 14.6 | 12,335 | 85.4 | 1,865 | 88.8 |
| 1930 | 16,553 | 2,891 | 17.5 | 13,662 | 82.5 | 2,634 | 91.1 |
| 1940 | 19,649 | 3,928 | 20.0 | 15,721 | 80.0 | 3,519 | 89.6 |
| 1950 | 25,779 | 7,210 | 28.0 | 18,569 | 72.0 | 6,149 | 85.3 |
| 1960 | 34,923 | 12,747 | 36.5 | 22,176 | 63.5 | 10,216 | 80.1 |
| 1970 | 49,050 | 22,004 | 44.9 | 27,046 | 55.1 | 17,379 | 79.0 |

SOURCE: Derived from Unikel (1978, 27).

*TABLE 11.3.*
*Population Growth of Metropolitan Area of Mexico City (MAMC) and Urban Area of Mexico City (UAMC), 1930–2000 (thousands)*

| *Year* | *UAMC* | *MAMC* | *UAMC/MAMC* |
|---|---|---|---|
| 1930 | 1,049.0 | 1,263.6 | 83.0% |
| 1940 | 1,559.8 | 1,802.7 | 86.5 |
| 1950 | 2,872.3 | 3,137.6 | 91.5 |
| 1960 | 4,910.0 | 5,186.8 | 94.7 |
| 1970 | 8,567.0 | 8,797.0 | 97.4 |
| 1980 | 13,853.0 | 14,569.8 | 95.1 |
| 1990 | 20,789.9 | 21,841.7 | 95.2 |
| 2000 | 28,113.3 | 30,860.7 | 91.2 |

SOURCE: Derived from Garza and Schteingart (1978).

NOTE: The UAMC refers to Mexico City and the Federal District (excluding the delegation of Milpa Alta, as well as several adjacent municipalities of the state of Mexico. The MAMC includes the UAMC, all other areas in the Federal District as well as a number of bordering urban areas. For the 1970–1980 period, 13 additional municipalities of the state of Mexico are included; for 1990–2000, 9 more municipalities in the state are included, one from the state of Tlaxcala and one from Hidalgo (Centro de Estudios Económicos y Demográficos 1975).

1930, and seemingly uncontrolled—and uncontrollable—population growth has continued to the present.

By measures of the urban area of the city, of the Federal District, or by a broader and more inclusive metropolitan definition, the current state and future trends of population growth clearly suggest the spatial imbalance in Mexico. One estimate places the population of Mexico City in 1980 at well over fourteen million, and projects for the year 2000 a population in excess of thirty million. The urban extension of this metropolitan area would continue from Cuernavaca in the south to the municipality of Tizayuca in the state of Hidalgo in the north (Garza and Schteingart 1978; 83).

However, the overwhelming presence of the capital city obfuscates several important trends and characteristics of spatial concentration in the country. First of all, while overall and urban population growth since 1940 has been very rapid, rural population growth has not (as is clear in Table 11-1). In fact, in at least one decade of the twentieth century (1910–1920) rural population experienced a decline. The violence of the revolutionary period provided the impetus for rapid out-migration to small urban centers in the north and especially toward the locus of power in the central valley (Unikel 1978). Principal migration trends for later periods were shaped in many ways by patterns that emerged at this time, as well as by responses to commercial linkage patterns in earlier decades (such as the railroads in the nineteenth century). However, in each decade an overriding phenomenon has been the process of rural-to-urban migration.

We will examine these migration patterns and the consequences for Mexico City in a later section of this chapter.

Another pattern of urban concentration emerges from a cursory examination of Table 11-2. As of 1970, the thirty-five largest cities of Mexico accounted for four-fifths of the total urban, and 35 percent of the total, population. While the largest four cities have increased their population rapidly, this is not to suggest that smaller cities have not fared well in recent decades. Cities in the 100,000 to 500,000 person range have grown rapidly as well. In addition, the total number of cities has increased in recent years. In 1940, there were 90 localities with at least 10,000 persons; in 1950, there were 141; in 1960, there were 195; and by 1970, there were 281 cities with 10,000 persons or more (Censos Generales de Población, VI through IX).

Thus, the overall pattern of urbanization in Mexico for the twentieth century has resulted in several discernible characteristics: the overwhelming primacy of Mexico City; the absolute expansion of that city (see Table 11-3); dramatic disparities in rural/urban growth rates; and the growth of secondary and tertiary urban centers.

The spatial disparities suggested here have far-reaching implications for more than just demographic characteristics, and have both intraurban and interregional manifestations as well as the interurban characteristics noted above. To understand the factors that have led to the dramatic lack of housing in Mexico City, for example, the factors that have created regional imbalances must be examined as well.

A great deal of literature exists on urban hierarchies and the role of large cities in national development, and while most efforts have focused on the implications of the growth of urban centers in relation to aggregate economic growth, recently the spatial focus has begun to be examined for the implications of urban concentration for social equity and distributional concerns. As Cornelius and Kemper point out:

> As students of the development process in Third World countries became more attentive to the extreme inequalities in wealth distribution which have accompanied aggregate economic growth in these countries in recent decades, metropolitan primacy was singled out increasingly as a key factor contributing to such 'misdevelopment' (1978, 9).

This regional component of inequality is demonstrated in Tables 11-4 and 11-5. Table 11-4 shows regional differences in gross domestic product over time as expressed in constant (1950) *pesos*. Expressed in per capita terms, the real increase in gross domestic product for the period 1950–1970 was a very respectable 3.03 percent annually. Given the rate of population growth over the same period this amount is quite significant. However, the disparities in regional growth are of equal significance, as can be judged by the rankings and absolute figures for regions over time. While the *rate* of growth of GDP for region VII (which contains Mexico

*TABLE 11.4.*
*Gross Domestic Product Per Capita by Region (1900–1970)*
*(1950 Pesos)*

| | *1900* | | *1940* | | *1950* | | *1960* | | *1970* | |
|---|---|---|---|---|---|---|---|---|---|---|
| *Region*[a] | *GDP* | *Rank* | *GDP* | *Rank* | *GDP* | *Rank* | *GDP* | *Rank* | *GDP* | *Rank* |
| I | 941 | (2) | 1,421 | (3) | 2,163 | (2) | 2,591 | (3) | 4,098 | (2) |
| II | 1,081 | (1) | 1,422 | (2) | 2,041 | (4) | 2,837 | (2) | 4,015 | (3) |
| III | 665 | (4) | 1,216 | (4) | 2,049 | (3) | 2,225 | (4) | 2,871 | (4) |
| IV | 581 | (5) | 660 | (5) | 983 | (5) | 902 | (6) | 1,330 | (6) |
| V | 421 | (7) | 607 | (7) | 887 | (6) | 1,080 | (5) | 1,693 | (5) |
| VI | 542 | (6) | 617 | (6) | 803 | (7) | 896 | (8) | 1,296 | (7) |
| VII | 887 | (3) | 2,869 | (1) | 3,141 | (1) | 4,512 | (1) | 5,965 | (1) |
| VIII | 395 | (8) | 507 | (8) | 769 | (8) | 927 | (7) | 1,247 | (8) |
| Nation | 613 | – | 1,165 | – | 1,593 | – | 2,125 | – | 3,104 | – |

SOURCE: Garza and Schteingart (1978, 58).

[a] The regions noted here are:
Region I (Northwest): Baja California, Nayarit, Sinaloa, and Sonora.
Region II (North): Coahuila, Chihuahua, Durango, and Nuevo León.
Region III (Gulf): Tamaulipas and Veracruz.
Region IV (North-central): Aguascalientes, San Luis Potosí, and Zacatecas.
Region V (Central-west): Colima, Guanajuato, Jalisco and Michoacán.
Region VI (Central): Hidalgo, Morelos, Puebla, Querétaro and Tlaxcala.
Region VII (Valley of Mexico): Federal District and the state of Mexico.
Region VIII (South and Southwest): Campeche, Chiapas, Guerrero, Oaxaca, Quintana Roo, Tabasco and Yucatán.

*TABLE 11.5.*
*Regional per Capita Gross Domestic Product as Percent of National GDP/CAP*

| *Region* | *1900* | *1940* | *1950* | *1960* | *1970* |
|---|---|---|---|---|---|
| I | 154% | 122% | 136% | 122% | 132% |
| II | 176 | 122 | 128 | 134 | 129 |
| III | 108 | 104 | 129 | 105 | 92 |
| IV | 95 | 57 | 62 | 42 | 43 |
| V | 69 | 52 | 56 | 51 | 55 |
| VI | 88 | 53 | 50 | 42 | 42 |
| VII | 145 | 246 | 197 | 212 | 192 |
| VIII | 64 | 44 | 48 | 44 | 40 |
| Nation | 100 | 100 | 100 | 100 | 100 |

SOURCE: Derived from Unikel (1978, 179 and 184).

*TABLE 11.6.*
*Distribution of Income and Households by Size of Municipality and Average Annual Income*

| *Size of Locality* | *Households (%)* | *Current Income (%)* | *Current Income (Pesos/Yr/Household)* |
|---|---|---|---|
| 10,000 or less | 12.46 | 5.31 | $23,618 |
| 10,001–100,000 | 37.79 | 20.84 | 30,586 |
| 100,000+ (excluding metropolitan areas) | 23.06 | 29.28 | 70,410 |
| Metropolitan Areas | 26.67 | 44.58 | 92,736 |
| TOTAL | 100.00 | 100.00 | 55,480* |

SOURCE: Secretaría de Programación y Presupuesto, *La distribución del ingreso y el gasto familiar en México* (August 1979).

*Mean current income for the entire sample.

City) has slowed (to 2.8 percent annually for the 1960–1970 period) to below the national mean (of 3.7 percent annually for the same period), the *absolute gap* in constant dollar terms between that region and other regions either remained the same or has increased markedly. For example, while region V had the second most rapid growth of GDP for the 1960–1970 period (at 4.4 percent annually) the gap between the two regions increased in absolute terms from $3,432 pesos in 1960 to $4,272 pesos in 1970. More dramatically, region V fell further behind national GDP per capita (from a gap of $1,045 pesos in 1960 to a gap of $1,411 pesos in 1970). Some regions (e.g., regions IV and VI) declined markedly in terms of their relation to national GDP per capita over the course of the twentieth century. In fact, from 1900 to 1970 only one region (that containing Mexico City) increased its "distance" positively from the national figures. It should come as no surprise that the region with the clearest initial advantage also has the greatest advantage at the end of the time frame.

The spatial dynamics of income inequality can be observed in the disparities between urban and rural income. Table 11-6 presents data from the 1977 Household Survey of Income and Expenditures. Localities were grouped in terms of the size of municipality. While one-eighth of the households live in areas with under 10,000 persons they account for only one-twentieth of current national income. At the opposite extreme, slightly over one-quarter of the households live in the three metropolitan areas (Mexico City, Monterrey, Guadalajara), yet these three represent 45 percent of income. More dramatically, two-thirds of all households in the top income decile live in these three areas, while only 1.6 percent of the top decile live in areas of less than 10,000 persons. To some extent this may be a function of underreporting of income in kind in nonurban areas, but the degree of disparity also suggests that the (inverse) relationship of size of locality and income level holds.

A further dynamic to consider in this analysis of the dimensions of inequality in Mexico is the nation's capacity to deal with issues of containment of urban size. Conscious policies of containment (across the Third World more generally) have been notoriously unsuccessful. Whether the policies are those of containment of urban size and decentralization (such as new towns, industrial parks, etc.) or policies of slum (and/or squatter) clearance, these policies rest, as Mohan suggests, on "dubious underpinnings" (1977, 439). In many ways, these policies go against the basic dynamics of economic forces. Garza and Schteingart note that in the case of Mexico, historical factors and public policies have led to the concentration and to the locational advantages of concentrated urban settlement:

> A circular, accumulative process has been set into motion: original locational advantages → new enterprises → public investments → more locational advantages → more enterprises → new infrastructural investments. . . . This process of concentration seems irreversible under present conditions (1978).

Both the independent dynamics of urban growth and the separate—although not unrelated—public policies of government have had important implications for the distribution of income in spatial terms and across income groups. Public policies, particularly in the form of service provision, have important consequences for income. As Danielson and Keles (1980, 271) have noted:

> In considering income and its distribution . . . we are concerned with public services as well as income derived from earnings, rent, and other conventional sources. . . . Widespread availability of public services can mitigate differences in conventional income. . . . On the other hand, defining the scope of the public sector narrowly increases the importance of conventional income. And concentrating municipal services in areas where earnings are relatively high reinforces income differences.

In the following section, we will consider the consequences of the provision of one public service—in the form of housing policy—on the distribution of income.

## Urbanization and the "Housing Problem" in Mexico

The rapid urbanization of Mexico in recent decades is largely a function of the shifts in population within the country. For example, one out of every three residents of metropolitan Mexico City is a migrant (Goldani 1977, 129). The tremendous income differential between urban areas and the impoverished countryside have made Mexico City a city of migrants. The impact of this migration flow on the structure of that city—and on other areas of the country—cannot be overestimated. Coupled with high rates of natural increase in the population, this migration has meant serious strains on all aspects of service provision. One principal consequence has been the creation of a serious housing shortage; the inability of large numbers of the poor to enter existing formal housing markets serves to exacerbate the problem.

Estimates as to the size of the housing deficit vary greatly and are a function, in part, of different criteria utilized to determine the shortfall. These estimates ranged in 1970 from a low of 2.3 million units (Silva Herzog 1973) to a high of 5.8 million units (Garza and Schteingart 1976). The explanation for the difference among estimates is the result of the importance the various authors attribute to the several components of the estimate. Low figures tend to underestimate both the replacement needs that result from deteriorating housing and the qualitative deficit that results from housing conditions that are below acceptable standards. Several factors account for the total estimated housing deficit:

1. The *quantitative* deficit that is provoked by natural population growth, formation of new households, shifts in migration, and the subdivision (overcrowding) of existing dwelling units. One estimate suggests that merely the quantitative deficit due to overcrowding was equal to 2.1 million units in 1970, of which 1.4 million units were in urban areas.
2. The *qualitative* deficit consists of the need to replace deteriorated housing that is in uninhabitable condition given a minimal standard—which presumes a roof, walls, and a floor. Puente Leyva (1970) estimates that for 1970 this included one-fifth of the urban housing stock (or 1.0 million units) and one-fourth of the existing rural housing stock (or 0.9 million units).

Thus, to absorb the existing housing deficit in 1970 would require the construction of 4.0 million housing units at a minimum. However, this absorption does not take into account the large number of housing units that have deteriorated between 1970 and 1980, which were deemed "satisfactory" in 1970. If one assumes a (reasonable) replacement rate of 3.5 percent per year for existing stock, by 1980 the replacement needs would have added approximately 4.3 million housing units to the 1970 deficit.[3] Just to keep abreast of new needs for the 1970–1980 period would have required no less than 8.9 million new units, without affecting the current deficit at all. This is more housing units than were constructed in the first four hundred years since the conquest of Mexico (Puente Leyva 1970, 276)!

An estimate for the growth of the housing deficit for urban areas through 1980 is provided in Table 11-7. The cumulative deficit indicated in column I is based upon an estimate of total new needs in housing (column II) less the number of units that can reasonably be expected to be met by households gaining access to existing housing markets. By this standard—and the estimates tend to be optimistic at best—the potential cumulative deficit for 1980 was over 6.0 million needed units.

*TABLE 11.7.*
*Estimated Housing Deficit in Urban Areas, 1969–1980*

| *Year* | *I* *Cumulative Deficit*[1] | *II* *Annual Needs*[2] | *III* *Potential Demand*[3] | *IV* *Unsatisfied Needs*[4] *(II–III = IV)* |
|---|---|---|---|---|
| 1969 | 2,422.5 | 398.9 | 160.9 | 238.0 |
| 1970 | 2,680.5 | 424.9 | 170.1 | 254.8 |
| 1971 | 2,935.3 | 443.9 | 179.5 | 264.4 |
| 1972 | 3,199.7 | 474.9 | 188.8 | 286.1 |
| 1973 | 3,485.8 | 507.2 | 199.2 | 308.0 |
| 1974 | 3,793.8 | 540.5 | 209.0 | 331.5 |
| 1975 | 4,125.3 | 574.5 | 220.5 | 354.0 |
| 1976 | 4,479.3 | 609.4 | 231.6 | 377.8 |
| 1977 | 4,857.1 | 645.4 | 243.7 | 401.7 |
| 1978 | 5,258.8 | 682.5 | 255.9 | 426.6 |
| 1979 | 5,685.3 | 720.0 | 269.1 | 450.9 |
| 1980 | 6,136.3 | 758.6 | 281.9 | 476.7 |

SOURCE: Puente Leyva (1970, 300–301).

[1]In each year, the unsatisfied need (column IV) is added to the previous cumulative deficit.

[2]Estimate of total new "socially necessary" housing to accommodate needs derived from population growth and replacement of totally deteriorated housing.

[3]Demand that corresponds to those individuals who have sufficient income to gain access to housing markets.

[4]Residual. Those who are unable to gain access and who, therefore, add to the cumulative deficit.

An examination of the housing deficit and housing quality within Mexico City yields equally dramatic results. Utilizing data from the IX General Census of Population (1970), housing needs were derived for the twelve delegations (districts) of the city and the additional twelve delegations of the Federal District. In addition, calculations were made for those household units in each district that contained at least a combined family income of 85 percent of the minimum wage. The assumption (somewhat generous) made here is that these families would be able to gain access to the private or public housing markets (column II). The difference (column III) is the population of each sector of the metropolitan area which by most standards is unable to gain access to housing markets because of low income. Table 11-8 provides a picture of the conditions in 1970 for the metropolitan area of the city.

Traditionally, there have been a number of residential responses to the lack of access to formal housing markets in the city. Low-income settlements of various residential classifications have grown tremendously in the city. Ward (1975, 330) suggests that *colonias proletarias* (literally proletarian communities) constituted 23.5 percent of the built-up area and 14.2 percent of the population of Mexico City in 1952. By 1970, they

*TABLE 11.8.*
*Housing Needs and Effective Demand in the Federal District (1970)*

| *Zones* | *Families Needing Housing** | *Effective Demand*** | *Families Excluded* |
|---|---|---|---|
| Mexico City | 102,374 | 82,941 | 19,633 |
| I | 16,474 | 14,365 | 2,109 |
| II | 9,514 | 8,086 | 1,433 |
| III | 5,470 | 4,801 | 669 |
| IV | 4,031 | 3,478 | 558 |
| V | 3,822 | 3,304 | 518 |
| VI | 3,688 | 3,109 | 579 |
| VII | 8,267 | 6,562 | 1,705 |
| VIII | 11,552 | 8,249 | 3,303 |
| IX | 13,455 | 10,861 | 2,594 |
| X | 7,877 | 5,511 | 2,365 |
| XI | 8,038 | 6,135 | 1,903 |
| XII | 10,182 | 8,480 | 1,902 |
| Federal District | 129,681 | 108,218 | 21,463 |
| Azcapotzalco | 15,331 | 13,207 | 2,124 |
| Coyoacán | 11,935 | 9,395 | 2,540 |
| Cuajimalpa | 1,480 | 1,200 | 280 |
| Gustavo Madero | 39,890 | 34,266 | 5,624 |
| Iztacalco | 13,755 | 11,612 | 2,143 |
| Iztapalapa | 16,600 | 13,919 | 2,681 |
| Magdalena Contreras | 2,402 | 1,990 | 412 |
| Milpa Alta | 1,259 | 812 | 447 |
| Alvaro Obregón | 14,935 | 12,244 | 2,691 |
| Tlahuac | 2,449 | 1,856 | 593 |
| Tlalpan | 4,664 | 3,772 | 892 |
| Xochimilco | 4,981 | 3,945 | 1,036 |
| Netzahualcoyotl | 16,133 | 14,305 | 1,828 |

SOURCE: IX Censo General de Población; INFONAVIT (1975, vols. 1 and 2).

*The terminology utilized here follows that used by INFONAVIT. The term "families needing housing" or "families without housing" is not meant to imply that these are families literally on the streets. Rather, these are families inhabiting housing already occupied by another family. This total, then, is new housing needs.

**Effective Demand is the number of families without housing who earn at least 85 percent of the minimum wage (as of 1970). The assumption is that they are not excluded from either government or popular housing with this income.

represented 35–40 percent of the population and 42 percent of the urban area, with an estimated annual growth rate of 10–15 percent over the intervening period. However, the low-income housing of the city is not an undifferentiated mass, and, in fact, clearly delineated housing responses can be identified.

One need only walk several blocks from the Zócalo, or central plaza, of the city to observe one long-standing response—extreme overcrowding in the downtown areas and the formation of what are locally referred to as *vecindades* (slums). Beginning as early as the turn of the century through the 1940s, these central zones provided the principal form of low-income housing. They can be characterized as areas in rapid deterioration of old colonial homes that have been subdivided to the point of containing ten to twelve families per housing unit, often in one room per family and sharing common services. Sudra and Turner (1973) estimate that approximately two million people live in these densely occupied areas, paying rents that account for as much as 25–30 percent of household income. Lomnitz notes in this regard:

> Vecindades are central-city slums, typically in the form of alleys containing 20 to 50 rented rooms each. Many of these slums are rent-controlled and have very little population turnover. The residents tend to form stable family networks (1977, 19).

Beyond this central zone, yet still within the heart of the city, a second more recent response to the lack of access to formalized housing by the urban poor has been the creation of what are commonly referred to *ciudades perdidas* (lost cities). Here again, the rise of this alternative housing has been a function of high demand for (relatively) low-rental accomodations in locationally advantageous sectors of the city. Turner (1971) has estimated the population residing in these areas to be some 200,000 persons. Like vecindades, these areas tend to be closer into the city, although more often in the interstitial zones of decaying urban areas. And also like vecindades, they are areas where rental housing tends to predominate, although often in single-family huts rather than rooms in larger structures. But unlike vecindades, these are areas where complete urban services are less prevalent. In one sense, ciudades perdidas are the successors of vecindad-style rental housing as the latter became saturated by the late 1940s and early 1950s (Ward 1975; 338). One study (Sudra and Turner 1973) offers some insight into the character of these dwelling areas. Shantytown dwellings in style, they often are formed on private land (59 percent) and originally were created as rental lots (68 percent). Invasion, a phenomenon associated with squatter settlements, is not prevalent (13 percent), and lot size (80–150 square meters) tends to be smaller than that of squatter areas. Owners either would sublet barren lots for individual construction (and rental) or they would provide irregular and skeletal infrastructural services (Ward 1975).

By far the largest housing alternative for low-income dwellers has become the creation of *colonias proletarias* or *populares,* either as a result of the formation of illegal subdivisions *(fraccionamientos clandestinos)* or as a result of land invasions *(colonias paracaidistas* or literally "parachute" communities). In both cases, land is "owner"-occupied (in a loose sense), although the tenure status of land is often illegal. In the former case, families have purchased lots from subdividers who either do not have clear title to the land themselves (although they have been known to provide pseudo-legal titles to purchaser) or who fail to provide legally required services. In the latter case, little initial pretense of legality is proferred by owner-invaders of public lands. While no truly accurate estimate of the number of residents of squatter settlements can be provided, estimates range upward of five million people in the greater metropolitan area (Brown 1972: Garza and Schteingart, 1976).[4]

The most striking example of squatter settlement growth is the district of Netzahualcoyotl, an area of approximately 56 colonias proletarias located in the southeastern portion of the city on the dried beds of Lake Texcoco. The initial population of the area formed in the town of San Juan Pantitlan; however, by the late 1940s and early 1950s large tracts were purchased at minimal prices by "developers" for subsequent sale to low-income dwellers. The original dwellers were able to obtain inexpensive land at prices of from 3–5 pesos per square meter with minimal down payments of as little as 50 pesos (or US $4) with extended terms (of up to ten years) from the "developers" (Cornelius 1975; Rosa 1975). By 1970, lots of approximately 150 square meters were selling from $20,000–35,000 pesos, or $200 pesos per square meter (US $16).

Several factors led to the rapid growth of the region and the increasing land values in the 1960s. Cornelius notes that a prohibition on new low-income subdivisions within the Federal District led to the growth of numerous subdivisions in the state of Mexico (1975, 48). In the early 1960s, the construction of a major highway route to Puebla created access to unused lands in the periphery of the city as well. Estimates of the population of the area in 1960 were approximately 60,000-65,000 persons (Ferras 1977; Rosa 1975); however, it is difficult to judge the accuracy of these figures because at the time the area had no legal status and basically was ignored. In April 1963, "municipality 120" was created by the state congress in recognition of the need for urban services in Netzahualcoyotl. By 1970, the population had exploded to 580,000 persons according to official census reports. By 1974, estimates placed the population at between 1.1 and 1.2 million persons, wtih a growth rate of 15,000 persons per month (Ferras 1977, 12).

In 1958, the *Ley de Fraccionamientos del Estado de México* was enacted which required developers, who subdivided and sold tracts of land, to provide the basic infrastructure. Those who had received authorization prior to that time were not bound by the new statute because it was

*TABLE 11.9.*
*Ciudad Netzahualcoyotl: Housing Characteristics (1970)*

| | | |
|---|---|---|
| Existing housing units: | 90,338 | |
| Owner occupied | | 59,935 |
| Rental/other than owned | | 30,403 |
| Units in deterioration | | 9,488 |
| Units without access to piped water | | 16,344 |
| Units with dirt floors | | 12,721 |
| Units without drainage | | 36,564 |
| Construction materials: | | |
| adobe | | 1,888 |
| tabique (plaster board) | | 80,847 |
| wood | | 2,685 |
| embarro (packed dirt) | | 261 |
| other | | 4,657 |
| Families "without housing":* | 16,133 | |
| Eligible for INFONAVIT (worker) housing | | 9,016 |
| Eligible for GOVERNMENT (employee) housing | | 516 |
| POPULAR housing, ineligible for assistance based on employment | | 6,601 |
| Those earning less than minimum wage** | | 2,637 |

SOURCE: Derived from INFONAVIT (1971a).

*Again, as in Table 11-8, the term "without housing" should be understood to mean total new housing needs. We are following the convention utilized both by the Census Division and INFONAVIT.

**And, therefore, unlikely to be able to enter the formal housing market(s) of the city.

not made retroactive (Cornelius 1975, 34). However, lack of enforcement of service provision throughout the 1960s meant that service levels, even subsequent to the official recognition and subsequent to the creation of several institutions aimed at responding to needs in the district[5], remained—and remain—abysmal. Table 11-9 provides some useful data on characteristics of the area as of 1970. As of 1974, there were twenty-five private telephones and twelve public telephone booths, of which nine belonged to public-sector concerns (a ratio of one phone for every 40,000 inhabitants). Other services, such as potable water, drainage, paved streets, garbage collection, market systems, schools, medical centers, etc. are lacking to the extreme—suggesting the relative failure of the state to cope with this growth. For example, Table 11-9 indicates the large number of households without access to piped water in any form; also, of those who had access to water: 24,892 had water outside of the unit, but in the building area; 19,944 had access to public water, but outside the building area; and only 29,158 had piped water inside the unit.

While we have focused on the rather spectacular growth and accompanying problems of one district within the metropolitan area, the conditions described are not markedly different from those that prevail in other colonias proletarias in terms of the quality of housing and access to public services. Indeed, the very fact that Netzahualcoyotl is a separate juridical unit would suggest some institutional commitment to the district that other areas would lack.

It is clear from the above description that there is great variety in the housing and residential land-use patterns of the urban poor. Thus, there would seem to be a need for different policy options for housing to account for these different needs and preference structures in the population, not only across different income groups but within the broad category of the low-income population as well. Following the work of John F.C. Turner (1971), Mohan (1977) has noted that approaches to housing and residential land-use policy need to be targeted to income sectors. We would add that this may be true within income groups as well. He suggests:

> We can divide land consumers into three operational income groups: the highest who do not need any help from policy makers; the middle-income group, who participate in the land market but who have access difficulties; and, last, the lowest income groups who are effectively shut out of the urban land market. The first group can be left to its own devices except that it should be taxed. . . . The thrust of land policy for [the second group] is provision of adequate financial institutions to provide mortgages . . . and provision of information . . . (464).

However, for the third group, the urban poor, the goal is to increase income "by providing more land as a consumption good to raise them to higher indifference curves" (Mohan 1977; 465). If, as Turner argues, the very poor are price-oriented and not location-oriented (except in terms of distance to work, which may still be a weak orientation), then the creation of access to housing or land markets at some minimal price—however improved in terms of service delivery—may not be a reasonable alternative to (possibly free) land already occupied. This would suggest that a common reaction to urban squatters (as well as slum formation in the form of *ciudades perdidas*), that is, the reaction of eradication coupled with relocation, may prove to be inappropriate. Similarly, several differing strategies may be necessary to account for differential needs and preferences of subsets within the urban poor. In the following section, we will examine the responses and strategies that have been employed in the case of Mexico.

## Housing Policy: The Public Sector Response

As we have noted, the responses to the "housing problem" in Mexico have taken a number of forms. One early response to the needs of the central-city poor was rent-control. Initially applied in 1942 to *vecindad* housing with rents of less than 300 pesos per month, the controls have been maintained since. However, as Cornelius (1975; 27) notes, this policy has had the consequence of hastening deterioration in these sectors as owners are reluctant to invest in the maintenance of *vecindades* for lack of profitability. With deterioration has come renewal in favor of commercial construction and new high-rise (middle- and upper-income) housing construction. Eviction and eradication, typical responses to land invasion in Mexico in earlier decades, have been replaced by policies that focus on land tenure rights and "regularization" of low-income peripheral zones of the city. Notes one leading scholar;

> In 1971 alone, the government formally "intervened" by expropriation and sale below market value in 186 *colonias proletarias* within the Federal District. In recent years, several hundred land titles have been distributed each month . . . and during a 40-month period from 1967 to 1970 more than 20,000 titles were distributed (Cornelius 1975, 203–4).

However, while the rate of "regularization" has increased markedly in recent years, service provision in these same areas has not kept pace.

When we examine actual housing construction as a means of resolving housing demands, we can distinguish among three basic housing markets: the private sector, the public sector, and self-constructed "popular" housing. Table 11-10 provides data from 1950 to 1974 which describes the contribution of each of these sectors to total housing construction. The data presented in this table are national in scope; however, a similar—if somewhat less pessimistic—picture holds true for Mexico City. As can be seen in Table 11-10, public-sector activity in housing construction did not account for a large proportion of total construction in the 1950s. The role of the public sector, however, increased dramatically over the period 1961–1970, and in the decade of the 1970s public-sector participation ranged from one-sixth to one-quarter of total construction. In spite of the growth of public-sector participation in recent years, popular housing continued to provide two-thirds of all new housing construction throughout the period. Private-sector housing construction declined relatively from over one-quarter of the total in the 1950s to approximately one-sixth by 1974. It would seem that the real change that is notable is the relative shift to public housing from private housing, while the vast majority of the population remains excluded from either market.

Public-sector activity in the area of housing construction has been concentrated in the capital. As a result, one finds relatively higher levels of public-sector participation. On the other hand, the cost of private-sector

*TABLE 11.10.*
*Participation of Various Sectors in Housing Construction (1950–1974)*
*(in thousands)*

| *Year* | *Public* | *Private* | *Popular* | *Total* |
|---|---|---|---|---|
| Units existing at beginning of period (1950) | | | | 5,259 |
| 1951–1960 | | | | |
| Number | 62 | 331 | 757 | 1,150 |
| Percent | 5.4 | 28.8 | 65.8 | 100 |
| 1961–1970 | | | | |
| Number | 175 | 503 | 1,199 | 1,877 |
| Percent | 9.3 | 26.8 | 63.9 | 100 |
| 1970 | | | | |
| Number | 21.9 | 33.0 | 147.0 | 201.9 |
| Percent | 10.8 | 16.3 | 72.8 | 100 |
| 1971 | | | | |
| Number | 33.1 | 23.7 | 154.2 | 211.1 |
| Percent | 15.7 | 11.2 | 73.0 | 100 |
| 1972 | | | | |
| Number | 36.1 | 56.5 | 161.9 | 254.5 |
| Percent | 14.2 | 22.2 | 63.6 | 100 |
| 1973 | | | | |
| Number | 50.5 | 41.6 | 169.8 | 261.9 |
| Percent | 19.3 | 15.9 | 64.8 | 100 |
| 1974 | | | | |
| Number | 82.0 | 50.9 | 178.0 | 310.9 |
| Percent | 26.4 | 16.4 | 57.3 | 100 |
| 1970–1974 | | | | |
| Number | 223.7 | 205.7 | 810.9 | 1,204.3 |
| Percent | 18.0 | 16.5 | 65.5 | 100 |

SOURCE: Evans (1974), as cited in Garza and Schteingart (1976).

housing is much higher within the city and Federal District such that—in spite of the larger role of the public sector—it has been calculated (Garza and Schteingart 1976, 37) that almost half of the households in the city are unable to gain access to either private financial instruments or public housing. Why public housing has failed to reach this proportion of the population is the subject of this section.

Throughout most of the institutional history of public-housing programs in Mexico, the thrust has been to assure housing for the working class and has utilized as its legal basis the Constitution of 1917. Article 123 (Section 12) provides not only a symbolic mandate, but also a clear statement of responsibility for working conditions and the fundamental right of housing for workers:

> In all businesses—agricultural, industrial, mining, or however classified—employers are obligated to provide workers with decent and sanitary housing . . . for which employers may charge rents that do not exceed the average catastral value of the land. . . .

The linking of housing to the work place proves to be of critical importance in current programs.

Most housing programs for the first thirty years of the "new republic" focused on (1) private credit markets providing access (mortgage credit) within the private sector; and (2) specific institutions of relatively minor importance that provided subsidized rental payments to employees. Public participation in the control or regularization of the prices, in terms of credit, or in land (in the housing sector) itself was indeed contemplated, but not actualized during this time period.[6]

More intensive participation by the public sector began in 1945 under President Avila Camacho with the creation of the *Banco de Fomento de la Habitación, S.A.* (Housing Promotion Bank). This institution for the first time contemplated the utilization of public capital for housing construction (in the Federal District only). A sum of 10 million pesos was authorized for use by several agencies, including the government of the Federal District (5.1 million pesos); the Department of Civil Service Pensions *(Dirección de Pensiones Civiles de Retiro)* for retired public employees (1.7 million pesos); the Mexican Institute of Social Security (IMSS, 1.7 million pesos); and private-sector finance and construction companies (1.5 million pesos). Reorganization of the bank in 1946 placed the earlier program within the National Urban Mortgage and Public Works Bank (*Banco Nacional Hipotecario Urbano y de Obras Públicas, S.A.* or BNHUOPSA). A Department of Housing was created within that institution (Gonzalez Prieto 1973).

However, it is the period since the 1950s that marked the real beginning of government action in housing policy in spite of the prior (1933) existence of BNHUOPSA. Housing policy during the period of 1950–1960 consisted primarily of: (1) lending programs; (2) rental subsidy programs; (3) programs oriented toward those who legitimately could gain access to the existing private mortgage markets based on income; and (4) programs that financed housing access for public employees. The principal focus of programs aimed at stimulating private-sector activities. However, the concept of "social-interest" or low-income housing was not completely disregarded—although the impact on newly emerging urban housing needs (and particularly on lower-income households) was not truly significant.[7] The effect, in many ways, was to provide financing capabilities for middle-income households, especially in urban areas.

The period from the 1960s suggests a new shift in the orientation of public policy toward housing in Mexico, away from rental subsidy and toward increased direct construction. The major institutional program in this period was the Housing Operation and Discount Fund (*Fondo de Operación y Descuento a la Vivienda* or FOVI), created in 1963 to carry out the Financial Housing Plan of that year. Again, the clear purpose of public-sector intervention in housing markets was seen as the stimulation of private initiative. Housing problems were seen and defined in terms of a "financial problem" of access to credit markets. The mandate grew out of increasing international concern for housing. This concern was evident in this case in the fact that much of the financing of FOVI was external (AID-IDB).[8] While the concern for social-interest housing is present in the FOVI program, the reliance on private institutional lending meant (and means) that the principal element of the popular sector that is reached is the very upper portion of lower-income groups. FOVI, and its complementary institution created at the same time (the *Fondo de Garantía y Apoyo* or FOGA), serve principally as the minimal support for social interest housing, mortgage guarantor for low-income housing lending in the private sector, and as a regulator of interest rates for low-income housing finance (INFONAVIT, 1976c).

This orientation of housing programs has had serious implications for the participation of the intended beneficiaries of the program. First, by framing the issue of the "housing crisis" purely as a problem of access to financial (private) credit markets the program places actions in acceptable terms for the private-banking sector. Social-interest housing, which during the 1960s had an average cost to the consumer of $60,000 pesos, excluded the vast majority of potential beneficiaries. Two-thirds of the urban families of Mexico in 1963 earned $1,500 pesos or less per month. The average cost of "low-income" housing was clearly outside of the realistic reach of this population (Puente Leyva, 1970, 262). Furthermore, by placing the financing in private-sector hands, the impact on land values (especially in Mexico City) exacerbates an already spiraling rate of housing cost increases. Since the early days the program has altered the price structure of housing, the effect of which is to assure the "credit acceptability" of the (private-sector managed) loans, while impeding further access for intended beneficiaries. The maximum scale price of FOVI units in 1970 was $80,000 pesos, at which 30 percent of the units were priced; the lowest price was $55,000 pesos, which included 41 percent of the units. In 1975, the maximum prices by various zones of the country were $117,000, $139,000, $153,000, and $164,000 pesos (the second zone includes Mexico City). In 1978, the maximum prices were $236,000, $290,000, $319,000, and $346,000 pesos for the various zones (FOVI 1978).

The exclusion is evident. Utilizing 1975 data on maximum housing prices for social-interest housing for Mexico City ($139,000 pesos) and data from the 1977 *Household Income and Expenditure Survey,* we see the following relationships.[9] A down payment of from 10–20 percent is required under the program guidelines ($14,000–$28,000 pesos), an unrealistic amount in itself. Assuming that the bank financed 80 percent, and assuming a fifteen-year (normal) mortgage at 9.0 percent interest, the monthly payments in the program would be $1,128 pesos (Garza and Schteingart 1976). Table 11-11 provides data on income distribution and housing expenditures from the 1977 survey mentioned above. Based on monthly expenditures for the various deciles for housing maintenance, the monthly payments suggested above would exclude all but the top three deciles. Even the minimum cost housing for the zone ($125,000 pesos) would exclude most households. Several studies have suggested various estimates of the proportion of household income that may be available for housing. A World Bank study (1972) utilizes the figure of 2 to 2.5 times annual income or 15 percent of monthly income as a reasonable estimate of available income for housing; in this case, all but the top four deciles would be excluded. Bergsman (1979) suggests that for urban households in poverty as much as 24 percent of monthly income may be utilized for housing; in this case again, all but the top four deciles would be excluded. Certainly, this program reaches the middle-income groups, but the urban poor fall well outside the range of the program.

Given the limited penetration of this program, it is not surprising that the advent to power of the Echeverría administration in 1970 marked the most fundamental change in housing policy in the fifty-three years since the formation of the new republic. The period of the 1970s witnessed the

*TABLE 11.11.*

*Size Distribution of Household Income and Housing Expenditures (1977)*

| *Deciles* | *Number of Households (millions)* | *Mean Annual Income (pesos)* | *% of Total Income in Decile* | *Annual Housing Expenditures (pesos)* | *% of Total Household Income*[a] |
|---|---|---|---|---|---|
| I | 1.1 | $6,818.2 | 1.08 | $605 | 8.87 |
| II | 1.1 | $13,963.6 | 2.21 | $1,456 | 10.43 |
| III | 1.1 | $20,400.0 | 3.23 | $1,712 | 8.39 |
| IV | 1.1 | $27,916.4 | 4.42 | $2,563 | 9.18 |
| V | 1.1 | $36,196.4 | 5.73 | $4,318 | 11.93 |
| VI | 1.1 | $45,163.6 | 7.15 | $5,704 | 12.63 |
| VII | 1.1 | $57,545.5 | 9.11 | $7,291 | 12.67 |
| VIII | 1.1 | $75,665.5 | 11.98 | $9,829 | 12.99 |
| IX | 1.1 | $107,945.5 | 17.09 | $17,660 | 16.36 |
| Xa | .55 | $158,421.8 | 12.54 | $21,799 | 13.76 |
| Xb | .55 | $321,512.7 | 25.45 | $49,513 | 15.40 |

SOURCE: 1977 Household Income and Expenditure Survey.

[a]For comparison, the average expenditure on housing as reported in the 1968 Household Income and Expenditure Survey was equal to 16.0 percent of total income, ranging from 11.8 percent in the lowest income sectors to 20.5 percent in the highest income sectors. This would suggest that relatively less of family income is expended on housing in the more recent survey.

creation of a number of new mechanisms of housing policy as well as the persistence of a multitude of existing programs. "Housing policy" in the current period is the responsibility of no less than 150 private institutions that facilitate finance credit for construction and/or purchase, as well as a plethora of public agencies involved in the housing game (Reyes Navarro 1973). Public involvement suggests the corporatist nature of the public sector as a variety of institutions structure loyalties and participation through specialized service programs. As one author puts it:

> At present, the number of agencies involved in the housing game is endless and includes, for example, the Departamento del Distrito Federal, PEMEX, CFE, CTM, STIC, Ferrocarriles Nacionales de México, la Comisión Constructora de Hospitales de la Secretaría de Salubridad, IMSS, ISSSTE, BANOBRAS, Crédito Ejidal, el Instituto Nacional de la Vivienda (INV), el Instituto Nacional para el Desarrollo de la Comunidad Rural y de la Vivienda Popular, FNV . . . (Reyes Navarro 1973). (Author's translation.)

And the list does not include the private sector at all.

It is into this confusion of programs and goals that an attempt was made to offer a more "integrated approach" to housing policy in the 1970s. Also, the rapid deterioration of the housing potential for large segments of the population prompted some response. Among the new institutional settings for housing policy created in the post 1970 period, several are noteworthy:

1. In 1970, the *Dirección General de la Habitación Popular del Distrito Federal* (DGHP-DDF) was created to develop housing programs and popular housing developments, as well as to carry out urban renewal and to coordinate and collaborate public/private action in resolving housing needs in the district.
2. In 1971, the *Instituto Nacional para el Desarrollo de la Comunidad Rural y de la Vivienda Popular* (INDECO) was created to substitute for the INV and symbolized the new government role in housing action of the Echeverría regime. The principal foci of the program are in the area of technical and consultative functions, although there is a clear emphasis on decentralization, public/private coordination, and planning, especially in the formation of a public-sector land base for housing action (the *reserva territorial*).
3. The major thrust of the new housing activity of the national government was the creation (in 1972) of the *Instituto del Fondo Nacional de la Vivienda para los Trabajadores* (INFONAVIT), a program that will concern us, in more detail later in this chapter.
4. As a complement to INFONAVIT, the new administration created the *Fondo de la Vivienda del Instituto de Seguridad y Servicios Sociales de los Trabajadores del Estado* (also in 1972) to serve the needs of public-sector employees. This program functions in much the same way as INFONAVIT, except that the government is the employer.
5. A third arm created to serve worker housing needs in 1972 was the *Fondo de la Vivienda para los Miembros de las Fuerzas Armadas* (FOVIMI), utilizing

much the same approach to housing as INFONAVIT and serving the needs of members of the armed forces.

6. Finally, at the municipal level, the *Fideicomiso para el Desarrollo Urbano de la Ciudad de México* (FIDEURBE) was created to facilitate the integration of squatter settlements in the urban periphery. The principal housing role of the institution results from its mandate to regularize land tenure for eventual financing and not from direct housing activity.[10]

Of all the programs created, the DGHP-DDF and FIDEURBE are the only ones that were created specifically to deal with urban squatters and nonsalaried employees. All of the others rely upon action through the employer/employee relationship as a primary mechanism for housing finance. While FIDEURBE was principally a program for the acquisition of land (for regularization), the DGHP-DDF provides the least costly housing of any program. Two programs instituted by the institution since 1972 are worth noting. In 1972, the insitution began a program of housing construction entitled the Basic Family Unit (Unidad Familiar Base) in which the lot size was fifty-six square meters (and the unit construction size was thirty-six square meters) at a total cost of $30,000 pesos. The down payment for the unit is $1,500 pesos (5 percent) and monthly payments were $242 pesos—by far the most accessible housing program for the urban poor at the time. Yet, the monthly payments would still absorb 21 percent of the minimum wage at that time and still remained outside the reach of the majority of the population earning less than the minimum wage. In 1976, the DGHP instituted a second program, the *Tapanco* housing unit (the term conveys the image of hutlike dwellings), as an alternative to their earlier program. The cost of the unit in 1976 was $37,500 pesos; down payments were $1,875; and monthly payments were $312 pesos or 16 percent of minimum wage (Parcero Lopez 1977; 47). Of particular interest is the fact that this new unit has incorporated the concept of housing expansion squatter settlement style. Lot size is ninety square meters and unit size is a mere twenty-seven square meters with one bedroom. Thus, substantial room for expansion of the dwelling unit is available as income permits. However, the inability of most of the urban poor to take advantage of even this program is evident. Assuming the ability to make the down payment, the monthly payments of $312 pesos would still require an income of approximately $1,700 pesos (at 20 percent of monthly income for housing). This effectively excludes 70 percent of the economically active population.

Among all of the programs designed to meet housing demands, the most important institution of the 1970s is INFONAVIT. In the first four years of its existence, INFONAVIT provided more than half of all public-sector housing in terms of funds invested, housing units constructed, or in terms of households benefited (Table 11-12). The passage of legislation authorizing the creation of INFONAVIT finds its roots in several previous actions. In 1970, a new labor law was enacted with far-reaching

*TABLE 11.12.*
*Housing Programs of the Public Sector (1972–1975)*

| | *Investment* | | *Units Completed* | | *Individuals Benefited* | |
|---|---|---|---|---|---|---|
| *Organization* | *Millions* | *(%)* | *Number* | *(%)* | *Number* | *(%)* |
| INFONAVIT | 10,556.9 | 58.1 | 62,976 | 56.5 | 403,906 | 59.0 |
| FOVISSSTE | 3,898.7 | 21.5 | 15,449 | 13.8 | 86,516 | 12.7 |
| BANOBRAS | 1,593.3 | 8.8 | 13,645 | 12.2 | 79,140 | 11.5 |
| INDECO | 882.4 | 4.8 | 7,725 | 7.0 | 46,745 | 6.8 |
| Departamento del D.F. | 672.3 | 4.0 | 11,156 | 10.0 | 65,395 | 9.5 |
| FOVIMI | 372.7 | 2.0 | 301 | 0.2 | 1,806 | 0.2 |
| Dirección de Pensiones Militares | 137.2 | 0.7 | 359 | 0.3 | 2,144 | 0.3 |
| FIDEURBE | 30.1 | 0.1 | — | — | — | — |
| TOTAL | 18,143.6 | 100.0 | 111,611 | 100.0 | 635,652 | 100.0 |

SOURCE: INFONAVIT (1975b).

Not included in this breakdown is FOVI, because housing units promoted by this organism are considered by the Subcomisión de Programación de la Vivienda to be within the private sector since it is that sector that provides principal financing.

consequences. Reviving a long dormant clause from Article 123 of the 1917 Constitution, the new labor code carried the rights of worker housing to a more explicit level. The original clause (Section 12 of Article 123) obligated employers to provide housing and sanitation facilities to workers in nonurban areas, or, more importantly, where the number of workers exceeded one hundred. It is the latter provision that created the precedent for action under INFONAVIT programs in the 1970s (INFONAVIT 1976c). Under the 1970 labor law, employer provision of housing is required within the following criteria:

1. If the firm (employer) is located "outside populated areas" (more than three kilometers)
2. If more than 100 workers are employed (regardless of whether the firm is in or out of populated areas)
3. The criterion of 100 workers only applies to those who have been with the firm for more than one year
4. Workers need to notify employers of their desire for housing
5. Only workers who formally belong to a union are eligible
6. Within three years an agreement must be reached between union and employer concerning housing arrangements (INFONAVIT 1976a)

Based upon the law, INFONAVIT was created to expand the letter of the law in order to "universalize the rights of workers." The program administers credit to workers under a variety of schemes or "credit lines." The majority of funds are allocated to direct financing of the construction of housing for workers (credit line #1). This activity accounts for two-thirds of total credit provided by INFONAVIT. Other credit activities (lines #2–5) envisage loans for the purchase of existing housing, refinancing of extant loans, housing rehabilitation, and individual construction. Funding of the program occurs principally through the participation of employers (in theory, mandatory) who contribute 5 percent of the sum of all workers' salaries to INFONAVIT. This sum is placed in an "account" in the name of each individual worker. After ten years, this account becomes available to the individual worker in the form of a savings account. In effect, this contribution by employers register both the firm and employees in the housing program. Workers eligible for the program must earn no more than five times the minimum salary (MS). Once registered, the worker may begin the process of application for INFONAVIT housing (or credit under the other lines of credit).

A number of criteria are employed in the determination of the priority of applicants, including preferences to those who are applying for direct housing finance, who are in the lower salary ranges (less than two MS), number of dependents, choice of housing, etc. Through 1976, the breakdown of housing construction credit by income meant that approximately 82 percent of credit went to workers earning up to two MS, 10 percent to those earning from two to three MS, 7 percent to those earning three to four MS, and 1.0 percent to workers earning more than four MS (INFONAVIT 1975).

The credit terms of INFONAVIT housing are rather unique. No down payment is required for participation, interest rates on the unpaid principal are 4.0 percent, and the amortization of the loan can be up to twenty years. However, there is no fixed amortization of the loan. Repayment is based upon a fixed percentage of employee income rather than a fixed amount over the entire period. Employers discount the fixed proportion directly from the worker's salary and this amount is deposited with INFONAVIT. For workers earning less than 1.25 MS, 14 percent of salary is withheld; those with larger incomes pay 18 percent of their salary. The proportion of income withheld does not change over time (except where individual income moves beyond 1.25 MS).

The INFONAVIT program has provided a valuable alternative in the housing market over existing programs. Coupled with other new programs, the penetration of housing alternatives for individuals within the formal sector has ben dramatic in the last decade. In the first year of its existence, INFONAVIT saw two million workers and over 100,000 firms registered. That number grew rapidly in the following several years, after which registration leveled off (see Table 11-13). Resources available to the program grew from slightly more than one billion pesos in 1972 to over $14 billion pesos in 1979, and given the nature of the repayment the amount available for future programs will increase more markedly in the

*TABLE 11.13.*
*Support for INFONAVIT Housing: Worker and Employer Participation*

| Year | Resources at End of Year (millions) | Annual Variations | Number of Workers (millions) | Number of Companies |
|---|---|---|---|---|
| 1972 | $1,305 | — | 2.0 | 114,622 |
| 1973 | 2,867 | $1,562 | 3.1 | 190,000 |
| 1974 | 4,074 | 1,207 | 3.8 | 229,000 |
| 1975 | 4,986 | 912 | 4.0 | 231,000 |
| 1976 | 6,391 | 1,405 | 4.0 | 231,000 |
| 1977 | 8,409 | 2,018 | 4.0 | 240,000 |
| 1978 | 10,654 | 2,245 | NA | NA |
| 1979 | 14,620 | 3,966 | NA | NA |

SOURCE: INFONAVIT, *Informes Anuales de Actividades, 1973–1980;* INFONAVIT, *Planes de Labores y Financiamientos, 1973–1980.*

next few years. Of equal importance is the fact that in comparison with other (public and private) housing alternatives it is clear that INFONAVIT provides both terms and access not afforded generally. Table 11-14 offers a comparison of programs of social-interest housing in terms of financing conditions. The improvements offered by INFONAVIT are evident.

However, it should be noted that the program—and other programs of so-called social-interest housing—does not reach the urban poor with any degree of success. The assumption of housing for those in the formal labor market and earning at least the minimum wage, excludes the majority of the population. Even housing provided under the DGHP program does not reach the truly needy. In the case of INFONAVIT, other problems have become apparent. Employer registration has not proceeded as rapidly as might be desired. While the first several years witnessed large numbers of employers registering, more recently the pace has slackened

*TABLE 11.14.*
*Conditions for Financing Social-Interest Housing**

| Institution | Down Payment | Interest Rates (%) | Term | Payment Period | Housing Costs (pesos) Low | Housing Costs (pesos) High |
|---|---|---|---|---|---|---|
| FOVISSSTE | None | 4 | 10–20 Years | Monthly | $170,000 | $400,000 |
| INFONAVIT | None | 4 | 10–20 Years | Monthly | 141,480 | 332,478 |
| FOVI | 10–20% | 9 | 10–15 Years | Monthly | 136,000 | 186,000 |
| DGHP-DDF | 5% | 6 | 15 Years | Monthly | 37,000 | |
| Private Banks | 10–20 Years | 9–10 | 10–15 Years | Monthly | 136,000 | — |

SOURCE: Fernandez, 1976.
*Data are from 1976.

considerably. The attempt to expand participation has confronted opposition or negligence, so much so that by 1976 only 27 percent of eligible workers had filled out the required information cards (Garza and Schteingart 1976). It is clear that even within existing positive efforts, much remains to be done.

In a broader sense this chapter has focused on housing policy within the context of a spatially concentrated system. We began by suggesting that both historical factors and public policies have led to the spatial concentration and to the cumulative locational advantages exemplified most clearly in the preeminence of Mexico City in the national system of cities. Conscious spatial policies of regional development in the past—aimed at speeding national development—are explicit manifestations of the impact of public policy on spatial inequality. Service provision policies, such as housing, may have equally important impacts on spatial concentration and income distribution.

In spatial terms it is evident that housing policy has been concentrated in the capital city, to a lesser extent in other metropolitan areas, and is almost absent in the rural context. Within the urban area of Mexico City, housing policy has had additional implications for the distribution of wealth. The continued focus on the public sector as the stimulant to private-sector actions, the overwhelming focus of housing policy on the "working poor," and the still-evident failure to reach the urban poor with existing policy instruments—all these suggest a rather dismal prospect for ameliorating the (housing) condition of the bottom deciles of the income ladder, even *within* the urban setting. Recognition of this is evident in recent government actions, the impacts of which remain in the future. In spite of the tremendous growth in the 1970s of institutional programs for the provision of new housing, for housing rehabilitation, and for urban renewal, resolution of the housing needs of the poor remains a long way off; yet, recognition of the need to combine housing construction programs with decentralized housing activity (as is the case in INFONAVIT), with greater emphases on rural housing and living conditions (as is the case in INDECO), and the need for regional strategies of employment and deconcentration (as is evident in the Global Plan) represent—as an integrated package—steps in the right direction.

# Notes

1. A rather strict definition of "urban" is utilized here: areas with a population of 15,000 or more. More flexible definitions (e.g., 10,000, 5,000, 2,500) would increase the urban population greatly.

2. Until 1877, Puebla was the second largest city of Mexico with a population in that year of approximately 70,000. Also, measured by a primacy index or rank-size rule, the imbalance we now associate with Mexico was not as apparent until the turn of the century. The emergence of Guadalajara as a major commercial center and its current dynamism are well described in Walton (1978).

3. It has been argued that the depreciation rate used here (3.44%) is too high when applied to Mexico because labor costs are low and therefore maintenance schedules tend to extend the life cycle of housing. This estimate is based upon the quality of construction materials and the physical condition of these materials. A more complete explanation of the weighing system and derivation of the depreciation rate used here can be found in Puente Leyva (1970, 274). However, even if a more conservative rate is utilized, the size of the new construction needs would continue to be extremely large.

4. For detailed examinations of the squatter phenomenon in Mexico City, the reader is referred to a number of excellent sources, including Brown (1972), Cornelius (1975), Lomnitz (1975) and Montaño (1976).

5. Principally, the several popular housing agencies: the *Fideicomiso de Netzahualcoyotl,* the *Procuradía de Colonias Populares,* FIDEURBE, AURIS, and the national agency aimed at "regularizing land tenure," the *Comisión para la Regularización de la Tenencia de la Tierra* (CORETT). However, the thrust of many of these programs is to (a) regularize land tenure, so that (b) public services can be introduced. The problem is that regularization leads to the privatization of the land (i.e., it becomes part of the private market) and land speculation, and as a consequence many of the lower-income sectors are excluded. In addition, the cost of service delivery is borne increasingly by users rather than developers, further excluding a segment more concerned with shelter than amenities. The end effect, then, is displacement.

6. The 1931 Ley de Trabajo in Article II, Section IV stated:

> "The Federal Executive and its component entities shall attend to the needs of workers, with regard to the length of employment, the location of said employment, and considering the economic possibilities of employers, by *regulating the conditions and terms* by which employers fulfill their obligations in reference to . . . [housing conditions]." (Author's translation and underlining.)

The Supreme Court struck down this clause in 1942 as unconstitutional because of the declared power to regulate the prices of housing (Gonzalez Prieto 1973).

7. "Social-interest housing," even in private lending institutions, was mandated as early as the 1950s. Five percent of reserves were to be held in housing bonds for investment in popular housing, rent, and construction loans. However, credit in private institutions retained a "productive" orientation (INFONAVIT 1976c).

8. The role of AID and the Interamerican Development Bank were critical in the post-1964 period. The attempt to stimulate private sector participation in housing pervades the philosophy of both of these organizations, and Mexican housing policy as well (Garza and Schteingart 1976).

9. It is important to bear in mind that the devaluation of the peso and the floating of the pesos in 1976–1977 had marked effects on prices of consumer goods, and consequently, on the housing market. Thus, utilizing both 1975 data and 1977 data may have the effect here of overestimating the potential participation of consumers in the housing market.

10. As Moreno Toscano (1979, 167) notes, FIDEURBE had disappeared by June 1977, the Procuraduría de Colonias Populares had been dissolved, and a coordinating body—the Comisión de Desarrollo Urbano—was created for regularizing land tenure.

## References


BANOBRAS (1970). *Mejoramiento de vivienda: programa buena vida.* Mexico: BANOBRAS.

Barkin, David (1978). "Regional Development and Interregional Equity: A Mexican Case Study." In Wayne Cornelius and Robert V. Kemper, eds. *Urbanization and Inequality: The Political Economy of Urban and Rural Development in Latin America.* Beverly Hills: Sage.

Bergsman, Joel (1979). "Income Distribution and Poverty in Mexico." Washington, D.C.: World Bank, mimeo.

Brown, Jane Cowan (1972). "Patterns of Intra-Urban Settlement in Mexico City: An Examination of the Turner Thesis." Ph.D. Diss., Cornell University, Ithaca.

COPEVI (1977). *Investigación sobre vivienda: la producción en la zona metropolitana.* Mexico: COPEVI.

Cornelius, Wayne A. (1975). *Politics and the Migrant Poor in Mexico City.* Stanford: Stanford University Press.

——— and Robert V. Kemper (1978). "Introduction." In Cornelius and Kemper, eds. *Metropolitan Latin America.* Beverly Hills: Sage.

Danielson, Michael and Rusen Keles (1980). "Urbanization and Income Distribution in Turkey." In E. Ozbudun and A. Ulsan, eds. *The Political Economy of Income Distribution in Turkey.* New York: Holmes & Meier.

Fernandez, Fernando (1976). "Vivienda para México." Mexico: INFONAVIT, mimeo.

Ferras, Robert (1977). *Ciudad Netzahualcoyotl: un banco en vías de absorción por la ciudad de México.* Mexico: El Colegio de Mexico.

FOVI (1978). *Programa financiero de vivienda.* Mexico: Secretaría de Hacienda y Crédito Público.

Garza, Gustavo and Martha Schteingart (1976). *La acción habitacional del estado de México.* México: El Colegio de México.

——— (1978). Mexico City: The Emerging Megalopolis." In Cornelius and Kemper, eds. *Metropolitan Latin America.* Beverly Hills: Sage.

Goldani, Ana María (1977). "Impacto de los inmigrantes sobre la estructura y el crecimiento del área metropolitana." In Humberto Muñoz, et al. *Migración y desigualdad social en la ciudad de México.* México: UNAM and El Colegio de México.

Gonzalez Prieto, Alejandro (1973). "Orígen y evolución del problema de la vivienda en México." *Boletín Informativo* (INFONAVIT), no. 16.

INFONAVIT (1973–1980). *Informes anuales de actividades.* Mexico: INFONAVIT.

——— (1973–1980). *Plan de labores y de financiamientos del Instituto del Fondo Nacional de la Vivienda.* Mexico: INFONAVIT.

——— (1975a). *Indicadores de la necesidad y demanda de vivienda urbana en la república mexicana* (3 vol). Mexico: INFONAVIT.

——— (1975b). *40 meses*. Mexico: INFONAVIT.

——— (1976a). *INFONAVIT, una nueva institución de la república, 1972–1976: los primeros pasos, I and II*. Mexico: INFONAVIT.

——— (1976b). *Fuentes legales de financiamiento a la vivienda popular*. Mexico: INFONAVIT.

Lomnitz, Larissa (1975). *Como sobreviven los marginados*. Mexico: Siglo 21.

——— (1977). *Networks and Marginality*. New York: Academic Press.

Mohan, Rakesh (1977). "Urban Land Policy, Income Distribution and the Urban Poor." In Charles Frank and Richard Webb, eds. *Income Distribution and Growth in Less Developed Countries*. Washington, D.C.: Brookings.

Molina Pasquel, Roberto (1974). "Una fórmula mexicana para el financiamiento de la vivienda." *Boletín Informativo* (INFONAVIT), no. 21.

Montaño, Jorge (1976). *Los pobres de la ciudad en los asentamientos espontáneos*. Mexico: Siglo 21.

Moreno Toscarno, Alejandra (1979). "La 'Crisis' en la Ciudad." In Pablo Gonzalez Casanova and Enrique Florescano, eds. *México, hoy*. México: Siglo 21.

Navarette, Ifigenia M. de (1970). "La distribución del ingreso en México." In David Ibarra, et al. *El perfil de México en 1980,* vol. I. México: Siglo 21.

Parcero Lopez, Juan (1977). "La vivienda en la ciudad de México y su marginación." *Vivienda,* 2:10.

Puente Leyva, Jesus (1970). "El problema habitacional." In David Ibarra, et al. *El perfil de México en 1980*. México: Siglo 21.

Reyes Navarro, Carlos (1973). "Las enfermedades urbanas." México: INFONAVIT, mimeo.

Rosa, Martín de la (1975). *Netzahualcoyotl: un fenómeno* (Testimonios del Fondo, no. 19). México: Fondo de la Cultura Economica.

Secretaría de Programación y Presupuesto (1979). *La distribución del ingreso y el gasto familiar en México*. México: Secretaría de Programación y Presupuesto.

Silva Herzog, Jesus (1973). *El problema de la vivienda en México*. México: Primero seminario de estudio del problema de la habitación en México, Instituto de estudios politicos, economicos y sociales.

Sudra, Tomás L. and John F. C. Turner (1973). "Housing Conditions and Priorities of the Lower-Income Sectors of the Population: Case Studies of Families in Metropolitan Mexico City." Unpublished report, Mexico City.

Turner, John F. C. (1971). "Government Policy and Lower-Income Housing Systems in Mexico City." Report, Mexico City and Cambridge, Mass.

Unikel, Luís (1978). *El desarrollo urbano de Mexico: diagnóstico e implicaciones futuras*. México: Centro de Estudios Económicos y Demográficos, Second edition.

Walton, John (1978). "Guadalajara: Creating the Divided City." In Cornelius and Kemper, eds. *Metropolitan Latin America*. Beverly Hills: Sage.

Ward, Peter (1975). "The Squatter Settlements, Slum or Housing Solution: Evidence from Mexico City." *Land Economics,* 52:3.

World Bank (1972). *Urbanization: Sector Working Paper*. Washington, D.C.: World Bank.

Wibel, J. and Juan de la Cruz (1971). "Mexico." In Richard M. Morse, ed. *The Urban Development of Latin America, 1750–1920*. Stanford: Center for Latin American Studies, Stanford University.

## CHAPTER 12

# *State Enterprise and Income Distribution in Mexico*

Raymond Hill

### I. Introduction

#### *Goals of State Ownership*

The theoretical justification economists give for the creation of state-owned enterprises (SOEs) is the correction of market failure. Consequently much of the existing literature on public enterprise is concerned with the problem of "natural" monopolies and efficient pricing rules. Apart from this kind of analysis, the work on public enterprise has focused mostly on administrative and organizational topics or is discussed in a political or historical context.

In contrast to the economist's perspective, a realistic assessment across countries would reveal a range of motives for the existence of state ownership, a range too wide to fit within any reasonably narrow view of market failure. Not only do the motives exceed the normal range of economists' arguments, but they are often so broad as to call into question the consistency (or existence) of any general strategy for state ownership. In Mexico, in particular, the motives for state ownership fit this description. Economic growth, stability, the elimination of bottlenecks, control over natural resources and vital public services, poor private performance, innovation and R&D, and finally, income distribution have all been suggested as objectives of state enterprise.

The Mexican government's complete control of electric power (through the Comisión Federal de Electricidad [CFE]) provides a good example. The CFE began as a supplement to private, foreign-owned electric enterprise. It seems originally intended to provide greater investment in regions where private firms were reluctant to expand, but even at the time of its creation plans had been discussed for much broader state intervention in this sector. The eventual buy-out of the private firms in 1960 was supported by substantial interests within the industrial sector. The principal argument of these industrialists seems to have been that the private electric firms were stunting Mexican growth through monopoly pricing (and, of course, inadequate supply). A more general view is that the politicization of the regulatory process had chilled all incentive for private expansion. Moreover, the absence of effective and coherent regulation permitted (or helped to create) an irrational variation in prices across classes of consumers which seemed arbitrary in the sense that price differences were related to neither efficiency nor equity. Immediately following nationalization, the structure of rates across classes of consumers and regions was revised. In sum, then, while market failure played a role in the state's entry into and nationalization of electric power, its motives were varied and complex. Redistributional concerns also played a role but were hardly the central issue.

### *Scope of this Chapter*

These comments are intended as an explanation for the approach taken in this chapter toward analyzing the effect of state enterprise on income distribution in Mexico. It would be convenient if income redistribution were an important and maintained goal of state ownership or if one could analyze the redistributional consequences of some consistent strategy. Absent such a well-defined path of analysis, this chapter is a search for significant patterns of redistribution which emerge from the panoply of goals.

I concentrate on three aspects of state ownership which might reasonably be expected to affect relative incomes in a fashion which is sufficiently general and significant to be of interest to policymakers. The first of these aspects is the regional pattern of state ownership, where I assume state ownership makes a positive contribution to regional income. The second is the possibility that workers in state enterprises earn higher wages than their counterparts in the private sector. The third is the relationship between subsidies to state enterprise and the incomes of consumers—either through direct subsidies to final output or through the prices of intermediate inputs. In the cases of regional policy and the pattern of price subsidies, redistribution has been an often articulated goal of public ownership. In the case of wage policy, higher wages for SOE employees seem to be "common knowledge." In all three cases an attempt at quantifying the effect of state ownership is reported even when success was limited. Given the multiplicity of goals for state enterprise, it is important to ask whether these specific effects can, in fact, be measured, particularly when one holds "all else equal."

### *Distribution and the Public Ownership of Capital*

One question that will *not* be addressed at any length in this chapter is how the state's ownership of capital per se affects income distribution. In other words, when we abstract from the issues of what the state does with the enterprises it owns—i.e., employment policy, and price setting, or locational decisions—does it matter that capital is in the hands of the state rather than private individuals? Is income distribution significantly affected by the fact that returns from capital enter the federal budget rather than the income of capitalists? There is considerable evidence that the distribution of wealth in thoroughly socialist economies is less concentrated than in market economies (although comparisons are fraught with conceptual and quantitative difficulties). There is no comparable evidence about distribution and the degree of state ownership among mixed economies, however. In the Mexican case, in particular, there is little reason to believe state ownership per se has a significant effect on distribution.

For state ownership to affect income distribution, it must reduce the wealth of private capitalists or increase the wealth of noncapitalists. As long as a substantial part of the economy and foreign assets are available for private investment, there is no reason to believe state ownership in limited sectors will reduce capitalist wealth or its rate of growth (in the absence of confiscation, which is discussed below).

What about noncapitalist wealth? Suppose we think of the returns from state capital being distributed through the fiscal system into the disposable incomes of all classes. Then, if capital accumulation by the state supplements private saving and investment, the wealth of noncapitalists would grow more rapidly ceteris paribus when the state invests in productive enterprise. As a result, the distribution of disposable income could improve over time, but the improvement would be subject to the following limitations:

1. Growth comes at the expense of current expenditure so that disposable income must fall and income distribution worsen for some generations.
2. Exactly how the distribution of income changes depends on how the returns from state capital are used in the fiscal system. Simply knowing that the state has more to spend (or less need to tax) tells us virtually nothing.
3. In many sectors state enterprise does not produce positive returns (see Section V of this chapter) so that the question of how those returns are used is moot. Of course, one reason for the absence of positive returns may be that the real return is "paid out" in higher wages and price subsidies. These possibilities are examined explicitly in Sections IV and V.

If the state acquires its capital by confiscation, then there would appear to be more direct consequences for income distribution. In Mexico, some degree of political coercion was involved in the acquisition of a number of enterprises, but owners—whether foreign or domestic—appear to have been compensated. Pure confiscation when it occurred was probably limited to the capitalized value of future monopoly profits. Moreover, in the case of the electric utilities, the largest foreign firm appears not to have been reluctant to accept the government's offer; and a number of more recent acquisitions (steel, for example) represent buy-outs of failing enterprise rather than anything resembling the expropriation of wealth from capitalists to the state.

In the case of oil, of course, the rents appropriated by the state are of tremendous significance. The importance of oil, however, is a matter of the state's ownership of natural resources and an accompanying windfall gain, not of state enterprise or capital accumulation. Moreover, just how those oil rents will affect distribution is not a simple story and is discussed in the paper by Socrates Rizzo in this volume.

In conclusion, in an open economy with substantial private capital and few instances of confiscation there is little reason to expect any significant effect on redistribution simply because the state acts as an entrepreneur. In the Mexican case, the fact that the state owns productive enterprise should matter much less than what it does with its capital.

## II. The Scope of State Enterprise in Mexico

The Cárdenas administration (1934–1940) is usually associated with the creation, in a significant way, of entrepreneurial activities by the state. It was during that period that the state acquired rural industrial enterprises and took over the petroleum and electric power sectors. Hansen (p. 44) (see the Bibliography) notes that the state was *already* in a position of dominance in the railway and banking sectors before the Cárdenas administration. Since the Cárdenas administration, state ownership has spread widely across sectors, but there has been no clear trend in, for instance, public capital formation as a percentage of gross domestic product (GDP), as Table 12-1 makes clear.[1]

*TABLE 12.1.*
*Public and Private Capital Formation*

| | *Percent Distribution* | |
|---|---|---|
| *Period* | *Public* | *Private* |
| (1) 1940–1946 | 52 | 48 |
| (2) 1947–1950 | 36 | 64 |
| (3) 1954–1960 | 26 | 74 |
| (4) 1961–1962 | 34 | 66 |
| (5) 1963–1969 | 36 | 64 |
| (6) 1970–1976 | 33 | 67 |

SOURCE: Lines (1)–(4), Hansen, p. 44. Lines (5) and (6), Villareal and Villareal, p. 40.

### *An Inventory of SOEs*

*Public enterprise* in Mexico includes organizations performing a wide array of economic activities. It also includes firms with mixed private and public ownership but under public control. The federal registers of decentralized, parastatal enterprises include more than the productive enterprises which form the subject matter of this chapter (i.e., research institutes, hospitals, local economic development councils, or public fiscal commissions).[2] To avoid confusion, I will refer to the latter as "nonproductive" in contrast to the "productive" SOEs.

In the 1979 registers there were 72 enterprises wholly owned by the state. These included the well-known *Petroleos Mexicanos* (PEMEX), *Comisión Federal de Electricidad* (CFE [Federal Electric Commission]), and the state trading company for agricultural products (CONASUPO), but the majority were nonproductive enterprises. There were 47 enterprises—almost all apparently of the productive sort—in which the state had a majority interest and a majority of the board of directors. There were an additional 58 firms, again virtually all productive, in which the state's share was between 25 and 50 percent. In addition, by my count there were 389 firms in which the state had an indirect ownership of 50 percent or more. This indirect ownership occurs through other SOEs, including state-owned financial institutions and through branches of the federal government.

These lists do not include approximately 60 state-owned credit institutions and 4 insurance companies.

### *Size and Sectorial Composition*

Table 12-2 gives several measures of the amount of activity carried out by SOEs compared to gross domestic product. Because of the relative capital intensity, the state's share is much higher measured by sales or value added than by employment. For 1977, the last year for which com-

*TABLE 12.2.*
*Output of State Enterprises*
*(Millions of 1960 Pesos)*

| | *1970* | *1971* | *1972* | *1973* | *1974* | *1975* | *1976* | *1977* |
|---|---|---|---|---|---|---|---|---|
| Total sales | | 27,813 | 29,538 | 34,819 | 41,023 | 44,225 | 45,642 | 48,797 |
| As % of GDP | | 9.1 | 9.0 | 9.8 | 10.9 | 11.3 | 11.5 | 11.9 |
| Wages and salaries | 8,888.1 | 9,837 | 10,797 | 11,462 | 12,802 | 14,775 | 14,351 | 15,727 |
| As % of GDP | 3.3 | 3.2 | 3.3 | 3.2 | 3.4 | 3.8 | 3.6 | 3.6 |
| Value added[a] | 18,186.3 | 19,556 | 22,607 | 23,661 | 26,966 | 32,891 | 32,274 | 34,997 |
| As % of GDP | 6.1 | 6.4 | 6.9 | 6.7 | 7.2 | 8.4 | 8.1 | 8.5 |

Source: "Tercer Informe de Gobierno," *Annex* I (1979).

[a]Total costs less "compra de bienes y servicios."

TABLE 12.3.
*State Enterprise by Sector*[a]

| | *Revenues* | *Wages and Salaries* | *Value Added*[b] |
|---|---|---|---|
| Electricity | 23,569 | 6717 | 21,715 |
| Railroads | 8,321 | 8206 | 12,231 |
| Communications and transportation | 6,077 | 2356 | 4,384 |
| Industry | 16,494 | 2890 | 7,430 |
| Agriculture | 4,066 | 741 | 1,501 |
| Commerce[c] | 23,456 | 942 | 7,148 |

SOURCE: "Tercer Informe de Gobierno," *Annex* I (1979).

[a] Does not include the sector "Desarrollo Social," which includes the national lottery, the Mexican Institute of Social Security (IMSS), the Social Service and Security Institute for State Workers (ISSSTE), and the National Institute for the Development of the Rural Community and Public Housing (INDECO).

[b] Sales of goods and services less purchases of intermediate inputs.

[c] Includes CONASUPO.

plete data were available, my crude measure of value added indicates that SOEs accounted for 9.9 percent of GDP. As noted, there is no marked long-term trend in the public sector share of total investment although it has been rising slowly over the last decade. In 1976 that share amounted to 45 percent of total investment and 9.0 percent of GDP. Decentralized enterprises, in turn, accounted for about 74 percent of total public investment (Villareal and Villareal).

The sectorial distribution of the activity of state enterprises for 1977 is given in Table 12-3. In the railroad and electric power industries the state has a monopoly position.

### *The Industrial Sector*

The 1976 Industrial Census (with data primarily from 1975) provides a rich source of information about state ownership in the industrial sector. The census covered 247 state-owned enterprises with 725 industrial establishments. Those enterprises employed 142,674 persons, or 8.7 percent of employment by firms covered in the general industrial census.

As Table 12-4 indicates, the publicly owned firms in the industrial sector were larger on average and more capital intensive than their private sector counterparts. Table 12-5 gives some indication of the relative importance of state enterprises by industry. In only two industries, tobacco and coal and oil, do SOEs account for more than half of total fixed assets; in eight industries they account for something between 10 and 50 percent; and in the remaining fourteen, less than 10 percent. In two of the two-digit industries there is no state participation.

## Financial Institutions

As noted, there are approximately sixty public financial entities known as national credit institutions. As of February 1980, their assets amounted to 494.4 billion pesos compared with assets of 900.3 billion in the private financial sector. Aside from the Bank of Mexico and *Nacional Financiera,* these institutions are relatively specialized, usually established to meet the financial needs of a particular region, a specific crop, or a given clientel. Two important examples are the *Banco Nacional de Crédito Ejidal* and the *Banco Nacional Hipotecario Urbanò y de Obras Públicas.*

TABLE 12.4.
*State Enterprise in the Industrial Sector: Firm Characteristics*

| | | Ratio of State Enterprise to Total Industry | | | |
|---|---|---|---|---|---|
| *Industry* | *Classification Number* | *Employees Per Firm* | *Assets Per Firm* | *Value Added Per Firm* | *Average Assets Per Employee* |
| Total | | 37.9 | 50.8 | 47.0 | — |
| Mining | | | | | |
| Coal and oil | 11 | 7.3 | 7.3 | 6.7 | 1.0 |
| Metals | 13 | 4.2 | 4.8 | 4.0 | 1.4 |
| Nonmetals | 14 | 18.6 | 39.2 | 45.9 | 1.2 |
| Salt | 15 | 0.5 | 0.2 | 0.1 | 4.9 |
| Processing | | | | | |
| Food | 20 | 80.3 | 128.8 | 84.8 | — |
| Beverages | 21 | 3.9 | 2.5 | 0.9 | 1.9 |
| Tobacco | 22 | 1.3 | 1.0 | 0.6 | 1.0 |
| Textiles | 23 | 11.4 | 15.0 | 11.3 | 1.2 |
| Clothing | 24 | 107.2 | 273.6 | 184.7 | 0.8 |
| Shoes and leather | 25 | *No state enterprise* | | | 1.4 |
| Lumber | 26 | 22.5 | 28.0 | 21.5 | — |
| Furniture | 27 | 28.1 | 14.3 | 10.9 | 1.0 |
| Paper | 28 | 4.0 | 4.8 | 4.8 | 1.3 |
| Printing | 29 | 19.1 | 21.7 | 18.3 | 2.3 |
| Chemicals | 30 | 5.6 | 6.3 | 5.3 | 1.9 |
| Oil refining | 31 | 3.2 | 6.3 | 6.5 | ? |
| Rubber and plastic | 32 | *No state enterprise* | | | |
| Nonmetallic | | | | | |
| Mineral processing | 33 | 25.4 | 31.6 | 57.3 | 4.9 |
| Basic metals | 34 | 5.4 | 5.9 | 5.6 | 0.9 |
| Metal fabrication | 35 | 43.6 | 58.9 | 87.5 | 1.6 |
| Nonelectrical machinery | 36 | 10.7 | 10.9 | 10.5 | 3.3 |
| Electrical machinery | 37 | 15.1 | 20.1 | 14.5 | 1.0 |
| Transportation equipment | 38 | 12.6 | 14.0 | 15.6 | 1.2 |
| Miscellaneous | 39 | 11.3 | 16.4 | 22.7 | 1.6 |

SOURCE: *Censo Industrial,* 1976, Secretaría de Agricultura y Recursos Hidráulicos (Mexico City, 1979).

The latter is primarily concerned with financing public works projects of state and municipal government and low-cost housing. In particular, normal commercial banking is overwhelmingly in the private sector. In spite of the ratio of private to public sector assets of roughly 2 to 1, checking and time deposits of the private sector were about six times those of the national credit institutions at the beginning of 1980.

One role of the national banks is to supply credit to governmental

*TABLE 12.5.*
*State Enterprise in the Industrial Sector: Relative Importance by Sector (1975)*

| *Industry* | *Classification Number* | *SOE Share (%) in*[a] *Employment* | *Fixed Assets* |
|---|---|---|---|
| Total | | 7.9 | 14.4 |
| Mining | | | |
| Coal and oil | 11 | 75.8 | 80.6 |
| Metals | 13 | 22.6 | 34.1 |
| Nonmetals | 14 | 17.9 | 36.0 |
| Salt | 15 | 4.5 | 0.6 |
| Processing | | | |
| Food | 20 | 9.9 | 21.7 |
| Beverages | 21 | 0.5 | 0.3 |
| Tobacco | 22 | 54.2 | 66.1 |
| Manufacturing | | | |
| Textiles | 23 | 9.0 | 7.9 |
| Clothing | 24 | 1.0 | 1.3 |
| Shoes and leather | 25 | *No state enterprise* | |
| Lumber | 26 | 13.8 | 17.1 |
| Furniture | 27 | 1.1 | 1.5 |
| Paper | 28 | 7.4 | 15.6 |
| Printing | 29 | 1.2 | 2.3 |
| Chemicals | 30 | 5.4 | 7.7 |
| Oil refining | 31 | 5.1 | 7.1 |
| Rubber and plastic | 32 | *No state enterprise* | |
| Nonmetallic minerals | 33 | 2.1 | 13.0 |
| Basic metals | 34 | 28.1 | 27.5 |
| Metal fabrication | 35 | 3.9 | 6.7 |
| Nonelectrical machinery and equipment | 36 | 1.5 | 4.1 |
| Electrical machinery | 37 | 3.7 | 4.9 |
| Transportation equipment | 38 | 19.0 | 21.1 |
| Miscellaneous | 39 | 0.5 | 0.7 |

SOURCE: *Censo Industrial,* 1976.

[a]Ratio of values from industrial census of Empresas de Participación Estatal y Organismos Descentralizados to those in general industrial census.

*TABLE 12.6.*
*Investments of Financial Institutions, February 28,1980 (Billions of Pesos)*

| | Total[a] | Private Institutions | Public Institutions |
|---|---|---|---|
| Obligations of the public sector | 47,608 | 20,526 | 25,878 |
| Federal government | 30,185 | 16,131 | 10,013 |
| State and municipal governments[b] | 13 | — | — |
| State-owned enterprise | 14,296 | 1,364 | 12,763 |
| Financial system[c] | 3,114 | 3,031 | 3,102 |
| Obligations of private sector | 26,339 | 22,993 | 3,815 |
| Firms | 22,279 | 14,687 | 3,148 |
| Financial system | 5,051 | 8,306 | 667 |
| External obligations | 217 | 99 | 118 |
| Governments and firms | 116 | — | 116 |
| Financial institutions | 101 | 99 | 2 |
| Totals | 75,155 | 43,618 | 29,811 |

*Source:* "Boletín Estadístico," Dec. 1979, *Comisón Nacional Bancaria y de Seguros.*

[a]The total is slightly more than the sum of the two columns because of an additional category, auxiliary organizations.

[b]Bonds of the State of Jalisco.

[c]Includes, for example, petrobonds.

institutions and to state enterprise. Direct information on the public-private division of credit is limited. However, Table 12-6 gives the obligations of public and private sector institutions held as investments by the public and private sectors of the financial system. The obligations of SOEs are largely in the hands of the national banks, while the obligations of private firms are disproportionately held by private institutions. Most of the banking system's financing is supplied through loans rather than investments, but the public-private allocation of loans is not available. Table 12-7 gives total credit (loans and investments) with separate figures for a number of sectors. Again the national banks supply a disproportionate share of credit to those sectors where government activity is highest. Compare, for example, the national-private breakdown for petroleum and electric power to that for manufacturing or, more specifically, to the electrical equipment industry (which has no state enterprise).

This pattern is also illustrated in the specific case of *Nacional Financiera,* the leading public credit institution. In 1973 the leading 15 recipients of *Nacional Financiera* credit (with about 77 percent of the total) were all public sector entities.[3] *Nacional Financiera* does supply credit to private institutions, however, and the sixteenth ranked recipient was the Small

*TABLE 12.7.*
*Credit to Firms and Individuals, Outstanding Stock, December 1979 (Millions of Pesos)*

| | *National Banks* | *Private Banks* |
|---|---|---|
| Total | 323.7 | 515.6 |
| Agriculture | 57.7 | 53.0 |
| Mining | 3.2 | 2.0 |
| Petroleum | 28.7 | 9.6 |
| Electric power | 24.2 | 1.4 |
| Manufacturing[a] | 47.4 | 90.8 |
| Nonmetallic minerals | 0.8 | 5.5 |
| Metal processing | 22.5 | 19.2 |
| Electrical equipment | 2.0 | 11.5 |
| Construction | 11.4 | 40.4 |
| Commerce | 4.3 | 135.2 |

SOURCE: Banco de México, *Informe Annual,* 1979, Cuadro 29.
[a]Does not include the three categories which follow it.

Business Guarantee and Promotion Fund which redistributed funds (presumably) largely to private firms.

*International Comparisons*

To complete this general description, we now examine how the scope of state enterprise in Mexico compares with other mixed economies.

Table 12-8 (from Lindblom 1977) gives the share of employment accounted for by state enterprise in a number of developed countries. Mexico would rank on the low end of that scale, although data limitations make the comparisons rather imprecise. In the industrial sector only, employment by SOEs covered by the industrial census was 7.9 percent of employment by all firms covered in the census. It is likely, however, that the coverage of firms in the general census was less complete than for the

*TABLE 12.8.*
*Share of Total Employment in Publicly Operated Market Enterprises*

| | | | |
|---|---|---|---|
| Austria | 13% | Belgium | 8% |
| Ireland | 13 | Netherlands | 8 |
| France | 12 | Norway | 6 |
| United Kingdom | 12 | Luxembourg | 5.5 |
| Italy | 11.5 | Canada | 5 |
| Sweden | 10.5 | Denmark | 5 |
| Finland | 10 | New Zealand | 5 |
| West Germany | 9 | Australia | 4 |
| | | United States | 3 |

SOURCE: Lindblom, 1977, p. 114.

census of SOEs. If we compared SOE employment from the census to independent data on industrial sector employment, the percentage falls to around 4 percent.

For all sectors of the economy, the percentage appears to be even lower. Villareal and Villareal report that total employment of budgetary controlled enterprises was 460,275 in 1976. This represents slightly less than 3 percent of total employment in that year.[4] As a check I also computed total SOE employment in 1975 from the consolidated income statement of the state enterprises on the assumption that labor costs per worker for all enterprises equaled the average in the industrial (SOE) sector. This computation provided an estimate that employment was just under 4 percent of the total. Compared to Lindblom's numbers, the various estimates of employment share rank Mexico on the low end of the scale in the vicinity of the United States or Australia.

We can also compare the Mexican experience to that of other developing countries in Latin America. Unfortunately, the only data available for other countries are on investment, so the comparisons will be in a different dimension from those with developed countries. Table 12-9 gives figures for public sector participation in total investment for a number of Latin American countries. The percentage of public investment and investment accounted for by SOEs is higher in Mexico than in any country but Bolivia. Within this group the shares of the public sector are fairly sensitive to state ownership of a relatively few very large-scale enterprises in mining, petroleum, railways, energy, or communications. Mexican state enterprises participate in all these sectors.

## III. Regional Consequences of State Ownership

State ownership can affect the regional distribution of income and employment directly through the conscious location of new plants in areas where growth is preferred. The Las Truchas Steel Complex in Michoacan is a notable example of such a policy. In Mexico, state participation in the energy and financial sector has also been a means of affecting the incentives for private locational decisions. In this section the latter policies are briefly described, and then some evidence on the regional distribution of SOEs in the industrial sector is presented.

### *Energy and Regional Policy*

The Industrial Development Plan contains a detailed and explicit structure of subsidies for natural gas, oil, and electricity for industrial use. Subsidies up to 30 percent (on prices already below world prices) are available to firms constructing new facilities or substantially expanding existing ones in the priority zones for port development and in some of the priority zones for urban development.

*TABLE 12.9.*
*Public Sector Shares in Total Investment for Latin America*

| | Year | Investment as a % of GDP | Public share in Investment: Public Sector | General Govt | Public Enterprise |
|---|---|---|---|---|---|
| Argentina | 1969 | 21.7 | 37.1 | 23.1 | 14.0 |
| Bolivia | 1968 | 20.8 | 50.7 | 11.6 | 39.1 |
| Brazil | 1968 | 17.7 | 39.0 | 24.8 | 14.2 |
| Costa Rica | 1968 | 17.6 | 17.8 | 10.5 | 7.3 |
| Panama | 1968 | 20.9 | 19.1 | 8.7 | 10.4 |
| Mexico | 1976 | 19.9 | 45.2 | 26.8 | 18.4 |

SOURCE: Non-Mexican data are taken from the United Nations. The Mexican total investment figures are from Villareal and Villareal, and SOE figures are from consolidated accounts of budgetary controlled enterprises.

The use of energy prices to affect regional development is not new. Nationalization of the electric utilities was followed by a large expansion in the supply of electric power and a change in the rate structure. Rates had previously varied considerably by region, with rural areas generally paying above-average rates. After nationalization the rate structure was simplified and rates to rural areas reduced, while those for more industrialized areas rose. In addition, the average rate across classes of consumers also rose, but rates to agriculture for irrigation were left unchanged (Wionczek, pp. 104 and 105).

### *National Banks and Regional Policy*

State participation in the banking sector involves two elements of regional policy. Among the national credit institutions there are over two dozen with regional (and some with regional and agricultural) specialization. In addition, *Nacional Financiera* administers several trusts devoted to financing industrial decentralization and regional development. Among these have been the National Border Program with assets in 1971 of 470 million pesos, the Trust Fund for Industrial Complexes, Parks and Cities and Commercial Centers (with assets of 49 million pesos in 1974), and the National Ejido Development (56.9 million pesos in assets in 1971). Unfortunately, the annual reports of *Nacional Financiera* and of the financial system as a whole do not permit a more detailed analysis of public sector credit allocation compared to private.

### *Location of Industry*

A natural question to ask about the performance of state ownership in Mexico is how the regional distribution of SOEs compares to the location of private industry. One possible role for state enterprises is to be an instrument for shifting employment and income from high-income to low-income regions or from already concentrated areas to regions where growth is preferred.

An alternative possibility is that SOEs have behaved much like private enterprise—responding to the same incentives which created regional income disparities or industrial concentration. Indeed, it is conceivable that the distribution of SOEs has been more "unequal" than that of private industry. This could have happened if, for example, the location of state enterprise is a highly political question and concentrated regions have a disproportionate influence in settling that question.

As it turns out, the available data fail to display any systematic relationship in the industrial sector between the location of state enterprise and income. Three tests support this conclusion.

Figures 12-1 and 12-2 are scatter diagrams of the level of SOE activity by state plotted against per capita GDP by state. "Activity" is measured by value added in Figure 12-1 and by the wage bill in Figure 12-2. Only the industrial sector is represented in these figures. The distribution is clearly not uniform across states—but it also fails to show any clear positive or negative relationship to per capita production. The data for these figures are given in Table 12-10.

Another cut at the data can be made by normalizing SOE activity on the regional distribution of private sector activity. Figures 12-3 and 12-4 show per capita GDP plotted against the ratio of SOE to private activity by region. Value added and employment are for those firms represented in the industrial census. Once more the scatter reveals no systematic relationship between location and income. By using value added, the correlation coefficient is $-0.113$; with employment it is $-0.136$. (The negative correlation coefficient indicates a slight tendency for the distribution of state enterprise to be more skewed toward poorer regions than private activity.)

In any of the scatter diagrams shown, some systematic relationship might be obscured by the random location of a relatively few very large state enterprises in a few industries. A final test was to control for industrial composition, giving the distribution within each industry equal weight by fitting the following regression:

$$r_{i,j} - \sum_j r_{i,j} = \alpha_0 + \alpha_1 y_j + \epsilon_{i,j}$$

The dependent variable is the ratio of SOE activity to private activity in region *j* and industry *i* minus that ratio in industry *i* for the entire economy. There are 122 such observations at the three-digit level of industry aggregation. The right-hand side variable is, again, GDP per capita in region *j*. As noted, this gives the same sort of correlation as shown in Figures 12-3 and 12-4 except that the regional distribution of each industry

**Figure 12-1. Regional Distribution of SOE Value-Added vs. GDP per Capita.**

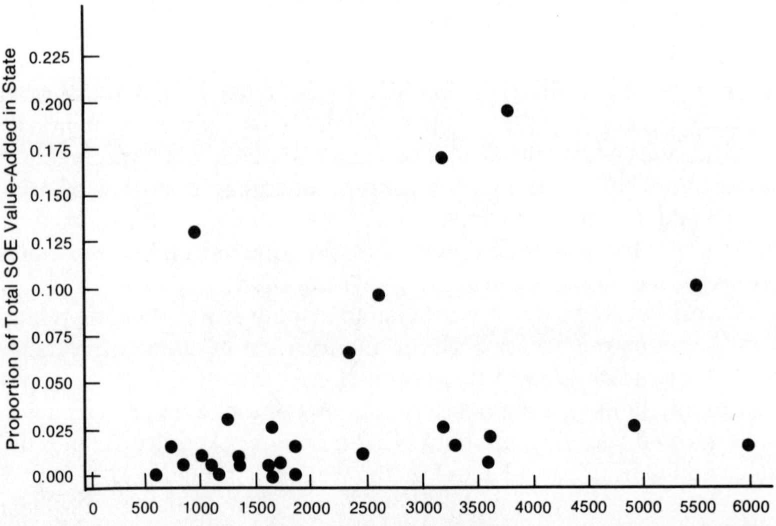


SOURCE: Table 12-10.

**Figure 12-2. Regional Distribution of SOE Wage Bill vs. GDP per Capita.**

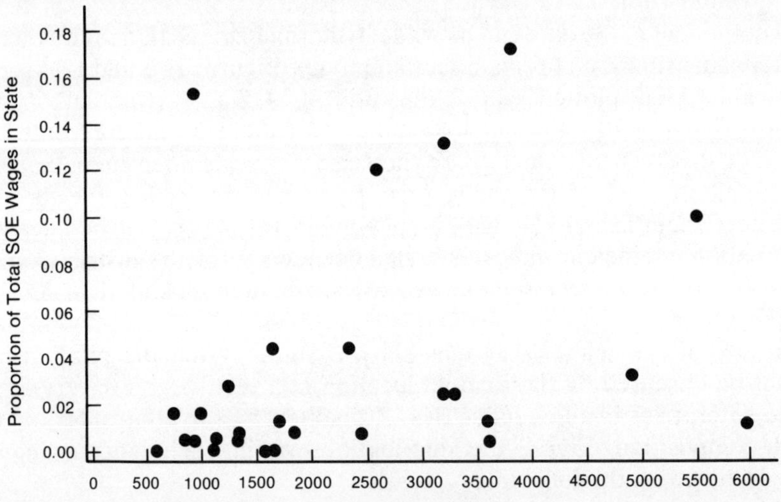


SOURCE: Table 12-10.

is equally weighted. Once more, no regional pattern is evident. By using either employment or value added as the measure of activity, the value of $\alpha_1$ is totally insignificant.[5]

### Summary

There are notable examples of the use of state ownership as part of regional policy and the decentralization of industry. In Mexico, as in

TABLE 12.10.
*Regional Distribution of State Enterprise and GDP Per Capita*

| | GDP Per Capita | Proportion of SOE Activity in State by: Value Added | Wage Bill | State |
|---|---|---|---|---|
| 1 | 589 | 0.000406 | 0.000257 | Tlaxcala |
| 2 | 764 | 0.013875 | 0.017018 | Oaxaca |
| 3 | 870 | 0.002765 | 0.003995 | Zacatecas |
| 4 | 937 | 0.001393 | 0.001965 | Quintana Roo |
| 5 | 949 | 0.132692 | 0.149856 | Hidalgo |
| 6 | 1007 | 0.011372 | 0.014738 | Michoacán |
| 7 | 1079 | 0.002726 | 0.001723 | Chiapas |
| 8 | 1146 | −0.000035 | 0.004586 | Guerrero |
| 9 | 1269 | 0.031500 | 0.026501 | San Luis Potosí |
| 10 | 1335 | 0.031202 | 0.046565 | Pueblo |
| 11 | 1343 | 0.008969 | 0.008914 | Guanajuato |
| 12 | 1469 | — | — | Querétaro |
| 13 | 1577 | 0.002813 | 0.001864 | Durango |
| 14 | 1634 | 0.000420 | 0.000379 | Morelos |
| 15 | 1652 | 0.001214 | 0.001558 | Yucatán |
| 16 | 1694 | 0.005313 | 0.011300 | Nayarit |
| 17 | 1819 | — | — | Aguascalientes |
| 18 | 1826 | 0.013656 | 0.008457 | Colima |
| 19 | 1842 | 0.001432 | 0.006296 | Tabasco |
| 20 | 2338 | 0.067462 | 0.042548 | Jalisco |
| 21 | 2465 | 0.008587 | 0.007839 | Chihuahua |
| 22 | 2618 | 0.093266 | 0.114947 | Veracruz |
| 23 | 2799 | — | — | Campeche |
| 24 | 3175 | 0.171382 | 0.129773 | México |
| 25 | 3188 | 0.024052 | 0.022577 | Tamaulipas |
| 26 | 3285 | 0.016492 | 0.024517 | Sinaloa |
| 27 | 3601 | 0.018249 | 0.013297 | Baja California Norte |
| 28 | 3615 | 0.003729 | 0.005716 | Baja California Sur |
| 29 | 3801 | 0.193207 | 0.191093 | Coahuila |
| 30 | 4910 | 0.026910 | 0.032532 | Sonora |
| 31 | 5508 | 0.101032 | 0.097498 | Distrito Federal |
| 32 | 5943 | 0.013920 | 0.011691 | Nuevo León |

SOURCE: *Censo Industrial,* 1976. GDP per capita, *Secretaría de Agricultura y Recursos Hidráulicos,* Mexico City, 1979, p. 83.

**Figure 12-3.**

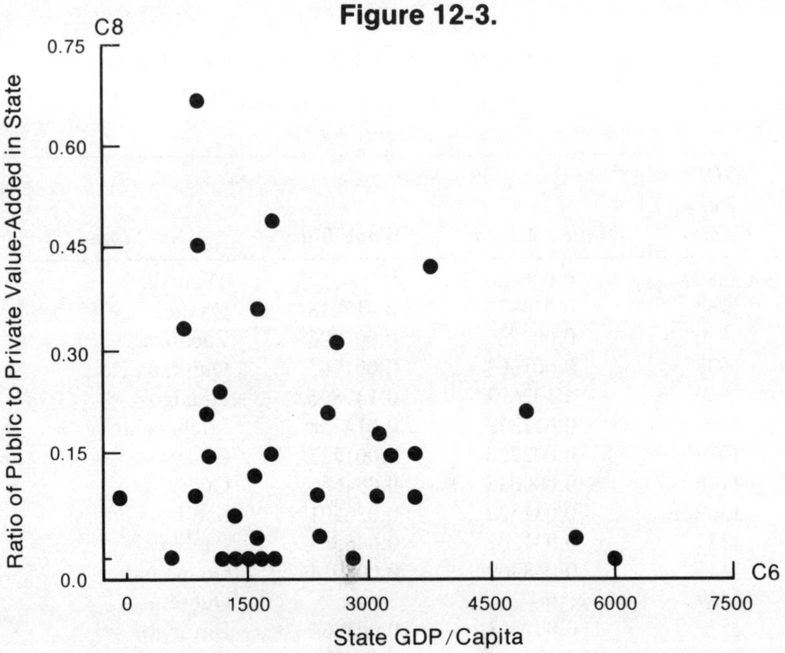


SOURCE: Table 12-10.

**Figure 12-4.**

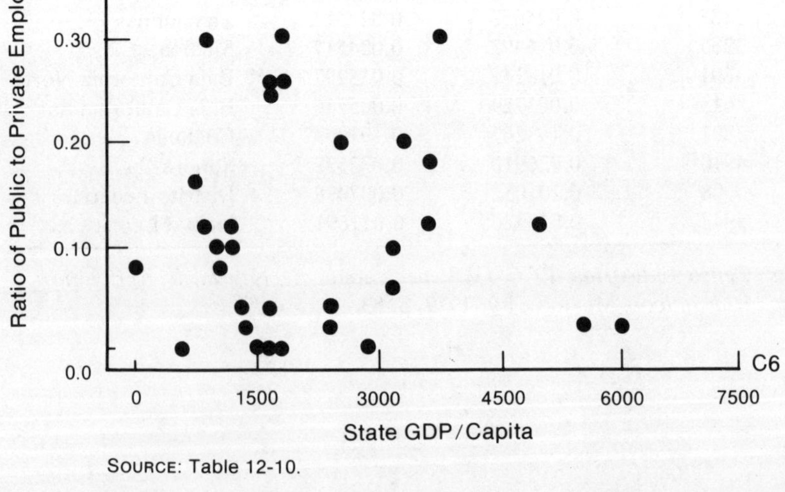


SOURCE: Table 12-10.

other countries, there is little quantitative evidence of the effect of policies which are intended to supply incentives for relocation (regional financing and electric power pricing, for example). With respect to the location of public enterprise, when we go beyond individual examples, the industrial census reveals little difference between public and private locational choice. A more detailed study of the success of regional policy is clearly possible. Of particular interest would be the consequences for the personal distribution of income of attempts to affect the regional distribution of industrial activity.

## IV. Relative Wages in the State Enterprises

In their study of Mexican state enterprises Villareal and Villareal asserted that "There is not a labor policy . . . unified to the non-public enterprise sector which makes public employees a privileged elite" (p. 7). The belief that state ownership leads to higher wages, relative to the private sector, is not unique to Mexico. I will not attempt to offer a complete theory of pressure on public sector wages. The general argument is that state ownership opens the enterprise to political pressure not to resist high wage demands. The firm's ability to take strikes, for example, may be impeded either by pressure from politicians on behalf of workers or on behalf of consumers if an argument can be made that the enterprise provides some "vital" public service.

In addition to the possibility that wages may be higher in public enterprises for workers of given skill and experience, one also encounters the argument that state enterprises are top-heavy in relatively highly paid managers.[6] In the analysis that follows we will be using an average of compensation per employee over all employees so that we shall not distinguish this potential effect of public ownership on wages. The industrial census, however, allows the calculation of the number of salaried to hourly workers for state relative to private firms. This simple statistic, calculated across two- and three-digit industries, reveals no pattern of top-heavy administration for state firms.

Whatever the cause of the "demand" for high wages, public enterprises are able to meet that demand in a way private firms cannot. They may have a monopoly in their sector, in which case labor appropriates some of the monopoly profits potentially available. In more competitive sectors, public firms are often released from the market constraint for an adequate—or even positive—return on capital. Subsidization of public enterprises will then amount, at least in part, to subsidization of wages of public sector employees.

### *The Problem of Measurement*

Documenting the effect of public ownership on wages is not easy. Often the only evidence available is observation of the collective bargaining

*TABLE 12.11.*
*Public and Private Compensation Per Worker*

| *Average Compensation Per Worker* | | | |
|---|---|---|---|
| *SOEs (1)* | *All Enterprises (2)* | *(1)/(2)* | *Industry No.*[a] |
| 39.517 | 38.6508 | 1.02242 | 11 |
| 60.056 | 51.7835 | 1.15975 | 13 |
| 105.739 | 87.1093 | 1.21387 | 14 |
| 43.244 | 12.0856 | 3.57810 | 15 |
| 55.243 | 34.2915 | 1.61098 | 20 |
| 35.739 | 35.3742 | 1.01032 | 21 |
| 44.954 | 57.9327 | 0.77597 | 22 |
| 58.534 | 45.7279 | 1.28005 | 23 |
| 70.545 | 31.2907 | 2.25451 | 24 |
| 35.696 | 28.2391 | 1.26407 | 26 |
| 15.753 | 15.7594 | 0.99960 | 27 |
| 76.886 | 62.6097 | 1.22802 | 28 |
| 59.028 | 53.1890 | 1.10977 | 29 |
| 60.083 | 47.6048 | 1.26213 | 33 |
| 78.940 | 72.1912 | 1.09349 | 34 |
| 55.363 | 46.8007 | 1.13296 | 35 |
| 52.937 | 52.5720 | 1.00694 | 36 |
| 71.070 | 60.4832 | 1.17504 | 37 |
| 78.787 | 65.8394 | 1.19666 | 38 |
| 59.629 | 49.1396 | 1.21345 | 39 |

SOURCE: *Censo Industrial*, 1976.

[a] See Table 12-5

result which follows a shift from public to private ownership. A straightforward comparison of compensation per employee leaves no doubt that wages are higher in state enterprise. Table 12-11 gives the ratio of public to total compensation per employee for each of the two-digit industries in the 1975 census. In seventeen of the nineteen industries the ratio is greater than unity. The same ratio was also calculated at the three-digit level by region to control for the possibility that SOEs are located in high-wage regions. On average SOE compensation was 36 percent higher than compensation for all firms. However, these simple comparisons of wage levels are clearly biased in favor of the hypothesis that public ownership causes higher wages, since (as we have seen) public sector firms tend to be larger and more capital intensive. Both these attributes could be correlated with high wages in the absence of state ownership.

To see why, we need to dwell for a moment on the theory of wage determination. One view is that wages are largely determined *institutionally*. That is, in an imperfect, segmented labor market characteristics of firms which affect their bargaining power vis-à-vis workers will determine interindustry wage differentials. For example, firms with monopoly power have more latitude to meet wage demands than firms in a competitive industry. As a result, an index of monopolization such as industry concentration should be associated with high wages. Also, firms with a low labor share in value added should be in a better position to pass on wage increases since they represent a smaller share of costs. If we fail to control for these institutional variables, then we attribute too much influence to public ownership. As an example, labor seems to have been in a very strong position in the electric power industry before nationalization for reasons that are related to the industry's structure (see Wionczek, pp. 84 and 102).

This suggests that we could fit a regression of wages by industry on concentration and labor share of value added and then add, as an explanatory variable, the proportion of state enterprise in the industry. A positive coefficient on the proportion of state enterprise would be evidence that state ownership leads to higher wages.

Unfortunately, such a test would be incomplete. We also expect wages to be determined by the human capital of employees—the skill and experience they bring to their job. Moreover, since the SOEs are relatively large and capital intensive, they may well hire workers with greater skill and experience. As a result, a variable measuring state participation in the industry would pick up these skill effects as well. Since we have no data on the skill levels of workers in public versus private firms, we must be cautious in interpreting the results of any statistical test. If, after allowing for institutional variables, the proportion of the industry controlled by public enterprise is *not* associated with higher wages (after allowing for institutional variables), then we can conclude that public ownership has no significant effect on wages. A positive conclusion is more problematical. We can add size and capital intensity as proxy variables to reflect any difference in average skill levels between private and public firms. The danger here is that if SOEs do pay higher wages for reasons unrelated to skill, higher capital intensity is a rational response by management to economize on high-priced labor. Hence, if the hypothesis of a positive effect of state ownership is true, *too much* influence will be attributed to size and capital intensity and too little to state ownership per se.

## *Econometric Results*

With these warnings in mind, we now refer to Table 12-12, which presents several specifications of a regression explaining compensation per employee across eighty three-digit industries. In all cases the proportion of industry employment accounted for by SOEs is significant at the 1 percent level of significance. The size of the SOE share coefficient is also

TABLE 12.12.
*Regression Results: Compensation Per Employee Across Three-Digit Industries*

| | Constant | Share of SOEs in Total Employment | Ratio of Hourly to Salaried Workers | Average Firm Size (Assets) | Labor Share of Value Added | Capital-Labor Ratio | $R^2$ |
|---|---|---|---|---|---|---|---|
| 1 | 44.9 | 26.3 | | | | | 0.08 |
| | (21.5) | (2.56) | | | | | |
| 2 | 69.6 | 28.4 | −5.85 | | | | 0.48 |
| | (19.6) | (3.67) | (7.78) | | | | |
| 3 | 65.3 | 23.0 | −5.33 | 0.199 | | | 0.59 |
| | (19.6) | (3.25) | (7.77) | (4.38) | | | |
| 4 | 61.6 | 21.5 | −5.53 | 0.212 | 10.2 | | 0.59 |
| | (11.4) | (2.95) | (7.61) | (4.43) | (0.87) | | |
| 5 | 59.6 | 20.3 | −4.80 | 0.075 | | 46.4 | 0.63 |
| | (16.0) | (2.98) | (7.09) | (1.25) | | (2.93) | |
| Mean of independent variables | | 0.095 | 4.26 | 12.9 | 0.45 | 0.11 | |

Mean of compensation per employee = 47.4 (thousand pesos)
Number of observations = 80

relatively large. Although the linear specification of the regressions is likely to be a crude approximation of the "true" functional relationship, the coefficient implies that wages in an industry rise about 4 percent for each ten-percentage-point increase in SOE share (evaluated at the mean wage and with the lowest estimated coefficient of SOE share).

The ratio of hourly to salaried workers is included to measure intraindustry differences in the average educational or skill mix of workers. This variable is negatively correlated with size and capital intensity and positively correlated with labor's share of value added.[7] Firm size and labor's share of value added are included as institutional explanations of relative wages. The latter variable is significant only when the ratio of hourly to salaried workers is omitted. Capital intensity is included as a proxy for relative skill level on the assumption that firms with high capital intensity hire relatively skilled workers. Size and capital intensity are, as one might expect, highly correlated. Including either variable reduces the coefficient of the SOE share variable, although it remains statistically significant.

What can we conclude from these regressions? The collinearity among the independent variables and the absence of a direct measure of average skill by industry prevents us from using the results to sort out successfully the institutional versus human capital explanations for wage determination. However, the robustness of the SOE share coefficient across various specifications supplies strong evidence that state ownership has a positive effect on relative wages. The significantly positive relationship persists when we allow for the fact SOEs are systemically different from the average industrial enterprise. Since some characteristics of SOEs (capital intensity and the ratio of hourly to salaried workers) will reflect *adjustments to* rather than *competing explanations* of higher wages, the results are all the more compelling.

In conclusion, that state enterprises pay higher wages, on average, than other firms in the industrial sector is unambiguous. To some extent this result is explained by characteristics of SOEs which imply that they would pay higher wages even if they were under private ownership. However, even after attempting to control for these characteristics, public ownership, per se, appears to have a positive influence on relative wages. Note that this evidence is entirely drawn from the industrial sector where SOEs are not typically in the position of state monopolies. This implies that higher wages are, relatively speaking, less a function of a protected monopoly position and more a function of state subsidies. In Section V we shall see that state subsidies to SOEs in the industrial sector are, in fact, significant.

## V. Subsidies and Output Prices: General Considerations

One direct channel through which SOEs can affect income distribution is the pricing of output. There are a number of pricing policies which give rise to redistributive effects, including subsidized output prices, efficient pricing rules, and perturbation of equilibrium in oligopolistic markets. The quantitative work in Section VI looks only at the first of these policies, but here I discuss each in general terms.

### *Implicit or Explicit Subsidies*

There are at least two enterprices for which the state has given formal, articulated pricing policies, PEMEX and CONASUPO. For PEMEX the pricing policy involves subsidization—relative to world prices—of output financed by the rents from oil production. For CONASUPO subsidies to output prices must be financed by subsidies from the federal government.

Subsidies to state enterprise are hardly limited to CONASUPO, however. Table 12-13 gives the revenues and operating profits for budgetary controlled enterprises by sector for the period 1970–1977. In this chapter I will assume that these other federal subsidies lower final output prices in a number of sectors where there is no articulated pricing policy. To argue that operating subsidies produce subsidies to output prices, one must

*TABLE 12.13.*
*Revenues (r)[a] and Operating Profit (p)[b] for State Enterprises*

| | 1970 | 1971 | 1972 | 1973 | 1974 | 1975 | 1976 | 1977 |
|---|---|---|---|---|---|---|---|---|
| Electricity | | | | | | | | |
| *r* | — | 6,505 | 6,957 | 7,748 | 8,941 | 11,878 | 14,001 | 18,673 |
| *p* | −1,859 | 932 | 523 | 304 | −802 | −3,233 | −2,435 | −1,783 |
| Railways | | | | | | | | |
| *r* | — | 2,625 | 2,825 | 3,159 | 3,823 | 5,486 | 5,406 | 7,934 |
| *p* | −770 | −486 | −1,226 | −1,598 | −2,681 | −2,310 | −3,661 | −4,898 |
| Communications and transportation | | | | | | | | |
| *r* | — | 1,661 | 1,916 | 2,280 | 2,710 | 3,592 | 4,324 | 5,944 |
| *p* | 461 | 401 | 502 | 628 | 310 | 378 | 552 | 1,078 |
| Industry | | | | | | | | |
| *r* | — | — | — | 4,538 | 5,811 | 9,108 | 10,636 | 14,688 |
| *p* | — | — | — | −408 | −1,402 | 652 | −1,677 | −3,136 |
| Agriculture | | | | | | | | |
| *r* | — | — | 1 | 1,731 | 1,787 | 2,613 | 2,876 | 4,066 |
| *p* | −7 | −10 | −6 | −155 | −166 | −376 | −1,069 | −439 |
| Commerce | | | | | | | | |
| *r* | — | 3,014 | 3,548 | 5,654 | 9,998 | 11,541 | 16,169 | 22,950 |
| *p* | −562 | −666 | −660 | −1,949 | −5,871 | −9,055 | −2,921 | −7,850 |
| PEMEX | | | | | | | | |
| *r* | — | 14,599 | 15,762 | 18,133 | 30,228 | 36,331 | 45,518 | 68,714 |
| *p* | 3,092 | 3,841 | 1,531 | 2,787 | 6,611 | 5,529 | 14,240 | 17,620 |
| Total[c] | | | | | | | | |
| *r* | — | 40,997 | 45,990 | 63,208 | 92,476 | 116,834 | 147,189 | 205,907 |
| *p* | 3,261 | 2,999 | 8 | −735 | −6,112 | −8,340 | 3,471 | −3,224 |

SOURCE: "Tercer Informe de Gobierno," *Annex* I (1979).
[a] Sales of goods and services.
[b] Operating profit for state enterprises (AHORRO).
[c] Total includes categories not represented in table (airlines, for example).

specify the counterfactual: What would prices have been in the absence of subsidies?

For example, SOEs in the textile industry have approximately 10 percent of sales in that market. With such a small market share it is highly unlikely that a subsidy affects prices significantly. If SOEs in that sector have operating deficits funded by the central government, our working assumption must be that they have higher costs than their competitors, either through outright inefficiency or through a more expensive wage bill, as discussed earlier. In the absence of subsidies these firms would either find ways to lower costs or go out of business.

On the other hand, for SOEs which dominate their market, one can reasonably suppose that subsidies do affect the price of output. The major uncertainty surrounding that conclusion is how such firms would behave in the absence of subsidies. It is always possible that recourse to state

*TABLE 12.14.*
*Subsidies by Sector as a Percent of Sales*

| | Estimated Capital Stock (1977)[a] (1) | Effective Subsidy as a % of Sales | |
|---|---|---|---|
| | | Without Return to Capital[b] (2) | With Return to Capital[c] (3) |
| Electricity | 10,073 | −25.5 | 37.6 |
| Railways | 21,865 | 45.2 | 85.7 |
| Communications and Transportation | 7,216 | −30.2 | −13.5 |
| Industry | 21,131 | 4.6 | 24.5 |
| Agriculture | 3,240 | 12.7 | 24.0 |
| Commerce | 9,198 | 34.6 | 40.3 |

SOURCE: "Tercer Informe de Gobierno," *Annex* I (1979).

[a]The capital stock is calculated by summing annual investment (in 1977 prices), assuming 10 percent depreciation per year. The annual investment series begins in 1970 for all sectors except industry, where it begins in 1973.

[b]Operating profit plus interest payments.

[c]Column (2) plus a 10 percent return on capital as a percent of sales.

funding is a *cause* of higher costs. In that case subsidies either support inefficiency or flow into wages. In practice, subsidies will probably affect both prices and costs. This means that the following estimates represent the maximum impact on price from state-funded deficits.

If one assumes a one-for-one pass-through of subsidies into prices in sectors dominated by state firms, how big are the numbers? The operating deficits given in Table 12-13 understate the size of the implicit subsidy since they ignore a return to capital. In Table 12-14 I have calculated the average percentage subsidy of output prices by (1) computing the average 1970–1977 deficit from Table 12-13, (2) adding a minimal return to an estimated capital stock, and (3) dividing that sum by average revenue. By using this measure, only in the communications and transportation sectors were there positive economic profits. The effect of including a minimal return to capital has the most dramatic effect, of course, in the most capital-intensive sectors. For electricity, the 25.5 percent profit margin on sales becomes a 37.6 percent subsidy when the return to capital is taken into account.

## *Partial and General Analysis*

To account precisely for the effect of subsidies on income distribution would require a full-blown general equilibrium model of the Mexican economy. Short of such a model there are several levels of partial analysis that provide successively better approximations to the effect of subsidies.

A first-level approximation can be derived from the relationship between income and final consumption of the subsidized goods. This requires only an estimate of the size of the subsidies and the relationship between consumption of the goods in question and income. At a second level, some subsidized output represents intermediate production which will be used as inputs into other goods. To estimate these indirect effects, we require an input-output matrix and the budgets of households by income decile. One other indirect effect may be of interest. If downstream industries which buy subsidized inputs are not competitive, then the possibility exists that the incidence of subsidies will be on profits as well as output prices. To the extent that subsidies appear downstream only in variable (as opposed to fixed) costs, standard models of monopoly or oligopoly would predict no incidence on profit margins. Most SOE intermediate production does seem to fall into the category of variable inputs for downstream users. Since prices will be lower, however, demand for these goods rises, and total profits increase on the larger volume of sales.

In this chapter, I examine only the first-level effects of subsidies on total consumption. The 1970 input-output matrix and the household survey provide the means of estimating the next level of indirect effects as well. Estimating the profits-price incidence is more problematical since it requires a systematic classification of market structure and elasticities of demand. Nevertheless, estimating the flow of subsidies into profits may well be tractable and worthwhile for a few specific industries. Concentrated industries which use subsidized energy intensively are obvious candidates for further investigation. Soft drink bottlers benefit from highly subsidized sugar prices and operate in a concentrated market as well. They also represent an industry where profits are likely to absorb a significant part of price subsidies.

## *Other Pricing Policies*

It is worth noting two other forms of pricing policy with potential effects on distribution.

An important strand of the literature on developed-country, state-owned or regulated enterprise deals with the variation of markups (above cost) over the differentiated output of the firm.[8] This variation has typically been studied as a problem of finding the optimal pattern of (positive and negative) markups subject to the condition that the firm break even. The consequences of such pricing policies have so far received very little attention.[9] This lack of attention has probably been a consequence, in part, of the lack of information about the relative incomes of consumers. Although such policies are not analyzed in this chapter, the household survey may provide a useful data base for such investigations.

Another pricing policy which lies beyond the scope of this chapter is the use of state enterprise to promote competitive pricing in oligopolistic industries. Schneider (1967) suggests that an important role of state-owned steel firms in Mexico has been to keep output levels in the industry higher than they would otherwise have been. Since this industry consists of a relatively few firms, he concludes that this policy has had the effect of eliminating oligopolistic profits and lowering prices.

## VI. Subsidies for Final Consumption

A first cut as measuring the effects of pricing policy is to examine the relationship between income and several classes of SOE output which go directly into final consumption. We look first at hydrocarbon fuels and electricity and later at expenditures at CONASUPO stores. These classes of consumption are chosen because subsidization is unambiguous and is virtually certain to be reflected in output prices.

### *Energy*

Figures 12-5 through 12-7 plot the semiannual expenditure of each decile on electricity, a combination of hydrocarbon fuels,[10] and gasoline, respectively. Since for most goods ("normal" goods in the theory of consumer behavior) consumption increases with income, a subsidy to final consumption will necessarily provide a larger peso benefit to the rich than the poor. Energy consumption is no exception. To have a comparative measure of the progressivity of these subsidies, the figures chart the incidence of taxes by decile alongside consumption. The left-hand bar for each decile gives a measure of the relative incidence of direct taxes for that decile.[11] The right-hand bar gives the same measure for total taxes (the sum of direct and indirect).

One interpretation of these figures is that they give the net redistribution for each decile under the assumption that subsidies are "paid for" at the margin in proportion to the percentage of total taxes paid by each decile (i.e., if the tenth decile pays $x$ percent of total taxes, it would pay $x$ percent of any subsidy as well). Thus a tax bar higher than a consumption bar implies a net loss for that decile. This method of presentation is illustrative only, of course, since we have no theory of how subsidies are actually paid for at the margin.

The consumption pattern for gasoline differs dramatically from those for household energy. Consumption for electricity and home heating fuels rises steadily through the seventh decile, where it peaks. Thus consumption (and the incidence of subsidies) for the top three deciles rises much more slowly than the incidence of taxes. Our simple assumption that subsidies are paid in proportion to average tax incidence implies that redistribution is from the tenth decile to the first eight, with the largest absolute amounts of redistribution going to middle-income households.

For gasoline, however, both the first and second derivatives of con-

Figure 12-5. Electricity Consumption and Tax Incidence.

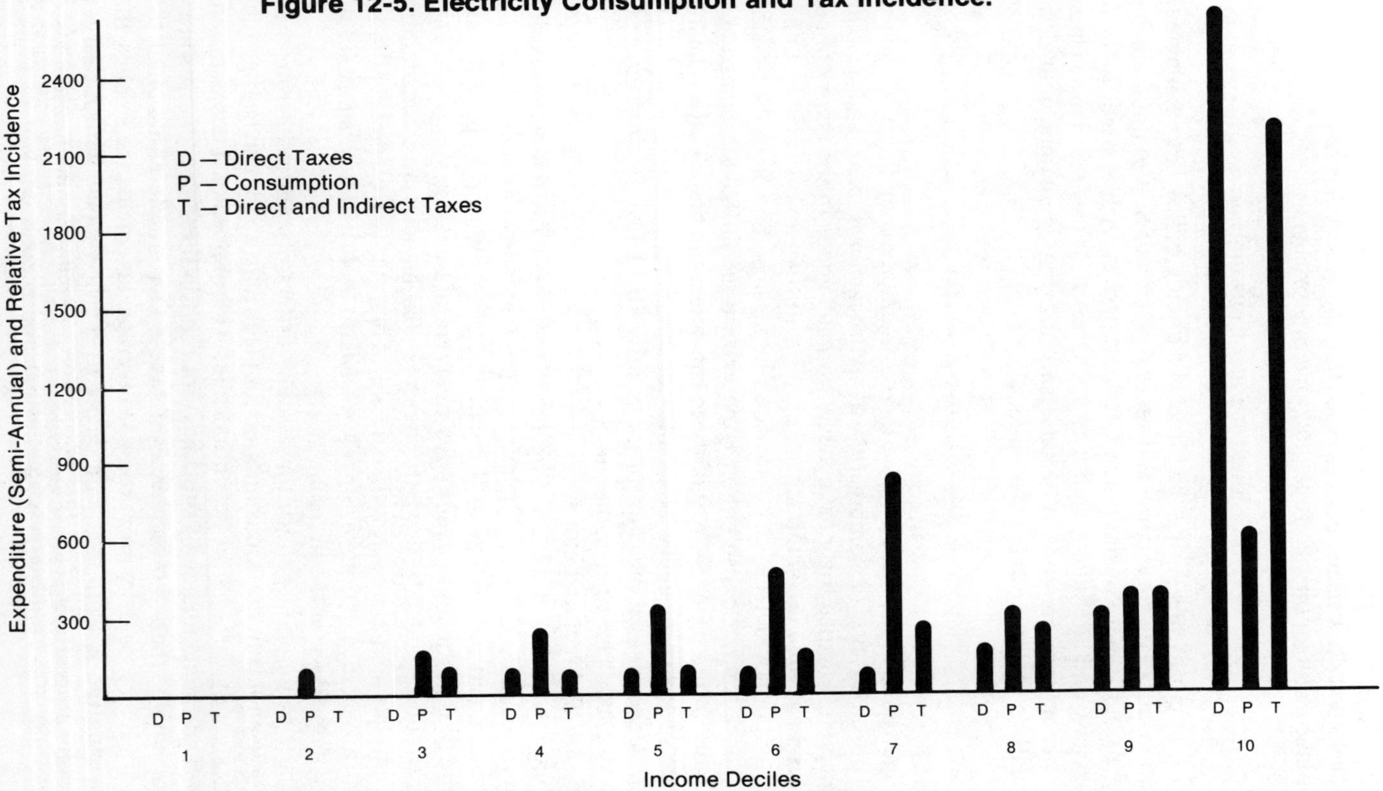


SOURCE: Consumption: household expenditure survey. Taxes: Chapter 4.

**Figure 12-6. Home Heating Fuel Consumption and Tax Incidence.**

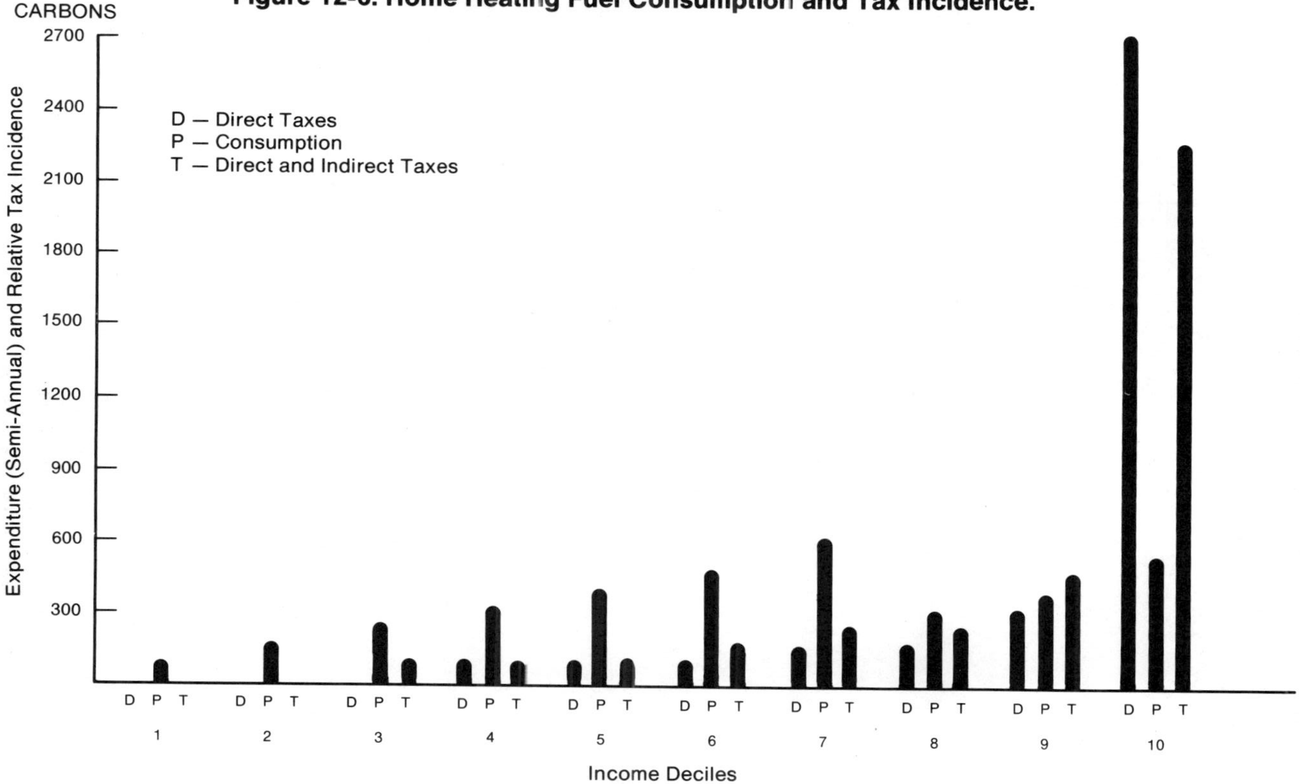


SOURCE: Consumption: household expenditure survey. Taxes: Chapter 4.

Figure 12-7. Gasoline Consumption and Tax Incidence.

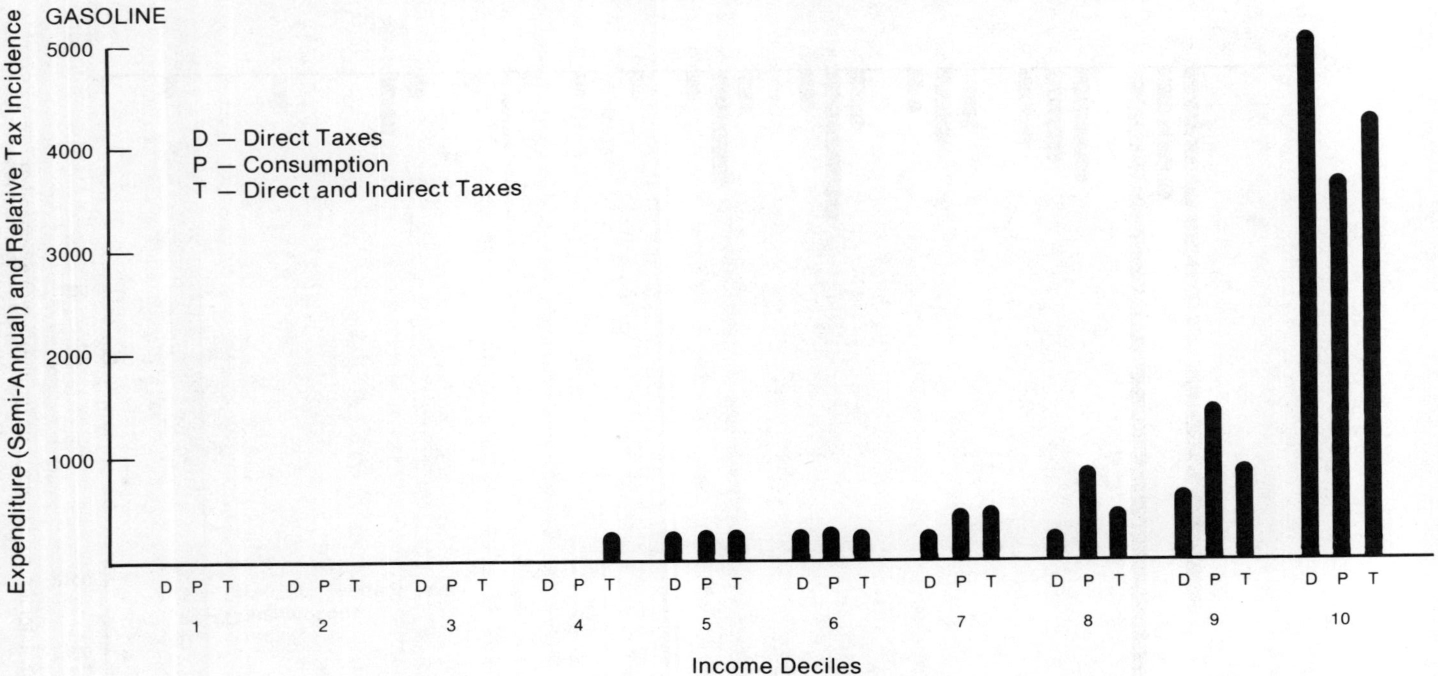


SOURCE: Consumption: household expenditure survey. Taxes: Chapter 4.

sumption with respect to income are positive. Tax incidence is still greater than the incidence of subsidies for the tenth decile, while the eight and ninth deciles enjoy virtually all the redistribution from the tenth. Since gasoline consumption is nil for the first four deciles, redistribution away from these households is implied by the tax incidence comparison. Moreover, total gasoline consumption for all deciles is approximately equal to total expenditure on the two other forms of energy. Thus, the weight of gasoline will ensure that subsidies to total energy consumption are significantly more progressive than expenditures on electricity or home heating fuels would suggest.

Subsidies to energy may be less progressive if one takes into account the possibility that they allow lower prices to be charged for public transportation, where fuel could be a significant part of total cost and low-income families may be relatively heavy users. Figure 12-8 plots the consumption of the (intracity) public transportation, taxi, and intercity bus and train categories of the expenditure survey by income decile. Clearly, the pattern is much more like home heating fuels than gasoline. Quantitatively, however, energy subsidies passing through public transportation consumption are much less important than the categories already discussed.[12]

## *CONASUPO*

CONASUPO is a state enterprise established to raise and stabilize income in the rural areas through purchases of agricultural products and to provide subsidized retail outlets for the sale of basic goods to low-income consumers. CONASUPO purchases totaled 26.0 billion pesos in 1978, of which 14.1 billion were imports; grain accounted for about 70 percent of purchases with the remainder in beans (frijol), soy products, and dairy products.

CONASUPO attempts to stabilize and raise agricultural income through a system of price guarantees and warehouses. The warehouses are intended to be located in low-income rural areas so that farmers can sell directly to CONASUPO and bypass monopsonistic middlemen. Their success in this role has been analyzed at length by Gil (1978) and Grindle (1977). Both authors suggest that politics rather than economic need has played a large role in the location of CONASUPO warehouses and that in some areas the outlets have become part of the system of local "bosses" *(caciques)*. As a result both authors are skeptical of the redistributive effect of CONASUPO on agricultural income.

As a retailer of basic commodities, CONASUPO has claimed an average subsidy on the goods it sells of 15 percent below the prices of private retailers. Gil reports the results of several surveys of CONASUPO prices in which the average subsidy was estimated to be anywhere from about 4 percent to about 22 percent. (The high end of the range is from a survey

**Figure 12-8. Public Transportation Consumption and Tax Incidence.**

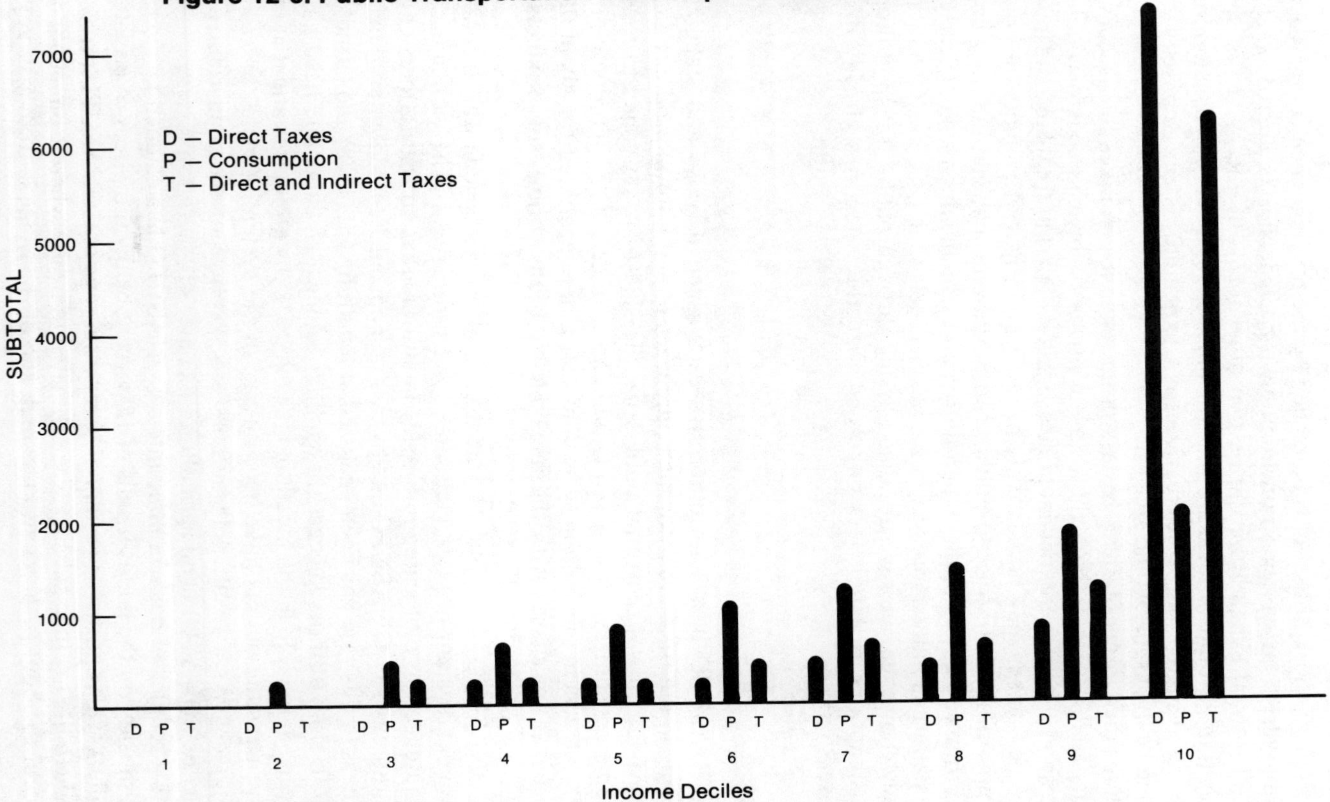


SOURCE: Consumption: household expenditure survey. Taxes: Chapter 4.

conducted by CONASUPO itself.) He also attempted to evaluate their effectiveness in redistribution by analyzing the locational pattern of the stores in the Mexico City urban area. He found a close relationship between the density of private food stores and CONASUPO outlets. Also, he was unable to find a systematic relationship across Mexico City neighborhoods between the density of CONASUPO relative to private stores and the percentage of the population at the bottom of the income distribution (measured by those earning less than 1000 or 2500 pesos per month). He concluded, as a result, that CONASUPO's customers were not significantly different from customers of private retailers.

The household expenditure survey provides us with more precise information concerning the relationship between CONASUPO purchases and income. Figures 12-9 and 12-10 are the bar charts of expenditures at CONASUPO by decile. The derivation of these charts is not quite as straightforward as for the earlier figures, however. The household expenditure survey includes a set of questions about the type of establishment in which each of a list of goods was purchased. The respondent could give three "typical" locations for each good. Figures 12-9 and 12-10 plot the mean family expenditure on each of these goods for families who typically bought those goods at CONASUPO. The numbers are subject to error to the extent that families who typically shop at CONASUPO also buy elsewhere and families who typically shop elsewhere occasionally buy at CONASUPO. To have some idea about the seriousness of this kind of error, the computations are first done only when CONASUPO was the first choice of location (Figure 12-9) and then when CONASUPO was any of the three choices (Figure 12-10).

Table 12-15 gives some of the data used to construct the bar charts. For each category of goods the top part of the table is the total weekly expenditure[13] of those families reporting CONASUPO as any of their three typical shopping places for the good divided by the number of families in the decile. This is our measure of mean family expenditure on each good for each decile. The bottom part gives the number of families who named CONASUPO as one of the three shopping places. The last two columns refer to total expenditures. In the top of the table total B is simply the sum of the preceding individual columns. Total A is a similar sum calculated only from those families who reported CONASUPO as their *first* choice. In the bottom the totals are, respectively, the number of families who reported CONASUPO as one of three or the first choice of location for any purchase at all.

Thus we have a proxy for expenditure at CONASUPO and actual figures on frequency of shopping by decile.[14] Mean expenditure for those families that frequent CONASUPO increases with income. Thus when we compound the frequency of shopping with expenditure data in Figures 12-11 and 12-12, the average incidence of CONASUPO usage is shifted even higher in the income distribution.

Figure 12-9. Consumption of CONASUPO Goods (first choice) by Decile.

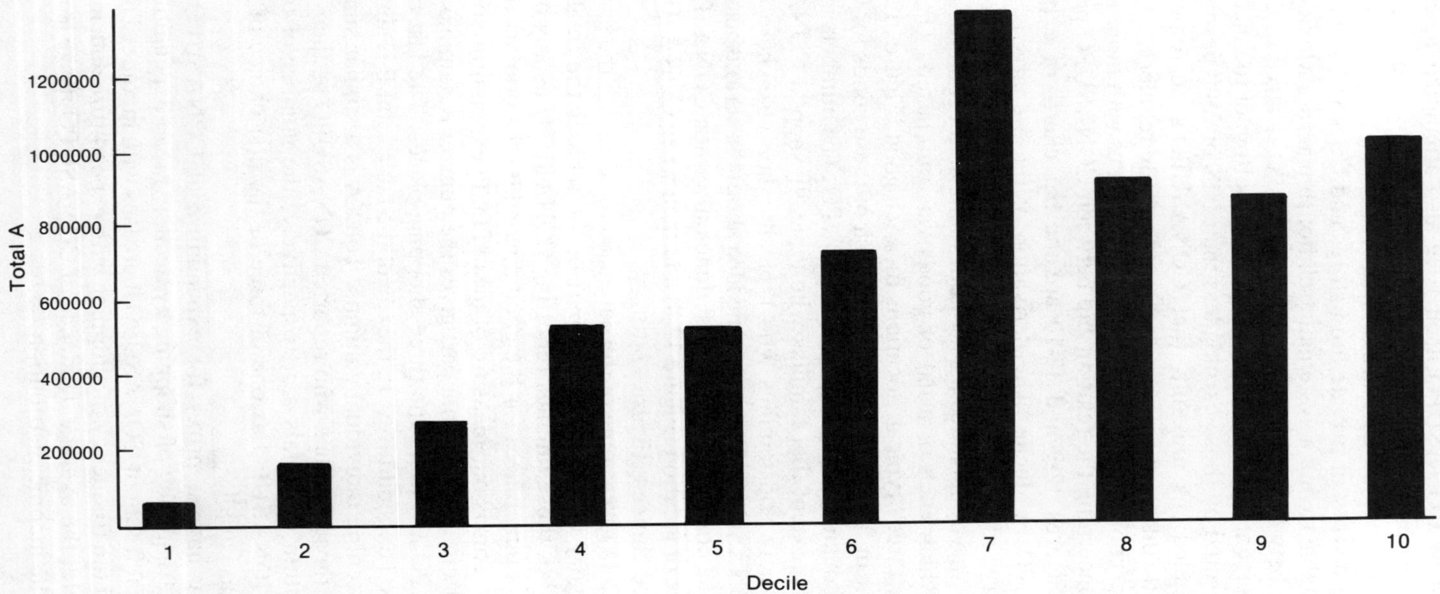


SOURCE: Table 12-15.

**Figure 12-10. Consumption of CONASUPO Goods (any choice) by Decile.**

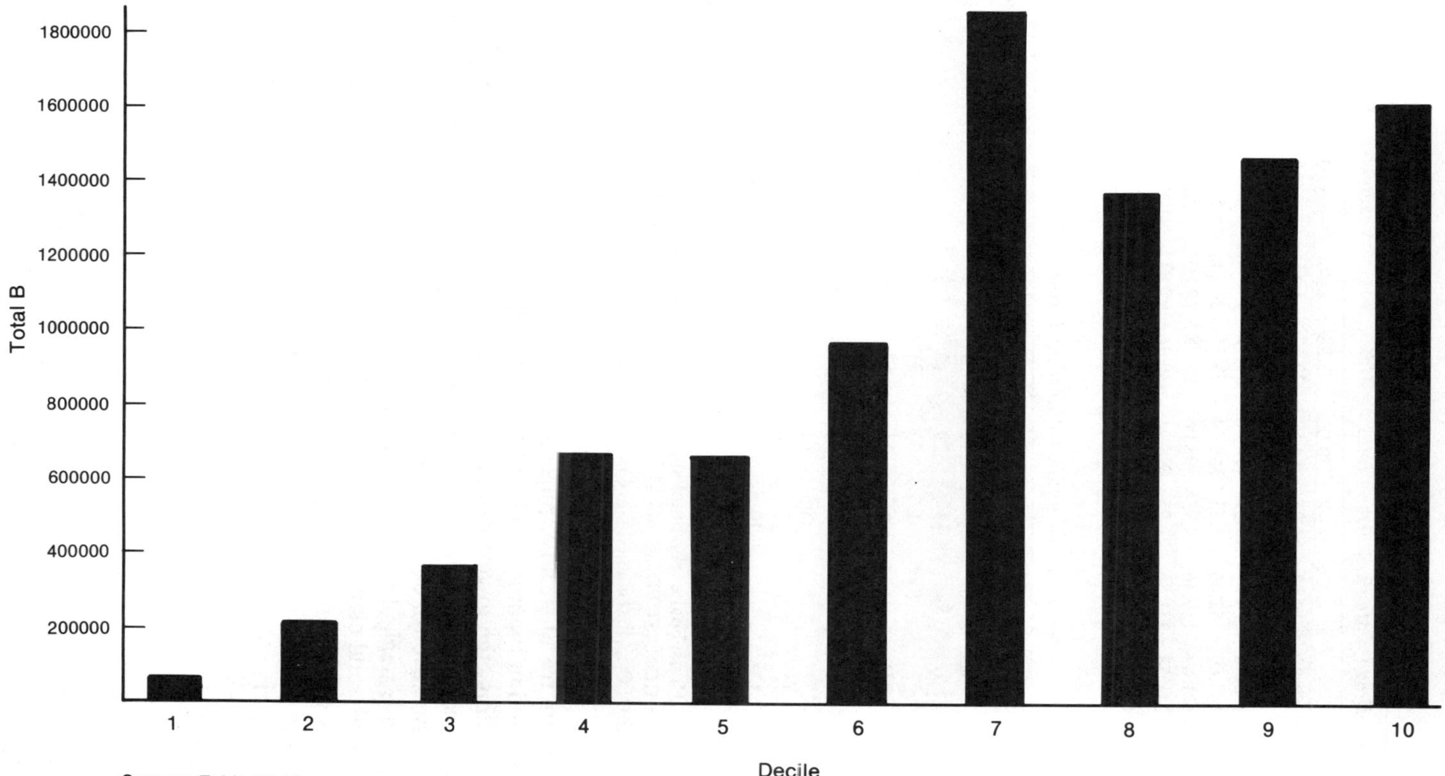


SOURCE: Table 12-15.

*TABLE 12.15.*
*Mean Expenditure Per Family*

| Decile | Bread | Meats | Fish | Eggs | Milk | Fruit | Vegetables | Total A | Total B |
|---|---|---|---|---|---|---|---|---|---|
| I | — | — | — | 20.06 | 5.88 | 1.86 | 6.50 | 32.83 | 34.30 |
| II | 50.98 | 12.03 | 4.25 | 64.53 | 20.57 | 1.11 | 4.64 | 127.38 | 158.11 |
| III | 53.90 | 43.04 | 2.56 | 100.90 | 37.17 | 15.70 | 26.94 | 219.27 | 280.22 |
| IV | 138.43 | 70.39 | 14.37 | 190.86 | 79.72 | 23.77 | 45.53 | 434.92 | 563.07 |
| V | 105.69 | 52.06 | 3.73 | 258.34 | 73.75 | 34.11 | 54.42 | 456.66 | 582.10 |
| VI | 121.47 | 119.36 | 4.73 | 394.06 | 95.88 | 19.60 | 52.02 | 605.13 | 807.12 |
| VII | 241.58 | 351.85 | 21.25 | 628.21 | 130.36 | 97.97 | 108.60 | 1172.91 | 1579.81 |
| VIII | 116.46 | 266.02 | 22.92 | 487.59 | 142.20 | 48.47 | 78.16 | 798.79 | 1161.82 |
| IX | 136.93 | 246.78 | 36.76 | 622.11 | 144.35 | 40.17 | 39.94 | 748.82 | 1267.03 |

*Number of Families Who Purchased at CONASUPO*

| Decile | Bread | Meats | Fish | Eggs | Milk | Fruit | Vegetables | Total A | Total B |
|---|---|---|---|---|---|---|---|---|---|
| I | 0 | 0 | 0 | 12 | 5 | 2 | 3 | 16 | 19 |
| II | 7 | 4 | 3 | 29 | 10 | 2 | 4 | 41 | 53 |
| III | 7 | 8 | 1 | 35 | 23 | 9 | 9 | 48 | 68 |
| IV | 12 | 11 | 5 | 51 | 37 | 18 | 13 | 67 | 93 |
| V | 14 | 9 | 2 | 77 | 33 | 11 | 12 | 98 | 120 |
| VI | 14 | 17 | 3 | 84 | 45 | 13 | 12 | 103 | 121 |
| VII | 22 | 28 | 8 | 101 | 50 | 29 | 26 | 124 | 153 |
| VIII | 12 | 24 | 7 | 74 | 55 | 17 | 18 | 100 | 130 |
| IX | 13 | 14 | 10 | 71 | 48 | 13 | 10 | 89 | 126 |
| X | 10 | 15 | 5 | 58 | 31 | 10 | 10 | 70 | 98 |

SOURCE: Household expenditure survey, 1977. Figures for individual goods and total B are based on CONASUPO as any of three typical places of purchase. Total A is based on CONASUPO as first-named place of purchase.

Again for illustrative purposes, the CONASUPO expenditure data are repeated in Figures 12-11 and 12-12, bracketed by tax incidence. Because of scaling, the lowest deciles simply disappear from the graph. The economic interpretation of this disappearance is that, in absolute terms, below the seventh decile CONASUPO subsidies decline with income until they are negligible for the lowest deciles. In absolute terms the sixth, seventh, and eighth deciles are the largest recipients of net transfers.

It is worth emphasizing that the expenditure figures may well overstate the receipt of subsidies for the higher deciles. As noted, expenditures were estimated from data on frequency of shopping at CONASUPO and separate data on expenditures in all types of shops. Even so, the frequency data alone support the conclusion that most redistribution ignores the lowest deciles.

**Figure 12-11. CONASUPO Consumption (first choice) and Tax Incidence.**

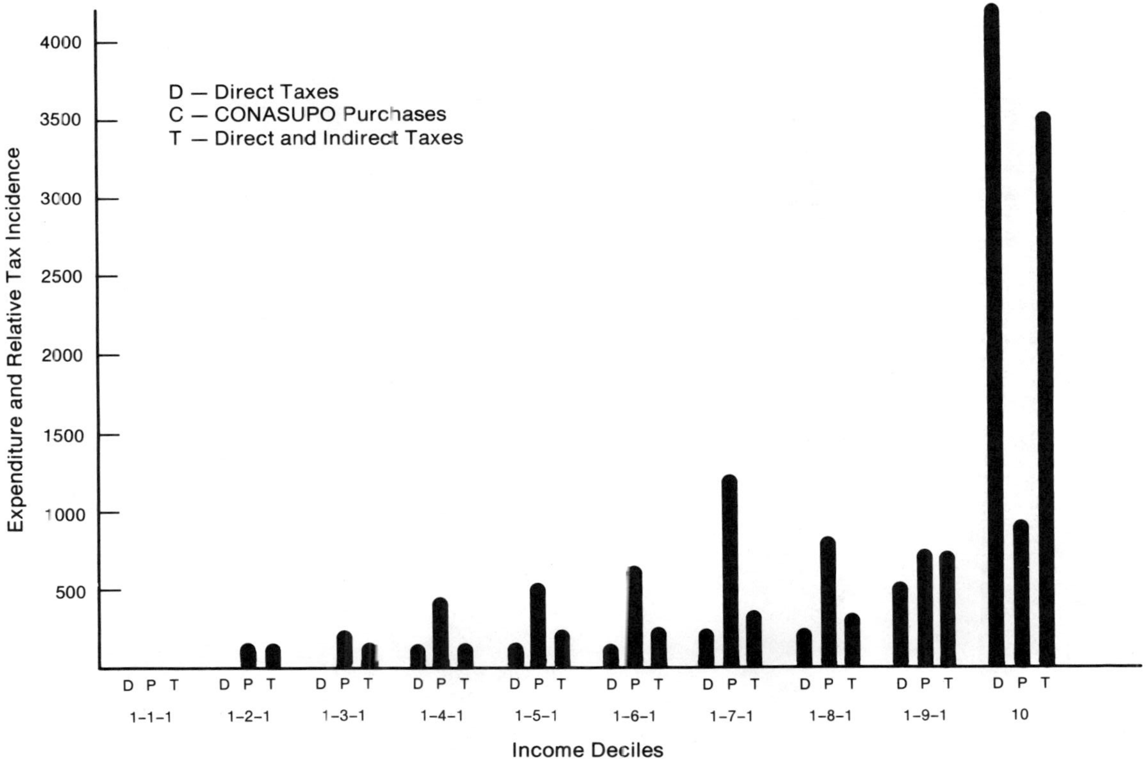


SOURCE: Consumption: Table 12-15. Taxes: Chapter 4.

Figure 12-12. CONASUPO Consumption (any choice) and Tax Incidence.

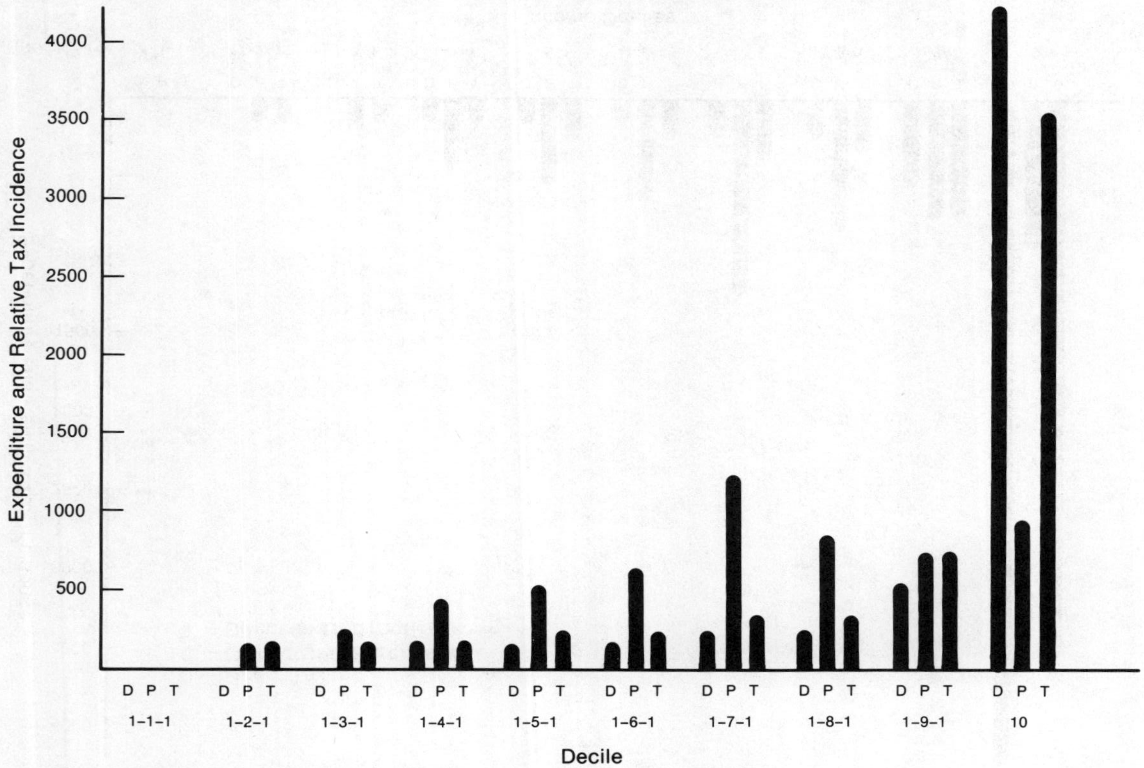


SOURCE: Consumption: Table 12-15. Taxes: Chapter 4.

## VII. Conclusions

State-owned productive enterprises account for about 8 percent of value added in Mexico and a relatively large share of national investment (about 18 percent in 1976, for example). The state holds a monopoly position in traditional sectors such as railroads and electricity but also owns all or part of firms spread throughout the industrial sector. This chapter is an attempt to find empirically significant effects of state ownership on income distribution. In that attempt we examined three dimensions along which public ownership could be a tool (or at least a cause) of redistribution: regional location of industry, relative wages of SOE employees, and, finally, subsidized output prices. The picture which emerges from these investigations contributes to a leitmotif of this volume: The detectable redistributive effects of state ownership tend to improve the position of the middle of the income distribution at the expense of the upper end and in disregard of the lower.

One contribution to this theme is the evidence that publicly owned firms appear to pay higher wages than their private sector counterparts, even after accounting for other systematic differences between public and private firms. These higher wages appear to be paid for through subsidies (at least to the extent of forgoing a market return to capital) from the federal budget. Since the benefit of higher wages goes only to those who are employed, the lowest deciles are not affected at all. Moreover, since SOEs tend to be large and capital intensive, the workers who receive these higher wages would tend to be in the upper deciles of the employed, wage-earning population.

This pattern of redistribution was also supported by our limited examination of price subsidies for energy and for CONASUPO. It is hardly surprising that subsidies tied to final consumption would tend to rise with income. It is noteworthy that the incidence of ad valorem subsidies would rise faster than the incidence of taxes through the seventh decile and that eighth and ninth deciles would still be *net* recipients of such subsidies were they paid for in proportion to average tax incidence. Finally, it is striking that subsidies to CONASUPO, which are ostensibly better targeted to low-income consumers, peak for the seventh decile and are significantly larger for the eighth and ninth together than for the first three deciles combined.

### *Further Research*

This chapter is largely exploratory. Redistribution is an important rhetorical justification for state ownership, but hard evidence on the redistributive effects of state enterprise is often lacking. The results presented in this chapter suggest some dimensions along which redistributive effects can be successfully documented. The results are far from definitive, but neither do they exhaust the data available.

The success of the regional incentives for the location of industry provided by the state financial sector is one problem worth pushing further. The developed economy evidence on such incentives appears to be mixed, and it is often unclear how the personal distribution of income is affected even if industry moves to low-income regions. The indirect consequences of price subsidies have yet to be explored, but the required information on family budgets and the input-output matrix are available. The incidence of subsidies on profits of downstream producers is more difficult, but it is a tractable and important problem. Also, there is much more to be done on the question of who enjoys CONASUPO subsidies. In particular, the regional information in the household expenditure survey will help explain why the upper-middle deciles are the principal CONASUPO patrons. Finally, our look at the wage policy of SOEs was limited to the industrial sector and lacked hard data on skill differences between the public and private sector. Extensions of this inquiry are clearly needed.

## Notes

1. Investment by SOEs is, of course, only a part of public investment. No data are available to trace the share of SOEs in total public investment over the entire time span of Table 12-1.

2. "Fideicomisos"—like independent fiscal authorities at the federal state, and local level of the United States.

3. *Nacional Financiera, Annual Report,* 1973, p. 8.

4. These data are from the *Secretaría de Agricultura y Recursos Hidráulicos*. I have interpolated between the 1970 and 1978 reported figures to estimate employment for 1975.

5. The best *t* statistic is 0.16.

6. See, for example, Gorre's comparison of private and nationalized insurance firms in France.

7. The correlation matrix is as follows:

| | *Compensation* | *SOE Share* | *Hourly-Salaried* | *Size* | *Labor Share* |
|---|---|---|---|---|---|
| SOE share | 0.28 | | | | |
| Hourly/salaried | −0.63 | 0.03 | | | |
| Size | 0.47 | 0.17 | −0.16 | | |
| Labor share | −0.21 | 0.18 | 0.36 | −0.31 | |
| Capital/labor ratio | 0.59 | 0.20 | −0.29 | 0.72 | −0.37 |

8. *Peak-load* and *Ramsey-optimal* pricing are examples.

9. One exception is Willig (1981).

10. Petroleum for household use and natural gas.

11. The tax bars give the *relative* incidence of taxes across deciles. The absolute size of the weights was chosen so that the average height of either set of tax bars equals the average height of the consumption bars. Thus if $c_{i's}$ is total consumption by the $i^{th}$ decile in the household expenditure survey and $t_i$ is the share of total taxes paid by the $i^{th}$ decile, the height of the tax bar is $t_i\Sigma c_i$. The data on tax incidence are from Chapter 4.

12. As a ball-park estimate of their magnitude we can use the fact that pruchases of goods and (nonlabor) services represented about 8.8 percent of the total cost of state enterprises in the transportation sector. Average per family consumption of public transportation was 955 pesos per family (semiannually). Multiplying this figure by 8.8 percent gives us 84 pesos as an order-of-magnitude estimate of the energy component of public transporation. This figure compares to average per family consumption (semiannually) of 655 pesos for gasoline and 655 pesos for heating fuels.

13. Expenditure is in centavos, not pesos. The figures are low since they are averages across all families, not just those who frequent CONASUPO.

14. Although the overall frequency may seem surprisingly low, it is roughly comparable to the number of CONASUPO stores relative to private food stores in Mexico City. (See Gil for evidence on the relative number of CONASUPO stores.)

## Bibliography

Bennett, Douglas, and Kenneth Sharpe. "The State as Banker and Entrepreneur." *Comparative Politics* (Jan. 1980). Vol. 12, No. 2 pp. 165–189.

Gil, Andres V. *CONASUPO: Observations About a Public Enterprise.* A.B. thesis, Princeton University, Princeton, N.J., 1978.

Gorre, Lucien. The Nationalization of Insurance in France. Unpublished paper, 1979.

Grindle, Merilee S. *Bureaucrats, Politicians, and Peasants in Mexico.* Berkeley: University of California Press, 1977.

Hansen, Roger D. *The Politics of Mexican Development.* Baltimore: Johns Hopkins Press 1971.

Lindblom, Charles E. *Politics and Markets.* New York: Basic Books, 1977.

Purcell, Susan K., and F. H. John. "State and Society in Mexico: Must a Stable Policy Be Institutionalized?" *World Politics* XXXII, No. 2 (Jan. 1980). pp. 194–227.

Reynolds, Clark. *The Mexican Economy: Twentieth Century Structure and Growth.* New Haven, Conn.: Yale University Press, 1970.

Schneider, Norman. *Government Competition in the Mexican Steel Industry*. Davis: University of California, 1967.

Secretaria de Agricultura y Recursos Hidráulicos. *Estadistica Basica para la Planeación Agropecuaria y Forestal*. Federal District of Mexico, 1979.

United Nations. "Public Enterprises: Their Present Significance and Their Potential in Development." *Economic Bulletin for Latin America* 16, No. 1 (1971).

Vernon, Raymond (ed.). *Public Policy and Private Enterprise in Mexico*. Cambridge, Mass.: Harvard Univ. Press, 1964.

Villareal, Rociode, and Rene Villareal. "Public Enterprises in Mexican Development Under the Oil Perspective in the 1980's." Paper presented at the Second Boston Area Public Enterprise Group Conference, spring, 1980.

Willig, R. D. "Social Welfare Dominance." *American Economic Review* 71, No. 2, (May 1981), 200–204.

Wionczek, Miguel S. "Electric Power: The Uneasy Partnership," in R. Vernon (ed.) *Public Policy and Private Enterprise in Mexico*. Cambridge, Mass.: Harvard University Press, 1964.

# CHAPTER 13

# *Social Security, Health, and Social Solidarity in Mexico*

Emilio Lozoya Thalmann

## Introduction

The following is a general review of some concepts of social security with reference to a specific case. Particularly emphasized are the effects social security can have on income distribution.

The analysis is based on the elementary conceptual principles of social security theory and its scope is that of an introduction to the subject for nonspecialists. Therefore, no formal proof of the theory is given and no direct use of quantitive analysis procedures is made. It is rather sought to present some elements of the transcendence and characteristics of social security—particularly in the case of Mexico.

A warning on the availability of information is pertinent. The Mexican social security system is made up of various institutions, whose information is not always homogenous in quality, concepts, and timeliness. It is true that there have been significant advances to facilitate the study of this sector and the institutions comprising it, and that, in turn, there have been

This article is the partial result of a research project on "Distribution of Income and Consumption" carried out by the author for the Sistema Alimentario Mexicano (Mexican Food System) at El Colegio de México. The author is indebted to Raúl Legaspi—research associate of the project—for his great help provided in the empirical phase; as well as to Alicia Contreras, Magda Jan, Martha Llamas del Moral, Rubén Reséndiz, and Miguel Angel Santín, for their assistance in handling the originally voluminous information.

My gratitude goes as well to Cassio Luiselli, Coordinator of the Sistema Alimentario Mexicano, for his enthusiastic support and for the stimulating discussions which drew away time from his already too busy schedule; and to the rest of the people working at the SAM who contributed to the elaboration of this project.

Also I would like to express my thanks to Constantino Lluch and Lance Taylor for their useful comments and methodological suggestions, as well as to the rest of the collaborators of the Princeton ITAM project and my colleagues at the Center of Economic Studies, El Colegio de México. As usual, I am entirely responsible for the errors and mistakes.

certain advances in the generation and analysis of information on income distribution. Nevertheless, information on the distribution of income is still insufficient for a parallel analysis with social security.

In addition, certain concepts must be defined. "Social security" is generally understood as including some concepts that are handled differently in this work. For these purposes, "health" is understood as the people's full enjoyment of their physical and psychic faculties, to which social security institutions contribute with their preventive, curative, and informative services. In turn "social security," within the context of this work, has to do mainly with economic benefit programs oriented to provide a worker with protection of his means of subsistence in periods of temporary or permanent physical incapacity as well as when he retires. Finally, "social solidarity," as a concept of the Mexican system, means the deliberate transfer of resources and services, mainly financed by the state, to low-income groups which in turn repay society with voluntary work.

In this analysis, the activities of the Mexican Social Security Institute (IMSS) stand out, not only because it is the main institution of the Mexican system but also because it has made the greatest achievements through its administration.[1]

The chapter is structured in the following way: the first section presents some theoretical considerations regarding the effect of social security services on the distribution of income; the second section covers the history and development of the social security system in Mexico, from colonial times to the period following promulgation of the Social Security Law in 1943; in the third section, health and social security services are analyzed—their objectives, benefits, recent behavior, and present situation—finishing with the application of the concept of social solidarity through the IMSS-COPLAMAR program; and finally, some conclusions are presented.

A selection of the most important statistics on the Mexican Social Security and Social Solidarity System are set out at the end of the chapter.

## Theoretical Considerations on the Impact of Social Security Services on Income Distribution

There is a close relationship between social security systems and the operation of a society, to such a degree that these systems produce economic and social effects on income distribution, supplementary to the effects of fiscal, monetary, and income policies through taxes, public expenditure, interest rates, prices, and wages. Thus the various elements affect the distribution between consumption, savings, and investment, with long-term consequences on the economic and political development of a specific country.

In turn productive structure characteristics, particularly technological organization, condition income distribution patterns to a large degree.[2]

With regard to the redistribution of income as an element of social equilibrium and economic efficiency, the problem can be considered through so-called "vertical" income redistribution, referring to transfers between population groups with different income levels. This is the traditional object of an analysis of the progressive or regressive impact of a tax policy within public finance, and, in the case of social security, basic reference can be made to the origins and destiny of implicit transfers between different deciles. It is a controversial theoretical issue whether the redistributive effect of social security depends upon the level of development reached by a country. It is estimated that in developing countries there is a transfer of resources towards the middle classes by means of the fiscal burden to the detriment of marginated groups.[3] Partial correction of this has been achieved in Mexico through specific schemes which will be commented upon below.

On the other hand, it is also relevant to study "horizontal" income redistribution, underlining instances of distribution between regions of different economic development, various branches of economic activity and employers and workers. With regard to the redistributive effect of social security, some outstanding characteristics are: redistribution between active and retired workers; between the covered and unprotected population; between the employed and the unemployed or underemployed; between the users and nonusers of its services, between healthy and sick insured person; between small and large families; between various risks with different incidences; between the beneficiaries of various branches of insurance; and between different generations in the course of time.[4] The flows between the foregoing also involve redistributive elements between groups with different income levels.

In a specific country, the significance of the redistributive impact of social security services depends upon factors such as: (1) the distinctive characteristics of the social security system; (2) the percentage of national income assigned to social security; (3) the production structure; and, (4) the possibilities for making a progressive income redistribution in accordance with the existing system of inequality and power distribution.[5]

With regard to the characteristics of social security services, the most interesting are those referring to the coverage of risks and benefits, the population groups that are protected, and the sources for financing the services.

With respect to financing sources in developing countries with embryonic and regressive taxation systems, as well as restricted groups tending to contribute in accordance with their benefit possibilities, the basic sources of financing are generally employers, workers, and the state, as in the case of Mexico. Here, the greater weight of the public sector in developing countries as a contributor and beneficiary should be emphasized. It should be mentioned that there are some theoretical problems regarding the options for considering the employer's contribution as a deduction from the profit margin, as a burden transferred to the consumer through prices, or, also as a factor in wage negotiations expressed in production costs. The problem presented by these cases is whether to consider those contributions as coming from employers or as in fact financed by other social groups.[6]

Both benefits granted and groups covered are generally of more limited scope in less-developed countries than in more advanced economies. In this regard there is, in turn, a theoretical problem with respect to the manner of measuring the transfers made by means of social security services, because the benefits are frequently granted in kind. In this sense, the lower-income strata consume a certain type of goods and services that, otherwise they would not consume—at least in socially acceptable proportions.[7] This gives rise to a real increase in the income of the most needy groups and modifies the consumption structure toward socially necessary services. It should also be emphasized that it is normally the middle- and low-income groups that make greater use of the benefits in kind. Such transfers acquire a shadow price that is quite different when valued in terms of the social benefits they entail.

The lesser a country's degree of development, the smaller tends to be the weight of social security in national income and the greater the need may be to change the unequal character of income distribution.[8] In such cases it is indispensable to balance the distribution of power among various pressure groups—which is not always particularly favorable—in order to carry out significant redistributional actions.

The main purpose of social security is not income distribution, *per se,* although it may serve this function in pursuit of its more general objectives; it is rather the furnishing of social services and medical assistance necessary for individual and collective welfare. Besides taxation, price, and wage policies, traditional income distribution strategies are based primarily on the creation of employment. However, when the real limitations of the incidence of an isolated economic strategy on income distribution are known, social measures acquire crucial relevance.[9] It is in this context that, even with conceptual difficulties in measuring the value of the transfers, social security is deemed to be a valuable supplementary mechanism producing economic and social effects on distribution.

Mexico's case presents most interesting characteristics, tending toward an intermediate position with elements that could be considered typical of both developed and underdeveloped countries. It is remarkable that, when considering the main elements of social security and solidarity, Mexican social security has been oriented towards persons enjoying a permanent and remunerated labor relationship. However, at the present time, it has developed solidarity plans which permit the channelling of resources toward marginated groups in an effective vertical distribution of income. The organized labor group—the basis and support of Mexican social security—received the benefits from modernization of the economy in a greater measure. It has been possible at the present time to provide services to other social groups, thus raising their levels of welfare.

In addition, it will be appreciated that Mexico has a tripartite financing system to which the state contributes with resources derived from the ordinary fiscal budget, supplemented by resources derived from the contributions of workers and employers.

The development and the present situation of social security in Mexico is described in the following section. The foregoing considerations will then be applied to a specific case and some corollaries on the implicit trends and requirements for increasing the effectiveness of a social security system as a supplementary mechanism for income redistribution will be reached.

## General Antecedents of Social Security in Mexico

### *The Colonial and the Independence Periods*

The background of social security in Mexico is as remote as the Mexican people's struggle to conquer their social rights. During the colonial period the search for security gave rise to *cofradías* (worker's brotherhoods), corresponding to the different crafts, which began to function in New Spain in 1538. This institution lasted throughout the colonial period. In spite of the decay of the handicrafts production system it was not until the *Reform* period of the late nineteenth century that these associations began to disappear. Their successor, almost secular in nature, appeared in the mutual assistance associations, which began to flourish under European influence.

During the *Restored Republic* the artisans and the incipient wage labor sector began to struggle for their interests and better working conditions. The unionization spirit and the mutual associations were the germ of the union. At the height of Porfirio Díaz's dictatorship, the first reforms to benefit the workers were attempted. The need of reform in the dominant political and social system was foreseen as a means to prevent a social explosion, and the first Labor Accidents Law was promulgated.[10]

### *The Revolutionary Period*

When the Revolution succeeded, workers took advantage of the liberties instituted by Francisco I. Madero to found various labor organizations. Labor legislation whose basic goal was worker protection, was directly influenced by the action of these groups. Their influence was decisive in the creation of Article 123 of the 1917 Constitution, a joint axis with Article 27 of the Mexican Social Constitutional Law.

Two labor reform bills were presented to the Chamber of Deputies in 1913 favoring the adoption of labor provisions to improve work relationships and to protect workers' rights. A group of representatives—on the basis of humanistic considerations—supported the necessity of regulating work injuries in the entire Republic. The "renovating" group of deputies proposed the amendment of the 1890 Code of Commerce, which would confer on the Federal Legislature competence in labor matters. This initiative became the first antecedent of the Federal Labor Law.

Venustiano Carranza, head of the Constitutional Army, issued two decrees in September 1916, setting out the urgency of putting into effect the political and social reforms postulated by the Mexican Revolution. He convened a Constituent Congress where the aspirations of the Mexican people were to be expounded for their conversion into a fundamental part of the Constitution, and, consequently, into an action program.[11]

On December 1, 1916, Venustiano Carranza delivered the proposed constitutional reforms to the Consitutent Congress at Querétaro, in which social security was expressed in revolutionary terminology for the first time.[12]

Constitutional Article 123 was approved at this Constituent Congress, thus converting Mexico into the first country in the world to include fundamental social rights by means of provisions regulating, among other aspects, employer-employee relationships in the text of its Constitution. Sections devoted to social security were included in that precept covering labor accidents and occupational diseases as well as the establishment of popular insurance plans, such as disability, life, involuntary interruption of labor, and accident funds, and of other funds with analogous purposes.

The origin of social security institutions in Mexico was mixed with the establishment of labor standards as in other parts of the world. Although the political philosophy of the 1917 Constitution opposed the laissez-faire liberal principle, state intervention was still limited to guarantee minimum justice in employer-employee relations.

The General Law of Civil Retirement Pensions, enacted in 1925, provided stability and certain continuity in the administrative apparatus of the state. This is an important antecedent of social security, since it guaranteed pension rights for advanced age and disability and annuities of relatives in case of death, to all officers and employees of the federal government, of the Federal District Department, and of the governments of Federal Territories.

## *The Revolution Institutionalized*

The National Revolutionary party, formed on the May 1, 1929 to integrate all the revolutionary groups and fractions, proclaimed in its declaration of principles that it would adopt a workers' security project that had been conceived by General Alvaro Obregón.[13]

In 1929, during the presidency of Emilio Portes Gil, Article 123 of the Constitution was amended, in order to clarify the concept of social security and declare it of public interest.[14] The Federal Labor Law of 1931 provided protection for labor accidents and sickness. Although the federal executive was granted exceptional powers in 1932 to issue a social security law, political circumstances such as the opposition of certain private groups and labor organizations prevented the president from exercising these powers.

The first effort in government action planning was made in 1934 with the First Six-year Plan, prepared by the party in power in view of the imminent presidential succession. As an immediate need, the plan provided the "introduction of obligatory insurance which shall include the main risks not covered by the Federal Labor Law" and for that purpose "a Social Security Law shall be passed in favor of wage earners, based on cooperation between concurrent entities, i.e., the state, workers, and employers in the proportion shown to be equitable by a study".[15]

During the term of President Lázaro Cárdenas, the nation's priorities were sovereignty over its natural resources and agrarian reform. Therefore, other programs like social security had to be postponed. The only social security laws issued by Cárdenas favored the military; the first established the Savings Bank for Officers of the Armed Forces (1936), the other improved the pension system (1939).[16]

Collective bargaining secured benefits for the working class that would later be imposed by law. In 1936 the oil workers formed a powerful organization (STPRM). Upon signing their first collective labor contract in 1942 they obtained old age and disability pensions and widowhood annuities.[17] The Railway Workers' Union signed its collective labor contract with the recently nationalized enterprise in 1938, and received a benefit package similar to the one obtained by the oil workers.[18]

Also created in 1938 was the Department of Public Welfare, converted into the Department of Health and Welfare (SSA) in 1943, which grouped all of the governmental agencies that had been attending separately to health and social-medical welfare problems.

### *Promulgation of the Social Security Law*

In the Second Six-Year Plan (1940–1946), prepared by the Mexican Revolutionary party prior to nomination of the party's candidate for the approaching electoral contest, it was provided that the social security law would be issued during the first year the plan was in force (1941) to cover the most important professional and social risks. It was also provided that in the institution created for that purpose, capital would be contributed by the employers and the state. The organized labor class would take part in its organization and administration.[19] This sector was experiencing deep discontent due to growing inflation caused by the monetary policy that had been adopted, by the economic readjustments produced by changes in the production system, and by a decrease in agricultural production for domestic consumption resulting from the maladjustment which followed the action of the agrarian reform.[20] As a result employer-employee relations experienced growing tensions.

Incoming President Manuel Avila Camacho prepared a series of legislative measures designed to strengthen his capacity to assuage employer-employee tensions.[21] In order to provide an administrative mechanism to face the complex labor and economic problems,[22] both the Federal Labor Law and the respective articles of the Constitution were amended. Also the Labor Department was transformed into the Department of Labor and Social Welfare, with an enlarged scope of jurisdiction. In addition, President Camacho appointed the Technical Drafting Commission for the social security law.[23] Under a new approach, the commission was formed on a tripartite basis. Made up of representatives of the federal government, employers, and workers, and including two representatives of the Congress, the commission worked under the direction and standards of Secretary of Labor and Social Welfare Ignacio García Tellez. At the same time, a favorable political climate was promoted in order to secure the consensus of the sectors directly involved in this case: the organized labor sector and the employers.[24]

A policy of national unity was consolidated by an agreement between the government and the major labor organizations, which encompassed 85 percent of the country's working class, establishing a series of temporary measures such as: the suspension of judicial disputes; the abolition of strikes and stoppages and their solution by conciliatory means and arbitration; and the lowering of the cost of living. The National Labor Council, entrusted with supervising compliance with the obligations acquired by labor organizations, was formed June 11, 1941.[25]

The Social Security Law was finally promulgated on January 19, 1943.

### *The Foundation and Structure of the Mexican Social Security Institute*

Once the law was enacted, its application had to be gradually put into operation to guarantee financial equilibrium and stability in the face of a complete absence of the infrastructure required to grant the corresponding benefits. At the same time, the leaders of the employer and employee sectors—and later the entire population—had to be made completely aware of the advantages and benefits deriving for the country's workers and employers from the obligatory imposition of social security,[26] in the face of reluctant attitudes adopted by some organized groups, especially in those cases where vested interests were affected.

Nevertheless, the Mexican government was committed in the face of the obligations it had contracted with the main labor organizations. On January 1, 1943 the Mexican Social Security Institute (IMSS) was created as a decentralized agency with legal capacity, and its director general as well as the members of the tripartite Technical Council were appointed.

This body immediately began to discuss, and to promote before the federal executive, the issuance of regulations to the Social Security Law. Simultaneously, the first obligatory affiliation of employers and workers in the Federal District was decreed, in order to begin rendering services on January 1, 1944. Thereafter, the system would be extended throughout the length and breadth of the Mexican territory, through incorporation into the obligatory social security system of the municipalities meeting the established requirements—and as far as the social and economic conditions of the different regions permitted.

The Law of the State Workers' Social Security and Services Institute (ISSSTE) allowed, as of January 1960, the fusion and regularization of some existing trade union type medical services for civil servants—plus the benefits provided since 1925 to the bureaucracy—reaching a base of 325,000 union workers and more than 50,000 supernumeraries, who, together with their families, totalled approximately 1.5 million beneficiaries.[27]

In the final days of President Echeverría's government, in June 1976, the Law of the Social Security Institute for the Armed Forces (ISSFAM) was promulgated to integrate the benefits and medical services they already enjoyed.

Finally, in order to coordinate all national level programs for attention to children and broaden the scope of action to the family group, the National System for Integral Family Development (DIF) was created in early 1977.

## An Analysis of the Health and Social Security Sector

### *Introduction*

The organization of Mexican health and social security services consists of formal bipartite or tripartite financing systems, and of systems charged to the ordinary fiscal budget attending to the marginal or informal sector of the population.

A study of the convenience of integrating health services into a centrally coordinated national system was recently commissioned by President José López Portillo. This measure would be congruent with the political philosophy of the global Development Plan—the main planning instrument of the present administration—which, in matters of health and social security, sets forth "to guarantee integral protection against damage and risks to its beneficiaries" and minimal health services "in order to give priority to the population in marginated rural and urban areas, particularly to the maternal-infantile group".[28] For this purpose, the General Coordination of Public Health was created in August 1980, as a presidential agency. Its main function is to coordinate sectoral strategies in health matters and to study the creation of a national system.

The population is classified in two service groups:

1. Defined sector, integrated by workers with contractual relations based on bipartite or tripartite financing systems. The corresponding institutions furnish both benefits in kind—by means of medical services—and in cash. According to the volume of their services, they occupy a preponderant position in the health sector as will be seen below.
2. Open sector, formed by informal, marginated sectors, through plans substantially engaged in furnishing health services, with financing systems charged to the ordinary fiscal budget.

The IMSS, ISSSTE, and ISSFAM are included in the first group. In addition, the National Oil Company (PEMEX), the National Railways of Mexico, and others, cover very specific populations.[29] In the case of IMSS, in addition to its ordinary schemes, marginated regions are served by means of a specific program financed with the resources of the federal budget (IMSS–COPLAMAR Program). The Department of Health and Welfare (SSA) and some other welfare services—operated by the state governments and not coordinated with the SSA itself—attend the second group.

An analysis of the sector's main components is set out below to clarify its structure and fundamental characteristics. Reference is first made to health services and then the financial and social benefits are analyzed.

During 1978, 1979, and 1980, the total budget of the four principal institutions integrating the health sector (IMSS, ISSSTE, SSA, and DIF), rose to $103, 128, and 178 current billion pesos, respectively. Of these institutions, the first two are social security institutions, and the medical services furnished by them are a part of the benefits in kind, whereas the other two are part of the government's public health service. Basic health programs (preventive and curative services, the formation and development of human resources, and population training), represented 43 percent of the budgeted resources in 1978, 36 percent in 1979, and 37 percent in 1980 (see Tables 13-1, 13-2, and 13-3).

It can be seen that, during the period analyzed, the IMSS contributed more than two-thirds of the resources assigned to this sector. A slight tendency toward a decrease in the ratio of health programs participation to the total annual expenditures of the sector's institutions can be observed. Although public sector expenditures registered an increasing participation in the gross national product (GNP), from 44 percent in 1978 to 53 percent in 1980, resources assigned to basic health programs as related to GNP decreased in relative terms during this period, from 2.1 percent in 1978 to 1.7 percent in 1980 (see Table 13-4).

This situation is consistent with what occurs in developing countries, whose social expenditures are seen to decrease as directly productive investment increases.[30] If the federal government had increased the resources for the basic health programs at the average nominal rate of growth of public spending (46 percent annually from 1978 to 1980), the expenditure on health would have reached more than the double than what was actually spent on these programs in 1980.

### *Expenditure Distribution by Health Programs and Institutions*

Distribution of the expenditures used in the basic health programs during the 1978–1980 period has been maintained without significant variations in the following proportions: (1) 85 percent on curative services (includes general and specialized outpatient care, general and specialized hospitalization, emergency treatment, and rehabilitation); (2) 9 percent on preventive services (vaccination, disease control, timely detection, nutrition, family planning, oral health, and others); (3) 5 percent on the formation and development of human resources (the formation and development of professional, technical, administrative, and health assistance personnel); and (4) 1 percent on population training (health orientation, information, and education). As can be seen, health services are mainly oriented toward population curative services.

The sector's institutional budget program structure from 1978 to 1980 likewise reflects the predominance of curative services, with greater weight in the case of social security (IMSS and ISSSTE) than in sanitary and welfare institutions. Revenues for sectorial expenditure devoted to curative services programs in 1980 were received in the following proportions: 66.3 percent from the IMSS's budgetary resources, 20.9 percent from the ISSSTE's, 11.4 percent from the SSA's, and 1.4 percent from the DIF's (see Table 13-3).

The curative services of the social security institutions are mainly furnished to insured persons and their beneficiaries, with the exception of the social solidarity programs discussed below. Curative services of social security institutions tend to be concentrated on low- and medium-income participants because the high-income groups more frequently use the services of private medicine, whereby the welfare of the beneficiary groups is increased.[31]

In relation to the sectorial budgetary sum intended for the preventive medicine programs during the 1979–1980 period, the participation of the IMSS in the sectorial expenditures for preventive services showed a tendency to rise—from 17.4 percent in 1978 to 32.20 percent in 1980. It should be noted that one of the basic reasons for this increasing tendency is the growing interest put into the family planning program, which had three times more budget in 1980 than in 1979 (see Table 13-3).

The work performed by the IMSS in this regard should be emphasized. Because of the role played by preventive services in health care, the institute furnishes these services to everybody without requiring the

TABLE 13.1.

*Total Budget Devoted to Basic Health Programs by the Main Institutions of the Health Sector during 1978*
*(Thousands of current Mexican pesos)*

| *Basic Health Programs* | *Main Institutions* | | | | *Total by Program* | |
|---|---|---|---|---|---|---|
| | *IMSS* | *ISSSTE* | *SSA* | *DIF* | *Absolutes* | *%* |
| 1. *Preventive Services* | 610,090 | 608,100 | 1,064,520 | 1,217,000 | 3,499,710 | 7.93 |
| | 17.43 | 17.38 | 30.42 | 34.77 | 100.00 | |
| 01. Control of Diseases Preventable by Vaccination | 397,570 | — | — | 34,000 | 431,570 | 0.98 |
| 02. Control of Transmissible Diseases | — | — | — | — | — | — |
| 03. Timely Detection of Diseases | 17,480 | — | — | — | 17,480 | 0.04 |
| 04. Voluntary Family Planning | 121,840 | 58,900 | — | — | 180,740 | 0.41 |
| 2. *Curative Services* | 27,523,960 | 4,798,000 | 4,959,580 | 595,700 | 37,877,240 | 85.83 |
| | 72.67 | 12.67 | 13.09 | 1.57 | 100.00 | |
| 01. General Outpatient Care | 5,661,400 | 2,303,100[1] | — | — | 7,964,500 | 18.05 |
| 02. Specialized Outpatient Care | 9,035,400 | — | — | — | 9,035,400 | 20.47 |
| 03. Training Hospitalization | 5,224,350 | 2,494,900 | — | — | 7,719,250 | 17.49 |
| 04. Specialized Hospitalization | –5,935,780 | — | — | — | 5,935,780 | 13.45 |

| | | | | | | |
|---|---|---|---|---|---|---|
| 3. *Training and Development of Human Resources for Health* | 1,402,340 | 438,500 | 541,190 | 93,300[2] | 2,475,330 | 5.61 |
| | 56.65 | 17.72 | 21.86 | 3.77 | 100.00 | |
| 4. *Training of the Population* | 87,680 | 17,600 | 174,320 | — | 279,600 | 0.63 |
| | 31.36 | 6.29 | 62.35 | — | 100.00 | |
| 01. Orientation and Information | — | — | — | — | — | — |
| 02. Health Education | — | — | — | — | — | — |
| Totals by Institution | | | | | | |
| Absolutes | 29,624,070 | 5,862,200 | 6,739,610 | 1,906,000 | 44,131,880 | 100.00 |
| % | 67.13 | 13.28 | 15.27 | 4.32 | 100.00 | |
| Total Budget | 52,421,550 | 35,803,000 | 12,460,560 | 1,991,300 | 102,676,410 | |
| % Health Programs/Budget | 56.51 | 16.37 | 54.09 | 95.72 | 42.98 | |

SOURCE: Estados Unidos Mexicanos. Presidencia de la República *3er. Informe de Gobierno. Sector Salud y Seguridad Social*. México, D.F.

[1]Includes specialized outpatient care

[2]Medical Education and Specialized Instruction

*TABLE 13.2.*

*Total Budget Devoted to Basic Health Programs by the Main Institutions of the Health Sector during 1979*
*(Thousands of current Mexican pesos)*

| *Basic Health Programs* | *Main Institutions* | | | | *Total by Program* | |
|---|---|---|---|---|---|---|
| | *IMSS* | *ISSSTE* | *SSA* | *DIF* | *Absolutes* | *%* |
| 1. *Preventive Services* | 1,524,000 | 285,100 | 1,511,100 | 943,600 | 4,263,800 | 9.29 |
| | 35.74 | 6.69 | 35.44 | 22.13 | 100.00 | |
| 01. Control of Diseases Preventable by Vaccination | 136,700 | 23,200 | 461,800 | 38,700 | 660,400 | 1.44 |
| 02. Control of Transmissible Diseases | 95,700 | 27,000 | 225,200 | — | 347,900 | 0.76 |
| 03. Timely Detection of Diseases | 154,700 | 22,000 | 61,400 | — | 238,100 | 0.52 |
| 04. Voluntary Family Planning | 280,100 | 18,400 | 127,100 | — | 425,600 | 0.93 |
| 2. *Curative Services* | 25,451,000 | 6,462,100 | 5,914,100 | 460,500 | 38,287,700 | 83.39 |
| | 66.47 | 16.88 | 15.45 | 1.20 | 100.00 | |
| 01. General Outpatient Care | 6,275,200 | 1,268,600 | 1,173,300 | — | 8,717,100 | 18.98 |
| 02. Specialized Outpatient Care | 3,818,400 | 442,300 | 939,600 | — | 5,200,300 | 11.33 |
| 03. General Hospitalization | 3,633,900 | 4,721,700 | 3,721,300 | — | 12,076,900 | 26.30 |
| 04. Specialized Hospitalization | 10,269,000 | — | — | — | 10,269,000 | 22.37 |

| | | | | | | |
|---|---|---|---|---|---|---|
| 3. *Training and Development of Human Resources for Health* | 1,968,000 | 166,400 | 664,900 | 50,700 | 2,850,000 | 6.21 |
| | 69.05 | 5.34 | 23.33 | 1.78 | 100.00 | |
| 4. *Training of the Population* | 148,000 | 7,900 | 361,000 | — | 511,900 | 1.11 |
| | 27.94 | 1.54 | 70.52 | — | 100.00 | |
| 01. Orientation and Information | 114,300 | 2,400 | 31,800 | — | 148,500 | 0.32 |
| 02. Health Education | 28,700 | 5,500 | 47,500 | — | 81,700 | 0.18 |
| Totals by Institution | | | | | | |
| Absolutes | 29,086,000 | 6,921,500 | 8,451,100 | 1,454,800 | 45,916,400 | 100.00 |
| % | 63.35 | 15.07 | 18.41 | 3.17 | 100.00 | |
| Total Budget | 67,370,100 | 42,498,100 | 16,030,200 | 2,585,300 | 128,480,600 | |
| % Health Programs/Budget | 43.17 | 16.29 | 52.72 | 56.27 | 35.74 | |

SOURCE: Estados Unidos Mexicanos. Presidencia de la República *4o. Informe de Gobierno. Sector Salud y Seguridad Social.* México, D.F.

TABLE 13.3.

*Total Budget Devoted to Basic Health Programs by the Main Institutions of the Health Sector during 1980*
*(Thousands of Mexican current pesos)*

| *Basic Health Programs* | *Main Institutions* | | | | *Total by Program* | |
|---|---|---|---|---|---|---|
| | *IMSS* | *ISSSTE* | *SSA* | *DIF* | *Absolutes* | *%* |
| 1. *Preventive Services* | 1,944,000 | 407,000 | 3,622,000 | 111,000 | 6,084,000 | 9.22 |
| | 31.95 | 6.69 | 59.53 | 1.83 | 100.00 | |
| 01. Control of Diseases Preventable by Vaccination | 191,000 | 196,000 | 1,281,000 | 2,000 | 1,670,000 | 2.53 |
| 02. Control of Transmissible Diseases | 172,000 | 50,000 | 1,050,000 | — | 1,272,000 | 1.93 |
| 03. Timely Detection of Diseases | 236,000 | 31,000 | 23,000 | — | 290,000 | 0.44 |
| 04. Voluntary Family Planning | 358,000 | 64,000 | 264,000 | — | 686,000 | 1.04 |
| 2. *Curative Services* | 37,107,000 | 11,673,000 | 6,408,000 | 808,000 | 55,996,000 | 84.85 |
| | 66.27 | 20.85 | 11.44 | 1.44 | 100.00 | |
| 01. General Outpatient Care | 11,020,000 | 3,988,000 | 1,188,000 | 86,000 | 16,282,000 | 24.67 |
| 02. Specialized Outpatient Care | 5,078,000 | 2,078,000 | 857,000 | 332,000 | 8,345,000 | 12.64 |
| 03. General Hospitalization | 5,394,000 | 5,083,000 | 4,220,000 | 2,000 | 14,699,000 | 22.27 |
| 04. Specialized Hospitalization | 13,235,000 | — | — | 328,000 | 13,563,000 | 20.55 |

| | | | | | | |
|---|---|---|---|---|---|---|
| 3. *Training and Development of Human Resources for Health* | 2,359,000 | 661,000 | 300,000 | 178,000 | 3,498,000 | 5.30 |
| | 67.44 | 18.90 | 8.57 | 5.09 | 100.00 | |
| 4. *Training of the Population* | 186,000 | 12,000 | 145,000 | 74,000 | 417,000 | 0.63 |
| | 44.60 | 2.88 | 34.77 | 17.75 | 100.00 | |
| 01. Orientation and Information | 146,000 | 2,000 | 33,000 | 4,000 | 185,000 | 0.28 |
| 02. Health Education | 40,000 | 10,000 | 91,000 | 70,000 | 211,000 | 0.32 |
| Totals by Institution Absolutes | 41,596,000 | 12,753,000 | 10,475,000 | 1,171,000 | 65,995,000 | 100.00 |
| % | 63.03 | 19.32 | 15.87 | 1.78 | 100.00 | |
| Total Budget | 91,368,000 | 63,811,000 | 19,486,000 | 3,706,000 | 178,371,000 | |
| % Health Programs/Budget | 45.53 | 20.00 | 53.76 | 31.60 | 37.00 | |

SOURCE: Estados Unidos Mexicanos. Presidencia de la República *5o. Informe de Gobierno. Sector Salud y Seguridad Social*. México, D.F.

*TABLE 13.4.*
*Percentage Participation of the Basic Health Programs[1] in the Public Sector Expenditure and in Mexico's Gross Domestic Product 1978–1980*
*(Millions of current Mexican pesos)*

| *Concept* | *1978* | *1979* | *1980* | *Rate of Average Annual Growth %* |
|---|---|---|---|---|
| *Absolute Data* | | | | |
| Basic Health Programs | 44,132 | 45,913 | 65,995 | 22.29 |
| Budget of the Federation | 937,397 | 1,266,878 | 2,018,598 | 46.74 |
| Gross Domestic Product | 2,122,800 | 2,767,800 | 3,821,500 | 34.17 |
| *Relative Data* | | | | |
| *Basic Health Programs* | | | | |
| % in relation to the budget | 4.71 | 3.62 | 3.27 | |
| % in relation to GDP | 2.08 | 1.66 | 1.73 | |
| *Budget of the Federation:* | | | | |
| % in relation to the GDP | 44.16 | 45.77 | 52.82 | |

SOURCE: Estados Unidos Mexicanos, Presidencia de la República, *Tercero, Cuarto y Quinto Informes de Gobierno* México, D.F., 1979, 1980 y 1981 respectivamente.

PIB: IMSS, Jefatura de Servicios de Planeación. Subjefatura de Programación y Estudios. *Cuadro:* (Indices de Preciose Base 1960). México, D. F., 1981.

[1]Includes programs of curative and preventive services, formation and development of human resources and training of the population.

beneficiaries to be social security dues payers. Thus, health services reach low-income groups, when otherwise they would be beyond their reach. An important contribution of the IMSS to income redistribution, to health levels, and the people's welfare can be appreciated as well.

With regard to the program for the formation and development of human resources for health, during the period under examination the average participation of the institutions was: IMSS, 64.9 percent; SSA, 17.1 percent; ISSSTE, 14.3 percent; and DIF, 3.7 percent. Two important aspects of this program can be seen: on the one hand, the IMSS participation as a percent of total rose from 56 percent of the program's sectorial expenditure in 1978 to 67.4 percent in 1980; and on the other hand, SSA's participation was 21.9 percent in 1978 and dropped to 8.5 percent in 1980 (see Tables 13-1, 13-2, and 13-3).

It is important to emphasize—with respect to the population training program—that the IMSS represented 31.4 percent of the total expenditures of this program in 1978, rising to 44.6 percent in 1980, because of an effort to orient users on how to care best for their health and also on how to get suitable medical attention (see Tables 13-1, 13-2, and 13-3).

In summary, three aspects of the participation of the institutions in basic health programs stand out; because of their relevance, they are described below:

(a) The IMSS and SSA have been the main contributors to the services and preventive programs, and it should be pointed out that the former has increased its relative participation during the period analyzed. Because of the IMSS orientation toward the entire population, it is one of the most suitable ways health services can redistribute income.

(b) The IMSS maintains its majority participation in the sectorial budget of the curative services program. As has been stated, the curative services of social security institutions tend to concentrate on the low- and middle-income groups—implying an effective means of redistribution among different income levels—as well as between the healthy and sick population.

(c) As the main social security institutions, the IMSS plays a major role in the total volume of health services in Mexico.

## *Nominal Coverage of Health Services*

In accordance with estimates made by the agencies with respect to coverage, the country has the potential for public health services for 62 million Mexicans, i.e., 92.2 percent of its total population. However, it should be pointed out that this figure could reflect overlaps of nominal coverage among institutions, because it includes the population located in the places where the medical units are located and in their zones of influence; it is not implied that services are literally furnished to that proportion of the population. There is not enough information available on effective coverage by institutions, but it is estimated at more than half of the nominal data. With regard to nominal coverage of the population, the IMSS is the most important institution in Mexico, by August 1981 it was furnishing health services to 42 million persons, made up of 25 million beneficiaries and 17 million people in marginated rural areas in coordination with the COPLAMAR[32] system (see Table 13-5). This means that, with respect to the extension of health, all the institute's services cover 62.4 percent of the country's total population.

On the other hand, as of the same date the Department of Health and Welfare covered 12 million persons, i.e., 17.8 percent of the total. The ISSSTE is in third place with 6 million beneficiaries, i.e., 8.9 percent of Mexico's population; the ISSFAM and others, with slightly more than 2 million beneficiaries, cover 3.2 percent of the total; and, finally, 7.8 percent of the people are attended by other agencies, by private health services, or are not covered at all (see Table 13-5).

By 1970 the health services of these institutions reached more than 21 million persons, i.e., approximately 43 percent of the country's total population, and it is estimated that by 1981 nominal coverage by national institutions had risen to 92.2 percent. It can be concluded from the foregoing that the coverage increase during this period has been over 100 per-

*TABLE 13.5.*
*Nominal Coverage by Institution*
*1981*
*(Estimated)*

| *Institution* | *Total* | *Urban* | *Rural* | *% in relation to the total* |
|---|---|---|---|---|
| | *(Millions of Persons)* | | | |
| Mexican Social Security Institute (IMSS)[1] | 25.0 | 25.0 | — | 37.1 |
| Solidarity IMSS | 3.0 | — | 3.0 | 4.5 |
| IMSS–COPLAMAR[2] | 14.0 | — | 14.0 | 20.8 |
| State Workers' Social Security and Services Institute (ISSSTE)[3] | 6.0 | 6.0 | — | 8.9 |
| Ministry of Health and Welfare (SSA)[4] | 12.0 | 7.1 | 4.9 | 17.8 |
| National Oil Company (PEMEX)[5] | 0.7 | 0.7 | — | 1.0 |
| National Railroads of Mexico[5] | 0.6 | 0.6 | — | 0.9 |
| Ministry of the National Defense[5] | 0.7 | 0.7 | — | 1.0 |
| Ministry of the Navy[5] | 0.2 | 0.2 | — | 0.3 |
| Other Institutior, and Private Services* | 5.2 | 4.0 | 1.2 | 7.7 |
| Total Population of the Country | 67.4 | 44.3 | 23.1 | 100.0 |
| Percentage[6] | 100.0 | 65.7% | 34.3% | |

SOURCES:

[1] Autoevaluación institucional para el primer. semestre. 1981. Jefatura de Servicios de Planeación. IMSS.

[2] Autoevaluación del Programa Nacional de Solidaridad IMSS–COPLAMAR, 1981.

[3] Projections based on Anuario 1979 del ISSSTE.

[4] Catálogos de Unidades Médicas de la Dirección General de Servicios Coordinados de Salud Pública del D.F. y de los Estados, 1980.

[5] Secretaría de Programación y Presupuesto. Coordinación General del Sistema Nacional de Información. Dirección General de Estadística 1970–1977.

Proyección por 1981. Jefatura de Servicios de Planeación, IMSS Depto. de Programación.

[6] Secretaría de Gobernación. Consejo Nacional de Población, 1980.

*Data obtained by subtraction.

cent. The institutions have contributed to the coverage increase in several ways, reflecting the socioeconomic development process and their own development capacity.

With regard to the population benefited by health services, the IMSS has grown from 9.9 million in 1970 to 42 million beneficiaries and solidarity-beneficiaries in 1981, representing a growth of 324 percent in 11 years. Approximately 60 percent of the population protected by the IMSS is located in urban and 40 percent in rural areas. This achievement is due to the emphasis given to rural regions programs during the last five years.

From 1970 to 1981 the coverage of the State Workers' Social Security and Services Institute (ISSSTE) grew from 1.3 million to 6 million beneficiaries, representing a more than fourfold increase. The ISSSTE's beneficiary population is completely urban.

The scope of the Department of Health and Welfare (SSA) grew from slightly more than 10 million persons in 1970 to 12 million in 1981, a 20 percent rate of growth. In 1981, 69 percent of the population protected by the SSA is located in urban and 31 percent in rural areas.

Out of the total urban population nominally protected, 56.4 percent is protected by the IMSS, 16 percent by the SSA, and 13.4 percent by the ISSSTE (See Table 13-5). Nominal coverage of the rural population is distributed as follows: IMSS (through the IMSS–COPLAMAR Program) covers 73.6 percent and the SSA 21.2 percent (see Table 13-5).

### *Institutional Participation in Achievement of Sectorial Service Goals*

Among the service goals achieved by the sector during 1980 is that 46.2 million doses of vaccine were applied in the preventive disease subprogram, almost 14 million outpatient care services were held for the control of transmissible diseases, and 5.9 million diagnoses for the timely detection of diseases. Especially notable are 9.5 million outpatient care services with voluntary recipients of family planning, and 55 million general and 16.4 million specialized outpatient care services held. The hospital system generated 2.3 million hospital discharges, trained 61,000 persons, and provided orientation to 26 million persons (see Table 13-6).

The IMSS and the SSA were the two strategic institutions involved in the achievement of the sectorial goals that were accomplished. For example, 95.3 percent of the vaccine doses applied were furnished by these two agencies (see Table 13-6).

In the control of transmissible diseases, of the total services held: the IMSS participated in 87.6 percent; the SSA in 10.2 percent; the ISSSTE in 2.1 percent; and the DIF in 0.1 percent.

The following contributions were made to the timely detection of disease subprogram: IMSS, 75.8 percent; SSA, 20.2 percent; and ISSSTE, 4.0 percent.

*TABLE 13.6.*
*Sectorial Operation Goals by Subprogram*
*1980*

| | *Sector* | | *IMSS* | | *SSA* | | *ISSSTE* | | *DIF* | |
|---|---|---|---|---|---|---|---|---|---|---|
| *Programs and Subprograms* | *No. Thousands* | *%* | *No. Thousands* | *%* | *No. Thousands* | *%* | *No. Thousands* | *%* | *No. Thousands* | *%* |
| *Preventive Services* | | | | | | | | | | |
| Control of Diseases Preventable by Vaccination | 46,218 (doses) | 100.0 | 20.627 | 44.6 | 23,415 | 50.7 | 2,107 | 4.6 | 69 | 0.1 |
| Control of Transmissible Diseases | 13,952 (services) | 100.0 | 12,220 | 87.6 | 1,421 | 10.2 | 296 | 2.1 | 15 | 0.1 |
| Timely Detection of Diseases | 5,950 (services) | 100.0 | 4,506 | 75.7 | 1,205 | 20.3 | 239 | 4.0 | n.d. | — |
| Voluntary Family Planning | 9,492 (services) | 100.0 | 7,216 | 76.0 | 2,094 | 22.1 | 182 | 1.9 | n.d. | — |

| | | | | | | | | | | |
|---|---|---|---|---|---|---|---|---|---|---|
| *Curative Services* | | | | | | | | | | |
| General Outpatient Care | 54,950 (services) | 100.0 | 41,295 | 75.2 | 4,311 | 7.8 | 9,232 | 16.8 | 112 | 0.2 |
| Specialized Outpatient | 16,365 (services) | 100.0 | 9,571 | 52.4 | 3,874 | 23.6 | 3,632 | 22.2 | 288 | 1.8 |
| General Hospitalization | 2,341 (discharges) | 100.0 | 1,605 | 68.6 | 477 | 20.4 | 244 | 10.4 | 15 | 0.6 |
| *Training and Development of Human Resources for Health* | | | | | | | | | | |
| Training and Development of Professionals and Technicians | 73 (persons) | 100.0 | 28 | 38.4 | 43 | 46.6 | 9 | 12.3 | 2 | 2.7 |
| *Training of the Population* | | | | | | | | | | |
| Health Education | 25,901 (persons) | 100.0 | — | — | 25,472 | 98.3 | 274 | 1.1 | 155 | 0.6 |

SOURCE: *5º Informe de Gobierno. Anexo Programático*. Secretaría de Programación y Presupuesto. México, 1981.

In regard to voluntary family planning, the IMSS made up 76 percent, the SSA 22.1 percent and the ISSSTE 1.9 percent of the sectorial figure.

The IMSS held 75.2 percent of general outpatient care services, ISSSTE 16.8 percent, SSA 7.8 percent, and DIF 0.2 percent. The specialized outpatient care subprogram sectorial goal was met with 52.4 percent by the IMSS, 23.6 percent by the SSA, 22.2 percent by the ISSSTE, and 1.8 percent by the DIF (see Table 13-6).

The greater proportion of hospital discharges, i.e., 68.6 percent in the sector, came from the IMSS; followed by the SSA with 20.4 percent, the ISSSTE with 10.4 percent, and the DIF with 0.6 peprcent.

Referring to the participation in the formation and development of human resources, IMSS participated with 46 percent, SSA with 36.1 percent, ISSSTE with 14.6 percent, and DIF with 3.3 percent. The participation of the IMSS in the subprogram of health education was 691,000 sessions, it being estimated that more than 7 millions persons attended.

## *Development in Recent Years*

With regard to subprograms of curative assistance, the sectorial participation behavior of the IMSS was preponderant and stable, the SSA's contribution to total sector services was stable, and the participation of the ISSSTE declined slightly during the period examined. Finally, DIF's participation in the sector was meager.

In most of the preventive service subprograms, the IMSS displayed an increasing tendency in its sectorial participation during 1978, 1979, and 1980. The participation of SSA in these same programs has shown little change, so that both institutions generate together the great majority of preventive services, while the ISSSTE displayed a slight tendency to grow (see Tables 13-6, 13-7, and 13-8).

It should be pointed out that sectorial efficiency in the use of resources has still to be improved, in order to render services to a larger proportion of the population with not many more financial resources. For example, hospital beds were being used in 1980 at 58.5 percent of the installed capacity. The IMSS had the highest productivity, with 72.4 percent of occupation, and SSA the lowest with 36.5 percent (see Table 13-14).

As it has been seen, a diversity of agencies are taking part in rendering health services in the country. As a consequence, a plan aimed at incorporating existing services into a national health system has been put forward. This measure, which is congruent with the rationalization objectives of the Global Development Plan, would be oriented toward an improvement in rendering services and increasing the coverage to a greater number of Mexicans.

It is considered that such integration of health services into a national system should be based on the IMSS system, because it is the one with the greatest human, material, and financial resources, in addition to covering more than two-thirds of the domestic population. Likewise, the IMSS has developed the most efficient administrative systems of the sector, which permits it to operate with higher productivity levels.

### *Coverage and Economic Benefits of Social Security Institutions*

Social security economic benefit programs are engaged in furnishing the worker with protection of the means of subsistence during periods of temporary or permanent physical disability and assuring him a dignified and adequate income at the end of his productive life when he goes into retirement. There are provisions in the various fields of insurance for this purpose, furnishing the insured person or his beneficiaries with cash benefits in proportion to his income level and the time he has paid dues to the social security system. Outstanding among them in Mexican social security are the provisions dealing with subsidies and assistance granted as compensation for wages lost due to periods of sickness, as well as pensions and annuities granted for permanent disability or old age retirement.

In addition, the Mexican social security system is characterized by an ambitious program of social benefits, oriented toward furnishing services to the general population—not only insured persons—that will permit the levels of welfare to be raised. By this means one of the specific contributions of social security favoring income redistribution is carried out by making preponderant use of the resources of society as a whole in favor of the popular classes. Among these social benefit services are those that have to do with training the people for productive activities, which are furnished to an open population. It is also worthwhile mentioning the activities related to spreading culture and promoting sports, by which the IMSS is carrying out relevant work at the national level.

With the exception of some special pension plans in operation in public enterprises, as in the case of Pemex and the National Railways, most of the subsidies and pensions granted at the national level originate in the services of the IMSS and ISSSTE, Mexico's most important social security institutions. In addition there is a specific agency for the armed forces (ISSFAM),[33] and some others of a regional nature implemented by state governments.[34] From 1971 to 1981 the economically active part of the population insured by the IMSS and the ISSSTE grew from 27.5 percent to 43.5 percent. While the IMSS protects workers involved in productive and service activities, employees of the federal government are attended to by the ISSSTE. The IMSS protected about 80 percent and the ISSSTE about 20 percent of all insured workers (ie., approximately 8.2 million persons) as of August 1981. By incorporation of groups that

*TABLE 13.7.*
*Sectorial Operation Goals by Subprogram*
*1979*

| *Programs and Subprograms* | *Sector* | | *IMSS* | | *SSA* | | *ISSSTE* | | *DIF* | |
|---|---|---|---|---|---|---|---|---|---|---|
| | *No. Thousands* | *%* | *No. Thousands* | *%* | *No. Thousands* | *%* | *No. Thousands* | *%* | *No. Thousands* | *%* |
| *Preventive Services* | | | | | | | | | | |
| Control of Diseases Preventable by Vaccination | 31,389 (doses) | 100 | 12,236 | 39.0 | 17,326 | 55.2 | 1,803 | 5.7 | 24 | 0.1 |
| Control of Transmissible Diseases | 8,813 (services) | 100 | 7,706 | 87.4 | 944 | 10.7 | 163 | 1.9 | n.a. | — |
| Timely Detection of Diseases | 5,697 (services) | 100 | 4,518 | 79.3 | 879 | 15.4 | 300 | 5.3 | n.a. | — |
| Voluntary Family Planning | 1,894 (services) | 100 | 1,252 | 66.1 | 487 | 25.7 | 155 | 8.2 | n.a. | — |

| | | | | | | | | | | |
|---|---|---|---|---|---|---|---|---|---|---|
| *Curative Services* | | | | | | | | | | |
| General Outpatient Care | 61,058 (services) | 100 | 45,350 | 74.3 | 5,148 | 8.4 | 10,077 | 16.5 | 483 | 0.8 |
| Specialized Outpatient | 17,349 (services) | 100 | 10,003 | 57.7 | 3,397 | 19.5 | 3,949 | 22.8 | n.a. | — |
| General Hospitalization | 1,916 (discharges) | 100 | 1,372 | 71.6 | 303 | 15.8 | 228 | 11.9 | 13 | 0.7 |
| *Training and Development of Human Resources for Health* | | | | | | | | | | |
| Training and Development of Professionals and Technicians | 113 (persons) | 100 | 92 | 81.4 | 17 | 15.1 | 4 | 3.5 | n.a. | — |
| *Training of the Population* | | | | | | | | | | |
| Health Education | 796 (persons) | 100 | 370 | 46.5 | 172 | 21.6 | 254 | 31.9 | n.a. | — |

SOURCE: *3er. Informe de Gobierno. Anexo Programático.* Secretaría de Programación y Presupuesto. México, 1979.

*TABLE 13.8.*
*Sectorial Operation Goals by Subprogram*
*1978*

| *Programs and Subprograms* | *Sector* | | *IMSS* | | *SSA* | | *ISSSTE* | | *DIF* | |
|---|---|---|---|---|---|---|---|---|---|---|
| | *No. Thousands* | *%* | *No. Thousands* | *%* | *No. Thousands* | *%* | *No. Thousands* | *%* | *No. Thousands* | *%* |
| *Preventive Services* | | | | | | | | | | |
| Control of Diseases Preventable by Vaccination | 32,748 (doses) | 100 | 12,175 | 37.2 | 19,720 | 60.2 | 824 | 2.5 | 28 | 0.1 |
| Control of Transmissible Diseases | 100 (services) | 100 | n.a. | — | n.a. | — | 100 | 100 | n.a. | — |
| Timely Detection of Diseases | 3,690 (services) | 100 | 3,686 | 99.0 | n.a. | — | 4 | 1.0 | n.a. | — |
| Voluntary Family Planning | 626 (services) | 100 | 540 | 86.3 | n.a. | — | 86 | 13.7 | n.a. | — |

| | | | | | | | | | | |
|---|---|---|---|---|---|---|---|---|---|---|
| *Curative Services* | | | | | | | | | | |
| General Outpatient Care | 65,204 (services) | 100 | 54,465 | 83.5[1] | 10,259 | 15.7 | n.a. | — | 480 | 0.8 |
| Specialized Outpatient | 1,940 (services) | 100 | n.a. | — | 1,940 | 100.0 | n.a. | — | n.a. | — |
| General Hospitalization | 2,152 (discharges) | 100 | 1,418 | 65.9 | 469 | 21.8 | 254 | 11.8 | 11 | 0.5 |
| *Formation and Development of Human Resources for Health* | | | | | | | | | | |
| Formation and Development of Professionals and Technicians | 111 (persons) | 100 | 93 | 83.8 | 15 | 13.5 | 3 | 2.7 | n.a. | — |
| *Training of the Population* | | | | | | | | | | |
| Health Education | 114 (persons) | 100 | n.a. | — | 114 | 100.0 | n.a. | — | n.a. | — |

SOURCE: 2º *Informe de Gobierno. Anexo Programático*. Secretaría de Programación y Presupuesto. México, 1978.

[1]Includes Specialized Outpatient Care

*TABLE 13.9.*
*Coverage of Social Security Institutions*

| *Concept* | *1971* | *1980* | *1981*[1] | *Variation 1971–1981* |
|---|---|---|---|---|
| Total insured persons (Thousands of persons) | 3,702 | 7,932 | 8,187 | 4,485 |
| Percentage of the IMSS | 87.3 | 80.3 | 80.1 | 74.2 |
| Percentage of the ISSSTE | 12.7 | 19.7 | 19.9 | 25.8 |

SOURCE: José López Portillo. *5° Informe de Gobierno 1981*. Presidencia de la Republica.

[1]To the Second Quarter of 1981.

*TABLE 13.10.*
*Beneficiary Population of Social Security with Respect to the Total*

| *Population* | *1971* | *1980* |
|---|---|---|
| 1. Total of country (thousands) | 47,500 | 67,400 |
| 2. Beneficiaries (thousands) | 12,015 | 29,533 |
| 3. Relation 2/1 | 25.3% | 32.8% |

SOURCE: *Memoria Estadística,* IMSS, 1979, José López Portillo, *5o. Informe de Gobierno, 1981*. Presidencia de la República.

had not been covered either on a regional or on a sectorial basis, the rate of growth of both institutions has been noticeably greater than that of the population (see Table 13-10).

During 1980 the economic benefit programs of both institutions absorbed resources totaling 44 billion pesos, that is 1.2 percent of the gross national product and 2.3 percent of the federation's budget (see Tables 13-12 and 13-13). Subsidy and pension subprograms represented only 49.8 percent of the total of that amount; in addition, the ISSSTE has a personal loan system which accounted for 44.1 percent of the total. Just as in the case of medical services, economic benefits represent a growing but small percentage of the GNP in comparison with what typically is devoted to these services in the developed countries.[35]

With regard to the above-mentioned programs, the IMSS handles almost all of the subsidy and assistance resources and cases. It is estimated that approximately 80 percent of all pensions have been granted by the IMSS, a proportion that is increasing over the years as a result of the growth and structure of the insured population. Various adjustment procedures of the amount of pensions—oriented toward protecting the pensioners from the effects of the inflationary process—are incorporated in the legislation corresponding to both institutions.

There has been a notable improvement in the financial situation of the IMSS in recent years, which has permitted it to make significant increases in the amounts of pensions, without compromising the medium- and long-term financial stability of the institution. Technical reserves guaranteeing future generations better retirement conditions have been created for such purposes in accordance with careful actuarial studies.

The technical reserves amounted to $8.032 billion pesos as of December 1980: $1.722 billion in the field of invalidity, old age, retirement and death pensions; $6.0 billion for work injuries; and $310 million for covering the institute's employer obligations. In turn, the institute's operational surplus amounted to $5.044 billion pesos in 1978, $8.736 billion in 1979, and $17.7 billion in 1980.

The branches of insurance referred to are financed with the following premiums: 9 percent of wages for general sickness and maternity (E and M), in which 5.625 percent corresponds to the employer, 2.25 percent to the employee and 1.125 percent to the state; 6 percent for invalidity, old age, retirement age, and death pensions (IVCM), in which the employer contributes with 3.75 percent, the employee with 1.5 percent, and the state with 0.75 percent; from 0.26 percent to 6.56 percent as a variable premium according to the risks of each enterprise for work injuries (RT), with the employer as the sole contributor; and finally 1 percent for nursery, the employer also being the only contributor.

These percentages are to be applied to the workers' average wage, and the amount so calculated is distributed among employers, workers, and the federal government in the approximate proportions of 62.5 percent, 25 percent, and 12.5 percent, respectively. Nevertheless, in some situations in which the insured person is in the double position of employer and employee, a bipartite scheme is applied wherein the financing is distrib-

*TABLE 13.11.*
*Coverage of Social Security Institutions*
*(Thousands of Persons)*

| | *Years* | | | | | | | |
|---|---|---|---|---|---|---|---|---|
| | *1971* | | *1980* | | *1981*[1] | | *Increments 1971–1981* | |
| *Concept* | *Absolute* | *Relative* | *Absolute* | *Relative* | *Absolute* | *Relative* | *Absolute* | *Relative* |
| Economically active population | 13,501 | 100.0 | 19,994 | 100.0 | 20,392 | 100.0 | 6,891 | 51 |
| IMSS insureds | 3,233 | 24.0 | 6,369 | 32.0 | 6,559 | 32.2 | 3,326 | 103 |
| ISSSTE insureds | 469 | 3.5 | 1,563 | 7.8 | 1,628 | 8.0 | 1,159 | 247 |

SOURCE: José López Portillo. 5o. Informe de Gobierno, 1981. Presidencia de la República.

[1]To second quarter of 1981.

TABLE 13.12.

*IMSS and ISSSTE Budget Devoted to Economic and Social Benefit Programs*
*(Millions of Pesos)*

| | *1980* | | | | | | *1981** | | | | | |
|---|---|---|---|---|---|---|---|---|---|---|---|---|
| | *Total* | | *IMSS* | | *ISSSTE* | | *Total* | | *IMSS* | | *ISSSTE* | |
| *Programs and Subprograms* | *Absolute* | *Relative* | *Absolute* | *Relative* | *Absolute* | *Relative* | *Absolute* | *Relative* | *Absolute* | *Relative* | *Absolute* | *Relative* |
| Economic benefits | 44,145 | 100.0 | 17,669 | 40.0 | 26,476 | 60.0 | 30,575 | 100.0 | 15,131 | 49.5 | 15,444 | 50.5 |
| Subsidies and assistance | 5,958 | 100.0 | 5,953 | 99.0 | 5 | 1.0 | 4,969 | 100.0 | 4,969 | 100.0 | n.a. | — |
| Pensions and retirement | 16,013 | 100.0 | 11,584 | 72.4 | 4,429 | 27.6 | 12,759 | 100.0 | 10,072 | 79.0 | 2,687 | 21.0 |
| Global indemnity | 341 | 100.0 | 121 | 35.5 | 220 | 64.5 | 112 | 100.0 | 84 | 75.0 | 28 | 25.0 |
| Account closures | 10 | 100.0 | 10 | 100.0 | — | — | 5 | 100.0 | 5 | 100.0 | — | — |
| Deposit refunds (FOVISSSTE) | 144 | 100.0 | — | — | 144 | 100.0 | 84 | 100.0 | — | — | 84 | 100.0 |
| Family allowances | 1 | 100.0 | 1 | 100.0 | — | — | 1 | 100.0 | 1 | 100.0 | — | — |
| Short-term loans | 21,578 | 100.0 | — | — | 21,678 | 100.0 | 12,645 | 100.0 | — | — | 12,645 | 100.0 |
| Social benefits | 2,933 | 100.0 | 2,438 | 83.1 | 495 | 16.9 | 2,609 | 100.0 | 2,279 | 87.4 | 330 | 12.6 |
| Social welfare and family integration | 1,311 | 100.0 | 1,070 | 82.0 | 241 | 18.0 | 1,367 | 100.0 | 1,252 | 92.0 | 115 | 8.0 |
| Instruction and training | 207 | 100.0 | 178 | 86.0 | 29 | 14.0 | 168 | 100.0 | 140 | 83.3 | 28 | 16.7 |
| Infant care | 1,389 | 100.0 | 1,190 | 86.0 | 199 | 14.0 | 1,038 | 100.0 | 887 | 85.5 | 151 | 14.5 |
| Old age care | 26 | 100.0 | — | — | 26 | 100.0 | 36 | 100.0 | — | — | 36 | 100.0 |

SOURCE: José López Portillo. 5o. *Informe de Gobierno, 1981*. Presidencia de la República.

*January–August.

## TABLE 13.13.

### *IMSS and ISSSTE: Goals Attained in Economic and Social Benefit Programs (Thousands of pesos)*

| Programs and Subprograms | 1980 | | | | | | 1981* | | | | | |
|---|---|---|---|---|---|---|---|---|---|---|---|---|
| | Total | | IMSS | | ISSSTE | | Total | | IMSS | | ISSSTE | |
| | Absolute | Relative | Absolute | Relative | Absolute | Relative | Absolute | Relative | Absolute | Relative | Absolute | Relative |
| Economic benefits | — | — | — | — | — | — | — | — | — | — | — | — |
| Subsidies and assistance | 4,752 | 100.0 | 3,662 | 77.1 | 1,090 | 22.9 | 3,248 | 100.0 | 2,522 | 78.0 | 726 | 22.0 |
| Pensions and retirement | 439 | 100.0 | 371 | 85.0 | 68 | 15.0 | 617 | 100.0 | 527[1] | 89.0 | 70 | 11.0 |
| Global indemnity | 12 | 100.0 | 10 | 83.0 | 2 | 17.0 | 7 | 100.0 | 4 | 57.0 | 3 | 43.0 |
| Account closures | 3 | 100.0 | 3 | 100.0 | — | — | 3 | 100.0 | 3 | 100.0 | — | — |
| Deposit refunds (FOVISSSTE) | 7 | 100.0 | — | — | 7 | 100.0 | 3 | 100.0 | — | — | 3 | 100.0 |
| Family allowances | 247 | 100.0 | 247 | 100.0 | — | — | 250 | 100.0 | 250 | 100.0 | — | — |
| Short-term loans | 612 | 100.0 | — | — | 612 | 100.0 | 475 | 100.0 | — | — | 475 | 100.0 |
| Social benefits | — | — | — | — | — | — | — | — | — | — | — | — |
| Social welfare and family integration | 9,079 | 100.0 | 9,560 | 94.0 | 519 | 6.0 | 15,683 | 100.0 | 15,204 | 97.0 | 479 | 3.0 |
| Instruction and training | 1,815 | 100.0 | 1,791 | 99.0 | 24 | 1.0 | 1,502 | 100.0 | 1,481 | 99.0 | 21 | 1.0 |
| Infant care | 2,490 | 100.0 | 2,485 | 99.0 | 5 | 1.0 | 1,786 | 100.0 | 1,781 | 99.0 | 5 | 1.0 |
| Old age care | 0.2 | 100.0 | — | — | 0.2 | 100.0 | 0.1 | 100.0 | — | — | 0.1 | 100.0 |

SOURCE: José López Portillo—*5o. Informe de Gobierno, 1981*. Presidencia de la República.

[1]The IMSS figures for this subprogram are derived from the master pension list which furnishes the monthly balance of those pensions in the process of settlement and do not include pensioners with partial permanent ability valued at less than 50%.

*TABLE 13.14.*
*Productivity in the Use of Resources*
*1980*

| | *Sector* | *IMSS* | *ISSSTE* | *SSA* | *DIF* |
|---|---|---|---|---|---|
| Available Hospital Beds | 59,304 | 28,639 | 5,493 | 24,704 | 468 |
| Hospital Discharges (thousands) | 2,426 | 1,602 | 231 | 578 | 14 |
| Average Hospital-Days per Discharge | 5.4 | 5.0 | 6.0 | 6.0 | 8.0 |
| Occupation % | 58.5 | 72.4 | 70.0 | 36.5 | 67.8 |

SOURCE: IMSS, Jefatura de Servicios de Planeación, Recursos Materiales en el Sector, mimeo, 1981.

uted in two equal parts: 50 percent for the account of the employer-employee and 50 percent for the federal government.

In relation to the destination of resources, in 1980 the expenditure in the branches of insurance reached $81.677 billion pesos, of which 65.3 percent related to sickness and maternity, 20.1 percent to invalidity, old age, retirement age, and death benefits, 13.4 percent to work injuries and 1.2 percent to nursery.

It should be mentioned that the surpluses were obtained through a basic rationalization of medical service expenditures, where the premiums break-even point requires lesser financial support from the invalidity, old age, retirement age, and death benefits. This has allowed the establishment of important surpluses to improve pensions, besides forming pertinent financial reserves. In this respect, the expenditure in pensions was $6.755 billion pesos in 1978, $8.648 billion in 1979, $11.658 billion in 1980 and it is estimated that in 1981 it will be $15.617 billion pesos, representing respectively 12.9, 11.2, 12.8, and 13.0 percent of the institute's budget.

The inflationary process during the last decade has put the efficiency of social security institutions and the solidarity bases supporting them to the test. The actuarial provisions at the beginning of the Mexican social security system were affected by levels of inflation previously unknown in the country. Their effect on pension purchasing power was acute, and the adjustments that were made in pension benefit amounts permitted transfers from active generations, which, with the support of pertinent studies, have allowed income redistribution and protection of the pensioners' standard of living.

The institute has increased the amount of pensions as its financial balance has improved. While not a legal requirement, political sentiment has led to increases such as those which have been given. As inflation continues, various organizations have suggested the convenience of creating dynamic pensions. Evaluations of the establishment of such a system should be carried out with utmost care in view of the risks of endangering the institution's future financial stability. Dynamic pensions require solid bases, such as surpluses and actuarial reserves much greater than those of the present system; in order to achieve them it would be necessary to weigh a possible increase in social security premiums against its effects on employment, inflation and general economic activity.

During 1980 approximately $3.0 billion pesos were devoted to the activities of the social benefit program; and almost 90 percent of the resources and services were furnished by the IMSS, which considers these activities of great importance because of their contribution to the improvement of the population's standard of living. The institute served a total of 1.8 million persons who attended sessions of the teaching and training subprogram, placing special emphasis on workers from the tourist industry, handicraft and farm workers.

The child care subprogram stands out in the social benefit program. It focuses on furnishing day-care center services to the children of insured mothers. This activity is included in a specific security branch, which is the most recent creation of the Social Security Law. The IMSS uses this means to subsidize working family income, by permitting the woman to continue in her productive activities with the assurance that her children are being attended to with the most painstaking care and scientific advances during her working day. It is worthwhile to point out that the payments to this type of security are contributed exclusively by the employers, who pay 1 percent of a worker's wages for this purpose (see Tables 13-12 and 13-13).

### *IMSS–COPLAMAR Program*

The role of the public budget as an instrument of income redistribution is of even greater inportance in the proportion that it is directly used in the production and distribution of goods and services for the population. In accordance with this thesis, the present government has broadened service programs for the marginated and low-income population through existing institutional structures, to avoid incurring the greater administrative expense implicit in the creation of specific operational agencies.

In this context, the General Unit for Coordination of the National Plan for Depressed Zones and Marginated Groups (COPLAMAR) was created in January 1977, to coordinate all federal action directed to serving these groups through various agencies promoting agricultural, agroindustrial, and handicraft development. Among the social welfare sectors undertaken by COPLAMAR are nutrition, housing, education, health and environmental protection.

The structure of income distribution—particularly of the marginated population—is seen to be more critical when measured with reference to access to consumer goods and services. As a result, in the distribution strategy planned by the state other economic and social measures besides the creation of employment were proposed. Among the former, price stability and increased productivity stand out. Nevertheless, in view of the known limitations of the actual effect of isolated economic measures, others of a social character were also included. These programs are focused on the effective production of services facilitating the direct access of the population to minimum levels of welfare.

Overcoming social margination is conceived of as the result of an action of such magnitude that it goes beyond the possibilities of isolated action by any federal agency. On the other hand, the intervention of COPLAMAR would permit coordination of the action of various agencies in accordance with a joint plan, for which a programmatic cooperation system—resting on three basic elements—was proposed.

Under this system, projects are assigned to (1) the agencies grouped into the Coordination Agreement and (2) the rest of the federal public administration agencies and units. Integration of the projects at the planning, execution, and evaluation stages in each zone is carried out by various public institutions. A nontransferrable budget is designated to cover programs and projects targeted to the depressed zones and marginated groups.

In accordance with these principles, on May 25, 1979, COPLAMAR and the IMSS entered into a Coordination Agreement, whose basic purpose was to foster the broadening of the coverage of social solidarity services and the consolidation of a community cooperation system for the benefit of the collectivities for which these services are intended.

The institute's structure coincided with the purposes of the agreement because of the following precedents:

(a) The new Social Security Law, enacted in 1973, is an instrument fostering the right to health as one of the measures suited for the achievement of the welfare minimums required by the large national groups.

(b) In accordance with the new law, the IMSS initiated the social solidarity program in 1974. At the moment the agreement with COPLAMAR was executed, the IMSS had already 30 field hospital clinics and 310 rural medical units, providing services to a population of approximately 3.8 million persons.

(c) The operative and administrative capacity of the IMSS has developed at a faster rate than the country's economic growth, particularly during the present administration, as can be seen from the fact that the population protected by the institute's services grew from 9.9 million beneficiaries in 1970 to 42 million in 1981, while the geographical coverage of IMSS action has been extended from 533 to 1,582 municipalities during the same years. There are now very few places in Mexico that do not as yet enjoy social security benefits.

In principle the agreement's goal was to furnish medical attention to 10 million solidarity beneficiaries through 2,000 rural medical units and 52 field hospital clinics. For this purpose, 1,796 rural medical units and 11 field hospital clinics were built in 1979, benefiting 19,696 locations in 1,038 municipalities. In 1980 and 1981 an additional stage was added to the group of units in operation in 1979; it included construction of 918 rural medical units and 30 fields hospital clinics. This means that by the end of 1981 the program will possess a total of 3,024 rural medical units, and 71 field hospital clinics by the middle of 1982. Present coverage in Mexico's low-income areas is estimated at 17 million solidarity beneficiaries. This population represents approximately 73.6 percent of the country's rural population, which is estimated to be 23.1 million persons. The program has surpassed its original proposals due to the receptiveness of the beneficiary population.[37]

The building and operation of these units was entrusted to the IMSS, through the coordination of the IMSS–COPLAMAR Program. This agency handles the program of Social Solidarity for Community Cooperation, which include both COPLAMAR's promotions and those directly made by the institute.

Total investment in the three stages of IMSS–COPLAMAR program will be $5.143 billion pesos and total operating costs $8.862 billion pesos, totaling $13.969 billion pesos during the 1979 to 1982 period. In the case of finance for solidarity programs, the federal government contributes 60 percent and the institute 40 percent. This represents an actual transfer from the ordinary system's dues payers to the solidarity beneficiary groups, whose contribution consists of voluntary labor for undertaking community benefit works. An operating budget of $4.766 billion pesos has been calculated for 1982.

The program's first level of medical attention includes family medical services, general outpatient consultation, and preventive services, while the second level comprises outpatient care and hospitalization in the four basic fields of medicine (internal medicine, surgery, pediatrics, and gynecology-obstetrics).

## Conclusions

1. The funadmental objective of social security is not redistribution of income but protection of the health and socioeconomic levels of the population. In this sense it is an auxiliary mechanism complementing more direct macroeconomic instruments, particularly taxation. Vertical and horizontal possibilities of income redistribution through social security are part of social programs complementing economic strategies whose isolated effect would be less effective.
2. There are three main sources financing social security; labor, employer, and state contributions. The latter contributes resources originating in the ordinary fiscal budget, and workers by deductions from their total income. In the case of employer contributions there are differences of opinion between

their social and private character, because of the employer's opportunity to include these contributions in the final price of his products.

3. In developing countries the tripartite financing of social security may work to the detriment of the marginated classes by transferring fiscal resources to middle classes with access to social security. This has had a tendency to correct itself in recent times in Mexico as programs open to noninsured groups and also as specific marginated group service plans (IMSS–COPLAMAR Program), provide virtually free medical care, under an effective income distribution formula, without requiring the payment of dues for such services in accordance with traditional financing schemes. By this means low- and middle- income groups are actually benefited.
4. Due to the dynamics of their growth and the volume of resources handled, social security institutions in less developed countries tend to occupy a predominant place in their economic structure. In Mexico, the Social Security Institute furnishes the preponderance of medical services as a part of its benefits in kind and is therefore the backbone of the national health system.
5. An important aspect of social security, with ambiguous effects on income distribution, is found in the case of pensions, which comprise a solidarity system between active workers and pensioners. There are transfers of income between both groups, in proportions that must be supervised by the institutions in order to assure medium- and long-term financial equilibrium, guaranteeing reasonable and sufficient pensions for new generations.
6. Mexican social security has experienced accelerated growth, covering by direct insurance more than 40 percent of the economically active population and over 70 percent of the total population including the coverage of the overall beneficiaries of the IMSS, the ISSSTE, and the IMSS–COPLAMAR Program. Nevertheless, the budget of the various social security organizations represents, through medical benefits, about 1.7 percent of Mexico's gross domestic product. This is a smaller proportion than what is devoted to the same purposes in the developed countries. It is estimated that the growth and modernization of the productive infrastructure will allow countries like Mexico to dedicate greater resources to social welfare.
7. For the first time in its history, in recent years the IMSS has achieved a sufficiently solid financial situation that has allowed it to form technical reserves of $8.032 billion pesos in accordance with existing legal outlines. The main objective of the reserves is to make certain that the financial burdens originated by obligations acquired in the present will not have a negative impact in the future.
8. In Mexico, social security will have greater redistributive effects through the social solidarity schemes that benefit most of the people. In this respect the director general of IMSS has quoted the president of the Republic warning: "Our country will not reach real progress if most of the people keep on lacking the minimum security and do not share, in justice, the goods of life."[38]

## Notes

1. In his 5th State of the Nation Address, the president of the republic recognized "the efficiency and honesty with which its present administration has managed one of the fundamental institutions of the Mexican Revolution."

2. H. Lydall, *A Theory of Income Distribution*. (Oxford, England: Clarendon Press, 1979).

3. F. Paukert, "Seguridad Social y Redistribución del Ingreso: estudio comparado," *Revista Internacional del Trabajo*, vol. 78, no. 5, November 1968.

4. See, for example: Lucila Leal de Araujo, "Los sistemas de seguridad social como mecanismo de redistribución del ingreso en los países en desarrollo," *Revista Mexicana de Seguridad Social*, año 1, no. 3, February 1972; and Organización Internacional de Trabajadores (1970): Efectos macroeconómicos de la seguridad social, Geneva.

5. F. Paukert, op. cit.

6. Organización Internacional de Trabajadores, op. cit.

7. Ibid.

8. F. Paukert, op. cit.

9. Sen, A., *On Economic Inequality* (Oxford, England: Clarendon Press, 1973).

10. IMSS, *El Seguro Social en México (Antecedentes y legislación, convenios, recomendaciones, resoluciones y conclusiones en materia internacional)*, México, 1971. Proi.

11. Jesús Silva Herzog, *Breve Historia de la Revolución Mexicana (La etapa constitucionalista y la Lucha de Facciones)*, Tomo II, Fondo de Cultura Económica (México, 1960), p. 252.

12. México a través de los Informes Presidenciales, *La Seguridad Social . . . por la Sria. de la Defensa*, IMSS, ISSSTE, Sria. de la Presidencia, Tomo 13 (México, 1976), p. 13.

13. Miguel García Cruz, *La Seguridad Social en México: Bases, evolución, importancia económica, social, polítícia y cultural, 1906–58*, Tomo I B. Costa-Amic Editor (México, c 1972), p. 58.

14. Ibid, p. 13.

15. *Partido Nacional Revolucionario*. Plan Sexenal del PNR (México 1934), p. 46.

16. Carmelo Mesa Lago, *Social Security in Latin America: Pressure Groups, Stratification, and Inequality* (Pittsburgh: University of Pittsburgh Press, 1978), p. 214.

17. Ibid.

18. Ibid.

19. Luis Medina, *Historia de la Revolución Mexicana: Período 1940–52: del Cardenismo al Avilacamachismo*, El Colegio de México (México, 1978), pp. 94–96.

20. María Antonieta Benejan, *Historia del Instituto Mexicana del Seguro Social: Los primeros años, 1943–1944*, Imp. Talleres Gráficos de Ediciones. Culturales, S.A. (México 1980), p. 33.

21. Medina, op. cit., pp. 292, 293.

22. María Antonieta Benejan. op. cit., pp. 33, 34.

23. García Cruz, op. cit., p. 72.

24. Ibid, pp. 72, 73.

25. Medina, op. cit., p. 305.

26. García Cruz, op. cit., p. 79.

27. Rómulo Sánchez Mireles, *El Movimiento Burocrático* (México: Fondo de Cultura Económica. 1960), pp. 206–7.

28. Secretaría de Programación y Presupuesto, *Plan Global de Desarrollo* (Mexico D.F., 1980), p. 193.

29. In October 1981, the National Railways's social security plan, which operated independently, was incorporated to the IMSS system.

30. See among others, F. Paukert, op. cit. (1973).

31. See among others, Leal de Araujo (1972).

32. COPLAMAR: General Coordination of the National Plan of Depressed Zones and Marginated Groups.

33. ISSFAM: Social Security Institute for the Armed Forces and the Navy.

34. For example, ISSTESON: the Social Security Institute in the Service of the Workers of the State of Sonora.

35. See, among others, Organización Internacional de Trabajadores, op. cit.

36. Memoria del Programa IMSS-COPLAMAR. COPLAMAR, Presidencia de la República, México, 1981.

37. "The IMSS-COPLAMAR formula is an unprecedented effort at social development because of its quantitative aspect, and it will soon signify a substantial advance in the solution of problems due to its qualitative consequences, if we combine them with other efforts in the areas of education, marketing, and health in general", in *La Filosofía Política de José López Portillo,* Secretaría de Programación y Presupuesto (Mexico, 1980).

38. Arsenio Farell Cubillas, "Informe de las activadades desarrolladas durante 1980 y programa de labores para 1981," in *Memoria Institucional,* 1980, IMSS, México. December 1980. p. 47.

## Bibliography

Benejan María Antonieta.—*Historia del Instituto Mexicano del Seguro Social.—Los primeros años 1943–1944.*—Imp. Talleres Gráficos de Ediciones Culturales, S.A.—Mexico, 1980.

Chávez Orozco, Luis.—"Orígenes de la Política de Seguridad Social".—*Sobretiro de la Revista Historia Mexicana,* vol. 16, no. 2, October-December 1966.

Farell Cubillas, Arsenio.—"Informe de las activadades desarrolladas durante 1980 y programa de labores para 1981", in *Memoria Institucional 1980 IMSS,* Mexico, December 1980.

García Cruz, Miguel.—*La Seguridad Social en Mexico.—Bases, evolución, importancia económica, social, poliítica y cultural, 1906–58,* Tomo I B. Costa-Amic Editor, Mexico (c. 1972).

Instituto Mexicano del Seguro Social.—*El Seguro Social en Mexico (Antecedentes y legislación, convenios, recomendaciones, resoluciones y conclusiones en materia internacional),* México, 1971.

Leal de Araujo, Lucila.—"Los sistemas de seguridad social como mecanismo de redistribución del ingreso en los paíes en desarrollo". *Revista Mexicana de Seguridad Social,* Year 1, no. 3, February 1972.

López Portillo, José.—*Quinto Informe de Gobierno,* Presidencia de la República, Mexico, 1981.

Lydall, H.—*A Theory of Income Distribution.* Oxford: Clarendon Press, 1979.

Medina, Luis—*Historia de la Revolución Mexicana: Período 1940–1952, del Cardenismo al Avilacamachismo.*—El Colegio de México, no. 18, México 1978.

Mesa Lago, Carmelo.— *Social Security in Latin America. (Pressure Groups, Stratification and Inequality).* Pittsburgh: University of Pittsburgh Press, 1978.

*Memoria del Programa IMSS-COMPLAMAR.* Presidencia de la República.—Coordinación General del Plan Nacional de Zonas Deprimidas y Grupos Marginados, México, 1981.

*México a Través de los Informes Presidenciales.*—La Seguridad Social . . . Tomo 13, Secretaría de la Presidencia, México, 1976.

Organización Internacional de Trabajaderes. *Efectos macroeconómicos de la seguridad social.* Geneva, 1970.

Partido Nacional Revolucionario.—*Plan Sexenal del P.N.R.* Mexico, 1934.

Paukert, F.—"Seguridad Social y Redistribución del Ingreso: estudio comparado," *Revista Internacional del Trabajo,* vol. 78, no. 5. November 1968. English version in Everett M Kassalow, editor, "The Role of Social Security in Economic Development," U.S. Department of Health, Education, and Welfare, Research Report no. 27, Washington, 1968.

Sánchez Mireles, Rómulo.—*El Movimiento Burocrático.* Fondo de Cultura Económica, Mexico 1960.

Sen, A. *On Economic Inequality,* Oxford: Clarendon Press, 1973.

Secretaría de Programación y Presupuesto.—*Plan Global de Desarrollo,* Mexico, 1980.

Secretaría de Programación y Presupuesto.—*Filosofía Política de José López Portillo.*—Mexico, 1980.

Silva Herzog, Jesús.—*Breve Historia de la Revolución Mexicana. (La Etapa Constitucionalista y la Lucha de Facciones)* Tomo II, Fondo de Cultrua Económica, México, 1960.

# CHAPTER 14

# *Distribution of Income, Food Consumption, and Fiscal Cost of Alternative Policy Options*

Nora Lustig

## Introduction

Malnutrition, especially in the form of a deficient intake of calories and proteins, is quite a common problem in the LDCs. In many of these countries it is the result of their overall poverty, but in others it is related more to inequality in the distribution of wealth and income. This seems to be the case of Mexico; according to the latest estimates made in 1979 by the *Instituto Nacional de la Nutrición* (National Nutrition Institute), the availability of calories and proteins in per capita terms would be sufficient to provide for adequate per capita intakes, if they were equally distributed. In this respect, one could say that malnutrition in Mexico is a problem that lies more on the distribution side than on the production side. This does not mean that increases in production of food are not necessary or helpful in the battle against malnutrition (in fact, they are essential), but it warns us against assuming that raising food production is sufficient. Several studies have shown that in countries where wealth and income are very concentrated, increasing the production of food does not solve the problem of malnutrition because the additional food that is produced may be bought by those who have the purchasing power in the country or abroad (food is exported).[1] In addition, when income is very concentrated and part of the population has incomes comparable to those of developed countries, their diet becomes more sophisticated and a large part of the resources are used for producing relatively more expensive food (like meat and dairy products), while at the same time staple commodities consumed by the poor (corn and beans, for example) are displaced.

Malnutrition in Mexico has been estimated to be quite high. For example the recent results obtained from the last rural Nutrition Survey[2] indicate that except for the northwestern states and part of the north-center the per capita daily caloric intake was not adequate; in terms of proteins the situation is even worse because only a small fraction of the north-west coast achieves an adequate intake (parts of Sinaloa, Nayarit and Jalisco). One the other hand, the institute has estimated that the national average daily availability of calories (2,600) and grams of protein (76) in per capita terms is sufficient to meet the recommended levels; this is an indicator that malnutrition in Mexico must be attributed above all to unequal distribution of purchasing power and resources.

The prevalence of widespread malnutrition together with the presence of what has been called the "agricultural crisis," which has manifested itself by a relative decline in agricultural production (especially of basic grains) accompanied by a substantial increase in imports starting around the mid-sixties,[3] led the government of López Portillo to launch a program called *Sistema Alimentario Mexicano* (Mexican Food System) whose two main objectives were to achieve "self-sufficiency" in staples (especially corn and beans) and improve the income and nutritional conditions of the rural as well as the urban poor. Self-sufficiency in the production of staples is associated with political independence in Mexico and with the possibility of devoting foreign exchange to noncompetitive imports such as basic capital goods to "complete" the industrialization process.

The idea of self-sufficiency should not be confused with autarky. The goal was to minimize the dependency on imports of basic foodstuff—especially corn and beans. In fact, it was an attempt to redefine Mexico's "comparative advantage" in such a way that at the same time that incomes of small *campesinos* and *ejidatarios* (although not the marginal *campesinos*) were raised, pressures on the balance of payments deficit due to food imports could be relaxed.[4]

The two objectives of the *Sistema Alimentario Mexicano* were to be achieved through the implementation of a *production strategy* and a *consumption strategy*.[5] The production strategy consisted of a series of measures to encourage production of staples, especially in the nonirrigated areas where most of the poorer peasants live. These measures included cheap credit, subsidized inputs (fertilizers and seeds), higher support prices and sharing the risks of the use of new techonology; they were intended to contribute to the self-sufficiency goal as well as to improve the income and nutrition of the Mexican *campesinos*. On the other hand, in the consumption strategy the idea was to implement policies that would enable the currently malnourished population to have a food intake equivalent to the *basic recommended diet*—a normative consumption basket estimated by the Mexican Food System, which fulfilled a series of nutrient requirements at the minimum cost. This could be achieved with different kinds of measures such as income transfers, food stamps, price subsidies, direct distribution, etc.[6]

At this point (October 1981) most of the policies of the production strategy have been implemented in a number of districts and have resulted in some increases in the production of corn and beans during 1980 and 1981. During 1980 the agricultural sector grew at a 7 percent rate and in 1981 it is expected to grow at an annual rate of 4.5 percent—in both cases surpassing the population growth rate. Although outputs for 1981 are not yet known with certainty, it has been estimated that corn production will reach over 13 million tons, a rise of 5.9 percent; for beans the expected increases are equal to 29.9 percent (with respect to 1980), reaching around 1.19 million tons.

The consumption strategy—on the other hand—has not yet been launched on a similar scale: up to now, it has focused on increasing the state distribution network for rural areas (DICONSA), in which thirteen of the twenty-seven food items contained in the basic recommended diet are sold at a price estimated to be 35 percent lower than the market rural prices;[7] and using CONASUPO stores for cheaper food in urban areas. However, the percentage of food that is marketed through these channels is still small, and thus the subsidy does not reach a large part of the malnourished population. Thus, from the consumption side the policy options are—so to speak—still open to discussion since those already in practice have not been implemented on a large scale; this means that the possible measures designed to increase the food intake of the malnourished should be analyzed and compared in the light of a set of criteria, so that the most "adequate" choice can be made. The purpose of this work is to contribute partially to this analysis.

The chapter is organized as follows: in the first section we begin by analyzing the relationship between income distribution and the prevalance of malnutrition in Mexico; in the second section we present an estimate of the redistributive requirements if all households were to be able to spend an amount on food equal to the basic recommended diet; in the third section a comparison is carried out in terms of their fiscal cost, among three different target-group oriented policy options (income transfers, food stamps, and food price subsidies); and in the last section we present a summary of the findings and introduce some other aspects that should be present when comparing the policy options.

## Distribution of Income, Food Consumption and Nutrition

As has been shown in other studies, income in Mexico has been—and still is—very concentrated and unequally distributed.[8] In Table 14-1, for instance, we can observe the results in the distribution of income obtained for the 1977 Income and Expenditure Survey (IES):[9] while the first decile

*TABLE 14.1.*
*Distribution of Household Income: 1977*

| *Deciles*[1] | *1977* |
|---|---|
| I | 1.08 |
| II | 2.21 |
| III | 3.23 |
| IV | 4.42 |
| V | 5.73 |
| VI | 7.15 |
| VII | 9.11 |
| VIII | 11.98 |
| IX | 17.09 |
| Xa | 12.54 |
| Xb | 25.45 |

SOURCE: Hernández L. y Córdova (1979, 507).
[1]Number of households in each decile: 1,100,000.

received only 1.08 percent of total income, the top one got 38 percent. These results may differ somewhat if one takes account of underreporting, which in this survey seems to be very high (see Appendix); nevertheless, some experiments that take account of this indicate that the concentration of income would still be very high even after the adjustment for underreporting is made. Bergsman, for example, has recalculated the distribution of income with two different assumptions on underreporting; under the "low inequality" estimate, the Gini coefficient with the 1977 data changes from .496 (unadjusted) to .476, while in the "high inequality" estimate it jumps to .569 (Bergsman 1980, 15). Moreover, in addition to the existence of "relative" poverty, according to the 1977 survey quite a large number of households in Mexico (between 40 percent and 50 percent) earned an income below the corresponding minimum wage for that year. To the extent that the minimum wage is supposed to represent a "well-being" threshold, this result indicates that a considerable portion of the Mexican population has not achieved this level yet. Moreover, the minimum wage in Mexico might not be adequate to cover the "basic needs" of a standard family and, in addition, it has been decreasing in real terms during the last four years.[10]

With respect to "who" and "where" are the poor in Mexico, it was found that the largest proportion of households below the corresponding minimum wage is in the central and southern Pacific region of Mexico, with most of the population working in agriculture as small peasants and/or *jornaleros* (literally, workers paid by the day). Poor households outside agricultural areas obtain their income mainly from the so-called informal sector: i.e., they do not have a permanent job and survive doing the hundred different kinds of small services that one can witness in any of the larger urban areas. (Lustig 1980a)[11]

The disparity in income among the different deciles reflects itself in distinct corresponding expenditure patterns (see Table 14-2). For instance, the percentage spent on food and beverages is relatively high for the bottom decile and it declines persistently as income rises; it goes from 61.6 percent of total expenditure for the first decile to around 22 percent for the top one. Moreover, from the total amount spent on food and beverages the first decile accounts for 1.6%, while the top 10 percent of the households buy 24.8 percent of the total (see Table 14-3).

Within the food category itself, the tendency as income rises is to move away from starches, especially derivatives from corn, toward a more protein-rich diet. This becomes evident if one looks at the rankings presented in Table 14-4. While for the first three deciles, maize in grain and beans occupy the first and second place, respectively, in terms of expenditure (22.3 percent and 7 percent of total food expenditure); from the IV decile onward and for the total of the population, beef occupies the first place. Such changes in the diet are mainly due to the changes in purchasing power, while things like habits and tastes have less influence on it. However, another important factor that may be influencing diet is the access to land; peasant households may consume larger proportions of corn and beans than rural wage earners or urban self-employed or wage earners of the same income, because they grow them themselves.[12] In addition, in some areas the diet may be influenced as well by supply conditions; in small towns, for example, meat is available only on certain days of the week.

The high concentration of income together with the large proportion of households with incomes below the corresponding minimum wage, and the noticeable differences in food consumption and diversity in diets, are all elements that suggest that in Mexico serious problems of malnutrition (especially in the form of undernutrition) may exist.

An attempt to measure the degree of malnutrition in relation to income was carried out by Flores (1973). Flores found that the cost of an "adequate" diet in 1970 was equal to 599 pesos per family in urban settings and 571 pesos in rural areas. Basing her analysis on the Income and Expenditure Survey of Secretaría de Industria y Comercio (1969), she argued that very few households spent more than 65 percent of their income on food; accordingly, she concluded, most of the famlies with an income below \$1,000 pesos per month ran the risk of being undernourished; in the 1970 survey this amounted to approximately 4.3 million families, or 22.6 million persons, i.e., around 49 percent of the country's total population.

Another rough estimate of the prevalence of malnutrition was made by Van Ginneken (1974). Using the 1968 Income and Expenditure Survey implemented by the Bank of Mexico, Van Ginneken calculated the dis-

*TABLE 14.2.*

*Consumption Patterns per Decile: 1977*
*(Percentages)*

| *Item* | *I* | *II* | *III* | *IV* | *V* | *VI* | *VII* | *VIII* | *IX* | *Xa* | *Xb* |
|---|---|---|---|---|---|---|---|---|---|---|---|
| Food and beverages | 61.58 | 58.31 | 59.74 | 57.66 | 54.45 | 50.44 | 44.86 | 42.42 | 34.94 | 23.83 | 20.18 |
| Clothing and shoes | 8.37 | 8.04 | 8.95 | 9.06 | 8.51 | 8.75 | 9.83 | 10.09 | 10.15 | 10.18 | 9.25 |
| Rent and house maintenance | 8.87 | 10.43 | 8.39 | 9.18 | 11.93 | 12.63 | 12.67 | 12.99 | 16.36 | 13.76 | 15.40 |
| Furniture and appliances | 7.58 | 6.84 | 7.03 | 6.77 | 6.50 | 7.31 | 7.51 | 7.51 | 7.09 | 8.35 | 8.73 |
| Health care | 4.43 | 4.21 | 3.79 | 3.30 | 3.20 | 2.58 | 3.11 | 2.92 | 2.69 | 3.01 | 3.09 |
| Transportation and communication | 2.91 | 3.37 | 3.69 | 4.29 | 4.98 | 5.58 | 7.18 | 8.41 | 10.72 | 17.13 | 18.29 |
| Entertainment | .44 | .69 | 1.06 | 1.24 | 1.84 | 2.89 | 3.17 | 3.55 | 3.64 | 5.21 | 5.48 |
| Education | .72 | .84 | .92 | 1.33 | 1.11 | 1.18 | 1.29 | 1.71 | 2.00 | 2.70 | 2.93 |
| Other goods and services | 4.06 | 6.27 | 4.98 | 5.60 | 6.50 | 5.98 | 7.83 | 7.68 | 8.82 | 9.54 | 9.39 |
| Transfers | 1.04 | 1.00 | 1.45 | 1.57 | 2.14 | 1.50 | 2.55 | 2.72 | 3.59 | 6.29 | 7.27 |
| Total | 100.00 | 100.00 | 100.00 | 100.00 | 100.00 | 100.00 | 100.00 | 100.00 | 100.00 | 100.00 | 100.00 |

SOURCE: Secretaría de Programación y Presupuesto, (1979a, 107–8).

*TABLE 14.3.*

*Distribution of Consumption among Deciles: 1977*

*(Percentages)*

| *Item* | *I* | *II* | *III* | *IV* | *V* | *VI* | *VII* | *VIII* | *IX* | *X* | *Total* |
|---|---|---|---|---|---|---|---|---|---|---|---|
| Food and beverages | 1.55 | 3.27 | 4.75 | 6.16 | 7.80 | 9.48 | 11.40 | 13.78 | 17.02 | 24.79 | 100.0 |
| Clothing and shoes | 0.74 | 1.77 | 2.78 | 4.01 | 4.99 | 6.43 | 9.29 | 12.29 | 18.56 | 39.16 | 100.0 |
| Rent and house maintenance | 0.85 | 1.62 | 2.89 | 4.15 | 6.43 | 8.54 | 10.18 | 13.51 | 18.52 | 33.30 | 100.0 |
| Furniture and appliances | 1.01 | 1.90 | 2.70 | 3.75 | 5.01 | 6.67 | 8.63 | 12.18 | 16.38 | 41.77 | 100.0 |
| Health care | 1.03 | 2.64 | 3.76 | 4.77 | 5.64 | 6.94 | 7.78 | 11.37 | 16.05 | 40.01 | 100.0 |
| Transportation and communication | 0.21 | 0.56 | 1.05 | 1.76 | 2.47 | 3.64 | 5.53 | 8.77 | 15.25 | 60.76 | 100.0 |
| Entertainment | 0.07 | 0.35 | 0.91 | 1.56 | 2.83 | 4.68 | 8.29 | 11.76 | 17.85 | 51.71 | 100.0 |
| Education | 0.35 | 0.76 | 1.31 | 2.51 | 4.04 | 4.59 | 6.55 | 9.90 | 17.26 | 52.72 | 100.0 |
| Other goods and services | 0.69 | 1.50 | 2.45 | 3.13 | 4.89 | 6.17 | 8.09 | 11.24 | 17.62 | 44.22 | 100.0 |
| Transfers | 0.21 | 0.56 | 0.81 | 1.52 | 2.38 | 3.41 | 4.98 | 8.33 | 14.62 | 63.19 | 100.0 |

SOURCE: Secretaría de Programación y Presupuesto, (1979a, 109).

TABLE 14.4.

*Ranking of Food Items According to Expenditure (1977)*

| Food items | Deciles I | II | III | IV | V | VI | National total |
|---|---|---|---|---|---|---|---|
| Maize in grain | 1 | 1 | 1 | 2 | 9 | 26 | 12 |
| Beans | 2 | 2 | 2 | 3 | 3 | 4 | 5 |
| Tomatoes | 3 | 4 | 4 | 5 | 5 | 6 | 6 |
| Coffee | 4 | 6 | 13 | 9 | 10 | 22 | 22 |
| Spices | 5 | 9 | 9 | 13 | 13 | 10 | 11 |
| Lard | 6 | 5 | 7 | 14 | 21 | 25 | 25 |
| Brown sugar | 7 | 7 | 14 | 16 | 20 | 24 | 26 |
| Beef | 8 | 3 | 3 | 1 | 1 | 1 | 1 |
| Chile (pepper) | 9 | 17 | 20 | 25 | 22 | 20 | 24 |
| Vegetable oil | 10 | 10 | 8 | 8 | 8 | 9 | 10 |
| Onion | 11 | 15 | 17 | 22 | 23 | 19 | 23 |
| Refined sugar | 12 | 16 | 24 | 24 | 29 | 33 | 30 |
| Eggs | 13 | 8 | 5 | 4 | 4 | 3 | 3 |
| Pork | 14 | 19 | 21 | 19 | 10 | 12 | 13 |
| Rice | 15 | 14 | 10 | 11 | 17 | 15 | 15 |
| Bread (sweet) | 16 | 13 | 16 | 10 | 12 | 13 | 2 |
| Refreshments | 17 | 11 | 6 | 7 | 6 | 5 | 8 |
| Corn tortillas | 18 | 22 | 12 | 6 | 2 | 2 | 4 |
| Potatoes | 19 | 21 | 18 | 20 | 18 | 16 | 17 |
| Unpasteurized milk | 20 | 12 | 11 | 12 | 16 | 17 | 20 |
| Soup noodles | 21 | 18 | 15 | 15 | 15 | 14 | 18 |
| Bread (white) | 22 | 20 | 19 | 18 | 11 | 11 | 14 |
| Crackers | 23 | 25 | 25 | 26 | 28 | 31 | 29 |
| Poultry | 24 | 23 | 22 | 17 | 7 | 8 | 9 |
| Other maize products | 25 | 24 | 23 | 21 | 24 | 23 | 32 |
| Banana | 26 | 26 | 31 | 31 | 30 | 30 | 33 |
| Wheat and rice flour | 27 | 29 | 30 | 29 | 32 | 35 | 34 |
| Cheese (fresh) | 28 | 28 | 28 | 28 | 26 | 21 | 28 |
| Sweets and desserts | 29 | 30 | 26 | 30 | 25 | 18 | 21 |
| Processed fish | 30 | 31 | 35 | 37 | 40 | 42 | 44 |
| Other milk | 31 | 27 | 27 | 27 | 27 | 27 | 27 |
| Processed vegetables | 32 | 37 | 37 | 39 | 39 | 36 | 37 |
| Fresh fish | 33 | 39 | 36 | 36 | 35 | 37 | 35 |
| Pasteurized milk | 34 | 33 | 29 | 23 | 14 | 7 | 7 |
| Instant coffee | 35 | 36 | 34 | 33 | 37 | 32 | 36 |
| Other meat | 36 | 38 | 38 | 34 | 33 | 29 | 16 |
| Other fruit | 37 | 34 | 32 | 32 | 30 | 28 | 19 |
| Cocoa, tea | 38 | 32 | 33 | 38 | 36 | 39 | 39 |
| Apple | 39 | 40 | 41 | 42 | 42 | 43 | 42 |
| Other banana | 40 | 42 | 40 | 41 | 43 | 44 | 47 |
| Baby food | 41 | 35 | 39 | 35 | 34 | 34 | 31 |
| Other cheese | 42 | 45 | 45 | 45 | 45 | 45 | 41 |

*TABLE 14.4.* (Continued)

| *Food items* | *Deciles* | | | | | | *National total* |
|---|---|---|---|---|---|---|---|
| | *I* | *II* | *III* | *IV* | *V* | *VI* | |
| Lemon | 43 | 44 | 44 | 40 | 38 | 38 | 40 |
| Orange | 44 | 41 | 46 | 46 | 46 | 50 | 45 |
| Avocado | 45 | 43 | 43 | 43 | 41 | 40 | 43 |
| Other bread | 46 | 46 | 42 | 44 | 44 | 41 | 38 |
| Butter | 47 | 50 | 48 | 47 | 48 | 48 | 46 |
| Cream | 48 | 48 | 47 | 49 | 47 | 46 | 48 |
| Lettuce | 49 | 49 | 50 | 50 | 50 | 47 | 50 |
| Carrots | 50 | 47 | 49 | 48 | 49 | 49 | 49 |

SOURCE: Lustig (1980a).

parities in nutritional intake, by quantifying the amount spent on each food item for the different family income strata; the quantities were then converted into calories and proteins. The straightforward application of this procedure yielded unrealistic[13] results, due possibly to the combination of reporting errors plus the fact that the prices used to obtain the quantities may not have corresponded exactly with the actual prices paid by the consumers. Thus, Van Ginneken standardized the results using as a base the estimated average per capita consumption of calories and proteins in Mexico for 1970, which according to estimates made by the Mexican Nutrition Institute, were 2,600 calories and 80 grams of protein per capita per day. Van Ginneken's calculations then actually measure the relative consumption levels of calories and proteins among income groups, more than the absolute levels. The results obtained appear in Table 14-5. Here one can observe the prevailing inequality in the caloric and protein intake. For example, the highest income group (families earning above 10,000 pesos per month in 1968) consumed almost twice as many calories and over 2.5 times more grams of protein than the lowest income strata (the families earning between zero and 300 pesos per month in 1968).

The nutrition recommendations given by the FAO during the early seventies were 2,120 calories and 45.5 grams of proteins per capita per day. With these recommended levels and the adjusted results based on the 1968 survey Van Ginneken concluded that around 40 percent of the families in agriculture and 26 percent of the rest, did not achieve these minima. As a result, the number of "undernourished" families totaled 2.5 million, equivalent to 13.5 million persons or 28 percent of the population of Mexico. One must bear in mind, however, that these estimates do not really reflect levels and thus should be taken only as a rough approximation.

An exercise analogous to Van Ginneken's was carried out by the author

*TABLE 14.5.*
*Daily per Capita Consumption of Calories and Grams of Protein per Income Stratum: 1968*

| | *Less than $300 pesos* | *$301–600* | *$601–1,000* | *$1,001–3,000* | *$3,001–6,000* | *$6,001–10,000* | *$10,001 or more* |
|---|---|---|---|---|---|---|---|
| Calories | 1,642 | 2,071 | 2,347 | 2,666 | 3,272 | 3,604 | 4,102 |
| Protein (grams) | 51 | 62 | 70 | 82 | 102 | 115 | 134 |
| Percent of population | 4.3 | 14.6 | 19.7 | 41.7 | 14.1 | 3.5 | 2.1 |

SOURCE: Van Ginneken (1974, 67).
NOTE: These calculations were made given an estimated national per capita average for 1970 of 2,600 calories and 80 grams of proteins.

with the information contained in the 1977 Income and Expenditure Survey. The results are shown in Table 14-6. According to the FAO recommendations (2,120 calories and 45.5 grams of protein per capita per day) around 20 percent of the Mexican population in 1977 would have qualified as undernourished. The levels recommended by the National Institute of Nutrition, however, are quite different: 2,600 calories and 80 grams of protein per capita per day. This would carry the percentage of the population that was undernourished up to 70–80 percent (see Table 14-6). A simple average of the two recommended levels would show that between 40 percent and 50 percent of the population is undernourished. On the other hand, the caloric and protein consumption is almost twice as high and 3.75 times higher, respectively, between the lowest 10 percent and the highest 5 percent of the population.

As a rough approximation, then, the undernourished population in 1977 would be comprised of those families who received an income that was below the average minimum wage. This is so because the latter in 1977 was 2,707 pesos per month, while the average household income for the fifth decile was equal to 2,693 pesos (see Table 14-6). That is, if the average 1977 minimum wage was indeed the threshold income to guarantee an adequate food intake.

Maintaining the distribution of income as a constant and assuming an increase in real country-level per capita income equal to 5 percent per year[14] (an optimistic assumption since it would require a GDP growth of around 8 percent per year), our results showed that families in the lowest decile would have to wait for 39 years, while the II, III, and IV deciles would have to wait for 21, 13, and 6 years, respectively, to reach an income equivalent to the 1977 minimum wage in real terms. If instead of 5 percent, real per capita income grew at 3 percent per year, it would take the bottom decile up to 64 years and 35, 21, and 10 years for the II, III, and IV deciles, respectively, to reach such an income. On the other end of the spectrum, if the entire rise in income went to the bottom 40 percent while the real income of the rest remained constant, it would take 2.5

TABLE 14.6.

*Daily per Capita Consumption of Calories and Grams of Protein per Decile: 1977*

| | *I* | *II* | *III* | *IV* | *V* | *VI* | *VII* | *VIII* | *IX* | *X* | *Xa* | *Xb* | *Total* |
|---|---|---|---|---|---|---|---|---|---|---|---|---|---|
| Calories | 1,833.5 | 2,152.12 | 2,309.02 | 2,315.77 | 2,443.13 | 2,525.10 | 2,756.15 | 2,782.62 | 3,064.77 | 3,386.79 | 3,174.97 | 3,643.13 | 2,600 |
| Protein (grams) | 36.62 | 46.52 | 53.74 | 57.67 | 67.70 | 75.66 | 84.64 | 87.91 | 101.05 | 123.06 | 111.29 | 137.50 | 75 |
| Household monthly income (pesos) | 406 | 944 | 1,431 | 2,005 | 2,693 | 3,412 | 4,398 | 5,779 | 8,204 | 16,962 | 11,787 | 22,137 | 4,623.25 |

SOURCE: Secretaría de Programación y Presupuesto (1979a, 79).

NOTE: These calculations were made given an estimated national per capita average for 1976 of 2,600 calories and 76 grams of proteins.

years to reach the required average for the first four deciles—if real per capita income grew at 5 percent per year, and 4.12 years if it grew at 3 percent.

In the introduction it was mentioned that, according to the National Nutrition Institute estimates, the daily availability of calories (2,600) and grams (76) of protein in per capita terms is sufficient to meet the recommended levels—if it is equally distributed. Thus, the problem of undernutrition does not lie so much on the "production side" as it does on the "distribution side." Increasing food production—though essential—does not by itself guarantee that nutrition standards will get better. The increments in food may be exported and/or go to the groups who have the purchasing power to buy it—and not necessarily to those who need it most. Therefore, to ensure that food goes to the latter, other additional mechanisms have to be designed and implemented.

### Basic Recommended Diet and Redistributive Requirements

Another way to calculate the nutritional gap and provide an estimate of the malnourished population is by means of a normative food consumption basket whose cost can be compared with the amount spent on food by different income groups. The gap between the two values, presuming that both have been derived from the same set of prices, gives an idea of the gap in food intake not measured, however, in terms of calories, proteins or any other nutrient but in the monetary unit. In order to calculate the deficit in nutrients it would be necessary to compute the gap, item by item, between actual consumption and that included in the recommended diet. In theory one could carry out both calculations, i.e., the aggregate and the itemized one, but this was impossible in practice because no reliable information exists on what the actual consumption is of each separate item. This information in principle could have been obtained either from the 1979 Nutrition[15] Survey directly or by converting into quantities the amounts in nutrition value recorded in the 1977 IES. However, when this was attempted the results turned out to be unrealistic; in the case of the Nutrition Survey the problem arises perhaps because the available results are preliminary and some adjustments and corrections have to be made before the data can be used.

In the case of the 1977 IES the problem lies perhaps in the prices used to transform the expenditures in pesos into quantities. If this is the case the assumption—that the set of prices used to calculate the recommended diet are the same as those implicit in the amount spent on food—is no longer valid. But, even if item by item prices should not be taken as equal, one could argue that—when aggregating over all the commodities—errors and differences may cancel each other out so that the gap in pesos between the actual and the recommended diet is more or less accurate.

The construction of the recommended consumption diet can be done in many different ways. Here we have chosen the Basic Recommended Diet (BRD) proposed by the *Mexican Food System* which is presented in Table 14-7. The BRD used by the *Mexican Food System* was computed using linear programming techniques; the objective function was to minimize the cost of the diet, subject to a series of constraints that included a list of nutrient requirements, consumption habits, etc.[16] The BRD obtained in grams was then converted into pesos multiplying each item by its corresponding 1977 (regional) price. This was carried out for nine regions and the results appear in column (3) of Table 14-8. The nine regions were taken from the regionalization used in the 1977 Income and Expenditure Survey: eight correspond to groupings of the Mexican states (excluding the three largest metropolitan areas), and the ninth to the metropolitan areas of Guadalajara, Monterrey, and Mexico City (the classification of states into regions is shown in Table 14-9).

The BRD in 1977 pesos calculated for each region with the corresponding prices was compared with the corresponding actual average per capita expenditure on food. This was done for 18 socioeconomic groups constructed in the following way: for each region households were divided in two groups according to whether they earned an income less than, or equal to the corresponding 1977 minimum wage (groups 1 and 2) or more (group 3). Afterward, those households that were placed in groups 1 and 2 were classified in two sectors: *rural* (group 1) and *urban* (group 2) households, according to whether the main activity of the head of the household was in agriculture or not.[17] Finally those households that had an income equal to, or below the corresponding 1977 minimum wage (by region and urban-rural) were selected. The minimum wage was used here as a threshold, given what was said in the previous section about the undernourished population in Mexico. Because this threshold, as we have mentioned, is based on somewhat weak grounds, we carried out an additional test; given the cost of the BRD, we computed the number of households above the minimum wage that spent a smaller amount on food than the cost of the BRD, and the number of households below the minimum wage that spent more than the BRD. The results were 10 cases in a sample of over 8,000. Thus, the minimum-wage threshold seems to be "safe" enough for our purposes.

For each socioeconomic group, the deficit between the BRD in pesos and the actual expenditure on food was calculated, and an estimate of the required income was provided. The required income measures the per capita income that would be sufficient to guarantee a level of expenditure on food equal to the BRD in pesos, and it was calculated as follows. For each socioeconomic group we estimated the corresponding "income elasticity"[18] for food, as the coefficient of a log-linear regression of per capita expenditure on food on per capita total expenditure. The information came from the 1977 IES; the coefficients were estimated using generalized least squares, to correct for heteroskedasticity, and the method of instru-

*TABLE 14.7.*

*Basic Recommended Diet*

| | *Net daily per capita intake (grams)* | *Gross daily per capita consumption (grams)* | *(percentage)* |
|---|---|---|---|
| *Corn* | *497.19* | *516.45* | *43.74* |
| Maize in grains | 221.48 | 240.74 | 20.39 |
| Tortillas | 268.25 | 268.25 | 22.72 |
| Dough | 7.46 | 7.46 | 0.63 |
| *Wheat* | *88.14* | *88.14* | *7.48* |
| Flour | 16.6 | 16.6 | 1.41 |
| Sweet bread | 16.78 | 16.78 | 1.42 |
| White bread | 30.0 | 30.0 | 2.54 |
| Crackers | 8.76 | 8.76 | 0.75 |
| Noodles | 16.0 | 16.0 | 1.36 |
| *Rice* | *18.0* | *18.0* | *1.52* |
| *Beans* | *52.0* | *52.0* | *4.40* |
| *Potatoes* | *23.04* | *28.1* | *2.38* |
| *Vegetables* | *35.59* | *40.9* | *3.46* |
| Tomatoes | 30.18 | 34.3 | 2.91 |
| Chili | 1.82 | 2.0 | 0.17 |
| Onions | 2.66 | 3.1 | 0.26 |
| Lettuce | 0.24 | 0.4 | 0.03 |
| Carrots | 0.69 | 1.1 | 0.09 |
| *Fruits* | *41.53* | *63.9* | *5.41* |
| Banana | 17.88 | 26.3 | 2.23 |
| Apples | 0.93 | 1.4 | 0.12 |
| Lemon | 4.77 | 7.7 | 0.65 |
| Oranges | 17.95 | 28.5 | 2.41 |
| *Dairy and meat* | *278.58* | *306.0* | *25.94* |
| Beef | 13.11 | 19.0 | 1.61 |
| Pork | 7.1 | 10.0 | 0.85 |
| Poultry | 6.72 | 12.0 | 1.02 |
| Other meat | 5.46 | 7.0 | 0.60 |
| Eggs | 25.52 | 29.0 | 2.46 |
| Milk (fresh) | 210.0 | 210.0 | 17.79 |
| Lard | 2.0 | 2.0 | 0.17 |
| Fish | 8.67 | 17.0 | 1.44 |

*TABLE 14.7.* (Continued)

| | *Net daily per capita intake (grams)* | *Gross daily per capita consumption (grams)* | *(percentage)* |
|---|---|---|---|
| *Others* | *67.0* | *67.0* | *5.67* |
| Vegetable oil | 17.0 | 17.0 | 1.44 |
| Sugar | 50.0 | 50.0 | 4.23 |
| TOTAL | 1,161.7 | 1,180.5 | 100.0 |

SOURCE: Mexican Food System (1980).

mental variables with per capita income as an instrument for per capita total expenditure, to correct for errors of measurement.[19] Using the estimated elasticity and given the required increment on food expenditure, one can estimate the required increase in income; applying this increment to current per capita income, the required income is estimated.

As will be seen in Table 14 8, the required increment in income (column 7) can be very high: i.e., for group 5.1 (region 5, rural sector) it is around 170 percent. In general it is highest in regions 4, 5, 6, 7 and 8, the poorest in the country, especially region 5.

In column 11 of Table 14-9 we have estimated the number of years that it would take for the per capita income in each region to reach the required level, assuming an optimistic growth in per capita income of 5 percent per year and no changes in the distribution of income. As it turns out, in the case of regions 4 and 5 the estimated number of years (column 11) would be around 13 and 21, respectively.

These simple experiments, in spite of their shortcomings and weaknesses, again indicate the need for the implementation of policy measures if the conditions of the poor in terms of food intake are to be improved in the short run. In what follows we will compare three possible policy measures in this direction in terms of their fiscal cost. These policies are income transfers, food stamps, and (food) price subsidies.

## Policy Options and Their Fiscal Cost

There are a number of measures that a government may implement to improve the nutritional standards of the undernourished. These range from redistribution of wealth and income to educational programs geared to change "bad" food consumption habits. As a global distinction, policies can be directed toward the entire population, such as (general) food price subsidies, or may be target-group oriented.The latter imply that the mea-

*TABLE 14.8.*

*Required Monthly per Capita Income by Region and Sector*

| (1) Region and Sector | (2) Actual expenditure on food* | (3) Recommended expenditure on food* | (4) Deficit* (3)-(2) | (5) Deficit in % (4)/(2) | (6) Expenditure-elasticity for food | (7) Required increment in income in % (5)/(6) | (8) Current income** | (9) Required increment in income** | (10) Required income** | (11) Estimated years |
|---|---|---|---|---|---|---|---|---|---|---|
| 1.1 | 7.54 | 10.40 | −2.86 | 37.93 | 1.1397 | 33.28 | 374.05 | 124.48 | 498.53 | 6.6 |
| 1.2 | 12.46 | 10.40 | — | — | 0.7910 | — | 492.99 | — | — | — |
| 2.1 | 7.12 | 9.69 | −2.57 | 36.09 | 1.4669 | 24.60 | 252.59 | 62.14 | 314.73 | 6.3 |
| 2.2 | 12.05 | 9.69 | — | — | 1.3990 | — | 490.83 | — | — | — |
| 3.1 | 6.76 | 10.18 | −3.42 | 50.59 | 1.2681 | 39.80 | 241.44 | 96.31 | 337.75 | 8.4 |
| 3.2 | 9.74 | 10.18 | −0.44 | 4.51 | 1.1753 | 5.30 | 368.55 | 19.53 | 388.08 | 1.0 |
| 4.1 | 5.41 | 10.09 | −4.68 | 86.50 | 1.2424 | 69.62 | 213.80 | 148.85 | 362.65 | 12.8 |
| 4.2 | 6.84 | 10.09 | −3.25 | 47.51 | 1.1397 | 41.69 | 321.08 | 133.86 | 454.94 | 8.0 |
| 5.1 | 3.59 | 9.84 | −6.25 | 174.09 | 1.0244 | 169.94 | 190.53 | 222.91 | 413.44 | 20.7 |
| 5.2 | 7.22 | 9.84 | −2.62 | 36.28 | 1.1786 | 30.78 | 284.38 | 87.53 | 371.91 | 6.34 |
| 6.1 | 6.44 | 10.20 | −3.76 | 58.38 | 1.0334 | 56.49 | 225.70 | 127.50 | 353.20 | 9.42 |
| 6.2 | 8.72 | 10.20 | −1.48 | 16.97 | 0.9364 | 18.12 | 358.05 | 64.88 | 422.93 | 3.21 |
| 7.1 | 6.35 | 10.36 | −4.01 | 63.14 | 1.1999 | 52.62 | 221.06 | 116.32 | 337.38 | 10.03 |
| 7.2 | 8.83 | 10.36 | −1.53 | 17.32 | 0.9631 | 17.98 | 386.79 | 69.54 | 456.33 | 3.27 |
| 8.1 | 6.10 | 9.86 | −3.76 | 61.63 | 1.2265 | 50.25 | 202.14 | 101.58 | 303.72 | 9.84 |
| 8.2 | 9.27 | 9.86 | −0.59 | 6.36 | 0.9371 | 6.79 | 326.35 | 22.16 | 348.51 | 1.26 |
| 9.1 | 8.61 | 10.37 | −1.76 | 20.44 | 0.7472 | 27.36 | 390.82 | 106.93 | 497.75 | 3.8 |
| 9.2 | 10.31 | 10.37 | −0.06 | 0.58 | 1.0858 | 0.53 | 512.80 | 2.72 | 515.52 | 0.12 |

SOURCE: Author's calculations. Based on the Income and Expenditure Survey, 1977 (Secretaría de Programación y Presupuesto).

NOTE: In Column (1), each i.j refers to region (i = 1, . . . 9) and to sector (j = 1, rural; and j = 2, urban), respectively.

*In daily per capita 1977 pesos; exclude alcoholic beverages and soft drinks; includes autoconsumption.

**In monthly per capita 1977 pesos.

*TABLE 14.9.*
*Regionalization and Corresponding Minimum Wages for 1977*

| *Region* | *States* | *Minimum Wage (pesos)* |
|---|---|---|
| 1 | Baja California Norte<br>Baja California Sur<br>Sinaloa<br>Sonora<br>Nayarit | $3185 |
| 2 | Tamaulipas<br>Nuevo León | 2694 |
| 3 | Coahuila<br>Chihuahua<br>San Luis Potosí<br>Zacatecas<br>Durango | 2684 |
| 4 | Aguascalientes<br>Colima<br>Guanajuato<br>Michoacán<br>Jalisco | 2460 |
| 5 | Hidalgo<br>Morelos<br>Puebla<br>Querétaro<br>Tlaxcala<br>México | 2619 |
| 6 | Tabasco<br>Veracruz | 2933 |
| 7 | Campeche<br>Quintana Roo<br>Yucatán | 2367 |
| 8 | Chiapas<br>Guerrero<br>Oaxaca | 2357 |
| 9 | Metropolitan Areas:<br>México<br>Monterrey<br>Guadalajara | 3066 |

SOURCE: *Secretaría de Programación y Presupuesto* (1979b).

sure will, in principle, only affect a particular preselected group of the population.[20] Among the target-group oriented policies the most common options are: direct free distribution of food, income transfers, food stamps and price subsidies. The choice between a general or a target-group oriented policy, and among the targeted policies must be based on a series of criteria such as the time required to implement the policy, associated fiscal cost, administrative cost, nutrition-effectiveness, political feasibility, etc.

In what follows we will obtain orders of magnitude in terms of the fiscal cost for three target-group-oriented policy options—income transfers, food stamps and price subsidies. In addition to fiscal cost, other criteria will be mentioned at a qualitative level, since some of them—for different reasons—are very hard to measure. In addition, we will also compute the fiscal cost associated with a general-price subsidy. As will be seen this measure turns out to be much more expensive than any of the others—in addition to the fact that it might be regressive in terms of income distribution—but since it is the easiest to handle, it is the policy most frequently implemented by governments.[21]

### *Income-Transfers*

This policy option entails a direct transfer of income to the population group currently undernourished. The amount of income to be transferred must be sufficient to cover the required expenditure on food and thus it will depend, among other things, on the marginal propensity to spend on food of the target group. It can be shown that the fiscal cost per unit of increment in food consumption is a fraction equal to *f* can be expressed as

$$FC_u = \frac{P_f}{m_p}\left[1 + C(1+f)\frac{e_p^d}{e_p^s}\right]$$

where

$P_f$ = (unitary) price of food
$m_p$ = marginal propensity to consume food of the target group
$e_p^d$ = demand-price elasticity for food of the target group
$e_p^s$ = excess-supply price elasticity for food faced by the target group.[22]
$f$ = required relative increment in food consumption by the target group

The unitary fiscal cost ($FC_u$) will be greater, the higher the price of food ($P_f$), the required increment (f) and the demand-price elasticity of the target group are, and the lower are the marginal propensity to spend on food ($m_p$) and the excess-supply price elasticity. When the commodity is partly imported and the subsidy does not discriminate between imports and domestic production, the $FC_u$ is evaluated for a $e^s = \infty$, which implies that $e_p^s = \infty$; the $FC_u$, then becomes equal to:

$$FC_u = \frac{P_f}{m_p}$$

In our calculations we have made this assumption since it is the case that part of the food in Mexico is imported, especially grains.

The total fiscal cost of an income transfer program in Mexico was calculated in the following way. The required marginal propensities to consume (column 2 of Table 14-10) were obtained multiplying our estimated income elasticities by the corresponding average propensity to spend. The inverse of the $m_p$'s give us the fiscal cost per unit of increment as a ratio of the price; these are shown in column 3 of Table 14-10. To obtain the fiscal cost associated with the required increment and evaluated at the relevant price, we can multiply the magnitudes in column 3 by the corresponding required increment in food expenditure (column 4 of Table 14-8). If this new magnitude is then multiplied by the size of the population (column 4 of Table 14-10) and by 365 (days), and then added over the eighteen socioeconomic groups, we get an estimate of the total fiscal cost per year associated with this particular policy; this has been calculated in column 5 of Table 14-10. As it turns out, the total fiscal cost of implementing the income transfer would have amounted to something like 2.56 percent of the 1977 Mexican GDP.

This magnitude seems quite high especially when compared with the proportion of government expenditure in total: in 1977 this was equal to 11.7 percent of the GDP. Moreover, the cost of this policy will be even higher when the administrative costs of implementing it are taken into account. However, one should bear in mind that we are calculating the fiscal cost of the income-transfer policy with a series of parameters that may be overestimating the "true" fiscal cost, but that put us on the "safe" side in terms of fighting undernutrition in Mexico. This is so because the calorie-protein threshold that was used is relatively high when compared with the FAO requirements for example. In addition since the BRD was calculated to fulfill many different nutrient requirements, it includes food items that are relatively expensive; moreover, the data on food expenditure may be underestimated because of reporting errors and inadequate measurement of autoconsumption. All these factors can yield an inflated version of the fiscal cost not only because the gap between actual expenditure on food and the BRD (in pesos) is overestimated, but because the size of the undernourished population may also be overestimated because the latter is sensitive to the magnitude of actual and recommended consumption. In any case, our main interest is to compare the fiscal cost of different policy options and since the former are all going to be calculated with the same data base—even if the absolute levels overestimate the true fiscal cost—one can still go ahead with the comparisons. Our next task, then, is to calculate the fiscal cost of a food stamp program.

## *Food Stamp Program*

Food stamp programs have been widely used in the United States.[23] Such a program provides participants with the opportunity of purchasing

*TABLE 14.10.*
*Fiscal Cost of Target Group-Oriented Policies: Income Transfers and Food Stamps**

| *(1)* | *(2)* | *(3)* | | *(4)* | *(5)* | |
|---|---|---|---|---|---|---|
| *Region and sector* | *Marginal propensity to spend on food* | *Fiscal cost per unit of increment/ price of food (in pesos)*** | | *Population (in thousands)* | *Total fiscal cost/year (in millions of 1977 pesos)* | |
| | | *IT* | *FS* | | *IT* | *FS* |
| 1.1 | .6664 | 1.50 | 1 | 1,298.1 | 2,032.6 | 1,355.1 |
| 1.2 | .4071 | 2.46 | 1 | 378.6 | — | — |
| 2.1 | .6152 | 1.63 | 1 | 394.1 | 602.5 | 369.7 |
| 2.2 | .6103 | 1.64 | 1 | 285.9 | — | — |
| 3.1 | .6016 | 1.66 | 1 | 1,761.8 | 3,650.1 | 2,199.2 |
| 3.2 | .5909 | 1.69 | 1 | 880.9 | 239.1 | 141.4 |
| 4.1 | .6435 | 1.55 | 1 | 2,495.7 | 6,607.9 | 4,263.1 |
| 4.2 | .6435 | 1.55 | 1 | 1,189.9 | 2,187.8 | 1,411.5 |
| 5.1 | .6500 | 1.54 | 1 | 3,036.4 | 10,677.2 | 6,926.8 |
| 5.2 | .6335 | 1.58 | 1 | 1,398.4 | 2,112.9 | 1,337.3 |
| 6.1 | .6000 | 1.67 | 1 | 2,163.3 | 4,958.1 | 2,968.9 |
| 6.2 | .4641 | 2.15 | 1 | 463.6 | 538.4 | 250.4 |
| 7.1 | .7783 | 1.29 | 1 | 934.9 | 1,765.2 | 1,368.4 |
| 7.2 | .5851 | 1.71 | 1 | 409.5 | 391.0 | 228.7 |
| 8.1 | .6227 | 1.61 | 1 | 2,179.2 | 4,815.1 | 2,990.7 |
| 8.2 | .4759 | 2.10 | 1 | 873.2 | 394.9 | 188.1 |
| 9.1 | .4202 | 2.38 | 1 | 1,120.4 | 1,712.9 | 719.7 |
| 9.2 | .5247 | 1.91 | 1 | 3,052.0 | 127.6 | 66.8 |
| TOTAL | | | | 24,315.9 | 42,803.9 | 26,785.8 |

SOURCE: Author's calculations in Column (4). Based on "Income and Expenditure Survey, 1977" Secretaría de Programación y Presupuesto (1979b).

NOTE: In Column (1) each i.j refers to region (i = 1, . . . , 9) and sector (j = 1, rural; j = 2, urban), respectively.

IT: income transfer

FS: food stamp

*These calculations were made under the assumption that food is partly imported.

**These are the fiscal costs per unit of increment as a ratio of the price of food.

a fixed amount of food at a lesser cost than market prices. If the consumers' indifference maps were known, then an optimal food stamp program could be implemented whose cost per unit of food reaching the target group would be less than the price of the food.[24] However, this is impossible in practice and thus one has to settle for a suboptimal program where the cost per unit of increment is equal to the price of food, i.e., where the cost of the food stamps equals the consumer's expenditure on food without the program. In the case where the programs have no effect on the supply price of food (e.g., when part of the food is imported), the fiscal cost per unit of increment as a ratio of the price of food of a suboptimal food stamp program would then equal unity.[25] (This is shown in column 3 of Table 14-10.)

The total fiscal cost is calculated in analogous fashion to that of the income transfer: the $FC_u = 1$ peso is multiplied by the food expenditure deficit (shown in column 4 of Table 14-8), and this quantity is then multiplied by population and by 365, to obtain the total fiscal cost per year. In comparison to the income-transfer whose cost was 2.56 of the 1977 GDP, the fiscal cost of the food stamp program would be 1.60 percent.

### *Food Price Subsidy*

A target-group-oriented food price subsidy provides beneficiaries with as much food as they wish to purchase at a reduced price. In general, a price subsidy would not be applied to all food but to some preselected commodities. However, state-owned food stores may be distributing all food items at a constant discount, and if only the target group is allowed to shop at such stores, this would be a real-world example of a target-group-oriented overall food price subsidy.

The fiscal cost per unit of increment as a ratio of the price of food associated with this policy is equal to:[26]

$$FC_u = \frac{1 + f}{e_p^d}$$

where $f$ is the required increment in food consumption (measured as a fraction of initial consumption).

Since it was not possible to calculate the price elasticities by region or sector (see Appendix), we have computed the fiscal cost of a food price subsidy for the target group at a national level, i.e., those households that earned an income less than or equal to the corresponding minimum wage. In order to carry out the comparisons with the fiscal cost of the income transfer and the food stamp program, we have recalculated the first using the propensity to spend on food estimated for the target group at a national level. As will be seen, using the latter increases the estimated total fiscal cost when compared with the fiscal cost of the income transfer

*TABLE 14.11.*
*Fiscal Cost of Different Policy Options**

| *Policy* | *General formula*** | *Unitary fiscal cost*** in 1977 pesos* | *Total fiscal cost**** (in millions of pesos/year)* | *Total fiscal cost as a % of 1977 GDP* |
|---|---|---|---|---|
| Income transfer | $\frac{1}{m_p}$ | 1.898 | 50,872.9 | 3.04 |
| Food stamp | 1 | 1 | 26,785.8 | 1.60 |
| Target-group price subsidy | $\frac{1+f}{e_p^d}$ | 1.814 | 48,621.4 | 2.91 |

SOURCE: Author's calculations. Based on Income and Expenditure Survey, 1977 *Secretaría de Programación y Presupuesto*, 1979b.

NOTE: $m_p = .5270$; $f = .42$; $e_p^d = .784$.

*These calculations were made on the assumption that part of the food is imported (i.e., $e^s \to \infty$).

**These are the fiscal costs per unit of increment as a ratio of the price of food.

***The total fiscal cost is obtained by multiplying unitary fiscal cost by the deficit (3.02), the target population size (24,315,900) and 365 days.

aggregated over regions and sectors (shown in Table 14-10); this may be due, however, to the difference between the marginal propensities to spend obtained at the regional and sectorial levels, and that estimated directly from the national data. Again, we are interested in comparing the orders of magnitude more than in the absolute levels, and thus this should not be viewed as a serious problem.

At the national level, per capita daily food expenditure by the target group was estimated at 7.15 pesos (1977), and the deficit at –3.02 pesos (1977).[27] This means that *f* is equal to .42. In Table 14-11 we summarize the fiscal cost per unit of increment and the total fiscal cost associated with the different policy options. As can be observed, the target group food price subsidy is less expensive in terms of its fiscal cost than the income transfer; however, it is somewhat more expensive than the food stamp program; as a percentage of the GDP, the fiscal cost of the income transfer would equal 3.04 percent while that of the food price subsidy and the food stamp program would be 2.91 percent and 1.60 percent, respectively.

However, an income-transfer has a big advantage in contrast with the other two policy options in that it allows for an increase in the consumption of other products different from foodstuffs and thus raises the "welfare" level of the target population by more than the other policies considered here.

It should also be mentioned that the required decline in the price of food to encourage an increase of 42 percent in the consumption of food on the part of our target group would be of an order of magnitude of 48 percent.[28] Such a decline may not be possible to sustain from either a practical or a political point of view.

*Intensity of Consumption and Fiscal Cost of Product-Specific Policies.*

So far we have dealt only with policy measures and the implied fiscal cost of increasing the consumption of food as a whole. This was done mainly to make comparisons among alternatives easy and more evident. In practice, however, price subsidies (or food stamps) may not be implemented for food as a whole and at a uniform rate. Thus, one policy question that confronts the state is: What products should be chosen for subsidies if the objective is to enable the poorer classes to benefit the most? This question becomes more important when a price subsidy cannot be target oriented because the government does not have the mechanisms to enforce it.

Thus, in this section we will introduce a criterion that could shed some light on what products should be selected for policy purposes. The discussion will be followed by some calculations of the expected fiscal cost of food stamps and price subsidies on specific products for the target group only—and for the entire population. The criterion for product selection proposed here is something that has been called the intensity of consumption (IC).

The concept of intensity of consumption is somewhat analogous to the Gini coefficient and is defined by the ratio of the shaded area in Figures 14-1, 14-2 and 14-3, divided—respectively—by the "perfect equality" triangle. In the horizontal axis of Figures 14-1, 14-2 and 14-3 the population is measured in percentage terms, whereas in the vertical axis we have the corresponding proportion of any particular product that is consumed. Whenever the IC coefficient is greater than unity it indicates that the consumption of that particular product is more "intensive"—i.e. more favored—by the lower-income groups (see Figure 14-1); the opposite is the case when the IC coefficient is less than one (see Figure 14-2); an IC equal to unity indicates that the proportion consumed is uniformly distributed; i.e., the share of consumption of that good is *identical* to the share of population (see Figure 14-3).

We have carried out the calculation of several IC coefficients for Mexico for several products that appear to be consumed relatively more by the poorer population[29] that could be part of a state-run distribution program more easily because they are not perishable goods. The results are shown in Table 14-12.

Thus, unprocessed corn and corn-derived products are very good candidates for a price subsidy. In fact, the corn *tortilla*—which is already sold at a lower price because its inputs are subsidized—has an IC coefficient

## Intensity of Consumption

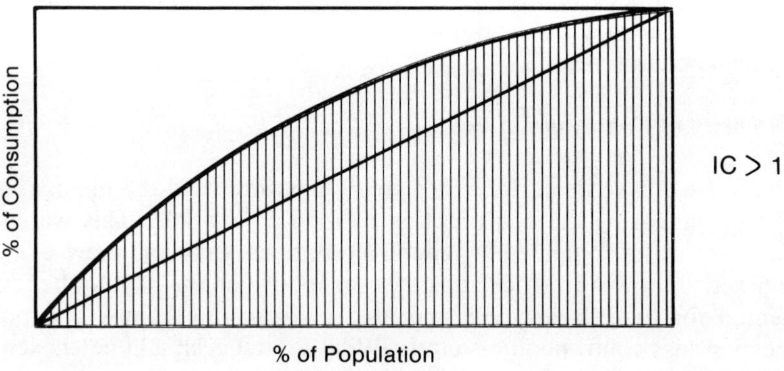


**Figure 14-1.**

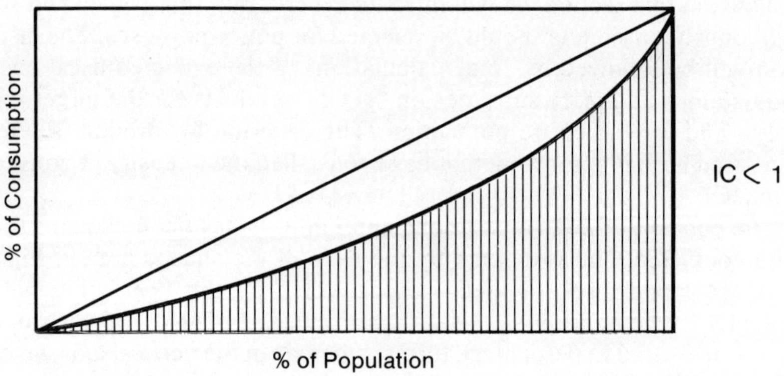


**Figure 14-2.**

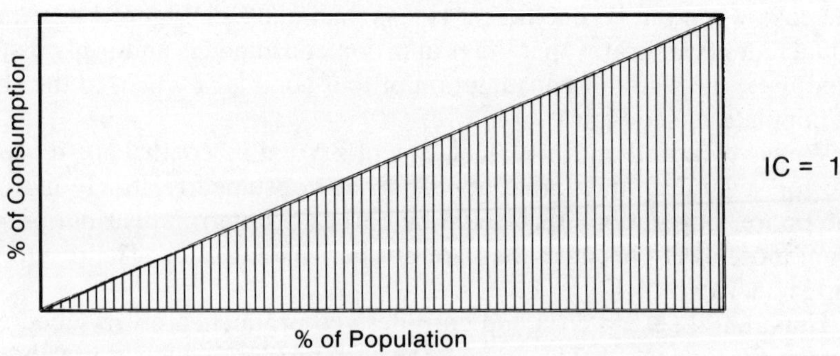


**Figure 14-3.**

*TABLE 14.12.*
*Intensity of Consumption Coefficients*

| *Food Product* | *IC* |
|---|---|
| Maize | 1.16 |
| Brown Sugar | 1.0062 |
| Lard | .9908 |
| Corn Flour | .9768 |
| Beans | .9605 |
| Corn Dough *(nixtamal)* | .9339 |
| Refined Sugar | .9075 |
| Rice | .8834 |

SOURCE: Author's calculations based on the 1977 Income and Expenditure Survey, *Secretaría de Programación y Presupuesto, (1976b).*

equal to .7965, i.e., lower than other corn products. The latter means that the benefits of a general subsidy accrue relatively less to the poorer classes than a subsidy on maize, corn dough or corn flour. However, this might be true[30] for the rural areas but not for the urban population, because the former tends to produce the *tortillas* at home and buy the inputs, whereas the latter buys the finished product. Thus, when designing policies, differences between the rural target population and the urban one should be taken into account.

We will now give some indication of the associated unitary fiscal cost of target-group-oriented and general-price subsidies for the list of products included in Table 14-12. There are three empirical problems in this calculation: one is that price-elasticities for specific products were calculated using the Frisch method and in this case the "want independence" assumption is hard to sustain; also, this method cannot be used in the presence of inferior goods; thus, we will not be able to obtain fiscal costs for some products; finally, since it was impossible to construct reliable data on the consumption gaps for specific products we cannot define what the required increment is in the expenditure for each good. Therefore, we chose a different road to carry out the comparisons starting by defining a certain decline in the price of the final product and then calculating the proportional increase in expenditure; the experiments were carried out assuming a 10 percent subsidy on the final price of each product. In Table 14-13 we present the results of such a subsidy on beans, corn dough *(nixtamal),* rice and corn *tortillas;* these calculations were not carried out for the rest of the articles that appear in Table 14-12 because the estimated price-elasticity was unavailable (they were either inferior goods or had nonsignificant coefficients).

From Table 14-13 we can observe that it is much more "cost effective" to subsidize products that have a high price-elasticity like corn *tortillas* and corn dough and to do it for the target group only; for the case of *tortillas* the unitary cost between the target-group oriented and the gen-

*TABLE 14.13.*
*Fiscal Cost of Product-Specific Policies*

| Product | *Price elasticity of target group* ($e_p^d$) | *Price elasticity of total population* ($e_p^d$) | *C Estimated rise in consumption* (f) | *Unitary cost of target-oriented subsidy (TOS)** | *Unitary cost of general subsidy (GS)** | *Unitary cost of food stamp ("optimal" program)* |
|---|---|---|---|---|---|---|
| 1. Beans | −.1618 | ns | .01618 | 6.28 | — | 1 |
| 2. Corn/dough *(nixtamal)* | −1.0145 | ns | .10145 | 1.086 | — | 1 |
| 3. Rice | −.4371 | −.1976 | .04371 | 2.388 | 5.161 | 1 |
| 4. Corn *tortillas* | −.9482 | −.4535 | .09482 | 1.155 | 2.305 | 1 |

SOURCE: Author's calculations. Based on the Income and Expenditure Survey, 1977, Secretaría de Programación y Presupuesto (1979b).

ns: not significant

*These calculations were made under the assumption that supply is infinitely elastic. The formula for TOS is given in the text in the previous section; the formula for GS is: $\frac{f}{e_p^d}\left(\frac{e_p^d}{e_g^d f} + 1\right)$.

They both are a measure of the unit fiscal cost per unit of increment as a ratio of the corresponding price. The simulated decline in price is of 10 percent.

eral subsidy doubles: it goes from 1.155 to 2.305. The difference in total fiscal cost will be even higher because in the general subsidy the unit cost has to be multiplied by total population and in the other case it is only the target population.

The corollary is that the government should choose to subsidize those goods with the highest priced target-group elasticities and with higher IC coefficients. In addition, the government should always strive to have target-group oriented subsidies since this not only is more cost effective but it is also more egalitarian.

Compared to price-subsidies an "optimal" food stamp program again would be the most cost effective[31]. To implement such an optimal program might not be possible because it would require a precise knowledge of the target population's preferences and thus the results here may be underestimating the cost of a feasible food stamps option.[32]

## Concluding Remarks

On the basis of the fiscal cost our results show that a *food stamp* program would be by far the most cost effective; it would cost almost 50 percent less than an income transfer, for example. The second most cost-effective policy is a *target-group oriented price subsidy;* the third one is the *income transfer* option. This ranking of the policies is surprising to us since the marginal propensity to spend on food—as well as the price elasticity for food—is bound to be less than unity and, as we saw in the formulas, this is the main reason why the income transfer and the price-subsidy will be higher in cost than the food stamp program. In cases where the target group is poor, however, the price elasticity and the marginal propensity to spend on food tend to approach one, and the three programs become almost equally cost effective. In general, a target-group-oriented price subsidy would be fiscally more cost effective than an income transfer the larger the price elasticity is, compared to the marginal propensity to spend. We must remind ourselves, however, that an income-transfer can improve the general standard of living more effectively.

The fiscal cost of a general-price subsidy for a specific product like corn *tortillas* for example, turned out to be (per unit of increment) twice as high as the target-group-oriented price subsidy (see Table 14-13). This shows how costly any kind of nondiscriminatory general-price subsidy is—in addition to the fact that it also benefits the higher-income classes who do not need it. If the *tortillas* could be sold at a lower price to the target group only, the difference in the fiscal cost could be employed in other subsidies to the target group.

From the fiscal cost perspective a food stamp program would be the most effective, and according to a series of studies it has been fairly successful in the United States from the point of view of nutrition—as well as of distribution of income.[33] However, its implementation in a country like Mexico may face a series of administrative difficulties especially in the process of identifying the target group and then effectively reaching it, since a large portion of the poor live in rural areas or are part of what is called the "informal" sector, and there are no official records kept on this population. On the other hand, food stamps are also more difficult to implement in LDCs because participants would have to accumulate sufficient cash to purchase a month's or even a week's supply and this may be very difficult precisely for those that most need the additional food.[34] In fact, a basic condition for implementing a cost-effective food stamp program is differential costing of the stamps for participants, in accordance with their expenditures on food; otherwise, those with the greatest need will refuse to participate in the program and participants who have a higher-than-average income will use only a fraction of the subsidy for added food consumption. In addition, the time costs (queuing, obtaining forms, etc.) involved in a food stamp program on the part of the beneficiary may not necessarily mean an automatic self-selection by the poor.

Given all the administrative difficulties, it may be more feasible to implement a target-group-oriented food price subsidy through the state-run distribution network (DICONSA and CONASUPO, mainly). The idea is that the location of these stores would work as a self-discriminatory scheme in favor of the poor. There is, however, the danger of encouraging the development of a "black market." On the other hand, the price subsidy system has an additional advantage compared with a general food stamp program, namely, that it may be easier to shape the diet in a more adequate direction by introducing a differential price-subsidy program. In fact, one of the problems with the calculations made in the previous section is that we analyze the impact of policies on overall food consumption without taking into account their compositional effect: that is, what the expected change in the diet would be after an income transfer, a food stamp program, or a price subsidy? This may be very important from a nutrition point of view since the additional food intake that arises from any such policies may not be of the most adequate kind. In this sense, a differential-price subsidy program where food items are subject to different discounts may turn out to be the best way to encourage consumption in adequate proportions. To calculate this, however, we would require estimates of the target group's demand price-elasticities for separate food items and accurate information on the actual consumption of them. As was mentioned before, up to now we do not have reliable information on the latter; nor do we have a satisfactory method to measure the former.[35] On the other hand, from the administrative point of view, the implementation of a differential-price subsidy scheme may be considered impractical. Also, the food stamp program could be implemented for only certain products and thus help reshape the diet in the same way as a product-discriminatory price subsidy would.

Thus, given the advantages and disadvantages of either program the decision is not an easy one to make. If the idea is to improve the nutritional level of those who need it most at the least cost—and without subsidizing those who are better off—then, in spite of all the administrative complications a product-selective food stamp program might do the job. However, one should not forget that an income transfer (i.e., negative income tax) is more effective in terms of its redistributive power and of the welfare impact on the poorer population.

Perhaps the choice among the different possible forms of food consumption studies should be made after experimenting with pilot projects in different areas of the country, since such experiments would provide a clearer picture on what inconveniences are associated with the implementation of any particular program.

The programs analyzed in this work focus mainly on the consumption side: i.e., how to improve the food intake by measures other than those affecting the income generating source. In terms of the latter, there are usually two broad lines followed to improve the conditions of the poor within the limits imposed by "reformist" changes: employment generation and measures designed to better the situation of the self-employed or small producers that have some access to land or other means of production (peasants, shopkeepers, etc). A study done by Benito (1979) has shown that when comparing a series of policy options for very poor peasant households in Mexico, the most cost-effective measures to improve nutrition conditions for these households were cheap credit (lower interest rates); and secondly, subsidized inputs, while the support price for corn and the market subsidy to corn turned out to be much more expensive. However, the corn subsidy would induce higher increases in net cash income and the income effect is an important one since, presumably, it will help peasants to improve their welfare by consuming other goods than food. As mentioned in the introduction, the Mexican Food System is already implementing all four kinds of policies (cheap credit, subsidized inputs, higher price supports, and subsidized corn) in some districts in the rural sector and thus it would be very useful to study the impact of this combination of policies on the incomes and nutrition of the peasants.

Our analysis (as well as that of Benito) of the impacts and associated fiscal costs of the different policy options have all been carried out within a partial equilibrium framework. It is a well-known fact that partial equilibrium analysis can be misleading because a lot of the relevant interactions are left out. An ongoing study to measure the impact of the price and subsidy policies recommended by the Mexican Food System on the distribution of income and food consumption has shown that policies designed to benefit the peasantry (subsidized inputs and price supports) should be accompanied by other measures, such as an increase in the wage rate or consumption subsidies, if the rest of the poor population is to benefit from the increases in food production.[36]

## Appendix

### *The Data*

The information that was used in this study comes from the 1977 Income and Expenditure Survey (IES) carried out by the *Coordinación General del Sistema Nacional de Información, Secretaría de Programación y Presupuesto*.[37]

In order to check the accuracy of the data recorded in this 1977 IES, we have compared some of the magnitudes it contains with those in the

*TABLE A.14.1.*
*Comparison of Income Expenditure Surveys of 1968 and 1977 with National Accounts*

| | | *1968* | *1977* |
|---|---|---|---|
| (1) | Population (thousands) | 45,803 | 62,172 |
| (2) | Disposable income N.A. (millions of pesos) | 314,025 | 1,482,018 |
| (3) | Private final consumption N.A. (millions of pesos) | 247,825 | 1,101,127 |
| (4) | Per capita disposable income N.A. [(3)/(2)] | 571 | 1,986 |
| (5) | Per capita private consumption N.A. [(3)/(1)] | 451 | 1,476 |
| (6) | Per capita income (surveys) | 374 | 864 |
| (7) | Per capita consumption (surveys) | 361 | 943 |
| (8) | (4) at 1968 prices | 571 | 693 |
| (9) | (5) " " " | 451 | 515 |
| (10) | (6) " " " | 374 | 302 |
| (11) | (7) " " " | 361 | 329 |
| (12) | (6)/(4) (percentage) | 82.93 | 43.51 |
| (13) | (7)/(5) ( " ) | 80.04 | 63.89 |
| (14) | Annual rate of growth of per capita income N.A. (1968–1977) | | 2.18 |
| (15) | Annual rate of growth of per capita income (surveys) | | 2.18 |

SOURCES: (1) Nacional Financiera, S. A. *La Economía Mexicana en Cifras,* México 1978; p. 5 (2), (3) 1968; Banco de México, S. A.; *Estadísticas de la Oficina de Cuentas de Producción 1960–1976.* 1977: Banco de México, S. A.; Subdirección de Investigación Económica y Bancaria; *Producto Interno Bruto y Gasto; Cuaderno 1970–1978;* México 1979. (6) y (7) SPP; *Encuesta Nacional de Ingresos y Gastos de los Hogares 1977;* Banco de México, *Encuesta Nacional de Ingresos y Gastos de las Familias; 1968* Banco de México, S. A., *Indicadores Económicos, Cuaderno Mensual; vol. 7: no. 9;* Agosto 1979, pp. 48–49.

National Accounts and in the 1968 IES. This comparison is in Table A.14-1. In rows (13) and (14) we can observe that the 1977 IES underestimates income and consumption per capita—when compared with the National Accounts—much more than the 1968 IES does. Moreover, the 1977 IES per capita income is lower in real terms than the per capita income for 1968 shown either by the National Accounts or the IES. The differences between the 1977 IES and the National Accounts may be due partly to definitional problems; since "income" is not the same concept in both sources.[38] However, the size of the discrepancy together with the observed decline in real per capita income between the two surveys, leads us to conclude that the 1977 IES may be suffering from rather serious underestimation problems.

Whose income has been underestimated is very difficult to say a priori, and to answer this question one has to rely mostly on "intuitive speculation."[39] Therefore, in this study no adjustments have been made in the information, and we tried to minimize the impact of measurement errors by using the instrumental variables method when estimating the regression coefficients.

### *Methodology: Income-Elasticities and Marginal Propensities to Spend*

To obtain the estimates for the expenditure-elasticities and the marginal propensities to spend on food, we proceeded in three stages.

First, the income-elasticities for each socioeconomic group, and for food and beverages and one for aggregate consumption, were estimated using Generalized Least Squares since the regressions were computed from grouped observations.[40] Second, the expenditure-elasticity for food was obtained by dividing each of the income-elasticities for food and beverages by the income-elasticity corresponding to the aggregate consumption function. This is called the instrumental variables method, and its use is recommended in those cases where the variables have been measured with errors. Given that—as we saw—income seems to be underestimated in the 1977 IES, we have estimated expenditure-elasticities using income as an instrument.[41] These expenditure-elasticities, however, will be considered as income-elasticities. Lastly, we calculated the marginal propensities to spend on food, multiplying the income-elasticities by the corresponding average propensity to spend out of total expenditure.

The function that was selected to carry out our estimations is of a log-linear form: the latter was chosen because of its simplicity and flexibility. In algebraic terms,

$$[\log g_i = a_i + b_i \log y + e]_j$$
$$[\log g = a' + b' \log y + e']_j$$

where i = Food and Beverages;

$$j = 1, \ldots, 30$$

where $g_i$ is the (weighted) per capita expenditure on good i; y, the (weighted) per capita income; and g is the (weighted) per capita total expenditure. As we already explained, the income-elasticity ($c_i$) is equal to $\bar{c}_i = \bar{b}_i/\bar{b}'$.

As mentioned in the text, the estimations were carried out for 27 socio-economic groups; 9 regions; 2 income classes; and, for one of the income classes, for two sectors. The regions are defined in Table 14-9 of the text; the two income classes correspond to all those households that earned an income less than or equal to the regional minimum wage, and those who were above this level; in turn, the first income class was divided into rural and urban, according to the main activity of the head of the household (agriculture and nonagricultural, respectively), since the 1977 IES does not have information on the size of the town where the household is located. In addition to this grouping, calculations were made as well for the national total and for the latter divided into two income classes: households with a monthly income less than or equal to the minimum wage, or above.

Commodities were grouped into seven large consumption categories: food and beverages; shoes and clothing; housing; education; health; transportation and communication; others. The regression results for food and beverages and for total expenditure are presented in Tables A.14-2 and A.14-3, respectively.[42] It can be observed from the tables that the coefficients turned out to be significant (at least at the 95 percent level) and the goodness of fit is generally quite acceptable. In Table A.14-4 we introduce the resulting income-elasticities and marginal propensities to spend for food and beverages. These were calculated according to the method described above and were used in the text to obtain the estimates of the fiscal cost associated with various food policy options.

*Methodology: Price-elasticities.*

Since we did not have the required information on prices, we proceeded to compute the price-elasticities using Frisch's method.[43] This method enables us to estimate price-elasticities from the income-elasticities, the average propensity to spend (budget shares) and the so-called flexibility of money.[44] The formula to estimate the direct price-elasticity can be written as follows:

$$e_{ii} = \bar{c}_i \left[ M_i - \frac{1 - M_i\bar{c}_i}{f} \right]_j$$

where i = food and beverage;
j = y≤MW; y>MW; national total;
where $e_{ii}$ is the direct demand price-elasticity for good i; $\bar{c}_i$, the income-elasticity for good i;. $M_i$, the budget share of good i; and, f the flexibility of money.[45]

As shown in the formula, to compute the price-elasticity one must have

*TABLE A.14.2.*
*Regression Results by Socioeconomic Group: Food and Beverages (1977)*

| *Socioeconomic Group* | *Intercept* | *Slope* | *t–ratio* | $R^2$ |
|---|---|---|---|---|
| 1.1 | .20818 | .92341 | 18.494 | .9448 |
| 1.2 | .18389 | .68647 | 13.346 | .9284 |
| 1.3 | .19344 | .68306 | 13.945 | .8329 |
| 2.1 | .64510 | .48885 | 5.246 | .5447 |
| 2.2 | − .48968 | .93986 | 7.753 | .7320 |
| 2.3 | − .34139 | .79846 | 19.100 | .9057 |
| 3.1 | .14320 | .75335 | 17.365 | .9291 |
| 3.2 | − .49500 | .99100 | 20.863 | .9498 |
| 3.3 | − .12444 | .77286 | 20.587 | .9177 |
| 4.1 | .49421 | .81021 | 15.274 | .9210 |
| 4.2 | −2.08180 | .92341 | 18.494 | .9448 |
| 4.3 | − .27675 | .82124 | 29.607 | .9564 |
| 5.1 | .27700 | .65200 | 13.583 | .8872 |
| 5.2 | − .30800 | .93300 | 34.215 | .9807 |
| 5.3 | .12919 | .65987 | 14.191 | .8378 |
| 6.1 | .5000 | .57300 | 7.442 | .7091 |
| 6.2 | .59451 | .60450 | 6.311 | .6548 |
| 6.3 | .53173 | .55952 | 5.165 | .4257 |
| 7.1 | .03908 | .88467 | 32.685 | .9798 |
| 7.2 | − .01813 | .87050 | 15.554 | .9098 |
| 7.3 | .18169 | .71876 | 20.381 | .9162 |
| 8.1 | .18199 | .73211 | 13.335 | .8811 |
| 8.2 | .14545 | .76881 | 13.317 | .8852 |
| 8.3 | .09754 | .78071 | 25.265 | .9424 |
| 9.1 | .34648 | .73062 | 6.012 | .6801 |
| 9.2 | − .45450 | .96410 | 18.924 | .9421 |
| 9.3 | .38392 | .59772 | 17.105 | .8851 |
| Y≦MW | 1.6000 | .67800 | 23.379 | .9525 |
| Y>MW | 3.8310 | .40800 | 19.429 | .9313 |
| National Total | 2.2010 | .64200 | 49.385 | .9817 |

SOURCE: Author's calculations. Based on the Income and Expenditure Survey, 1977 Secretaría de Programación y Presupuesto, (1979b).

NOTE: The i.j's in the first column correspond to region (i = 1, . . . , 9); and, income strata and sector (j = 1, rural and Y≦MW; j = 2, urban and Y≦MW; j = 3, Y>MW). MW: Minimum wage and Y: income per household.

an estimate of the f-parameter in addition to the others that are obtained from the regression estimates and the 1977 IES. There are several ways to estimate the f-parameter. Here we chose to do a direct calculation introducing an exogenously known price elasticity. The formula is as follows:[46]

$$f = \frac{\bar{c}_i\,[1 - M_i\bar{c}_i]}{e_{ii} + M_i\bar{c}_i}$$

*TABLE A.14.3.*

*Regression Results by Socioeconomic Group: Total Expenditure (1977)*

| *Socioeconomic Group* | *Intercept* | *Slope* | *t–ratio* | $R^2$ |
|---|---|---|---|---|
| 1.1 | .68497 | .81021 | 15.274 | .9210 |
| 1.2 | .51679 | .86786 | 22.195 | .9284 |
| 1.3 | .52887 | .86355 | 23.158 | .9322 |
| 2.1* | 1.23667 | .67180 | 77.702 | .7295 |
| 2.2 | 1.23667 | .67180 | 7.702 | .7295 |
| 2.3 | .61237 | .84353 | 18.738 | .9023 |
| 3.1 | 1.26208 | .59407 | 9.675 | .8027 |
| 3.2 | .60800 | .84300 | 15.543 | .9131 |
| 3.3 | .63191 | .82317 | 34.380 | .9689 |
| 4.1 | .68497 | .81021 | 15.274 | .9210 |
| 4.2 | .37001 | .88813 | 22.839 | .9631 |
| 4.3 | .57390 | .81011 | 21.638 | .9213 |
| 5.1 | .68500 | .81000 | 15.274 | .9210 |
| 5.2 | .66200 | .79200 | 10.456 | .8262 |
| 5.3 | .03474 | 1.00769 | 52.481 | .9860 |
| 6.1* | 1.20127 | .64556 | 8.343 | .7682 |
| 6.2 | 1.20127 | .64556 | 8.343 | .7682 |
| 6.3 | .35721 | .91007 | 16.359 | .8814 |
| 7.1 | .73527 | .73726 | 10.883 | .8433 |
| 7.2 | .39224 | .90388 | 17.727 | .9290 |
| 7.3 | 1.07096 | .69542 | 9.807 | .7168 |
| 8.1 | – .49970 | .78580 | 13.790 | .9423 |
| 8.2 | .65481 | .82041 | 11.146 | .8438 |
| 8.3 | .82533 | .74626 | 21.275 | .9207 |
| 9.1 | .13104 | .97780 | 14.004 | .9202 |
| 9.2 | .94230 | .88790 | 13.200 | .8879 |
| 9.3 | .19554 | .96275 | 67.280 | .9917 |
| Y≦MW | 3.37300 | .64200 | 20.710 | .9121 |
| Y>MW | .91300 | .85300 | 38.773 | .9819 |
| National Total | 1.479 | .83500 | 55.667 | .9849 |

SOURCE: Author's calculations. Based on the Income and Expenditure Survey, 1977, Secretaría de Programación y Presupuesto (1979b).

NOTE: The i.j's in the first column correspond to region (i = 1, . . . , 9); and, income strata and sector (j = 1, rural and Y≦MW; j = 2, urban and Y≦MW; j = 3, Y>MW). MW: Minimum wage and Y: income per household.

*These estimates had very low $R^2$'s. Thus, we used the results obtained for the same income stratum but in the other sector.

*TABLE A.14.4.*

*Income-Elasticity and Marginal Propensity to Spend by Socioeconomic Groups: Food and Beverages 1977*

| | *Income-Elasticity* | *Marginal propensity to spend* |
|---|---|---|
| 1.1 | 1.1397 | .6664 |
| 1.2 | .7910 | .4071 |
| 1.3 | .7910 | .2930 |
| 2.1* | 1.4669 | .6152 |
| 2.2 | 1.3990 | .6103 |
| 2.3 | .9466 | .2993 |
| 3.1 | 1.2681 | .6016 |
| 3.2 | 1.1753 | .5909 |
| 3.3 | .9389 | .3442 |
| 4.1* | 1.2424 | .6435 |
| 4.2 | 1.1397 | .6435 |
| 4.3 | 1.0137 | .4148 |
| 5.1* | 1.0244 | .6500 |
| 5.2 | 1.1786 | .6335 |
| 5.3 | .6548 | .2300 |
| 6.1* | 1.0334 | .6000 |
| 6.2 | .9364 | .4641 |
| 6.3 | .6148 | .2197 |
| 7.1 | 1.1999 | .7783 |
| 7.2 | .9631 | .5851 |
| 7.3 | 1.0336 | .4177 |
| 8.1* | 1.2265 | .6227 |
| 8.2 | .9371 | .4759 |
| 8.3 | 1.0462 | .4300 |
| 9.1 | .7472 | .4202 |
| 9.2 | 1.0858 | .5247 |
| 9.3 | .6208 | .1871 |
| Y≤MW | 1.0561 | .5270 |
| Y>MW | .4783 | .1688 |
| National Total | .7689 | .2856 |

SOURCE: Author's calculations. Based on the Income and Expenditure Survey, 1977, Secretaría de Programación y Presupuesto (1979b).

NOTE: See Table A.14.3.

MW: minimum wage; Y: income per household.

*Corrected for aggregation test.

*TABLE A.14.5.*
*Demand Price—Elasticities for Food and Beverages*
*1977*

| | *Y≦MW* | *Y>MW* | *National total* |
|---|---|---|---|
| Price elasticity | – .7840 | – .4762 | – .5922 |
| Frisch parameter | – 1.1944 | – 1.2880 | – 1.7915 |

SOURCE: Author's calculations. Based on the Income and Expenditure Survey, 1977, Secretaría de Programación y Presupuesto (1979b).

Y = monthly household income (1977 pesos).

MW = minimum wage (1977 pesos).

In this study we estimated three f–parameters: one using an exogenous (demand) price-elasticity for corn and wheat equal to –0.1; a second one with a price-elasticity for beans, rice and potatoes equal to –0.3; and, a third one with an elasticity equal to the weighted average of the previous two.[47]

The calculations of the price-elasticities for food and beverages were made only for the national total and the two income classes (less than or equal to, and over the minimum wage). The regional estimates were left out because we would have required exogenous price-elasticities by region to compute the corresponding f-parameter. The estimated price elasticities are presented in Table A. 14-5.

A word of caution, however, must be attached to these results. The Frisch method ı ·quires *want-independence* among goods, i.e., the marginal utility derived from the consumption of any good must be independent of the quantity consumed of any other good.[48] This assumption may hold for broad categories of commodities but it is very unlikely to hold for disaggregated goods. When no want-independence exists, the Frisch method yields biased estimates.[49] In addition, the method assumes that all consumers face the same set of prices, and inferior goods cannot be dealt with.

In spite of all these shortcomings and problems—and until better alternatives are found—we have chosen to use the price-elasticities estimated by using the Frisch method since the assumption of want-independence could be applicable, given the broad categories we defined.

## Notes

1. See, for example, Ramírez et al. (1975); McCarthy (1978); United Nations (1979).

2. *Instituto Nacional de la Nutrición* (1979).

3. For a discussion of the technical causes and political economy of the agricultural crisis see Luiselli (1979) and Martín del Campo (1979), for example.

4. The issue of comparative advantage has been part of theoretical and practical discussions worldwide for more than a century and a half. Those who argue in favor of a specialization in terms of "comparative advantage" base their ideas on a belief in the workings of Smith's "invisible hand". The problem is that it is often forgotten that comparative advantage is not "God given" but that it can be constructed and *changed* over time. For example, an ongoing research on United States agricultural policy shows that in the 1920s and 1930s U.S. agriculture was in disarray and the country became a net importer of grains. Then came a period of intensive government intervention (in 1938, for example, one-third of all farm income was government payments) which led—in less than 20 years—to a complete transformation of U.S. agriculture (Darryl McLeod, unpublished Ph.D. dissertation, Department of Agricultural Economics, University of California, Berkeley; a summary was presented at the "First Workshop on Terms of Trade Policy and Income Distribution," organized by the *Sistema Alimentario Mexicano* on September 25–26, 1981).

5. There is also a *marketing strategy*.

6. For further details on this subject see Sistema Alimentario Mexicano (1980).

7. Until recently the number of DICONSA rural stores was 4,780 and it is expected that by the end of 1972 they will rise to 14,000.

8. See, for example, Navarrete (1960), Cline (1972), Kalifa (1977), Hernández y Córdova (1979) and Bergsman (1980).

9. This survey was carried out by the Secretaría de Programación y Presupuesto (1979), Coordinación General del Sistema Nacional de Información.

10. Banco de Mexico (1977, 1978, 1979, 1980).

11. The fact that we are using deciles of population to indicate the degree of inequality does not mean that we embrace a *gradational* theory of the determination of income distribution. Our contention is that a theory that explains the distribution of income has to center on the social organization of production that determines the laws of generation and appropriation of the economic surplus; under such a theory it would be argued "that the location within class relations establishes limits of variations on income, on the location within exchange and technical relations, and on personal characteristics" (Wright 1979, 65). This means, for example, that no worker—independently of how skilled he/she is—can get an income higher than the highest of the capitalists' income. We are aware that class structure might be "insufficient" to explain the degree of inequality and that other variables such as demand and supply conditions, institutional power, market segmentation differential skills, etc., have to be introduced to understand inequality within classes. However, again, these variables—in our view—affect inequality on a secondary level, the first being the location within class structure itself. This implies, for example, that improving the levels of education, nutrition, health, etc., of the poor population—although they should definitely be goals on their own—cannot be taken as the best alternatives to reduce inequality in the distribution of income or, moreover, to change substantially the ability of the poorest classes to generate higher-income levels for themselves as a group.

12. It has been observed that autoconsumption (of corn and beans, mainly) is much higher for households in agriculture than for the rest (keeping income constant). See Lustig (1980a, 26).

13. The higher income strata showed a caloric consumption of over 5,000 units per capita per day—which is biologically impossible.

14. These calculations were made using the formula: $Y_{t+r} = Y_t (1+g)^r$. For a more detailed discussion of how these experiments were carried out see Lustig (1980b).

15. This Nutrition Survey was carried out by the *Instituto Nacional de la Nutrición;* the results have not been published yet.

16. The details on the computation of the BRD are contained in the Document of Project No. 3, Mexican Food System, Office of Advisors to the President.

17. The rural-urban categorization based on the size of the town could not be made because the 1977 survey does not have this information.

18. The income-elasticities are actually expenditure-elasticities but the latter were considered as the "best" estimate of the income elasticity. (See Appendix.)

19. A more detailed description of the method is included in the Appendix.

20. In general, any policy will affect more people than those considered to be part of the target group because of the indirect effects of a policy: employment creation, inflationary pressures, etc.

21. See Reutlinger and Selowsky (1976, 81).

22. The excess supply faced by the target group equals total food supply minus the consumption of the rest of the population; thus, the excess-supply price elasticity depends, not only on the global-supply price elasticity, but also on the demand-price elasticity of the rest of the population ($e_r^d$). In algebraic terms it is equal to:

$$e_p^s = \frac{e^s}{x} + \frac{(1-x)e_r^d}{x},$$

where $x$ is the proportion of total food consumed by the target group, and $e_r^d$ the demand-price elasticity of the rest.

23. For a survey of evaluations of the U.S. Food Stamp Program, see Taylor et al. (1980, 39–54).

24. See Reutlinger and Selowsky (1976, 47–48).

25. Ibid., (1976, 50).

26. We maintain the assumption that part of the food is imported so that $e^s \rightarrow \infty$.

27. These two magnitudes were obtained by weighting the regional-sectorial ones by the respective population; the information is in Tables 14-9 and 14-10.

28. This criterion was suggested by McCarthy (1978) in a study on nutrition planning for Pakistan.

29. According to our estimates these goods are: maize in grain; brown sugar; pork lard; maize flour; coffee; beans; maize dough *(nixtamal);* refined sugar; rice. All these products fulfill the condition that, of total expenditure, 30 percent or more corresponds to the target population (those who earn an income less than or equal to the corresponding minimum wage). See Lustig (1980a, 28).

30. One has to bear in mind that these results as well as the previous ones are partial equilibrium results and that under a general equilibrium results framework we might encounter quite different results.

31. For a description of an "optimal" food stamp program see Reutlinger and Selowsky (1976)

32. For a thorough discussion on the miscroeconomics of food stamps and food subsidies in general see Taylor et al. (1980, 11–15).

33. On this point see Taylor et al. (1980).

34. Unless the stamps are given out free.

35. The Frisch method used to estimate the price elasticity for food can only be applied confidently to broad consumption categories (see the Appendix on this).

36. This project is carried out by William Gibson, Lance Taylor, and the author and is sponsored jointly by the Mexican Food System and *El Colegio de México*. In this project, the Mexican Food System's price and subsidy policies are simulated in a multisectorial and multisocial-classes general equilibrium model for Mexico that assumes price clearing behavior for agriculture and quantity clearing for the nonagricultural sectors; for the latter the model is estimated under two different price closures: mark-up and Sraffian or reproduction prices.

37. For additional information on the definition of concepts see *Secretaría de Programación y Presupuesto* (1979a).

38. National Accounts do not have an estimate of personal, disposable income, but only of national disposable income. In addition, private consumption is estimated as a residual.

39. Bergsman (1980) has estimated the distribution of income resulting from two different underreporting assumptions: one "low-inequality" and one "high-inequality," which give a range within which the "true" distribution may lie.

40. The Generalized Least Squares method introduces a weighting system that gets rid of heteroskedasticity, a common problem when grouped observations (group means) are used. For further details on this subject see Cramer (1973, 144–146).

41. See Goreux (1960).

42. The remaining estimates as well as those for specific food products (58) may be obtained directly from the author.

43. Frisch (1959, 177–196).

44. The flexibility of money (also called the Frisch parameter), is defined as the proportional increase in utility when money income changes; it is an elasticity measured by the ration of the two proportions.

45. See Pinstrup-Andersen et al. (1980, 132).

46. Ibid., (1980, 136).

47. The exogenous price-elasticities were obtained from Duloy and Norton (1973, 317). The choice among them was done comparing the magnitudes of the f-parameter with those appearing in similar studies.

48. When this assumption applies to all arguments, the utility function becomes additive.

49. See Brandt and Goodwin (1980); and Pinstrup-Andersen (1980).

## References:

Banco de México, S. A. (1974) *La Distribución del Ingreso en México. Encuesta sobre los ingresos y gastos de las familias, 1968*. Fondo de Cultura Económica, México, D.F.

Banco de Mexico, S.A. *Informe Anual,* various issues, México, D.F.

Benito, C. (1979) "Policies for food production and consumption in underdevelopment: The case of Mexico," *Journal of Policy Modeling,* vol. I, no. 3.

Bergsman, J. (1980) "Income Distribution and Poverty in Mexico," *Working Paper # 234-A (#176-B-15),* World Bank, Washington, D.C., March.

Brandt, J. A. and J. B. Goodwin (1980) "The Impact of Increasing Food Supply on Human Nutrition: Implications for Commodity Priorities in Agricultural Research and Policy: Comment," *American Journal of Agricultural Economics,* August.

Cline, W. R. (1972) *Potential Effects of Income Redistribution Economic Growth. Latin American Cases.* New York: Praeger Publishers.

Cramer, J. S. (1973) *Econometría Empírica,* Fondo de Cultura Económica, México, D.F.

Duloy, J. K. and R. D. Norton (1973) "CHAC, Programming Model of the Mexican Agriculture" in *Multilevel Planning: Case Studies in Mexico,*ed. by L. M. Goreuz and A. S. Mann, Amsterdam: North Holland.

Flores, A. M. (1973) *La Magnitud del Hambre en México,* Impresos Modernos, México, D.F.

Frisch, R. (1959) "A complete scheme for computing all direct and cross demand elasticities in a model with sector," *Econometrića,* no. 27

Goreux, L. M. (1960) *Boletin Mensual de Economía y Estadísticas Agrícolas,* FAO, vol. 9, no. 10, October.

Hernández, E. y H. Córdova. (1979) "Estructura de la Distribución del Ingreso en México," *Comercio Exterior,* vol. 29, no. 5, May.

Instituto Nacional de la Nutrición (1979) *Segunda Encuesta Nacional de Alimentación,* México, D.F.

Kalifa, S. (1977) "La distribución del ingreso en México: una reconsideración del problema distributivo," (Spanish translation of unpublished doctoral dissertation in Economics), Cornell University, Ithaca, N.Y.

Luiselli, C. (1979) "Agricultura y alimentación: premisas para una nueva estrategia," in *Panorama y Perspectivas de la Economía Mexicana,* ed. by N. Lustig, El Colegio de México. México. México, D.F.

Lustig, N. (1980a) "Polílitcas de Consumo y Distribución del Ingreso," *Demografíay Economía.* vol. 16, no. 2 (50).

———. (1980b) "Distribución del Ingreso y Consumo de Alimentos en México" *Demografía y Economía,* vol. 14, no. 2 (42).

Martín del Campo, A. (1979) "Transformación Agraria y Nuevas Opciones para el Desarrollo" in *Panorama y Perspectivas de la Economía Mexicana,* ed. by N. Lustig, El Colegio de México. México, D. F.

McCarthy, D. (1978) "Food and nutrition planning: Pakistan," *International Nutrition Policy and Planning Program,* Center for International Studies, Massachusetts Institute of Technology, Discussion Paper no. 12.

Navarrete, I. (1960) *La Distribución del Ingreso y el Desarrollo Económico en México,* Universidad Nacional Autónoma de Mèxico. Mexico, D. F.

Pinstrup-Andersen, P. et al. (1980) "The impact of increasing food supply on human nutrition: Implications for commodity priorities in agricultural research and policy," *American Journal of Agricultural Economics,* 58, August.

Ramırez et al. (1975) "Aspectos socioeconómicos de los alimentos y la alimentación en México," *Comercio Exterior,* vol. 21 no. 8, Agust.

Reutlinger, S. and Selowsky, M. (1976) *Malnutrition and Poverty: Magnitude and Policy Options.* Baltimore: Johns Hopkins University Press.

Sistema Alimentario Mexicano (1980) "Medidas Operativas Agrarias y Pesqueras, Estrategias de Comercialización, Transformación, Distribución y Consumo de la Canasta Básica Recomendable," México, D. F.

Secretaría de Programación y Presupuesto (1979a) *Encuesta Nacional de Ingresos y Gastos de los Hogares, 1977: Primera observación,* México, D. F.

Secretaría de Programación y Presupuesto (1979b) *Encuesta Nacional de Ingresos y Gastos de los Hogares, 1977: Informe Metodológico,* México, D. F.

Taylor, L. et al. (1980) "Food subsidy programs: a survey," Massachusetts Institute of Technology, mimeo, December.

United Nations (1979) *World Food Council Report.*

Van Ginneken W. (1974) "Mexican income distribution within and between rural and urban areas," World Employment Programme Research, Working Paper No. WEP 2–23, Geneva.

Wright, E. O. (1979) *Class Structure and Income Determination,* New York: Academic Press.

# CHAPTER 15

# *Food Marketing and Income Distribution*

Leopoldo Solís

## I. Introduction

The aim of this chapter is to examine the problems inherent in an economic policy whose objectives are to redistribute income in favor of the lowest-income groups. Current indications show poverty to be a phenomenon that is mainly rural. The cost of expanding the rural share in the distributive scale of income, however, is enormous. Even in urban zones, it is extremely difficult and costly to achieve effective redistribution results in the two lower deciles of the distribution scale. Hence, the idea of modernizing the marketing system—that is, instituting a policy of commercial development that is directed toward upgrading the functioning of the basic commodities market—is an effective step toward redistributing income.

This chapter explores the problems involved in modernizing the marketing system for basic commodities, taking data from research in progress on the nature of the processes of commercial intermediation in Mexico. Since the topic is extremely wide in scope, I have restricted myself to the marketing of grains and perishables. In the former, the Mexican public sector has undertaken a major effort to improve the price producers receive through a program of price guarantees, striving also to improve retail marketing conditions. With regard to improving marketing conditions, it must be noted that positive steps are being taken with the beginning of the construction of the new wholesale markets in Puebla and Mexico City, among other places.

Section II examines the process of marketing fruits and vegetables; Section III analyzes the marketing of grains; and Section IV, the marketing of food at the retail level, including the state-owned distribution system CONASUPO. Section V shows the distributive effects of the development of different marketing channels through the use of a general equilibrium model with the disaggregated commercial sector. Finally, Section VI reflects on the examined facts and points to certain directions that are indicated for further research.

**Figure 15-1.**

**Price Indexes in Tomatoes, Potatoes, and Chiles**

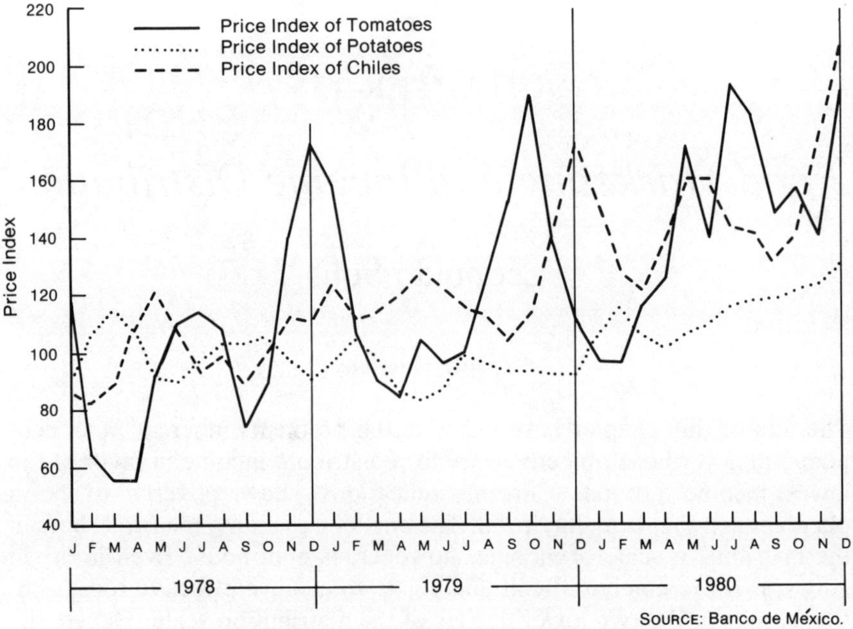


SOURCE: Banco de México.

**Price Indexes in Onions, Oranges, and Avocados**

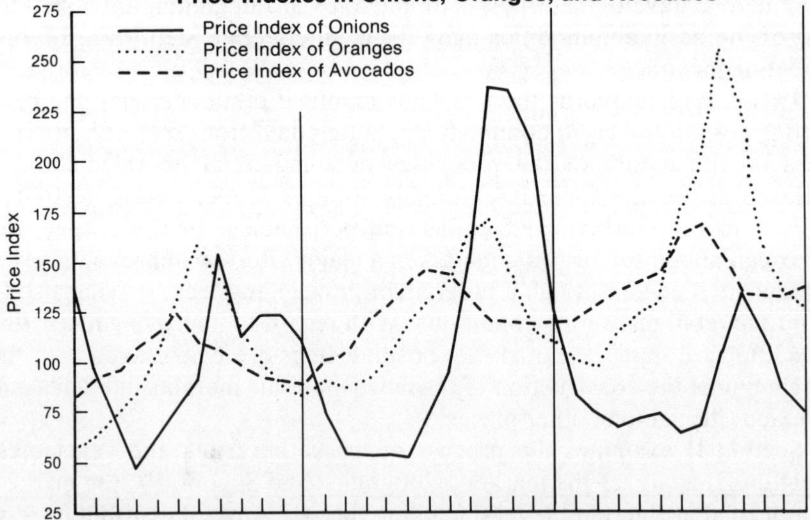


SOURCE: Banco de México.

## II. Characteristics of Marketing Fruits and Vegetables

The poor distribution of income that is characteristic of the country makes consumption of foods of high nutritional value difficult for the poorer sectors of the population. At the same time that demand increases for the goods their purchasing capacity allows them to consume, price fluctuations appear—seasonal and market-provoked. These fluctuations imply transfers of income from the rural producers to the urban consumers and middlemen, thus worsening the living conditions of groups of the population that are already acutely poor. To describe how market mechanisms work in this process, and to examine subsequent attempts to correct the deficiencies in the intermediation process, is no easy matter. It can be said, though, that the situation is indeed serious and that it merits attention. Two features of marketing patterns are particularly serious: on the one hand, the poorest farmers market their products under the worst conditions, while on the other hand, urban products are sold in rural zones at the highest prices—that is, with the highest trade margins. The result is that the low-income rural strata buy the worst quality of goods at the highest prices.

The possibilities for improving the marketing of perishables—mainly fruits and vegetables—are very limited. This is true not only because of the structural obstacles caused by segmented and isolated markets, but also because of the volatile reactions of a market of this type, which a government enterprise would find difficult to overcome unless it were highly efficient. But then, government regulation to improve and develop the functioning of the market is not easy either.

The main characteristic of this type of market and the cause of instability in agricultural prices is due to the lack of coordination in the shipments of fruits and vegetables. This results in market breakdowns and transfers of the income of small and medium-scale farmers to other economic agents: the oligopsonic urban wholesalers and urban consumers.

Let us look first at how the rural price of perishable crops presents a "U"[1] pattern over a period of time (see Fig. 15-1). At the start of the harvest, when only a few producers have the product available, intermediaries are willing to pay high prices. At this moment, it is said that a seller's market exists. As other producers appear with their mature crop, the price falls—at times, it even collapses—leading to a market controlled by the buyers. If for any reason, there is a significant increase in output, the price may drop to such a level that the producer does not even recover his production costs. When such a situation occurs, the product is left in the field without harvesting it. Finally, at the end of the crop cycle, when only a few producers are harvesting, the relationship is reversed and, once again, it becomes a seller's market.

It is precisely in the trough of the curve of the "U" pattern, when the

## Figure 15-2.

### Supply/Price Ratio in Serrano Chiles at Retail

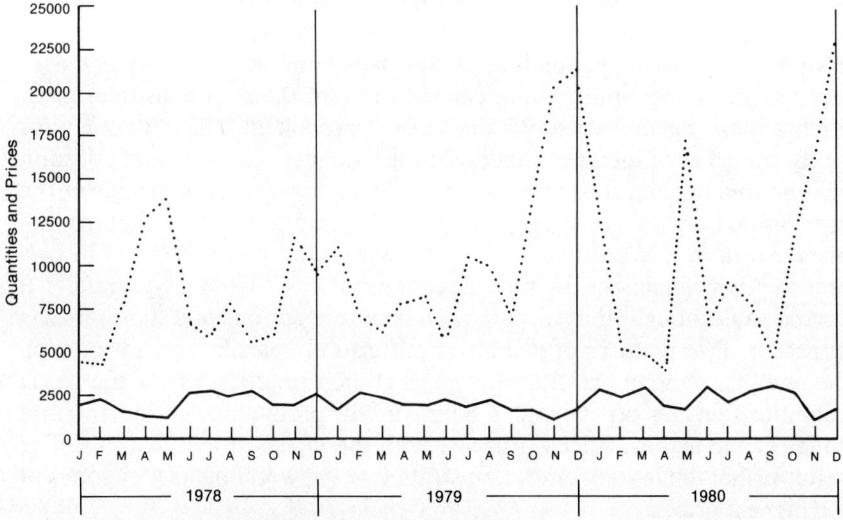


—— Quantities of Serrano Chiles at Retail in Tons
........ Prices of Serrano Chiles at Retail in Pesos per Ton

SOURCE: Banco de México.

### Supply/Price Ratio in White Potatoes at Retail

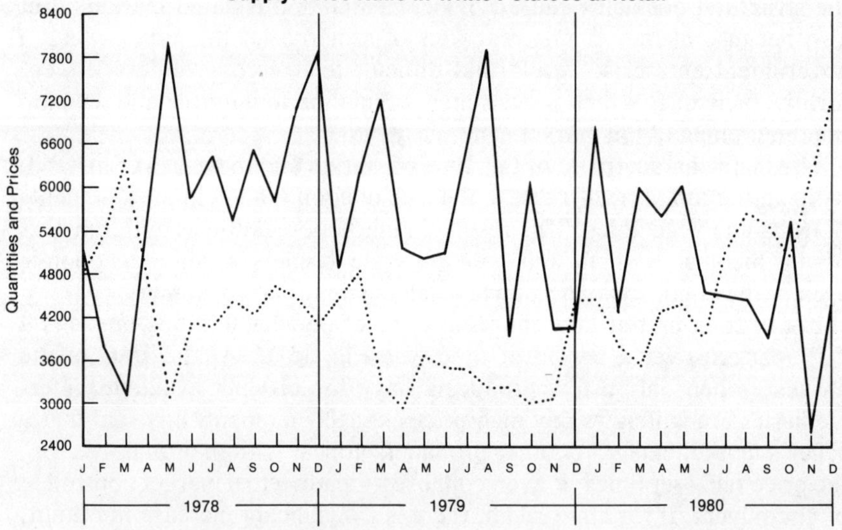


—— Quantities of White Potatoes at Retail in Tons
........ Prices of White Potatoes at Retail in Pesos per Ton

SOURCE: Banco de México.

rural producer and the urban consumer, respectively, sell and buy the greatest part of the crop at the lowest price. For the producer, this represents the possibility of not recovering the cost of production; for the consumer, it means being able to acquire a greater volume of agricultural products at an especially favorable price. Hence, the income of producers remains conditioned by a process of uncertainty which, in turn, limits the programming of investments, the adoption of technological changes, and does not allow for suitable planning in output. Thus, the instability of prices is a relevant feature of the market, meriting special attention.

In Mexico's case, since production comes from various regions and is harvested at different times of the year, the conditions of a buyer's market tend to be prolonged, to the detriment of the average price level at which the majority of the producers sell their crops.

Figure 15-2 presents the ratios between prices and quantities, incorporating the price behavior previously indicated: when the quantity goes up, the price goes down, and vice versa, except in cases of seasonal consumption. The association between prices and producing zones also becomes clear.

Figure 15-3 shows the ratio between price fluctuations and the number of producing zones supplying Mexico City. There exists an inverse ratio between these two variables: when the number of producing zones increases, the price decreases, and vice versa. In some cases, the reaction in prices is not easy to explain. For example, toward the end of August, the harvest of green chiles is intensified, but prices do not begin to drop until September. Naturally, these lags exist when the stock of products can be preserved; such is the case with bananas, onions and others

Although this method of analysis is rather simple, and presents limitations (among others, one cannot distinguish the importance of the different producing zones supplying Mexico City), it is only a first step in approaching an everyday phenomenon in the marketing of fruits and vegetables in Mexico.

According to Schramm, who found a close relationship between price fluctuations and marketing risks, "the unpredictability of prices is because almost all the products can be harvested at any time of the year, and the information remains fragmentary. Thus, many potential suppliers will enter or leave the market on a more or less valid basis, depending on their past successes or failures or their future price expectations".[2]

Despite Schramm's implicit assumption of the high mobility of productive resources, it is evident that the lack of coordination among producers in shipping produce leads to price instability. The more perishable the product is and the less diversified its production, the more drastically the prices fluctuate. Such is the case of tomatoes and oranges (see Fig. 15-5). This instability raises a question: Why doesn't the normal arbitrage of the market buffer price fluctuation? Theoretically, prices reflect the informa-

**Figure 15-3.**

**Supply/Price Ratio in Round Red Tomatoes at Retail**

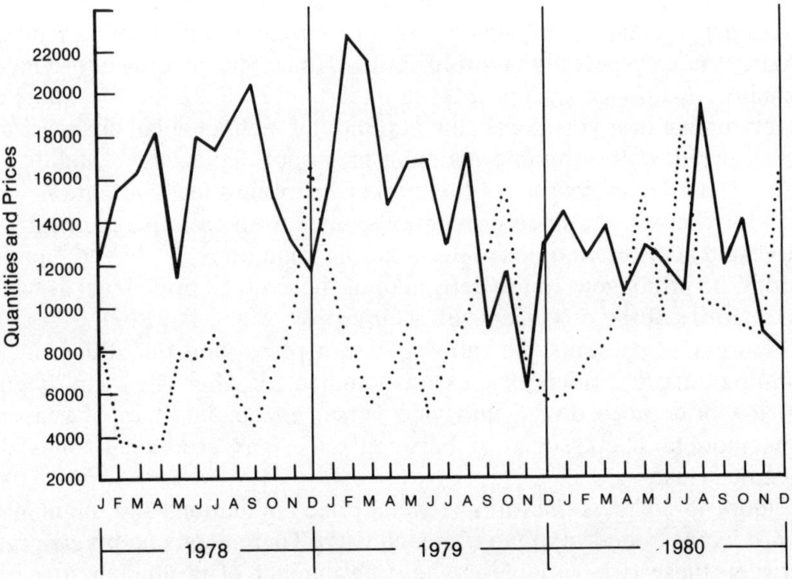


Quantities of Round Red Tomatoes at Retail in Tons
Prices of Round Red Tomatoes at Retail in Pesos per Ton

SOURCE: Banco de México.

**Supply/Price Ratio in Green Sour Cherry Tomatoes at Retail**

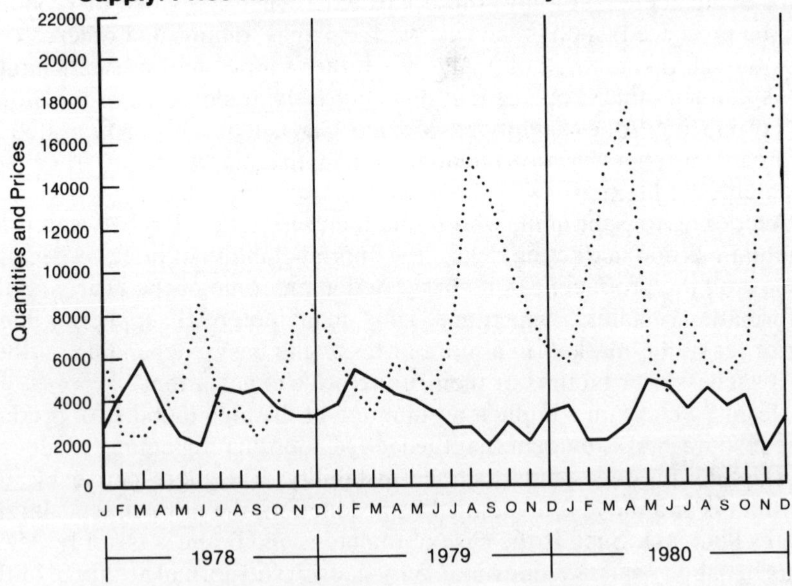


Quantities of Green Sour Cherry Tomatoes
Price of Green Sour Cherry Tomatoes

SOURCE: Banco de México.

**Figure 15-4.**

**Ratio of Number of Producing Zones to Price of Bananas**

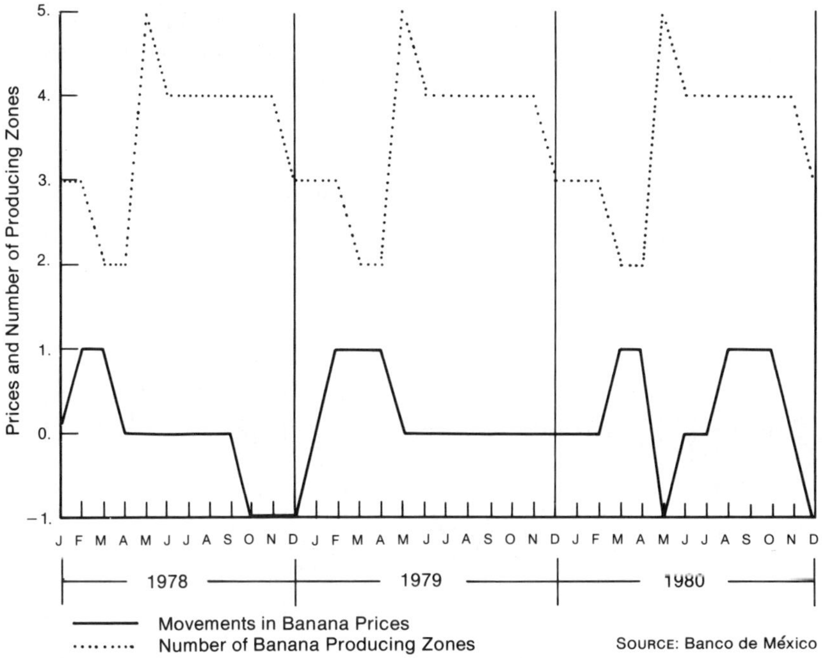


SOURCE: Banco de México

**Ratio of Prices to Number of Tomato Producing Zones**

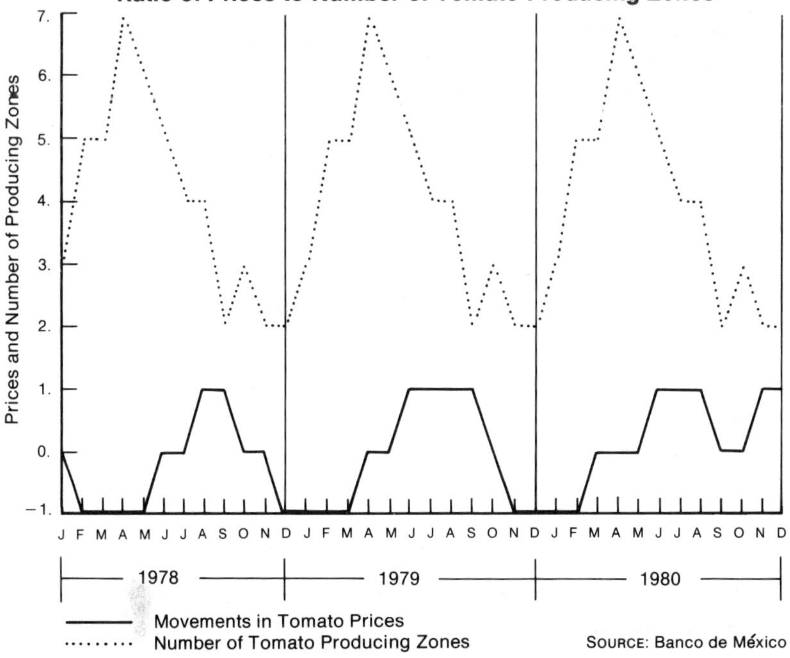


SOURCE: Banco de México

tion available in a competitive market and tend to differ for an amount not greater than the cost of transporting goods or of substituting one consumer product for another.[3] The absence of a futures market in the marketing of perishable goods is an obstacle to arbitrage. On the other hand, it seems clear that information is disseminated very imperfectly. I suspect that the cost of such dissemination is very high, and one of the most

**Figure 15-5.**

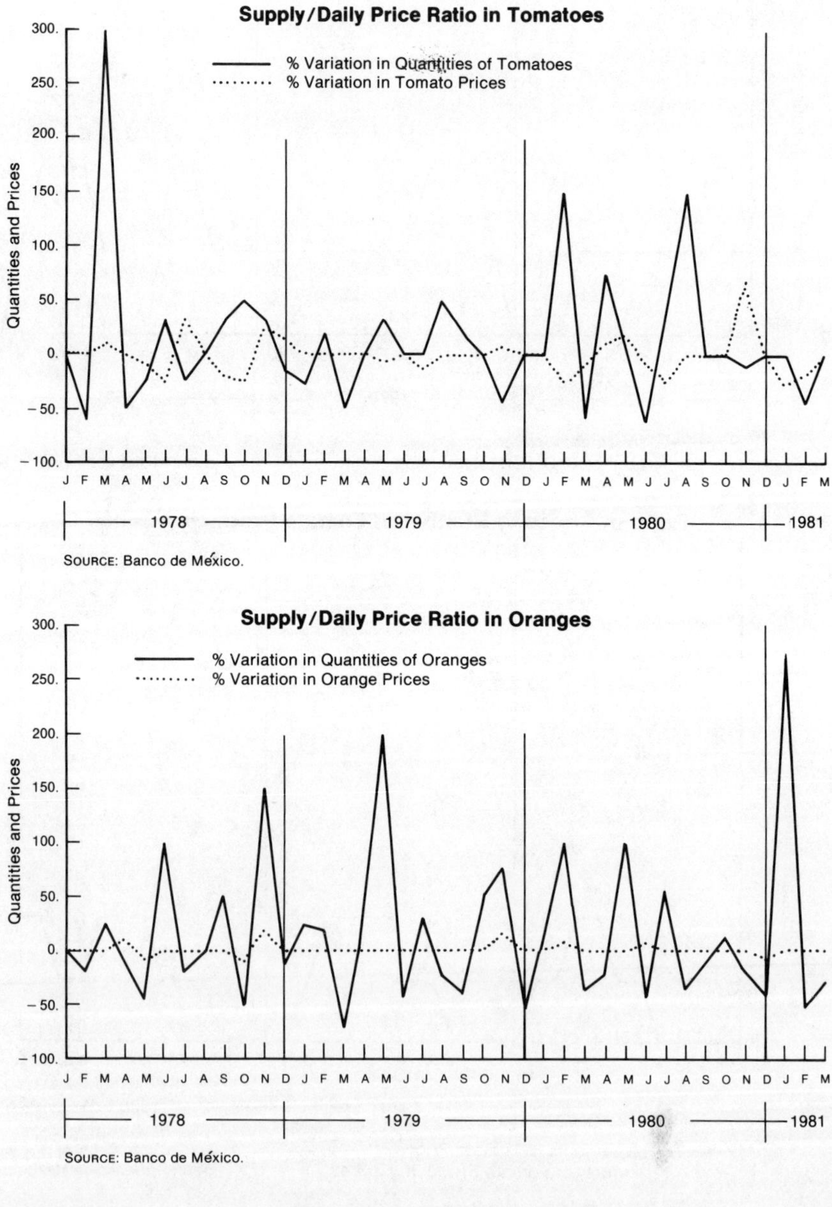

important reasons is the heterogeneity of the products. For instance, the tomatoes cultivated for export in Sinaloa, have very little in common with those cultivated in Morelos for local consumption.

Prices in the perishables market are determined by the random quantities offered during a very short period—a day or a week. Thus, the "U" pattern is noticeable only in periods that encompass the whole crop cycle, in which a strong volatility can be appreciated in the very short run in price quotations and other market conditions. It can be argued that the majority of urban consumers concentrate their purchases in seasonal perishables, which means that they buy at the bottom of the "U." In other words, the quantity bought by urban consumers resembles an inverted "U" for the same harvest season. Thus, it becomes possible to think that this lack of arbitrage in prices over time means that urban consumers buy the greatest part of the harvest when prices are below the median, so that there exists a redistribution of income from the agricultural producers to the urban consumers.

The question, then, is: Apart from the argument of heterogeneity, why are transaction costs so high? Baligh and Richartz[4] assure us that to the extent that a greater number of intermediaries exist—mainly wholesalers—the variance in the income of each of them increases. Therefore, it is to the benefit of each of them to have a commercial service capacity in excess of what they would normally have, and thus be able to take advantage of the possible peaks of demand that may appear. But when an excess in the commercial service capacity of these wholesalers exists, it implies voluminous inventories and high costs of operation. Moreover, given the uncertainty these merchants face, their marketing margins are high, resulting in a decrease in the real income of producers as well as consumers. The distribution structure of wholesalers reflects the situation of agricultural producers: a few of large size, and numerous small and medium wholesalers. Although wide-line wholesalers have already appeared in fruits and vegetables, like those that have forward linkages with distribution transport—they supply hotels, restaurants, institutional dining facilities, etc.—the ones that predominate are those that have backward linkages with transport facilities; they directly produce and carry out contracts in association with producers giving them preferential advantage in their access to the market, to the detriment of smaller farmers of lower income without such links.

The existence of large consumption centers has given rise to large-scale, wide-line wholesalers and has also encouraged the appearance of big supermarket chains, due to the need to handle efficiently a large volume of products and maintain a wide assortment. Both perform functions of load concentration and separation, and assortment creation. In addition, they receive perishables from producers and suppliers, distributing them to far greater numbers of buyers—thus increasing transaction costs.

The instability of prices in fruits and vegetables (which is only one particular aspect of the structure of Mexico's agricultural marketing system) results in producers—especially small- and medium-scale farmers—receiving a lower price than the average, with the differential remaining in the hands of other economic agents. This, in turn, worsens the current state of income distribution in the country.

## III. Features of Marketing Grain

One important feature of grain markets in developing countries is the existence of government-owned marketing enterprises. These institutions pursue numerous targets, some of which may contradict each other. Among the objectives most frequently mentioned are: to improve the bargaining power of agricultural producers in domestic and international markets; to improve marketing organization and practices; to stabilize prices and income; to obtain funds for agricultural research; to promote services for agricultural extension; to maintain adequate reserves of basic goods for food security; to provide low-priced food to urban consumers, etc. Briefly, what is sought is to raise the living standards of individuals, improving the distribution of income.

With respect to one of the objectives sought, some studies have shown that price policies tending to increase production and raise rural income have little effectiveness. Agriculture and price policies have placed emphasis on improving the well-being of the population. In turn, this has led institutions—developed for the purpose of marketing grains—to act with certain tendencies that favor the urban population. They try to keep the price of food down, considering that it is desirable and that doing so will combat poverty (despite the fact that it is known that the most severe poverty is concentrated in the rural zones) improve the nutrition level of the population, reduce the rate of inflation and, above all, make greater industrial development possible by maintaining the cost of labor at a relatively low level.[5]

When the stabilization of prices is sought with the idea of benefiting production, the desired effects are not usually obtained. Actually, such price stabilization is only useful in nominal values—not in real terms. Moreover, producers must perceive and effectively receive the changes in price—changes that should be transmitted throughout the marketing system of agricultural products. But the ineffectiveness of this system often makes it work in a regressive way by worsening the distribution of income—that is, favoring the wealthier producers.

On numerous occasions, price-guarantee policies work against general-price stability. Prices of agricultural products may not follow the trend of urban prices, causing the deterioration of the exchange ratio for farmers and, as a result, increasing the instability of real prices.[6]

When purchase prices are boosted without raising prices to the consumer, via subsidies, an inflationary impact results by way of the fiscal deficit. This endangers the objective of overall price stability: concern with urban welfare acts to the detriment of rural living standards. Nonetheless, these marketing institutions have tried to improve the channels for marketing grains through systems of information and the process of market planning.

Before going any further into the matter, we may ask ourselves to what degree are the natural markets for grain and cereals efficient. For example, García,[7] in his study on the corn market in Veracruz, concludes that ". . . despite imperfections or departures from the competitive regime, the system of marketing is working more or less effectively." Oscar Vera,[8] in considering the same topic, points out that the intervention of CONASUPO cannot be efficient when functioning with the high operating costs this institution has for implementing the price-support policies in Mexico. Vera specifies that, during the 1973–1975 period, CONASUPO sales doubled, while its operating costs tripled, reaching 34.5 percent of the value of its sales in 1975. Vera also points out that ". . . the subsidy to CONASUPO, which comes from the federal government, represented 72.2 percent of the income of the enterprise in 1975 . . . and, the obvious beneficiary of this situation (the expansion in operations) seems to have been CONASUPO itself, through its own bureaucratic apparatus."[9] The author goes on to say ". . . in general, the average effectiveness ratio for the three commodities studied (corn, wheat and beans) was 0.256, which can be seen as the average transfer for the producer and consumers for each peso of subsidy to CONASUPO—that is, in real terms, and on the average, only one-fourth of such subsidy reached the pretended beneficiaries." In concluding, Vera states that ". . . the programs (of CONASUPO) cannot be justified in economic terms. . . . Their main policy goal (CONASUPO's) seems to have been to avoid the scarcity of food and channel a subsidy to the urban consumer."[10] Nonetheless, Table 15-1 shows that the degree of intervention of CONASUPO has continued to increase in recent years.

At this point it seems prudent to cite Schuh's[11] comment that "many policies for transferring income from one sector to another through interventions in the commodities market by means of price policies—the effects of which are very fleeting—should be replaced by an effective fiscal system that mobilizes resources more directly."

Aside from this, there is a recent additional factor in the Mexican economy that has a negative effect on the rural producer in his relation to the urban consumer. This factor is the massive grain imports that Mexico has used to feed the large and growing urban middle class. The process is a result of importing grain at a rate of exchange that is actually less that the real value of the foreign currency. That is, keeping a currency overvalued—either through foreign loans or with oil earnings—subsidizes the consumption of imported goods (in this case, grains) to the detriment of

*TABLE 15.1.*
*Share of* CONASUPO* *Industries in the Production and Marketing of Basic Products*

| *Products* | *Sales* | *Unit* | *1977* | *1978* | *1979* | *1980* | *1981* | *1982*** |
|---|---|---|---|---|---|---|---|---|
| Wheat | Consumo Nacional | Thousands | 2,250 | 2,319 | 2,360 | 2,380 | 2,491 | 2,512 |
| Flour | ICONSA | of tons | 167 | 149 | 220 | 246 | 385 | 285 |
| | Participación | % | 7.4 | 6.4 | 9.3 | 10.3 | 10.8 | 10.5 |
| Salt | Consumo Nacional | Thousands | — | — | — | 800 | 824 | 849 |
| | ICONSA | of tons | — | — | — | 30 | 77 | 77 |
| | Participación | % | — | — | — | 3.7 | 9.3 | 9.1 |
| Cooking | Consumo Nacional | Thousands | — | — | — | 822 | 3,047 | 3,047 |
| Oils and | ICONSA | of tons | — | — | — | 320 | 565 | 565 |
| Solids | Participación | % | — | — | — | 14.0 | 18.5 | 18.5 |
| Pasta | Consumo Nacional | Thousands | 120 | 123 | 127 | 130 | 134 | 137 |
| for Soup | ICONSA | of tons | 7 | 7 | 9 | 9 | 13.4 | 13.4 |
| | Participación | % | 5.8 | 5.7 | 7.1 | 6.2 | 10.0 | 9.8 |
| Balanced | Consumo Nacional | Thousands | 3,500 | 3,600 | 3,700 | 3,800 | 3,914 | 4,031 |
| Foods | ICONSA | of tons | 85 | 105 | 77 | 96 | 106 | 106 |
| | Participación | % | 2.4 | 2.9 | 2.2 | 2.5 | 2.7 | 2.6 |
| Milk | Consumo Nacional | Thousands | — | 155.3 | 181.0 | 205.6 | 233.6 | 265.3 |
| Concen- | LICONSA | of tons | — | 33.6 | 43.0 | 47.5 | 103.5 | 119.4 |
| trate | Participación | % | — | 21.0 | 24.0 | 34.0 | 44.3 | 45.0 |
| Powdered | Consumo Nacional | Thousands | — | 31.5 | 36.6 | 42.6 | 49.6 | 57.8 |
| Milk | LICONSA | of tons | — | — | — | 4.6 | 7.3 | 12.2 |
| | Participación | % | — | — | — | 10.8 | 14.7 | 21.1 |
| Corn | Consumo Nacional | Thousands | 661 | 681 | 698 | 890 | 975 | 1,024 |
| Flour | MINSA e ICONSA | of tons | 198 | 237 | 280 | 303 | 319 | 344 |
| | Participación | % | 30.0 | 35.0 | 40.0 | 34.5 | 32.7 | 33.6 |

SOURCE: *IV Report to the Nation* (Mexican Food System (SAM) (ICONSA) (LICONSA) (MINSA)). Manager's Office of Control, CONASUPO.

*A government-subsidized retail distribution system of basic products.

**Projections

the domestic producers that have to compete with these subsidized imports.

## IV. Marketing Food at Retail

In examining the marketing of foods on general and the effect this has on distribution, let us take a brief look at retail marketing.[12]

In 1976, Mexico had 180,700 food stores with an annual sales average of US $30,000—almost equal in number to those existing in the United States (189,000), where the annual sales average was US $140,600. Mexico had 2.9 establishments per 1,000 inhabitants in 1977, while the U.S. had only 0.9 establishments for an equal number.[13] The conclusion is that

54,800 food stores would have been more than enough to supply the market in Mexico, with the same marketing organization as in the U.S.

The concentration of marketing activity is very pronounced.[14] Multiple stores (various retail establishments belonging to the same owner—usually supermarkets), representing 1.2 percent of the total number of retail food establishments were responsible for 32 percent of retail food sales in 1976. On the other hand, purchasing groups and voluntary chains—so important in Europe—have no meaning whatsoever in Mexico. A major part of commerce is carried out by supermarkets with sales areas of more than 2,500 square meters, which sell one-third of the total amount of food sold, and whose average sales are high under any international comparison.[15] Supermarkets whose sales areas cover between 400 and 2,500 square meters, representing 0.2% of the total number of retail food establishments account for 14.1% of retail food sales. Thus, it is not strange that the Gini coefficient is so high (0.829). Actually, in 1976, 2% of the total number of retail food establishments accounted for 50% of total sales, with 5% selling 60% of the total referred to. These percentages are surpassed only in France.

The concentration in food retailing, together with its dispersion and fragmentation[16], has resulted in a very inefficient marketing system—with higher prices for the poorest consumers. At the same time, it helps to explain the extremely high share it represents in the gross domestic product.[17] We shall attempt to describe this set of circumstances in the following paragraphs. Initially we must show that, faced with the prevailing situation, the public sector has tried to bring cheap food within reach of low-income groups, setting up a costly distribution system.

## *Official Marketing*

CONASUPO maintains a large participation in the industrialization and marketing of basic commodities: powdered milk, milk concentrate, corn flour, cooking oils and solids, wheat flour, bread, pasta for soup, salt, and balanced food (see Table 15-1); plus corn, wheat, sugar, beans, rice, coffee, and other consumer products prepared by its affiliates and by other companies.

DICONSA, its retail affiliate, has a national network of stores that in 1980 numbered 1,987 in 500 cities of more than 10,000 inhabitants, 4,074 in rural zones (including 3,606 rural stores, 110 mobile units, 165 PIDERs and 37 DIF centers,[18] among others), with plans to expand this distribution network significantly. DICONSA has a 9 percent share of total sales in basic commodities (1980), with between 5 and 9 percent of the country's families using DICONSA affiliates as their main place to shop for cereals, groceries and milk, and a somewhat lower percentage for eggs, fruits, vegetables and meat. However, their operations barely touch the lowest-income groups.

**Figure 15-6. Cumulative Percentage of Food Buying by Families According to Income Strata and Establishment, Nationwide.**

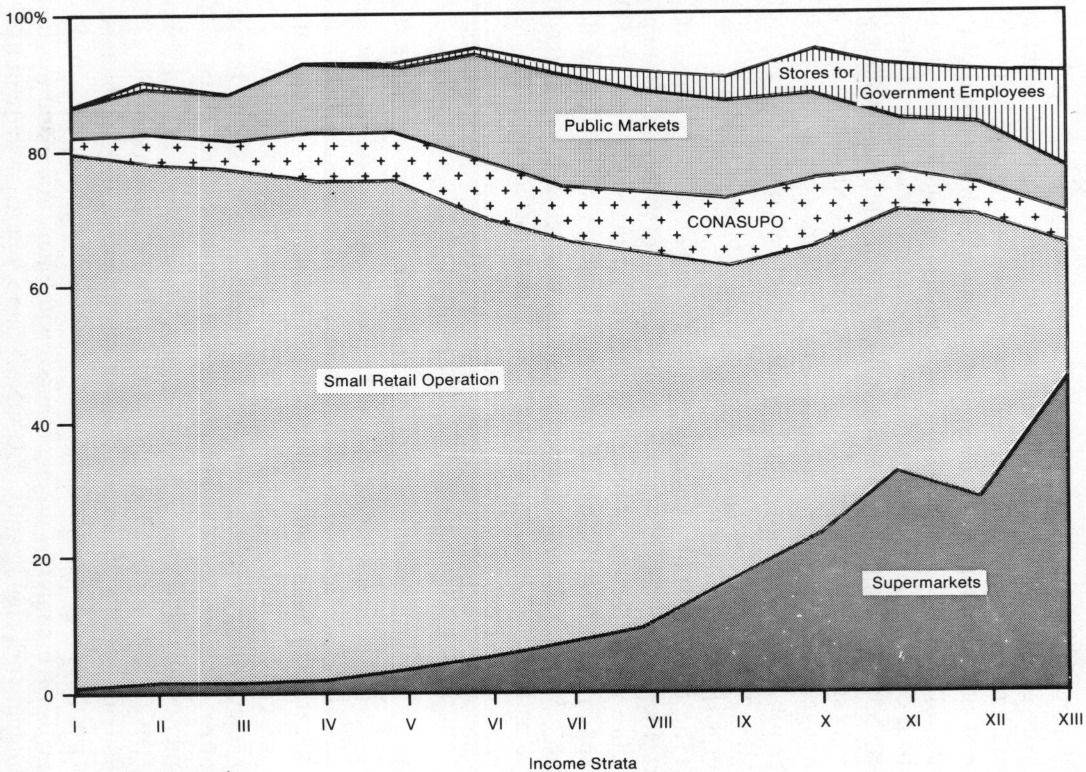


SOURCE: Banco de México.

From income and spending surveys showing points of food buying, information was taken for Figure 15-6, which demonstrates that CONASUPO retail outlets benefit the medium-income strata more than lower-income groups.

IMPECSA is the counterpart of CONASUPO in wholesale activities connected with basic commodities, supplying goods to small-scale retailers in order to improve their efficiency. It has 3,500 affiliates, with 210 wholesale warehouses that supply 350 basic products to urban zones, and 25 to rural zones. Again we see that the government's policies in this sector tend to benefit the urban sector of the economy more than the rural zones.

### *Private Retailing*

Private self-service chains have been very successful. In 1975, there were 2,396 of these establishments. Integrated chains—operating on the basis of branches—have numerous supermarkets that handle an average of 8,000 food products (up to a total of 66,000 articles throughout the store) in selling areas of over 10,000 square meters. These chains have contracts with agricultural producers. For example, the most important chain in Mexico acquires between 70 to 80 percent of its fruit and vegetable operation directly from the producer.[19] Self-service chains supply medium- and high-income groups and exert a great influence on the distribution of groceries and cereals. They have less influence on the distribution of meat and eggs, and still less influence on fruit and milk, but are rapidly gaining ground and capturing a larger share of the market.

Convenience chain stores are small self-service operations that sell basic products, are located near the consumer, and have extended store hours. These chains are newcomers to the Mexican market and handle between 500 to 1,000 products.

Independent wholesalers and retailers usually operate on a small scale, with a high participation in food distribution. More than 80 percent of families buy their fruit, vegetables, meat and milk from these outlets, while around 50 to 60 percent buy their cereals and eggs there.

Other types of commercial operations such as mobile markets, public markets, and small neighborhood operations have less importance. Prices in mobile markets tend to be somewhat lower than other alternatives, while public markets specialize in fruit, vegetables and meat for lower- and middle-income groups. Small neighborhood operations sell their products at prices 7 to 30 percent higher on the average than the bottom market price.[20]

### *Marketing of Perishables*

It is surprising that price levels of perishables are sometimes higher in supermarkets than in public markets.[21] Expressed in indexes, their behavior over time shows a former with respect to the latter (see Table 15-2 and

*TABLE 15.2.*

*Price Indexes[1] of Fruit[2] and Vegetable[3] Prices in Supermarkets and Public Markets in Mexico City*

| | | *Fruit* | | *Vegetables* | |
|---|---|---|---|---|---|
| *Year* | *Month* | *Supermarkets* | *Public Markets* | *Supermarkets* | *Public Markets* |
| 1977 | January | 100.00 | 100.00 | 100.00 | 100.00 |
| | February | 93.18 | 101.01 | 89.41 | 100.81 |
| | March | 96.03 | 108.63 | 85.31 | 101.24 |
| | April | 102.01 | 106.51 | 78.37 | 101.62 |
| | May | 103.24 | 103.73 | 64.70 | 93.74 |
| | June | 111.38 | 110.30 | 61.21 | 91.08 |
| | July | 132.83 | 134.51 | 64.48 | 89.89 |
| | August | 144.55 | 174.47 | 67.58 | 88.47 |
| | September | 131.53 | 176.59 | 73.46 | 96.36 |
| | October | 120.06 | 147.84 | 75.86 | 87.08 |
| | November | 103.43 | 143.29 | 83.81 | 105.14 |
| | December | 105.38 | 138.37 | 105.06 | 126.82 |
| 1978 | January | 107.89 | 134.29 | 101.15 | 130.43 |
| | February | 122.70 | 143.79 | 79.70 | 106.54 |
| | March | 130.99 | 152.65 | 76.51 | 102.48 |
| | April | 142.99 | 161.96 | 88.65 | 114.29 |
| | May | 153.65 | 180.40 | 100.92 | 127.64 |
| | June | 166.46 | 187.28 | 103.25 | 138.63 |
| | July | 159.61 | 188.54 | 94.52 | 124.73 |
| | August | 144.69 | 174.29 | 112.47 | 131.37 |
| | September | 136.05 | 162.49 | 92.78 | 108.20 |
| | October | 132.77 | 154.66 | 104.98 | 122.31 |
| | November | 130.94 | 151.91 | 128.78 | 146.39 |
| | December | 124.86 | 151.01 | 126.35 | 157.40 |
| 1979 | January | 129.44 | 158.26 | 121.03 | 154.06 |
| | February | 135.09 | 156.55 | 102.93 | 134.23 |
| | March | 149.07 | 175.45 | 87.84 | 125.22 |
| | April | 159.56 | 181.53 | 89.14 | 123.15 |
| | May | 174.15 | 195.96 | 96.65 | 130.68 |
| | June | 172.46 | 206.97 | 94.41 | 127.66 |
| | July | 187.35 | 216.85 | 109.02 | 134.82 |
| | August | 205.06 | 240.73 | 136.97 | 170.19 |
| | September | 205.44 | 266.89 | 142.96 | 173.17 |
| | October | 152.74 | 215.87 | 163.00 | 184.75 |
| | November | 139.12 | 188.02 | 167.95 | 174.62 |
| | December | 127.95 | 183.80 | 157.28 | 171.49 |
| 1980 | January | 136.02 | 180.96 | 136.72 | 167.57 |
| | February | 149.49 | 181.88 | 122.12 | 163.29 |

*TABLE 15.2.* (Continued)

| | | *Fruit* | | *Vegetables* | |
|---|---|---|---|---|---|
| *Year* | *Month* | *Supermarkets* | *Public Markets* | *Supermarkets* | *Public Markets* |
| | March | 161.03 | 189.45 | 123.60 | 158.11 |
| | April | 170.42 | 199.22 | 135.10 | 176.22 |
| | May | 175.69 | 205.60 | 142.46 | 177.12 |
| | June | 218.45 | 258.90 | 121.65 | 156.26 |
| | July | 259.16 | 281.36 | 144.51 | 174.17 |
| | August | 326.64 | 338.09 | 151.78 | 174.26 |
| | September | 287.78 | 330.38 | 146.32 | 165.56 |
| | October | 254.18 | 287.13 | 164.46 | 175.30 |
| | November | | | 191.15 | 200.21 |
| | December | 242.02 | 255.89 | 206.65 | 236.00 |
| 1981 | January | 240.94 | 257.38 | 229.19 | 261.59 |
| | February | 272.89 | 283.12 | 223.43 | 262.39 |
| | March | 289.18 | 288.09 | 237.17 | 266.82 |
| | April | | | 239.93 | 262.74 |

SOURCE: Banco de México, S.A.

[1]The index is calculated as the geometric average of prices on the quoted products.

[2]The products included in the fruit index were oranges and bananas.

[3]The products included in the vegetable index were: onions, *jalapeño* and *serrano* chiles, white and yellow potatoes, green and red tomatoes.

Fig. 15-7). This is valid for fruit and vegetables, with the exception of certain products such as green chiles and Tabasco bananas. Over a period of time, the competitiveness of supermarkets improves and cushions price rises. Actually, this is explained by supermarkets fixing their prices according to marginal cost pricing, taking into account the monopolistic features that come into being once the customer is inside the store.[22]

Nonetheless, there are cases that seem to constitute an exception. When fruits and vegetables experience a rapid hike in price, the effect is more readily apparent in supermarkets than in public markets. On the other hand, when the contrary is true, such a phenomenon reverses itself (see Fig. 15-8). This can be explained by the hypothesis that supermarkets maintain a constant markup on their purchase price, have a more stable volume and require a few days to line up perishables, requiring a higher purchase price in order to ensure the volume they need. The stands in public markets, on the other hand, can dispose of products on the same day and can acquire ripe fruit that wholesalers have to get rid of at lower prices, even though their margins are higher. When the market falls, it operates in the opposite sense, and prices in supermarkets are lower.[23]

According to the research of Martínez[24] on establishments that sell fruit

**Figure 15-7.**

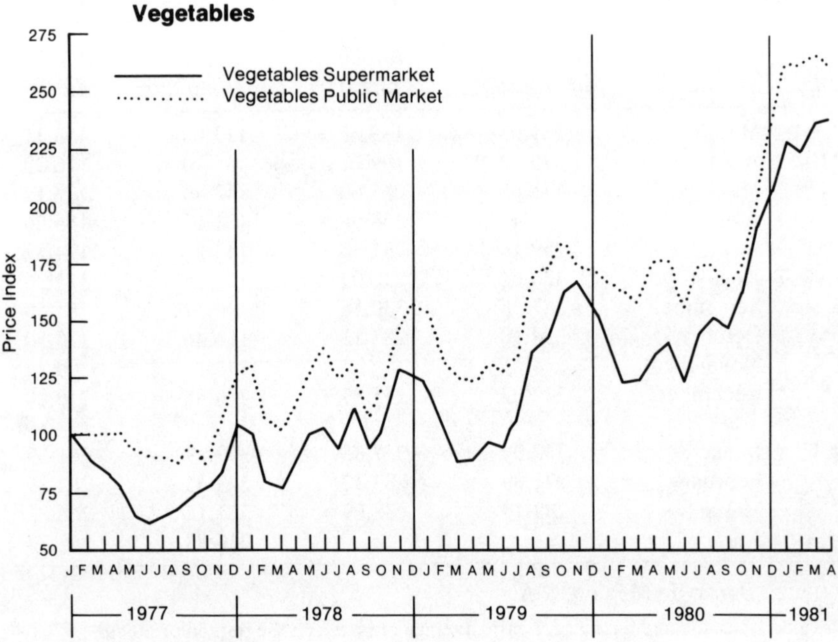


SOURCE: Banco de México.

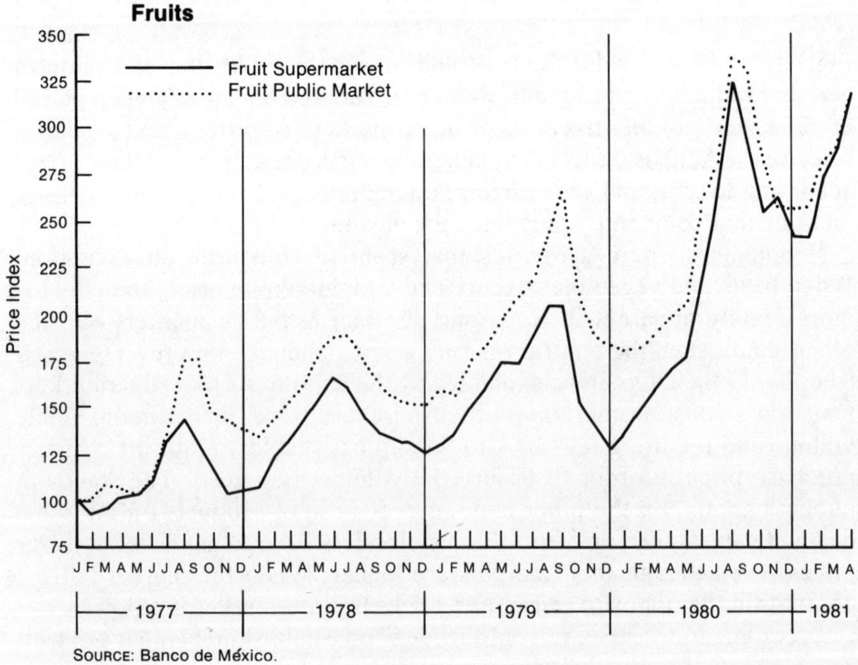


SOURCE: Banco de México.

**Figure 15-8. Behavior of Prices in Mexico City.**

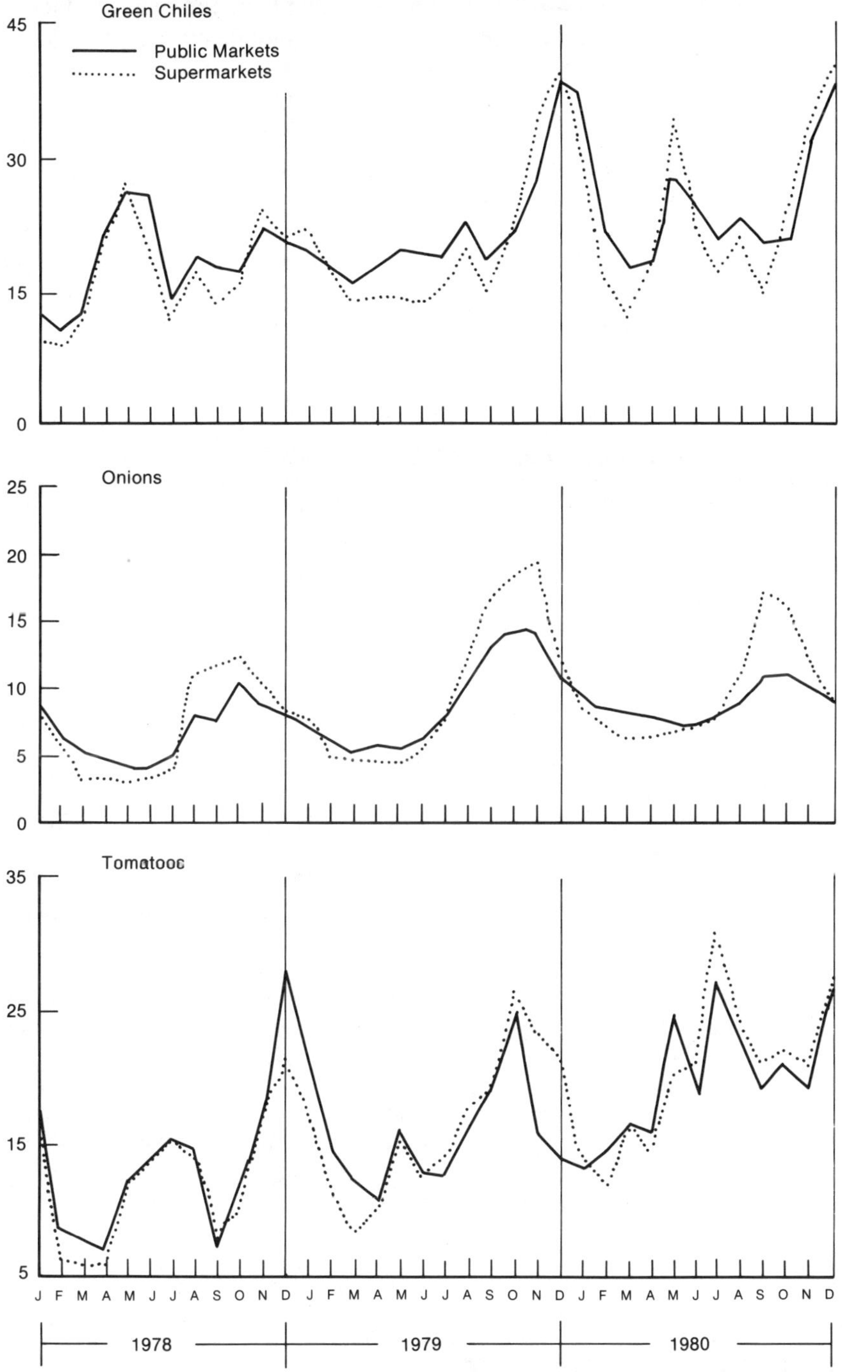


SOURCE: Banco de México.

and vegetables in the city of Puebla, it is usually the stands of small retail operations located in poorer neighborhoods that have the highest marketing margins. Those that have the lowest are the mobile markets that move from neighborhood to neighborhood.[25] Furthermore, he wanted to establish the relationship between the size of the establishment and the marketing margin on the assumption that prices could be lower in larger establishments on account of economies of scale and superior bargaining power at the purchase-wholesale level. However, he was unable to support this statistically.[26]

Although the initial hypothesis would seem to have ample validity, the information available for Mexico City only allows the establishment of annual averages of gross marketing margins for supermarkets and public

*TABLE 15.3.*
*Marketing Margins of Fruit and Produce at Retail*

| *Product* | *Year* | *Wholesale Prices* | *Annual average in pesos per kg.* *Public Markets* | *Annual average in pesos per kg.* *Super-markets* | *Annual average in pesos per kg.* *Public Markets* | *Annual average in pesos per kg.* *Super-markets* |
|---|---|---|---|---|---|---|
| Onions | 1977 | 4.7 | 6.3 | 6.3 | 34.04 | 34.7 |
| | 1978 | 4.9 | 6.7 | 6.9 | 36.73 | 40.82 |
| | 1979 | 5.7 | 8.7 | 9.6 | 52.63 | 68.42 |
| | 1980 | 4.0 | 8.8 | 9.5 | 120.00 | 137.50 |
| | 1981 | 14.7 | 23.7 | 29.3 | 61.22 | 99.32 |
| Green Chiles | 1977 | 7.21 | 14.53 | 11.55 | 101.53 | 60.19 |
| | 1978 | 10.79 | 18.45 | 16.70 | 70.99 | 54.77 |
| | 1979 | 11.86 | 21.96 | 20.11 | 85.16 | 69.56 |
| | 1980 | 11.20 | 25.30 | 24.40 | 125.89 | 116.07 |
| Tomatoes | 1977 | 5.56 | 8.70 | 9.29 | 56.50 | 67.10 |
| | 1978 | 9.02 | 13.15 | 11.98 | 45.80 | 32.80 |
| | 1979 | 10.00 | 15.42 | 15.94 | 54.70 | 59.40 |
| | 1980 | 13.06 | 19.70 | 19.72 | 50.80 | 53.80 |
| Yellow Potatoes | 1977 | 4.80 | 5.90 | 7.40 | 22.92 | 54.17 |
| | 1978 | 5.60 | 8.70 | 11.20 | 55.36 | 100.00 |
| | 1979 | 5.30 | 8.70 | 9.60 | 64.15 | 81.30 |
| | 1980 | 6.90 | 9.80 | 12.50 | 42.03 | 81.16 |
| Tabasco Bananas | 1977 | 0.93 | 3.67 | 3.14 | 294.95 | 237.63 |
| | 1978 | 1.30 | 4.46 | 3.79 | 243.08 | 191.54 |
| | 1979 | 1.90 | 5.73 | 5.09 | 201.58 | 167.89 |

SOURCE: Banco de México, S. A.

markets (assuming that both are supplied by "La Merced," the capital's main wholesale market; see Table 15-3). Nor does the survey made in Puebla, although providing more detail on purchase prices from wholesalers, permit a well-grounded generalization. The concept of scale is extremely elusive in this context,[27] and the practice of marginal cost pricing in supermarkets[28] raises the margins for inelastic articles.

### *Marketing of Food in Grocery Stores*

Grocery stores represent a category worthy of our attention. Those located in low-income areas had sales per square meter of 243 pesos daily in 1978, while those situated in medium- and high-income zones almost doubled that figure (451 and 422 pesos, respectively). Neighborhood stores sell mainly basic food products that are under official price control. Their mix is determined basically by the demand of the consumers in each income group, by the profit margin on the product and by their distribution structure.[29]

In the study on groceries previously cited in the text it was stated that stores attending to the needs of lower-income consumers have alternative supply channels that can save them between 7 and 27 percent—when they associate themselves with a voluntary chain; but, in practice, this is rarely done.

Some retailers supply themselves at self-service chains or at a CONASUPO outlet, thus increasing the marketing chain by two retail transactions. These stores operate with high profit margins, use inadequate equipment, handle slow-turnover products and keep little stock. In low-income zones, grocery stores constitute the principal source of supply for prepared foods, despite their being sold at higher prices. The explanation for their importance is their proximity and the ease in attending to the basic needs of families of little means who—because of their limited budget—make frequent small purchases, thus raising transaction costs. In these stores sale per square meter are low, partly because they are usually adaptations of the owner's home, with intensive unpaid family help, representing up to four-fifths of the labor used, and with very low opportunity cost. Similarly, the low turnover of inventory indicates an inefficient use of capital.

Stores located in medium-income zones have higher marketing margins due to better purchasing prices. The sales ratio per square meter is higher, they have a more commercial attitude, a higher turnover, a sounder financial situation, and a larger sales volume. They compete with self-service chains and with each other. Grocery stores located in high-income zones supplement self-service chains. They fulfill the consumer's last-minute needs for fresh products and those requiring more complicated handling (bakery goods, soft drinks, milk products, etc.) than the standard prepared foods.

Summing up, this section points to the fact that distortions in retailing show themselves in the form of high social costs: the poor pay higher prices for their food. The poor majority of Mexico's inhabitants buy sparingly, while the wealthier minority accounts for the major part of food purchasing.[30] The great number of small retailing operations sell little in quantity, while the large retailers deal in considerable volume. All this results in an unequal distribution of the benefits of marketing, to the detriment of the lower-income strata of the population.[31]

### V. Distributive Effects Under Different Marketing Schemes

This section takes a broader look at the question we have been dealing with: To what extent will marketing development work a favorable influence on the redistribution of income to low-strata groups? To this end, the Banco de México—the central bank—has promoted the development of a general equilibrium model for the marketing sector.[32] The idea is to use it to analyze the allocation of resources, changes in distribution and variations in employment, as well as assess antipoverty policies and price fixing on food products.

The principal features of the model are those of a static Walrasian general equilibrium model, which determines simultaneously the prices and quantities of equilibrium. The model divides the marketing sector into eight components: wholesalers, public markets, grocery stores, CONASUPO outlets, supermarkets, specialty stores, department stores and other retailing outlets. It differentiates between twenty-one productive sectors, twenty-six consumer goods, three sectors that demand nonconsumer goods, twelve types of consumers, and three production factors (see Table 15-4).

Activity levels are represented by the equation $Q_j = \min(A_j, V_j)$, with $j = 1, 2, 3, \ldots n$ and where $A_j$ represents the demand of intermediate inputs and $V_j$, the components of aggregate value.[33] The utility levels of the consumer are given by a Cobb-Douglas utility function:

$$U(x) = \sum_{i=1}^{n+3} b_i \log X_i$$

with $i = 1, 2, 3 \ldots, n$, and where $b_i$ is the part of income that assigns the consumer to the good i and $X_i$ is the quantity of the good i.

Due to the characteristics of the text, only a part of the different aspects contemplated by the model will be analyzed, i.e., such variables as: variations in employment; changes in income; level of consumer utility; and purchasing share of consumers by type of good and by type of establishment. For this, only ten consumer goods will be considered (bread, tortillas, cereals, milk and milk products, eggs, other groceries, fresh fruit, fresh vegetables, meat, and fish); four types of establishments (public markets, supermarkets, grocery stores, and CONASUPO outlets); ten types of consumers (those that represent home aggregates in the Mexican

*TABLE 15.4.*

*Production Sectors, Commerce Sectors, Nonconsumption Demand Sectors, Consumption Goods, Factors of Production, and Type of Consumers*

*Production sectors*

1. Agriculture
2. Livestock
3. Forestry
4. Fishing and hunting
5. Mining
6. Petroleum and petrochemicals
7. Alcoholic beverages
8. Soft drinks
9. Tobacco and tobacco products
10. Food products
11. Textiles
12. Wood products
13. Chemical products
14. Nonmetal production
15. Basic metals
16. Machinery
17. Automobiles
18. Electric energy
19. Transportation
20. Services
21. Construction

*Commerce sector*

22. Wholesalers
23. Public markets
24. Grocery stores
25. CONASUPO
26. Supermarkets
27. Specialty stores
28. Department stores
29. Other retailers

*Nonconsumption Demand sectors*

30. Government
31. Imports–exports
32. Fixed investment and inventory accumulation

*Consumption goods*

33. Bread
34. Tortillas
35. Cereals
36. Milk and milk products
37. Eggs
38. Other groceries

*TABLE 15.4.* (Continued)

39. Fresh fruits
40. Fresh vegetables
41. Meat
42. Fish
44.
43. Nonalcoholic beverages
45. Tobacco and tobacco products
46. Clothing
47. Shoes and shoe repair
48. Furniture and accessories
49. Household fabrics
50. Household appliances
51. Glassware and dishware
52. Medical products
53. Automobiles, parts, and repairs
54. Transportation
55. Household accessories
56. Educational articles
57. Articles for personal care
58. Services

*Factors of production*
59. Rural labor
60. Urban labor
61. Capital and other factors

*Type of consumers by sector and income level (per month)*
62. Urban poor (0–1,800 pesos)
63. Rural poor (0–1,800 pesos)
64. Urban low income (1,801–3,150 pesos)
65. Rural low income (1,801–3,150 pesos)
66. Urban low-middle income (3,151–5,725 pesos)
67. Rural low-middle income (3,151–5,725 pesos)
68. Urban middle income (5,726–13,400 pesos)
69. Rural middle income (5,726–13,400 pesos)
70. Urban upper income (13,401 pesos and up)
71. Rural upper income (13,401 pesos and up)

economy—in the rural as well as the urban sector—which are divided into five groups each, according to income level); and three production factors (urban employment, rural employment, and "capital and other factors").

In order to examine the effects on the variables mentioned, simulations are made that change the marketing structure prevailing in Mexico by means of varying the number of establishments (public markets, grocery stores, supermarkets, and CONASUPO outlets), or by applying full modernization to the marketing sector through the reduction of wholesale costs.

*TABLE 15.5.*
*Number of Establishments by Type of Simulation*

| *Simulations* | *Type of Establishment* | | | | |
|---|---|---|---|---|---|
| | *Public Market* | *Grocery Store* | CONASUPO | *Super-market* | *Department Store* |
| ORIGINAL | 20 | 98 | 8 | 5 | 1 |
| 1 | 10 | 45 | 14 | 12 | 3 |
| 2 | 16 | 32 | 16 | 19 | 5 |
| 3* | 16 | 32 | 16 | 19 | 5 |
| 4 (increases CONASUPO retail store) | 20 | 98 | 25 | 5 | 1 |

*Wholesalers were made more efficient by multiplying $a_{22,j}$ times 0.6, except for public market and grocery store.

Table 15-5 shows four simulations numbered 1 to 4. In simulation 1, public markets and traditional grocery stores diminish, while retail outlets of CONASUPO, supermarkets, and department stores increase in number; in simulation 2, public markets diminish somewhat less than in simulation 1, with grocery stores diminishing more, while CONASUPO outlets, supermarkets, and department stores increase; simulation 3 attempts to assess marketing development by means of reducing wholesale costs, multiplying the wholesale margin by 0.6, accompanied by a decrease in public markets and grocery stores, and an increase in CONASUPO outlets, supermarkets, and department stores; and, last, simulation 4 raises the number of CONASUPO outlets and preserves the number of the other retail operations that appear in the original equilibrium.

Tables 15-6 to 15-10 show, respectively, the effects on consumer utility, establishment activity, and the factor price. Thus, the figures represent percentage changes of values obtained in each of the simulations vis-à-vis those of the original equilibrium, with negative signs indicating decreases, and positive, increases.

On the basis of the results from the simulations, it was found that a policy stressing participation of government food outlets (CONASUPO stores) is inferior, in terms of consumer utility, compared to a policy of full modernization of marketing channels—that is, reducing wholesale costs (simulation 3, see Table 15-6). In the first case, rural poverty is becoming more acute with the decrease of utility in consumer decile groups 2, 4, 6, 8 and 10;[34] in contrast, urban consumers of medium-high strata groups benefit from an increase in their utility level. In the second case—that is, simulation 3—all consumers except group 10 raised their utility level, especially those with low incomes. Furthermore, if we compare the increases in utility of the consumers in simulation 3 with those

*TABLE 15.6.*

*Level of Utility: Type of Consumer and Type of Simulation (Percentage Change with Respect to the Original Equilibrium)*

| *Type of Consumer* | *Level of Utility* | | | |
|---|---|---|---|---|
| | *Simulations* | | | |
| | *1* | *2* | *3* | *4* |
| Consumer | | | | |
| 1 | .0047439 | .0085147 | .057734 | .010085 |
| 2 | .000216 | .000456 | .00487 | −000336 |
| 3 | .018013 | −.01359 | .05670 | .010373 |
| 4 | .0003747 | .000656 | .00103 | −.00028 |
| 5 | −.00344 | .00357 | .07641 | .0018082 |
| 6 | .0042514 | .0007488 | .001427 | −.00034 |
| 7 | −.005012 | −.02535 | .017278 | .032620 |
| 8 | .000067 | .000242 | .007168 | −.000349 |
| 9 | −.00556 | −.008577 | .046654 | .0018303 |
| 10 | .0007886 | .0013324 | −.002638 | −.0005167 |

SOURCE: Banco de México, S.A.

*TABLE 15.7.*

*Spending Share: Type of Consumer by Type of Good in Grocery Stores (Percentage Change)*

| | | | *Simulation* | | | |
|---|---|---|---|---|---|---|
| | | | *1* | *2* | *3* | *4* |
| Consumer 1 | Type of good | 1 | −.012 | −.019 | −.008 | .003 |
| | | 2 | −.009 | −.016 | −.005 | −.001 |
| | | 3 | −.037 | −.072 | −.061 | −.023 |
| | | 4 | −.009 | −.016 | −.005 | −.001 |
| | | 5 | −.037 | −.072 | −.046 | −.023 |
| | | 6 | −.037 | −.072 | −.061 | −.023 |
| | | 7 | −.485 | −.936 | −.787 | −.302 |
| | | 8 | −.485 | −.936 | −.787 | −.302 |
| | | 9 | .000 | .000 | .000 | .000 |
| | | 10 | −.787 | −.787 | −.787 | −.973 |
| Consumer 2 | Type of good | 1 | .000 | .000 | .000 | .000 |
| | | 2 | .000 | .000 | .000 | .000 |
| | | 3 | .000 | .000 | .000 | .000 |
| | | 4 | .000 | .000 | .000 | .000 |
| | | 5 | .000 | .000 | .000 | .000 |
| | | 6 | .000 | .000 | .000 | .000 |
| | | 7 | .000 | .000 | .000 | .000 |
| | | 8 | .000 | .000 | .000 | .000 |
| | | 9 | .000 | .000 | .000 | .000 |
| | | 10 | .000 | .000 | .000 | .000 |

*TABLE 15.7.* (Continued)

| | | | *Simulation* | | | |
|---|---|---|---|---|---|---|
| | | | *1* | *2* | *3* | *4* |
| Consumer 3 | Type of good | 1 | .057 | .021 | .014 | −.019 |
| | | 2 | .057 | .021 | .014 | −.019 |
| | | 3 | −.010 | −.051 | −.051 | −.020 |
| | | 4 | −.020 | −.069 | −.069 | −.020 |
| | | 5 | −.010 | −.051 | −.050 | −.020 |
| | | 6 | −.010 | −.051 | −.051 | −.020 |
| | | 7 | −.436 | −.839 | −.839 | −.013 |
| | | 8 | −.417 | −.817 | −.817 | −.014 |
| | | 9 | .000 | .000 | .000 | .000 |
| | | 10 | .000 | .000 | .000 | .000 |
| Consumer 4 | Type of good | 1 | .000 | .000 | .000 | .000 |
| | | 2 | .000 | .000 | −.001 | .000 |
| | | 3 | .000 | .000 | .000 | .000 |
| | | 4 | .000 | .000 | .000 | .000 |
| | | 5 | .000 | .000 | .000 | .000 |
| | | 6 | .000 | .000 | .000 | .000 |
| | | 7 | .000 | .000 | .000 | .000 |
| | | 8 | .000 | .000 | .000 | .000 |
| | | 9 | −.000 | .000 | .000 | .000 |
| | | 10 | .000 | .000 | .000 | .000 |
| Consumer 5 | Type of good | 1 | −.195 | −.291 | −.292 | −.011 |
| | | 2 | −.016 | −.121 | −.123 | .026 |
| | | 3 | −.042 | −.124 | −.126 | −.013 |
| | | 4 | −.072 | −.159 | −.161 | −.013 |
| | | 5 | −.042 | −.124 | −.126 | −.013 |
| | | 6 | −.042 | −.124 | −.126 | −.013 |
| | | 7 | −.455 | −.986 | −.100 | −.086 |
| | | 8 | −.372 | −.984 | −.984 | .000 |
| | | 9 | .000 | .000 | .000 | .000 |
| | | 10 | .000 | .000 | .000 | .000 |
| Consumer 6 | Type of good | 1 | .000 | .000 | .000 | .000 |
| | | 2 | .000 | .000 | .000 | .000 |
| | | 3 | .000 | .000 | .000 | .000 |
| | | 4 | .000 | .000 | .000 | .000 |
| | | 5 | .000 | .000 | .000 | .000 |
| | | 6 | .000 | .000 | .000 | .000 |
| | | 7 | .000 | .000 | .000 | .000 |
| | | 8 | .000 | .000 | .000 | .000 |
| | | 8 | .000 | .000 | .000 | .000 |
| | | 9 | .000 | .000 | .000 | .000 |
| | | 10 | .000 | .000 | .000 | .000 |

*TABLE 15.7.* (Continued)

| | | | Simulation | | | |
|---|---|---|---|---|---|---|
| | | | *1* | *2* | *3* | *4* |
| Consumer 7 | Type of good | 1 | −.075 | −.159 | −.031 | −.065 |
| | | 2 | .065 | .158 | .325 | −.026 |
| | | 3 | −.021 | −.021 | −.021 | −.021 |
| | | 4 | −.075 | −.075 | −.075 | −.020 |
| | | 5 | −.021 | −.021 | −.021 | −.021 |
| | | 6 | −.021 | −.021 | −.021 | −.021 |
| | | 7 | −1.000 | −1.000 | −1.000 | −1.000 |
| | | 8 | −.478 | −.652 | −1.000 | .052 |
| | | 9 | .000 | .000 | .000 | .000 |
| | | 10 | .000 | .000 | .000 | .000 |
| Consumer 8 | Type of good | 1 | .000 | .000 | .000 | .000 |
| | | 2 | .001 | .000 | .000 | .000 |
| | | 3 | .000 | .000 | .000 | .000 |
| | | 4 | .000 | .000 | .000 | .000 |
| | | 5 | .000 | .000 | .000 | .000 |
| | | 6 | .000 | .000 | .000 | .000 |
| | | 7 | .000 | .000 | .000 | .000 |
| | | 8 | .000 | .000 | .000 | .000 |
| | | 9 | .000 | .000 | .000 | .000 |
| | | 10 | .000 | .000 | .000 | .000 |
| Consumer 9 | Type of good | 1 | −.209 | −.211 | −.211 | −.017 |
| | | 2 | −.238 | −.245 | −.247 | −.020 |
| | | 3 | −.108 | −.108 | −.108 | .000 |
| | | 4 | −.108 | −.109 | −.382 | .000 |
| | | 5 | −.108 | −.108 | −.108 | .000 |
| | | 6 | −.108 | −.108 | −.108 | .000 |
| | | 7 | −1.000 | −1.000 | −1.000 | .000 |
| | | 8 | −1.000 | −1.000 | −1.000 | .000 |
| | | 9 | .000 | .000 | .000 | .000 |
| | | 10 | .000 | .000 | .000 | .000 |
| Consumer 10 | Type of good | 1 | .000 | .000 | .000 | .000 |
| | | 2 | .000 | .000 | .000 | .000 |
| | | 3 | .000 | .000 | .000 | .000 |
| | | 4 | .000 | .000 | .000 | .000 |
| | | 5 | .000 | .000 | .000 | .000 |
| | | 6 | .000 | .000 | .000 | .000 |
| | | 7 | .000 | .000 | .000 | .000 |
| | | 8 | .000 | .000 | .000 | .000 |
| | | 9 | .000 | .000 | .000 | .000 |
| | | 10 | .000 | .000 | .000 | .000 |

SOURCE: Banco de México, S.A.

*TABLE 15.8.*
*Spending Share: Type of Consumer by Type of Good in Supermarket (Percentage Change)*

| | | | Simulation | | | |
|---|---|---|---|---|---|---|
| | | | *1* | *2* | *3* | *4* |
| Consumer 1 | Type of good | 1 | .608 | .506 | .264 | −.188 |
| | | 2 | 1.333 | 1.807 | 1.874 | −.104 |
| | | 3 | 1.333 | 1.807 | 1.874 | −.104 |
| | | 4 | 1.334 | 1.808 | 1.874 | −.104 |
| | | 5 | 1.333 | 1.807 | 1.874 | −.104 |
| | | 6 | 1.334 | 1.808 | 1.874 | −.104 |
| | | 7 | 1.333 | 1.807 | 1.874 | −.104 |
| | | 8 | 1.333 | 1.808 | 1.874 | −.104 |
| | | 9 | .000 | .000 | .000 | .000 |
| | | 10 | 6.725 | 6.725 | 6.725 | 6.725 |
| Consumer 2 | Type of good | 1 | .000 | .000 | .000 | .000 |
| | | 2 | .000 | .000 | .000 | .000 |
| | | 3 | .013 | .000 | .000 | .000 |
| | | 4 | .000 | .000 | .000 | .000 |
| | | 5 | .000 | .000 | .000 | .000 |
| | | 6 | .000 | .000 | .000 | .000 |
| | | 7 | .000 | .000 | .000 | .000 |
| | | 8 | .000 | .000 | .000 | .000 |
| | | 9 | .000 | .000 | .000 | .000 |
| | | 10 | .000 | .000 | .000 | .000 |
| Consumer 3 | Type of good | 1 | .847 | 1.253 | 1.194 | −.059 |
| | | 2 | .847 | 1.253 | 1.194 | −.059 |
| | | 3 | .847 | 1.253 | 1.194 | −.059 |
| | | 4 | .847 | 1.253 | 1.194 | −.059 |
| | | 5 | .847 | 1.253 | 1.194 | −.059 |
| | | 6 | −.582 | 1.371 | 1.488 | −.059 |
| | | 7 | .847 | 1.253 | 1.194 | −.059 |
| | | 8 | .847 | 1.253 | 1.194 | −.059 |
| | | 9 | .000 | .000 | .000 | .000 |
| | | 10 | .000 | .000 | .000 | .000 |
| Consumer 4 | Type of good | 1 | .000 | .000 | .000 | −.792 |
| | | 2 | *** | *** | *** | *** |
| | | 3 | .000 | .000 | .000 | .000 |
| | | 4 | .000 | .000 | .000 | .000 |
| | | 5 | .000 | .000 | .000 | .000 |
| | | 6 | .000 | .000 | .000 | .000 |
| | | 7 | .000 | .000 | .000 | .000 |
| | | 8 | .000 | .000 | .000 | .000 |
| | | 9 | .000 | .000 | .000 | .000 |
| | | 10 | .000 | .000 | .000 | .000 |

TABLE 15.8. (Continued)

| | Type of good | Simulation 1 | 2 | 3 | 4 |
|---|---|---|---|---|---|
| Consumer 5 | 1 | 2.689 | 3.604 | 3.836 | .328 |
| | 2 | .474 | −.485 | −.815 | −.093 |
| | 3 | .474 | −.484 | −.815 | −.093 |
| | 4 | .474 | −.485 | −.814 | −.093 |
| | 5 | .474 | −.485 | −.814 | −.093 |
| | 6 | .474 | −.485 | −.814 | −.093 |
| | 7 | 1.509 | −.108 | −.684 | −.158 |
| | 8 | .392 | −.513 | −.825 | −.143 |
| | 9 | −.023 | −.023 | −.023 | −.023 |
| | 10 | .000 | .000 | .000 | .000 |
| Consumer 6 | 1 | .000 | .000 | .000 | .000 |
| | 2 | .000 | .000 | .000 | .000 |
| | 3 | .000 | .000 | .000 | .000 |
| | 4 | .000 | .000 | .000 | .000 |
| | 5 | .000 | .000 | .000 | .000 |
| | 6 | .000 | .000 | .000 | .000 |
| | 7 | .000 | .000 | .000 | .000 |
| | 8 | .000 | .000 | .000 | .000 |
| | 9 | .000 | .000 | .000 | .000 |
| | 10 | .000 | .000 | .000 | .000 |
| Consumer 7 | 1 | −.136 | −1.000 | −.519 | −.022 |
| | 2 | −.079 | .174 | −.487 | −.157 |
| | 3 | −.231 | .158 | −.434 | −.223 |
| | 4 | −.136 | .255 | −.519 | −.022 |
| | 5 | −.136 | .037 | −.519 | −.022 |
| | 6 | −.136 | −.037 | −.519 | −.022 |
| | 7 | .158 | .266 | −.479 | −.061 |
| | 8 | .220 | .444 | −.479 | .008 |
| | 9 | −.005 | .037 | .000 | .000 |
| | 10 | .000 | .049 | .000 | .000 |
| Consumer 8 | 1 | .000 | 2.595 | .000 | .000 |
| | 2 | .000 | 1.475 | .000 | .000 |
| | 3 | .000 | −.815 | .000 | .000 |
| | 4 | .000 | .254 | .000 | .000 |
| | 5 | .000 | −.166 | .000 | .000 |
| | 6 | .000 | .015 | .000 | .000 |
| | 7 | .000 | −.188 | .000 | .000 |
| | 8 | .000 | .085 | .000 | .000 |
| | 9 | .000 | .066 | .000 | .000 |
| | 10 | .000 | .412 | .000 | .000 |

*TABLE 15.8.* (Continued)

| | | | *Simulation* | | | |
|---|---|---|---|---|---|---|
| | | | *1* | *2* | *3* | *4* |
| Consumer 9 | Type of good | 1 | .594 | −.735 | .606 | .029 |
| | | 2 | .594 | .600 | .606 | .029 |
| | | 3 | .594 | .363 | .606 | .029 |
| | | 4 | .594 | .952 | .606 | .029 |
| | | 5 | .594 | .622 | .606 | .029 |
| | | 6 | .258 | .614 | −.137 | −.032 |
| | | 7 | .258 | −.397 | −.128 | −.032 |
| | | 8 | .252 | −.110 | −.128 | −.032 |
| | | 9 | .000 | .092 | .000 | .000 |
| | | 10 | .000 | .004 | .000 | .000 |
| Consumer 10 | Type of good | 1 | .000 | 3.260 | .000 | .000 |
| | | 2 | .000 | 1.366 | .000 | .000 |
| | | 3 | .000 | −.836 | .000 | .000 |
| | | 4 | .000 | 2.113 | .000 | .000 |
| | | 5 | .000 | −.398 | .000 | .000 |
| | | 6 | .000 | −.471 | .000 | .000 |
| | | 7 | .000 | .391 | .000 | .000 |
| | | 8 | −.033 | .035 | .000 | .000 |
| | | 9 | .000 | −.157 | .000 | .000 |
| | | 10 | .000 | −.057 | .000 | .000 |

SOURCE: Banco de México, S.A.

*TABLE 15.9.*
*Spending Share: Type of Consumer by Type of Good in Public Market (Percentage Change)*

| | | | *Simulation* | | | |
|---|---|---|---|---|---|---|
| | | | *1* | *2* | *3* | *4* |
| Consumer 1 | Type of good | 1 | −.041 | −.364 | −.463 | −.568 |
| | | 2 | −.111 | −.557 | −.467 | −.360 |
| | | 3 | −.111 | −.574 | −.467 | −.360 |
| | | 4 | −.041 | −.364 | −.463 | −.567 |
| | | 5 | −.111 | −.557 | −.467 | −.360 |
| | | 6 | −.041 | −.368 | −.463 | −.567 |
| | | 7 | −.111 | −.557 | −.467 | −.360 |
| | | 8 | −.111 | −.557 | −.467 | −.360 |
| | | 9 | .000 | .000 | .000 | .000 |
| | | 10 | 8.074 | 8.074 | 8.074 | 8.074 |

TABLE 15.9. (Continued)

| | | | Simulation | | | |
|---|---|---|---|---|---|---|
| | | | *1* | *2* | *3* | *4* |
| Consumer 2 | Type of good | 1 | .000 | .000 | .000 | .000 |
| | | 2 | .000 | .000 | .000 | .000 |
| | | 3 | .000 | .000 | .000 | .000 |
| | | 4 | .000 | .000 | .000 | .000 |
| | | 5 | .000 | .000 | .000 | .000 |
| | | 6 | .000 | .000 | .000 | .000 |
| | | 7 | .000 | .000 | .000 | .000 |
| | | 8 | .000 | .000 | .000 | .000 |
| | | 9 | .000 | .000 | .000 | .000 |
| | | 10 | .000 | .000 | .000 | .000 |
| Consumer 3 | Type of good | 1 | −.061 | −.424 | −.422 | −.472 |
| | | 2 | −.061 | −.422 | −.422 | −.472 |
| | | 3 | −.061 | −.422 | −.422 | −.472 |
| | | 4 | −.061 | −.422 | −.422 | −.472 |
| | | 5 | −.061 | −.422 | −.422 | −.472 |
| | | 6 | −.061 | −.422 | −.422 | −.472 |
| | | 7 | −.061 | −.291 | −.369 | −.472 |
| | | 8 | −.061 | −.290 | −.369 | −.472 |
| | | 9 | .000 | .000 | .000 | .000 |
| | | 10 | .000 | .000 | .000 | .000 |
| Consumer 4 | Type of good | 1 | .000 | .000 | .000 | .000 |
| | | 2 | .000 | .000 | .000 | .000 |
| | | 3 | .000 | .000 | .000 | .000 |
| | | 4 | .000 | .000 | .000 | .000 |
| | | 5 | .000 | .000 | .000 | .000 |
| | | 6 | .000 | .000 | .000 | .000 |
| | | 7 | .000 | .000 | .000 | .000 |
| | | 8 | .000 | .000 | .000 | .000 |
| | | 9 | .000 | .000 | −.087 | .000 |
| | | 10 | .000 | .000 | .000 | .000 |
| Consumer 5 | Type of good | 1 | −.248 | −.571 | −.469 | −.568 |
| | | 2 | −.818 | .383 | .323 | −.027 |
| | | 3 | −.219 | −.621 | −.531 | −.618 |
| | | 4 | −.247 | −.571 | −.469 | −.568 |
| | | 5 | −.011 | .383 | .323 | −.027 |
| | | 6 | −.219 | −.621 | −.531 | −.618 |
| | | 7 | −.011 | .383 | .323 | −.027 |
| | | 8 | −.011 | .373 | .323 | −.027 |
| | | 9 | .000 | .000 | .000 | .000 |
| | | 10 | .000 | −.000 | −.155 | .000 |

TABLE 15.9. (Continued)

| | | | *Simulation* | | | |
|---|---|---|---|---|---|---|
| | | | *1* | *2* | *3* | *4* |
| Consumer 6 | Type of good | 1 | .000 | .000 | .000 | .000 |
| | | 2 | .000 | .000 | −.012 | .000 |
| | | 3 | .000 | .000 | .000 | .000 |
| | | 4 | .000 | .000 | .000 | .000 |
| | | 5 | .000 | .000 | −.670 | .000 |
| | | 6 | .000 | .000 | .000 | .000 |
| | | 7 | .000 | .000 | .000 | .000 |
| | | 8 | .000 | .000 | .000 | .000 |
| | | 9 | .000 | .000 | .000 | .000 |
| | | 10 | .000 | .143 | .000 | .000 |
| Consumer 7 | Type of good | 1 | −.286 | −.861 | −.819 | −.273 |
| | | 2 | −.063 | −.885 | −.851 | −.240 |
| | | 3 | −.236 | −.885 | −.851 | −.399 |
| | | 4 | −.286 | −.861 | −.819 | −.273 |
| | | 5 | −.063 | −.885 | −.851 | −.240 |
| | | 6 | −.062 | −.885 | −.851 | −.240 |
| | | 7 | −.305 | −.762 | −.628 | −.532 |
| | | 8 | −.034 | −.770 | −.658 | −.311 |
| | | 9 | .000 | −.013 | .000 | .000 |
| | | 10 | .000 | .000 | .000 | .000 |
| Consumer 8 | Type of good | 1 | .000 | .000 | .000 | .000 |
| | | 2 | .000 | −.018 | .000 | .000 |
| | | 3 | .000 | .000 | .000 | .000 |
| | | 4 | .000 | .000 | .000 | .000 |
| | | 5 | .000 | .000 | .000 | .000 |
| | | 6 | .000 | .000 | .000 | .000 |
| | | 7 | .000 | .000 | .000 | .000 |
| | | 8 | .000 | .000 | .000 | .000 |
| | | 9 | .149 | .149 | .149 | .149 |
| | | 10 | .000 | .000 | .000 | .000 |
| Consumer 9 | Type of good | 1 | −.138 | 1.000 | −1.000 | −1.000 |
| | | 2 | −.086 | −1.000 | −1.000 | −1.000 |
| | | 3 | −.138 | −1.000 | −1.000 | −1.000 |
| | | 4 | −.138 | −1.000 | −1.000 | −1.000 |
| | | 5 | −.086 | −1.000 | −1.000 | −1.000 |
| | | 6 | −.138 | −1.000 | −1.000 | −1.000 |
| | | 7 | .107 | 1.444 | 1.411 | .568 |
| | | 8 | .107 | 1.444 | 1.411 | .568 |
| | | 9 | .000 | .000 | .000 | .000 |
| | | 10 | .000 | .000 | .000 | .000 |

TABLE 15.9. (Continued)

| | | | Simulation | | | |
|---|---|---|---|---|---|---|
| | | | *1* | *2* | *3* | *4* |
| Consumer 10 | Type of good | 1 | .000 | .000 | .000 | .000 |
| | | 2 | .000 | .000 | .000 | .000 |
| | | 3 | .000 | .000 | .000 | .000 |
| | | 4 | .000 | .000 | .000 | .000 |
| | | 5 | .000 | .000 | .000 | .000 |
| | | 6 | .000 | .000 | .000 | .000 |
| | | 7 | .000 | .000 | .000 | .000 |
| | | 8 | .000 | .000 | .000 | .000 |
| | | 9 | −.007 | .000 | .000 | .000 |
| | | 10 | .000 | .000 | .000 | .000 |

SOURCE: Banco de México, S.A.

TABLE 15.10.

*Spending Share: Type of Consumer by Type of Good in CONASUPO (Percentage Change)*

| | | | Simulation | | | |
|---|---|---|---|---|---|---|
| | | | *1* | *2* | *3* | *4* |
| Consumer 1 | Type of good | 1 | .797 | 1.035 | 1.204 | 1.102 |
| | | 2 | .559 | .765 | .912 | 1.118 |
| | | 3 | .558 | .764 | 1.044 | 1.118 |
| | | 4 | .198 | −.134 | −.437 | .126 |
| | | 5 | .559 | .765 | .912 | 1.118 |
| | | 6 | .198 | −.134 | −.437 | .126 |
| | | 7 | .559 | .765 | .912 | 1.118 |
| | | 8 | .559 | .765 | .912 | 1.118 |
| | | 9 | .000 | .000 | .000 | .000 |
| | | 10 | −.874 | −.874 | −.874 | −.874 |
| Consumer 2 | Type of good | 1 | .000 | .000 | .000 | .000 |
| | | 2 | .000 | .000 | .000 | .000 |
| | | 3 | .000 | .000 | .000 | .000 |
| | | 4 | .000 | .000 | .000 | .000 |
| | | 4 | .000 | .000 | .000 | .000 |
| | | 5 | .000 | .000 | .000 | .000 |
| | | 6 | .000 | .000 | .000 | .000 |
| | | 7 | .000 | .000 | .000 | .000 |
| | | 8 | .000 | .000 | .000 | .000 |
| | | 9 | .000 | .000 | .000 | .000 |
| | | 10 | .000 | .000 | .000 | .000 |

*TABLE 15.10.* (Continued)

| | | | *Simulation* | | | |
|---|---|---|---|---|---|---|
| | | | *1* | *2* | *3* | *4* |
| Consumer 3 | Type of good | 1 | −.624 | −.577 | −.418 | .444 |
| | | 2 | −.624 | −.577 | −.418 | .445 |
| | | 3 | −.624 | −.560 | −.418 | .445 |
| | | 4 | −.624 | −.577 | −.418 | .444 |
| | | 5 | −.624 | −.577 | −.418 | .445 |
| | | 6 | −.544 | −.683 | −.683 | .444 |
| | | 7 | .000 | .733 | .733 | 1.267 |
| | | 8 | .000 | .733 | .733 | 1.267 |
| | | 9 | .000 | .000 | .000 | .000 |
| | | 10 | .000 | .000 | .000 | .000 |
| Consumer 4 | Type of good | 1 | .000 | .000 | −.792 | .000 |
| | | 2 | .000 | .000 | .000 | .000 |
| | | 3 | .000 | .000 | .000 | .000 |
| | | 4 | .000 | .000 | .000 | .000 |
| | | 5 | .000 | .000 | .000 | .000 |
| | | 6 | .000 | .000 | .000 | .000 |
| | | 7 | .000 | .000 | .000 | .000 |
| | | 8 | .000 | .000 | .000 | .000 |
| | | 9 | .000 | .000 | .000 | .000 |
| | | 10 | .000 | .000 | .000 | .000 |
| Consumer 5 | Type of good | 1 | −.363 | −.090 | −.726 | 5.003 |
| | | 2 | −.362 | −.090 | −.728 | 5.008 |
| | | 3 | −.365 | −.092 | −.727 | 5.000 |
| | | 4 | .514 | 1.106 | 1.285 | .331 |
| | | 5 | −.362 | −.089 | −.739 | 5.005 |
| | | 6 | −.367 | −.090 | −.727 | 5.000 |
| | | 7 | −.364 | −.091 | −.727 | 5.000 |
| | | 8 | *** | *** | *** | *** |
| | | 9 | .000 | .000 | .000 | .000 |
| | | 10 | .000 | .000 | .000 | .000 |
| Consumer 6 | Type of good | 1 | .000 | .000 | .000 | .000 |
| | | 2 | .000 | .000 | .000 | .000 |
| | | 3 | .000 | .000 | .000 | .000 |
| | | 4 | .000 | .000 | .000 | .000 |
| | | 5 | .000 | .000 | .000 | .000 |
| | | 6 | .000 | .000 | .000 | .000 |
| | | 7 | .000 | .000 | .000 | .000 |
| | | 8 | .000 | .000 | .000 | .000 |
| | | 9 | .000 | .000 | .000 | .000 |
| | | 10 | .000 | .000 | .000 | .000 |

*TABLE 15.10.* (Continued)

| | | | *Simulation* | | | |
|---|---|---|---|---|---|---|
| | | | *1* | *2* | *3* | *4* |
| Consumer 7 | Type of good | 1 | .037 | −.505 | −.968 | 1.183 |
| | | 2 | .731 | −.201 | −.600 | 6.594 |
| | | 3 | .032 | −.505 | −.968 | 1.183 |
| | | 4 | .032 | −.505 | −.968 | 1.183 |
| | | 5 | −.215 | −.505 | −.968 | .914 |
| | | 6 | −.215 | −.505 | −.968 | .914 |
| | | 7 | .077 | −.591 | −.923 | 1.039 |
| | | 8 | .734 | −.200 | −.600 | 6.595 |
| | | 9 | .000 | .000 | .000 | .000 |
| | | 10 | .000 | .000 | .000 | .000 |
| Consumer 8 | Type of good | 1 | .000 | .000 | .000 | .000 |
| | | 2 | .000 | .000 | .000 | .000 |
| | | 3 | .000 | .000 | .000 | .000 |
| | | 4 | .000 | .000 | .000 | .000 |
| | | 5 | .000 | .000 | .000 | .000 |
| | | 6 | .000 | .000 | .000 | .000 |
| | | 7 | .000 | .000 | .000 | .000 |
| | | 8 | .000 | .000 | .000 | .000 |
| | | 9 | .000 | .000 | .000 | .000 |
| | | 9 | .000 | .000 | .000 | .000 |
| | | 10 | .000 | .000 | −.469 | .000 |
| Consumer 9 | Type of good | 1 | −1.000 | −1.000 | −1.000 | .333 |
| | | 2 | −1.000 | −1.000 | −1.000 | .208 |
| | | 3 | −1.000 | −1.000 | −1.000 | .333 |
| | | 4 | −1.000 | −1.000 | −1.000 | .333 |
| | | 5 | −1.000 | −1.000 | −1.000 | .208 |
| | | 6 | −1.000 | −1.000 | −1.000 | .333 |
| | | 7 | −1.000 | −1.000 | −1.000 | .556 |
| | | 8 | −1.000 | −1.000 | −1.000 | .556 |
| | | 9 | .000 | .000 | .000 | .000 |
| | | 10 | .000 | .000 | .000 | .000 |
| Consumer 10 | Type of good | 1 | *** | *** | *** | *** |
| | | 2 | *** | *** | *** | *** |
| | | 3 | .000 | .000 | .000 | .000 |
| | | 4 | .000 | .000 | .000 | .000 |
| | | 5 | .000 | .000 | .000 | .000 |
| | | 6 | .000 | .000 | .000 | .000 |
| | | 7 | .000 | .000 | .000 | .000 |
| | | 8 | .000 | .000 | .000 | .000 |
| | | 9 | .000 | .000 | .000 | .000 |
| | | 10 | *** | *** | *** | *** |

SOURCE: Banco de México, S.A.

corresponding to other simulations, the efficiency of the policy of marketing modernization still comes out ahead.

On the other hand, the results obtained in simulation 4 reflect the composition of CONASUPO customers as to income strata and the fact that it barely makes a showing in rural areas. In other words, the expected results were confirmed—that is, little impact on low-income groups, due to relatively few purchases made in this type of establishment.

If it is considered socially desirable that low-income individuals buy in establishments with lower prices (CONASUPO outlets and supermarkets), then the modernization of marketing channels has greater influence on reaching this objective—since it means lower prices in nearby stores. Simulation 3 in Table 15-8 demonstrates that consumer groups 1 and 3 register the highest percentage of purchases in CONASUPO outlets and supermarkets,[35]—as well as the lowest percentage of purchases in grocery stores and public markets—of all the simulations. It also becomes apparent, however, that this target was not fully reached in rural zones; consumers of groups 2, 4 and 6 show no change whatsoever in their percentages of purchases. With this fact, it proves once again how difficult it is to implement redistributive policies in favor of the low-income strata of the population located in rural areas.

Concerning the activity level of the establishment being examined, it was found that simulation 3 was the one that comes closest to the social objective sought in purchasing places. In this case, supermarkets and CONASUPO outlets show greater increases in activity, while the opposite result occurs in public markets and grocery stores (see Table 15-11).

Continuing with the remuneration of factors, it was observed that the policy of modernizing marketing channels was the one with the greatest impact—on capital as well as urban labor (see Table 15-12). Despite this, with the price of rural labor not varying in any of the simulations, it was confirmed that difficulties do exist for implementing policies designed to raise the living standards of rural groups.

*TABLE 15.11.*

*Level of Activity: Type of Simulation and Type of Establishment (Percentage change with respect to the original equilibrium)*

| | *Level of Activity* | | | |
|---|---|---|---|---|
| | *Simulation* | | | |
| *Type of Establishment* | *1* | 2 | 3 | 4 |
| Public market | −.16995 | −.2392 | −.22909 | −.05552 |
| Grocery store | −.09936 | −.13475 | −.11223 | −.01653 |
| CONASUPO | −.13844 | −.33077 | −.53028 | .63458 |
| Supermarket | .15306 | .09829 | −.04647 | −.04522 |

SOURCE: Banco de México, S.A.

TABLE 15.12.

*Price of Factors: Type of Factor and Type of Simulation*
*(Percentage change with respect to the original equilibrium)*

| | *Simulation* | | | |
|---|---|---|---|---|
| *Type of factor* | *1* | *2* | *3* | *4* |
| Rural labor | 0 | 0 | 0 | 0 |
| Urban labor | −.00302 | −.00503 | .15384 | .00169 |
| Capital and other factors | −.00009 | .00014 | .07422 | .00065 |

SOURCE: Banco de México, S.A.

In accordance with the foregoing, and since the assumptions of the model are rigid, the tentative proposition emerges that a policy of fully modernizing marketing channels seems superior to subsidizing the government distribution network. Nonetheless, the difficulty of implementing a redistributive income policy in favor of low-income groups remains very much in evidence, especially in rural areas. However, this does not mean that the problem will be pushed aside; instead we should recognize that this is simply the first step in tackling the problem.

## VI. Conclusions and Final Remarks

In the case of perishables, the Puebla survey has shown that, in terms of size, small stores have marketing margins of 30 to 40 percent. As the size of the selling area increases, the profit margin diminishes to almost 20 percent; at that point, the margin begins to increase in self-service chains where, occasionally, it exceeds 100 percent. Thus, the margin again tends to behave in the form of a "U," according to the size of the store.

Facts that reinforce the impressions that appear throughout the text are found in information processed at the Banco de México, in which families were classified by income strata and were related to groups of consumer goods, and to the type of establishments where they were purchased.

The results show that more than 60 percent of families in the low strata buy food in public markets or small retail operations (with the latter standing at around 30 percent). This takes on more relevance when we become aware of the fact that it is these small retail operations that show greater marketing margins.

The type of establishment frequented most by all families is the public market, where more than 40 percent of families from all income strata buy.

On the other hand, the establishments showing the lowest marketing margins—mobile markets that move from neighborhood to neighborhood—are frequented only by about 10 percent of low-income families.

Outstanding also is the fact that establishments of a social nature with lower prices and less marketing margins—such as stores for government employees and those CONASUPO outlets—capture only 1 percent of families, and these tend to be in the medium- and high-income strata. This can be explained by the selective policy concerning customers that is enforced in stores for government employees, and the location of CONASUPO outlets in zones inhabited mainly by persons in the medium-income strata. Hence, simulation 4 applied in the marketing sector model results in a slight impact on the living standards of low-income groups, and exerts no influence on the price of rural labor. For this reason, it is better to implement a policy that will improve marketing channels. In this sense, the current practice of building new wholesale markets seems to be a better alternative.

Regarding supermarkets, a trend has been noted showing that as people's income rises, they tend to frequent these stores in greater proportion, which leads us to assume that this type of establishment is designed to meet the consumption needs of the medium- and high-income strata of the population. Indeed, as family income rises, purchases of fruit and vegetables become more diversified as far as establishments are concerned, and although supermarkets' margins are high, the fluctuations in sales prices are less abrupt than in other segments of the market, such as in public markets which show more flexibility in handling assortments.

On the basis of the spending structure described previously, it may be said that the public market is the type of establishment that supplies fruit and vegetables to the majority of income strata in Mexico's population. However, price behavior outpaces supermarkets and the scale is too small to show any improvement in growth.

In addition to the above, another phenomenon that stands out is the fact that, after public markets, low-income families prefer to buy food from small retail operations in their neighborhoods where marketing margins are quite high—while families of higher income gravitate toward supermarkets, where prices are, as a whole, usually lower. In other words, the former group frequents establishments of medium and high margins, while the latter group diversifies its purchases in establishments of medium to low prices, benefiting to a greater degree from more efficient marketing channels.

In summary, the fact that the price swings of agricultural perishables predominantly affect small producers, and the fact that they belong to low-income families in the rural sector which operates with higher transaction costs, both produce an implied transfer of income from the rural to the urban sector. This mechanism benefits, on the one hand, the intermediaries involved and, on the other hand, the medium- and high-income strata of the urban sector that benefit mainly through the type of establishments in which they make their purchases.[36]

In conclusion, I would like to underline the fact that serious difficulties exist for raising the living standards of the poorest strata of the population, because of the mechanisms described in the foregoing pages and because of the results of the marketing sector model—but this does not mean that the effort should be abandoned.

## Notes

1. R. Anson, "Overview of a developing country's fruit and vegetable production and domestic market system: The case of the role and prospects of the Mexican small farmer." Instituto Tecnológico y de Estudios Superiores de Monterrey, November, 1977.

2. Gunter Schramm, "Input and Marketing Constraints in Irrigation Planning: Mexico." *Land Economics,* vol. 55, no. 4, November, 1979, p. 440.

3. Armen A. Alchian, "Information, Martingales and Prices." *Swedish Journal of Economics,* 1974, p. 109.

4. Helmy Baligh and Leon Richartz, *Vertical Market Structures* (Boston: Allyn and Bacon, 1967). Mentioned by Louis P. Bucklin, "Problems in the Evolution of Urban Wholesale Markets in Developing Countries," 1979. Mimeographed.

5. For a detailed analysis see E. Jones Blalock, "Food Subsidies as a Policy Instrument in Developing Countries: Problems and Issues." March, 1981. Mimeographed.

6. Usually, the poorer farmers are net buyers of corn. Therefore, an increase in the real price of the staple, through an increase in the guaranteed price of it, has an adverse effect on them. Overall, the incidence of a price stabilization policy on the development of the agrarian sector for the case of Mexico can be seen in the first chapter of my book *Economic Policy Reform in Mexico* New York: Pergamon Press, 1981.

7. P. Garcia, "Market Linkages of Small Farms: A Study of the Maize Market in Northern Veracruz." Cornell University, 1978. Mentioned by Oscar Vera, "An Appraisal of Price Policy for Selected Agricultural Commodities in Mexico," Master's thesis, University of York, 1980.

8. Op. cit.

9. Ibid, p. 203.

10. Ibid, p. 216.

11. Edwin Schuh, "Approaches to 'Basic Needs' and to 'Equity' that Distort Incentives in Agriculture", p. 323, in T. Schultz (ed.) *Distortions of Agriculture Incentives.* Bloomington: Indiana University Press, 1978.

12. See A. C. Nielsen Report No. 3. The Grocery Marketing Scene, a Nielsen World-wide Review. Nielsen Plaza; Northbrook, Illinois, 1978.

13. The comparison made of the commercial structure of Mexico to that of the U.S., shows the influence of the U.S. example on the commercial establishments of Mexico.

14. Undoubtedly, there are some countries whose development is more advanced than Mexico's,—for example Belgium and France—whose levels of commercial food are higher, although their structure is different. On the one hand, concentration may be increased by the opening of supermarkets that represent a higher retail percentage without involving a great number of outlets, which operate together with the traditional stores of less percentage

importance. On the other hand, the concentration can be the result of new supermarkets that will eventually replace the small stores, obtaining as a result a much more homogeneous commercial structure. The more developed countries are in the second situation while those that are not as developed are in the first situation.

15. Nielsen, op. cit.

16. This means that the scale of operation of the majority of marketing establishments is quite reduced since, in many cases, the sales area is less than 15 square meters, and the assortment of products is extremely limited, which results in excessive specialization.

17. See Consuelo Meyer "Observations on Marketing Activity in Mexico" published at the Centro de Estudios Históricos at Colegio de Mexico; "Mexican Extremes." México, 1971, pp. 191–224; and Leopoldo Solís and Aurelio Montemayor "Modernizing Marketing and Economic Development," published at Secrétaría de Comercio y Desarrollo. México, 1977.

18. Selected types of rural and urban food stores.

19. Because of their size, scale and efficiency these producers are less affected by the market instability shown in the second section of this chapter.

20. Franz M. Baan et al. "Some aspects of grocery retailing in Mexico City." *Comercio y Desarrollo,* no. 6, 1978, pp. 45–51.

21. It is surprising to discover the extent to which supermarkets do not pass on to the consumer, via price reductions, the benefits obtained in operating with enormous economies of scale—physical as well as monetary. Hence, the hypothesis can be formulated that in Mexico the prices of basic commodities are fixed by the most inefficient economic units (in the sense that for the goods referred to, prices in the supermarkets and in neighborhood stores are similar).

22. That is, as far as margin is concerned, it is more economic for the consumer to buy at supermarkets than other alternatives. Customers usually arrive at this type of establishment in their cars, pay in cash or with a credit card, receive attention that is more or less impersonal, the products are well presented, and purchasing alternatives are numerous. Hence, once the customer is inside, these factors mean that supermarkets exercise a certain monopoly.

23. Moreover, examining the wholesale and consumer price indexes, we find a similar phenomenon: when prices rise, the effect is more pronounced on the consumer price index than on the wholesale price index, while when the situation is the opposite, the phenomenon is reversed.

24. Nestor M. Martínez, "The retail operation in Puebla." An attempt at an empirical analysis. Instituto Tecnológico Autónomo de México, Thesis, 1980.

25. For a more detailed analysis see Martínez, *op. cit.,* pp. 50–51.

26. Naturally, this rests on the assumption of homogeneity of the product.

27. The expression "elusive" refers to the difficulty of defining the operational scale under which the outlets operate in Mexico, due to the fact there is a great variety of types (supermarkets, neighborhood stores, mobile markets, etc.), sales volume, and sales area.

28. R. H. Holton "Price discrimination in supermarkets." In *Economics of Retailing,* K. A. Tucker and B. S. Yamey (eds.), Penguin Education, pp. 27–46.

29. Baan, *op. cit.*

30. There are two factors that provide a better explanation of the low purchases by low-income groups: a) The relative distance between the stores with lower marketing margins and the low income of the consumers; b) The limited income of these population sectors creates secondary factors (storage and moving capacities), which prevents them from buying larger quantities of perishable goods to be used for the entire week. To get a better idea of this concept, see Leopoldo Solís and Aurelio Montemayor "Modernizing Marketing and Economic Development," Secretaría de Comercio y Desarrollo. Mexico, 1977.

31. This situation suggests two alternative policies: (a) Improvements of the efficiency of the outlets with larger marketing margins through technical advice, low interest rates on loans, organized purchase of merchandise by the merchants themselves, etc.; (b) Increasing the number of more efficient outlets in order to eliminate the inefficient ones. Although the second option seems better for Mexico, the fact should not be forgotten that small outlets are a major source of employment and their elimination would cause problems in the labor market.

32. T. Kehoe, J. Serra, and L. Solís, "Megamex: A General Equilibrium Model of the Mexican Economy," mimeographed, 1981. Available on request.

33. The intermediate input used, by hypothesis, are in fixed proportions:

$$A_j = \min \frac{\chi_{ij}}{a_{ij}}$$

where $\chi_{ij}$ represents the physical quantities of input i used in the production of merchandise j, and $a_{ij}$ is the minimal input of i per unit of j. The production of aggregate value is as follows:

$$V_j = c_j K_j^{\alpha_j} L_{j,u}^{\beta_j} L_{j,r}^{\gamma_j}$$

with $\alpha_j + \beta_j + \gamma_j = 1$, where $c_j$ is the efficiency parameter, $K_j$ the capital used in the production of j, and $L_{j,u}$ the urban labor used in the production of j, and $L_{j,r}$ the rural labor used in the production of j; what is involved then is a Cobb-Douglas function.

34. The decrease of utility in simulation 4, the interpretation of which is applicable to the other 3, results from the variation in relative prices that diminishes the consumer's real income. In other words, if there is a 5 percent increase in profit, it means a 5 percent increase in income if the prices remain constant.

35. Groups 1 and 3 of consumers register the highest variations in sales percentages, because the improvement in efficiency is strongly reflected in the outlets frequented by these consumer groups.

36. The fact that not all consumer groups pay higher prices is due to the fact that their purchase place is different and because of this price fluctuations affect consumer welfare in many different ways.

# CHAPTER 16

# *Production and Participation in Rural Areas: Some Political Considerations*

Carlos Salinas de Gortari

## I. Introduction

In the countries considered as underdeveloped or in the process of development, the rural sector is of major importance. This is true from an economic perspective, since it is the basic sector for providing foodstuffs and essential inputs into urban industrial growth, as well as part of the foreign exchange necessary for the imports required in the development process. From the political viewpoint, it is also true since the majority of the population of these countries usually lives in the rural sector and—in view of the system of extraction of surpluses that is applied to the sector to favor the industrialization process—it is an area in which strong political tensions converge with deeply rooted social differences.

The rural sector has been studied mainly for its contribution to economic development, stressing the aspect of productivity and disregarding those relative to distribution of income and social equilibrium. Similarly, the economic studies and even those of a political nature have been developed from an aggregate perspective, often ignoring the attitudes and particular behavior of the individuals, groups and communities that shape the rural sector.

In practical terms, the importance of the production of food in the short and medium term, and the need for political stability for such production, have been incentives for the state to introduce and to stimulate development programs in this sector. That is, public spending has been used as an appropriate instrument in developing countries for fulfilling a double objective: create the infrastructure necessary for increasing the productivity of the rural sector and achieve, at the same time, political support from the sectors benefited by such action.

Since the majority of developing studies, however, have to address several priority objectives—in addition to stimulating the rural sector—in a situation of scarce resources for fostering development, priority has usually been given to urban-industrial growth under the well-known model of import substitution.[1]

Within this context, the case of Mexico is an important example among developing countries. In order to increase growth rates, Mexico has followed since the fifties a model that stresses the development of the urban-industrial sector while neglecting the rural sector. This provoked a situation in which, during the seventies, 42 percent of the population lived in the rural sector and only generated 11 percent of the gross domestic product (GDP), demonstrating the serious problems of low productivity and an inequitable distribution of income.

In 1940, the rural population of Mexico presented 61 percent of the total population; in 1980, it was estimated at 33 percent. However, this figure does not represent a reduction in the number of inhabitants and rural communities, since in absolute terms the population increased by 80 percent, causing strong pressures on available farming land. In addition, the rural population is dispersed in more than 100,000 communities of less than 2,500 inhabitants, complicating their access to the country's social services and development programs.

In Mexico, public investment has been used as one of the main instruments of intervention by the state in the economy. In 1981, public investment represented 43.8 percent of the total investment.[2] As in many developing countries, however, emphasis has been placed on allocating public resources to developing urban-industrial projects, resulting in serious economic and political repercussions on the rural areas. During recent decades, the rural sector has evidenced a relative reduction in the part of public investment allocated to the development of agricultural production—as well as that channeled to the sector for improving living standards. The decline in these resources, their excessive concentration in a few areas, and the resulting social inequities, have been the cause of serious problems in the development of this sector.

The peculiarities of the historical process of Mexican development—especially as it concerns the rural sector—have allowed the political system to achieve some success in dealing with social unrest among the peasants. Thus, the Revolution of 1910 and the agrarian movements that followed during the decade of the twenties acted as a means of resolving the social tensions that had been building up in the rural sector. It was during this decade that the rural movement began to be organized by the state, associating itself with the political party of the Revolution—the Revolutionary National party—created in 1929.[3]

The thirties saw a decline in the efficiency of the political apparatus for maintaining stability in the rural sector. As a result, it was between 1934 and 1940 that the system responded to rural restlessness with the broadest agrarian reforms that have ever taken place in the history of Latin America, except for Cuba and, it was in the 1940s and the beginning of the

1950s that investment rose in the rural sector, resulting in sharply increased agricultural production. Notwithstanding, investment in the rural sector was concentrated mainly in the large irrigation lands thus benefiting certain regions, such as the northwest.

The Mexican government introduced a series of rural development programs at the beginning of the sixties, in order to curb the rate of migration to urban areas and increase the rural income of those who remained in the countryside. The purpose of these programs was mainly to raise output and stressed the participation of peasants from rainfed lands. These programs sought to increase rural productivity and to obtain cheaper food for urban areas. Implicit in them was the objective of awakening a sense of loyalty toward the regime among the peasants who received the benefits.

However, the necessary resources for financing the rural development programs were seriously affected by the demand for resources to finance the significant growth of basic inputs for development, mainly energy, whose availability has had a strategic importance equal to that of food.

In addition, it is necessary to take into account that the effect of public spending on the distribution of income does not depend only on the level of expenditures, but also on the efficiency with which the corresponding spending policies are implemented. The resources must be effectively utilized in accordance with the proposed original aims and be in agreement with the aspirations of the general population. To achieve this, experience has taught us that it is not enough to draw up well-designed programs; as important—or more important still—is the way in which they are administered and introduced into the rural sector.

At the beginning of the seventies, certain programs were implemented which, lacking adequate administrative support, wasted resources and failed to meet the targets set. In recent years, the greater financial ease that a surplus of oil resources provided the Mexican government allowed it to launch ambitious programs for rural development. Nevertheless, the complexity of the objectives pursued as a whole affected the conditions of their effective implementation.

At present—and in the context of the overall austerity in public spending that the economic crisis has brought on—emphasis must be placed on organization and peasant participation in programs for rural development; this must be done not only to improve the efficiency with which resources are used but also with regard to the fairness with which their benefits are distributed. Although this aspect in the implementation of public spending is basic for guaranteeing results, its importance has been commonly ignored in discussions on public spending and the distribution of income.

The purpose of this chapter is to stress the analysis of public spending at a micropolitical and social level. We will first discuss the importance of an analysis focusing on the implementation phase of public spending. An effective application of development programs is as crucial to its economic results as its proper design. Furthermore, it is basically in the study of the rural communities that the political effects—also implicit in the governmental programs—can be assessed.

In the next section we will present the basic considerations that guided the research on which this chapter is based. In particular, we will refer to the importance of collective participation for the implementation of development programs and the need to adopt a contextual analysis in order to correctly identify its possible determinants. We will then introduce the development programs evaluated in the research, followed by a discussion on the results obtained in terms of the impact of leadership on political participation and the effects of political support for the system.

Finally, we will present some political recommendations for the implementation of development programs, in order to guarantee the government the achievement of its goals.

## II. Program Implementation and Political Goals

The approach of the majority of papers on the distribution of income has been from a general level of analysis, neglecting the importance of the ways in which programs are implemented at the local level. It is at this stage of applying public policies, however, that serious obstacles can arise for effectively attaining the well-being sought for the population, and where the impact of public spending is weakened.

Although the proper administration of programs for rural development can increase production and improve the distribution of income in the rural sector, it is necessary to examine what it means for the government in terms of political support to allocate such resources. In this sense, we will measure the effectiveness of public spending for building political support.

As Sidney Verba clearly indicated, "It is not enough for a political system to be instrumentally efficient—that is, maintain an efficient economic system, respond to the demands of different groups, etc. It must also gain and maintain the support of its citizens; . . . A system that does not obtain the basic support of the country's inhabitants can maintain itself for a time, but it will have serious problems for survival if its instrumental efficiency breaks down.[4]

This fundamental consideration is not unknown in the political pragmatism and revolutionary origin of the Mexican political system. Thus, in structuring and adapting new technology to development programs—where collective participation is needed for carrying them out—a causal model similar to the one shown in Figure 16-1 is implicit in certain actions of the public sector.

The technological structuring of new development programs is designed to increase the collective participation of its beneficiaries. The state expects that this will produce a more efficient use of available resources and result in increased productivity and output. At the same time,

**Figure 16-1. Causal Model Implicit in Certain Programs of the Public Sector.**

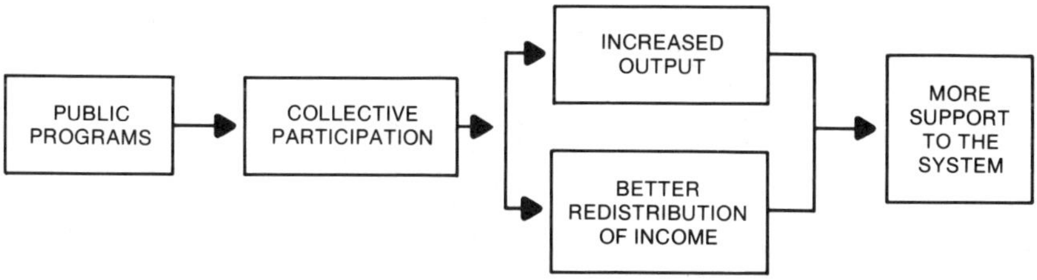


collective participation will provide a better redistribution of the resources channeled to the program, since the participants will benefit from them. They can adapt them to their needs, thus improving the degree of efficiency in the allocation of resources and the distribution of income.

Politically, the government expects to derive—from this increment in production and improvement, income redistribution—an increase in political support for the system. This proves to be essential in light of the political reform, which has given greater play to political parties and opened a wider electoral democratization of the country.[5] Within this logic, the government would expect to capitalize on its economic efforts in votes, since the competition for votes will be more strenuous in the coming years. Thus, public spending comes to play a fundamental political role: that of strengthening the Mexican democratic system—tied to effective economic development.

Although economic studies of cost-benefit analysis have been made on some programs, the relationship existing between development programs, the political system and the attitude and political actions of the beneficiaries—especially in the rural sector—have not been assessed in Mexico, nor in Latin America.

The assessment required is strictly one of political economy. In other words, to the extent that these programs seek the double objective of increasing productivity and support for the system, their costs and benefits—economic as well as political—must be assessed, especially at the level of the community where they are applied.

## III. Initial Considerations in the Study of Rural Communities

The main purpose of the research mentioned above was to try to analyze, on the basis of a specific study, the political impact of the participation and organization required by public programs to raise rural output and income. On the basis of the case studies of some rural communities, several analytical arguments were derived. This chapter will focus particularly on those political propositions.[6]

Several studies[7] have confirmed that the greater the participation of peasants in rural development programs, the greater their income can be,

Figure 16-2. Contextual Factors that Influence Political Participation.

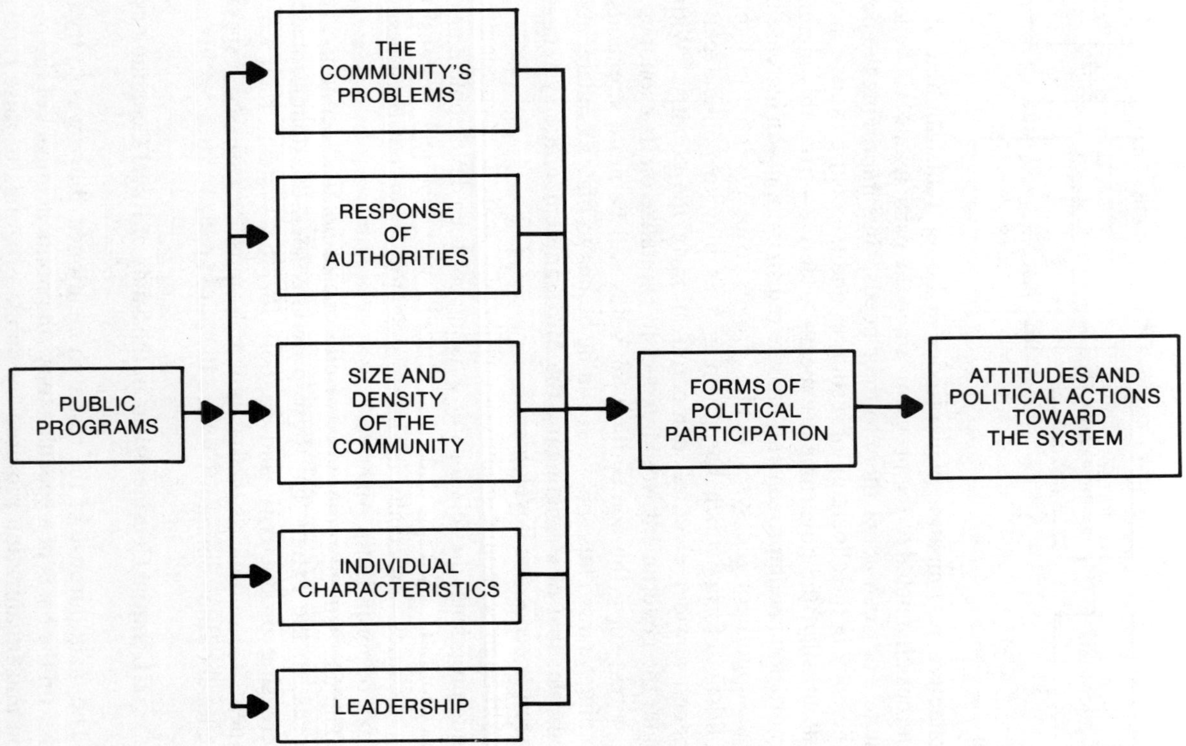

since the participants obtain a double benefit: (1) that which the project will yield once it is finished; and (2) the income obtained from their participation in the construction of the same.[8]

The present research was directed toward assessing the hypothesis implicit in the development scheme of the Mexican government, and which is derived from Figure 16-1: The greater the participation stimulated by development programs, the greater the support for the political system will be. The dependent variable was the support for the political system, while the independent variable was participation.

As we observed during the research, the concept of participation has undergone important modifications in recent years. Empirical studies have discerned several different modes of political participation within the framework of systemically supportive activities. These are distinguished here from the type of political participation that has traditionally been studied in rural areas—the violent or radical type. Outstanding among these supportive activities are voting, participating in the solution of community problems, and petitioning government officials.

The studies carried out by Verba, Nie and Cornelius,[9] among others, have made it possible to detect and analyze the elements that determine, in turn, the different forms of political participation. As can be seen in Figure 16-2, the forms of political participation that stimulate an active involvement in development programs can be explained by contextual factors that operate at the community and individual level. Among the most important are: the individual characteristics of the inhabitants; the size and density of the community; the response of the authorities to the petitions of the participants; and the leadership factor, which has been singled out as one of the most relevant within the literature.[10]

Thus, we assume that the capacity of public spending for increasing productivity in the rural sector and distributing its benefits fairly—in order to achieve political support for the system—will depend on the government's capacity to increase peasant participation in the implementation of programs. Our assumption thus states that these participatory attitudes are affected by contextual elements in rural communities, among which the leadership factor is outstanding and which influence attitudes toward the political system.

To continue with the analysis—mainly in terms of the political aspect—it was considered essential to determine the relevant unit for the study. In other words, should this study be made on a national basis, as has traditionally been the case, or on a regional one? Or should the focus be at the most disaggregate level of community and individual, where changes of attitudes and political actions that take place in the individuals and in their communities when development programs are implemented, and the interrelationship to the political system is most notable. The choice was to make a "contextual analysis," which would make it possible to determine the actions and attitudes of the individuals in the environment in which they live.[11]

Once the programs to be studied (presented below) had been selected and it was decided that it was necessary to make the analysis at the community and individual level, four communities were chosen with the following characteristics:

(A) First, a community that has received in abundance—and, without having requested it—public works and benefits from government spending.

(B) Second, another community that would stand out for having obtained—as the result of efforts and pressures exerted—benefits from the federal government.

(C) Third, one that would show no interest in obtaining benefits from the government, nor the government in providing any.

(D) And last, a community that would have mobilized in an autonomous way to pressure the government in order to obtain benefits, but was oriented by the action of political organizers autonomous from the community.

## IV. Rural Development Programs

A number of rural programs were tried in Mexico during the seventies: community development, collectivization, new methods of communication, establishing property lines, setting up small kilns, livestock extension, family orchards, etc. Our selection criteria for development programs, however, required the active participation of the community's inhabitants for their execution.

Two programs stood out at the national level with these characteristics:

(1) The National Roadbuilding Program, set into action by the Ministry of Public Works, resulted in the construction of at least 1,500 federal roads, making intensive use of manual labor, and requiring the constant and active participation of the inhabitants in the areas where they were built. The benefits were twofold: income received from working on the project, and the opportunity of having a permanent means of communication for the community involved.

(2) The second program selected for study was the Puebla Plan, developed by the International Center for Improving Corn and Wheat Crops (CIMMYT) and the Ministry of Agriculture and Livestock. The objective of this program was to develop a technology that would increase yields of small-scale farm operations in rain-fed zones. Its most relevant characteristic, however, consisted in having the basic requisite of organized participation of peasants in its execution.

Thus, these programs corresponded to the requirements of the research being carried out, since they covered the basic criterion of selection which was the participation of the peasants. Moreover, they were relevant for the participants, since there were two fundamental repercussions on their daily life—allowing them to increase the production of their food, and endowing them with a means of communication for moving their surplus output to market and introducing goods into their communities that were not produced locally.

The results of the programs are favorable in aggregate terms: the national economy benefited by the communication that was established as well as the savings in foreign exchange and imports that the National Roadbuilding Program made possible; also, the Puebla Plan employed a significant number of participants who were able to raise the average yield of their crops significantly. Modern technologies that require the participation of peasants in programs for rain-fed zones increase efficiency in the use of resources and basic inputs.

Yet, when the results are disaggregated, we observe that the impact on the economic situation of the participants at the specific level of the community did not produce any substantial increase in income nor a significant participation derived from the impetus provided by the programs.

The economic assessment of the results of these programs seems satisfactory in terms of production and marketing, but deficient in terms of income distribution. Furthermore, it does not supply information on the secondary objective sought by the state in these programs—that is, to determine whether they achieved an awakening of loyalty toward the state among the participants.

Relevant is the fact that an attempt has been made to modify the traditional technological packages for the rural environment, which previously, and under the influence of the "green revolution," were designed to increase output—but not to provide more jobs or to stimulate a fairer redistribution of resources. Thus, the two programs examined in the research showed that the state had advanced at an aggregate level in the development of a new technology that insists on participation as a means for increasing efficiency and improving the redistribution of income. Still, it is a long way from achieving the important mission of dispersing the benefits of this new technology at the community level.

## V. Political Participation and Leadership

To a great degree, the impact of these programs depends on the generation of adequate collective participation. At the same time, from the political standpoint, traditional mass participation through the electoral process is not sufficient to fortify democracy in the country. It is fundamental that new ways of political and economic organization be developed that will lead to the convergence of democratic political and cultural development with the aims of improving living standards and income distribution.

The study showed that participation was not unidimensional, but that it adjusted itself quite well to the political behavior patterns that have been encountered in other countries. This was true not only for participants living under the traditional mores of rural areas, but refers to those who migrate to urban zones as well. Thus, the results from the pioneering work done by Verba and Nie[12] are confirmed in the sense that similar patterns of political participation exist under cultural contexts that are very different.

Indeed, the most relevant forms of participation encountered in this study were voting, petitioning public officials and participating in the solving of the community's problems. The first of those mentioned, although crucial at the national level, is in fact an individual form of participation that has no direct effect on the development programs; the second, whose purpose is to obtain economic benefits through contacts with public officials, does not imply, however, a direct participation in the activities linked to programs that would make it possible to take better advantage of them; the third—solving the community's problems—requires a collective organization that, when accompanying a specific public program, can contribute substantially toward an improved administration and control. This latter means of participation stands out from the rest for assuring success in the implementation of development programs. Indeed, it is cited as an essential element by Montgomery and Murray[13] for obtaining the multiplier effect from inputs to development programs.

It was necessary to determine what effect the different contextual variables of a community have on the form of participation that is generated. At the same time, it was found that there is no direct positive relationship between participation and support of the system; and furthermore, that participation could even be negative for the system. Thus, it was concluded that the causes and possible effects should be analyzed separately. The community that participated in the most active manner was the one that displayed the least support for the system. Similarly, in the area selected, the community that was most benefited by the state in the mid-seventies recorded one of the lowest correlations between participation and support. The fact that the government may have supplied abundant resources through public works did not generate the attitudes of support for the system that were expected.

There are contextual variables that can influence participation although without great certainty. At the community level, the most important variables that could positively affect participation were the following:[14]

(1) Small and highly dense communities

(2) Socioeconomic homogeneity

(3) Stability of residence
(4) Conflictual origin of the community such as land takeovers
(5) Existence of voluntary organizations
(6) Lack of internal political divisions
(7) Important common problems and needs
(8) Successful outcomes from contact with public officials

Inasmuch as these variables only very partially explained the variations in participation, it was necessary to place them in interaction with other variables, mainly that of leadership. However, what remained clear was that the response of the government to the petitions and requests of participants and communities can become an important explanatory variable of participation, since the way in which the government provided its benefits seems to have discouraged participation by generating, instead, frustration and distrust.

Some personal traits of the inhabitants of the community, such as a higher socioeconomic level, a positive attitude toward collective work or an understanding of common problems, can also be included as factors that induce a more active participation.[15]

In addition to the fact that leadership is one of the variables that can affect participation, it also acts as a variable that defines and, in certain cases, modifies the influence of personal and contextual variables on participation and support. Leadership, then, becomes an explanatory variable of major importance.

Few systematic studies have been made of political leadership, and fewer still of its impact on political participation. Nonetheless, we have drawn up a typology of local leadership, to detect some of the variables affecting it (see Figure 16-3):

(1) Local leadership without external orientation. We differentiate between traditional leaders (*caciques*[16]) and local reform leaders.
(2) A local leader with external orientation of an official nature (extension agents[17]), whose attitude may be moderate or radical.
(3) A local leader oriented by external leaders not of an official nature.

Within the new field of political analysis on leadership, the characterization of local leadership based on the influence from external leadership took on some importance. The results of the research enabled us to determine that the typology derived from the interaction of local leader-external leader was more varied than the initial hypotheses suggested; as a result, five types of outside orientators were designated.

Although it was recognized that the contextual situation in which the leader operates affects his attitudes and actions, the influence of external leadership is observed as a variable that accelerates the transformation process of the local leader. In other words, it is not necessary to wait until conditions change in the normal course of development for the local

**Figure 16-3. Impact of Outside Leadership on the Local Leadership of Rural Communities.**

| | EXTERNAL LEADERSHIP | | | | |
|---|---|---|---|---|---|
| | ABSENT | | PRESENT | | |
| | | | OFFICIAL | NONOFFICIAL | |
| | | | NORMAL EXTENSION AGENT | RADICAL EXTENSION AGENT | OUTSIDE ORGANIZER |
| LOCAL LEADERSHIP | CACIQUE | DEVELOPMENT LEADER | NORMAL PROMOTER | RADICAL PROMOTER | LOCAL ORGANIZER |

**Figure 16-4. The Filter-Effect of Local Leadership on the Variables that Affect Participation.**

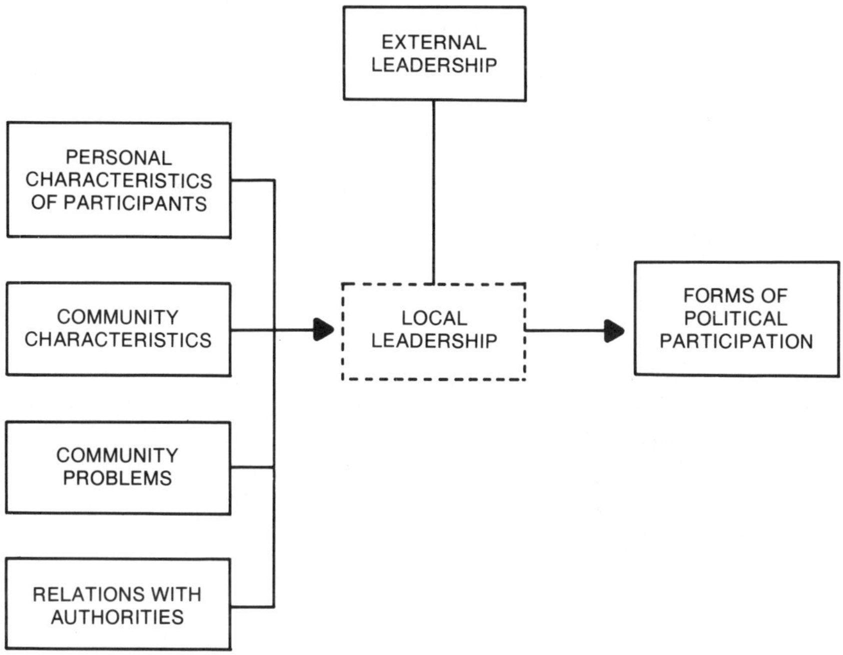


leader to modify his actions. The orientation and politicization of the external leader can speed up this process with important results in participation and the relationship of the participants to the system (see Figure 16-4).

In terms of participation, the local organizer and the radical extension agent exert sharp influence, making use of the favorable characteristics of the community and of the individuals to stimulate participation. Such external leaders can orient the local leader and the community toward problem solving, in addition to the simple act of voting. That form of participation, although basic for achieving a multiplier effect in development programs, does not, however, seem to go hand in hand with attitudes of support to the system. This is mainly due to the fact that the orientation of external radical leaders is deliberately directed against the government.

The foregoing leads us to an explanation for the opposing relationship found between participation and support. Understanding it is important for the state, if it wishes to modify the elements that prevent participation and result in lack of support for the system.

On the other hand, the *cacique* and the normal promoter, although managing to stimulate attitudes of support for the system, did not have the desire to or did not have sufficient impact in the community to mobilize

**Figure 16-5. Impact of Local Leadership on Participation in and Support for the System.**

Modes of Participation and Support for the System

| | | CACIQUE | DEVELOPMENT LEADER | NORMAL PROMOTER | RADICAL PROMOTER | LOCAL ORGANIZER |
|---|---|---|---|---|---|---|
| VOTING | MORE SUPPORT TO THE SYSTEM | ★ | | ★ | | |
| | LESS SUPPORT | | | | ★ | |
| CONTACT WITH PUBLIC OFFICIALS | MORE SUPPORT | | | | | |
| | LESS SUPPORT | | ★ | | | |
| SOLUTION OF COMMUNITY PROBLEMS | MORE SUPPORT | | | | | |
| | LESS SUPPORT | | | | | ★ |

political participation different from the symbolic vote in electoral processes[18] (see Figure 16-5).

The crucial role of leadership in the interrelationships indicated between participation and support, and the determination of the variables that affect participation explain the fact that the presence of development programs with labor-intensive techniques to stimulate participation was not enough to create a permanent attitude of active involvement. Taken as such, these programs did not generate a participatory attitude that would activate the inhabitants of the communities to seek a solution to their problems and make more efficient use of the resources at their disposal.

Despite the influence of a very critical leadership, even in the most independent community, no attitudes directed toward a violent and immediate change in the system were detected among the rural inhabitants. Nonetheless, the state should generate new forms of organization that would result in economic and political benefits, as well as greater efficiency and well-being in the rural sector.

## VI. Political Recommendations

These considerations serve as a basis for suggesting a series of recommendations that could aid the government in transforming the advances in efficiency and productivity of its programs into political support. From an economic standpoint the government mainly seeks to achieve three objectives with its programs: a rise in production; increases in employment; and, improvements in the distribution of income. The results obtained at an aggregate level from the rural development programs studied in our research indicate that the government was *relatively* successful in simultaneously obtaining the aforementioned objectives. However this has not always been the case. That is why it is essential for the government to continue introducing this type of programs, but placing them and adapting them within the economic and social reality in which they are to be carried out.

The problems observed at the community level of rural programs introduced by the government in the mid-seventies are not peculiar to investments with technology that require participation. The failure to comply with what was offered, the lapse that occurred between the petition or the offer to undertake the project and its initiation, and the corruption involved in its administration were to be found in many other types of programs as well.

In order for the programs requiring peasant participation to maintain the relative success they have had and surmount the difficulties observed, it is necessary to modify their introduction and the ways of participation. A policy of promotion of rural welfare is needed—one that is clear and coherent and that takes into account the aspects and requirements of public investment. Otherwise, these programs are too costly, and tremendous amounts of resources are wasted.

What was shown in the work mentioned was the importance of adopting and promoting new ways of organization and production in the countryside at a local level. This could not only lead to a potential solution to the structural problems of the countryside, but could also guarantee the well-being of the population. In this sense the process of rural modernization requires new forms of politico-economic participation that, without becoming disruptive, would really transform the situation, removing local and national obstacles to development, and allowing the rural sector to become a real force—one that can renegotiate its relationship to society.

### *The Introduction of Programs*

The government has to realize that if its programs are introduced late or incompletely into the rural sector—no matter how ambitious they may be—the results will be counterproductive in terms of support. The timeliness and efficiency in introducing a program requires the decentralization of decisions on the disbursement of funds. In other words, sufficient resources of the investment programs must be delegated to a responsible official—at the local level—in order to guarantee the timely and complete execution of such programs.

The above means that the government must have at its disposal a group of development administrators—at the national as well as the local level—that are receptive to the problems that can appear when the programs are introduced into the communities. To ignore this aspect and continue assuming that the magnitude of the program and its good design at an aggregate level are sufficient conditions for its success is to disregard the daily problems that appear in the introduction of development programs and the unfavorable effect that can be created in the attitudes of rural inhabitants.

### *The Importance and Need of Participation*

A program that requires mass participation in its execution does not guarantee by itself that results will be satisfactory. It is necessary to recognize that additional elements are required so that participation can be successful. Most important among these elements is leadership. Organization and collective participation with the characteristics we have described herein are essential in development programs because they make it possible to achieve several objectives simultaneously.

First, participation increases productivity and efficiency in the programs themselves. Furthermore, the participation of rural inhabitants, not only in the execution but in the administration of programs, makes it possible to reduce margins of corruption. That is why it is essential that rural economic policy consider suitable mechanisms that will guarantee not only the economic well-being of the peasants and the efficient implementation of programs, but also strict control of the institutions and persons in charge of carrying them out—thus avoiding the squandering of resources, corruption, and the failure to meet the demands of the communities or the aims of the programs. Similarly, participation oriented in a proper way will lead to a favorable change of attitude among the participants. In addition to achieving objectives of efficiency and fairness, participation has a fundamental political significance: it is at the center of democratic development.

### *The Importance of the Extension Agent*

The government will not be able to achieve the economic, social and political objectives it intends to accomplish through public programs if it does not have a group of extension leaders. This group is essential for the decision making necessary for an efficient and timely introduction of programs. At the same time, they play a basic role in orienting participants toward the most important way of participating in the development process: permanent participation in solving the problems of a community. Lastly, the government needs participants in order to translate the benefits of programs into attitudes of support for the political system.

It is not enough, however, to merely create groups of extension agents to achieve objectives; it is necessary that these individuals have characteristics that are appropriate. Among these, the following can be mentioned: first, the extension agent has to have a personality that does not have any paternalistic feelings toward the participants and—at the same time—has to accept that he needs them and that he can even learn from them. This learning process is essential, since the participants know the risks and benefits of changing their methods of production because of prior experiences—and their decisions are rational ones. Furthermore, it is necessary that the extension agent live in and coexist with the community in a permanent way and that he considers his work not as fulfilling a bureaucratic assignment, but regards it in terms of a commitment in a social context. In other words, he must have the highest of motivations.

As a result, the role of the extension agent must not be one of rank, but of decentralized decision making—that is, the extension agent is a coordinator and an orientator, not a boss in a hierarchical organization. Rank does not seem to be an element that contributes to the commitment of the extension agent in this new role. The decentralization of decisions is also an essential element. The extension agent must have the authority to put into effect the aims of the program in a timely way. Concurrently, decision-making processes in the execution of the program must also be decentralized, such that participants can modify decisions. The feedback between extension agents and participants is fundamental.

The extension agent must take advantage of the informal organizations that have traditionally existed in the community, and use, as well as adapt, the forms demanded by the programs themselves, such as those that banks require to grant credit. These organizations, however, must be used as an instrument for stimulating participation and not as an end in itself.

It is necessary that the extension agent recognize the problematic situation of the particular community in which development programs are going to be introduced, so that he may determine—on the basis of contextual factors—what elements can be used to promote participation and support for the system.

The leader's scale of values is a critical element in the integration of groups required by the state. The conflicts derived from socioeconomic realities indicate that, in order to be effective, the action of the extension agent cannot be apolitical. He has to recognize the basic problems individuals face in order to motivate them toward wider participation and broader commitment to rural development programs, so that they can decide on the position they will take. In other words, government extension agents require a clear mandate from the government on the basic objective that is to be pursued—or the way it is to be achieved—and recognize that in its implementation, certain groups will be affected. As a result, both the extension agent and the participants will have to take sides. The state can not ignore the fact that participation in development programs will have political repercussions.

The extension agent referred to here can work with several communities, provided he can rely on local groups and local leaders, and that his work is not spread over an excessive number of communities with which it would be impossible to coexist.

These suggestions are made in a tentative vein. Since this is a new field in which systematic research has barely begun, they need to be verified by means of comparative studies in other areas. More research will have to be carried out in other communities in which assessments can be made on the presence of leaders supportive of the government's endeavor and the impact these leaders have on the attitudes of the peasants. It would also be a good idea to repeat this same research in other development programs in other zones that are culturally and geographically homogeneous in order to confirm the results.

Meanwhile—and in light of the scarcity of studies on the topic in the rural context—it is considered that the research carried out made it possible to show that there is a marked difference between the success of development programs at an aggregate level and their impact at the specific level of the community. The efficient use of scarce resources at a macroeconomic level does not necessarily translate into successful results at a microeconomic level.

Thus, leadership should not be disregarded as a political instrument that can increase the efficiency of a political project at the local level and augment support for the system. An adequate and intensive use by the government of orientation work carried out by leaders in communities is a basic element for eliminating the efficiency-legitimacy disjunction—that is, of the political economy that the state could face in the Mexican rural media.

Programs incorporating these elements should be designed not only at a general level, but also in strategic terms, since what is implied by the dynamic elements at work is that there is a dual leadership role to be played: A political leadership that acts in the same direction as the economic leadership so that the development project maintains its unity and feasibility. This integration is a fundamental challenge that requires a political concept and strategy in which political organizations—including partisans—participate in a convergent manner with institutions of agricultural development and agrarian regulation. In Mexico, the political organization that has these bases is the *PRI*—the Institutional Revolutionary party—and it has been the only political party capable of articulating the demands of the rural sector with the centers of political decision.

In a mixed economy where market coverage is very broad, it is essential to strengthen the social sector of the economy and make it more efficient in order to improve living standards and income distribution. This is especially true of rural areas, but it must be done within a logic that is decentralized and not through populist or totalitarian mechanisms of control. The integral modernization of the Mexican countryside is feasible using only the present forms of land ownership that have evolved from the Revolution of 1910—that is, small plots and *ejidos*. The organization of social forms of production can be a source of permanent benefit to the peasants, as can the gradual grouping of small plot owners into more extensive areas of exploitation.

The political system must lay down the guidelines for this transformation process, developing better organizational forms that lead to rural modernization, thus reestablishing one of the ideological pillars of the Mexican Revolution—to do away with injustice in the country's rural areas.

## Notes

1. For a detailed description of the Import-Substitution Model and the loss of the relative importance of the agricultural sector see Leopoldo Solís, *La Realidad Económica Mexicana: Retrovisión y Perspectivas. Siglo 21,* Editores, México, 1970.

2. *Sistema de Cuentas Nacionales,* Secretaría de Programación y Presupuesto.

3. For a systematic study of the Institutional Revolutionary party see Luis Javier Garrido. *El Partido de la Revolución Institucionalizada: La Formación del Nuevo Estado en Mexico.* (1928–1945). Siglo 21. Editores, México, 1982.

4. Sidney Verba, *Small Groups and Political Behavior.* (Princeton: Princeton University Press, 1961), p. 6.

5. See the documents presenting the purposes and scope of the political reform in Mexico. *Reforma Política,* Comisión Federal Electoral, 1977.

6. The empirical findings that sustain the arguments presented here can be found in Carlos Salinas de Gortari, *Producción y Participación Política en el Campo,* Mexico: Universidad Nacional Autónoma de Mexico, 1980.

7. This hypothesis has been empirically proved by Ivan Restrepo and Salomón Eckstein. *La Agricultura Colectiva en Mexico.* Siglo 21, Editores, 1975, chap. 8.

8. In those cases in which the participants do not receive monetary income for work on a program, the benefit is calculated by the reduction in the cost of the project represented by not having to hire personnel from outside the community to execute it.

9. Sidney Verba, op. cit. Wayne Cornelius, "The Political Sociology of Cityward Migration in Latin America: Toward Empirical Theory," pp. 95–147 in Francine F. Rabinovitz and Felicity M. Trueblood (Eds.), *Latin American Urban Research,* vol. 1 (Beverly Hills: Sage Publications, 1974). Norman H. Nie, G Bingham and Keneth Prewith, "Social Structure and Political Participation: Developmental Relationships," *American Political Science Review,* 63 (2, 3), 1969), 361–78.

10. Kenneth Landa F., "Towards the Explication of the Concept of Leadership in Terms of the Concept of Power," *Human Relations,* 12, 4, (1960), 345–363; David C. Korter, "Situational Determinations of Leadership Structure," *Journal of Conflict Resolution,* 6, 3, (Sept. 1962), 222–225. Glen Paige, *Political Leadership: Readings for an emerging field,* (New York: Free Press, 1977).

11. See F. Frey, "Cross Cultural Survey Research in Political Science," pp. 173–296 in R. Holt and J. Turner, (Eds.), *The Methodology of Comparative Research,* (New York: Free Press, 1970).

12. Sidney Verba and Norman Nie, *Participation in America: Political Democracy and Social Equality,* (New York: Harper & Row, 1972).

13. John Montgomery, *Technology and Civic Life,* (Cambridge: Massachusetts Institute of Technology Press, 1974). Charles Murray A. *A Behavioral Study of Rural Modernization,* (New York: Praeger Publishers, 1977).

14. See chap. 9 in Carlos Salinas, *Producción Política en el Campo.* México: Universidad Autónoma de México, 1980.

15. See chap. 8, op. cit.

16. Persons in a community who exercise substantial influence in political and administrative matters.

17. The extension agent is a person sent by the government to introduce the program to the communities and provide them with the technical advice needed to improve both the quality and the quantity in agricultural production.

18. See chaps. 10 and 11, op. cit.

# About the Contributors

PEDRO ASPE is president of the National Institute of Statistics, Geography, and Information in the Ministry of Program and Budget.

HERMINIO BLANCO is professor of Economics at Rice University.

JAVIER BERISTAIN is rector of the Instituto Tecnológico Autónomo de México.

FRANCISCO GIL DÍAZ is subdirector of the economic investigation division of the Bank of Mexico.

RAYMOND HILL is a vice president in the investment banking division of Lehman Brothers Kuhn Loeb.

NORA LUSTIG is professor of Economics at the Colegio de México.

ROBERT MCCLEERY is in the Department of Economics at Stanford University.

RICHARD J. MOORE is an assistant professor of Public and International Affairs at Princeton University.

RAUL RAMOS is in the Department of Economics at Stanford University.

JESÚS F. REYES HEROLES is director general of planning in the Ministry of Public Policy.

CLARK REYNOLDS is a professor in the food research institute at Stanford University.

SOCRATES C. RIZZO is director general of economic and social programs in the Ministry of Program and Budget.

CARLOS SALINAS DE GORTARI is minister in the Ministry of Program and Budget.

PAUL E. SIGMUND is a professor of Politics at Princeton University.

LEOPOLDO SOLÍS is deputy director general of the Bank of Mexico.

EMILIO LOZOYA THALMANN is deputy undersecretary in the Ministry of Labor and Social Welfare.

# Index